Intimate Relationships

DISCARD

DATE DUE	
NOV 2 6 1996	
OCT 1 6 199_	
NOV	

P9-CCZ-157

McGraw-Hill Series in Social Psychology

CONSULTING EDITOR, Philip G. Zimbardo

Intimate Relationships

Second Edition

❖

Sharon S. Brehm
*State University of New York
at Binghamton*

McGraw-Hill, Inc.
New York   St. Louis   San Francisco   Auckland   Bogotá
Caracas   Lisbon   London   Madrid   Mexico   Milan
Montreal   New Delhi   Paris   San Juan   Singapore
Sydney   Tokyo   Toronto

INTIMATE RELATIONSHIPS

Copyright © 1992, 1985 by McGraw-Hill, Inc. All rights reserved.
Printed in the United States of America. Except as permitted under the
United States Copyright Act of 1976, no part of this publication may be
reproduced or distributed in any form or by any means, or stored in a
data base or retrieval system, without the prior written permission of
the publisher.

2 3 4 5 6 7 8 9 0 DOC DOC 9 0 9 8 7 6 5 4 3 2 1

ISBN 0-07-007443-7

This book was set in Palatino by Better Graphics, Inc.
The editors were Christopher Rogers and Jean Akers;
the production supervisor was Kathryn Porzio.
The photo editor was Anne Manning.
R. R. Donnelley & Sons Company was printer and binder.

Cover credit: Painted by Jan Vermeer: Girl Interrupted at Her Music.
Copyright The Frick Collection, New York.

Credits appear on pages 485–488, and on this page by
reference.

Library of Congress Cataloging-in-Publication Data

Brehm, Sharon S.
    Intimate relationships / Sharon S. Brehm. —2nd ed.
        p.   cm.—(The McGraw-Hill series in social psychology)
    Includes bibliographical references (p.   ) and index.
    ISBN 0-07-007443-7
    1. Family life education.   2. Interpersonal relations.
    I. Series.
    HQ10.B735   1992
    306.7'07—dc20   91-14504

AUSTIN COMMUNITY COLLEGE
LEARNING RESOURCE SERVICES

About the Author

———— ❖ ————

Sharon S. Brehm is Professor of Psychology and Dean of the School of Arts and Sciences and of Harpur College at the State University of New York at Binghamton. She received her Ph.D. from Duke University and completed an internship in clinical psychology at the University of Washington Medical Center in Seattle. She has been a Fulbright Senior Research Scholar in Paris and has given talks in England, France, Germany, Israel, Italy, and Switzerland as well as in the United States. In addition to numerous articles and chapters, she has published seven books—including *The Application of Social Psychology to Clinical Practice*, a recognized classic in the field, and a popular textbook, *Social Psychology*, co-authored with Saul Kassin. The first edition of *Intimate Relationships* received wide acclaim for its usefulness in the classroom and as a sourcebook for researchers.

This book is dedicated to Ellen Berscheid and Elaine Hatfield for their pioneering contributions to the study of attraction, love, and relationships. Their intellectual leadership and personal encouragement have made it possible for others to follow in their footsteps.

For love, all love of other sights controls,
And makes one little room, an everywhere.

John Donne

Contents

———— ❖ ————

Foreword

———— ❖ ————

During the many decades when American psychology was held captive by a limited scientific doctrine of behaviorism, the pathfinders who dared to venture beyond these intellectually limited boundaries and explore new horizons were largely social psychologists. They valued the personal perspectives of the human actor in life's dramas, honored the alternative interpretations of reality held by different observers, and defended the subtle interplay of dynamic forces between and within cultures, social situations, and individual psyches.

Long relegated to a subordinate position within psychology's status hierarchy for these points of view, social psychology has steadily moved to the center of contemporary psychology. It did so by establishing a cognitively flavored brand of psychology, which, in recent years, has become the banner flown by mainstream psychology. Social psychology was the home of generalists within psychology, a haven for scholars interested in understanding the depth and breadth of the nature of human nature. It was neither too shy to ask the big questions that have intrigued social philosophers for centuries, nor too orthodox to venture into alien territories with new methodologies that have provided empirically grounded answers to the more philosophical questions. Finally, social psychologists have become the vanguard of the movement to extend the boundaries of traditional psychology into realms vital to contributing solutions for real-world problems, the areas of health, ecology, education, law, peace and conflict resolution, and much more. Indeed, it is not immodest to declare that nothing of human nature is too alien to social psychological inquiry and concern.

Our McGraw-Hill Series in Social Psychology celebrates the fundamental contributions being made by researchers, theorists, and practitioners of social psychology to a richer understanding of the human condition. The authors of each book in the series are distinguished researchers and dedicated teachers, committed to sharing a vision of the excitement inherent in their particular area of investigation with their colleagues, graduate students, and seriously curious undergraduates. Taken as a whole, the series will cover a wide path of social psychological interests, allowing instructors to use any of them as supplements to their basic textbook or, for the more daring, to organize a challenging course around a collection of them.

While reading Sharon Brehm's new edition of her successful text, *Intimate Relationships*, I could not help but think of the many people I've met—men and women, young and old, gay and straight—who despite apparent accomplishment and success felt that their lives had become empty and meaningless. If you ask those individuals about their feelings (and, being an inordinately curious person, I do tend to ask), their responses show a striking consistency. The problems they point to, the reason for their season of discontent, almost always involve their intimate relationships. They feel perplexed, bewildered, even, about how relationships are formed, developed, and enriched. They have specific concerns about issues of communication, power, jealousy, envy, expectations, and selfishness. And they long to experience and understand the dynamics of attraction, romance, love, and sometimes sexuality. *Intimate Relationships* deals with each of these topics in depth, and blends Brehm's insights with her analysis of what psychologists have learned from years of systematic study of people as they go into, through, and out of such relationships.

There is no better first step for those who want to establish a life style that builds from a core of enriched friendship and loving relationships than to explore the perspectives and information that Sharon Brehm has gathered for us in this book. What is remarkable is the unique combination of the scholarly and pragmatic that Brehm presents. The breadth of scientific research and current theory on a wide array of issues that are part of intimate relationships is carefully developed as the intellectual scaffolding from which practical advice can be extracted and put to use in building optimal personal relationships.

In her sensitive analysis of this core of human existence, Brehm combines social-psychological theory and research along with a practical focus on ways to improve intimate relationships and cope with their dissolution. Her approach reveals her sophisticated comprehension of the nuances of these complex issues, her ability to pose the right questions, and her appreciation for the appropriate place for a critical reading of the available empirical evidence. She tells us when common sense conceptions about intimate relationships are informative and when they are wrong, though appealing.

The study of intimate relationships is a relatively new topic in social psychology, which typically has dealt with groups and dyads in more structured contexts, as they cooperate or compete, negotiate and bargain, conform or comply. The rising interest among social psychologists in the topics of interpersonal attraction, liking, love, romance, sexuality, and marriage is part of the field's emerging concern for developing the richest possible conception of human actors at play on all of life's stages. But the audience for this book goes well beyond the student of social psychology. When we enlarge our perspective to consider the social and cultural contexts in which intimate relationships take place, students of sociology are also included, as are those in family studies, home economics, and communication studies. Researchers too will find this a useful volume for keeping them up to date on the latest theory and research in this rapidly expanding area. And those professionals who counsel people experiencing problems in their relationships will find valuable sound guidance in their pursuit of solutions that are too often difficult to find.

So each of these readers will be taken on a fascinating journey where the destination is clear—a comprehensive scholarly understanding of all the elements that go into intimate relationships—and the process of getting there will engage the reader both intellectually and emotionally. In this book, the life of the mind and the cares of the heart lie, quite comfortably, close together.

Philip G. Zimbardo
Series Editor

Preface

———— ❖ ————

The first edition of this text started out under a rather peculiar designation. A "chicken-and-egg book" my first editor called it, meaning that in order to have a healthy commercial life it would need to generate courses that would use it as well as secure adoptions from existing courses. Fortunately, there seem to have been a sufficient number of instructors ready to hatch new courses on relationships or modify existing ones to include a greater emphasis on relationships. This second edition owes its existence to the warm welcome the first one received from instructors, students, and researchers.

In writing this edition, I have kept the original structure of the book as a whole relatively unchanged. The number of chapters (15) remains the same, and Chapters 3 through 13 continue to follow a developmental sequence from the beginning of a relationship to its ending and aftermath. To make this sequence even clearer to the reader, this large middle section is now divided into four multi-chapter parts (Getting Together, Progress and Fairness in the Relationship, Relationship Issues, When a Relationship Ends). As in the first edition, Part I consists of an introduction to the study of relationships and a chapter on research methods, while the final part includes a chapter on therapeutic interventions and then a concluding essay on the present status of intimate relationships in our society and some possible future trends.

Within this basic structure, however, the content of the chapters themselves has changed a great deal. Since the 1985 publication of the first edition, the amount of research and theory on relationships has expanded enormously. Where I once had to stretch to find relevant materials, now I have had to be selective. In general, I have tried to retain enough coverage of previous research to provide an adequate foundation for more recent work. Nevertheless, almost all of the chapters have been extensively revised and some have been rewritten entirely. Although this level of revision requires considerable time and effort from both author and publisher, it allows this edition, like the first one, to function as a comprehensive introductory text, suitable for a range of different approaches to the study of intimate relationships.

As approaches will differ, so too will the audience for this book vary. Researchers will find it a helpful compendium of information and citations; for clinicians, it can serve as a concise overview of developments in the field. But the primary audience for whom this book is intended consists of undergraduate students and their instructors. Written in clear, everyday language, the text provides numerous examples from everyday life. It does not, however, avoid complex issues involving research findings and theoretical interpretations. In short, the text sustains the personal appeal of the subject matter *and* maintains rigorous standards of scholarship.

This combination is, I believe, particularly appropriate for the study of intimate relationships. While teaching my own course on relationships, I have seen the intense curiosity that students bring to such a course and how their curiosity motivates them to master the material presented. They welcome the opportunity to consider new ideas and compare alternative perspectives. Students also appreciate having thorough, well-organized summary sections to help them review after having read a chapter and before taking an exam. The chapter summaries provided in this edition, changed significantly from the summary outlines in the first edition, were developed in response to student feedback about the summary format they found most useful.

In addition to thanking my students for their suggestions about how I could improve this textbook, I would like to express my gratitude to those reviewers who commented on the book at various stages in the revision process: Andrew Barclay, Michigan State University; Kelly Brennan, SUNY–Buffalo; Jeff Bryson, San Diego State University; Scott Fuller, Santa Rosa Junior College; Jane Ellen Kestner, Youngstown State University; Phillip R. Shaver, SUNY–Buffalo; and Robert Weiss, University of Oregon.

I have also enjoyed the great good fortune of having the superb assistance of Christine Averill and Marianne Sharsky in preparing the final manuscript. And, from start to finish, I have appreciated the opportunity to work with Christopher Rogers, Jean Akers, and all the other members of the especially fine editorial staff of the College Division at McGraw-Hill.

Sharon S. Brehm

Intimate Relationships

PART ONE

———— ❖ ————

Introduction to the Study of Intimate Relationships

1

$\mathcal{R}$elationships $\mathcal{T}$oday

---------- ❖ ----------

Defining Intimate Relationships ◆ Marriage ◆ *Marriage and Happiness* ◆ Divorce ◆ *Divorce and Stress* ◆ *Why Has the Divorce Rate Increased?* ◆ Cohabitation ◆ *Cohabitation and Marital Outcomes* ◆ Being Single ◆ *The Problems and Rewards of Being Single* ◆ Past and Present: An Overview ◆ Chapter Summary

T alk to a friend. Listen to a song. Watch a movie. Chances are that at some point the topic of relationships will appear in the conversation, the lyrics, or the plot. Relationships get a lot of attention because, for most people, their relationships with the people they love, the people they care about, are a central aspect of their lives: a source of great joy when things go well, a cause of great sorrow and disappointment when things go badly. Most of us have an almost insatiable curiosity about relationships. We want to understand how they get started, how they develop, and how, sometimes, they end in a haze of anger and pain. When it comes to relationships, we are all embarked on a lifelong voyage of discovery.

This book is a part of that process of discovery. Drawing on the work of various disciplines in the social sciences (such as psychology, sociology, communication studies), it describes what social scientists have learned about relationships through their research. This more scientific view of relationships provides a somewhat different perspective than you might find in conversations with your friends, in song lyrics, or in the movies. But this book is *not* a how-to manual. There is no magic formula for a satisfying relationship. Instead, each of us must bring his or her beliefs, values, and personal experiences to bear on the information presented here. The purpose of this book is to help you arrive at your own conclusions about relationships.

To set the stage for the discoveries to come, we need to define our subject matter. What are "intimate relationships"? How do they differ from other kinds of social interactions? Next, we examine some important changes that have occurred in four major social categories: marriage, divorce, cohabitation, and being single. If we are to improve our relationships in the future, we must first understand where we are today and how we got there.

DEFINING INTIMATE RELATIONSHIPS

People have all kinds of relationships with each other. They have parents and/or children; they work with others on the job and or at school; they encounter grocery clerks, physicians, and office receptionists; they have friends; they may be dating, living with a lover, or married. Out of this vast array of relationships, this book will concentrate on the last two categories. We will call interactions with friends, dates, lovers, and spouses "intimate relationships." Only relationships between adults are considered here, though later in this book (Chapter 13) we will examine the effects on children when their parents' marriage fails to endure.

But even when we restrict our focus to friendships and romantic relationships between adults, we have still not defined what an intimate relationship is. There are, in fact, many possible definitions (Perlman & Fehr, 1987). Most definitions, however, emphasize one or more of the following three characteristics: behavioral interdependence, need fulfillment, and emotional attachment.

Behavioral interdependence refers to the mutual impact that partners have on each other (Berscheid & Peplau, 1983). In an interdependent relationship, our lives are not parallel tracks; they are intertwined. What each partner does affects what the other partner wants to do and can do. Interdependence between intimates is frequent (partners often affect each other), strong (partners have a meaningful impact on each other), diverse (partners influence each other in many different areas of life), and enduring (partners influence each other across a significant time period). When relationships are interdependent, behavior has implications for the partner as well as for the self.

Another way to define intimate relationships is in terms of the psychological needs they serve. Weiss (1969) has suggested that people have five important needs that can be met only through relationships with others:

1. The need for intimacy—someone with whom we can share our feelings freely
2. The need for social integration—someone with whom we can share our worries and concerns

3. The need for being nurturant—someone whom we can take care of
4. The need for assistance—someone who will help us out
5. The need for reassurance of our own worth—someone who will tell us that we matter

In close, rewarding, intimate relationships, partners meet each other's needs—disclosing feelings and sharing confidences, discussing practical concerns, helping each other, and providing reassurance.

Emotional attachment—people's feelings of love and affection for each other—is another important characteristic of intimate relationships. As we will see in Chapter 4, love has even more possible definitions than intimate relationships. It does appear, however, that love can exist in the absence of either behavioral interdependence or need fulfillment. In a summer's romance, emotional attachment is intense, but the effects on one's long-term goals and choices are often minimal. In a one-sided love affair, the person in love encounters rejection and even humiliation rather than kindness and reassurance. Behavioral interdependence can also stand alone. Spouses in an "empty-shell" marriage closely coordinate the practical details of their daily lives (who takes the children to the doctor, who does the shopping, what car should be purchased), but live in a psychological vaccum in which their more intimate psychological needs are not met and feelings of love have disappeared. Thus, although our most satisfying and meaningful intimate relationships include all three of these defining characteristics— behavioral interdependence, need fulfillment, and emotional attachment—there are many intimate relationships based on only one or two of these characteristics.

Focusing on adult relationships defined in this way excludes many relationships from our consideration: those with parents or children, with colleagues at work or school, with casual acquaintances, and with people we encounter during daily business transactions. Nevertheless, this definition still covers a large territory. Intimate relationships vary on such dimensions as:

- *Intensity*. Some intimate relationships are very intense; others are quiet and tranquil; some are just plain dull.
- *Commitment*. Some partners have a strong commitment to a long-lasting relationship; others are merely dropping by for a brief stay.
- *Emotion*. Feelings about relationships run the gamut from ecstatic joy to agonizing despair.
- *Sexuality*. Sex and psychological intimacy are independent factors. Some intimate relationships are sexual; some are not. Some sexual relationships are psychologically intimate; others are not.

- *Gender.* As we will see throughout this book, men and women often take different approaches to intimate relationships. And intimate relationships occur between same-sex partners as well as between partners of the opposite sex.

There is, then, no one kind of intimate relationship. Indeed, perhaps the most fundamental lesson about relationships is one we can learn at the outset: They come in all shapes and sizes. This variety is a source of great complexity; it is also a source of endless fascination.

MARRIAGE

For many people, marriage is the ultimate expression of an intimate relationship: a public vow of the intention to establish a lifelong partnership. Americans like to get married. Relative to Europeans, more of us marry, and we marry at a younger age (Skolnick, 1978). Divorce has surprisingly little effect on this preference for the married state. Some 80 percent of divorced individuals remarry (Burgess, 1981; Norton, 1987), although the remarriage rate has declined over the past several decades (Bumpass, Sweet, & Castro Martin, 1990) and is higher for men than for women (Norton & Moorman, 1987). Reflecting the high social value of marriage, homosexual couples—who are denied the legal right to marry—have petitioned state and municipal governments for "domestic partnership" legislation that will grant unmarried couples some of the benefits of marriage—such as property rights, life insurance, health benefits, and access to pensions (Isaacson, 1989). Some type of domestic partnership legislation can now be found in New York State; San Francisco; Madison, Wisconsin; and West Hollywood, California (Seligmann, 1990).

The consistent popularity of marriage throughout American history does not mean that the marriage rate has stayed absolutely constant. There has been some variation. As you can see from Figure 1.1, marriage rates shot up after World War II and then declined. There was also a dip in the marriage rates in the mid-1970s, after which these rates remained relatively stable. For the young adults of today, it is estimated that 90 percent will marry, which represents a small decline from previous rates of 95 percent (Norton, 1987).

But there have been some dramatic changes in American marriages. Perhaps the most dramatic concerns the age when people get married. Since reaching a historic low in the late 1950s, age at marriage has climbed steadily upward for both men and women (see Figure 1.2). The average age at marriage for men is now almost 26, and the average age

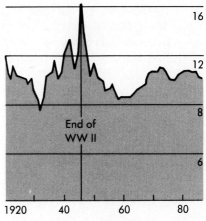

FIGURE 1.1

Marriage rates per 1,000 people. Data Sources: U.S. Census Bureau,
(*Newsweek*. Special Edition.)   National Center for Health Statistics

for women is approaching 24. Although typically the man is older than
the woman, there also appears to be a slight decrease in the average age
differential between men and women in their first marriage.

FIGURE 1.2

Age at marriage. (*Newsweek*.
Special Edition.)

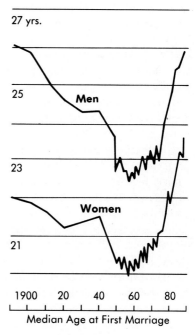

Median Age at First Marriage

Data Source: U.S. Census Bureau

Compared with marriages that took place a generation ago, today's newlyweds are older, are more likely to have children from a previous marriage, and more frequently have similar commitments to both career and family. (Hazel Hankin/Stock, Boston)

Another important change in marriage concerns the occupational status of husbands and wives. In 1940, only 27.4 percent of women worked outside the home, and of these only one-third were married. By 1987, 56 percent of women were employed in the work force, and of these 54.7 percent were married (Footlick, 1990). Increasingly, it's work and marriage that go together like a horse and carriage—for women as well as men. And increasingly, particularly among college graduates, men and women have similar commitments to career and family (Regan & Roland, 1985).

The third dramatic change in marriage is one with which you or your friends may have direct experience: stepfamilies. By the mid-1980s, 46 percent of marriages were remarriages for at least one partner (London & Wilson, 1988), and some 16 percent of married-couple households in the United States included at least one spouse who had a child by a former marriage (Norton, 1987). It is now estimated that among children born in the 1980s, as many as a third of them will live with a stepparent by age 18 (Kantrowitz & Wingert, 1990). Getting married today is often a family affair.

Marriage and Happiness

People certainly think that marriage is satisfying and rewarding. When over 300 couples, the vast majority of whom said they were happy, explained why their marriage had lasted, they selected items that clearly reflect the benefits of an enduring marriage (Lauer & Lauer, 1985). Table 1.1 lists the 15 most frequent responses given by husbands and wives. In general, research on the relationship between marital status and personal well-being confirms the widespread belief in the benefits of marriage. Overall, married people are happier than those who have never married, are separated or divorced, or are widowed (Campbell, 1981; Veroff, Douvan, & Kukla, 1981; Wilson, 1967). Married people also tend to be healthier (Lynch, 1977) and to live longer (Berkman & Syme, 1979). Recently, however, a statistical analysis of a large number of studies on

TABLE 1.1 WHAT KEEPS A MARRIAGE GOING?

When asked about the factors that contribute to an enduring marriage, married respondents gave these reasons, listed in order of frequency.

Men	Women
My spouse is my best friend.	My spouse is my best friend.
I like my spouse as a person.	I like my spouse as a person.
Marriage is a long-term commitment.	Marriage is a long-term commitment.
Marriage is sacred.	Marriage is sacred.
We agree on aims and goals.	We agree on aims and goals.
My spouse has grown more interesting.	My spouse has grown more interesting.
I want the relationship to succeed.	I want the relationship to succeed.
An enduring marriage is important to social stability.	We laugh together.
We laugh together.	We agree on a philosophy of life.
I am proud of my spouse's achievements.	We agree on how and how often to show affection.
We agree on a philosophy of life.	An enduring marriage is important to social stability.
We agree about our sex life.	We have a stimulating exchange of ideas.
We agree on how and how often to show affection.	We discuss things calmly.
I confide in my spouse.	We agree about our sex life.
We share outside hobbies and interests.	I am proud of my spouse's achievements.

SOURCE: Lauer & Lauer, 1985.

marriage and well-being suggested that the effect of marriage on happiness and satisfaction, while evident, may be quite small (Haring-Hidore, Stock, Okun, & Witter, 1985).

But what about gender? Who benefits the most from marriage, men or women? In most previous research, the bulk of the evidence appeared consistent with Durkheim's (1897) early proposition that marriage is a greater advantage for men than for women (Bernard, 1972; Gove, 1972a, 1972b, 1973; Hamilton, 1929; Horwitz, 1982; Kessler & McRae, 1984; Knupfer, Clark, & Room, 1966; Morgan, 1980; Radloff, 1975; Sporakowski & Hughston, 1978; Veroff et al., 1981). But, in a recent study, a different conclusion has been drawn by Wood, Rhodes, and Whelan (1989). These investigators maintain that it is important to separate measures of *positive* well-being (such as happiness, life satisfaction, morale, positive feelings, and general well-being) from other measures (such as overall psychological adjustment, mental illness, psychosomatic symptoms, and physical health) that include *negative* aspects of well-being. Using a procedure that assessed positive and negative aspects separately, they found that on at least some measures of positive well-being (i.e., happiness and life satisfaction), women had higher scores than did men, and that this difference is greater among people who were married than among people who were not married. These findings indicate that, in terms of positive feelings, women benefit more from marriage than do men. However, Wood et al. do not dismiss the other side of the argument. They acknowledge that women also *suffer* more in marriage than do men, reporting more negative feelings and distress. According to these investigators, "women may be more responsive than men to emotional highs *and* lows, particularly when involved in close relationships" (p. 260; emphasis added). Thus, in examining who derives the greater benefit from marriage, Wood et al. emphasize that the answer depends on how you ask the question. Women seem to get more of the highs, but men appear better able to avoid the lows.

But even if we ask the question in terms of positive feelings, there is some evidence that the relationship between marriage and happiness is not as strong as it used to be and that married women are not as happy as they once were. Reviewing U.S. national surveys conducted from 1972 to 1986, Glenn and Weaver (1988) found that the happiness of married women had declined, while the happiness of never-married men had increased. Putting these two trends together, Glenn and Weaver determined that the difference in happiness between married and never-married individuals had narrowed. This reduction was most pronounced among young men (ages 25–39). In surveys taken between 1972 and 1976, there was a sizable gap of 20.5 percentage points between the proportion of married men and the proportion of never-married men of this age range saying they were "very happy." But in surveys taken between 1982 and 1986, this gap had narrowed to only 5.7 percentage points. In their concluding comments, Glenn and Weaver (1988) offer a rather pessimistic interpretation of their results.

> We should entertain the possibility that, in an increasingly individualistic and hedonistic society, an increasingly hedonistic form of marriage is having diminished hedonistic consequences for those who participate in it. (p. 323)

What Glenn and Weaver cannot assess, however, is whether the survey results from the 1980s are best understood as part of a continuing set of societal trends that are having a negative impact on the benefits of marriage or whether these data may represent the crest of societal forces that have now diminished. We will return to this issue in the conclusion of this chapter, when we survey a broad range of behavioral and attitudinal changes that have taken place in American society. One of the most dramatic of these changes, with far-reaching consequences for the lives of millions of people, has been what some have called the "divorce epidemic."

D*IVORCE*

When you look at the figures, the term "divorce epidemic" does not seem an exaggeration. As illustrated in Figure 1.3, the divorce rate in the United States climbed steadily from the late 1960s to the early 1980s. Since then, it has declined slightly but still remains high. Projecting current rates into the future, researchers have estimated that around 50 percent of today's *first* marriages will end in divorce; for *second*

FIGURE 1.3

Divorce rates per 1,000 people. (*Newsweek.* Special Edition.)

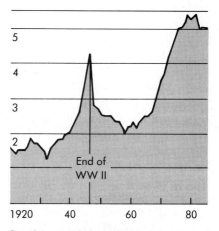

Data Sources: U.S. Census Bureau, National Center for Health Statistics

marriages, estimates of the likelihood of divorce go as high as 60 percent (Cherlin, 1983; Furstenberg & Spanier, 1984). Although divorce rates increased in virtually all Western countries during this same period, the United States has the dubious distinction of leading the pack (Phillips, 1988). Some countries continue to have a very low divorce rate. For example, the divorce rate in Japan is less than 25 percent of that in the United States (Cornell, 1989).

When London and Wilson (1988) took a demographic snapshot of divorced couples in the United States, they found that:

> The typical couple who divorced in 1985 had been married nine years and six months. The wife was 24 years old at marriage—the husband, 27. At the time of the divorce, the wife was 34 years old, and the husband 36. On average, divorced couples have one child. (p. 22)

Overall, younger people are more likely to divorce than older ones, and divorce is more common early in a marriage (particularly the first two or three years) than later on (Bumpass et al., 1990; London & Wilson, 1988).

Although the current divorce rate represents a significant change in our society, the ending of large numbers of marriages after a relatively short period is not unique to the United States at the end of the twentieth century. In former times, many marriages were terminated by the early death of one of the partners. The hazards of childbirth made it especially likely that a married woman would die young and her husband would remarry. As historian Lawrence Stone puts it, divorce could be considered "a functional substitute for death: both are means of terminating marriage at a premature stage" (1988, p. 21). In addition, many marriages in the past were ended by desertion, without a legal divorce ever being obtained. Those young men encouraged to "Go West!" often left wives and children behind. Actually, the average duration of marriage seems to have increased "from about fifteen to twenty years in preindustrial Europe to about thirty-five years in 1900, and then to almost fifty years today" (Phillips, 1988, p. 393). And when anything has the possibility of lasting a longer time, it also has an increased possibility of breaking down. Taken in their broader historical context, the current high rates of divorce in the United States seem less deviant, less shocking. Nevertheless, what has clearly changed is the *way* that marriages end.

Divorce and Stress

One can, of course, argue that divorce is a definite improvement over the finality of death and the uncertainty of desertion. For those who experience it, however, divorce is often devastating. Admissions into a psychiatric facility, automobile accidents, alcohol abuse, and homicide are all greater for separated or divorced individuals than for people who are married, have never been married, or have been widowed (Bloom, Asher, & White, 1978). Divorce also appears to be associated with increased suicide rates (Stack, 1989, 1990). Overall, a report issued by the National Institutes of Mental Health concluded that "the single most powerful predictor of stress-related physical as well as emotional illness is marital disruption" (cited in Somers, 1981, p. 182).

Although both men and women experience the negative effects of divorce, conflicting findings have produced a debate about whether men (Bloom et al., 1978; Cargan & Melko, 1982; Chiriboga, Roberts, & Stein, 1978) or women (Clarke-Stewart & Bailey, 1989; Espenshade, 1979; Freedman, 1978; Raschke, 1977; Veroff et al., 1981) suffer more. One way to reconcile these inconsistent results is to consider that there may be two different kinds of stress associated with the loss of a marital partner: economic hardship and emotional deprivation (Knupfer et al., 1966). There is clear evidence that women suffer more economic hardship than men after a divorce (Weitzman, 1985) or after the death of a spouse (Atchley, 1975, 1977). On the other hand, widowers appear to have more difficulty maintaining social ties than do widows—with, for example, their children and grandchildren—and may, therefore, feel more socially and emotionally isolated (Berardo, 1970; Stroebe & Stroebe, 1983). As will be discussed later in this book (see Chapters 11 and 13), heterosexual men tend to rely heavily on their female partners for intimacy and emotional support; heterosexual women, however, seem more likely to establish emotionally close relationships with female friends and relatives as well as with male partners. Thus, the loss of a spouse through either divorce or death may lead to more emotional deprivation for men than for women.

These possible gender differences in the effects of divorce could also affect people's motives for remarrying. According to Farrell and Markman (1986), the need for financial security may play an important role in women's decision to remarry, while the need for emotional security may influence men's desire to remarry. In any case, marital satisfaction is higher in first marriages than in remarriages, and remarried men are more satisfied than remarried women (Vemer, Coleman, Ganong, & Cooper, 1989). Compared with divorced individuals, however, those who remarry are happier (Weingarten, 1985).

Why Has the Divorce Rate Increased?

Questions about *why* people behave in a certain way often create a strong desire for an answer. We like to understand what causes things to happen. In many cases, however, it is exceedingly difficult, even impossible, to know for certain why something took place. And so it is with the increase in divorce over the past 25 years. We cannot know exactly why it happened. But a number of possible reasons for the "divorce epidemic" have been suggested.

One leading candidate involves the changing status of women in our society (Phillips, 1988). Cross-cultural comparisons indicate that the level of socioeconomic development and women's participation in the labor force have a U-shaped relationship with divorce rates (Trent & South, 1989). Divorce is frequent at the two opposite ends of the continuum: (1) where the level of development and female labor force participation is low and (2) where the level of development and female labor force participation is high. It seems likely that these two societal conditions involve very different kinds of divorce. In the first, women's status is very low and men have easy access to divorce. In the second, women are less economically dependent on men, perhaps making divorce a more financially acceptable alternative for both spouses.

A recent study by Greenstein (1990) provides a careful examination of the relationship between marital disruption and women's employment in the United States. Greenstein distinguishes between the "independence hypothesis" described above, which postulates that paid employment increases a person's freedom to choose divorce, and a "stabilization hypothesis" proposing that people invest earned income into marriage-related assets (possessions, children) that, in turn, increase their commitment to the marriage. The first hypothesis predicts an increased divorce rate among women who work outside the home, while the second predicts a decrease. Greenstein's research provides some support for both hypotheses. On the one hand, women who worked 35 or more hours per week had a *higher* divorce rate than those who worked fewer hours. On the other hand, women who earned more money had a *lower* divorce rate than those who earned less. Combining these two effects, the greatest risk of divorce was found for low-income wives who worked 35 to 40 hours a week. Among these individuals, paid employment may be neither liberating nor stabilizing. Instead, it may be just another stressor that makes life more difficult and marital conflict more likely.

Another possible reason for the increase in the divorce rate involves the expectations that people have about the benefits of marriage. In 1968, Slater noted that:

> Spouses are now asked to be lovers, friends, and mutual therapists in a society which is forcing the marriage bond to become the closest, deepest, most important and most enduring relationship of one's life. Paradoxically, then, it is increasingly likely to fall short of the emotional demands placed upon it and be dissolved. (p. 99)

Twenty years later, Phillips (1988) expressed a similar point of view:

> The same stress on romantic love, emotional intensity, and sexual satisfaction that has long been associated with premarital and extramarital relationships has spilled over into marriage. . . . The higher these emotional expectations rise, the less likely they are to be fulfilled. (pp. 623–624)

Perhaps, then, people are simply asking too much of marriage.

Some of the possible causes of the increased divorce rate began as effects of this increase. In order to accommodate people's increasing desire to divorce, divorce laws were changed to make divorce easier to obtain. As the prevalence of divorce increased, people's attitudes toward divorce became more tolerant, which reduced the social barriers against divorce (Thornton, 1989). And divorce, like many other social customs, is passed down from one generation to another. Adults who as children experienced the divorce of their parents are themselves more likely to divorce (Glenn & Kramer, 1987). Like the declining strength of the relationship between happiness and marriage that was described earlier, the increased divorce rate appears to be part of some larger pattern of societal change. Cohabitation is another aspect of this larger pattern of change.

COHABITATION

For homosexual partners who want to live together, cohabitation—living together without being legally married—is the only option. Heterosexual partners, however, have a choice: They can live together with or without being married. And, increasingly, they are choosing cohabitation, at least for a while (Thornton, 1988). As you can see from Figure 1.4, the recent increase in unmarried-couple households in the United States is enormous. In 1988, there were five times as many unmarried couples living together as in 1970. According to Glick and Spanier (1981), this development reflects a real change in societal living arrangements. It cannot be accounted for by landlords taking in tenants, or by greater honesty in reporting one's living situation.

Glick and Spanier also report some general characteristics of cohabiting heterosexual couples:

- If they have never been married, cohabiting individuals tend to be young (i.e., under 30).
- Many cohabiting individuals have been previously married, and their age varies widely.
- Cohabitation is more likely in large metropolitan areas than in small towns or rural settings.
- Young cohabiting couples tend to be well educated.

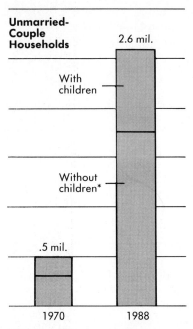

Unmarried-Couple Households

2.6 mil.

With children

Without children*

.5 mil.

1970   1988

*Under age 15
Data Source: U.S. Census Bureau

FIGURE 1.4
Living together. (*Newsweek*. Special Edition.)

- Most cohabiting couples are white, though the proportion of co-habiting couples is higher among blacks.
- Many cohabiting couples have low incomes.
- Among many cohabiting couples, both partners work.

This list of characteristics indicates that cohabitation is an alternative chosen by many different types of people. Some couples who live together without being married are young people, in school or just starting out on their careers. Others are older people, many of whom have been married previously. Cohabitation can be chosen because of personal desires to live together, but sometimes economic reasons are more important in the decision. Although many cohabiting couples have a sexual relationship, many others live together in friendship or out of convenience.

Both Figure 1.4 and the analysis by Glick and Spanier are based on data collected by the U.S. Census Bureau, which defines cohabitation in terms of sharing the same residence. This is not, however, the only way to define it. Many couples engage in what might be called "quasi-cohabitation": They continue to maintain separate residences but spend most of their free time and nights together. This kind of arrangement is often found among college students (Macklin, 1978). Whether they share a whole house or just a bed, cohabitation among young adults seems to be an "increasingly common aspect of courtship" (Tanfer, 1987, p. 493). And this is occurring not only in the United States. Of couples married in Great Britain in 1987, 58 percent of the men and 53 percent of the woman said they already lived with their partners (Brindle, 1989).

Cohabitation and Marital Outcomes

Since cohabitation on such a wide scale is a relatively recent development, the study of its effects has only begun. It is already clear, however, that these effects are different from what might have been expected. Before the recent surge in cohabitation, it was thought by some that cohabitation might be a way for people to determine more rationally whether they should get married. From this perspective, cohabitation would be a "trial marriage," and the result of the trial should be better marriages—happier and more enduring. As it has turned out, however, the idea of a trial marriage was more convincing in the abstract than in reality.

Young people who cohabit tend to emphasize the immediate benefits of cohabitation—such as emotional security, freedom from parental constraint, and the conveniences of domestic living and a readily available sexual partner—although at least some of them do seem aware that cohabitation can be used to test out their own feelings about the conflicts between personal freedom and interpersonal commitment (Ridley, Peterman, & Avery, 1978). Among older people, cohabitation may be viewed as an alternative to marriage, particularly among divorced individuals who are reluctant to remarry but still desire some of the benefits of living with someone.

Reflecting this complicated array of people's motives for cohabiting, research on the relationship between cohabitation and subsequent marital satisfaction has obtained mixed findings. For example, one study by Watson (1983) found that married couples in their first year of marriage who had "shared a bedroom and/or a bed" before their marriage reported *less* marital satisfaction than did those who had not. However, a replication with a similar group of subjects from the same locality (Victoria, British Columbia) did not obtain any difference in marital satisfaction between those who had cohabited and those who had not (Watson & DeMeo, 1987). Moreover, a three-year follow-up of subjects from both studies found no difference in marital satisfaction as a function of whether the couple had cohabited before marriage. One possible problem with this set of studies is the high rate of cohabitors involved: 64.3 percent in the original study and 75.2 percent in the replication.

Research by Newcomb also obtained conflicting findings. An earlier study found no significant difference in either marital satisfaction or the divorce rate between those who had cohabited before marriage and those who had not (Newcomb & Bentler, 1980). In a later study, however, with a larger and younger group of subjects, females who had cohabited before marriage were more likely to divorce than those who had not, but there was no difference in the divorce rate for cohabiting and noncohabiting males (Newcomb, 1986). Unfortunately, the way the 1986 study was conducted prevented Newcomb from distinguishing between people who had cohabited with their spouse before marriage and those who had cohabited with someone else.

As a further example of the lack of clarity surrounding the relationship between cohabitation and marital outcome, consider a 1987 study by White. The group of married cohabitors in this study was restricted to those who had married the person with whom they had cohabited, excluding individuals who had multiple cohabiting partners before marriage. When this group was compared with married couples who had not cohabited before marriage, the cohabiting couples had longer-lasting marriages than those who had not cohabited. However, this positive effect of cohabitation did not stand up to a more careful analysis. When demographic factors such as age at marriage were taken into account, there was no difference between the two groups (White, 1989).

Given all these confusing findings, what can we conclude about the relationship between cohabitation before marriage and marital outcomes? Actually, a more consistent pattern is just beginning to emerge. In light of White's reanalysis, there is no evidence that cohabitation before marriage has a *positive* association with marital satisfaction or stability. The hope that trial by cohabitation would improve marriage has not been confirmed by experience. What is more difficult to assess is whether cohabitation before marriage is associated with *poorer* marital adjustment. A number of investigators believe that, on balance, there is reasonably strong support for this relationship (Bennett, Blanc, & Bloom, 1988; Trussell & Rao, 1989). But what about those studies that find no difference between married couples who have cohabited and those who have not? And what about gender and racial differences? The higher divorce rate for cohabitors obtained by Newcomb (1986) occurred only among women, and, in another study, the association between cohabiting before marriage and reduced marital satisfaction was far stronger for wives than for husbands (DeMaris & Leslie, 1984). Furthermore, premarital cohabitation has been found to be associated with less marital happiness among black newlywed couples but not among white couples (Crohan & Veroff, 1989). At this point, the safest conclusion we can draw is that while premarital cohabitation does not seem to help, it may or may not hurt.

The question, though, is why would cohabiting with the person one later marries *ever* hurt? Could having a cohabiting relationship create beliefs, attitudes, and behaviors toward the partner that later interfere with establishing a satisfying, enduring marriage? Perhaps, but there is an alternative explanation that emphasizes the personal characteristics of those who cohabit rather than the cohabiting experience itself. Might those who are most likely to cohabit also be those who would be most likely to have trouble maintaining a good marriage? Newcomb (1987) suggests that both of these explanations could account for any tendency for cohabitation to be associated with poorer adjustment in marriage. For example, compared with heterosexual married couples, as well as living-together gay and lesbian couples, heterosexual cohabiting couples appear to be less committed to the relationship (Kurdek & Schmitt, 1986). This lower level of commitment could be produced by the cohabiting experience itself, or it could reflect personal inclinations that existed before the live-in relationship was established. Either way, a lower level of commitment could have a negative effect on a subsequent marriage. Finally, any negative association between cohabitation and marital satisfaction might simply be a matter of time. As will be seen later in this book (Chapter 11), marital satisfaction tends to decline over time. Since cohabitation before marriage starts the relational clock running earlier, those who marry after living together may be at a disadvantage compared with less experienced, more idealistic couples.

BEING SINGLE

During the same period that the age at marriage was rising, that the divorce rate was increasing, and that the number of heterosexual cohabiting couples was expanding, another major demographic shift was taking place in the United States: The proportion of never-married individuals in the population was growing much larger. As you can see from Figure 1.5, 18.9 percent of adult men (age 18 and older) and 13.7 percent of adult women in 1970 had never been married. By the mid-1980s, those proportions had increased to slightly over a quarter of adult men and almost a fifth of adult women. Obviously, this demographic change is related to some of the other changes discussed in this chapter. When young people wait until a later age to marry, the number of never-married individuals in the society becomes larger. Moreover, the increased acceptability of premarital cohabitation probably also contributes to a willingness to delay marriage and, therefore, helps expand the never-married segment of the population.

In fact, however, age at marriage as well as cohabitation is a relatively minor ingredient in the increase of never-married individuals in the United States. The major factor is the post–World War II baby boom. From 1945 to 1957, more babies were born each year than in the immediately preceding year. This created a huge bulge in the demographic pipeline. At every step along the way, the baby-boom generation will be the largest group in the country—as children, young people, middle-

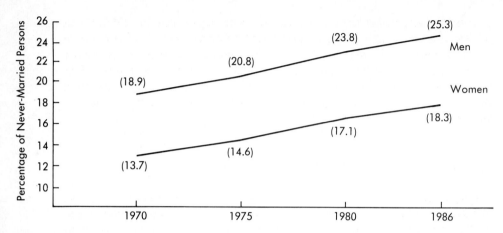

FIGURE 1.5
Never-married persons as a percentage of population. (U.S. Bureau of the Census.)

aged individuals, and the elderly. Thus, the proportion of never-married individuals will be smaller in the 1990s than in the 1980s, simply because all of the baby boomers will be "thirty-something" and "forty-something." By that age, most of them will have married, some will be divorced, and some will have remarried.

But "being single" is not the same as never having married. For example, many divorced and widowed individuals consider themselves, and are regarded by others, as being single. Cohabiting never-married individuals, on the other hand, often view themselves as "partnered" rather than "single." And what about never-married adults living at home with their parents? Although many of them probably would classify themselves as single, cultural awareness of being single seems to have developed only when large numbers of unmarried individuals established their own independent households. One hundred years ago, there were many unmarried people in the United States, but most of them lived with other family members and so were less likely to be perceived as part of a distinct social category. Among all those who might now be included in this social category, single parents may regard this classification with the most ambivalence. They are single in terms of being unmarried, but as they struggle to raise their children and survive financially, they must have a hard time identifying with all those media images of the free-spending, self-indulgent, "swinging singles" life.

Given these considerations, being single is probably best defined as a way of life and a state of mind. By this definition, the single person is unattached and independent. Singles are not committed to a long-term partnership with another adult, and they do not depend primarily on others for their financial security. These are the basic characteristics of being single. Other features may be typical, such as living alone and being employed, but they are not necessary. It is also possible that a person could self-identify as single in some aspects of life and not in others. The single parent on a date, for instance, probably feels much like any other single person. At home, however, awareness of his or her many responsibilities as a parent may make the term "single" seem less than fully appropriate. Being single, then, is more psychological than demographic; it is based on the way people lead their lives and see themselves.

The Problems and Rewards of Being Single

What is it like to be a single person? In general, it is probably neither so good nor so bad as our cultural myths would suggest. When Cargan and Melko (1982) compared some of the myths with some of the facts, they found that some agree while others do not. Their comparison is summarized in Table 1.2. Researchers have also examined the single life in terms of gender. And, similar to the mixed results of research on gender and divorce, investigators have drawn different conclusions about gender and being single. Some have concluded that being single is more difficult for women (Simenquer & Carroll, 1982), and others that it is more difficult for men (Knupfer et al., 1966). As was suggested in the previous discussion of divorce, the type of hardship involved may be the crucial factor in determining gender differences in the quality of life as a single person.

TABLE 1.2 THE SINGLE LIFE: MYTH VERSUS FACT

Myth	Fact
Singles (especially men) are tied to their mothers' apron strings.	No evidence for this.
Singles are selfish.	Like other people: some are, some aren't.
Singles are rich.	On the average, married people have more money.
Singles are happier.	On the average, married people are happier. Singles have more symptoms of stress (anxiety, depression) than married people.
Singles have more free time.	True.
Singles have more fun.	True.
Singles have a swinging sex life.	Depends on how you define it. Married people have more frequent sex. Singles have more variety.
Single people are lonely.	True, especially divorced singles.

SOURCE: Adapted from Cargan & Melko, 1982.

First, let us consider single women. Just as divorced women are more likely to suffer economic hardship, so are other single women. While there are, of course, some very rich single women and some very poor single men, on the average women make less money than men: 69 cents on the dollar. On average, then, single women are more likely to face financial hardships than are single men.

Single women may also suffer more from cultural stereotypes. Though positive attitudes toward both not marrying and being divorced increased dramatically from the mid-1950s through the mid-1970s (Thornton, 1989; Veroff et al., 1981), married people are still regarded, more favorably than those who are not married (Ganong, Coleman, & Mapes, 1990). And, at least in some circumstances, single women may be viewed more negatively than single men. After all, "old maid" is a far harsher term than "bachelor." In addition, single women's own beliefs may be a source of distress. Though the difference may be declining, there is a general tendency for women to value and desire marriage more than men (Thornton & Freedman, 1982). Thus, women who never marry or those who divorce may be more likely than their male counterparts to view themselves as having failed in a major life task.

It is also the case that single women who want to marry may have fewer opportunities than single men to do so. As will be described later in this book (see Chapter 6), women of the baby-boom generation were caught in a "marriage squeeze," where there were more marriage-eligible women than men. Among some young people today, the squeeze is on the other foot, with an excess of marriage-eligible white men compared with white women. However, young black women who wish to marry a black man continue to face a shortage of potential marriage partners: The mortality rate among black men is the highest of any group in the United States. In addition, black men more often marry white women than black women marry white men (Staples, 1981). Regardless of race, women over 40 are at a disadvantage should they wish to marry or remarry. Although the age difference between young people getting married for the first time is relatively small (on average, the man is about two or three years older than the woman), older men who marry or remarry prefer younger women—marrying partners who are, on average, some five to eight years younger. Moreover, the average life expectancy of men is shorter than that of women. Thus, as a woman ages, the number of unmarried men of her age or older grows smaller and smaller. To be sure, there are plenty of unmarried *younger* men, but the number of couples in which the woman is both over 40 and older than the man remains small.

Overall, then, single men would seem to have an easier time of it in terms of their economic situation, the way they are perceived by others, their own evaluation of themselves, and (at least for some) their marriage possibilities should they wish to marry or remarry. But never-married heterosexual men may be subject to the same feelings of emotional deprivation that divorced men and widowers often experience. The tendency for heterosexual men to establish close, confiding relationships only with their female partners may account, at least in part, for the consistent finding that never-married men are less happy and less well adjusted than never-married women (Knupfer et al., 1966; Macklin, 1980; Srole, Langner, Michael, Kirkpatrick, Opler, & Rennie, 1978; Veroff et al., 1981; but see Kessler & McRae, 1984, for a different conclusion). However, this difference between never-married men and never-married women appears to be declining. In the national surveys mentioned earlier in this chapter, the percentage of never-married women in the 1970s who described themselves as "very happy" exceeded that of never-married men who described themselves this way by 8.6 percentage points (Glenn & Weaver, 1988). But by the 1980s, this difference had narrowed to just 2.4 percentage points. These findings suggest that despite the different issues and problems they may face, never-married men and never-married women have, increasingly, a lot in common.

Presumably, some of these commonalities can be found among the larger group of singles as well. For example, friends are extremely

TABLE 1.3 THE TEN PILLARS OF HAPPINESS

Rank	Single Men	Single Women	Married Men	Married Women
1.	Friends and social life	Friends and social life	Personal growth	Being in love
2.	Job or primary activity	Being in love	Being in love	Marriage
3.	Being in love	Job or primary activity	Marriage	Partner's happiness
4.	Recognition; success	Recognition; success	Job or primary activity	Sex life
5.	Sex life	Personal growth	Partner's happiness	Recognition; success
6.	Personal growth	Sex life	Sex life	Personal growth
7.	Finances	Health	Recognition; success	Job or primary activity
8.	House or apartment	Body and attractiveness	Friends and social life	Friends and social life
9.	Body and attractiveness	Finances	Being a parent	Health
10.	Health	House or apartment	Finances	Being a parent

SOURCE: Freedman, 1978.

important to all those who are single. Indeed, when Freedman (1978) examined what makes people happy, he found that the item "friends and social life" was the single most important determinant of happiness among singles—both males and females (see Table 1.3). In contrast, having good friends and an active social life was a relatively poor predictor of the happiness of married individuals. For both groups, their happiness was closely bound up with their intimate relationships. Only among singles, however, was friendship more important than being in love.

PAST AND PRESENT: AN OVERVIEW

In many respects, this chapter has recited a litany of changes that have occurred in American society since the 1960s: Age at marriage has risen, the relationship between marriage and happiness appears to have weakened, more women are employed outside the home, stepfamilies are more common, the divorce rate has increased, cohabitation has become widespread, and being single has become a generally recognized social category. Not all of these changes have followed exactly the same time course. For example, the divorce rate, which accelerated sharply in the 1970s, leveled off in the 1980s. However, women's participation in the labor force, especially among mothers with young children, continued to increase throughout the 1980s. Nevertheless, the overall pattern that emerges is of enormous societal change that is gradually beginning to slow down.

According to Thornton (1989), a similar pattern emerges in respect to societal attitudes related to these various behavioral changes. Beginning in the 1960s, attitudes about the appropriate roles for men and women became more egalitarian; attitudes toward divorce, childlessness, remaining single, and cohabitation became more accepting; and sexual attitudes became more permissive. Again, there were some differences in timing. Although most of these attitudes experienced the most change up to the mid-1970s and have remained relatively stable ever since, acceptance of cohabitation continued to increase during the 1980s, while there is some evidence that young people's attitudes toward extramarital sex became *less* permissive in the 1980s. Despite some variations, however, the pattern of attitudinal changes closely resembles the pattern of behavioral changes: earlier dramatic shifts are now slowing down.

In examining the changes that have taken place, Thornton makes a crucial distinction. Although Americans have become far more tolerant than they used to be about getting a divorce, not marrying, and not having children, they have not rejected marrying and having children.

As Thornton notes:

> The data clearly suggest that the vast majority of Americans still value marriage, parenthood, and family life. Most Americans still plan to marry and to have children, and optimism for achieving success in marriage remains high. . . . What has changed in these areas of family life has been an increased tolerance for behavior not previously accepted, but not an increase in active embracement of such behavior. (p. 891)

Thornton characterizes the fundamental dynamic involved in these changes as "the relaxation of the social prescriptions for family behavior and an expansion of the range of individual choice" (p. 887). As cited earlier in this chapter, Glenn and Weaver (1988) expressed a similar idea, calling American society "increasingly individualistic and hedonistic" (p. 323). This shift in emphasis from socially defined roles to personally defined goals has been repeatedly observed by social scientists surveying recent American social history (Bellah, Madsen, Sullivan, Swindler, & Tipton, 1985; Veroff et al., 1981).

The evidence for the general pattern seems beyond dispute. But what factors contributed to that shift? One could argue, for example, that many of the changes in American society since the 1960s are inevitable products of our level of socioeconomic development. After all, there is a general trend for more singles, more divorce, and later age at marriage among more industrialized and more affluent countries (South, 1988). Similarly, the percentage of the population living in urban areas is a strong predictor of the divorce rate (Breault & Kposowa, 1987). From this perspective, the changes that have occurred are not specific to the United States but can be expected in any highly developed country.

On the other hand, a quick look back at the divorce statistics reviewed earlier in this chapter indicates that there are some important differences among highly developed countries. The U.S. divorce rate is higher than those in European countries and much higher than Japan's. Perhaps, then, recent changes toward greater freedom and tolerance in our intimate relationships require a strong base of individualism to build on. The Western countries, on the whole, are often said to emphasize individual liberty more than non-Western countries. And America has long been regarded as the most individualistic of nations (Tocqueville, 1840; Triandis, McCusker, & Hui, 1990). It is also hard to imagine that the baby boom itself didn't play an important role. Can it be entirely accidental that most of the behavioral and attitudinal changes we have been considering began in the 1960s when the first cohort of the baby-boom generation reached college age and subsided in the 1980s when the last cohort was in its twenties? Taken together, these three factors (socioeconomic development, a strong tradition of individualism, and a large proportion of young people in the population) may not fully account for all the recent changes in marriage, divorce, cohabitation, and being single—but they certainly seem the most obvious possibilities.

Regardless of how it all got started, the most personally relevant question concerns where it is going to end. Have these major societal changes involving intimate relationships leveled out and reached a plateau? Or is this just some kind of a pause before even more "individualistic and hedonistic" behaviors and attitudes develop? Or have we reached some kind of limit, and the changes that occur in the immediate future will be in the direction of a greater sense of community and solidarity with others? No one knows. But as you read this book, you should keep these alternatives in mind. As you learn more about intimate relationships, you will want to consider what the future may hold—for you and the ones you love.

CHAPTER SUMMARY

Defining Intimate Relationships

This book focuses on adult friendships and romantic relationships. An intimate relationship is defined as including at least one of the following three characteristics: behavioral interdependence (the mutual impact that partners have on each other), need fulfillment (such as intimacy, nurturance, reassurance), and emotional attachment. Intimate relationships vary in terms of intensity, commitment, emotion, sexuality, and gender.

Marriage

It is estimated that some 90 percent of today's young people will eventually marry and that 80 percent of divorced individuals will remarry. Since the late 1950s, the age at marriage has steadily increased. Increasingly, both men and women are committed to both career and family. Stepfamilies now make up a significant proportion of married-couple households in the United States.

Marriage and Happiness. Overall, married people are happier than those who have never married, who are separated or divorced, or who are widowed. The association between marriage and happiness may, however, be small in magnitude. Previous research on gender differences in benefiting from marriage indicated that men benefit more than do women. But recently it has been proposed that the difference between married and unmarried individuals is greater for women than for men on measures of *both* positive well-being and emotional distress. Moreover, the difference in happiness between married and never-married people declined over the period from 1972 to 1986, as the happiness of married women declined and the happiness of never-married men increased.

Divorce

The divorce rate in the United States increased sharply from the late 1960s to the early 1980s and has remained relatively stable since then. It is estimated that 50 percent of today's first marriages will end in divorce and up to 60 percent of today's second marriages. Younger people are more likely to divorce than older people, and divorce is more common early in marriage. In former times, divorce was relatively rare; marriages were more often ended by the early death of one of the spouses or by desertion.

Divorce and Stress. Divorce is associated with higher rates of psychiatric disorder and mortality from a variety of causes. The results of research on possible gender differences in experiencing stress after a divorce are inconsistent. It is clear, however, that divorced (and widowed) women are more likely than divorced (and widowed) men to suffer financial hardship. On the other hand, men who lose a marital partner may suffer more from social isolation and emotional deprivation than women. In any case, remarried men are more satisfied than remarried women, although marital satisfaction is generally higher in first marriages than in remarriages.

Why Has the Divorce Rate Increased? There are a number of possible reasons why the divorce rate has increased so dramatically in the United States over the past 25 years. First, women's increased participation in the labor force would seem to make divorce more economically feasible for women and economically easier for men. Recent research, however, indicates that the risk of divorce is greatest for low-income wives working 35 or more hours a week—suggesting that the effects of paid employment upon divorce may be more stress-related than a matter of financial independence. Second, people's expectations about the benefits of marriage may be so high that few marriages can meet them. Third, some of the consequences of an increased divorce rate may continue to keep this rate at a high level: Current divorce laws make it easier to obtain a divorce, attitudes toward divorce are more tolerant, and the children of divorce are more likely to get divorced.

Cohabitation

Among heterosexual couples, cohabitation (living together without being legally married) has increased at a rapid rate. People choose cohabitation for various reasons: convenience as well as emotional attachment. Many college couples engage in "quasi-cohabitation"—maintaining a separate residence but spending free time and nights together.

Cohabitation and Marital Outcomes. It was once thought that co-habitation might serve as a trial marriage, filtering out incompatible couples and producing longer-lasting marriages. This does not seem to be the case. Many younger couples choose cohabitation for more imme-diate benefits rather than for a test of the quality of their relationship. Divorced individuals may choose cohabitation because they are reluc-tant to marry again. Research on the relationship between cohabitation and subsequent marital outcomes has obtained mixed findings. Overall, however, there is no evidence that premarital cohabitation is associated with longer-lasting or more satisfying marriages. And there is some evidence that premarital cohabitation is associated with reduced marital satisfaction and with a higher divorce rate. This association appears to be stronger for females than for males and may be stronger among black newlyweds than among white newlyweds. But some studies have found no difference between married couples who cohabited before marriage and those who did not. If premarital cohabitation is associated with poorer marital outcomes, at least for some couples, the explanation could involve the effects of the cohabiting experience itself, personal characteristics of those who choose to cohabit, and/or the negative association between the length of a relationship and satisfaction with it. For whatever reason, it does appear that cohabiting heterosexual cou-ples are less committed to the relationship than are married heterosexual couples or living-together homosexual couples.

Being Single

During the post–World War II baby boom (1945–1957), more babies were born each year than in the immediately preceding year. This created a huge bulge in the demographic pipeline and resulted in a large number of young, never-married people from the 1960s through the mid-1980s. The number of young, never-married people will be smaller in the 1990s. But being single is not simply a matter of being young and never married. For example, divorced and widowed individuals can be consid-ered as singles. Being single is probably best defined as a way of life and state of mind: not committed to a long-term partnership with another adult and not primarily dependent on others for financial security. It is possible that a person could self-identify as single in some aspects of life and not in others.

The Problems and Rewards of Being Single. Men and women may encounter different kinds of problems in being single. Single women are more likely to encounter financial hardships than are single men. They may also suffer more from negative stereotypes about unmarried women and from their own views of the importance and value of marriage. In addition, some single women who wish to marry (or remarry) face a shortage of eligible men: women of the baby-boom generation, black women who wish to marry a black man, and women over 40 who wish to marry an older man. Among young whites, however, unmarried men face a shortage of unmarried women. Moreover, like divorced and widowed men, never-married men may suffer social isolation and emotional deprivation. In most earlier studies, never-married men were found to be less happy and less well adjusted than never-married women. Recently, however, the difference between never-married men and never-married women has narrowed. Whatever the problems they experience, single men and women value their friends. Among singles, the quality of their friends and social life is a stronger predictor of happiness than whether or not they are in love.

Past and Present: An Overview

In terms of both behaviors and attitudes, American society underwent dramatic changes between the 1960s and the 1980s. Though some of these changes continue, most have subsided. The basic theme that emerges from these changes is a shift in emphasis from socially defined roles to personally defined goals. Factors that may have contributed to this shift include a high level of socioeconomic development, the traditional emphasis in the United States on individualism, and the large proportion of young people during these years as a result of the baby boom.

2

Research Methods

❖

Students often dread chapters on research methods, regarding them as an ordeal to be endured before getting to "the good stuff." Most readers of this book, for instance, are probably interested in topics like love, sex, and jealousy—and do not have any great, burning desire to understand research designs, procedures, and measures. All too often, chapters on research methods seem irrelevant to what students really want to know.

But the method of inquiry is not irrelevant to those who seek answers to important questions. Consider, for example, the famous fictional detective Sherlock Holmes. As his friend and colleague Dr. Watson was to discover over and over again, Holmes' methods were the heart of his success. When Holmes entered a case, he was confronted with a large number of "facts": what people said to him, what the scene of the crime looked like, what he could find out about the history of the people involved. As a detective, his task was to sift through all these facts in order to come up with the solution to the mystery. He had to ignore some facts that Dr. Watson thought were very important. He had to focus on some facts that Dr. Watson thought should be ignored. And he had to ask some questions ("Why *didn't* the dog bark?") that Dr. Watson thought were silly. What guided Holmes in his detective work was his method of investigation, and by sticking to his method, he was able to tell the difference between misleading clues and solid evidence.

Scientific research is, in many ways, just like detective work. Like detectives, scientists have to sift among clues and figure out which ones are useful and which ones are red herrings. Like Sherlock Holmes, scientists too rely primarily on certain methods of inquiry to help them solve a mystery.

It is, therefore, impossible to separate what we know from how we know it. For the detective, not all clues are equal. For the scientist, not all facts have the same weight. How do we tell the difference? The answer to this question lies in applying a systematic set of methodological principles to gather evidence and to evaluate it. Researchers who study intimate relationships have applied these principles in order to obtain information on the topics discussed in this book. As you read this book, you should apply these principles in order to evaluate the "facts" before you. This chapter provides an overview of research methods that will be useful to you in your investigation. It is by no means a complete review of research methods in the social sciences. For more detailed examinations, there are a number of excellent sources (Aronson, Brewer, & Carlsmith, 1985; Cook & Campbell, 1979; Jones, 1985; Kazdin, 1980). Comprehensive reviews of methodological issues in the study of intimate relationships are also available (Harvey, Christensen, & McClintock, 1983; McCarthy, 1981) as well as a review of new research and procedures (Clark & Reis, 1988). Even though only basic principles are described here, becoming familiar with them will help you do your own detective work: deciding what evidence seems compelling and what seems less so. You will also be equipped to go beyond this book and explore additional research on those topics of particular interest to you. And you will have made an important advance toward the possibility of conducting your own research on intimate relationships.

FINDING A QUESTION

The first step in any scientific endeavor is to ask a question, and this step is both the easiest and the hardest one for any scientist. It is easy to ask a question because there are many sources of possible questions. Social scientists, for instance, take many of their questions directly from their observations of themselves and of other people. It is probably not at all accidental that as the divorce rate has increased among social scientists, there has been an increasing amount of social science research on divorce. Questions can also come from previous research: Research that tries to answer one question may create a whole set of new questions. In addition, questions come from theories. If a theory says that certain things should happen under certain conditions, the scientist will want to see if the theory is right in its predictions. Typically, in research on intimate relationships, all three sources of questions will be involved.

Social scientists will put together their personal observations, their knowledge of previous research, and their theoretical perspectives to come up with a question.

So to ask a question is easy. Indeed, it is hard to imagine that there is anyone who hasn't had at least some questions about intimate relationships. Asking a *good* question, however, is more difficult. A good question is both interesting and precise; it puts things in a new light—opens up possibilities we had not thought of before—and does it in such a clear way that we have a chance of coming up with the answer. Sherlock Holmes' question about why the dog did *not* bark was a good question. The question was clear, it was possible to answer it, and nobody else had thought of it.

In general, there are two major types of questions that researchers ask. First, researchers can want to describe some event or series of events as they naturally occur. We may, for instance, be curious about how married couples talk together when they disagree on an issue. In this case, our goal will be to describe this process as fully and accurately as we can. Second, researchers can focus on causal connections between events. We may want to know which factors will help a couple resolve a disagreement and which ones will cause the disagreement to get worse.

Descriptive research is more open and more exploratory than causal research. In order to do descriptive research, we try to have as few preconceived ideas as possible. In order to investigate a cause-effect sequence, we must start out with some idea about what this sequence is. In descriptive research, we want to let the reality speak to us. In causal research, we want to test our ideas about reality. These differences between descriptive and causal research are important, but they can be—and often are—exaggerated. On the one hand, it is not possible to do research without some ideas about what you are studying; no one can look at everything or everyone. By selecting what we will examine, we automatically impose our ideas on reality. On the other hand, investigators seeking to understand a causal connection often run across a piece of stubborn reality that they did not expect, does not fit into their theoretical framework, and, for the moment, can only be described. Thus, most social science research contains at least a hint of both types of questions, though one type may receive greater emphasis than the other. Indeed, most of the issues that we will consider in this book should be examined in both ways: trying to get a picture of what naturally occurs *and* trying to see if our ideas about causal factors are correct.

FINDING SUBJECTS

Research on intimate relationships studies the behavior and feelings of people who are currently in relationships, have been in relationships in the past, and/or want to be in relationships in the future. We can work with separate individuals, or we can conduct research with both partners. We can study specific types of relationships (e.g., cohabitation versus marriage), or we may want to examine differences between people who are happy in their relationships and those who are not. But whatever aspect of relationships we study, we need people to participate as *subjects* in our research.

Most research on intimate relationships has obtained subjects in one of two ways. The first approach involves the use of a *convenience sample*. Here, subjects are obtained in whatever way is convenient for the researcher. For example, university professors who study intimate relationships frequently work with college students, whereas clinical psychologists may study distressed couples who come into their clinics. Sometimes, researchers advertise through the mass media or local community organizations, asking for volunteers to participate in their research. Although some specific characteristics may be required of subjects (e.g., dating partners who have not known each other more than a year), researchers who use convenience samples typically do not concern themselves with their subjects' demographic characteristics (socioeconomic class, age, place of birth, etc.).

In contrast, demographic characteristics are crucial for researchers who use a *representative sample*. These researchers want to make sure that the subjects they study are representative of the entire population of people who are relevant to the research question. For example, if we want to know something about marriage, we would need, in theory, a sample that is representative of all married people—all ages, all nationalities, all socioeconomic backgrounds. No such study has ever been conducted, and probably never will be. However, some studies have been able to obtain samples that are representative of the adult population of individual countries.

There is no question that if we want to find general principles that apply to a large population, we are better off working with a representative sample than a convenience sample (Sears, 1986). With a convenience sample, there is always the danger that whatever results we obtain only apply to people who have the same characteristics as our subjects—only to students at a certain university, clients in a certain clinic, volunteers from a certain area of the country, etc. The problem with representative samples, however, is that they are difficult—and expensive—to obtain; many researchers have neither the money nor the personnel to contact people dispersed across a large geographical area. Morever, researchers are typically limited in the kind of research they can conduct with subjects in a representative sample. If a group of researchers decides to share the expenses of obtaining a representative sample, the researchers will also have to share their subjects' time. Each researcher may, therefore, end up with only a very brief period in which to conduct his or her research.

Thus, in finding subjects, researchers usually face a difficult choice.

In a representative sample, subjects reflect the basic demographic characteristics (gender, age, race, etc.) of the entire population of people that the researchers wish to study. (Jean-Claude LeJeune/Stock, Boston)

They can work with convenience samples, getting more detailed information that may or may not apply to the larger population of interest. Or they can go to the trouble and expense of obtaining a representative sample but find themselves restricted to limited information from each subject. Each choice has both a clear advantage and a clear disadvantage. Our job, when we evaluate research using either type of subject sample, is to be aware that each is, by itself, imperfect.

Indeed, for most aspects of social science research, there are no perfect, problem-free choices available, and our understanding has to depend on a cumulative, gradual building up of knowledge. The best hope for a glimpse of truth, of the underlying reality, comes through the work of many investigators studying the same topic in different ways (Houts, Cook, & Shadish, 1986). Each single study—each single picture of the reality we want to understand—is always imperfect, but if we have a series of pictures, each taken from a different angle, we may gradually begin to see what is really there.

FINDING A DESIGN

Once we have a question that we want to research and have some idea about how we are going to obtain subjects, we can consider the type of design that will best allow us to answer our question. This section describes several types of designs commonly used in research on intimate relationships.

Correlational Designs

A correlation allows us to answer the question: Do X and Y go together? Correlations can range between $+1.00$ and -1.00. If X and Y are perfectly *positively* correlated (as X goes up, so does Y; as X goes down, so does Y), we will obtain a correlation of $+1.00$. If X and Y are perfectly *negatively* correlated (as X goes up, Y goes down; as X goes down, Y goes up), we will obtain a correlation of -1.00. When X and Y have no relationship at all, we will obtain a correlation of 0. Examples of correlational patterns are provided in Figure 2.1.

We can ask an enormous number of specific questions based on this general question about whether things go together. For example, we can ask whether feelings about fairness in the relationship (see Chapter 7) go together with feelings of relationship satisfaction: Do people who feel fairly treated in their relationship also feel satisfied? We can also ask about whether the feelings and characteristics of one partner are correlated with the feelings and characteristics of the other partner. For example, Chapter 9 looks at the issue of whether heterosexual men who are high in the need for power have female dating partners who are dissatisfied with the relationship. In the first example we look at how things go together within an individual, in the second at how things go together across individuals.

Correlational designs are the most commonly used designs in research on relationships. Unfortunately, however, results based on correlational studies are frequently misinterpreted. Correlations tell us about an association that exists between two things; correlations do *not* tell us about the causal connections between these two things. In fact, many different causal connections are possible when we have a correlation:

- X may cause Y—in the example of fairness and satisfaction, it could be that when we feel fairly treated, this causes a certain level of satisfaction, *or*

- Y may cause X—it could be that a certain level of satisfaction with a relationship causes us to feel fairly treated, *or*

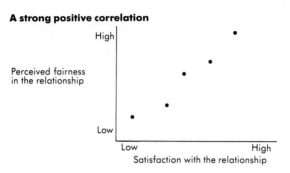

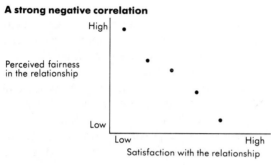

FIGURE 2.1
Correlational patterns.

- Some third factor could cause both X and Y—perhaps being in a particularly good mood influences feelings of both fair treatment and relationship satisfaction.

Thus, if we have only a simple correlation, we have only a statement about an association, and we cannot know what causal connections are involved.

Sometimes, however, we have more than a simple correlation. A number of complicated and sophisticated statistical analyses have been developed (e.g., partial correlations, multiple regression, path analysis) that help rule out various possible alternative causal connections among correlational findings. The details of these procedures go considerably beyond the level of this book, and the interested reader should consult an advanced statistics text (Dwyer, 1983; Pedhazur, 1982). For present purposes, the important point is that these procedures enable us to get closer and closer to making a causal statement based on correlational data. Although we should be very careful not to turn a simple correlation into a causal connection, we should also realize that, using the appropriate statistical techniques, it is possible to make some reasonable statements about causation within a correlational design.

Experimental Designs

In the best of all possible worlds, we would prefer to investigate ideas about causation within an experimental design. Experiments are ideally suited to making causal statements because in an experiment we (as experimenters) control one of the variables in the study. Thus, instead of asking "Do X and Y go together?" we ask "If we change X, what will happen to Y?" In other words, we manipulate the *independent variable* and see what effect, if any, this has on the *dependent variable*.

To illustrate the difference between an experiment and a correlation, consider the following two variables: (1) similarity in attitudes and beliefs and (2) liking someone. Our idea is that people who are similar to each other in attitudes and beliefs will tend to like each other (see Chapter 3). If we wanted to test this notion in a correlational design, we might ask couples about their attitudes and about how much they like each other. We would expect, if our idea were correct, that the more similar couples would like each other more—a positive correlation. But we do not know from this result if similarity has led to liking. It could be that liking someone leads to sharing his or her attitudes and opinions. Alternatively, some third factor, such as spending a lot of time together, may lead to both liking and attitude similarity.

With an experiment, however, we can make a much clearer test of our causal idea, our causal *hypothesis*. We could, for instance, have subjects come into the laboratory, where we would describe to them another individual whom they will meet later in the experiment. In this description, we would tell some of our subjects that the person they will meet shares many of their attitudes. Other subjects would be told that the person has attitudes very different from theirs. With this one exception, the descriptions would be the same. We would then ask subjects to tell us, based only on the information we have given them, how much they believe they will like the person they expect to meet. If we found that subjects who expected to meet another person who shared their attitudes liked this person more than subjects who expected to meet someone who did not share their attitudes, our hypothesis would be confirmed. The beauty of this kind of experimental logic is that the subjects in both groups have identical experiences *except* for the information they receive about the similarity or dissimilarity of attitudes. Thus, we have a true test of whether an individual's perception that he or she shares similar attitudes with another person will increase liking for that person.

Given the clarity with which experiments allow us to test our causal ideas, it may seem strange that anyone would ever use anything other than an experimental design. Unfortunately, the same factor that defines an experiment also limits its use: the manipulation of the independent variable. Researchers can control the information that subjects receive in the laboratory about people they have never met, but they cannot manipulate many of the truly important factors in intimate relationships. We cannot create love in the laboratory. We don't know how to do it. We probably could create jealousy between partners participating in laboratory research, but it would be unethical to do so. For the most part, laboratory experiments are limited to examining relatively emotionless interactions between strangers. Yet, in the study of relationships, we often want to understand intense encounters between intimates.

Comparing correlational and experimental designs, we can see that each has an advantage that the other lacks. With a correlational design, we can study events in the real world—commitment to a relationship, feelings of love and jealousy, degree of sexual involvement—and see what goes together. But correlational designs are limited in what they can tell us about the causal relationship between events. With an experimental design, we can test our ideas about causal connections, but we are extremely limited in the types of events we can study. Just as in our choice of subject samples, we have no perfect solution, and, again, this makes it crucial that we study the same topic in different ways, from different perspectives.

Developmental Designs

In developmental designs, we try to study the effects of time or a sequence of events over time. We may want to know, for example, if people's feelings of loneliness differ at different ages (see Chapter 12). There are three major types of developmental designs.

Cross-sectional designs. The most common type of design used to study questions of how things change or develop over time is called a *cross-sectional design*. To conduct a cross-sectional study on the relationship between loneliness and age, we would survey people of different ages, ask them about their feelings of loneliness, and examine the association we obtained between age and such feelings.

Cross-sectional designs are, then, correlational designs, and we want to think very carefully about what kind of causal connection might

In a cross-sectional design, researchers examine the responses from subjects of different age groups. For example, to see if musical preferences differ according to age, we could ask 20-year-olds and 60-year-olds to evaluate various entertainers. (*left*, Mark Anderson/ Camera Press-Globe Photos; *right*, Jeff Albertson/Stock, Boston)

be involved in any results we obtain from a cross-sectional study. At first it may seem that we have fewer problems here than with other kinds of correlations. After all, feelings of loneliness cannot change our chronological age. It is also hard to think of a third factor that could affect both aging and feelings of loneliness. It would appear, therefore, that aging itself must cause any changes in loneliness that we observe.

What you have just read is an example of the kind of logical trap into which many students and many researchers have fallen. To see this trap, and be able to avoid it, think of what could happen if we set out to study the relationship between musical preferences and age. Suppose we find that older people prefer mood music and crooners, while younger people like rock'n'roll and rock stars. Have we discovered that aging changes people's tastes in music? If you like Janet Jackson today, will you come to love Frank Sinatra as you grow older? Maybe, but maybe not. What we may have discovered in this correlation between age and musical taste is that people had different experiences with music depending on when they grew up. The difference in musical taste between a 60-year-old and a 20-year-old today may not be due to their different ages, but, instead, to the fact that Sinatra was the the rage when the 60-year-old was 20. Perhaps, then, the fact that older people prefer different music than do younger people actually indicates that musical taste remains constant over age: What we like in our youth determines what we will like when we are older.

Thus, cross-sectional designs are vulnerable to a specific kind of third variable effect: the social, cultural, and political events a person has lived through. Whenever we find a correlation between age and anything, we must question whether it is really age that is involved or a difference in what different age groups have experienced.

Longitudinal designs. Since we can never be sure with cross-sectional designs whether we are studying age or history, we might want to conduct a study in which people's history is the same but their age changes. The only way to do this would be to select a group of people, all of the same age, and follow them as they grow older. So, for instance, we might start with a group of people all of whom are 20 years old today and follow them over the next 40 years to see whether their musical tastes change as they age. If these people liked Janet Jackson at 20, but preferred Sinatra at 60, this would demonstrate that their tastes actually did change and would suggest that age was the cause of it.

Unfortunately, even with a *longitudinal design,* we have only a "suggestion," not "proof." We could argue that growing up with Janet Jackson makes one especially susceptible to Frank Sinatra in old age! Or, maybe, just when the group we are studying reaches 60, there's a great Sinatra revival and everyone—young and old—gets caught up in it. Even though we tried to control for historical effects by making sure that all our subjects had the same general historical experiences, we may still end up studying history rather than age.

If we are extremely persistent in our efforts to rule out historical factors, we can combine longitudinal and cross-sectional designs. We could start out with people who are 20 today and another group of people who are 40 today, and follow both groups until they reach 60. If, at age 60, members of both groups showed a distinct preference for Sinatra, then we might really begin to believe that—regardless of historical experiences—older people like crooners.

Sherlock Holmes, however, would still not be satisfied. He might remind us that while this combination design sounds wonderful in theory, there are lots of practical problems with it. The biggest practical problem is simply the time it takes to study people over time. The researcher must be willing to wait many years before the results are in. The subjects must be willing to stay in the study over its entire duration. Although it is possible to find patient researchers, keeping subjects committed to the research is much harder.

In fact, every longitudinal study suffers from what is called *subject attrition*—loss of subjects over time. Subjects move away and cannot be located; subjects get bored and just don't want to participate in the study anymore. And the longer the study goes on, the greater the problem becomes. With many longitudinal studies, we end up with a small and very select group of people who have stayed with the study. Indeed, we have to wonder if these people are at all representative of their age group. Perhaps in a longitudinal study of intimate relationships, the subjects who stay with the study have some particular interest in, or even some particular problems with, intimate relationships. If so, whatever results we obtain may only apply to people who have this particular interest or problem.

Retrospective designs. Given the difficulties of maintaining contact with subjects over the course of a longitudinal study, maybe we should go backward rather than forward. Why don't we just ask people about their past experiences rather than trying to follow them through the future? We can, of course, do this, and, in fact, many studies of intimate relationships use this kind of *retrospective design*. Sometimes long periods of time are involved ("What was it like when you were dating before you got married?"); sometimes very short periods are examined ("What kinds of interactions did you have with your spouse over the last 24 hours?").

Retrospective designs seem marvelously flexible. If we are worried about historical influences, we can ask people of different ages to retrospect to a common, younger age—and see if there are similar developmental patterns regardless of present age. Indeed, if we all had perfect recall, retrospective designs would be the perfect solution to all our problems. Unfortunately, of course, none of us has perfect recall. As we will see later in this chapter, there are many difficulties with asking people about their lives. These difficulties increase dramatically if we ask people about events that took place long ago. Whenever we rely on retrospective reports, we cannot know whether we are getting a clear picture of the past or a picture from the present imposed on the past.

This review of developmental designs forces us, then, back to the same conclusion we reached before. Each type of design is, in itself, imperfect, but each type can also contribute important information—a critical angle—on our research question. The angle on time provided by developmental designs is particularly crucial in research on intimate relationships. Our significant relationships with others are frequently long-term events, and if we want to understand relationships, we must attempt to understand their development through time.

FINDING A SETTING

Equipped with our research question, subjects, and a design, we have still to find a setting in which to conduct our investigation. Usually, the major choice in finding a setting is between conducting the research in the laboratory and conducting it in a natural, everyday environment, such as a couple's home. As always, each choice has advantages and disadvantages. Staying in the lab offers the advantage of greater control over extraneous, irrelevant factors. The researcher can guarantee the privacy of his or her subjects, control the exact experiences they will have, and arrange the physical environment itself to fit the particular purposes of the research. Going to the couple's home offers the advantage of obtaining more typical behavior, as subjects will usually feel more comfortable and relaxed in their own home.

The disadvantages of these two settings are mirror images of their advantages. The laboratory may elicit artificial behavior that tells us little about what people really do. On the other hand, so much may be going on in people's homes that factors quite irrelevant to the research question may heavily influence what subjects say and do. It seems clear that subjects do behave differently depending on whether research is conducted in the lab or in their home, and we need to be sensitive to the possible impact of the setting we have chosen on the results we obtain (Gottman, 1979; O'Rourke, 1963).

Another choice of setting that must be made does not involve the actual physical place where the research takes place, but the type of approach the researcher takes to collecting data. In essence, this choice is between a naturalistic (or unstructured) approach and a controlled (or structured) approach. Usually, research that takes place in the laboratory will be more structured than research that takes place in the home, but this is not necessarily the case (Harvey et al., 1983). It is possible to be unstructured in the lab (e.g., letting couples talk about whatever they want) as well as structured in the home (telling subjects exactly what we want them to do).

The advantages and disadvantages of these two approaches are quite similar to those of the two physical settings described previously. A structured approach gives the researcher more control over irrelevant factors but is necessarily more artificial. An unstructured approach provides more realistic, more typical behavior but runs the risk of being influenced by irrelevant factors. Although the exact amount of structure varies widely in research on intimate relationships, most of this research requires at least some structure. If, for example, we were interested in studying jealousy (see Chapter 10), just waiting around for subjects to talk about jealousy or to get jealous on their own would not be a very good way to proceed. It might never happen!

A final choice of setting is relevant only for researchers who are taking a fairly structured approach. Within such an approach, the investigator has to decide whether to study "real" or "as if" behavior. If our researcher interested in jealousy wanted to study "real" jealous behavior, it would be necessary to arrange the situation such that subjects actually did get jealous. As noted earlier, there are obvious ethical problems with this kind of experimental manipulation. For example, if subjects were induced to feel jealous about their partner's supposed interest in another person, this experience might affect their jealous feelings in real life once the experiment was over.

Some real behavior is, therefore, very difficult to study. It may be fairly rare, so if we wait around for it to happen, we may never see it. It may be unpleasant and/or very intimate, so it would be unethical to arrange for it to happen. Does this mean we cannot study topics such as jealousy, or conflict, or sexual interaction? As it turns out, we can study such topics, but we are limited in how we can study them. One method is to ask subjects to tell us about what has happened to them. Such studies based on self-reports can be very informative and very important in helping us answer our research question, but (as we will see in the next section) self-report data have a number of drawbacks. Another approach is to have subjects role-play the behavior we're studying—to act "as if " they were jealous, or were having an argument, or were getting involved sexually with someone.

Role-play studies vary a great deal in how realistic they are. At one extreme, some studies have subjects read over stories concerning the relevant behavior and instruct the subjects to imagine that what they read is happening to them. Such presentations lack the vivid impact of reality and allow subjects to respond in a cool, collected fashion to events that elicit a considerable emotional charge when they really take place. At the other extreme, some studies—usually called *simulations*—examine the actual behavior of subjects within a hypothetical situation. For example, an investigator might tell both partners of a couple to imagine that they were angry with each other and then observe how they behave toward each other. This approach creates a more realistic atmosphere, but subjects still know that it is only pretend. Subjects' knowledge that they are playing a role, rather than having an actual experience, detracts from the value of role-play research. Although role-play studies are a more ethically acceptable way of studying emotionally charged topics, we may learn what subjects think they should do in these situations rather than what they really would do. We have protected our subjects, but we may have lost the psychological reality we want to study.

*C*OLLECTING DATA

At this point in our examination of research methods, we turn to procedures for collecting data. Three major types of research measures are described here: people's own reports about their thoughts, feelings, and behaviors; observations of people's behavior; and couples' reports in which self-report and observation are combined.

Self-Reports

The most popular way to study intimate relationships has been to ask people about their experiences, to collect *self-reports* (Harvey, Hendrick, & Tucker, 1988; Olson, 1977). Researchers have used a variety of formats to obtain self-report data: asking subjects to fill out questionnaires, conducting interviews with subjects, having subjects make detailed self-recordings of their behavior in their home environment. No matter what the exact format is, all self-reports can be described in terms of three comparisons:

- *Retrospective versus concurrent.* Does the self-report require the subject to report on something that has happened in the past or to keep track of what is happening in the present?
- *Global versus specific.* Does the self-report ask the subject to report feelings or behaviors in general, overall terms (e.g., "How active is your sex life?") or in specific terms (e.g., "How many times in the past week did you have sexual intercourse?").
- *Subjective versus objective.* Does the self-report call for a subjective, feeling-based judgment (e.g., "How satisfying is your relationship?") or an objective, fact-based response (e.g., "Did your partner give you a present for your birthday?").

There are numerous advantages to collecting self-report data in research on intimate relationships. Self-reports tell us about the meaning that relational events have for the subject; this meaning may be considerably more important than any kind of "objective" reality that could be reported by outside observers (Fiske, 1975). Consider, for example, all those "little things that mean a lot." An observer who sees Margaret bring ice cream home for Kathy may regard Margaret's behavior as mildly pleasant and rewarding to Kathy, but nothing more. If, however, Kathy happens to absolutely adore—and constantly crave—the specific kind of ice cream that Margaret brings her, Margaret's gift will mean a lot more to Kathy than an outside observer could possibly understand.

Another advantage to self-report data is that self-reports are easy to obtain. An investigator does not need expensive equipment, research assistants, or an elaborate laboratory facility. All that is needed is paper, pencil, and some willing subjects. However, when we evaluate evidence based on self-reports, we must take into account three major potential problems:

Subjects' understanding of the researcher's terms. Although self-reports obtain information directly from the subject about the subject's experiences, this information is always structured in terms of the researcher's questions. If the subject misinterprets what the researcher intended to ask, then the researcher will inevitably misinterpret the subject's response. A striking example of how such a problem might occur is found in a study by Berger and Wenger (1973) on the meaning of the term "virginity." These researchers found that 40.9 percent of their subjects (male and female) accepted "she brings herself to climax" as a possible definition of loss of virginity in a woman! Thus, even such an apparently simple question as "Are you a virgin?" could be misunderstood and lead to false conclusions. Undetected differences in people's comprehension of terms referring to sexual behavior has been cited as a major problem in research on AIDS (Catania, Gibson, Chitwood, & Coates, 1990).

Difficulties in recall or awareness. There is considerable controversy about how much and how well people can remember and report on things that have happened to them (Ericsson & Simon, 1980; Nisbett & Wilson, 1977; Smith & Miller, 1978). There does, however, seem to be general agreement that people are more accurate when they report specific, objective events that have occurred recently. People are more likely to be inaccurate—and fill in what they don't remember with their present beliefs and opinions—when we ask them to make global, subjective reports about things that happened long ago.

Bias in subjects' reports. Another problem with self-report data involves systematic bias in subjects' reports. For example, researchers have found that partners in a relationship tend to have an "egocentric bias": they seem more aware of their own contributions to joint tasks and less aware of their partner's contributions (Ross & Sicoly, 1979; see also Chapter 6). In research on marital power, some studies have found what we might call a "powerlessness bias"—with each partner regarding the other as more powerful (Olson & Cromwell, 1975; see also Chapter 9). These biases are very interesting in their own right, as they tell us about general perspectives that couples take on their relationship. However, such biases interfere with accurate reporting by couples on what really goes on between them.

Perhaps the most well-known bias in all of psychological research is the one that comes from people wanting to have a good opinion of themselves and make a good impression on others. It has long been known that in answering questions people will be affected by the *social desirability* of their responses. In general, we would all prefer to paint a good picture of ourselves rather than an accurate picture, warts and all. Edmonds (1967) has suggested that this bias toward answering in a socially desirable way may affect reports on satisfaction with and happiness in marriage. To measure this tendency, he developed a "marriage conventionalization" scale (see Table 2.1). Edmonds assumed that there is no such thing as a perfect marriage, without any faults or problems, and that people who said their marriage was perfect were distorting the truth in the direction of what was maximally socially desirable. When this scale was correlated with a standard, widely used scale of marital satisfaction, there was a high positive correlation between the two (Edmonds, Withers, & Dibatista, 1972). These data suggest that self-

TABLE 2.1 MARRIAGE CONVENTIONALIZATION SCALE

Each of the following questions is answered by indicating whether it is *true* or *false* in regard to your marriage (or other type of relationship).

1.   There are times when my mate does things that make me unhappy.
2.   My marriage is not a perfect success.
3.   My mate has all of the qualities I've always wanted in a mate.
4.   If my mate has any faults I'm not aware of them.
5.   My mate and I understand each other perfectly.
6.   We are as well adjusted as any two persons in this world can be.
7.   I have some needs that are not being met by my marriage.
8.   Every new thing I have learned about my mate has pleased me.
9.   There are times when I do not feel a great deal of love and affection for my mate.
10. I don't think anyone could possibly be happier than my mate and I were and are with one another.
11. My marriage could be happier than it is.
12. I don't think any couple could live together in greater harmony than my mate and I.
13. My mate completely understands and sympathizes with my every mood.
14. I have never regretted my marriage, not even for a moment.
15. If every person in the world of the opposite sex had been available and willing to marry me, I could not have made a better choice.

To determine your score on this scale, give yourself 1 point when you have responded *false* to questions 1, 2, 7, 9, and 11, and 1 point when you have responded *true* to any of the other questions. The maximum high score is, thus, 15. Such a score would mean either that you have an extraordinarily happy relationship, or that you are concerned to present your relationship in a very positive way even if it is not quite as perfect as your answers would indicate.

SOURCE: Adapted from Edmonds, 1967.

reports on marital satisfaction should be taken with a relatively large grain of salt—or that there are a lot more perfect, problem-free marriages out there than Edmonds wants to believe!

Observations

The other way to collect information about intimate relationships is to rely on the reports of observers. An observer may be a trained investigator working on the research project or an "ordinary person" who knows the subject. In either case, it is important to make sure that the observer's reports are *reliable*—that is, that other observers would see the same thing. Indeed, most studies that use trained investigators as observers go to great lengths to ensure that there will be high *interrater reliability* (good agreement between at least two observers). Such studies develop written manuals to teach their observers what and how to observe, conduct extensive practice sessions with observers to make sure their reports agree, and, frequently, check on this agreement throughout the course of the study. Even with these elaborate precautions, however, there are problems in getting and maintaining interrater reliability (O'Leary & Kent, 1972). Reliability may be high in the beginning of the study but decline over time. Reliability may also be affected by the observers' motivation. For example, agreement between observers tends to be greater when they know they are being supervised than when observations are being checked without the observers' knowledge. And even reliable observations can be misleading. Pairs of observers who work together over long periods of time may develop their own, peculiar ways of observing and recording. Left to themselves, these observers may make observations that are highly reliable, but their observations will not agree with those made by newly trained observers who are going by the book. In short, it is not easy to capture "objective reality"—that is, a reality that everyone sees in the same way.

There are many different methods of observation. Some studies involve direct observations of ongoing behavior; others use audio and/or video recordings so that observations can be made at a later time. The amount of time during which observations are made also varies widely. Observations may continue over long periods of time (days or even weeks) or occur for only very short periods of time (minutes). One method of observation, called *time-sampling*, uses short periods of observation to obtain a sample of behavior that actually occurs over a long period of time. In time-sampling, an investigator first specifies those times at which the behavior of interest could occur. For example, if we were studying a married couple, these times might be in the morning before they went off to work, in the evenings when they were together again, and throughout the weekend. Then, we would randomly sample short time periods from these relevant times: observing, for instance, only 15 minutes at a time, but having these 15 minutes of observation occur at different times on different days.

Time-sampling was developed to try to avoid the disadvantages of both long and short periods of observation. With long observation periods, we must employ a number of observers; otherwise, there is the risk of inaccurate observations brought about by observer fatigue. With short observations, the observed behavior may not be typical of the way the subject usually behaves. Even time-sampling, however, faces a fundamental problem if we are interested in relatively rare events (e.g., jealousy, arguments, consoling a partner after a misfortune): The event may not occur while the observations are being made.

Regardless of the method of collecting observations or however long someone is observed, most observations involve one or more of the following four types of data collection.

Narratives. Here the observer records in writing everything he or she observes. Narratives tend to be rich in interesting detail; unfortunately, they also tend to have low reliability between observers.

Ratings. When observers make ratings, they observe subjects for some period of time and then try to characterize what they have seen in relatively global (and usually subjective) terms. For example, the observer might watch a couple discussing some topic they disagree on and rate this interaction as either "constructive, problem-solving" or "argumentative, hostile." With carefully developed rating scales and extensive training of observers, it is usually possible to obtain reasonable interrater reliability on ratings.

Coding. Coding procedures focus on highly specific behaviors (e.g., who initiated the discussion, the amount of time each participant spoke in the discussion, the physical movements made by each participant during the discussion). It is generally easier to get higher interrater reliability with codings than with either narratives or ratings, but the use of complex coding schemes (where many specific behaviors must be observed) will require extensive training of observers.

Sequential observations. Although many observational studies focus on the behavior of a single individual, there is also a great deal of interest in observing the sequence of interaction between individuals (e.g., Gottman, 1979; Kenny, 1988; McClintock, 1983). Through the use of complex coding schemes and sophisticated data analysis procedures, investigators are able to examine the effects of the behavior of each of two people on the subsequent behavior of the other person. For example, when Susan smiles during the course of a conversation, does this affect how often John smiles later in the conversation? Unfortunately, most sequential analyses are restricted to very short periods of time and hence fail to tell us about more long-term interactional patterns. Furthermore, it is considerably more complicated and, therefore, less common for investigators to examine "higher-order interaction sequences," where the interaction itself affects a person's subsequent behavior. When Susan smiles and John smiles back immediately, does John tend to smile more later on than when Susan smiles but John does *not* smile back immediately?

The major purpose of collecting data through observations instead of through self-reports is to try to avoid the disadvantages of self-reports. By using observations, the researcher attempts to capture an objective picture of reality, a picture that is not affected by misunderstanding of what the investigator wants to know, by recall problems, or by distortion due to the biases of the subject.

But observations, too, have their imperfections and limitations. Some of the difficulties are related to specific observational methods and types, and have already been mentioned. In addition, there are some general disadvantages common to all observational research. Two disadvantages of observational methods are exactly opposite to the advantages of self-reports. First, observation by an "outsider" cannot tell us what is going on inside a person's mind. When Margaret brings Kathy some ice cream, we know what happened but not what it means to the people involved. Second, observational studies are expensive. They often require equipment and a group of trained observers.

Observational research also runs into the problem of *reactivity:* People may change their behavior when they know they are being observed (Webb, Campbell, Schwartz, Sechrest, & Grove, 1981). Sometimes, these changes may be quite deliberate, as in the following incident from a doctoral student's research, described by Cromwell and Olson (1975). While working with one of the couples participating in this research, the experimenter had to leave the room for a moment. Although she had no intention of recording what happened in her absence, she forgot to turn off the audiotape when she left, and the couple was unaware that their conversation was still being recorded. When the experimenter later listened to the tape, she realized what had happened. To her surprise (and, presumably, dismay), she heard the couple engage in an animated conversation that ended with one partner saying to the other, "She's coming back; we'll have to be more careful." Note that there is some disagreement among researchers about the extent to which couples can actually fake their responses while being observed (Cohen & Christensen, 1980; Vincent, Friedman, Nugent, & Messerly, 1979). But we do know that many people monitor and at least attempt to change their behavior when they know they are being observed. After all, people are just as concerned about creating a good impression when their behavior is being observed as when they fill out a questionnaire or answer the questions of an interviewer.

Even when there is no deliberate attempt to act in more socially desirable ways, the presence of an observer may influence subjects' behavior. Kenkel (1961) found that the sex of the observer affected his married subjects' behavior (with subjects behaving differently with a female observer than with a male one), though the subjects themselves were probably unaware of this. In order to avoid such problems of reactivity, some investigators have devised elaborate, "high-tech" methods of observation. Christensen (1979), for example, asked families in his research to agree to having microphones placed unobtrusively in a room where the family often talked together. The microphones were hooked up to a tape recorder and timer, which were set in such a way that during whatever 4 hours of the day the family was most likely to be together in the designated room, the tape recorder was on for a 15-minute period. Although the family specified the 4-hour period, the timer randomly selected the 15-minute recording time. Thus, the family did not know on any given day which 15-minute period would be recorded. Presumably, it would be too much of a burden to try to create a good impression for 4 hours a day over a number of days, and so the family should soon begin to act naturally in spite of being observed. Though Christensen's technique for getting nonreactive observations is quite clever, one has to wonder how many families would agree to such a scheme. We may end up with very natural behavior from some very unusual families!

Couples' Reports

The final kind of data collection to be considered in this section involves obtaining reports from couples. In couples' reports, each partner self-reports on his or her own behavior and also acts as an observer of his or her partner's behavior. Couples' reports, then, combine the two major ways to collect data. (For other ways to combine self-reports and observations in the study of relationships, see Ickes & Tooke, 1988.) Many researchers have found that there is not very high agreement between partners' reports (Christensen et al., 1983; Clark & Wallin, 1964; Elwood & Jacobson, 1982; Jacobson & Moore, 1981). For example, a husband may report having behaved in an affectionate manner toward his wife, but his wife may not have perceived his actions to be affectionate. Better agreement tends to be obtained when partners of a couple have a chance to practice making their ratings, and when they are asked to report on objective, specific events rather than to make global, subjective assessments. However, as Christensen, Sullaway, and King (1983) have pointed out, global, subjective assessments may be more important for our understanding of the relationship than accurately reported, objective, specific events.

Couples' reports offer a replay of the basic contrast between self-report measures and observations: the tension between meaningfulness and accuracy. It is perfectly possible for people to report totally inaccurate information (e.g., saying that they have not had sex with their partner "for months" when in fact they had sex two weeks ago) that is nonetheless extremely meaningful (the person is reporting his or her feelings of extreme sexual deprivation). It is also possible for meaningfulness to be misleading. For example, the stereotype that husbands should be more powerful than wives may cause both spouses to under-estimate the actual power a wife has. The stereotype is very meaningful to such a couple, but the wife's actual power in day-to-day interactions may be much greater than what both partners report.

Thus, it is simply not possible for us as students, researchers, and good detectives to say that because information is unreliable (i.e., be-cause partners disagree about what they did, or because a couple's reports disagree with the observations of a trained investigator), it has no value. Instead, as numerous researchers in the area of intimate relationships have emphasized (Kelley, 1977; Levinger, 1977; Olson, 1977; Olson & Cromwell, 1975), the lack of reliability itself acts as a vital clue to the questions we need to ask. What does it mean when Betty and Tom do not agree on what Betty did? What does it mean when Betty and Tom agree perfectly well, but Hercule Poirot and his crew of trained observers see Betty's behavior entirely differently? By searching out the reasons why these reports and observations differ, we may stumble upon a picture of reality that is much more important than we could ever obtain from the facts of life on which we can all, easily, agree.

ANALYZING DATA

The details of statistical procedures for analyzing data go well beyond the purposes of this chapter, and the interested reader should consult a statistics text (e.g., Keppel, 1982; Kerlinger, 1979; Winer, 1971). It is useful, however, to take a brief look at two general issues that arise when data collected on intimate relationships are analyzed.

First, we should realize that most research on intimate relationships involves *aggregation,* the putting together of information (Riskin & Faunce, 1972). Sometimes, the researcher asks subjects themselves to aggregate data. When we ask questions such as "How generally satis-fied are you with your relationship?" we require subjects to put together a number of specific feelings and events in order to come up with one, general, aggregate response. But sometimes the researcher takes the responsibility of putting together information. We might, for example, combine all the negative, unpleasant feelings a subject reports in con-trast to the combination of all the positive, pleasant feelings. Re-searchers will often use statistical techniques to determine whether and how strongly various bits of information go together.

The point is that however we go about aggregating data, we must be careful in interpreting the combinations that are created. Whenever subjects or investigators make assumptions about what fits together, this can lead to mistaken conclusions. For example, not all pleasant events are equal, and if we treat them as though they are, we may come up with an inaccurate picture of how pleasant a relationship really is. Statistical analyses have the advantage of testing the fit among bits of information, but the disadvantage of sometimes putting together information in ways that do not make sense to the human observer. It could be that happily married couples are characterized by both loving each other and wearing blue socks, but does that last bit of information really help us understand marital happiness? When we aggregate information, we need to use all our senses: common, theoretical, and statistical.

The second issue about data analysis that needs to be mentioned concerns the statistical significance of results. Through statistical analysis, we can determine how likely it is that the data we obtained (e.g., the correlation we got, or the effect of our manipulated independent variable in an experiment) could have occurred by chance. The standard convention is that if a result could have occurred by chance only 5 or less times in 100 possible occurrences, it is considered a *significant result*. If it could have occurred by chance between 5 and 10 times in 100 occurrences, it is a *trend*. Otherwise (i.e., if the chance probability is greater than 10 in 100), the result is nonsignificant and is disregarded. All of the research results reported in this book are significant results or trends; nonsignificant results are not reported. This does not mean, however, that a result reported here could not have occurred by chance. When a result is significant, it simply means that chance occurrence is unlikely, not that chance occurrence is impossible. The best way to be sure that any finding is meaningful and not a chance event is for that same, statistically significant result to be obtained by several different investigators working with different subjects. When a result is *replicated* in this way, our confidence in it is vastly increased.

BEING ETHICAL

Possible ethical problems in conducting research on intimate relationships have been mentioned at several points in this chapter. What needs to be stressed, however, is that all types of research in this area involve important ethical dilemmas. Even if all we do is to ask subjects to fill out questionnaires describing their relationships, we need to think carefully about how this research experience might affect them and their partners. According to Rubin and Mitchell (1976), participating in research on intimate relationships is likely to have the following effects:

- Subjects may arrive at a new awareness of and a new judgment about relationship factors. For example, subjects who have never been jealous before may become more likely to get jealous after answering a questionnaire about jealousy.

- Subjects may discuss the research with their partners and, through these discussions, come to feel better or worse about the relationship. For example, couples who fill out Rubin's (1973) Loving Scale (see Chapter 4) may ask each other about their answers, and may be delighted or disappointed when they hear how their partner responded.

When research goes beyond questionnaires or relatively naturalistic observation, it may have an even greater lasting impact on couples. O'Leary and Turkewitz (1978b) have noted that conflict simulation tasks, in which partners are instructed to come to a mutual decision on topics on which they disagree, may increase the level of conflict in the relationship even after the research task itself is completed. Having an argument in the laboratory may well increase the possibility of having an argument at home.

All researchers need to weigh the possibility of these effects on subjects and do everything they can to safeguard their subjects' welfare. Researchers working with partners in distressed relationships should be especially careful. It is helpful in such research to consult with a clinician trained in couples' therapy (see Chapter 14) to make sure that the research procedures are not harmful. In any research, detailed information must be provided to all potential subjects before the research begins so that they may make an informed decision about whether to participate in it.

Once their role in the research has ended, subjects are entitled to and should receive prompt feedback from the researcher, describing any and all experimental manipulations that took place as well as going over all research procedures to make sure that subjects fully understand the purpose of the research. Additionally, once all subjects have participated and results of the study have been determined, subjects should receive a report on the overall outcome. In research on intimate relationships, comparative information about the average responses of all the people in the study may be especially valuable, as subjects sometimes have unwarranted concerns that their behavior was unusual.

Finally, Rubin and Mitchell (1976) have recommended that investigators conducting research on intimate relationships make available to all their subjects information about where they could obtain couples' counseling should they desire to do so. In conveying this information, the researcher must be careful not to imply to subjects that there is something wrong with their relationship. To avoid this implication, such information should be given in a calm, matter-of-fact way that clearly indicates that the researcher gives this information to all couples simply because he or she believes that all couples should know where they could seek help should they ever feel the need to do so.

In our necessary concern with treating subjects well and protecting them from any harmful effects, we must not overlook the other side of the ethical issue: the ethical imperative to gain more understanding of important areas of human behavior. Intimate relationships can be a source of the grandest, most glorious pleasure human beings experience; they can also be a source of terrible suffering and appalling destructiveness. It is, I believe, an inherently ethical response to try to learn how the joy might be increased and the misery reduced.

CHAPTER SUMMARY

Finding a Question

Research questions can come from a number of sources: personal experience, the results of previous research, and theoretical predictions. A good question is precise, can be answered, and raises new issues for consideration. In general, researchers conduct two types of research: descriptive explorations and specific tests of causal hypotheses. Often, a single study will involve both approaches.

Finding Subjects

Convenience samples are composed of subjects who are easily available to the researcher. Findings based on convenience samples may not generalize to other people. Representative samples are selected to reflect the characteristics of the population of interest in terms of demographic characteristics such as age, nationality, and socioeconomic background. It is expensive to select and contact a representative sample, and the time available with each subject is often short.

Finding a Design

Correlational Designs. A correlation is an association between two variables. Correlations can be positive or negative. Correlation is *not* causation. Any given association can be caused in a number of different ways.

Experimental Designs. In an experiment, the researcher manipulates the independent variable to see what effect this has on the dependent variable. Experiments allow us to examine specific cause-and-effect relationships. But, for practical or ethical reasons, many events cannot be studied experimentally.

Developmental Designs. In developmental designs, researchers attempt to study the effects of time or a sequence of events over time. Three kinds of developmental designs are discussed. Cross-sectional designs select subjects from different age groups or time periods, and compare them. It is often difficult to be sure what causes differences obtained in cross-sectional research. Longitudinal research follows the same group of subjects across time. Longitudinal studies often suffer from subject attrition, loss of subjects over time. Retrospective designs rely on subjects' recall of past events, but this recall may be inaccurate.

Finding a Setting

Research can be conducted in a laboratory or in real-world, everyday settings such as a couple's home. Laboratory research emphasizes control but pays the price of artificiality. Real-world settings can promote more natural behavior, but control over extraneous variables is reduced. Data collection may be highly structured or relatively unstructured. Role-play studies allow researchers to examine highly emotional events in an ethical manner but may fail to tell us what people really do in such situations.

Collecting Data

Self-Reports. Asking subjects directly about their thoughts, feelings, and behavior is widely used in research on intimate relationships. The advantages of self-reports are their convenience and the information they provide on the way subjects view themselves and others. Disadvantages include subjects' misunderstanding of the researcher's terms, difficulties in recall or awareness, and biases in subjects' reports. The desire to present oneself in a favorable light, called social desirability, is a common bias. Overall, self-reports are more accurate when they focus on recent, specific, and objective events than when they focus on global, subjective impressions of events long past.

Observations. When we observe people's behavior—rather than ask them to report it—reliability is a crucial issue. When interrater reliability is high, different observers agree on their observations. Time-sampling is often used in observational research: A set of different, usually brief, observations are made at randomly selected times drawn from a longer period of interest. Four types of observational measures are described: detailed narratives, global ratings, coding of specific behaviors, and sequential observations. Observational methods allow researchers to avoid the problems of self-reports, but they pose their own problems. The meaning of a behavior is not always clear, observational methods are expensive to employ, and subjects being observed may modify their behavior.

Couples' Reports. Couples' reports combine self-reports and observational techniques. Here, each partner is asked to report on his or her own thoughts, feelings, and behavior—and to act as an observer of the other partner's behavior. Often, the self-report of one partner does not agree with the observation by the other partner. Discovering that partners disagree can, however, be an important step in understanding their relationship.

Analyzing Data

Virtually all research involves aggregation, the putting together of pieces of information. Sometimes, subjects do their own aggregation by reporting a summary of their thoughts and feelings. Other times, the researcher aggregates subjects' responses into overall, combination measures. When data are analyzed statistically, results that could occur by chance less than 5 times in 100 are called significant. Even significant results, however, could occur by chance. Finding the same result with different investigators and different subjects, called replication, is the best safeguard against mistaking chance results for the real thing.

Being Ethical

Conducting research on intimate relationships is likely to have an influence on subjects' relationships. By participating in research, subjects may become more aware of various aspects of their relationships. Research involving couples may stimulate discussions between the partners about their relationship. Behavior engaged in during a study could spill over into the real lives of couples. Because of these possible effects, the welfare of subjects must be carefully guarded in research on relationships. All subjects must receive adequate information about the study before deciding whether or not to participate. Subjects are also entitled to a full explanation of research procedures once the study is completed, as well as a report on the results obtained. It has also been recommended that subjects participating in research on relationships be informed about the availability of couples' counseling. Properly conducted, research on relationships has the potential to contribute to more enduring and satisfying relationships.

PART TWO

— ❖ —

Getting Together

3

Interpersonal Attraction

❖

ow do intimate relationships get started? What sets the wheels of friendship or romance in motion? Obviously, the specifics vary widely. Relationships can begin under all kinds of circumstances—in the classroom, on a blind date, at work, on the playing field, in a grocery store. But psychologically the first big step toward a relationship is always the same: *interpersonal attraction,* the desire to approach someone. Feelings of attraction are not the same as love, nor do they guarantee that love will develop. Attraction does, however, open the door to the possibility.

Perhaps because attraction plays such a crucial role in so many different kinds of relationships, there has been an enormous amount of research on it

(Berscheid, 1985; Hendrick & Hendrick, 1983). The present chapter does not attempt to examine all of this material. Instead, we will focus here on several major factors that appear to be particularly important in the beginning of an intimate relationship. But first let us consider some basic principles about how attraction works.

THEORIES OF ATTRACTION: A MATTER OF REWARDS

According to most theories of attraction, we are attracted to individuals whose presence is rewarding to us (Clore & Byrne, 1974; Lott & Lott, 1974). Two major types of rewards influence attraction: *direct* rewards produced by an individual and rewards *by association*. Direct rewards refer to all the positive consequences we obtain from being with someone. When a person showers us with attention and encouragement, we enjoy these rewarding behaviors. When a person is witty and intelligent, we take pleasure in these rewarding characteristics. And when a person is able to give us access to desired external rewards such as money or status, we are pleased with the opportunities presented. The more of these rewards that a person provides for us, the more we should be attracted to that individual.

But what about just being in someone's company under pleasant circumstances? There you are, having a great time, and Chris is right there with you. Will you be attracted to Chris even though Chris is not responsible for the happy occasion? Many researchers think this is a distinct possibility (Byrne & Murnen, 1988). In attraction by association, the other person takes on the emotional tone of the surrounding situation. Having met Chris under happy circumstances, we experience a positive emotional response when we next interact with Chris.

These two kinds of reward—direct and by association—highlight the interactive nature of attraction (Gifford & Gallagher, 1985; Wright, Ingraham, & Blackmer, 1985). Attraction involves the needs, preferences, and desires of the person who becomes attracted; the perceived characteristics of the person who is seen as attractive; and the situation in which these two individuals find themselves. Our own needs can affect how we perceive others and react to the situation. The perceived characteristics of another person can influence our own desires and reactions in the situation. And the situation itself can modify our preferences and our perceptions. Attraction is based on rewarding experiences with another person, but those rewarding experiences can come about in a variety of ways. We consider a number of possible routes to attraction in this chapter, starting with a basic prerequisite—being there.

*P*ROXIMITY: LIKING THE ONES WE'RE NEAR

According to the lines of one popular song, being there is all there is: "If you can't be with the one you love, honey, love the one you're with." But long before songwriter Stephen Stills gave us this piece of rather cynical advice, social scientists were aware of the central role of proximity in fostering interpersonal attraction. Indeed, proximity is fundamental if a relationship is to develop. With the exception of fantasy relationships such as those fans have with movie stars and rock singers, our friendships and love relationships grow out of daily interactions with those around us. To meet people is not necessarily to love them, but to love them we must first meet them.

Two classic studies in social psychology vividly demonstrated the strong association between physical proximity and interpersonal attraction. The first of these studies (Festinger, 1951; Festinger, Schachter, & Back, 1950) examined the friendship patterns among military veterans and their wives living in two student housing projects at the Massachusetts Institute of Technology. It was found that people who lived closer to each other were much more likely to become friends than were those whose apartments were further apart. The exact location of people's apartments also had an effect on what friendships they formed. For example, within the buildings of one of the projects (Westgate West), friendships were highly dependent on whether residents lived in centrally located apartments or in apartments toward the end of the floor. People living in apartments located in the middle of the hallway (#3 and #8 in Figure 3.1) could easily interact with everyone else living on their particular floor and, in fact, had more friends who also lived on this floor than did the people living in less centralized apartments. In contrast, those residents living in apartments located near the entrance to the stairways (#1 and #5 in Figure 3.1) interacted with and made friends with people living on the floor above them. Thus, whenever we choose the exact place where we will live or work or go to school, we also take a major step toward determining who the significant others in our life will be. We know we are choosing a location; we may not fully realize we are also choosing people.

FIGURE 3.1
Schematic diagram of a building in Westgate West. (Festinger, Schachter, & Back, 1950.)

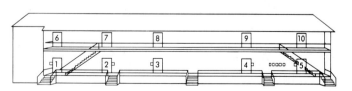

The second classic study of the effects of proximity was conducted by social psychologist Theodore Newcomb (1961). Newcomb was able to do what most social psychologists only dream about: He created his own experimental social world. In order to investigate the way that strangers become friends, Newcomb set up a dormitory near the campus of the University of Michigan. During each of two years, 17 college students (all male) lived there rent free in return for participating in Newcomb's research on friendship formation.

During the first year of the project, there was no evidence that physical proximity influenced interpersonal attraction. When roommates were compared with nonroommates, liking did not differ. During the second year (with an entirely different set of people living in the house), proximity did affect attraction, roommates liking each other more than nonroommates. This effect of proximity was so strong that it occurred in spite of an experimental manipulation in room assignment. Although rooms had been assigned randomly the first year, room assignments in the second year were based on residents' values and attitudes as expressed prior to their living in the dormitory. Half of those who were to live with roommates (there were also single rooms in the house) were assigned to live with people whose initial attitudes agreed with theirs; the other half were assigned to live with people whose initial attitudes were very different. Regardless of these assignments, however, the general effect of proximity still held: Roommates were more likely to become close friends than nonroommates.

These findings from Newcomb's research show us both the power and the weakness of proximity as a determinant of attraction. Sometimes proximity does not have an effect, as during the first year of the study. At other times, it is a very strong force, overcoming initial differences between people. It is important to realize, however, that the effects of proximity, when they do occur, are not always positive. Sometimes, we just hate the ones we're with!

The negative effects of proximity have been called "environmental spoiling" (Ebbesen, Kjos, & Konecni, 1976). The notion of environmental spoiling rests on the obvious truth that any time we live close to others, we will encounter people whose lifestyles differ from ours and some whose lifestyles actively conflict with ours. Our neighbors may play loud music when we want silence or object to our playing loud music when they want silence. They may look with horror on our unmowed lawn, while we fight off the unwelcome attentions of their German shepherd. Living close to each other provides the necessary setting for such conflicts to occur and for hostility to develop.

In their study of the residents of a middle-class condominium complex in California, Ebbesen et al. demonstrated both the positive and negative effects of proximity. Although the individual housing clusters were small, each containing only 3 percent of the people in the complex, 62 percent of people's friendships with other residents were with those in the same cluster. Disliking someone was even more strongly affected by proximity: 70 percent of the people who were disliked lived in the same cluster as the people who disliked them. In short, proximity provides the opportunity for social interactions but does not determine the quality of these interactions. On the other hand, long-term *lack* of proximity may make it more difficult to sustain attraction and commitment to another person. According to Rindfuss and Stephen (1990), married couples who do not live together are more likely to get divorced than those who share a residence. For these couples, separation did *not* make the heart grow fonder.

Personal Space: Coming Closer

Personal space is another spatial factor that can influence interpersonal attraction. Each of us has a preference for how much physical distance we want to maintain from others. This preference differs among individuals and is influenced by cultural and situational factors (Hall, 1966; Hayduk, 1983). But when our personal space is violated by someone's coming closer than we expect or desire, our attraction toward that individual is affected. Consider, for example, an experiment by Storms and Thomas (1977) in which a male experimenter sat either very close to a male subject (6 inches away) or at a normal distance (30 inches away). Toward half the subjects, the experimenter behaved in a pleasant, friendly manner; toward the other half, however, he was rude and distinctly unfriendly. After their interaction with the experimenter, subjects were asked to evaluate him. Their responses indicated that a personal space violation intensifies our initial reaction toward someone. The friendly experimenter who sat close was liked *more* than the friendly one who sat at a normal distance. But the unfriendly experimenter who sat close was liked *less* than the unfriendly one who sat at a normal distance. Like proximity, personal space violations do not determine whether we have a positive or negative response. They do, however, magnify the intensity of our feelings (Knowles, 1980).

Familiarity: Repeated Contact

Proximity and personal space are both spatial concepts that refer to the location of another person relative to us. In contrast, *familiarity* refers to frequency of contact. Proximity is necessary for familiarity to develop, but being near someone does not guarantee that we will interact frequently with that person. According to folk wisdom, familiarity breeds contempt. The research evidence, however, does not agree. Often, familiarity breeds attraction. Repeated contact with something or someone—called *mere exposure*—increases our positive response (Zajonc, 1968). In one study, for example, subjects had a series of brief (no more than 35 seconds), severely constrained (no talking was allowed), face-to-face contacts with others (Saegert, Swap, & Zajonc, 1973). Mere as it was, this exposure proved sufficient to increase attraction. Subjects liked those they had seen more often more than those they had seen less frequently.

But the power of familiarity to increase attraction is not unlimited. *Extreme* familiarity can decrease attraction (Harrison, 1977). And if people strongly dislike someone to begin with, repeated exposure can increase their hostility (Perlman & Oskamp, 1971). For instance, student exchange programs do not always have desirable effects. Perhaps because of all the stresses and strains of adjusting to a foreign culture, longer stays in a host country are sometimes associated with increasingly negative attitudes about that country (Stroebe, Lenkert, & Jonas, 1988). When rewards are in short supply, repeated reminders of one's deprivation can be distinctly unpleasant and unattractive.

PHYSICAL ATTRACTIVENESS: TO SEE YOU IS TO LIKE YOU

There is considerable evidence that people are attracted to individuals who are physically attractive (Berscheid & Walster, 1974b; Hatfield & Sprecher, 1986b). At least when we first meet people, our response will usually be more positive toward those who are highly physically attractive than toward those who are less good-looking. This effect is particularly strong when we consider an individual's *perception* of another's looks. Numerous studies have found a strong association between how attractive people perceive someone else to be and their positive evaluation of that person as someone they would want to meet or to date (Brislin & Lewis, 1968; Byrne, Ervin, & Lamberth, 1970; Curran & Lippold, 1975; Tesser & Brodie, 1971). Similar findings, though not quite so strong, have been obtained for the association between "objective" physical attractiveness (i.e., ratings made by independent judges) and favorable responses by others (Byrne et al., 1970; Byrne, London, & Reeves, 1968; Curran & Lippold, 1975; Stroebe, Insko, Thompson, & Layton, 1971; Walster, Aronson, Abrahams, & Rottman, 1966). But why is there a bias for beauty? Four major possibilities have received the most attention.

What Creates the Bias for Beauty?

Since people, as well as objects, are more rewarding to be with when we find their appearance pleasing, *aesthetic appeal* is one possible reason why we like those who are physically attractive more than those who are less attractive. But sheer viewing pleasure is probably not all that is involved. Another possible explanation of the bias for beauty is that people overgeneralize from appearance, assuming that those who are attractive on the outside are also nicer on the inside and have remarkably good future prospects (Dion, 1986; Warner & Sugarman, 1986). This overgeneralization is called the *what-is-beautiful-is-good stereotype* (Dion, Berscheid, & Walster, 1972). Some of the factors involved in this stereotype are listed in Table 3.1. In general, the what-is-beautiful-is-good stereotype appears to be particularly strong for life outcomes that result from having the right family connections (Kalick, 1988). The unattractive, it seems to be assumed, can earn a good life, but the beautiful are likely to have it handed to them on a silver platter.

This stereotype can influence attraction in at least two ways. First, if we believe that someone is good as well as beautiful, we have doubled the potential sources of rewards available from being with that person. Second, it is possible that our beliefs produce the reality we expect. If we

TABLE 3.1 WHAT IS BEAUTIFUL IS GOOD

Male and female subjects judged that physically attractive people (males and females) were more likely than physically unattractive people to have the following characteristics:

Sexually warm and responsive	Sensitive
Kind	Interesting
Strong	Poised
Outgoing	Sociable
Nurturant	Exciting dates
	Better character

These same subjects also believed that the future for physically attractive people would differ in the following ways from the future of physically unattractive individuals:

More prestige	Be more competent in marriage
Have a happier marriage	
Have more social and professional success	Have more fulfilling lives

SOURCE: Findings from Dion, Berscheid, & Walster, 1972.

believe that beauty on the outside signals goodness on the inside and act accordingly, our positive responses to beautiful people may enable them to develop the expected personal characteristics (Langlois, 1986). But are the beautiful, in fact, better? Overall, the answer is *no*. Talent and virtue are not found any more often among the very good-looking than among those who are less physically attractive (Hatfield & Sprecher, 1986b). There is, however, a more specific possible benefit of beauty. Perhaps the bias for beauty perpetuates itself. Since physically attractive individuals are more likely to have a history of positive social encounters, perhaps they develop especially good social skills that allow them to continue to elicit these positive responses from others.

The third possible explanation for the bias for beauty is, then, that the physically attractive *are more socially skilled*. And, indeed, some studies have found that physically attractive individuals are more skillful in their verbal communications with others (Chaiken, 1979; Goldman & Lewis, 1977). But physical attractiveness and social skills are not always packaged together. In a study of college seniors, the relationship between physical attractiveness and social skills was different for men and women (Reis, Wheeler, Spiegel, Kernis, Nezlek, & Perri, 1982). For male subjects, there was a positive relationship between self-reports of their social skills (assertiveness, self-confidence in their social abilities, not fearing rejection by the opposite sex) and physical attractiveness. For female subjects, however, their social skills were *negatively* related to physical attractiveness, with the more attractive women reporting fewer social skills. Among these young women, however, greater physical attractiveness and greater social skills were each separately associated with increased positive social interaction.

These findings suggest that physical attractiveness may serve to magnify social pressures to conform to sex-role stereotypes of the active male and the passive female (Dion & Stein, 1978). People may respond to physically attractive males in such a way as to promote their active, assertive social skills, thereby ensuring that there will be a general tendency for attractiveness and skills to go together. In contrast, people may respond to beautiful females by discouraging assertive social behavior, leaving females one of two independent routes to social success: to be beautiful *or* to be skillful. It is important to emphasize, however, that the physically attractive women in the study by Reis et al. were *not* socially withdrawn individuals who were unhappy with their social lives. Indeed, these women were more satisfied and pleased with the *quality* of their social interactions than were less attractive females. Among the men who participated in this study, level of physical attractiveness did not affect social satisfaction. In a more recent study, it was found that compared with their less attractive peers, physically attractive women had greater social self-esteem, while physically attractive men had less social self-esteem (O'Grady, 1989). Overall, then, phys-

Research has demonstrated a clear bias for beauty: people are particularly attracted to individuals who are especially good-looking. Several reasons for this bias are described in the text. (AP/Wide World)

ically attractive women may be less socially assertive than physically attractive men, but they experience at least as many social rewards—and perhaps more.

The fourth possible explanation of the bias for beauty involves the social profit that may be derived from *associating with physically attractive individuals*. Are we hoping that the glitter will rub off? Research on this possibility indicates that both gender and timing influence the effects of being evaluated along with a beautiful person.

In situations where two individuals of the same sex are observed together, assimilation is the rule (Geiselman, Haight, & Kimata, 1984; Kernis & Wheeler, 1981). A person of average attractiveness is seen as more attractive in the presence of someone who is very good-looking and as less attractive in the presence of someone who is quite unattractive. Among opposite-sex pairs, the rule stays the same for men, who benefit from being seen with an attractive woman (Sigall & Landy, 1973). But evaluations of women are not affected by the looks of their male partner (Bar-Tal & Saxe, 1976). For women, only their own looks seem to matter.

But what if individuals are observed separately, one after another?

Focusing on same-sex comparisons, research on sequential presentations has usually found a contrast effect (Cramer, Weiss, Steigleder, &
Balling, 1985; Wedell, Parducci, & Geiselman, 1987). In a contrast effect,
we gain from comparison with a less attractive individual but lose from
comparison with someone who is more attractive than we are. Consider,
for example, the effects of viewing highly attractive nude centerfolds.
Compared with subjects who viewed abstract art slides or pictures of
average-looking nude women, male and female subjects who had
looked over very attractive centerfolds from *Playboy* and *Penthouse* maga-
zines later gave a more negative evaluation to the picture of a nude
woman of average attractiveness (Kenrick & Gutierres, 1989). In another
study, these investigators found that male subjects who viewed very
attractive female nudes gave lower ratings on the sexual attractiveness
of and their feelings of love for their own female sexual partner than did
male subjects who viewed abstract art slides. Women's ratings of their
own male sexual partners were not, however, influenced by having
viewed highly attractive male nudes.

To summarize, there are four possible reasons for why physically
attractive individuals usually receive a more positive response from
others: aesthetic appeal, the what-is-beautiful-is-good stereotype, better
social skills, and the desire to increase one's own perceived attractiveness by association. To some degree or another, all of these factors
probably make some contribution. But what about the eye of the beholder? Do some people have a stronger bias for beauty than others? In
the next section, we consider individual differences in this bias.

Who Has a Bias for Beauty?

Imagine that you are talking to a close friend about the kind of people
you like to date. Would you mention physical attractiveness? If so,
would you say it was a very important factor or a relatively trivial one?
Research indicates that what you have to say about physical attractiveness probably will depend on your gender. Men are much more
likely than women to emphasize their interest in having a physically
attractive romantic partner (Berscheid, Dion, Walster, & Walster, 1971;
Buss & Barnes, 1986; Nevid, 1984). But what men and women *say* is not
necessarily matched by what they *do*. Consider, for example, a study by
Sprecher (1989). When male and female college students received information about a person of the opposite sex, this person's physical attractiveness was the primary determinant of attraction, and men and
women did not differ in the degree to which they were influenced by
physical attractiveness information. But when asked how much physical
attractiveness had determined their ratings, men said it played a greater
role in determining their feelings of attraction than did women. Similarly, when subjects were interviewed after they had a prearranged date

as part of a study, women were actually influenced at least as much as men by their partner's physical attractiveness—and sometimes more (Byrne et al., 1970; Coombs and Kenkel, 1966). According to Feingold's (1990) analysis of the relevant research, the tendency for physical attractiveness to influence romantic attraction more among men than among women affects both estimates and actual behavior. However, the difference between men and women is considerably stronger when they are estimating the importance of physical appearance than when they are actually attracted to someone.

But even if men usually feel freer than women to acknowledge their preferences for a physically attractive partner, not all men place the same value on physical appearance. Research on the personality trait of *self-monitoring* clearly indicates that some men are much more concerned than others about this characteristic (Snyder & Simpson, 1987). Self-monitoring refers to people's tendency to regulate their social behavior to meet the demands of social situations (Snyder, 1974; Snyder & Gangestad, 1986). High self-monitors are ready, willing, and able to tailor their behavior to make a good impression on others. In contrast, low self-monitors are more consistent across situations, as they strive to be true to their own beliefs and desires. People are divided into high and low self-monitors on the basis of their scores on the Self-Monitoring Scale, which is reprinted in Table 3.2. Although there is controversy about whether this scale measures one or more personality traits (Briggs & Cheek, 1988; Lennox, 1988), research on the relationship between self-monitoring and interpersonal attraction has treated self-monitoring as a single, general dimension of personality.

As we have seen, men can profit socially from being paired with an attractive woman. Thus, high self-monitoring men, who by definition seek social success, should be particularly interested in having a good-looking dating partner. And they are. When researchers presented male subjects with dating choices that pitted physical attractiveness against a good personality, high self-monitors chose on the basis of appearance, while low-self monitors chose on the basis of personality (Snyder, Berscheid, & Glick, 1985). Self-monitoring also appears to affect other aspects of intimate relationships. Low self-monitoring men are more cautious about getting involved in a romantic situation than are high self-monitors (Glick, 1985). Among both male and female undergraduates, those who are high self-monitors seem less committed to their current dating partner than those who are low self-monitors (Snyder & Simpson, 1984). Overall, then, there is some suggestion that being a high self-monitor is associated with a somewhat superficial approach to intimate relationships—an emphasis on the partner's appearance, a greater readiness for getting involved, and a tendency for less commitment. Because some of the research on this topic has relied exclusively on male subjects, it is unclear whether the full pattern applies only to men or to both men and women.

TABLE 3.2 THE SELF-MONITORING SCALE

For each of the following questions, indicate whether it is *true* or *false*.

1. I find it hard to imitate the behavior of other people.
2. At parties and social gatherings, I do not attempt to do or say things that others will like.
3. I can only argue for ideas which I already believe.
4. I can make impromptu speeches even on topics about which I have almost no information.
5. I guess I put on a show to impress or entertain others.
6. I would probably make a good actor.
7. In a group of people I am rarely the center of attention.
8. In different situations and with different people, I often act like very different persons.
9. I am not particularly good at making other people like me.
10. I'm not always the person I appear to be.
11. I would not change my opinions (or the way I do things) in order to please someone or win his or her favor.
12. I have considered being an entertainer.
13. I have never been good at games like charades or improvisational acting.
14. I have trouble changing my behavior to suit different people and different situations.
15. At a party I let others keep the jokes and stories going.
16. I feel a bit awkward in company and do not show up quite as well as I should.
17. I can look anyone in the eye and tell a lie with a straight face (if for a right end).
18. I may deceive people by being friendly when I really dislike them.

To determine your score on this scale, give yourself 1 point when you have responded *false* to questions 1, 2, 3, 7, 9, 11, 13, 14, 15, and 16, and 1 point when you have responded *true* to questions 4, 5, 6, 8, 10, 12, 17, and 18. Now count your total points. Among college students, the average score is about 10 or 11. Higher scores indicate that your behavior is responsive to changes in the situation; lower scores indicate that your behavior tends to remain constant regardless of situational demands.

SOURCE: Adapted from Snyder & Gangestad, 1986.

Adding Up the Gains and Losses

Although its strength may vary between individuals, the bias for beauty is real. Good-looking individuals have a distinct social advantage. Physically attractive individuals, particularly women, have more dates with the opposite sex than do less attractive individuals (Berscheid et al., 1971; Krebs & Adinolfi, 1975; Reis, Nezlek, & Wheeler, 1980; Walster et al., 1966). They also report a more active sex life (Curran & Lippold, 1975). Physically attractive men have more opposite-sex friends than do less attractive men (Berscheid et al., 1971; Reis et al., 1980; Reis et al., 1982; White, 1980b), although it is not clear whether the same edge in opposite-sex friendships holds for physically attractive women (Kaats & Davis, 1970: Reis et al., 1980). Indeed, it has been suggested that because of the greater social acceptance received by highly physically attractive individuals, they may be less at risk for mental illness than those who are physically unattractive (Archer & Cash, 1985; Farina et al., 1977; Napoleon, Chassin, & Young, 1980). You should note, however, that this proposition is based on correlational evidence and is quite controversial. Perhaps, for example, the causal connection goes the other way, with the experience of emotional distress reducing physical attractiveness (Mueser, Grau, Sussman, & Rossen, 1984).

Given the clear social advantages experienced by physically attractive individuals, it is surprising that one's appearance has only a small impact on a person's optimism and confidence (Abbott & Sebastian, 1981). One possible reason for this may lie in how extremely attractive individuals interpret their social interactions. Aware of the effect their beauty has on others, they may hesitate to believe what people say to them (DePaulo, Tang, & Stone, 1987; Sigall & Michela, 1976). In fact, physically attractive people who believe that they have been observed tend to discount the praise they receive for their performance (Major, Carrington, & Carnevale, 1984).

There is yet another reason why physically attractive individuals do not benefit from the social bias for beauty as much as we might expect. Although usually positive, stereotypes about beautiful people can also be negative. Good-looking women are more likely to be seen as egotistical and vain (Dermer & Thiel, 1975), and good-looking men as unintelligent (Byrne et al., 1968). Thus, highly physically attractive individuals have certain social advantages, but these can be offset by envy and, sometimes, hostility (Krebs & Adinolfi, 1975).

In the Long Run

This apparent balance between gains and losses raises a most important question. What happens in the long run to beautiful people? The what-is-beautiful-is-good stereotype suggests that life is kinder to those with better looks. But is it? To answer this question, researchers conducted a longitudinal study (Berscheid, Walster, & Campbell, 1972). First, they obtained ratings of college yearbook pictures from years past. Then they interviewed the now middle-aged college graduates to see how their lives had turned out. On one life event, there was a difference. The more physically attractive people among their subjects were more likely to have gotten married. In other respects, however, physical attractiveness was not a significant factor. There was no relationship between youthful good looks and either marital satisfaction or middle-aged happiness. This study suggests, then, that over time, beauty is *not* destiny.

SIMILARITY: LIKING PEOPLE WHO ARE JUST LIKE US

One of the most basic principles that has come from the study of interpersonal attraction is the rule of homogamy: Like attracts like. This section will describe some of the many ways in which "birds of a feather flock together."

Demographic Similarity

Looking over the research literature on homogamy, one is struck by the fact that people who form relationships with each other appear similar on almost every objective variable one can think of. Physical health, family background, age, religion, and education are only a few of the many demographic characteristics that have been found to be similar between members of heterosexual couples (Burgess & Wallin, 1953; Hendrick, 1981; Warren, 1966). Despite all this evidence of homogamy, it is a bit difficult to figure out exactly what it means. We can think of such findings as indicating that people survey a large number of other people but tend to be attracted primarily to those who are similar to them. There is, however, another perfectly plausible explanation. It could be that we tend to be around only those who are similar to us (e.g., attending the same church or school; living in the same neighborhood). If so, then demographic similarity between couples could indicate the effects of proximity rather than true preference for a similar other.

In the real world, it is difficult to separate proximity from preference. But in an artificial social world, specially designed to study the acquaintanceship process, this is easily done: You gather together a group of people who have never met, find out about their characteristics, then put them together for a time, and see if in fact initial similarity leads to liking. These were, in essence, the steps followed by Newcomb (1961), whose "experimental dormitory" was described earlier. Using an index of "objective" similarity based primarily on demographic factors (e.g., age, major college interest, urban versus rural background), Newcomb found that objectively similar students did like each other more.

Newcomb was also interested in whether objective similarity was important only early in a relationship or if it could affect attraction even after people knew each other fairly well. His results on this issue were mixed. For his second group of subjects (Year II), the effects of objective similarity declined steadily over time. With his Year I subjects, objective similarity had a more enduring effect. The relationship between similarity and liking was strong initially, then weakened, but then recovered and was quite strong even after more than three months of living together in the same house. This suggests that, for some people at least, similarity of demographic factors can have a persisting influence on attraction. Similar conclusions have been reached in research on teenage friendships (Kandel, 1978) and on married couples (Heaton, 1984).

Personality Similarity

Another way in which people may be similar to each other is in terms of their personalities (e.g., dominating, submissive, nurturing). Although Nias (1979) has criticized the work in this area, suggesting that findings have generally been weak and are frequently inconsistent from one study to another, other investigators have argued that there is reasonable evidence that people with similar personalities are attracted to each other (Barry, 1970; Boyden, Carroll, & Maier, 1984; Tharp, 1963). Furthermore, similarity in personality may continue to play a significant role in long-term enduring relationships (Schullo & Alperson, 1984; Thelen, Fishbein, & Tatten, 1985). For example, husbands and wives with similar personalities report greater marital happiness and satisfaction than do spouses with differing personalities (Antill, 1983; Caspi & Herbener, 1990; Meyer & Pepper, 1977; Skolnick, 1981). The effects of personality similarity on attraction may have both cognitive and emotional components. People who are similar to each other in the way that they structure and organize their thoughts and perceptions (called *cognitive complexity*) are more attracted to each other and more satisfied with their relationship than those who differ in cognitive complexity (Neimeyer, 1984; Neimeyer & Neimeyer, 1983). Similar mood states may also enhance attraction. Research has consistently indicated that nondepressed individuals are more attracted to others who are nondepressed than to those who are depressed; greater attraction toward mood-similar others has sometimes been found for depressed individuals (Locke & Horowitz, 1990) but not always (Rosenblatt & Greenberg, 1988).

Physical Attractiveness Similarity

Similarity in level of physical attractiveness has also received considerable attention in research on interpersonal attraction. As we have seen, there is a clear tendency for people to like physically attractive others more than those who are less attractive. A number of investigators have proposed that, in addition, there might be a tendency for people to like others who are similar to them in physical attractiveness. It seems reasonable. Surprisingly, however, the early returns were quite mixed. Some laboratory studies did find evidence for the *matching hypothesis* that people would prefer others of similar levels of physical attractiveness (Berscheid et al., 1971; Stroebe et al., 1971). But other studies failed to find such a preference (Huston, 1973; Walster et al., 1966).

When researchers ventured into the real world outside the laboratory, they discovered an entirely different picture (Feingold, 1988). Over and over again, in all kinds of couples, there was evidence of a match in physical attractiveness:

- Same-sex friends (Cash & Derlega, 1978)
- Dating couples (Critelli & Waid, 1980; Silverman, 1971)
- Couples going steady or engaged (Murstein, 1972b)
- Serious dating couples, cohabitants, engaged or married couples (White, 1980b)
- Couples getting married, based on wedding pictures (Shephard & Ellis, 1972)
- Married couples (Murstein & Christy, 1976; Price & Vandenberg, 1979)

Social scientists have also considered whether being similar in physical attractiveness would affect the progress and quality of a relationship. An interesting study by Folkes (1982) made use of a situation where physical attractiveness may be especially important: a professional dating service. The procedure of the Los Angeles dating service Folkes studied was to give clients demographic information about prospective dates plus a photo and a five-minute videotape of the potential date responding to some interview questions. If a client indicated interest in someone, the dating service then asked the other person for permission to release his or her name to the interested party. Using the five-step relationship development scale shown in Table 3.3 and judges' ratings of physical attractiveness (based on the same photos and videotapes that clients saw), Folkes obtained a clear relationship between similarity in physical attractiveness and progression of the relationship: The more similar that couples were, the more their relationship progressed.

TABLE 3.3 BEHAVIORAL INDEX OF RELATIONSHIP PROGRESS

Step 1	One client interested in meeting, but other client would not allow release of his or her name.
Step 2	Potential partner does allow release of name.
Step 3	Phone contact between the two clients.
Step 4	Clients have one date.
Step 5	Clients have two or more dates.

SOURCE: Based on Folkes, 1982.

Other investigators have also found that similarity in physical attractiveness may promote the development of a relationship. Murstein (1972b) reported a low but significant correlation between the degree of physical attractiveness similarity and courtship progress for his sample of going-steady and engaged couples: The more similar couples were more likely to indicate that their relationship had gotten closer over the six months of the study. Similarly, White (1980b) found that for both casual and serious daters, degree of similarity in physical attractiveness predicted changes in love for partner and likelihood of breaking up over a nine-month period: More similar couples reported increased love for each other and were less likely to break up. This association between physical attractiveness similarity and relationship progress was not found for the cohabitants and engaged or married couples in White's study, nor did Murstein and Christy (1976) find any relationship between physical attractiveness similarity and the adjustment of married couples.

This pattern of findings suggests that similarity in physical attractiveness may serve as a screening device. In initial encounters, it may foster attraction; later, it could strengthen attachment. Among committed couples, however, a match has already been achieved, and so physical attractiveness similarity does not continue to influence the progress of their relationship—unless, of course, that match were to fade away. In a study of sexual difficulties among married couples, Margolin and White (1987) found that those husbands who reported the greatest incidence of sexual difficulties believed that they had preserved their own attractiveness but that the attractiveness of their wives had declined. Wives' reports of their sexual difficulties were not, however, associated with a perceived "attraction gap" between themselves and their husbands.

At this point, we need to go back and tie up a loose thread in our understanding of the relationship between physical attractiveness similarity and attraction. Why was the evidence in favor of the matching hypothesis so weak in the laboratory but so strong in the real world? There are a number of possible reasons (Aron, 1988). First, the lab may

Attraction is strongly influenced by similarity. People who are similar in background characteristics, personality, physical attractiveness, and attitudes are more likely to be attracted to each other than are those who are dissimilar. (Michael Hayman/Photo Researchers)

not be a good place to test the matching hypothesis. In this artificial environment, subjects may indulge in "fantasy" choices of a "dream date" rather than select the more realistic options they would take in real life.

Second, being together may affect how people look. After all, people can—and, no doubt, do—change their appearance through the magic of makeup, clothes, and hairstyle in order to attain a level of physical attractiveness similar to that of their partner. It is even possible that couples just naturally grow to look alike. When undergraduates in one study were asked to figure out who married whom, they did a miserable job with college yearbook photos taken 25 years earlier when the couples under scrutiny were first married (Zajonc, Adelmann, Murphy, & Niedenthal, 1987). With current photos, however, the undergraduates made fairly accurate judgments. After 25 years of living together, spouses bore a strong resemblance to one another. However, subsequent research by Hinsz (1989) found greater similarity in appearance for both engaged and married couples, compared with random pairings of individuals. According to Hinsz, this similarity is not a matter of time spent together, nor is it simply a reflection of matching on level of physical attractiveness. Instead, he proposes that early and repeated exposure to our own appearance and genetically similar family members creates a strong preference for appearance similarity in others, which includes but is not limited to similarity in level of physical attractiveness.

Attitudinal Similarity

One of the major research areas in the study of similarity and attraction focuses on attitudinal similarity—how similar people are in their opinions, beliefs, and evaluations. There is a great deal of evidence that we will be more attracted to someone *we believe* has attitudes similar to our own than to someone we believe is attitudinally dissimilar (e.g., Brislin & Lewis, 1968; Byrne, 1971; Sachs, 1976; Stroebe et al., 1971; Tesser & Brodie, 1971).

There is also evidence that we will be more attracted to someone who *actually* is attitudinally similar. For instance, Byrne et al. (1970) selected students according to their attitudes, and matched up half of them with an attitudinally similar, opposite-sex partner and the other half with an attitudinally dissimilar, opposite-sex partner. All the couples then went out on a "Coke date." (For some readers, it may be necessary to note that in the late 1960s when this study was conducted, a "Coke date" involved having a soft drink together.) When subjects privately evaluated their partners after the date, there was a clear effect of similarity on attitudes: Highly similar couples were more attracted to each other than dissimilar couples.

This study also found a positive relationship between physical attractiveness (as rated by judges) and attraction. Indeed, attraction appeared to be an additive combination of both factors. Evaluations of the partner were most favorable when the partner was both physically attractive and attitudinally similar. In a follow-up at the end of the semester, subjects who had been paired with partners who were both attractive and similar were the most likely to remember their partners' names and to express a desire to date them again.

One of the most extensive examinations of the relationship between attitudes and attraction took place in Newcomb's (1961) "experimental dormitory," that specially created artificial world that has contributed so much to our understanding of interpersonal attraction. Both perceived and actual attitude similarity were examined. Perceived similarity and liking were found to be consistently associated from the beginning of the school year on. As we begin to interact with a stranger, we make an initial evaluation (usually based on relatively superficial characteristics such as physical appearance and/or demographic similarity). If we find ourselves attracted to that person, we will then infer that he or she has attitudes similar to ours. In other words, the initial attraction gives rise to the perceived similarity, which in turn strengthens the attraction (Marks & Miller, 1982).

The "time line" for the association between actual attitudinal similarity and attraction in Newcomb's study was quite different. This association was not evident from the beginning but increased steadily throughout the period students were living together. As we come to know people, we discover whether they actually do share our attitudes, and if they do, we will tend to like them. Actual attitude similarity is also related to marital happiness (Hendrick, 1981), another indication of the enduring importance of having similar opinions. Thus, while we always hope that someone we find attractive will view the world the way we do, *actual* agreement on beliefs and values may be crucial for satisfaction in long-term relationships.

Although most psychologists regard attitudinal similarity as a major factor in interpersonal attraction, Rosenbaum (1986) disagrees. In his view, similarity does not produce attraction, but *dissimilarity* does lead to repulsion—the desire to avoid. Rosenbaum emphasizes that similarity is expected and may not even be noticed. Dissimilarity, however, is usually unexpected and therefore gets our attention. Perhaps, then, we react to new acquaintances by avoiding those who are dissimilar rather than approaching those who are similar. Although Rosenbaum's attempt to make a wholesale substitution of the "repulsion process" for the "attraction process" may be too extreme, it is possible to combine both of them into a two-step process (Byrne, Clore, & Smeaton, 1986; Smeaton, Byrne, & Murnen, 1989). According to this model, people first avoid dissimilar others, and then approach similar others. These two stages are diagrammed in Figure 3.2. You should note that this model could be applied to various types of interpersonal similarity and not just to attitudes.

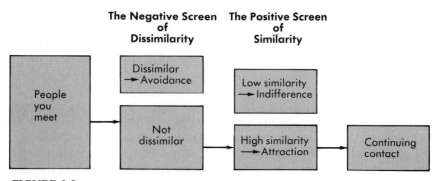

FIGURE 3.2
A two-step model of the attraction process. (Based on Byrne, Clore, & Smeaton, 1986.)

Why Is Similarity Attractive?

Whether it comes first in the attraction process or after an initial win-nowing based on dissimilarity, similarity raises an interesting question: Why do people like it so much? One answer is that it is reassuring (Byrne & Clore, 1970). We feel better about ourselves when we meet others just like us. There are, however, some other possible explana-tions for why similarity increases attraction. For example, perhaps per-ceived similarity produces expectations that the other person will like us, and so we just jump the gun and like them first (Aronson & Worchel, 1966; Condon & Crano, 1988). Or maybe what we are really attracted to is not similarity but an ideal. Usually, our ideals are reasona-bly close to the way we see ourselves—only better. Based on their research, Wetzel and Insko (1982) concluded that meeting ideal stan-dards had a greater impact on attraction than did similarity. But some-times our ideal friends or lovers are not available. Perhaps, then, we seek our ideal but have to settle for what we can get, and this turns out to be someone very similar to us instead of better (Kalick & Hamilton, 1986, 1988). Thus, despite the overwhelming evidence that birds of a feather do flock together, exactly how and why they get that way remain interesting questions for future research.

ATTRACTION AS A BALANCING ACT

As important as similarity is in interpersonal attraction, there are other ways in which people could fit together. In this section, we consider three possibilities: complementary fits between opposite personality types, a complementary exchange of personal resources, and the quid pro quo of reciprocity.

Complementarity in Personality

Complementarity in personality typically refers to a good fit between different personalities. If complementarity increases attraction, then we would expect, for example, that people with dominant personalities would like those with submissive personalities and vice versa. Prover-bially, opposites attract, and initially some researchers believed this was so (Winch, 1958). Later research, however, has yielded little evidence that personality complementarity increases attraction (Barry, 1970; Fish-bein & Thelen, 1981; Meyer & Pepper, 1977; Nias, 1979; Tharp, 1963). Complementary *behaviors*, however, may sometimes increase attraction (Strong et al., 1988). A person who behaves in a dominant way in a particular situation may get along better with a person who behaves submissively in that same situation.

Complementarity in Resources

Another way in which differences could fit together involves the personal resources that people possess. Probably the most widespread and best-documented example of resource complementarity is that between beauty and money (Murstein, 1972b). Traditionally, beautiful women have been expected to marry rich men. In an early study of this arrangement, Elder (1969) examined the relationship between the physical attractiveness of female high school students and their subsequent socioeconomic position as adults. He found that, particularly among those who came from working-class families, young women who were highly attractive in high school were more likely than their peers to marry men who were financially and professionally successful. But in this day of female employment, the beauty-for-money trade seems out of place. Surely, it must be a thing of the past. Actually, however, it appears to be alive and well—at least in the "dating marketplace" as represented by the personals ads in the print media and commercial dating services. Most studies of this marketplace have indicated that the primary resource offered by females and sought by males is physical attractiveness, while the primary resource offered by males and sought by females is economic status (Green, Buchanan, & Heuer, 1984; Harrison & Saeed, 1977; Koestner & Wheeler, 1988). In one study that failed to support this general pattern, three out of the four pieces were still in place for heterosexual advertisers. Men were more likely than women to indicate in their ads that they sought physical attractiveness and offered financial assets, and women were more likely than men to offer physical attractiveness (Deaux & Hanna, 1984). In this study, however, women were not more likely than men to seek financial assets.

But why might the beauty-for-money trade continue to flourish? According to some, the answer is evolution (Buss, 1988b; Buss & Barnes, 1986; Kenrick & Trost, 1989). The logic of this argument is as follows. Since reproductive success is the key to the survival of a species, natural selection should favor those mating patterns that promote the survival of offspring. Among humans, fertility is a function of the mother's age. In addition, the mother's health affects her fertility, the outcome of her pregnancy, and her ability to care for the child. Therefore, the chances for reproductive success should be increased for men who mate with younger adult women rather than older women and with healthy rather than unhealthy women. In the absence of more direct evidence, men may rely on physical appearance to estimate age and health, with younger and healthier women being perceived as more attractive. For women, mate selection is said to depend on their need for a provider male to take care of them during the long period of pregnancy and nursing. Women, then, should perceive powerful men who control resources that could contribute to the well-being of mother and child as especially attractive.

In a cross-cultural study involving respondents from 33 different countries, Buss (1989) found that the basic features of the traditional heterosexual exchange of beauty and money were widely endorsed. Men in most countries rated "good looks" in a mate as more important than did women, while women rated "good financial prospect" and "ambition and industriousness" as more important than did men. In all the countries included in this study, men preferred to be older than their spouse, while women preferred to be younger.

These results, however, do not prove that the evolutionary account of how the beauty-for-money trade developed is correct. Like other proposals in *sociobiology* (the application of the principles of evolutionary biology to explain social behavior), this view of the complementary fit between men's and women's mate preferences relies on the advantages of hindsight. Sociobiologists start with what is and work backward to how it got to be this way. In the absence of explicit rules for determining which accounts will be rejected and which ones accepted, it sometimes seems that an evolutionary-based explanation can be tailored to fit any given aspect of the status quo.

More specifically, the evolutionary-based explanation for the traditional heterosexual money-for-beauty trade ignores alternative explanations for that particular aspect of the status quo. Perhaps, for example, women have been forced to obtain desirable resources through men because they have been denied direct access to political and economic power (Caporael, 1989; Howard, Blumstein, & Schwartz, 1987). Moreover, it is difficult to see how an evolutionary-based account can explain the existence of *homosexual* relationships between an older, richer individual and a younger, more physically attractive person. Homosexual relationships do not contribute to the survival of the species; they are, however, subject to many of the same social and psychological factors that influence heterosexual partnerships.

Apart from the continuing debate about how best to explain the development of the apparent complementary fit between financial and appearance resources, there are some serious questions about the strength and endurance of the basic pattern itself. As we saw earlier in this chapter, men are far more likely than women to *say* that physical attractiveness is an important factor in their selection of a romantic partner. But sex differences in the *actual* influence of physical attractiveness on physical attractiveness are not as strong. Even if we restrict our examination to what men and women say they prefer in a mate, it is clear that many of the same characteristics are perceived as attractive by both sexes. In Buss's cross-cultural study, for example, both sexes rated "kind-understanding" and "intelligent" as more important than earning power and attractiveness. This similarity in the mate preferences expressed by men and women was also demonstrated when undergraduates were asked to judge 101 acts on how effective they would be in attracting members of the opposite sex (Buss, 1988a). Some acts were

TABLE 3.4 THE TOP 10 MALE AND FEMALE ACTS JUDGED MOST EFFECTIVE IN ATTRACTING OPPOSITE-SEX PARTNERS

10 Most Effective Male Acts	*10 Most Effective Female Acts*
1. He displayed a good sense of humor.	1. She displayed a good sense of humor.
2. He was sympathetic to her troubles.	2. She kept herself well-groomed.
3. He showed good manners.	3. She was sympathetic to his troubles.
4. He kept himself well-groomed.	4. She showed good manners.
5. He made an effort to spend a lot of time with a particular woman.	5. She showered daily.
6. He offered to help her.	6. She kept physically fit to create a healthy appearance.
7. He showered daily.	7. She made up jokes to make men laugh.
8. He kept physically fit to create a healthy appearance.	8. She made an effort to spend a lot of time with a particular man.
9. He exercised.	9. She wore stylish, fashionable clothes.
10. He wore attractive outfits.	10. She offered to help him.

SOURCE: From Buss, 1988a.

judged differentially effective for men and women, but the majority were viewed as equally effective for both sexes. Table 3.4 displays the "top 10" acts judged to be the most effective for men when they wanted to attract women and the "top 10" judged to be most effective for women when they wanted to attract men. As you can see, many of the same actions come highly recommended for both men and women.

Reciprocity and Consistency

So far we have discussed attraction that is based on proximity, physical attractiveness, similarity, and complementarity. Reciprocity—I'll give you back whatever you give me—is also important in social interactions. We like people who like us (Backman & Secord, 1959; Curtis & Miller, 1986) and who say nice things about us (Byrne & Rhamey, 1965; Sachs, 1976).

Beyond the general principle of liking those who like us, there may be an even more general rule of "liking likers." In a series of studies, Folkes and Sears (1977) demonstrated a clear tendency for people to be more attracted to individuals who liked things than to those who expressed negative opinions. This effect was totally independent of reciprocity, as subjects in these studies only observed and did not have any personal interaction with the people they evaluated. Note, however, that being a liker can have some drawbacks. Highly critical dislikers tend to be viewed as "brilliant but cruel," but bubbly likers may be seen as very nice but a little dim (Amabile, 1983).

Balancing acts in interpersonal attraction can get quite complex. According to *balance theory*, people desire consistency among their thoughts, feelings, and social relationships (Heider, 1958; Newcomb, 1959). When two people interact, reciprocity maintains balance. But what happens when there are three people involved? In order to answer this question, Aronson and Cope (1968) conducted the following experiment. Undergraduate subjects met first with an experimenter who either was polite and nice to them or was harsh and rude. After this experience, subjects observed the experimenter's supposed supervisor (who had not been present during the earlier interaction between the subject and experimenter and had no knowledge of this interaction) treat the experimenter in a pleasant or unpleasant manner. Subjects were then given an opportunity to help the supervisor on a task unrelated to the rest of the experiment.

Before reading on, you might want to see if you can figure out what the results of this experiment would be. When would subjects have been more likely to help the supervisor? If we always like pleasant and nice people ("likers"), then perhaps subjects would always be more likely to help if the supervisor was being nice, regardless of what kind of experience they had had with the experimenter. Or, perhaps, only the subjects who had had a totally pleasant experience (i.e., positive interaction with the experimenter, and observation of positive interaction between the experimenter and supervisor) would be likely to help out the supervisor.

In the actual experiment, the subjects who had had a totally pleasant experience were indeed quite helpful. But so were those who had a negative interaction themselves and observed a negative interaction between the experimenter and supervisor. Both findings are consistent with the notion that we prefer to keep thoughts, feelings, and relationships in balance. We like the friend of a friend *and* the enemy of an enemy.

*B*ARRIERS: LIKING THE ONES WE CANNOT HAVE

According to the theory of psychological reactance (J. Brehm, 1966; S. Brehm & J. Brehm, 1981), all individuals have a set of specific behavioral freedoms—actions, thoughts, and feelings that they feel free to engage in. Reactance theory states that when a person's specific freedom is threatened with being taken away, or is actually taken away, the person should become motivated to reestablish the freedom. Briefly put, reactance theory describes how and why we desire something more once we think we may have lost it. We can, of course, also desire *someone* more once we think we may have lost him or her. This section will examine the ways in which barriers to relationships—threats to the freedom to have a relationship—can increase attraction.

External Barriers

Probably the most obvious obstacles to relationships are those barriers that are created by people or conditions external to the relationship itself. Lovers can be parted by parental disapproval or geographical distance, and such partings may, at least initially, only serve to increase the attachment. If this reminds you of *Romeo and Juliet,* you are in good company. A group of social scientists also thought of Romeo and Juliet and decided to investigate Shakespeare's hypothesis (Driscoll, Davis, & Lipetz, 1972).

In this study, married and unmarried couples reported on their feelings of romantic love and the amount of parental interference they had experienced. These reports were gathered at two different times, 6 to 10 months apart. Looking first at subjects' initial reports, Driscoll et al. found a positive relationship between love and interference: The more parental interference subjects reported, the more love they expressed for their partner. Although this correlation was obtained for both married and unmarried subjects, it was stronger among unmarried couples. But what happened over the course of the study? Did changes in perceived interference from parents track changes in love? For unmarried couples, the answer is yes. Those who reported more parental interference later in the study also expressed more love; those who reported less parental interference than had been the case earlier reported less love. Among married couples, however, changes in parental interference were not related to changes in love for the partner.

Not all research on parental reactions to their children's romantic involvements has found a Romeo-and-Juliet effect. Sometimes, children appear to be more conforming to their parents' opinions, getting more involved in relationships their parents support and less involved in those to which their parents object (Parks, Stan, & Eggert, 1983). Other times, parental approval or disapproval may have little impact on the progress of their children's relationships (Leslie, Huston, & Johnson, 1986). This diversity of research findings indicates the need for further research to specify when and how parental reactions can affect their children's attraction to a romantic partner (Whyte, 1990).

Research on another kind of external barrier has focused on a disappointing moment in the dating game. In what they called "a country and western application to psychology," Pennebaker and his colleagues (1979) examined the relationship between the passage of time and the attractiveness of potential dating partners. They took their hypothesis from the song by Mickey Gilley that claims "the girls all get prettier at closing time." Interviews with men and women in three bars in Austin, Texas, suggested that they did, and so did the boys. Patrons were asked to rate the attractiveness of everyone present in the bar at 9 P.M., 10:30 P.M., and (right before closing) midnight. While their ratings of members of their own sex did not change appreciably across time, the perceived attractiveness of the opposite sex increased, especially from 10:30 P.M. to midnight. As reactance theory would predict, patrons faced with the threat of going home alone found those still available more desirable.

Subsequent research on this phenomenon has yielded mixed results. There is some evidence that it may sometimes be stronger for men than for women (Sprecher et al., 1984), and that it may occur in some bars but not in others (Nida & Koon, 1983). Although recent research by Gladue and Delaney (1990) did find that the attractiveness of the opposite sex increased at closing time for both men and women, these investigators were not able to identify the psychological process involved. In this study, ratings of opposite-sex bar patrons, alcohol consumption, and the stated desire to meet the opposite sex all increased over the course of the evening. However, the increase in ratings of the opposite sex occurred independently of the other two factors. Thus, the perception that others "get prettier at closing time" does not seem to be a matter of being too drunk to see straight. But the lack of a strong association between ratings of the opposite sex and stated desire to meet the opposite sex also raises doubts about the original explanation based on reactance theory. Like the Romeo-and-Juliet effect, the closing-time phenomenon needs further research to determine more precisely when and how it occurs.

Barriers in the Relationship

Another type of barrier resides not in the environment, but in the person with whom we might want to have a relationship. It has long been the commonsense wisdom of the dating game that a person will be more desirable if he or she "plays hard to get." Walster, Walster, Piliavin, and Schmidt (1973) made a concerted effort to demonstrate this "hard-to-get effect"—that is, to show that choosy, selective people would be seen as more attractive than others who were less discriminating. After five studies, Walster et al. had to conclude that the hard-to-get effect was, indeed, hard to get. In fact, they were not able to get it at all, though they did find that people preferred potential dates who were "selectively hard-to-get": someone who expressed attraction to them, together with a lack of interest in other potential partners.

Along with other researchers (Rodin, 1982), Wright and Contrada (1986) have pointed to a number of possible problems in the studies conducted by Walster et al. First, they note that it is important to distinguish between our response to a person who is hard to get (who is selective and choosy about whom he or she goes out with) and someone who is personally rejecting (a person who has explicitly stated that he or she will not go out with us). Playing hard to get is not the same as slamming the door in someone's face. Wright and Contrada also emphasize that extremely hard-to-get people may be viewed as arrogant and conceited, and this would take away from their attractiveness.

With these notions in mind, Wright and Contrada conducted a set of experiments on the hard-to-get effect. In these studies, subjects were presented with descriptions of people of the opposite sex who were characterized as very selective, moderately selective, or nonselective about whom they would go out with. This research indicated that we do find selective, choosy people more attractive than those who will go out with almost anyone. But selectivity can go too far. Subjects tended to see those who were very selective (saying they would only go out with "exceptional" people) as conceited and were more attracted to a moderately selective individual. Female subjects were particularly likely to react negatively to a male who was described as extremely selective, suggesting that it may be less socially acceptable for males than for females to play, or actually be, *very* hard to get.

EXPECTATIONS: LIKING THE ONES WE EXPECT TO LIKE

The earlier section on physical attractiveness suggested that our expectations about beautiful people may affect our reactions to them, which, in turn, may affect the kind of behavior they learn to engage in. More generally, there is the possibility that when we expect to be attracted to someone, we act in ways that elicit attractive behavior from them. This view of interpersonal attraction highlights the importance of self-fulfilling prophecies—by the way we act, we obtain reactions that confirm our expectations (Darley & Fazio, 1980; Miller & Turnbull, 1986).

A study by Snyder, Tanke, and Berscheid (1977) provided dramatic evidence of the power of expectations in interpersonal attraction. Subjects in this experiment were pairs of unacquainted male and female college students. Care was taken to ensure that subjects did not have a chance to meet or see each other before the experiment, and they remained in separate rooms throughout the study. Each pair of subjects was given some background information about their partner, and the males also received a photograph supposedly of their partner. In fact, these photographs were not of their partners; they were prepared ahead of time by the experimenters and were of females who never participated in the study. Half of the male subjects received a photograph of a physically attractive woman, and half received one of a physically unattractive woman.

After seeing the photograph and reading over the demographic information, males rated their impressions of their female partners. Subjects (males and females) then had a chance to have a brief audio-only (over headphones) conversation. Independent judges later rated these conversations, with one set of judges listening only to the male portions and another set listening only to the female portions.

Snyder et al. were interested in three major aspects of the behavior of subjects in this experiment. First, they looked at the males' impressions based only on the photograph and demographic information. As we would expect from the research on physical attractiveness, males displayed a strong what-is-beautiful-is-good stereotype. Those males who expected to interact with a physically attractive female expected her to have more socially desirable personality characteristics.

Second, Snyder et al. investigated the verbal behavior of males during the audio conversation and found that these subjects acted consistently with their expectations. Males who believed their conversational partner was physically attractive (and, therefore, also expected her to have many other socially desirable characteristics) were themselves more sociable and outgoing toward their partners; males who believed their partner was physically unattractive (and possessed fewer socially desirable characteristics) were less friendly. So far, then, Snyder et al. were able to demonstrate that we behave in accordance with our expectations: We act friendlier toward people we expect to like.

The third, and most important, aspect of this experiment had to do with the verbal behavior of the female subjects. Remember, male subjects' beliefs about the physical attractiveness of their partners were based on false information supplied by the experimenters. Thus, *actual* physical attractiveness of the female partners did not differ between the two groups of males; only the men's expectations were different. This difference, however, was enough to create different behavior on the part of the females in the study. Women who had interacted with males who had formed positive expectations about them were rated as having more socially desirable personality characteristics by judges who had not heard anything said by the male subjects.

These findings demonstrate that when we expect people to be beautiful, they will, in fact, behave beautifully . . . and when we expect them to be unappealing, they will behave in an unappealing fashion. In interpersonal relationships, we tend to reap what we sow. If we are friendly and positive and upbeat, we will find many attractive people in the world; if we are cold and critical and cynical, we will find very few attractive people. By our expectations and our own behavior, we can determine not only our own attractiveness, but the attractiveness of those around us.

CHAPTER SUMMARY

Theories of Attraction: A Matter of Rewards

According to most theories, we are attracted to individuals whose presence is rewarding to us. Two major types of reward influence attraction: direct rewards produced by an individual (rewarding behaviors, rewarding characteristics, access to external rewards) and rewarding associations in which we connect the presence of an individual with a positive experience not directly produced by that individual. Attraction is an interactive process—involving personal needs, another's perceived characteristics, and the situation.

Proximity: Liking the Ones We're Near

Proximity provides the opportunity for social interactions but does not determine the quality of these interactions. We select our friends, and our enemies, from those around us.

Personal Space: Coming Closer. When people violate our personal space by coming closer than we expect or desire, our initial reactions are intensified. Those we like, we like more; those we dislike, we dislike more.

Familiarity: Repeated Contact. In general, familiarity breeds attraction. Even when we have only brief, constrained contact (mere exposure), we usually like more those with whom we have interacted frequently. But there are limits. Extreme familiarity can decrease attraction, and repeated contact with someone we do not like can increase hostility.

Physical Attractiveness: To See You Is to Like You

In general, people are more attracted to individuals who are highly physically attractive.

What Creates the Bias for Beauty? Four possible reasons for the bias for beauty were examined. First, there is the sheer, aesthetic appeal of an attractive appearance. Second, there is the what-is-beautiful-is-good stereotype, in which attractive people are assumed to possess many other desirable personal characteristics. Third, there is some evidence that beautiful people may possess greater social skills. Active, assertive social skills appear to be more commonly associated with physical attractiveness among men than among women. Physically attractive women, however, may find social interactions more rewarding than do attractive men. The fourth possible reason for the bias for beauty is the desire to obtain social benefits from associating with good-looking individuals. In general, a person of average attractiveness is more likely to gain (assimilation) from being associated with beautiful people when there is a joint appearance and more likely to lose (contrast) when the beautiful people are seen first.

Who Has a Bias for Beauty? Men are more likely than women to say that the physical attractiveness of a potential date is important to them and to respond more favorably to more physically attractive members of the opposite sex. However, this sex difference is greater for estimations than for actual behavior. The personality trait of self-monitoring is associated with differential emphasis on physical attractiveness in a dating partner. Men high in self-monitoring (who say they tailor their behavior to meet social demands) are more likely than those low in self-monitoring (who say they are true to their own internal standards) to value physical attractiveness over a good personality. Low self-monitoring men are more cautious about getting involved in romantic situations. High self-monitors (male and female) appear less committed to their dating partners.

Adding Up the Gains and Losses. Despite all the social advantages of being physically attractive, extremely good-looking individuals also experience some losses. They appear to discount the praise they receive if their evaluators have had a chance to see them. They suffer from negative stereotypes, as well as benefiting from positive ones.

In the Long Run. Perhaps because the gains and losses from being physically attractive tend to cancel each other out, long-term life satisfaction appears much the same for very attractive and not so attractive individuals. Good-looking people are, however, more likely to get married.

Similarity: Liking People Who Are Just Like Us

Demographic Similarity. In a new environment, those who have similar backgrounds like each other more than those who come from different backgrounds.

Personality Similarity. People with similar personalities like each other more than do people with differing personalities. Both cognitive and emotional components may be involved in the positive effect of personality similarity on attraction.

Physical Attractiveness Similarity. In the lab, evidence on the matching hypothesis was mixed. In the real world, the evidence is strong that people who are attached to each other (as friends, dating partners, or spouses) have similar levels of physical attractiveness. The discrepancy between laboratory and real-world results may reflect the artificial conditions of lab experiments. It is also possible that being together can affect people's looks—as they strive deliberately to achieve a better match in appearance or just naturally grow to look alike.

Attitudinal Similarity. Both perceived and actual attitude similarity increase attraction. But attitude dissimilarity may also play an important role, as we avoid those whose beliefs and opinions differ from ours. It has been suggested that people may first screen out those who are dissimilar and then, among those who are left, become attracted to those who are more similar.

Why Is Similarity Attractive? There are many possible reasons why similarity is attractive. Similar people reassure us about ourselves. We also assume similar others will like us, and so we go ahead and like them. But perhaps we are more attracted to people who meet our ideals, though we may have to settle for those who are similar rather than better.

Attraction as a Balancing Act

Complementarity in Personality. There is little evidence that opposite personalities attract each other.

Complementarity in Resources. The traditional, heterosexual, complementary exchange of personal resources involves female beauty and male economic prowess. Some have argued that this exchange reflects evolutionary processes. Others contend that this exchange reflects the division of resources imposed by society. Despite their different emphases on physical attractiveness and financial assets, men and women find many of the same attributes attractive in opposite-sex partners.

Reciprocity and Consistency. Reciprocity plays an important role in interpersonal attraction: We tend to like those who like us. The desire for consistency also extends to three-person groups: We like the friends of our friends and the enemies of our enemies.

Barriers: Liking the Ones We Cannot Have

According to the theory of psychological reactance, people react to threats to or eliminations of their behavioral freedoms by becoming motivated to reestablish those freedoms. If we believe we have the freedom to have something, we will want it more should we fear we are about to lose it.

External Barriers. Barriers against attraction can come from outside the two people involved. Parents can interfere with their children's romantic attachments. In some cases, this interference can boomerang and create more attraction. Closing time at a bar can also act as an external barrier against securing a date for the evening. In some localities at least, the girls and the boys all get prettier at closing time.

Barriers in the Relationship. Barriers can also be erected by the person to whom we are attracted. Initially, the hard-to-get effect (liking those who are less available) was hard to get. Subsequent research has indicated that we respond most favorably to those who are moderately hard to get: not indiscriminate, but also not conceited.

Expectations: Liking the Ones We Expect to Like

In a self-fulfilling prophecy, our actions create reactions that confirm our original expectations. When we believe that individuals are attractive, we will act in a friendly manner, and they, in response, will behave in ways that are, in fact, more attractive. In interpersonal relationships, what goes out often comes back around.

4

Love and Romance

------ ❖ ------

What is love?
William Shakespeare
Twelfth-Night

S hakespeare's question is one that most people have asked at some time in their lives. And there have been a host of answers; *love* has more entries in *Bartlett's Familiar Quotations* than any other word except *man* (Levinger, 1988). Is it the noble passion for God and humanity described by Paul in 1 Corinthians 13, "Love bears all things, believes all things, hopes all things, endures all things"? Or is it the selfish, self-seeking desire described in one of William Blake's poems, "Love seeketh only self to please, to bind another to its delight"? Or is it the teenage heartthrob of a Bruce Springsteen song, "Ooh, Ooh I gotta crush on you"? Is it all of these things, or none of them?

In this chapter, we examine what social scientists have to say about love. They have much more to say now than they did even a few years ago, as research on love has increased dramatically (Shaver & Hazan, 1988). But, still, do not expect any quick and easy answer to Shakespeare's question. Love is a very complex form of human behavior. This complexity makes it hard to study and difficult to understand. It is also part of what makes love so fascinating.

Our exploration of love in this chapter looks at it from three different angles. First, we consider the history of love, the way it varies across cultures and historical periods. Then, we examine different ways to categorize the types of love experienced in adult intimate relationships. In the final section, we discuss several factors that contribute to differences among individuals in how they love. By the time you finish this chapter, you still will not know *exactly* what love is, but you should have a much better understanding of the range of possibilities.

A BRIEF HISTORY OF LOVE

In North America, we have inherited a rich and, at times, contradictory legacy about love. On the one hand, love is a constant: "Cases of romantic love can be found at all times and places and have often been the subject of powerful poetic expression" (Stone, 1988, p. 18). On the other hand, there are immense differences in how different societies have viewed the experience of love (de Rougemont, 1956; Gathorne-Hardy, 1981; Hunt, 1959). Consider, for example, these dimensions:

- *Cultural value:* Desirable versus undesirable
- *Sexuality:* Sexual versus nonsexual
- *Sexual orientation:* Homosexual versus heterosexual
- *Marital status:* Married versus not married

As you will see, the social construction of what love is, or should be, has drawn upon these dimensions to create some strikingly different patterns.

Ancient Greece

According to Sophocles, a Greek dramatist of fifth century B.C., love is both passionate and frightening:

> . . . Love is not love alone,
> But in her name lie many names concealed;
> For she is Death, imperishable Force,
> Desire unmixed, wild Frenzy, Lamentation.

For the Greeks such passion was a form of madness and had nothing to do with marriage or family life. But the ancient Greeks did have an alternate concept of love that was far more positive. In platonic love, the lover was thought to attain transcendence and ecstasy through nonsexual adoration of the beloved. This kind of love, however, was reserved almost exclusively for love between two men, usually one older and the other younger. Though there are examples in Greek literature of loving marriages, such examples are rare and tend to be based on quite early periods of Greek culture (Bardis, 1979). Indeed, sociologist Safilios-Rothschild (1977) claims that even in modern times it is widely believed in Greece that marriage destroys love.

Roman Antecedents

The early Romans took much of their view of love from the ancient Greeks. Love was seen as an undesirable torment that occurred outside of marriage. Later, however, the Romans began to develop a new perspective in which love was considered a game—to be played with great concentration but not to be taken seriously. Roman society was also one of the first to institutionalize divorce. Indeed, the last century of the Roman Empire, with what Gathorne-Hardy (1981) calls its "epidemic of divorces," has been characterized as the closest historical approximation to the current marital situation in the United States.

Courtly Love

In the twelfth century in the south of France, yet another tradition of love developed. Called "courtly love," it required knights to pay homage to their lady love while troubadors sang the praises of romance. Courtly love was a far cry from the Greek and Roman idea of love as a disastrous madness to be avoided if at all possible. It was equally different from the Roman concept of love as play. The knights who enlisted in the Court of Love around Eleanor of Aquitaine and other aristocratic women sought love as a holy grail, and they were extremely diligent in their devotion. It was all very idealistic, very elegant, and—at least in theory—nonsexual. It was also explicitly adulterous. In courtly love, the male partner was expected to be unmarried and the female partner married—to someone else! Among the aristocracy of the Middle Ages, courtly love was to be a peak experience; marriage, in contrast, was a deadly serious matter of politics and property.

A Time of Transition

For the next 500 years, it was the common assumption that passionate love, though it could be desirable and ennobling, was essentially doomed. Either the lovers would be prevented from being with each other (frequently because they were married to other people), or death would overtake one or the other (or both) before their love could be fulfilled. It was not until the seventeenth and eighteenth centuries that Europeans, especially the English, began to connect love with marriage and to believe that a "happy ending" was possible for romantic passion. There was support in the Hebrew scriptures for this connection:

> So Jacob served seven years for Rachel, and they seemed to him but a few days because of the love he had for her. (Genesis 29)

And there was also, as noted earlier, some precedent in ancient Greek literature. But, as a widespread cultural standard, this was a new idea.

Even to the present day, a close connection between romantic love and marriage has always been limited in application. Continental Europe did not take to this association as rapidly or as thoroughly as England. And in England itself, though members of the aristocracy

Royal marriages often serve to promote romantic ideas about marriage but are themselves usually based on concerns about politics and property. (UPI/Bettmann)

(Victoria and Albert in the nineteenth century; Charles and Diana in our day) promoted the idea of marrying for love, their own marriages were, in fact, usually based on political and economic concerns. Moreover, it was not until very recently that marrying for love began to gain widespread acceptance outside England, Europe, and North America (Xiaohe & Whyte, 1990). In many societies today, it is still the exception rather than the rule.

In Our Time

The acceptance of and enthusiasm for marrying for love has been most complete in North America. Perhaps because of the absence of an aristocratic class and the force of egalitarian ideas, the notion that individuals (not families) should choose marriage partners because of emotional attachment (not economic concerns) has become the dominant principle in our society. This principle shows no sign of weakening. Indeed, it has intensified. When college undergraduates were asked in 1967 whether they would marry someone with whom they were *not* in love, 64.6 percent of the men and 24.3 percent of the women said no (Kephart, 1967). By 1984, the verdict was overwhelming among both males and females: 85.6 percent of the men and 84.9 percent of the women said no (Simpson, Campbell, & Berscheid, 1986). Among heterosexuals, one marries for love, and when in love, one marries. Among homosexuals, there is considerable resentment that legally recognized marriage is not available.

Despite this strong belief that love and marriage should go together, the association has its critics.

> All societies recognize that there are occasional violent emotional attachments between persons of opposite sex, but our present American culture is practically the only one which has attempted to capitalize these and make them the basis for marriage. Most groups regard them as unfortunate and point out the victims of such attachments as horrible examples. Their rarity in most societies suggests that they are psychological abnormalities to which our own culture has attached extraordinary value just as other cultures have attached extreme value to other abnormalities. The hero of the modern American movie is always a romantic lover just as the hero of the old Arab epic is always an epileptic. A cynic might suspect that in any ordinary population the percentage of individuals with a capacity for romantic love of the Hollywood type was about as large as that of persons able to throw genuine epileptic fits. However, given a little social encouragement, either one can be adequately imitated without the performer admitting even to himself that the performance is not genuine. (Linton, 1936, p. 175)

Linton is, of course, arguing from an old tradition—the early Greek and Roman view of love as madness. He is also making an assumption—that there is only one kind of love. Consider all the different views of love you have just read about:

- Love is madness and a torment.
- Love is not possible in marriage.
- Love happens only between people of the same sex.
- Love should not involve sexual contact.
- Love is a game.
- Love is a noble quest.
- Love is doomed.
- Love leads to happiness.
- Love and marriage go together.

Are these just different perspectives on the same phenomenon? Or are there different kinds of love? Increasingly, social scientists are suggesting that the cultural and historical variations in love may reflect a basic psychological fact: A diversity of loving experiences can occur among human beings. In the next section, we consider the various types of love that have been emphasized in recent theory and research.

TYPES OF LOVE

In his influential book *Liking and Loving*, Zick Rubin (1973) set the stage for later typologies of love by distinguishing between two kinds of affectionate attachments. To see the difference between liking and loving, take a look at the items listed in Table 4.1. When Rubin asked college students to respond to statements like these, they said that items like the first three described their friends, while items like the last three

TABLE 4.1 RUBIN'S (1973) LIKING AND LOVING SCALES: SOME EXAMPLE ITEMS

Rubin's Liking Scale
1. My partner is one of the most likable people I know.
2. My partner is the sort of person that I would like to be.
3. I have great confidence in my partner's good judgment.

Rubin's Loving Scale
1. I feel I can confide in my partner about virtually everything.
2. I would forgive my partner for practically anything.
3. I would do almost anything for my partner.

applied to their romantic partners. On the basis of these results, Rubin proposed that liking and loving are distinct and, to some extent, mutually exclusive reactions to an intimate relationship. We like our friends. We love our lovers. It sounds reasonable and is consistent with findings obtained by other investigators besides Rubin (Pam, Plutchik, & Conte, 1975).

Some researchers, however, have discovered that the difference between liking and loving is not always clear-cut. Dion and Dion (1976b) gave Rubin's two scales to people involved in different kinds of relationships: casual daters, exclusive daters, engaged couples, and married couples. They found that casual daters did report more liking than loving, but that liking and loving were about equal in the other three kinds of relationships. In another study, subjects rated some items on the Loving Scale (e.g., "One of my primary concerns is my partner's welfare") as highly characteristic of loving *and* liking (Steck, Levitan, McLane, & Kelley, 1982). Perhaps one reason why the boundaries between liking and loving are not always so sharp is that Rubin took a rather strong view of liking and a rather mild view of loving. This possibility is reflected in the distinction we consider next.

Companionate and Passionate Love

Many social scientists maintain that all love is divided into two parts: companionate and passionate (Hatfield, 1988; Peele, 1988). *Companionate love* is a secure, trusting attachment—similar in many ways to what Rubin called liking. *Passionate love* is a state of high arousal, filled with the ecstasy of being loved by the partner and the agony of being rejected. If you examine the Passionate Love Scale in Table 4.2, you can see that it describes a much more emotionally intense version of love than Rubin's Loving Scale.

Arousal. Because of its intensity, passionate love is the stuff of great drama. What would novelists, playwrights, poets, and scriptwriters do without it? Actually, were we not so accustomed to it—in fictional accounts and, perhaps, in our own lives—we would regard passionate love as a distinctly odd aspect of human behavior. Passionate love isn't always a state of pure pleasure. In fact, it is often shot through with anxiety and obsession (Hindy, Schwarz, & Brodsky, 1989). Yet the agony just seems to increase the ecstasy. How could this be?

According to Elaine Hatfield* and Ellen Berscheid, the answer lies in arousal (Berscheid & Walster, 1974a; Walster, 1971). Drawing on Schachter's (1964) two-factor theory of emotion, Hatfield and Berscheid

* Earlier work by Professor Hatfield appears under the name E. Walster.

TABLE 4.2 THE PASSIONATE LOVE SCALE (SHORT FORM)

This questionnaire asks you to describe how you feel when you are passionately in love. Some common terms for this feeling are: passionate love, infatuation, love sickness, or obsessive love. Please think of the person whom you love most passionately *right now*. If you are not in love right now, please think of the last person you loved passionately. If you have never been in love, think of the person whom you came closest to caring for in that way. Keep this person in mind as you complete this section of the questionnaire. (The person you choose should be of the opposite sex if you are heterosexual or of the same sex if you are homosexual.) Try to tell us how you felt at the time when your feelings were the most intense.

Answer each item in terms of this scale:

1	2	3	4	5	6	7	8	9
Not at all true				Moderately true				Definitely true

1. I would feel deep despair if _____ left me.
2. Sometimes I feel I can't control my thoughts; they are obsessively on _____.
3. I feel happy when I am doing something to make _____ happy.
4. I would rather be with _____ than anyone else.
5. I'd get jealous if I thought _____ were falling in love with someone else.
6. I yearn to know all about _____.
7. I want _____—physically, emotionally, mentally.
8. I have an endless appetite for affection from _____.
9. For me, _____ is the perfect romantic partner.
10. I sense my body responding when _____ touches me.
11. _____ always seems to be on my mind.
12. I want _____ to know me—my thoughts, my fears, and my hopes.
13. I eagerly look for signs indicating _____'s desire for me.
14. I possess a powerful attraction for _____.
15. I get extremely depressed when things don't go right in my relationship with _____.

Higher scores on the PLS indicate greater passionate love.

SOURCE: Hatfield & Rapson, 1987.

characterize passionate love as consisting of (1) physiological arousal and (2) the belief that this arousal is caused by a reaction to the beloved. Sometimes, the connection between arousal and love is obvious. It isn't particularly surprising, for example, that sexually aroused men report more love for their romantic partners than do those who are not aroused (Dermer & Pyszczynski, 1978; Stephan, Berscheid, & Walster, 1971). But the two-factor theory of passionate love allows for an unexpected twist.

Arousal can be attributed to the wrong source—*misattributed*—and, thereby, create all kinds of interesting complications.

According to Hatfield and Berscheid, passionate love is produced, or at least intensified, when feelings of arousal in the beloved's presence are explained solely by that presence. The actual, also arousing, effects of other aspects of the situation are ignored. This process has been called *excitation transfer* (Zillmann, 1978, 1984). Arousal caused by one stimulus is transferred and added to that elicited by a second stimulus. The combined arousal is then perceived as caused by only the second stimulus.

Suppose, for example, that Dan is afraid of flying, but his fear is not particularly extreme and he doesn't like to admit it to himself. This fear, however, does cause him to be physiologically aroused. Suppose further that Dan takes a flight and finds himself sitting next to Judy on the plane. With heart racing, palms sweating, and breathing labored, Dan chats with Judy as the plane takes off. Suddenly, Dan discovers that he finds Judy terribly attractive, and he begins to try to figure out ways that he can continue to see her after the flight is over. What accounts for Dan's sudden surge of interest in Judy? Is she really that appealing to him, or has he taken the physiological arousal of fear and mislabeled it as attraction?

This possibility that fear might be mislabeled as sexual attraction was first examined by Dutton and Aron (1974), who conducted their experiment near two bridges located in a scenic tourist spot. One bridge was suspended over a deep gorge; the bridge swayed from side to side, and walking across it would make most people quite nervous. The other bridge was more stable and not far off the ground; most people would be perfectly comfortable walking across it.

As unaccompanied males (limited to those between 19 and 35 years of age) walked across these bridges, they were met by a research assistant, who was either male or female. The research assistant would ask each person to participate in a brief experiment in which he answered a few questions and wrote a brief story in response to a picture he was shown. When this was completed, the research assistant noted that if the subject wanted more information about the study, he could give the assistant a call at home.

The picture that the male subjects in this experiment told a story about was from the Thematic Apperception Test (TAT), and it is possible to score these stories in terms of sexual imagery. Dutton and Aron found that those male subjects who were met on the suspension bridge by a female research assistant had the highest sexual imagery scores for their stories. In addition, these subjects were more likely to call the assistant at her home. Fear had fueled attraction.

Or had it? Some researchers have argued that it is not necessary to rely on complicated processes like misattribution and excitation transfer to explain why romance blossoms in the midst of fear (Kenrick & Cialdini, 1977; Riordan & Tedeschi, 1983). Instead, they say, fondness for those who are with us in a time of distress comes from the comfort we take from their presence (Epley, 1974; Schachter, 1959). Because having them with us helps to reduce our distress, their presence is rewarding. Thus, the link between fear and love is just another example of how social rewards create attraction and strengthen attachment.

Subsequent research, however, indicated that a reward-based explanation could not provide an adequate explanation for the relationship between arousal and romance. In one study, male subjects ran in place for either 2 minutes or 15 seconds (White, Fishbein, & Rutstein, 1981). Subjects then saw a videotape of a young woman whom they expected to meet later in the experiment. Through the wonders of makeup, this young woman appeared either very attractive or very unattractive. When subjects gave their impressions of the woman they had seen on the videotape, it was found that both arousal and the characteristics of the female were important. For the attractive woman, high arousal led to greater attraction; for the unattractive woman, high arousal led to *less* attraction.

These results were replicated in a somewhat more elaborate second experiment. Here, White et al. had male subjects listen to one of three kinds of tape-recorded material:

- *Negatively arousing.* A description of the brutal mutilation and killing of a missionary while his family watched.
- *Positively arousing.* Selections from Steve Martin's album, *A Wild and Crazy Guy.*
- *Neutral.* A boring description of the circulatory system of a frog.

As in the first experiment, subjects then viewed a videotape of an attractive or unattractive female whom they expected to meet later, and indicated their impressions of how attractive she was. Once again, attraction was found to be affected by both arousal and the attractiveness of the woman. Subjects who were aroused (by positive, funny material as well as by the negative, horrible material) found the attractive woman more attractive than did subjects in the neutral condition. In contrast, aroused subjects perceived the unattractive woman to be less attractive than did the nonaroused subjects.

Taken together, these two studies demonstrate that the association between arousal and romance is not a simple matter of rewards. The men who participated in the first study did not experience any physical or emotional discomfort; there was no distress to be reduced by the woman's videotaped presence. In the second study, it did not matter whether arousal was created by a positive or a negative stimulus. In both studies, the same principle applied: Arousal intensified subjects' initial emotional reaction, positive *or* negative, to a member of the opposite sex.

The implications of this research are startling. Is love totally at the mercy of airplanes, bridges, exercise, and Steve Martin comedy routines? Fortunately, for our peace of mind, the answer is no. Misattribution and excitation transfer have their limits (Marshall & Zimbardo, 1979; Maslach, 1979; Reisenzein, 1983). One limit is imposed by the passing of time. A long delay between initial arousal and subsequent emotional response wipes out the possibility of excitation transfer. Initial arousal dissipates, and no leftover excitation is available for misattribution (Cantor, Zillmann, & Bryant, 1975; Zillmann, Johnson, & Day, 1974).

Another limit may be set by attributional clarity (White & Kight, 1984). If excitation transfer depends on *mis*attribution, knowing the real reason for our initial arousal will short-circuit the process. When Dan thinks, "Oh boy, here I go again, afraid of flying," he won't be able to mistake his fear as sexual attraction to Judy. Some researchers, however, question whether misattribution is necessary for one source of arousal to fuel another kind of emotional response (Allen, Kenrick, Linder, & McCall, 1989). Instead, they propose that what may be involved is a simple process of response facilitation. Whenever arousal is present, no matter what its source or the degree of our awareness of that source, our most likely response to the situation will be energized. According to this perspective, it does not matter whether Dan knows that his initial arousal was elicited by his fear of flying. In Judy's presence, his dominant response is sexual attraction, and this response will be automatically strengthened by any arousal added to it. In essence, then, the debate between the misattribution and response-facilitation explanations of arousal carryover effects centers on the issue of cognitive control. Further research is necessary before that debate can be fully resolved. In the meantime, think about its possible implications for your own life. When you walk out of a gym and encounter a most attractive person, will you dismiss your state of arousal as simply the result of a good workout and walk on by? Or might you fall in love anyway?

Thought. The two-factor theory of passionate love emphasizes the role of our thoughts and beliefs in accounting for arousal. Thoughts may also influence passionate love in other ways. Take, for example, Tesser's (1978) model of self-generated attitude change. This model proposes that the more we think about an issue, the more extreme our attitudes on that issue will become. Suppose you are mildly in favor of a certain political candidate. Tesser would predict that if you think about this candidate for a while, you will grow even stronger in your favorable opinion. The same intensification effect also holds for negative evaluations. Thinking about a political candidate whom you mildly oppose should increase your opposition.

Tesser and Paulus (1976) investigated the role of self-generated attitude change in love. At each of two testing sessions two weeks apart, they asked unmarried college undergraduates about their love for their dating partners and how much they thought about their dating partners. The results of this study indicated that love and thought work both ways. The more you love someone, the more you will think about him or her; the more you think about someone you love, the more you will love him or her.

Some questions have been raised about the interpretation of the results obtained by Tesser and Paulus (Bentler & Huba, 1979; Smith, 1978; Tesser & Paulus, 1978), and certainly further examination of the relationship between love and thought is necessary. However, the Tesser and Paulus study does suggest a way to account for the obsessive quality of passionate love affairs. As thought and love strengthen each other, the passionate lover falls ever more deeply in love and grows ever more obsessed with thoughts of the beloved. This type of obsessive intensification is perhaps particularly likely in relationships where the partners have little real information about each other—because they are just getting to know each other or are kept apart by circumstances (Beach & Tesser, 1988). In the absence of concrete, complicated knowledge of another, we are free to develop an oversimplified idealization.

And, indeed, idealization may be a critical factor in passionate love. On the basis of a careful examination of the works of such diverse figures as Stendhal, the nineteenth-century French novelist, and Teresa of Avila, the sixteenth-century Spanish mystic, I have proposed that "the core of passionate love lies in the capacity to construct in one's imagination an elaborated vision of a future state of perfect happiness" (Brehm, 1988, p. 253). Others take a similar view. Person (1988) states that "love is an act of the imagination" (p. 20) and that "passionate love seeks a transcendence akin to religious experience" (p. 86). The distinguished Latin American author Mario Vargas Llosa has analyzed Emma Bovary, the central character in Flaubert's great novel *Madame Bovary* and a classic literary example of passionate love, in terms of "the importance that the imaginary has for Emma" (1986, p. 182). And several researchers have suggested that the major difference between love and friendship involves characteristics associated with imaginative activity—such as mystery and fascination (Aron, Dutton, Aron, & Iverson, 1989; Davis & Todd, 1982). In general, this understanding of passionate love suggests that people fall in love with their own imagined constructions rather than with the concrete reality of another human being.

All of the factors described thus far as potential contributors to the experience of passionate love seem to imply that this experience will be

Love can last a lifetime. But, for most people, companionate love seems to endure longer than passionate love. (Hazel Hankin/Stock, Boston)

relatively short-lived. After all, the natural course of arousal is to decline, and an idealized view of the beloved is difficult to maintain once contact with the beloved is frequent and routine. But it appears that passionate love sometimes does last for quite some time (Hatfield, Traupmann, & Sprecher, 1984). Consider, for example, the following statement made by a man who was passionately in love for years:

> I lived in constant fear of divorce. . . . I would do everything I could think of to try and win her affection. . . . She was unpredictable. I could never be sure of how she'd react. . . . From the day I met her until the day she died, she was the most beautiful woman on earth. . . . She was a real queen and she ruled my emotions for a quarter of a century. (Tennov, 1979, pp. 53–54)

This man's experience suggests that the ultimate limit on passionate love might be imposed, not by time, but by certainty. If hope is completely lost, passion dies; if love is secure and taken for granted, passion fades. But if the beloved's commitment remains uncertain, arousal is constantly recharged and idealization can flourish. Under these conditions, passionate love can last a lifetime.

Trust. But for most people, it probably doesn't. For most people, companionate love is likely to have more endurance than intense, passionate attachments. Less emotionally intense, companionate love is also more stable and, perhaps, deeper. Companionate love can exist between friends as well as lovers. It rests on a foundation of respect, admiration, and trust. Indeed, interpersonal trust may be its single best defining characteristic (Holmes & Rempel, 1989). Companionate love involves both kinds of interpersonal trust described by Johnson-George and Swap (1982): trust in the other person's *reliability* (the likelihood that he or she will do what he or she promised) and *emotional trust* (the security that each person will act to protect the other's welfare). The questionnaire developed by Johnson-George and Swap to measure these aspects of trust is displayed in Table 4.3.

Attachment Styles

Although the distinction between passionate and companionate love is widely employed in research and theory on love, there are several other ways to categorize different types of love. One approach emphasizes *attachment style*, the way that a person interacts with significant others. According to Shaver, Hazan, and Bradshaw (1988), attachment style is often relatively constant across the life span. Thus, the way a person relates to an adult intimate partner should resemble the sort of relationship experienced with one's parents. Basing their research on a paradigm developed to study parent-child relationships (Ainsworth, Blehar, Waters, & Wall, 1978), Hazan and Shaver (1987) asked adult subjects to select the one attachment style that best described their feelings and experiences (see Table 4.4). Subjects also answered a variety of more specific questions about the nature and quality of their romantic relationships.

Among those participating in this research, 56 percent selected the secure style of attachment as the best descriptor of their feelings and experiences, around 25 percent chose the avoidant description, and some 20 percent opted for the anxious/ambivalent characterization. This distribution is within the range of that obtained for children in a number of different cultures (van Ijzendoorn & Kroonenbrg, 1988), and similar percentages have been obtained for other samples of adults (Mikulincer, Florian, & Tolmacz, 1990; Pistole, 1989). In the research by Hazan and Shaver (1987), those adults who reported a secure style of attachment described their romantic relationships as involving happiness, friendship, and trust. Those with the avoidant style emphasized a fear of closeness. Individuals with an anxious/ambivalent style reported a love life full of emotional extremes, obsessive preoccupations, sexual attraction, desire for union with the partner, desire for reciprocation from the partner, and love at first sight. The anxious/ambivalent style thus seems to resemble passionate love, while the secure style is similar to what others call companionate love. Individuals with an avoidant style seem reluctant to commit to a love relationship at all. Perhaps because of this, avoidant males report distinctly low levels of distress after the breakup of a romance (Simpson, 1990).

TABLE 4.3 THE SPECIFIC INTERPERSONAL TRUST SCALE

Although this scale has been validated only in regard to persons of the same sex, many of the items may also apply to opposite sex relationships. You may want to answer the items twice, thinking first of a person of the same sex for whom you have a great deal of trust and then thinking of a person of the opposite sex with whom you have a significant relationship. As you read each item, put the name of the person about whom you are thinking in the blanks. As you think about each statement, rate it on the following scale:

1	2	3	4	5	6	7	8	9
Strongly disagree								Strongly agree

Make sure you use the appropriate scale for your sex. Males should use the first set of twenty-one items; females should use the second set of thirteen items.

THE SIT SCALE FOR MALES

Overall Trust

1. If _____ gave me a compliment I would question if _____ really meant what was said.
2. If we decided to meet somewhere for lunch, I would be certain _____ would be there.
3. I would go hiking with _____ in unfamiliar territory if _____ assured me he/she knew the area.
4. I wouldn't want to buy a piece of used furniture from _____ because I wouldn't believe his/her estimate of its worth.
5. I would expect _____ to play fair.
6. I could rely on _____ to mail an important letter for me if I couldn't get to the post office.
7. I would be able to confide in _____ and know that he/she would want to listen.
8. I could expect _____ to tell me the truth.
9. If I had to catch an airplane, I could not be sure _____ would get me to the airport on time.

Emotional Trust

10. If _____ unexpectedly laughed at something I did or said, I would wonder if he/she was being critical and unkind.
11. I could talk freely to _____ and know that _____ would want to listen.
12. _____ would never intentionally misrepresent my point of view to others.
13. If _____ knew what kinds of things hurt my feelings, I would never worry that he/she would use them against me, even if our relationship changed.
14. I would be able to confide in _____ and know that he/she would want to listen.
15. If _____ didn't think I had handled a certain situation very well, he/she would not criticize me in front of other people.
16. If I told _____ what things I worry about, he/she would not think my concerns were silly.

Reliableness

17. If my alarm clock was broken and I asked _____ to call me at a certain time, I could count on receiving the call.

18. If _____ couldn't get together with me as we planned, I would believe his/her excuse that something important had come up.
19. If _____ promised to do me a favor, he/she would follow through.
20. If _____ were going to give me a ride somewhere and didn't arrive on time, I would guess there was a good reason for the delay.
21. If we decided to meet somewhere for lunch, I would be certain he/she would be there.

THE SIT SCALE FOR FEMALES

Reliableness

1. If I were injured or hurt, I could depend on _____ to do what was best for me.
2. If _____ borrowed something of value and returned it broken, _____ would offer to pay for the repairs.
3. If my alarm clock was broken and I asked _____ to call me at a certain time, I could count on receiving the call.
4. If _____ agreed to feed my pet while I was away, I wouldn't worry about the kind of care it would receive.
5. If _____ promised to do me a favor, he/she would follow through.
6. If _____ were going to give me a ride somewhere and didn't arrive on time, I would guess there was a good reason for the delay.
7. I would be willing to lend _____ almost any amount of money, because he/she would pay me back as soon as he/she could.

Emotional Trust

8. If _____ couldn't get together with me as we had planned, I would believe his/her excuse that something important had come up.
9. I could talk freely to _____ and know that he/she would want to listen.
10. _____ would never intentionally misrepresent my point of view to others.
11. If _____ knew what kinds of things hurt my feelings, I would never worry that he/she would use them against me, even if our relationship changed.
12. I would be able to confide in _____ and know that he/she would not discuss my concerns with others.
13. I could expect _____ to tell me the truth.

For males only: For items 1, 4, 9, and 10, reverse your scores: change 1s to 9; 2s to 8; 3s to 7; 4s to 6; 5s stay the same; 6s to 4; 7s to 3; 8s to 2; 9s to 1.

For males and females to determine your scores: For each factor (Overall, Emotional, and Reliableness for males; Reliableness and Emotional for females), add together your score for each item under that factor. You can then compare your scores with the following average scores for the several hundred college students studied by Johnson-George and Swap:

	Males	*Females*
Overall	54–84	—
Emotional	37–63	41–57
Reliableness	28–44	46–66

SOURCE: Johnson-George & Swap, 1982.

TABLE 4.4 ATTACHMENT STYLES

Which of the following best describes your feelings? (Make your choice before reading the labels given at the end of this table.)

A. I find it relatively easy to get close to others and am comfortable depending on them and having them depend on me. I don't often worry about being abandoned or about someone getting too close to me.

B. I am somewhat uncomfortable being close to others; I find it difficult to trust them completely, difficult to allow myself to depend on them. I am nervous when anyone gets too close, and often love partners want me to be more intimate than I feel comfortable being.

C. I find that others are reluctant to get as close as I would like. I often worry that my partner doesn't really love me or won't want to stay with me. I want to merge completely with another person, and this desire sometimes scares people away.

The first type of attachment style is described as "secure," the second as "avoidant," and the third as "anxious/ambivalent."

SOURCE: From Shaver, Hazan, & Bradshaw, 1988.

Colors of Love

In his typology of love, Lee (1977, 1988) uses color as a metaphor for ways of loving. According to Lee, there are three primary love styles (eros, ludus, and storge), which, like primary colors, form the basis for other combinations. Though the number of secondary styles is vast, Lee emphasizes three in particular: mania, agape, and pragma. These six ways to love (see Table 4.5) differ in the intensity of the loving experience, commitment to the beloved, desired characteristics of the beloved,

TABLE 4.5 STYLES OF LOVING

Eros	The Erotic lover searches for a person with the right physical appearance, and is eager for an intense relationship.
Ludus	The Ludic lover is playful in love and likes to play the field.
Storge	The Storgic lover prefers slowly developing attachments that lead to lasting commitment.
Mania	The Manic lover is demanding and possessive toward the beloved, and has a feeling of being "out of control."
Agape	The Agapic lover is altruistic, loving without concern for receiving anything in return.
Pragma	The Pragmatic lover searches for a person with the proper vital statistics: job, age, religion, etc.

SOURCE: Based on Lee, 1977, 1988. Reprinted from Brehm & Kassin, 1990.

and expectations about being loved in return. Research on Lee's types suggests that storge is similar to companionate love, and mania to passionate love (Hendrick, Hendrick, & Adler, 1988). Eros seems to partake of the best of both: a passionate, yet secure, style of loving.

Components of Love

Sternberg's *triangular theory of love* also focuses on three primary ingredients, which can combine to produce a range of ways of loving. According to Sternberg (1986), love consists of:

- Intimacy, the emotional component, which involves feelings of closeness
- Passion, the motivational component, which reflects romantic, sexual attraction
- Decision/commitment, the cognitive component, which includes the decisions people make about being in love and the degree of their commitment to their partner

These three components are the building blocks of love, and various combinations create eight major types of relationships. As you can see from Table 4.6, companionate love is included here. Passionate love has two representatives: the pure passion of infatuation and the intimate passion of romantic love (Sternberg, 1988).

TABLE 4.6 THE TRIANGULAR THEORY OF LOVE: TYPES OF RELATIONSHIPS

	Intimacy	Passion	Decision and Commitment
Nonlove	Low	Low	Low
Liking	High	Low	Low
Infatuated love	Low	High	Low
Romantic love	High	High	Low
Empty love	Low	Low	High
Companionate love	High	Low	High
Fatuous love	Low	High	High
Consummate love	High	High	High

SOURCE: Based on Sternberg, 1986. Reprinted from Brehm & Kassin, 1990.

An Overview

Given all these different ways to divide the pie, how many types of love are there? It is still hard to tell. Recent efforts to integrate various typologies and come up with an overall set of categories has generated inconsistent results (Hendrick & Hendrick, 1989; Levy & Davis, 1988). It does appear that the contrast between passionate and companionate love may well be the most important distinction, though there is growing empirical support for the usefulness of the tripartite division of adult attachment styles (Collins & Read, 1990; Feeney & Noller, 1990). Like Shakespeare, social scientists have discovered that attempting to answer the question "What is love?" is by no means an easy task.

*I*NDIVIDUAL DIFFERENCES IN LOVE

Most typologies assume that any given person can experience a number of different types of love. Most of us, for example, have experienced both companionate and passionate love—sometimes with different people and sometimes with one person. It also seems likely that many of us have experienced several of the styles of love described in Table 4.5 and the types of relationships listed in Table 4.6. On the other hand, a strict interpretation of the concept of attachment styles would suggest that it is, in fact, an individual difference measure: that each person learns one style in childhood and engages in that style throughout his or her lifetime. However, Shaver et al. (1988) explicitly disavow such a strict interpretation, noting that "there is continuity in attachment behavior, but there can also be significant change" (p. 86). But if attachment style is not a necessary constant across time and relationships, what is? In this section, we examine some characteristics of individuals that might exert a relatively enduring influence over their love experiences.

Gender

Probably the most powerful individual difference that affects how we experience love is that of gender. A considerable body of research shows that males and females construct their realities of love in very different terms (Dion & Dion, 1985; Hendrick, 1988; Peplau & Gordon, 1985).

Most of the research on gender differences in love has surveyed the responses of heterosexual couples on one or more of three scales: Rubin's Loving and Liking Scales (see Table 4.1) and a scale measuring romanticism. There are a number of different romanticism scales (see Table 4.7 for some examples). In general, romanticism scales focus on four beliefs: that love will find a way to conquer all, that for each person there is a one-and-only romantic match, that the beloved will meet one's highest ideals, and that love can strike at first sight (Sprecher & Metts, 1989). You should also note that whereas the Loving and Liking Scales refer to a person's feelings about a specific other person, romanticism scales ask about general attitudes and opinions. Thus, it is quite possible to like Melinda and love Ken but not believe in romance.

On the Loving Scale, some investigators have found that females report more love than males (Black & Angelis, 1974; Dion & Dion, 1975). Other studies, however, have not found any gender difference on love (Cunningham & Antill, 1981; Rubin, 1973). Other than noting that there are no reports of males obtaining higher scores than females, it is not possible to draw a conclusion about whether gender differences exist in love as measured by this scale.

Gender differences on the Liking Scale are more consistent, though not universal. Most investigators have found that females report more liking for their partners than do males (Black & Angelis, 1974; Dion & Dion, 1975; Rubin, 1973). All of the studies obtaining this finding were conducted with American college students. The one study in which no gender difference was obtained was conducted in Australia with a large number of people who varied widely in age, education, and occupation (Cunningham & Antill, 1981). It may be, therefore, that the gender difference in liking occurs primarily among American college students.

A similar situation exists when one looks at gender differences on romanticism scales. A number of studies of American college students (Fengler, 1974; Hobart, 1958; Kephart, 1967; Knox & Sporakowski, 1968; Spaulding, 1970; Sprecher & Metts, 1989) have found that males are more romantic than females, but, again, there was no difference between the sexes in the Australian survey by Cunningham and Antill. Moreover, a cross-sectional study of young adults, their parents, and their grandparents specifically points to the influence of age on a romantic view of life (Hieger & Troll, 1973). Among the young adults in this study, males were more romantic than females, but when all the subjects were considered together, females were more romantic than males. Thus, greater romanticism among males may be restricted to younger individuals.

The Australian survey of Cunningham and Antill was one of the few studies to examine the relationship among love, liking, and romanticism. These investigators found that all three tended to be positively correlated with each other, and that, in general, this positive association was greater for males than for females. These findings would seem to support Rubin's (1973) suggestion that in the area of love and romance, females make finer discriminations about their feelngs.

In addition to using these scales, researchers have also asked people about their specific romantic experiences and sensations. Responding to such questions, females usually report having been in love more fre-

TABLE 4.7 ROMANTICISM SCALES

For all the following scales, agreement with the items marked with an asterisk * and disagreement with the other items indicates a romantic attitude.

The Gross Romanticism Scale (1944; revised by Hobart, 1958)

1. Lovers ought to expect a certain amount of disillusionment after marriage.
2. True love should be suppressed in cases where its existence conflicts with the prevailing standards of morality.
*3. To be truly in love is to be in love forever.
4. The sweetly feminine "clinging vine" girl cannot compare with the capable and sympathetic girl as a sweetheart.
*5. As long as they at least love each other, two people should have no trouble getting along together in marriage.
*6. A girl should expect her sweetheart to be chivalrous on all occasions.
*7. A person should marry whomever he loves regardless of social position.
*8. Lovers should freely confess everything of personal significance to each other.
9. Economic security should be carefully considered before selecting a marriage partner.
10. Most of us could sincerely love any one of several people equally well.
*11. A lover without jealousy is hardly to be desired.
12. One should not marry against the serious advice of one's parents.

The Romantic Love Complex Scale (Spaulding, 1970)

Items 3, 5, 6, and 8 from the Gross Romanticism Scale.

quently than males (Dion & Dion, 1973; Kephart, 1967). Females also report more intense romantic sensations (such as "euphoria" in Dion & Dion, 1973; "wanting to run, jump, scream" in Kanin, Davidson, & Scheck, 1970) and more vivid memories of past romantic partners (Harvey, Flanary, & Morgan, 1986). Moreover, females tend to view their partners more favorably (Dion & Dion, 1975; Kanin et al., 1970), suggesting that they may idealize the person they love more than do males. And though females view love as more rewarding than do males, they also indicate having had more experiences of loving someone without being loved in return (Dion & Dion, 1975).

On the other hand, when couples are asked when they first fell in love with their partner, males report falling in love earlier than do females. This finding has been obtained both with dating couples (Kanin et al., 1970) and with newlyweds (Huston, Surra, Fitzgerald, & Cate, 1981). For that extremely dramatic event of falling in love "at first sight," there appears to be no difference between males and females (Kanin et al., 1970).

There has also been some research examining gender differences in types of love. Although some research has found that females report

*1.   A person can't help falling in love if he/she meets the right person.

*2.   Happiness is inevitable in true love.

*3.   True love leads to almost perfect happiness.

*4.   Love is an "all-or-nothing" feeling; there is no in-between.

*5.   When one is in love, the person whom he/she loves becomes the only goal of his/her life. One lives almost solely for the other.

*6.   There is only one real love for a person.

*7.   True love is known at once by the people involved.

The Romantic Idealist Factor (Fengler, 1974)

*1.   If I were in love with someone, I would marry him regardless of what his social class and family background was.

*2.   A deep love for one another can compensate for differences in religious and economic background.

*3.   I don't particularly care one way or the other whether I get married.

4.   Affection and emotional support in marriage are likely to prove valuable only if both spouses come to marriage with a similar social, religious, and economic background.

5.   The main function of the family today is to educate, protect, and provide status for its children.

6.   An ideal marriage would be where the spouses share the same social and economic background, the same religion, have close relations with parents and where both see the proper rearing of children as their social duty.

more passionate love experiences than do males, the difference appears to be weak, and in many studies it does not occur at all (Hatfield & Rapson, 1987; Hatfield & Sprecher, 1986a). Since a scale to measure companionate love has not yet been developed, gender differences in this type of love have not yet been assessed. Most studies have not found any gender differences among the three attachment styles of secure, avoidant, and anxious/ambivalent (Feeney & Noller, 1990; Shaver et al., 1988). The most extensive research on possible gender differences in the way that people love has focused on Lee's six love styles. Using the 42-item scale they developed to measure these styles, Hendrick and Hendrick (1986) found that women had higher scores than did men on storge, mania, and pragma, while men had higher scores on ludus. No gender differences were found on agape, and the results for eros have been inconsistent across different studies.

Only a few studies have examined how feelings of love affect actual behavior. In one early investigation, Rubin (1973) studied gaze behavior between dating couples. First he divided couples into two groups according to their scores on his Loving Scale: strong love couples, who expressed strong feelings of love for each other, and weak love couples, who expressed much weaker feelings of love. When the conversations of these couples were then observed, it was found that strong love couples looked at each others' faces *simultaneously* more often than did weak love couples. This "lovers' gaze" between strong love couples was replicated in a subsequent study and shown to be independent of the time spent talking to each other (Goldstein, Kilroy, & Van de Voort, 1976). Neither of these studies found any sex differences in how often males and females looked at their partners.

On the other hand, research by Dion and Dion has suggested that there may be important gender differences in the way love affects our behavior. In one study (1976a), they investigated the "Honi phenomenon." The Honi phenomenon was first discovered in 1949 when psychologist Hadley Cantril was studying perceptual illusions. Cantril was interested in how subjects perceive other people who walk through a room that actually is physically very peculiar (see Figure 4.1) but is arranged so that it looks like a normal room. Most people who watch someone walk through this room (called the "Ames room") perceive the person to alter in physical size. But Cantril found that when he was having a female subject observe her husband walk through the Ames room, she reported much less size distortion of her husband than was typical. Since this subject was nicknamed "Honi" (presumably, pronounced "Honey") by her husband, Cantril called this resistance to the

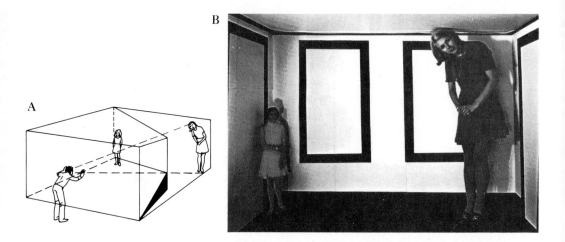

FIGURE 4.1

The Ames room. The diagram (A) shows the actual construction of the Ames room as compared with the way people will perceive it. The photograph (B) shows the room as it appears to a person looking through the peephole. The illusion results from the fact that people expect rooms to be rectangular and have flat floors. (Photo by Robert Berger from Science Digest © Hearst Corporation)

typical size distortion elicited by the Ames room "the Honi phenomenon."

Dion and Dion decided to examine the Honi phenomenon more
thoroughly. They had 50 couples in various types of relationships (married, engaged, steady dating, casual dating) observe each other walk
through the Ames room; these subjects also observed a stranger walk
through the experimental room. Subjects then completed Rubin's Loving and Liking Scales as well as a scale of interpersonal trust, and all
three scales were combined to form a measure of attachment to the
partner. The scores on this attachment measure were examined to see if
they were related to subjects' perceptual experiences. For males, there
was no relationship. Degree of attachment did not affect how distorted
their partners appeared relative to the distortion perceived for a
stranger. For females, however, more attachment was associated with
less distortion perceived in their partners' physical appearance. These
results suggest that, at least among women, love can change how
someone is perceived.

In a later study, the Dions found another gender difference in the
way that love affects behavior (Dion & Dion, 1979). This study involved
heterosexual couples who performed a group memory task; couples sat
in a square and pronounced word pairs sequentially around the table.
Subjects were then asked to recall these words. When an index combining the subjects' scores on Rubin's Loving and Liking Scales was examined (Dion, 1983), it was found that feelings toward the partner did not
affect males' recall. For females, however, more positive feelings toward
the partner were associated with better recall of their partners' words.
Thus, it appears that females who were strongly attached to their partners paid more attention to them than to other members of the group.

This section has described a number of gender differences in love
and romance—so many, in fact, that it may be hard to keep track of
them all. Table 4.8 summarizes these findings. Although no one knows
exactly why various differences between men's and women's romantic
experiences have been found, there are a number of possible explanations. First, it is important to realize that some of these apparent differences may not actually exist or may be quite limited if they do. Perhaps,
for example, women just feel freer to report the intensity of their romantic feelings, idealization of the partner, and experiences of unrequited
love. It is also possible, as noted earlier, that at least some of these
differences may be restricted to young men and women or to certain
cultures. Moreover, there is a tendency, though far from absolute, for
more gender differences to occur in older studies than in more recent
ones. Perhaps there is greater similarity in men's and women's love
experiences than there once was.

But what if, for the sake of speculation, we take these findings more
seriously? If so, the most likely explanation would appear to involve the

TABLE 4.8 GENDER DIFFERENCES IN LOVE AND ROMANCE

Females More Than Males	Males More Than Females	Apparently about Equal
Liking*	Romanticism*	Love
Discriminating among love, liking, and romanticism	Falling in love earlier in a relationship	Love at first sight
Frequency of being in love	Ludus	Passionate love
Intensity of romantic sensations		Attachment style
		Agape
More vivid memories of past partners		Eros
Idealization of partner		Looking at each other
Finding love rewarding		
Experiences of unrequited love		
Storge		
Mania		
Pragma		
Greater attachment leading to resistance of perceived distortion of partner's physical appearance		
Greater liking leading to better recall of what partner said		

*These gender differences may appear only among young adults.

importance of love. Men seem to have a more carefree attitude than women—endorsing a ludic love style, having romantic attitudes, and being willing to fall in love earlier in a relationship. Women, on the other hand, seem to take love more to heart, be more cautious about it, and be influenced by it more. Love appears to be more important to women than to men. If it is, this may reflect socialization practices that continue the traditional emphasis on women's role in loving and taking care of others. It could also reflect economic reality. Even today, men's average earnings are considerably higher than women's average earnings. Since, as we have seen, North Americans expect love to lead to marriage, falling in love can have far greater consequences for a woman's long-term socioeconomic status than for a man's.

Age

It is very difficult to conduct a precise examination of the effects of age on love and romance. One problem we face is that a number of different variables tend to be mixed together: As people age, they tend to have relationships that have lasted longer and to have had more relationships. So if we do find that some aspect of love increases with the age of the people we interview, we do not know whether it is really the age of our respondents that makes the difference or if it is length of their present relationships, the extent of their previous romantic experience, or some combination of such variables. There are complex statistical analyses that will allow us to separate these factors, but most studies have not made use of these techniques.

A second problem involves linear and curvilinear effects. If there is a linear relationship between two factors (say, age and romanticism), a simple correlation will describe this adequately. We might find, for example, a negative correlation, indicating that as age increases, romantic attitudes decrease. But what if the relationship is more complex? What if romanticism decreases only up to a certain time in life and then increases? This is called a curvilinear relationship, or more specifically, a U-shaped curvilinear relationship (see Figure 4.2). We cannot describe this kind of effect in terms of a simple correlation. Indeed, if we analyze findings like this with a correlational analysis, the correlation will appear to be around 0, and we would interpret this to mean that there is no relationship between the two variables of romanticism and age. In fact, in our example, there is a relationship, but it is not a linear one.

Both of these problems appear in the research that has attempted to examine the relationship between age and love or romance. For instance, Knox and Sporakowski (1968) found that when they questioned college students, seniors tended to be less romantic in their views of love

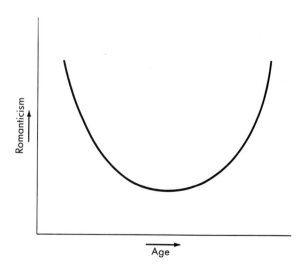

FIGURE 4.2
Possible U-shaped relationship between age and romanticism.

than freshmen. Hieger and Troll (1973), who dealt with a wider span of ages, also found a decline: The grandparents in their sample were less romantic than the young adults. However, when Knox (1970) interviewed a sample of people of differing ages, he found that romanticism was less for people who had been married for 5 years than for high school seniors, but greater for people who had been married for 20 years or more. Similarly, Munro and Adams (1978) found that married couples whose children had left home expressed stronger beliefs in "romantic power" (i.e., love as a powerful interpersonal force) than did respondents who were at an earlier stage in life (high school students, young marrieds without children, married couples with children).

With the clear exception of Hieger and Troll's (1973) unromantic grandparents, these data suggest that romanticism may have a curvilinear relationship with age: decreasing from the young adult years to middle age, then increasing. Such a relationship could explain why Cunningham and Antill (1981) failed to find a correlation between age and romanticism in their survey of a broad cross-section of the Australian public. These investigators only report simple correlations for their data and did not examine their results for curvilinear effects. But even if there is, in fact, a curvilinear (U-shaped, as in Figure 4.2) relationship between people's age and their endorsement of romantic ideas, we still cannot know for certain if age is really what is involved. It could be that it is not getting past middle age that makes at least some individuals more romantic, but being in a relationship that has lasted 20 years or more. Perhaps if we asked older divorced individuals to tell us their beliefs about romance, they would be considerably less romantic than married people who had just celebrated their silver anniversary.

Personality

One of the most widely discussed aspects of love is the possibility that people's self-esteem (their evaluation of self-worth) influences the way they view the one they love. Sigmund Freud (1922), the founder of psychoanalysis, believed that we cloak our beloved in the clothes we wish for ourself, that we project onto the person we love those characteristics that form our own ego ideal. Thus, for Freud, falling in love was, at its core, a substitute for personal achievement. Freud's view of the substitute nature of love set up an interesting and highly influential general principle: Love depends on being dissatisfied with ourself. When we love ourself (when we are "narcissistic" to use Freud's term), we have no available psychological energy for loving others.

The notion that loving others is directly opposed to having high regard for oneself came rather quickly under attack from other psychotherapists. In particular, a group of scholars who sought to modify Freud's theory (and, therefore, are called "neo-Freudians") proposed exactly the opposite view of how our love for self affects our love for others. The neo-Freudian approach to love emphasized that if we are to love others, we must first be secure and comfortable about ourself (Horney, 1939; Sullivan, 1947). Individuals with low self-regard were considered to be hypersensitive to rejection and unable to love.

Do we, then, love from weakness or from strength? These two views stemming from the Freudian versus neo-Freudian debate have created a polarity that still runs through most inquiries on the psychology of love. Reik (1944), for example, suggested that there are two *stages* in loving someone. The first stage—the desire and inclination to fall in love—comes from a need "to escape from internal discontent" (p. 34). In contrast, the second stage—where we actually love another person in a committed, enduring fashion—requires personal courage and security about the self. In another version of the weakness-versus-strength polarity, Fromm (1956) distinguished between immature and mature *types of love*. In immature love, the lover exploits the beloved in order to satisfy the lover's needs; in mature love, the lover has a genuine concern for the beloved's welfare. A similar distinction was drawn by Maslow (1954, 1968) in terms of "deficit love" and "being love." In Maslow's work, the type of love is closely associated with the *type of individual* who loves. Those who are more "self-actualized"—more personally secure and open to challenging experiences—are said to be more likely to engage in "being love" than those who are less secure. Maslow, then, brought us right back to the terms of the original debate between Freud and the neo-Freudians: Do self-esteem and other aspects of personality influence our love for others? Rather than continue the theoretical argument, social scientists decided to collect some data.

Initial research on the possible association between love and personality focused on interpersonal attraction. It was hypothesized that people low in self-esteem should have a greater need for positive encounters with others and, therefore, should react more favorably to such encounters. In one study, female subjects who felt bad about themselves as a result of receiving negative feedback about their personality liked a male confederate who had been friendly to them more than did subjects who felt good about themselves as a result of receiving positive feedback (Walster, 1965). However, subsequent research employing similar experimental procedures was unable to replicate these findings (Jacobs, Berscheid, & Walster, 1971). These studies used bogus feedback, rigged by the experimenter and unrelated to the subjects' actual level of self-esteem. But even when actual self-esteem was used to categorize subjects as high versus low in evaluations of their own self-worth, there was still very little evidence that self-esteem had any effects on how much subjects liked other people (Sprecher & Hatfield, 1982).

The possibility that our own self-esteem may affect the level of self-esteem we prefer in others has also been investigated. Here, the results were decidedly mixed. Of the four studies examining this version of the matching hypothesis (see Chapter 3), two found that people prefer others who have a similar level of self-esteem (Kiesler & Baral, 1970; Lloyd, Paulsen, & Brockner, 1983), while two other studies (both by Walster, 1970) did not find any evidence of a match on self-esteem. Thus, when it comes to liking other people in the context of heterosexual dating, the context examined in most of the studies described in this section, how we feel about ourself seems to have little, if any, effect on how we feel about others. But interpersonal attraction and liking are not the same as love. Perhaps if we looked more specifically at people's love experiences, we might find that self-esteem and other aspects of personality make a difference.

The most systematic investigation of this possibility has been conducted by Dion and Dion (1985, 1988). Using their own Romantic Love Questionnaire and Rubin's Loving Scale, these researchers obtained information about the history of subjects' romantic involvements (for example, the frequency, duration, and intensity of these experiences), the emotional and physical symptoms occurring when they were in love (such as euphoria and difficulty in sleeping), and their attitudes about romance in general as well as about a specific relationship. In addition to self-esteem, three other personality variables were investigated by Dion and Dion:

1. *Internal versus external locus of control.* The internal-external personality dimension refers to the difference between those people who generally see themselves as controlling what happens to them in life (internals) and those who generally see external events such as luck and powerful others as controlling their life outcomes (Rotter, 1966).

2. *Defensiveness.* This is the tendency to put oneself in the best possible light by claiming to behave in highly socially desirable ways (Crowne & Marlowe, 1964).

3. *Self-actualization.* Based on Maslow's theory, this personality dimension refers to the difference between those people who see themselves as acting in accord with their own personal standards free from the need to submit to external social pressures (high self-actualizers) and those who see themselves as more heavily influenced by the need to conform to others.

The results of the research by Dion and Dion on the relationship between personality and love can be summarized as follows. First, internals appear to take a much more cautious, rational approach to romantic love than do externals. Externals were more likely to report having been romantically attached, holding an idealistic view of romantic love, and seeing romantic attraction as being mysterious and volatile

(Dion & Dion, 1973). Surprisingly, however, externals did not report greater intensity in their love affairs than did internals. Second, defensiveness appears to play a crucial mediating role in the relationship between self-esteem and love experiences (Dion & Dion, 1975). Individuals who were *high* on self-esteem and *low* on defensiveness reported the greatest frequency of being in love and of having experienced unrequited love. In contrast, those who were high on *both* self-esteem and defensiveness reported the lowest frequencies of both loving and losing. These findings indicate that people who are self-confident, secure, and not anxious about social disapproval have more frequent and—perhaps because of their willingness to take risks—more unsuccessful experiences in loving. Third, Dion and Dion (1988) propose that both high *and* low self-actualizers can have highly meaningful loving relationships:

> People who are genuinely self-accepting and high in self-actualization do seem to be more open to the experience of romantic heterosexual love. On the other hand, individuals lower in these qualities report greater esteem and affection for their partner, perhaps because they have greater needs and appreciation for affection from a member of the opposite sex. (p. 272)

So where does this leave us on the issue of whether we love from strength *or* from weakness? The best answer, it appears, is that it is a bad question. We love from both. High levels of self-esteem, personal security, and independence can contribute to love by freeing us to pursue it. We do not have to be so afraid of appearing foolish or being rejected. On the other hand, our need for love is not especially pressing, and we may have a tendency to take those who love us for granted. Lower levels of self-esteem, personal security, and independence can contribute to love by prompting us to seek it. We need it more and may be most grateful when it is received. On the other hand, our concerns about appearing foolish or being rejected may inhibit us from active efforts to express our feelings and establish a loving relationship.

It should also be noted that in order to better understand the connection between personality and love, we need to take the situation into account. Personality involves relatively stable characteristics of the individual that endure across different situations. But personality is not impervious to life experience. Your self-esteem may, in general, be quite high. But put you through a week in which you fail an important exam, are rejected by your romantic partner, and break your leg in a fall, and probably your self-esteem would suffer a decline. Thus, to say that people high in some personality variable have such-and-such experiences in love does *not* necessarily imply that these people are set in stone, never to take a different view of themselves or have different kinds of intimate relationships. Moreover, many behaviors are affected by both personality and the situation (Kihlstrom, 1987; Snyder & Ickes,

1985). Take, for example, seizing an opportunity to meet someone you find attractive. Research has shown that it is easier to approach a potential partner when we have a good excuse to do so (Bernstein, Stephenson, Snyder, & Wicklund, 1983). Not everyone who asks to borrow someone else's class notes is interested in academic performance! Such self-protective strategies might be particularly attractive to people who are relatively low in self-esteem and self-confidence. When the circumstances allow them to disguise their true motives, they may find it easier to take the romantic initiative. Thus, by selecting or constructing situational circumstances that best fit our personal inclinations, it may be possible to optimize our romantic outcomes—regardless of our personality.

CHAPTER SUMMARY

A Brief History of Love

Different societies have taken different perspectives on love. Four dimensions on which views of love differ are cultural value, sexuality, sexual orientation, and marital status.

Ancient Greece. The ancient Greeks took a negative view of love, seeing it as a kind of madness. A more positive alternative, platonic love, was usually restricted to male homosexuals and was not supposed to involve sexual activities. The Greeks believed that marriage and love were usually mutually exclusive.

Roman Antecedents. Romans too viewed love as an undesirable madness, but they also saw it as a game. There was a high divorce rate during the last century of the Roman Empire.

Courtly Love. Originating in the twelfth century in southern France, courtly love between an unmarried knight and a married lady was viewed as an idealistic, nonsexual quest.

A Time of Transition. Modern ideas about love and marriage began around the seventeenth century, particularly in England. For the first time, love and marriage were widely viewed as compatible and desirable.

In Our Time. The social norm that people should marry for love is most accepted in North America. This norm has been criticized by those who hold the traditional view of love as madness and, therefore, a poor basis for marital commitment.

Types of Love

According to Zick Rubin, liking and loving are distinct and, to some extent, mutually exclusive reactions to an intimate relationship. Not all research, however, has supported a clear distinction between the two.

Companionate and Passionate Love. Companionate love is a secure, trusting attachment. Passionate love is a state of high arousal, which varies from agony to ecstasy. The two-factor theory of passionate love holds that it requires (1) diffuse arousal and (2) the belief that this arousal is caused by the presence of the beloved. In some circumstances, arousal can be attributed to the wrong source (misattributed) and fuel the process of excitation transfer. In excitation transfer, arousal caused by one stimulus is transferred and added to that elicited by a second stimulus; the combined arousal is then perceived as caused by only the second stimulus. Excitation transfer accounts for how an impersonal source of arousal (fear of flying, exercise) can enhance romantic attraction. Excitation transfer does not occur when there is a long delay between the first stimulus and the second one. There is debate about whether excitation transfer will occur when people are aware of the true source of their initial arousal.

According to Tesser's model of self-generated attitude change, thinking about something intensifies our attitudes about it. Research indicates that the relationship between thought and love is a two-way street: More thought is associated with more love, and more love is associated with more thought. Idealization of the beloved, which may come about because of the process of self-generated attitude change, may play a crucial role in passionate love. Passionate lovers appear to strive toward idealistic ideas of the beloved's perfection. Passionate love can last for a long period, perhaps particularly if the beloved's commitment remains uncertain. However, companionate love seems more likely to last longer. Trust may be the most important aspect of companionate love—trust in the other's reliability to fulfill promises and in the other's concerns for one's own welfare.

Attachment Styles. According to Shaver and his colleagues, attachment style—the way one relates to significant others—is often relatively continuous across a person's life span. When adult subjects were asked which of three attachment styles described them best, most of them chose the secure style, though sizable minorities chose the avoidant and anxious/ambivalent styles.

Colors of Love. Lee proposes that there are three primary ways of loving, but many secondary styles. Research usually focuses on the six styles displayed in Table 4.5.

Components of Love. The triangular theory of love also focuses on three primary ingredients, which are said to combine to produce eight possible relationship types. The three components of love postulated by this theory are intimacy, passion, and decision/commitment.

An Overview. Research attempting to develop a more comprehensive understanding of the types of love is ongoing. At present, the simple division between companionate and passionate appears to offer the best characterization.

Individual Differences in Love

Individual differences are relatively enduring characteristics of individuals that exert an influence across different situations.

Gender. There are many gender differences in love experiences, as summarized in Table 4.8. The exact reasons for these differences are unknown. Possibly, they reflect a gender difference in what men and women are willing to report, rather than actual differences in experiences. Perhaps they indicate that love is more important to women than to men because of socialization practices, economic concerns, or both.

Age. It is difficult to examine the influence of age on love because age is associated with many other factors (such as having had more relationships and having had relationships that lasted longer). The available research suggests the possibility that romanticism may have a curvilinear association with age, decreasing at first and then increasing.

Personality. The role that self-esteem plays in people's love experiences has received a great deal of attention. It now appears that people low in self-esteem do not react more positively to friendly overtures than do those high in self-esteem. The evidence for the matching hypothesis (that people would be more attracted to those with a similar level of self-esteem) is mixed. Dion and Dion have conducted a series of studies on the relationship between love and various personality factors—including self-esteem, internal-external control, defensiveness, and self-actualization. Their research suggests an important distinction between the confidence to pursue love relations and the need for these relations. High levels of self-esteem, personal security, and independence appear to contribute to the former, while lower levels contribute to the latter. By constructing situational circumstances that best fit our personal inclinations, it may be possible to optimize romantic outcomes regardless of personality.

5

Sexuality

———— ❖ ————

Predictors of Premarital Sexual Activity • *Contraception and Safe Sex* • Gender Differences in Sexual Attitudes • *Men's and Women's Perceptions of Sexuality* • Sex and Satisfaction • *Sex and Marital Happiness* • *Sex and Love among Dating Couples* • *Sex and Equity in the Relationship* • Relationships between Same-Sex Partners • *Relationship Issues* • *Love in the Time of AIDS* • Sex and Communication: Talk to Me, Talk to Me • Chapter Summary

When were you born? That may seem a strange question to ask at the beginning of a chapter on sexuality, but actually it isn't. Over the last several decades, dramatic changes in sexual attitudes and behavior have taken place in the United States (Thornton, 1989). People born at different times have encountered radically different cultural norms about sexuality. Consider, for example, a person born in 1940 whose teenage years were spent in the 1950s, a time of restrictive sexual norms, especially for women. Compare the early lessons about sexuality that person received with the experiences of those born in 1960. Reaching 18 at the height of the "sexual revolution" in 1978, these individuals encountered far more permissive attitudes about sexual activity. And now think about someone born in 1970, whose teenage years were spent during a time of more conservative political values and growing concern about the dangers of sexually transmitted diseases, particularly AIDS. In matters of sexuality, those who were 18 in 1958 lived in a very different world than did people who were 18 in 1978, while the sexual climate surrounding individuals who were 18 in 1988 was different from that in either of the earlier eras.

Although examining a shorter time period than our examples, research by Gerrard (1987b) provides a good illustration of how sexual activity has changed in parallel with larger societal trends. When Gerrard first surveyed a sample of college women enrolled in required sophomore-level classes in 1973–1974, she found that 35 percent reported they were sexually active. By 1978–1979, the percentage had increased to 51 percent, but it had declined to 37 percent by 1983–1984. Among these predominantly middle-class white females, sexual activity had waxed and waned over the course of the decade. National survey data collected from a sample of female teenagers in the United States document a similar, though less dramatic, development over time (Hofferth, Kahn, & Baldwin, 1987). After an appreciable increase in sexual activity during the 1970s, there was a leveling off among whites and a slight decline among blacks during the early 1980s. In both decades, however, teenage girls, white and black, continued to become sexually active at younger and younger ages. (You should note that research on rates of sexual activity usually focuses on unmarried females because their sexual behavior varies more across time and place than does the sexual activity of married individuals or of unmarried males.)

Changes in sexual attitudes and behaviors are not, of course, rare events. From one culture to another, from one time period to another, views about sex have shifted, sometimes drastically. Consider, for example, the following historical variations. The Romans were famous for orgies, the early Christians for celibacy, the Elizabethans for bawdiness, the Puritans for moral strictness, the Victorians for repressed sexuality, and the Edwardians for playboys. Moreover, the dominant sexual ethic has never fully controlled people's actual behavior. During the Elizabethan era, there were many who lived lives of strict propriety. In Victorian England, there were many who lived lives of outrageous indulgence. In short, sexual norms have always been subject to change, and sexual behavior has always been difficult for society to dictate (Brundage, 1987).

In this chapter, we examine the social psychology of sexuality. What factors contribute to an individual's decision to become sexually active? How do men and women differ in their attitudes about sex? And what is the role of sexuality and sexual orientation in intimate relationships?

PREDICTORS OF PREMARITAL SEXUAL ACTIVITY

In general, a person's values and attitudes are the best predictors of premarital sexual behavior. Teenagers who engage in sex at an early age place greater value on independence, express less concern about academic achievement, are less religious, and report that they are influenced more by the opinions of their friends than by those of their family

(Jessor, Costa, Jessor, & Donovan, 1983). Premarital sexual activity is also more likely among teenagers who view dating as important in their lives and express strong desires for a partner (Newcomb, Huba, & Bentler, 1986). In this study by Newcomb et al., the importance of dating was associated with (1) confidence about being popular with and attractive to the opposite sex, (2) a positive and accepting view of oneself, and (3) more experiences involving stressful physical or family-related events. Thus, the importance of dating, a predictor of premarital sexual activity, was correlated with both positive factors (social and personal confidence) *and* negative experiences (stress). Similar findings were obtained in research on unmarried pregnancies (Robbins, Kaplan, & Martin, 1985). The likelihood of becoming a parent out of wedlock increased for males and females whose parents had a lower socioeconomic status, who had more difficulties in school, and who were *more* popular among their peers. It appears, then, that socially successful teenagers who confront stressful life circumstances may be more likely than others to become sexually active and to run the risk of unmarried pregnancy.

Family structure is also related to premarital sexual activity. Research by Newcomer and Udry (1987) indicated, however, that the influence of family structure may differ for girls and boys. These investigators found that white adolescent girls growing up in homes without a father present were more likely to engage in premarital sex than were girls living with a father. But the boys who reported the highest level of premarital sexual activity were those who had experienced a change from an intact family, with both mother and father present, to a home without a father. Newcomer and Udry suggest that males become sexually active in response to parental loss of control during the breakup of a family, while paternal absence per se (regardless of when it occurred) appears to prompt female premarital sexual activity. Not all researchers, however, regard the connection between father absence and female premarital sex as particularly strong. When Miller and Bingham (1989) surveyed a national sample of 15- to 19-year-old females, they found that many other factors were better predictors of the level of premarital sexual activity reported by their subjects. Regardless of family structure, younger teenagers and those who were highly religious were less likely to have engaged in premarital sex.

Premarital sexual activity among adolescents also differs according to gender and race (Brooks-Gunn & Furstenberg, 1989). Boys report higher levels of sexual activity than do girls, and black girls report higher levels than do white girls. In addition, teenage pregnancies are higher among blacks than among whites (Furstenberg, Brooks-Gunn, & Chase-Lansdale, 1989). It has been estimated that in 1984, 19 percent of white women and 41 percent of black women became pregnant by age 18. According to Furstenberg et al., the educational and economic disadvantages experienced by young mothers diminish to some extent over time, but the children of young mothers "are distinctly worse off throughout childhood than the offspring of older childbearers" (p. 313, italics deleted).

Contraception and Safe Sex

In light of the enduring negative consequences for the children of teenage pregnancies and the perhaps shorter-lived but still significant problems faced by teenage mothers, there is a pressing need for more responsible sexual behavior among adolescents. But the need for more thought and less impulse in sexual activities is not restricted to teenagers. Today, the United States faces an epidemic of sexually transmitted diseases from herpes to gonorrhea—and, of course, AIDS (acquired immune deficiency syndrome). Transmitted through sexual intercourse, blood transfusions, pregnancy, and the use of contaminated needles by intravenous drug users, AIDS takes a terrible toll in human suffering and produces staggering costs for research and health care (Backer, Batchelor, Jones, & Mays, 1988; Shilts, 1987). As of the summer of 1990, some 130,000 cases of AIDS had been reported, with more than 80,000 deaths. Though accurate predictions are hard to come by because we are

The quilt memorializing AIDS victims on display in Washington, DC. It is estimated that by the mid-1990s, hundreds of thousands of people in the United States will have died from AIDS. (AP/Wide World)

still learning about the course of this disease and the benefits of new treatments are just beginning to take effect (*Manchester Guardian Weekly*, 1989; Thompson, 1990), the U.S. Centers for Disease Control have estimated that by the end of 1992 the cumulative total of AIDS cases in the United States could reach 365,000. By that time, it is believed that more than 250,000 people may have died and costs of medical care for the survivors will run into billions of dollars.

Increasingly, physicians and scientists trying to combat the AIDS epidemic in the United States discuss it in terms of three waves. The first wave decimated the gay male community but has now diminished. Some cities have seen a 65 to 85 percent reduction in sexually transmitted diseases among gay and bisexual men (Segal, 1987), and the incidence of new cases of AIDS among gay males is usually very low (Watkins, 1988). The second wave, which is still rising, involves inner-city drug users, their sexual partners, and their newborn infants. The third wave, which some believe will appear over the next five years, would involve heterosexual young adults. Preliminary results from a study of college campuses by the American College Health Association indicated that perhaps 2 out of every 1000 college students are infected with the HIV virus. This rate is considerably higher than what was expected.

We know from the experience of the gay male community that sexual behavior can be modified. Among older gay and bisexual males, "AIDS education and prevention campaigns have resulted in the most profound modification of personal health-related behaviors ever recorded" (Stall, Coates, & Hoff, 1988, p. 878). On the other hand, efforts to promote the safe-sex use of condoms among intravenous drug users appear to have met with little success, and there is growing concern that younger gay males may be engaging in risky sexual practices (Griggs, 1990). Among a sample of largely heterosexual college students, Carroll (1988) found that there was more talk than action in response to the fear of AIDS. Although more than 40 percent of sexually active subjects said that they had modified their sexual behavior because of concerns about AIDS, their reports of actual sexual behavior failed to confirm these claims. DeBuono and her colleagues (1990) also found little evidence that sexually active college women had decreased risky sexual practices, although use of condoms had increased during the period from 1975 to 1989.

These studies on the sexual behaviors of college students raise a crucial issue. Why is it that among well-educated, reasonably affluent young Americans, considerable high-risk sex still occurs? There is, of course, no one, easy answer to such a question. But there are some rather obvious possibilities. First, sex is not the easiest behavior to regulate—particularly for young men and women with vigorous sexual appetites. Second, the mixture of sex and alcohol, a commonplace on college campuses and in pickup bars, makes regulation even more difficult.

A third factor is the *illusion of unique vulnerability*—believing that bad things happen to others, but not to you (Lehman & Taylor, 1987; Perloff, 1987). This illusion interferes with taking appropriate measures to prevent foreseeable dangers. In one study of sexually active female undergraduates, those who perceived themselves as less likely than other women to get pregnant were also less likely to use effective contraception (Burger & Burns, 1988). Similarly, gay males who underestimated the risk of getting AIDS from unsafe sex were more likely to engage in high-risk sex (Bauman & Siegel, 1987). If you think you are invulnerable, you may not bother to take precautions.

A fourth factor contributing to the practice of safe or unsafe sex is a person's general attitude toward sex. In research on contraceptive use by heterosexuals, it has been found that sexual attitudes and feelings have a strong influence on that behavior (Gerrard, 1987a). Negative reactions to sex—such as guilt, anxiety, and negative evaluations of sexual situations—are associated with failure to use contraceptives (Andres, Gold, Berger, Kinch, & Gillett, 1983; Byrne & Fisher, 1983). Note the irony of these findings. People with negative attitudes toward sex are *less* likely to engage in sex. But if they do engage in sex, they are *more* likely to engage in *unsafe* sex (Fisher, 1986). Why? One possible reason is that people who are uncomfortable about sex know less about safe-sex practices (Goldfarb, Gerrard, Gibbons, & Plante, 1988). Since Goldfarb et al. found that those individuals can learn this information as well as people who have more positive attitudes toward sex, the lack of information among those with negative sexual attitudes appears to reflect active avoidance of such material. It is also possible that the tendency for men to rely on women to use contraception (Geis & Gerrard, 1984) creates an impression-management problem for women. Women, especially those with negative attitudes and feelings toward sex, may fear that if they practice contraception or ask a man to use a condom, they will appear overly experienced and eager (Marecek, 1987). Unfortunately, for some individuals the need to appear sexually naive may take precedence over the determination to avoid an unwanted pregnancy or a deadly disease.

GENDER DIFFERENCES IN SEXUAL ATTITUDES

The effects of sexual attitudes extend far beyond decisions about whether to engage in sex and whether to practice safe sex. Attitudes also influence the kind of sexual experiences people find satisfying and the conditions that elicit an interest in having sex. Some of the strongest differences in sexual attitudes are associated with gender. On average, men are more permissive in their sexual values and attitudes than are women (Hendrick & Hendrick, 1987; Snyder, Simpson, & Gangestad, 1986). Men are also more likely than women to enjoy sex without intimacy; women prefer sexual activities to be part of a psychologically intimate relationship (DeLamater, 1987; Whitley, 1988). These gender differences are strikingly apparent in extramarital affairs (Glass & Wright, 1985; Thompson, 1984). Men participating in such affairs emphasize the sexual element over emotional involvement, while women place more emphasis on their feelings. Women's involvement in an extramarital affair is more likely to reflect marital unhappiness, but men's involvement seems relatively unrelated to how happy they are with their marriage. These very different perspectives and concerns may well increase the likelihood of misunderstanding and conflict.

In addition, men and women differ in the sexual roles with which they are comfortable (Grauerholz & Serpe, 1985; Griffitt, 1987). Consistent with traditional gender stereotypes, men are more likely than women to be comfortable in a proactive role, where they exercise control by making the decision to initiate sexual activity. Women are more likely to be comfortable in a reactive role, where they exercise control by accepting or refusing another's sexual initiative. In the past, role differences between men and women also included a double standard. Traditional norms called for a more negative evaluation of sexually active women than of sexually active men.

But recent research looking for this double standard has failed to find it. When Mark and Miller (1986) had male and female undergraduates judge men and women of varying sexual experience, sexually active men and women received equivalent evaluations. Similarly, a survey of undergraduate opinions found that respondents regarded sexual intercourse as equally acceptable for both men and women, although men had actually engaged in it more (Jacoby & Williams, 1985). The young adults in this study did not advocate a double standard based on gender. They did, however, endorse a "selfish standard" based on experience. Both males and females reported that they preferred partners who had some sexual experience, but not too much. Surprisingly, this preference was found not only among the sexually inexperienced, but among the sexually experienced as well. Apparently, many people grant themselves more sexual freedom than they give to their partners.

Men's and Women's Perceptions of Sexuality

As we have seen, men typically have more permissive sexual attitudes and more sexual experience than do women. It might be expected, then, that men would perceive the world as a sexier place to be than would women. Among heterosexual men, such perceptions might be restricted to perceptions of women's sexuality, or they might be quite general, involving perceptions of men's sexual attributes as well. Research on these two possibilities provides stronger evidence for the first, more restricted, proposition than for the second, more general, one (Abbey, 1982; Abbey & Melby, 1986). When men and women interacted with a woman or just observed or read about her, men rated her as a more sexual person (endorsing such descriptors as "sexy" and "seductive") than did women. The relative tendency of men to characterize another man in sexual terms has varied across studies. Consistently, however, the highest ratings on sexually relevant descriptors have been found for men's perceptions of a woman.

It has been proposed by some researchers that men's tendency to perceive women in sexual terms may increase the risk of date rape. If a man perceives a woman as "sexy" and "seductive," he may hear a *yes* when she is saying *no*. Consider, for example, a study in which college students read 11 hypothetical scenarios describing various dating events (Muehlenhard, 1988). Across scenarios, male subjects perceived greater willingness on the part of the female character to engage in sex than did women—and more justification for the male character to have sex with a woman against her wishes. But the events that transpired on the date affected the perceptions of both male and female subjects. Perceptions of sexual eagerness on the part of the female character and of rape justification for the male character were highest when the woman initiated the date and went to the man's apartment. It is not clear whether these results reflect subjects' concerns about the risks that women may actually run or whether their perceptions are based on some remnant of the traditional double standard holding that women who take an active interest in a member of the opposite sex are necessarily available for sex, voluntarily or involuntarily. In any event, of the 540 college undergraduates who participated in this study, the vast majority (77.5 percent) stated that it was never justifiable for the man to have sex with the woman against her will.

*S*EX AND SATISFACTION

Having considered those factors that may contribute to the decision to engage in premarital sexual activity and some gender differences in views of sex, we now examine the association between sex and satisfaction in a relationship. The role of sexual activity in marital satisfaction is described first and then its role in dating relationships. At the end of this section, connections between feelings of being treated fairly in a relationship and sexual satisfaction are explored.

Sex and Marital Happiness

One of the earliest questions asked in research on relationships focused on the association between frequency of sexual activity and relationship satisfaction: "Do happily married couples have more sex?" Even the very first investigation of this issue suggested that the answer might be more complicated than one might think. In their pioneering study of marital relationships, Terman, Buttenweiser, Ferguson, Johnson, and Wilson (1938) found that frequency of sexual intercourse did not correlate with marital happiness. However, a close correspondence between desired and actual frequency of intercourse *was* associated with marital satisfaction. Individuals who stated that their actual frequency of sexual intercourse was very close to the level of sexual activity they preferred were more likely to report that they were happy in their marriage.

More recent research on the relationship between sex and marital happiness has also discovered some interesting complications. For instance, Howard and Dawes (1976) reported that although neither sexual activity nor number of arguments was in itself associated with the marital happiness reported by couples in their study, a combination of sex and arguments (specifically, the rate of sexual interaction minus the rate of arguments) did predict marital contentment. Thus, it seems that those couples who had a positive balance in what Gottman et al. (1976b) call the "marital bank account" (more positive/sexual deposits than argumentative withdrawals) tended to be happier with each other. The

Happy couples enjoy spending time together—in bed and out of it. (Barbara Alper/Stock, Boston)

importance of the *relative* balance is further demonstrated by the fact that in the Howard and Dawes study, sexual activity and arguing were positively correlated. Those couples who had more sex also had more arguments. It appears, then, that couples who argue a lot can be very happy with each other, providing they get together in some more positive way *more often.*

A third study on the relationship between sex and marital satisfaction examined two groups of married couples: (1) happily married couples who volunteered to participate in the study and (2) unhappily married couples who had come to a mental health clinic for marital counseling (Birchler & Webb, 1977). The happily married couples in this study did have a greater frequency of sexual interaction than the unhappily married couples. They also were more likely to report joint participation in leisure-time activities such as sports, hobbies, and social events. This suggests the at first rather surprising notion that having sex may have a lot in common with liking to play golf with each other. Both indicate that the two individuals enjoy doing things—together!

The results of these studies point out that we cannot assume that frequent sexual activity is some kind of magical ingredient in creating a happy marriage. Moreover, having frequent sex in marriage is not necessarily the same thing as having good sex. Having good sex would seem to depend on:

- Each individual having his or her needs met by a partner who respects the other's specific sexual desires.
- Having the proper balance of positive and negative interactions in the relationship, so that there are more positives than negatives.
- Enjoying being with each other, in bed and out of it.

Thus, for most couples in long-term relationships, the quality of their sexual interactions will reflect the more general quality of their relationship. If respect, caring, and enjoyment are absent, so, in the long run, will sexual satisfaction decline.

Sex and Love among Dating Couples

Like the 1938 study of marriage by Terman et al., the Boston Couples Study was a landmark in the history of research on relationships. This study, which began in 1972, originally involved 231 dating couples recruited from colleges in the Boston area. Through repeated contacts with subjects over the two years of the project, detailed information was obtained about a wide variety of relationship issues. Results from the Boston Couples Study have been described in a number of different

publications, many of which will be cited in this book. The most extensive review of the study's findings on sexual issues is provided by
Peplau, Rubin, and Hill (1977).

Peplau et al. divided the sexually active couples participating in the
Boston Couples Study into two types, depending on when their sexual
relationship had begun. "Early-sex couples" had engaged in sexual
intercourse relatively early in their relationship; "later-sex couples" had
engaged in sexual intercourse relatively late in their relationship. Compared with early-sex couples, later-sex couples reported more love for
each other and more guilt about sexual activities. In addition, women in
later-sex couples reported less sexual satisfaction than did women in
early-sex couples. Overall, then, neither group of couples had all the
advantages. Those who waited longer to begin sexual activities had the
advantage of more love but paid the price of more guilt and of less
sexual satisfaction for the woman. Those who began sex early paid the
price of less love but had the advantages of less guilt and more sexual
satisfaction for the woman.

In terms of the endurance of the relationship, however, there was
no difference between the two groups. When they were last contacted,
two years after the study had begun, neither early nor late timing was
related to whether the couple was still together. There is some evidence,
however, that the dating relationships of sexually active couples endure
longer than do nonsexual dating relationships. This evidence comes
from a study by Simpson (1987), who collected information from undergraduates engaged in dating relationships and then contacted them
again three months later to see whether their relationships were intact.
Of the 222 subjects who participated at both times in the study, 42
percent reported the breakup of their relationship within the three-
month period. Among those whose relationships were still intact, 77
percent of the female subjects and 87 percent of the male subjects had
indicated in the initial testing session that they were having sex with
their dating partner. Among those whose relationships had broken up,
51 percent of the women and 52 percent of the men had said they were
not having sex with their dating partner.

It is important to interpret Simpson's findings with some caution.
Three months is a very short time period in the life of a college dating
relationship, and we do not know whether these results would hold up
over a longer period. We also do not know what caused the association
between sex and relationship stability. It should be noted, however, that
this association remained strong even after various other factors (such as
subjects' satisfaction with their relationship, closeness to their partner,
length of their relationship, and sexual attitudes) were taken into account. Thus, these findings may confirm commonsense expectations of
a two-way street between sex and the quality of a relationship. Just as
romantic relationships that are more rewarding are probably more likely

to lead to sex, so do sexual activities increase the rewards available in the relationship. But this does not mean that adding sex to a poor relationship can make it into a good one, nor that sex by itself can guarantee the long-term survival of a relationship. Indeed, research on premarital pregnancies indicates that loving relations early on in a relationship do not necessarily translate into enduring positive regard (Surra, Chandler, Asmussen, & Wareham, 1987). In this study, newlywed couples who experienced a premarital pregnancy before they were mutually committed to getting married recalled very high levels of affection and love early in their relationship. Their current levels of affection and love, however, were lower than those reported by newlyweds who had not experienced a premarital pregnancy.

Sex and Equity in the Relationship

In Chapter 7, we consider equity theory as one explanation of why some relationships are satisfying and some are not, why some relationships endure and others do not (Walster, Walster, & Berscheid, 1978). Though the theory itself will not be considered in detail until Chapter 7, this section of the present chapter reviews the research relating equity principles to sexual behavior and satisfaction.

Equity theory emphasizes that what we get out of a relationship (outcomes) and what we put into it (inputs) are both important in influencing how we feel about the relationship. The theory also assumes that we pay attention to our own inputs and outcomes and to those of our partner as well. Thus, an equitable relationship is one in which both partners get about the same amount of benefit from the relationship relative to what they put into maintaining the relationship. If one partner obtains a larger proportion of benefits relative to his or her contributions, this person is described as "overbenefited." If, on the other hand, a person obtains a smaller proportion of benefits relative to his or her contribution, this person is called "underbenefited."

With these definitions in mind, let us look first as the association between equity and premarital sex. In a study by Walster, Walster, and Traupmann (1978), it was found that individuals in dating relationships who described their relationship as equitable also said that they were more content in the relationship than people who felt they were underbenefited *or* overbenefited. In addition, the equitable relationships were more likely to last longer. When asked about their sexual experiences, partners in equitable relationships reported "going further" sexually and were more likely to indicate that they had had intercourse because *both* of the individuals wanted to. It seems, then, that couples who feel they have an equitable relationship also feel they have a more satisfying, stable, and mutually responsive relationship; this total context of security and trust is associated with increased sexual expression.

Another study examined the relationship between feeling equitably treated and being sexually satisfied (Traupmann, Hatfield, & Wexler, 1983). Among the college students who took part in this research, those who perceived their relationships as equitable reported more sexual satisfaction across a variety of measures (e.g., overall sexual satisfaction, satisfaction after sex, perception of partner's satisfaction after sex). However, on all these measures, the difference between those who characterized their relationship as "equitable" and those who felt over-benefited was extremely small. Indeed, male subjects who felt over-benefited often reported somewhat greater satisfaction than equitably treated males. Among both males and females, feeling underbenefited was associated with the lowest level of sexual satisfaction. A similar pattern has been found with newlywed couples. Individuals who felt equitably treated *or* overbenefited expressed considerably more sexual satisfaction than those who regarded themselves as underbenefited (Hatfield, Greenberger, Traupmann, & Lambert, 1982).

Equity theorists have also investigated extramarital relationships. Walster, Traupmann, and Walster (1978) recount their use of a *Psychology Today* questionnaire that was completed and mailed in by 62,000 people! From this huge number of replies, Walster et al. selected a smaller sample of 2000 males and females, representing all age groups and a variety of intimate relationships. Their examination of extramarital sexuality was based on the replies of respondents who were married or living together (about 1200 people, the vast majority of whom were married).

Two questions from the questionnaire were most relevant to extramarital sex: (1) How many, if any, extramarital affairs did the respondents report? and (2) If they had had such a relationship, when did they have it? Answers to both questions revealed an association between feeling underbenefited and engaging in extramarital relationships. On the average, underbenefited individuals reported having a greater number of extramarital relationships than did either over-benefited individuals or people who felt their marriage was an equitable one. Moreover, among respondents who had had extramarital affairs, underbenefited people had their first affair earlier in their marriage (after an average of 9 to 11 years) than people who felt themselves to be overbenefited or in an equitable relationship (12 to 15 years).

In light of these results, Walster et al. (1978) suggested that lack of equity in the relationship may be one prominent reason why people have extramarital affairs; people who feel they are not getting the benefits to which they feel entitled are the ones most likely to turn, and to turn earlier, to other relationships. While overbenefited individuals are also in an inequitable relationship and may feel some discomfort (see Chapter 7), they do not appear to experience the dissatisfaction of those who are underbenefited. As we have seen, their level of sexual satisfaction is high and they have little interest in seeking sexual relationships outside the marriage. Although most people would probably say that they would prefer an equitable relationship, people's sex lives seem to go perfectly well when they think they are getting more out of the relationship than they think they really deserve.

RELATIONSHIPS BETWEEN SAME-SEX PARTNERS

Most of the research on romantic and/or sexual relationships focuses on relationships between *heterosexuals*, individuals whose exclusive or primary sexual preference is directed toward members of the opposite sex. In this section, we consider the romantic and sexual relationships of *homosexuals*, individuals whose exclusive or primary sexual preference is directed toward members of the same sex. Sexual orientation, be it heterosexual or homosexual, is not the same as sexual behavior. For various reasons, people of a given sexual orientation may engage in sexual activities with a member of the nonpreferred gender. An act does not an orientation make. What does make an orientation, according to Money (1987), is love:

> A person with a homosexual status is one who has the potential to fall in love only with someone who has the same genital and bodily morphology as the self. For a heterosexual, the morphology must be that of a person of the other sex. For the bisexual, it may be either. (pp. 385–386)

Relationship Issues

Comparisons between heterosexual and homosexual relationships indicate that there are many similarities. For example, when Oberstone and Sukoneck (1976) studied homosexual and heterosexual women, they found no difference in adjustment or general lifestyle patterns. Research by Peplau, Cochran, Rook, and Padesky (1978) on lesbian couples highlighted two major factors that influenced the way these individuals evaluated their relationship:

1. *Dyadic attachment.* The need for sharing and intimacy
2. *Personal autonomy.* The need for some aspects of one's life to be independent of the relationship

Obviously, the interplay, and sometimes conflict, between attachment and autonomy is a critical element in all intimate relationships—female and male, homosexual and heterosexual.

Studies of homosexual men have also found great similarities between homosexual intimate relationships and heterosexual ones. In research by Jones and Bates (1978), homosexual male couples described successful homosexual relationships in conventional heterosexual terms. Successful homosexual relationships were depicted as involving greater appreciation of the partner and of the couple as a unit, less conflict, more positive feelings about love and relationships, and future plans for activities as a couple. These are, of course, the same kinds of factors mentioned by heterosexual couples.

Dailey (1979), too, was impressed by the similarities among his sample of married couples, nonmarried heterosexual couples, and homosexual couples (male and female). These groups did differ on a few of the many measures taken in this study. Homosexuals had a lower level of relationship adjustment than the heterosexual couples, though all exhibited high levels of overall adjustment; nonmarried heterosexuals reported greater sexual satisfaction than the other couples, though again all groups reported high levels of satisfaction. But the number of such differences was small, and few of them appeared to indicate significant problems. On the whole, these different groups were very similar in terms of how successful they were in maintaining committed relationships.

The research evidence on this point is, then, clear and consistent. If we want to describe what goes on in a relationship between two homosexual individuals—what makes for the success of that relationship and what may lead to problems—we do not have to use a different language. We can use the same terms as we would in describing a relationship between two heterosexuals. In our intimate relationships, we are all much more similar than we are different.

Love in the Time of AIDS

It would, however, be foolish and remarkably insensitive to claim that there are no differences between homosexual and heterosexual relationships. Homosexual couples still face considerable social stigma and legal barriers. Homophobia—negative, emotional reactions toward homosexual persons—is still quite strong, particularly toward gay males (Triplett & Sugarman, 1987; Williams & Jacoby, 1989). Legally, homosexuals are prohibited from marriage, which creates all sorts of difficulties for tax returns, joint ownership of property, guardianship/adoption of children, pension plans, insurance coverage, and wills. As indicated in

Chapter 1, domestic partnership legislation passed in some states and cities will extend some of these benefits of marriage to unmarried couples, both homosexual and heterosexual. However, unless they are specifically included in antidiscrimination statutes or guidelines, homosexuals remain virtually the only group in our society that can be legally denied housing and employment solely on the basis of personal characteristics unrelated to financial status or job performance.

But for all the distress they cause, these problems pale in comparison with the devastating effects of AIDS. The earliest documented case of acquired immune deficiency syndrome in the United States occurred in 1968 (Cochran & Mays, 1989). It was not until the 1980s, however, that significant numbers of cases began to appear, and even then, there was much confusion about the nature of the disease and the threat it posed (Shilts, 1987). At the time this book is being written, there are still huge gaps in our knowledge about AIDS and the HIV (human immunodeficiency virus) infection that causes it. Table 5.1 summarizes some facts about AIDS based on current information; these facts, however, are subject to change in light of future scientific discovery.

But we do not have to wait for scientific discoveries to consider the impact of AIDS on the gay community. As described earlier in this chapter, the overwhelming majority of the victims of the first wave of the AIDS epidemic were gay males. By 1987, 10 percent of the general population said they knew someone with AIDS (Segal, 1987). Among gay males, particularly those living in large urban areas, the percentage who knew someone with AIDS has to be much greater. For these individuals, this has been a time both of unbearable sorrow, as more and more friends and lovers get sick and die, and of incredible fear that they might be next. Although their risk of infection is the lowest of any group in society, lesbians too feel the psychological brunt of the AIDS epidemic as they witness the suffering and death of many close male friends.

As noted earlier, the first wave of the AIDS epidemic has passed. New cases of AIDS among gay males involve, for the most part, individuals who were infected some time ago. We do not yet know how all these experiences will affect intimate relationships between gay males. Before AIDS, gender differences in homosexual relationships were very similar to gender differences in heterosexual relationships (Bell & Weinberg, 1978; Harry & DeVall, 1978; Peplau & Gordon, 1983). Like heterosexual women, lesbians made a strong connection between sex and psychological intimacy and were far more likely than homosexual males to have monogamous relationships. Like heterosexual men, gay men had more permissive attitudes about sex and were far more likely than homosexual females to have sexually unrestricted relationships and engage in promiscuous behavior. Thus, homosexuals were like heterosexuals—only, perhaps, more so.

TABLE 5.1 SOME FACTS ABOUT AIDS

1. *Can you get AIDS from casual contact?* There is no documented case of the transmission of AIDS from casual contact, even among families of AIDS patients.

2. *Are dental and medical personnel at greater risk for HIV infection?* Because HIV can be transmitted from direct contact of blood with an open sore, dental and medical personnel must take special precautions to protect themselves.

3. *Can a person be infected with HIV and still test negative?* Yes, there is a "window" of at least a few weeks between becoming infected and producing enough antibodies to be detected by a test for HIV.

4. *Can a person be infected with HIV and not have any symptoms of AIDS?* Although the average length of time between infection and developing the disease is about 8 years, this interval varies greatly among individuals. Lui et al. (1988) report a range of 4 to 15 years prior to the onset of the disease.

5. *Can a person be infected with HIV and never develop AIDS?* Most scientists believe that, in the absence of treatment, any person who is infected with HIV will eventually develop AIDS.

6. *If a person thinks that he or she might be infected, should this person get tested?* Absolutely. It is important to know whether you are infected in order not to infect others. In addition, taking AZT (currently the most effective treatment for AIDS) is now recommended for individuals who are HIV-infected but have not shown any symptoms of AIDS. This treatment can delay the onset of the disease.

7. *Are all babies who test positive for HIV at birth actually infected with HIV?* No. For reasons that are not presently understood, some babies who test positive will later be found not to be infected. For both babies and adults, it is crucial to have more than one test to establish a firm diagnosis.

8. *Is AIDS always fatal?* Up to now, it has been assumed that AIDS is a fatal disease. But new treatments are being rapidly developed, and there is the possibility that AIDS will become a chronic disease, like diabetes or high blood pressure, that can be managed. Although this possibility has not yet been realized, it is seen as a reasonable hope for the future by many of those involved in the research and treatment of AIDS.

We can assume that the lesbian preference for monogamous relationships remains, and may account, at least in part, for the high levels of attachment and satisfaction found among lesbian couples (Kurdek, 1989a). But what about gay males? The biology of AIDS does not require monogamy. It is possible to practice very safe sex (for example, mutual masturbation) with multiple partners, while unprotected sex with a single, infected partner is distinctly unsafe. On the other hand, the social psychology of AIDS may have strengthened gay men's motivation to establish enduring relationships. As in all times of plague, the AIDS epidemic has seen its fair share of selfish, uncaring actions. That is not surprising. What is remarkable is the degree to which people have been able to help each other, support each other, and band together in the face of catastrophe (Omoto & Snyder, 1990). AIDS is one of the most deadly diseases in human history (Lui, Darrow, & Rutherford, 1988), but it has been met with great courage by many of its victims and those who love them.

SEX AND COMMUNICATION: TALK TO ME, TALK TO ME

According to a *Time* magazine article, "Talk [was] the sex of the 80s" (Corliss, 1989, p. 65). Perhaps because of the fear of AIDS that makes talk much safer than sex, perhaps because of the continuing high rate of divorce that makes people doubt their ability to sustain a commitment, people appear to be focusing as never before on the need to talk to each other. Widespread recognition of the importance of communication is a relatively new development among the general public, but it has long been a major theme among therapists and counselors (Lederer & Jackson, 1968; Messersmith, 1976). One study, for example, found that in a sample of 100 married couples (the vast majority of whom said they were happily or very happily married), 50 percent of the husbands and 77 percent of the wives reported at least one sexual difficulty (Frank, Anderson, & Rubinstein, 1978). In discussing their results, Frank et al. concluded that many of these sexual difficulties reflected more general interpersonal problems in the relationship, a number of which may well be created or aggravated by poor communication. Thus, sexual problems may, in fact, be communication problems. As the head of a university clinic for sexual dysfunction put it, "The problem is what is happening with their mouths, not with their groins" (quoted in Gelman, 1987).

Not only can failing to communicate about relationship issues spill over and impair sexual relations, failing to communicate about sex itself can affect both sexual and relational satisfaction (Cupach & Comstock, 1990). The importance of good sexual communication was highlighted in a study by Masters and Johnson (1979), which compared the sexual experiences of heterosexuals and homosexuals. In terms of sexual efficiency (defined as reaching orgasm easily and consistently), there was little difference between the homosexual and heterosexual couples who participated in this study, in which couples were observed in sexual activities as well as interviewed about their reactions. Masters and Johnson concluded, however, that the subjective quality of the sexual experience (greater psychological involvement, more total body contact, more enjoyment of each aspect of the sexual experience, and more responsiveness to the needs and desires of the partner) was greater for homosexuals (male and female) than for heterosexuals.

Masters and Johnson credited the high subjective quality of the sexual interaction between homosexual couples to three main factors:

1. *Intragender empathy.* Since each person in a homosexual sexual encounter is of the same sex, partners have a better understanding of how to satisfy each other. Heterosexual couples lack the advantage of intragender empathy.
2. *Self-centeredness of techniques.* Nonintercourse techniques require less effort at coordination with the partner. Since, on the average, homosexual couples emphasize nonintercourse activities more than do heterosexual couples, heterosexual couples are faced with a greater need for coordination.
3. *Communication.* In this study, homosexuals talked more easily and openly about their sexual feelings than did heterosexuals. They would ask each other what was desired, and they would comment on whether what was being done was pleasurable. In contrast, Masters and Johnson noted a "persistent neglect of the vital communicative exchange" by heterosexual couples and their "potentially self-destructive lack of intellectual curiosity about the partner" (p. 219).

The major point that Masters and Johnson wish to make is quite clear. It is not that homosexual sexual activity is somehow inherently better than heterosexual sexual activity. It is that understanding the other person's needs and desires is crucial for high-quality sexual experiences. Homosexuals can obtain this understanding to some extent without communicating with each other; being of the same gender, their guesses about what the other person would like will often be relatively accurate (though some therapists believe that the effectiveness of intragender empathy has been exaggerated; see Brown & Zimmer, 1986). Homosexuals also have a greater interest in nonintercourse techniques (for example, masturbation of the partner and oral-genital sex), which require less coordination. And yet homosexual couples in the Masters and Johnson study were very good communicators.

Unfortunately, heterosexual couples who lack intragender empathy and, therefore, have a greater need for communication show less motivation and skill in talking about sexual desires and preferences. Instead, they appear to assume some kind of inherent male expertise that makes communication unnecessary. This assumption puts an unfair burden on the male; it also reduces the likelihood of sexual pleasure for both partners as neither has much knowledge of what the other enjoys. To compound the problem, heterosexual couples place a heavy emphasis on intercourse, a technique that requires more coordination between partners. Zilbergeld (1978) has called the assumption of male expertise and the emphasis on intercourse the "fantasy model of sex." Table 5.2 summarizes Zilbergeld's description of the beliefs on which this fantasy rests. Although these beliefs focus primarily on the male role in sexual interaction, both males and females in our society are likely to subscribe to them.

TABLE 5.2 THE FANTASY MODEL OF SEX

The equipment:	All you need is a penis. In Fantasyland, penises come in only three sizes—large, gigantic, and so big you can barely get it through the door.
The partner:	The women in Fantasyland are all gorgeous and perfectly formed. They want sex all the time, and want to be handled roughly, no matter how much they request gentleness.
The feelings:	Men should not have, or at least not express certain feelings. Aggressiveness, competitiveness, anger, and the other feelings associated with being in control are OK, but weakness, confusion, fear, vulnerability, tenderness, compassion, and sensuality are allowed only to girls and women.
The performance:	In sex, as elsewhere, it's performance that counts. The three A's of manhood are "Achieve, Achieve, Achieve."
The responsibility:	The man must always be the one to take charge of and orchestrate sex.
The desire:	A man constantly wants and is always ready to have sex. Men are like machines, and can perform any time the button is pushed.
The goal:	All physical contact must lead to sex. Cuddling, hugging, kissing, holding, and caressing are neither valuable nor pleasurable in their own right; they are useful only in paving the way for sex.
The main thing:	There is only one main thing—intercourse. All other forms of sex are only preliminaries. Oral sex is not sex. Only intercourse is sex.
The main thing (Part II):	An erection is everything.
The vigor:	Sex must be hard-driving and drive women into paroxysms of pleasure. Sex should not be slow or leisurely, with time for resting, talking, laughing.
The natural expertise:	There is no necessity for learning any new skills, talking about sex, or taking any corrective measures, for there is nothing to learn and nothing to correct.

SOURCE: Radlove, 1983; adapted from Zilbergeld, 1978.

It is interesting to compare the fantasy model of sex with a more realistic view of sexual communication. Table 5.3 outlines a particularly helpful discussion by Scoresby (1977) of the sorts of sexual communication problems that can arise and some suggested solutions to them. There are two major differences between the fantasy model and Scoresby's approach. In the fantasy model, the responsibility for good sex is seen as belonging to the man; Scoresby's perspective assumes from the outset that both partners share responsibility. Moreover, the fantasy model views sex as a "natural expertise" with nothing to learn and nothing to correct. Scoresby regards sex as a learning experience—where partners are constantly learning more about themselves and about each other. In short, the fantasy model not only is unrealistic but also inhibits personal and relational growth. Seen more realistically, good sex takes more effort but also offers far greater rewards.

CHAPTER SUMMARY

Dramatic changes in sexual attitudes and behaviors are not rare. Recently, the United States has gone through a period of permissive attitudes and increased sexual activity (the "sexual revolution" of the 1960s and 1970s). In the 1980s, there was a return to more conservative attitudes and reduced sexual activity at least among some segments of the population. However, females continue to experience their first sexual encounter at younger and younger ages.

Predictors of Premarital Sexual Activity

In general, a person's values and attitudes are the best predictors of premarital sexual activity. Some evidence indicates that socially successful teenagers who confront stressful life circumstances may be particularly likely to become sexually active and to run a greater risk of unmarried pregnancy. Family structure may also be related to premarital sexual activity, though the importance of father absence in contributing to increased sexual activity among female adolescents has been disputed. Premarital sexual activity among teenagers is higher for boys than for girls and for blacks than for whites.

Contraception and Safe Sex. The potential dangers of unsafe sex practices include unwanted pregnancy and a variety of sexually transmitted diseases including AIDS. The first wave of the AIDS epidemic involved gay males; the second wave involves IV drug users and their sexual partners. There is discussion of a third possible wave involving heterosexual young adults. Sexual behavior can be changed; safe sex is now practiced widely in the gay male community. At present, however, it appears that heterosexual college students talk more about safe sex

TABLE 5.3 SEXUAL COMMUNICATION PROBLEMS AND SOME POSSIBLE SOLUTIONS

Elements of Sexual Communication	Common Problems	Possible Solutions
Emotional bond and communicating desire	1. Failure to talk openly with each other. 2. Repeated lack of orgasm by female. 3. Tension and lack of relaxation. 4. One demanding the other to perform. 5. Excessive shyness or embarrassment. 6. Hurried and ungentle performance. 7. Absence of frequent touching, embracing, and exchanges of intimacy.	1. Increase each person's ability to self-disclose feelings. 2. Spend increased positive time alone together. 3. Avoid threatening to dissolve the relationship. 4. Check for angry conflict and reduce if possible.
Sexual responsibility	1. Only one person initiating. 2. Excessive modesty that restricts full expression. 3. Failure to freely consent or refuse invitations. 4. Blaming each other for sexual failure. 5. Double standard for males or for females. 6. Existence of beliefs that males and females differ sharply about feelings. 7. Insistence by one on exceeding the desired sexual limits of the other. 8. Feeling of pressure to perform by either or both.	1. Review training and education about sex to see if cultural training has disparaged positive sexual expression. 2. Discuss how previous experience and early training may affect each person. 3. Examine current relationship to see if excessive dominance is present. 4. Reduce criticism each may have for the other. 5. Seek professional help for the purpose of helping each feel accepting of sexual desires and asserting personal responsibility.

than actually practice it. Some possible reasons why safe-sex practices are not more prevalent among young, well-educated individuals include youthful sexual appetites, the influence of alcohol, and an illusion of unique invulnerability. Sexual attitudes are also important. Individuals who have a generally negative attitude toward sex are less likely to have sex, but if they do have sex, they are more likely to have unsafe sex.

Elements of Sexual Communication	Common Problems	Possible Solutions
Optimal variation	1. Repeatedly feeling that sex has become monotonous. 2. Feeling bored by having to participate in intercourse. 3. Excessive experimentation that violates the preferences of one or both. 4. Hurried and mechanical intercourse. 5. Lack of a set of sexual preferences.	1. Discuss what each prefers, why and when. 2. Stay within the sense of propriety felt by each person unless excessively restrictive. 3. Focus on varied feeling states as opposed to variations in techniques. 4. Acquire additional information about sexual techniques.
Physical performance	1. Existence of physical dysfunction: a) impotence, b) premature ejaculation, c) retarded ejaculation, d) failure to be orgastic, e) vaginismus, f) sensation of pain.	1. Seek competent professional help. 2. Examine each person's individual life or relationship for sources of tension and stress and reduce if possible. 3. Increase the amount of care, warmth, and nurturance rather than criticizing or ridiculing. 4. Evaluate and improve all elements of the sexual relationship.

SOURCE: Scoresby, 1977.

Gender Differences in Sexual Attitudes

On average, men are more permissive in their sexual values and attitudes than are women. Men are also more likely to enjoy sex without intimacy, while women prefer sex to be part of a psychologically intimate relationship. Men tend to be more comfortable with a proactive sexual role, and women tend to be more comfortable with a reactive sexual role. Traditionally, the double standard has called for more negative evaluations of sexually active women than of sexually active men. It appears, however, that such a double standard is no longer endorsed by today's college students. There is evidence of a preference among college students for sexual partners who have some, but not too much, sexual experience.

Men's and Women's Perceptions of Sexuality. When men's and women's views of an individual's sexuality are compared, the highest ratings of sexuality are found for men's perception of a woman. It has been proposed that men's tendency to see women in sexual terms may increase the risk of date rape. The vast majority of college students believe that it is never justified for a man to have sex with a woman against her will.

Sex and Satisfaction

Sex and Marital Happiness. Compared with unhappy couples, happy couples report a greater congruence between the level of sexual activity they desire and the level of sexual activity they actually have. Marital satisfaction is also associated with having a positive balance in the "marital bank account," such as having more sex than arguments. In general, happy couples engage in more frequent joint activities—including, but not limited to, sex.

Sex and Love among Dating Couples. The timing of when a couple has sex (early in the relationship versus later on) is associated with feelings of love and guilt, as well as with the woman's sexual satisfaction. Early-sex couples report less love, less guilt, and more satisfaction for the woman. Timing does not appear, however, to be related to the endurance of the relationship. Recent research has found that at least over a short period, sexually active couples are more likely to maintain their relationship than sexually inactive couples. The exact cause for this finding is not clear. Among married couples, those who had experienced an early premarital pregnancy reported lower current levels of love and affection than did those who had not experienced a premarital pregnancy.

Sex and Equity in the Relationship. Partners in an equitable relationship report more extensive sexual involvement and emphasize the importance of both persons' needs and desires. Individuals who regard themselves as underbenefited in their relationship—receiving a smaller proportion of rewards relative to contributions—report low levels of sexual satisfaction and appear to be more likely to engage in sexual activities outside the relationship.

Relationships Between Same-Sex Partners

Sexual orientation refers to a person's exclusive or primary preference for a sexual partner who is of the same or opposite sex. Sexual orientation is not the same as sexual behavior.

Relationship Issues. There are many similarities in the relationship issues that confront homosexual and heterosexual couples.

Love in the Time of AIDS. There are also some important differences between homosexual and heterosexual relationships. Homosexual couples have fewer legal rights and are faced with unpleasant or even frightening homophobic reactions. In the last decade, AIDS has been, by far, the most devastating problem with which gay males have had to cope. Some basic facts on AIDS are summarized in Table 5.1. Before AIDS, gender differences in homosexual relationships resembled those among heterosexuals. Lesbians were more likely to prefer monogamous relationships, and gay males were more likely to prefer sexually unrestricted relationships. In response to AIDS, gay males adopted safe-sex practices, which have dramatically reduced the rate of new infections. The long-term effects that the AIDS epidemic may have on gay males' relationship preferences are not yet known.

Sex and Communication: Talk to Me, Talk to Me

Sex and communication have a close relationship. On the one hand, difficulty in communicating about general relationship problems can spill over and impair sexual relations. On the other hand, good communication is essential for sexual satisfaction. Masters and Johnson suggest that communication is particularly important for heterosexuals because they lack intragender empathy and emphasize intercourse, which requires good coordination. And yet it appears that heterosexuals have more difficulty than homosexuals in establishing good sexual communication. One reason for this difficulty may be the tendency for heterosexuals to assume an inherent male expertise in sexual matters. This assumption and other false beliefs about the male role in heterosexual activities are incorporated in the "fantasy model of sex" outlined in Table 5.2. A more realistic model of sex, see Table 5.3, emphasizes that both partners share the responsibility in sexual activities and that sex is a learning experience.

PART THREE

———— ❖ ————

Progress and Fairness in the Relationship

6

Relationship Development

❖

Stage Theories of Relationship Development ✦ A Social Exchange Model of Relationship Development ✦ *Rewards and Costs* ✦ *Expectations* ✦ *Alternatives* ✦ *Investments* ✦ Commitment to the Relationship ✦ *When Commitment Fails* ✦ Chapter Summary

*I*ntimate relationships differ widely in how they begin. Some people fall madly, passionately in love the first time they meet. Others begin as friends, only to end up as lovers. Friendships can get started in the course of one briefly shared experience, or they can grow out of years of daily interaction. But no matter how they begin, all relationships change over time—sometimes for better, sometimes for worse. In this chapter, we focus on this change over time—the development of relationships.

There are two major approaches to the study of relationship development: stage theories and social exchange. Stage theories take a *qualitative* approach, making a sharp distinction between different phases in a relationship. In contrast, a social exchange perspective takes a *quantitative* approach, emphasizing the cumulative effect of gradual changes. For stage theories, the difference between point 1 and point 2 in a relationship is one of kind; for social exchange, the difference is one of degree. This chapter examines both of these approaches to relationship development.

STAGE THEORIES OF RELATIONSHIP DEVELOPMENT

According to *stage theories* of relationship development, relationships go through a specific set of stages in a certain order. The two-step theory of attraction described in Chapter 3 is a stage theory, with a first stage of repulsion based on dissimilarity and a second stage of attraction based on similarity. Another two-step model divides the path from attraction to love into immediate versus delayed effects (Berg, 1984; Neimeyer & Neimeyer, 1983). This model holds that a variety of characteristics produce initial repulsion or attraction, while another set of characteristics determine whether an established relationship remains casual or grows into a close and meaningful attachment (Davis & Oathout, 1987; Duck, 1977).

Perhaps the best-known two-stage theory was proposed by Kerckhoff and Davis (1962). In their research, "short-term couples," who had been together for less than 18 months, were compared with "long-term couples," who had been together for more than 18 months. Both types of couples were studied over a seven-month period. Kerckhoff and Davis found that for short-term couples, agreement on values was the best predictor of progress in the relationship. For long-term couples, however, personal need complementarity best predicted progress toward a more permanent commitment. As you may recall from Chapter 3, complementarity in personal needs or in personality refers to a compatible fit between differences—such that, for example, dominant individuals would get along with submissive individuals. In general terms, the findings of Kerckhoff and Davis implied that similarity was an important factor early in a relationship, while complementarity became more important later on. Despite its intuitive appeal, however, there is little supporting evidence for this particular two-stage model; investigators who tried to replicate the results of the original study were unable to do so (Levinger, Senn, & Jorgensen, 1970).

Other stage theories include more than just two stages. Reiss (1960) described the progress of a relationship in terms of four stages: initial rapport, mutual self-revelation, mutual dependency, and personal need fulfillment. Once this sequence has been completed for some issues, says Reiss, it may begin all over again for other issues. In another multistage theory, Lewis (1972, 1973) proposed that relationships begin with attraction based on similarity, which creates good rapport. According to Lewis, the relationship then goes through the following stages: mutual self-disclosure, empathic understanding of the other person, role compatibility, and, finally, commitment to the relationship and identity as a couple.

Another well-known stage theory was developed by Bernard Murstein (1976a, 1986, 1987). This theory, called *stimulus-value-role* (SVR) *theory,* proposes that intimate relationships proceed from a stimulus stage, where attraction is based on external attributes such as physical appearance, to a value stage, where attachment is based on similarity of values and beliefs. The final transition is to a role stage, where commitment is based on successful performance of relationship roles, such as husband and wife. Although Murstein states that all three factors have some influence throughout a relationship, each one is said to become prominent during only one stage (see Figure 6.1). A summary of the four major stage theories described here is provided in Table 6.1.

In evaluating any stage theory, the critical question involves *sequence.* For example, does the value stage always precede the role stage? Or might a couple work out roles before exploring whether their values are compatible? A number of investigators have concluded that the evidence for a fixed sequence of stages in intimate relationships is quite weak (Leigh, Homan, & Burr, 1987; Rubin & Levinger, 1974; Stephen,

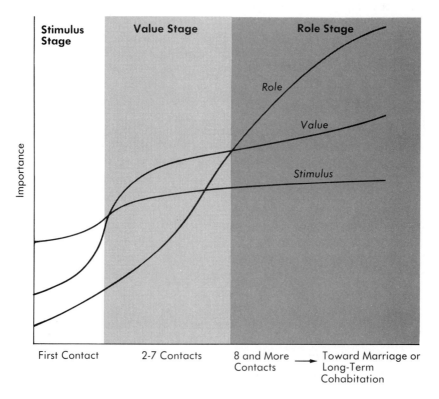

FIGURE 6.1
Stages of courtship in SVR theory. (Murstein, 1987.)

TABLE 6.1 STAGE MODELS OF RELATIONSHIP DEVELOPMENT

Stage in the Relationship	The Wheel Theory of the Development of Love (Reiss, 1960)	Filter Theory (Kerckhoff & Davis, 1962)	A Model of Premarital Dyadic Formation (Lewis, 1972, 1973)	SVR Theory (Stimulus-Value-Role) (Murstein, 1976a)
Early				Attraction based on external stimulus attributes (e.g., physical attractiveness)
		Similarity in values	Similarities	Value similarity
	Rapport		Rapport	
	Mutual self-revelation		Mutual self-disclosure	
	Mutual dependency		Emphatic understanding of the other person	
	Personality need fulfillment	Need complementarity	Interpersonal role fit (e.g., need complementarity)	
	(Can then recycle, going back to rapport)		Dyadic crystalization (e.g., commitment, identity as a couple)	Successful performance of roles in the relationship (e.g., wife, husband)
Late				

1987). The difficulty in coming up with a fixed sequence of stages for all relationships is illustrated by a series of studies on newlywed couples (Surra & Huston, 1987). Based on subjects' retrospective accounts of how their relationship developed, this research found a variety of different patterns of development for couples' progress toward marriage. "Stages," then, are probably best viewed as "phases" that take place at different times for different couples.

A SOCIAL EXCHANGE MODEL OF RELATIONSHIP DEVELOPMENT

Social exchange theory is based on an economic model of human behavior. This perspective assumes that just as a person's behavior in the marketplace is motivated by a desire to maximize profits and minimize losses, these same motives determine behavior in social interactions (Blau, 1964; Homans, 1961; Thibaut & Kelley, 1959). Social exchange provides a general framework for analyzing all kinds of relationships—with coworkers as well as friends, with a teacher as well as a spouse. There are five major components to this framework: rewards, costs, expectations, perceived alternatives, and investments. We will go over each of these components one by one, but before we begin, take a look at Figure 6.2, which displays the social exchange "map" as a whole.

Rewards and Costs

The fundamental premise of social exchange theory is that relationships that provide more rewards and fewer costs will be more satisfying and will endure longer. In an intimate relationship, rewards include companionship, love, consolation in times of distress, and sexual gratification if the relationship is a sexual one. Anticipated rewards are important as well (Levinger & Huesmann, 1980). Increasing involvement and intimacy with another may be desired for the sake of potential rewards in the future. But intimate relationships also involve costs: time and effort spent to maintain the relationship, compromises to keep the

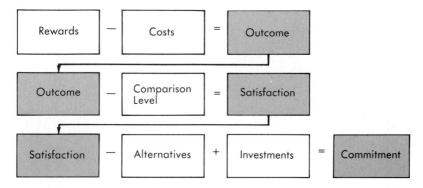

FIGURE 6.2
Factors that influence satisfaction and commitment in a relationship.
(Brehm & Kassin, 1990.)

peace, suffering in time of conflict, and outside opportunities that have to be given up if the relationship is to continue. As indicated in Figure 6.2, rewards minus costs yield the outcome of the relationship.

Research on the social exchange process between couples has pointed out both the complexity and the importance of rewards and costs in relationships. For happily married partners, some investigators have found that rewards are more important than costs in predicting the level of marital satisfaction (Jacobson, Waldron, & Moore, 1980); others, however, have indicated that costs are more important (Wills, Weiss, & Patterson, 1974). For unhappily married couples, the results are also contradictory. Margolin (1978) found that only pleasing behaviors received during a week's time correlated with the marital satisfaction of the distressed couples in her study, while displeasing behaviors were the best predictors of satisfaction for the unhappy couples in Jacobson et al.'s research. These studies, then, agree that rewards and costs in a relationship affect how we feel about the relationship. They disagree, however, on what (rewards or costs) is more important for whom (happy versus unhappy couples).

There is more consistency in the research findings when happy and unhappy couples are compared directly on the quality of their interactions. Across a number of studies, happy couples have been shown to act in more positive, more rewarding ways toward each other than unhappy couples (Billings, 1979; Birchler, Weiss, & Vincent, 1975; Gottman, 1979; Jacobson, Follette, & McDonald, 1982; Margolin & Wampold, 1981; Vincent, Weiss, & Birchler, 1975).

Happy couples have also been found to act in less costly, negative ways, though it should be noted that all married couples—happy or unhappy—tend to be more negative with each other than they are with strangers (Birchler et al., 1975; Vincent et al., 1975). Different types of negative behaviors may also be noticed differently by distressed couples. For example, Barnett and Nietzel (1979) found that happy and unhappy couples differed in their levels of negative task-oriented behavior, but not negative emotional behavior. This finding stands in sharp contrast to the extensive work by Gottman (1979), who emphasizes that the greatest difference between happy and unhappy couples occurs in the area of negative emotional behavior.

The reason for this apparent contradiction probably lies in the different research strategies employed by the two sets of investigators. Barnett and Nietzel employed self-recordings obtained from their subjects. As we would expect, unhappy couples were very sensitive to when their partners did something they did not like. They may, however, have been less aware of how much negative emotional interaction was also going on. Gottman's research group relies primarily on observations of couples, at home and in the lab; this method of study ensures that when negative emotional behaviors occur, they will be recorded (by the observers). On the other hand, because of limited observation time in the home and the artificial nature of the laboratory setting, Gottman's approach is less likely to detect the importance of negative behavior involving the daily transactions of marital life (e.g., the spouse failing to carry out his or her assigned chores, or interfering with the other spouse's efforts to accomplish some task). It seems likely that, in fact, unhappy marriages are characterized by both negative emotional *and* negative task-oriented behaviors.

The importance of rewards among premarital, dating couples has also been demonstrated (Lloyd, Cate, & Henton, 1984; Rusbult, 1983). Lloyd et al. found that the reported level of rewards in the relationship was a reasonably good predictor of whether a dating couple remained together during the seven months of their study. Although after seven months over 40 percent of these relationships (mostly among college sophomores) had broken up, this was less likely to happen for couples whose initial reward level had been high. In Rusbult's study, the way that rewards *changed* over the seven months of her investigation was strongly associated with whether or not couples stayed together: "Stayers" experienced a greater increase in rewards as the relationship progressed than did "leavers."

Costs in the relationship were not measured by Lloyd et al. In Rusbult's research, costs were not related to satisfaction during the earlier stages of the subjects' relationships. However, for the later stages (after about three months into the study), satisfaction dropped considerably for those subjects who reported that costs were increasing in the relationship. These results suggest that although the level of rewards is continually important in relationships, costs may only become a factor after "the honeymoon" is over.

Perception of rewards and costs. Although theories of social exchange are modeled after theories of economic exchange, the human equation is necessarily far more complex than typical financial transactions. As consumers in the economic marketplace, we can determine the worth of an item by referring to its price. And when several of us look at a price tag, we will all read the same figures. As participants in the social marketplace, we have no such ready indicators of agreed-on value. Instead, we are all faced, every day, with complexities that would boggle the mind of even the most sophisticated financial experts.

First, there is the problem of determining the cost of any specific behavior to be exchanged with another person. Perhaps the most striking example of the difficulty in setting a price on what we have to exchange comes from the research of Ross and Sicoly (1979) on the *egocentric bias.* These investigators had spouses independently rate how they divided responsibility for 20 activities relevant to married life (e.g., cleaning house, caring for children, planning leisure-time activities). Subjects rated each item by putting a slash at the appropriate point on a 150-mm straight line, the endpoints of which were labeled "primarily husband" and "primarily wife."

Since having to take responsibility for daily tasks can usually be considered a "cost," each partner was in effect saying how much he or she had to "pay" for each mutually beneficial activity. If we were dealing with mutually agreed-on prices, we would expect the combination of the husband's price (how much he felt he was responsible from 0 to 150) and the wife's price (how much she felt she was responsible from 0 to 150) to add up to the total price of 150 for each item. That such rational pricing is not the hallmark of marital relationships was clearly demonstrated. When the two prices were added up across all the items, the average total for 73 percent of the couples came to *over* 150. Thus, in nearly three-quarters of these couples, at least one of the spouses was overestimating his or her contribution to these daily activities.

The operation of the egocentric bias has some important implications for relationships. First, couples who display this bias should also tend to disagree about their contributions, with each partner taking more credit than the other will allow. Such disagreements might well increase the likelihood of conflict and misunderstanding. Second, taking excessive credit for a necessary chore can be viewed as a selfish behavior and, therefore, have a negative impact on the partner's satisfaction. Third, taking excessive credit for a particularly enjoyable outcome could also be seen as selfish and decrease the partner's satisfaction. Subsequent research has provided support for all three of these propositions. Couples whose perceptions of each other's behaviors agree report more satisfaction than those who disagree (Christensen, Sullaway, & King, 1983); generosity in recognizing the partner's efforts is associated with higher levels of relationship satisfaction (Thompson & Kelley, 1981); and exaggerating one's own responsibility for a positive outcome is associated with lower levels of relationship satisfaction (Fincham & Bradbury, 1989).

The egocentric bias involves perceptions of the role of one's own and the partner's behavior in producing a given outcome. Perceptions of the meaning and value of an outcome are also important. Have you ever given a present that you thought was wonderful to someone who was obviously *not* thrilled to receive it? In such circumstances, you and the other person disagree about the worth of the present. Research by Wills et al. (1974) suggests that this kind of disagreement may be a fairly common occurrence. In this study, seven married couples kept track of their behavioral exchanges over the course of 14 days. The interactions were tabulated in terms of four categories based on the dimensions of positive versus negative and task-oriented (instrumental) versus emotional (affectional).

1. *Instrumental positive:* e.g., taking out the garbage
2. *Instrumental negative:* e.g., leaving one's dirty clothes for the partner to wash
3. *Affectional positive:* e.g., kissing the partner
4. *Affectional negative:* e.g., having an argument

Wills et al. found that among negative behaviors, both instrumental actions and affectional gestures were similar in their importance to both husbands and wives. Among positive behaviors, however, there was a major gender difference. Instrumental positive actions were more important to husbands than affectional positive behaviors; for wives, it was just the opposite.

But what are the consequences of this kind of disagreement? As Wills et al. discovered, placing different interpretations on our actions can interfere with our efforts to please the partner. To make sure that the measures they were using were sensitive to changes in behavior, Wills

Husbands and wives are similar in their perceptions of the importance of both task-oriented and affectional negative behaviors. Among positive behaviors, however, task-oriented actions are more important to husbands and affectionate gestures more important to wives. (Sandra Weiner/The Image Works)

et al. instructed all the husbands during the last two days of the study to increase their positive affectional behavior toward their wives; the wives were not informed of this instruction. When Wills et al. looked at the wives' reports for this period, they found that husbands had increased their positive affectional behaviors; they had also, however, increased their positive instrumental behaviors, even though they had not been instructed to do so.

This pattern of results suggests that husbands may have had some difficulty discriminating between affectional and instrumental behaviors. More serious than lack of discrimination, however, was actual substitution of one class of behaviors for another. Wills et al. found that for one of their couples, the wife's report after the first day following the instruction failed to show any increase in her husband's positive affectional behavior. When the husband was contacted by phone to see if the instructions had been clear, he was considerably annoyed, saying that "he certainly had complied with the instruction . . . by *washing his wife's car*" (p. 810). Thus, this husband believed that washing his wife's car was a perfectly good way to communicate his affection for her, even though his wife saw his actions as nonemotional, instrumental assistance that failed to convey affection. He gave her something that was more valuable to him than to her.

Research on the egocentric bias and on people's perceptions of the meaning and value of their interpersonal actions highlights a basic fact about social exchange. The language may seem to come straight from a certified public accountant—rewards and costs, gains and losses—but the reality is more complex. The entries in the social exchange account are based on a psychological arithmetic—involving motives, beliefs, and emotions. Partners do not necessarily see each other and their relationship in the same way, and differing perceptions can make it harder to develop satisfying transactions. Furthermore, rewards and costs do not occur in a psychological vacuum. The following sections describe how our expectations about the balance sheet we deserve and our beliefs about available alternatives to the present relationship also affect our satisfaction with the outcome of any given reward-cost equation.

Expectations

The outcome of a relationship, the difference between rewards and costs, is not necessarily the same as satisfaction with the relationship. In their classic description of social exchange processes, Thibaut and Kelley (1959) proposed that if we want to predict how satisfied people will be in a relationship, we must take into account their experiences and expectations: the kinds of outcomes they have received in past relationships and, based on this previous experience, the kinds of outcomes they expect to receive in the future. Thibaut and Kelley called this average, expected outcome for relationships the *comparison level* (or CL) and indicated that it varies widely among individuals. Some people have a high comparison level; they expect to have positive relationships with others in which the rewards far outweigh the costs. Other individuals have a low CL, expecting troublesome and unrewarding social relations. From a social exchange perspective, relationship satisfaction is determined by both outcomes and CL. For those expecting very little (a low CL), low rewards may be acceptable; for those expecting a great deal (a high CL), many rewards may be insufficient.

Alternatives

The comparison level for relationships reflects the influence of the historical context on any specific relationship. We have had relationships in the past that affect our expectations about what we should be able to obtain in the present and future. The broader social context of a relationship also needs to be considered. According to Thibaut and Kelley (1959), people have a *comparison level for alternatives* (or CL_{alt}). CL_{alt} refers to the kind of outcomes people think they would receive in some other, alternative relationship or lifestyle. Just as CL affects satisfaction with the relationship, so does CL_{alt} affect commitment to the relationship. If a person perceives the rewards available in another relationship to be high, that individual should be less committed to remaining in his or her present relationship (Berg, 1984; Berg & McQuinn, 1986; Green & Sporakowski, 1983). But when people believe they have few alternatives (low CL_{alt}), they tend to stay in their present relationship—even if it is a dissatisfying one that falls below expectations (CL).

Outcomes, CL, and CL_{alt}: Putting them together. In considering both CL and CL_{alt}, there are several points to keep in mind. First, you should note that these concepts refer to subjective points of view. The person who has high expectations could be living out a fantasy rather than responding to past reality and future probabilities. The individual who thinks that there is a wonderful alternative relationship out there could be completely wrong. As far as the existing relationship goes, however, whether the person is right or wrong does not matter; it is the person's *beliefs* that affect his or her behavior in the present relationship.

Second, you should think carefully about the relationship between CL and CL_{alt}. In many cases, the two will be similar. People who have high expectations for relationships may often think of themselves as having positive alternatives available. It is, however, quite possible for the two to differ dramatically. Imagine a man who has had a difficult life, has a dim view of the quality of the relationships that he can expect,

TABLE 6.2 RELATIONSHIP OUTCOMES AND COMPARISONS: A LOVE FOR ALL SEASONS

| | Outcomes (Rewards − Costs) | | | |
| | Positive | | Negative | |
	High CL	Low CL	High CL	Low CL
High CL_{alt}	Rewarding Expected Good options[1]	Rewarding Unexpected Good options	Unrewarding Unexpected Good options[4]	Unrewarding Expected Good options
Low CL_{alt}	Rewarding Expected Poor options	Rewarding Unexpected Poor options[2]	Unrewarding Unexpected Poor options	Unrewarding Expected Poor options[3]

[1] Summer

Matilda has had a wonderful history of relationships. Everyone she has been interested in has been even more interested in her. Matilda, therefore, has very high expectations about the level of relationship satisfaction that she should experience. In her present relationship with Herman, her expectations are more than met. Herman is a prince among men—just as Matilda thinks of herself as a princess. Even though she cannot imagine wanting to leave Herman, it does occur to Matilda from time to time (even princes have their bad moments) that there are many other men around who would love to be with her. Matilda is a very happy woman; she feels great security and freedom in her relationship with Herman.

[2] Fall

Marty has a marvelous relationship with David. They seem to suit each together so well and enjoy each other tremendously. Marty is especially grateful for this relationship since he never expected to have one this good. His early history of dating was a disaster. It seemed that whatever was the wrong thing to do, he promptly did

and has settled for a relationship that is not very pleasant. Then, suddenly, Ms. Wonderful steps onto the scene and is madly in love with our hero. Once Ms. Wonderful makes her love known, our hero has, at least initially, a low CL (negative expectations in general) but a high CL_{alt} (positive alternative available). One of the most impressive aspects of Thibaut and Kelley's formulation of social exchange is how many different kinds of relationships can be described using just three items: outcome, CL, and CL_{alt}. Table 6.2 provides a complete matrix as well as some fanciful descriptions of some of the most interesting combinations.

A societal CL_{alt}: Sex ratios. Usually, we think of alternatives as specific to the individual. Sally, who has a relationship with Joe, believes she also could be happy with Ken. But sometimes broad societal trends can affect alternatives. Consider, for example, the overall sex ratio in a it. Sometimes, usually late at night after one of the rare times when he and David have not gotten along as well as they usually do, Marty remembers those disasters of the past and realizes that David is the only man he's ever met who really loves him. Momentarily—happy as he generally is—he feels a bit trapped.

3 Winter

Larry is in complete despair. He hates his relationship with Joan—just hates it. At first, it was OK. They had both just gotten divorced, and they needed each other's support in adjusting to their new lives. But now they have gotten much more comfortable in the "single life," and it has become obvious that—other than being divorced—they don't have an interest, value, or belief in common. Larry wants to leave the relationship, but where will he go? He hasn't met anyone else he is attracted to who is also attracted to him—and he is scared to be on his own. He knows that's silly, but he is scared, so scared that he stays in a relationship where there is much more pain than joy.

4 Spring

Another rotten night! Sometimes Debbie doesn't want to think about how many rotten nights she and Elizabeth have had lately. Debbie can't even figure out how she got into such a situation. In the past, her relationships have been pretty good; maybe not paradise, but good. Now, this one is hell. She has put it off as long as possible, but really there is only one thing to do. She has got to break it off with Elizabeth. That means she will be back on her own, but Debbie knows she has survived perfectly well on her own before and will again. "Besides," she remembers, "there was that good-looking woman at the party Saturday . . . Lucy, that's her name, Lucy . . . she was very attractive and fun to talk to . . . and she was interested enough in me to make sure I knew where she worked. . . ." Suddenly, Debbie feels a whole lot better.

---

society (Guttentag & Secord, 1983; Secord, 1983). The *sex ratio* is the number of men per 100 women in a specific population. When the sex ratio is high, there are more men than women; when the sex ratio is low, there are fewer men than women. A sex ratio of 100 indicates equal numbers of men and women. Sex ratios have varied greatly in different times and different places. On the Western frontier in the United States during the nineteenth century, the sex ratio was high; women were scarce. In Europe after World War I, the sex ratio was low; millions of young men had died on the battlefields.

A few years ago, *Newsweek* magazine reached an astonishing conclusion about sex ratios in the United States. In an article entitled "Too Late for Prince Charming" (1986), it claimed that sex ratios were so low that white, college-educated women born in the 1950s who were unmarried at the age of 40 were more likely to be killed by a terrorist than to get married. After some critical scrutiny from researchers, it now appears that the study on which *Newsweek* based its claim was seriously flawed and the results greatly exaggerated ("Women," 1987).

Behind the sensationalism, however, are some real and important facts about sex ratios in the United States. In reality, there was a "marriage squeeze" during the 1970s and 1980s. When the number of unmarried women over 18 years of age was compared with the number of unmarried men who were two years older, sex ratios were low: fewer men than women. (Younger women are compared with slightly older men because, on average, first marriages involve couples where the man is two to three years older than the woman). But why were sex ratios low during this period? As noted in Chapter 1, the answer lies in the bulge in the demographic pipeline created by the post–World War II baby boom, which lasted from 1945 to 1957. During this period, more babies were born each year than in the preceding year: for example, more in 1952 than in 1951, and more in 1953 than in 1952. Since women born in 1953 would tend to marry men born in 1951, there were more females "on the market" than there were males.

Since the baby boom ended, things have changed. For those born in the 1970s, who are now college age, the sex ratio among marriage-eligible whites is high: more men than women (Kennedy, 1989). This reversal of the baby-boom pattern is produced by two factors. First, birthrates have been relatively stable since 1958, so that the number of babies born each year has not fluctuated greatly. Second, since men tend to marry at an older age than do women, this increases the excess of young unmarried men. Among whites, the 24-year-old woman in 1995 who is interested in getting married will have more alternatives than will her male peers.

As was also described in Chapter 1, however, two groups of women are likely to encounter low sex ratios in the United States regardless of whether they are baby boomers or not: white women over 40 and black women of all ages (Guttentag & Secord, 1983). There are a number of reasons for this pattern:

- Men over 40 who remarry tend to marry women who are five to eight years younger rather than two to three years younger, thus shrinking the pool of men available for older women.
- The mortality rate for men is greater than that for women and the difference increases with age.
- Black males have particularly high mortality rates across all age groups.
- Black men marry white women more often than black women marry white men (Tucker & Mitchell-Kernan, 1990).

The effects of sex ratios on people's behavior are probably fairly subtle. People don't generally check the actuarial charts before going on a date, getting married, or filing for divorce. But when sex ratios differ greatly from parity, they do set a tone, which could influence people's feelings and choices. Knowing that the number of eligible partners is small could make a person feel discouraged and decide to withdraw socially. Such knowledge could also create a desperate clinging to any relationship, even a destructive one. However, the effects of a low CL_{alt}—whether specific to an individual or influenced by broad societal trends—are not necessarily negative. The unattached individual who sees few opportunities for establishing a romantic relationship can invest his or her energies in developing a rich and rewarding life of work, friends, and family. For those with a low CL_{alt} who are already in a relationship, being more committed to that relationship can motivate constructive efforts to create a strong and meaningful partnership. To "have no alternatives" can be a terrible situation. But to always be pursuing alternatives rather than ever making an enduring commitment seems a prescription for a shallow and, ultimately, unsatisfying life.

Investments

Part of the process of becoming committed to a relationship involves making an *investment*. Although a variety of definitions of investment have been proposed (Lund, 1985), most emphasize the key concept of irretrievability (Kelley, 1983; Rusbult, 1980a, 1980b, 1983). An investment is something an individual puts into a relationship that he or she could not recover should that relationship end. Past costs of the relationship are investments in the future of that relationship. If the relationship ends, we cannot go back and retrieve what we have invested.

In general, investments strengthen commitment. If a relationship has been satisfying, we feel our investments have paid off. We want to stay in the relationship because it is rewarding. But what if we have invested a great deal in a relationship that is *unsatisfying*? If we leave, we forfeit our investment. So what do we do? What we might do is stay and invest even more in a continuing attempt to turn things around. Brockner and Rubin (1985) call this process *entrapment*: Commitments to a failing course of action are increased in an effort to justify investments already made. Paradoxically, bad investments can strengthen attachment rather than weaken it.

Dissonance and relationships. The idea that we all want to be able to justify our previous actions is a central part of one of the major theories in social psychology—the theory of cognitive dissonance

(Brehm & Cohen, 1962; Cooper & Fazio, 1984; Festinger, 1957; Wicklund & Brehm, 1976). According to this theory, dissonance is an uncomfortable, unpleasant state that arises from discrepancies that occur among our thoughts, feelings, and behavior. For example, suppose that you think of yourself as a very loving person but find yourself behaving in a harsh and cruel way toward your partner. The image of yourself as loving and the realization that you have acted cruelly are dissonant—the one contradicts the other. Dissonance theory states that because dissonance is uncomfortable, you will be motivated to reduce it by somehow resolving the discrepancy that has arisen.

The basic way to reduce dissonance is through justification. For example, if you believed that you had no choice but to be cruel to your partner—in the extreme case: someone was holding a gun to your head—this belief would justify your action immediately. Or you might believe that your partner, by being cruel to you, forced you to be cruel in return just to protect yourself. Again, such a justification would reduce dissonance. Indeed, if before you ever behaved in a cruel fashion, you firmly believed that you were forced to do so and had no choice in the matter, dissonance would never be created in the first place.

However, you might not think that you were forced or provoked to act the way you did. In this instance, you are confronted squarely with a self-concept that is in direct conflict with a *voluntary* behavior. Dissonance theory predicts that in these kinds of circumstances, "something has to give," and that what will give will be whatever is easiest to change. Behavior, once we have done it, is hard to change. You were cruel to your partner; you saw it, your partner saw it, perhaps others saw it too. You would really have to distort reality in order to deny that you acted in a cruel and harsh way. But you *could* change your self-concept; it only exists within your own mind. Perhaps you start to think of yourself as an "assertive person," who stands up for his or her own rights. Or perhaps you begin to see yourself as tough and pragmatic in the pursuit of important goals—the "you can't make an omelet without breaking eggs" sort of approach. In any event, you undergo a change in how you see yourself. You probably would not start to think of yourself as mean and cruel—virtually no one actually thinks of themselves this way—but you would develop a self-concept that would justify your behavior and be consistent—instead of dissonant—with it.

Dissonance theory helps us understand the process of entrapment created by bad investments. According to the theory, it is dissonant to choose to exert great effort that produces unsatisfying consequences. But how can we reduce dissonance in this situation? As indicated in our discussion of the theory, it is usually hard to deny the behavior itself. Evaluations and attitudes, however, are easier to change. What if we distort the consequences? What if we maintain that, actually, the outcome we received was pretty good? The belief that we voluntarily exerted great effort that produced satisfying consequences does *not* arouse dissonance. Applying this logic to relationships, dissonance theory predicts that trying hard to establish or maintain a relationship that turns out to be unsatisfying will create dissonance, which will be reduced by developing a more favorable attitude toward the relationship. Thus, we modify our attitudes to justify our suffering, to make it seem worthwhile.

This relationship between making an effort and developing positive regard was demonstrated in a study by Aronson and Mills (1959; see also Gerard & Mathewson, 1966). Subjects (all females) in this experiment had agreed to take part in a group discussion on the psychology of sex. Before the discussion began, however, some of the subjects were asked to take what was supposedly a preliminary screening test. Some subjects (high-effort condition) took a screening test that involved reading aloud to a male experimenter twelve obscene words and two vivid descriptions of sexual activity. This version of the test was deliberately designed to be very embarrassing and uncomfortable for subjects. Other subjects (low-effort condition) were asked to read only five mildly sexual words, and a final group of subjects (no-effort condition) was not asked to participate in any such screening test.

All subjects then were told that since the group discussion was already in progress, for this first session they could listen in over headphones but not participate. In fact, all subjects heard a prerecorded script prepared by experimental assistants, and this arranged discussion on sexual behavior in lower animals was extremely dull and boring. After listening to the discussion, subjects were asked to evaluate the group members and the discussion itself. The results of this study showed clear support for the dissonance theory prediction. Subjects who had undergone the effortful, uncomfortable screening test were much more favorable in their evaluations than subjects who had only a mild test or no test at all.

Real relationships in the real world are, of course, quite different from artificial laboratory experiments that can use experimental assistants, faked screening tests, and prerecorded group discussions. However, the relevance of the Aronson and Mills (1959) study for real relationships is direct and obvious. We often do invest a great deal of time and effort in trying to meet someone, or trying to attract someone, or trying to keep someone attracted. To then admit that this effort was pointless—that the person is a bore or the relationship a disaster—contradicts all that effort. But if we can believe that the person is really a gem and the relationship is worthwhile, then the effort is justified. People do, of course, pay a price for making themselves feel better in this fashion. The favorable attitude they develop to justify their efforts strengthens their commitment—and makes further efforts more likely. In short, dissonance reduction can create entrapment.

The second application of dissonance theory to intimate relationships involves the effects of our knowledge of the ongoing, present costs of the relationship. For example, suppose we have strong political differences with a partner, or strong differences in lifestyle preferences (neat versus messy; early to bed versus night owl). Now if these differences are extreme enough and unpleasant enough, we might decide to terminate the relationship. But what about those instances where the differences are unpleasant, but not enough to make us break up? Do the differences simply act as costs, subtracting from our satisfaction—or might they have a different, less obvious effect? These were the kinds of questions that Cohen (reported in Brehm & Cohen, 1962) considered in a study of male college students.

Cohen's subjects were all involved in serious dating relationships and had indicated that they were considering becoming engaged during an upcoming Christmas break. At the first session of the study, subjects were asked to complete questionnaires, which included measures of various "objective" aspects of the relationship (e.g., religious disagreement between the subject and his partner) as well as of subjective aspects (e.g., love for the partner). The second session of the study was held after the break. Subjects were asked to respond again to the subjective questions according to how they felt at the present time.

The subjects of major interest are those who did become engaged over the Christmas break (20 of the original 30). On the basis of their answers to the *objective* questions at the first session, Cohen divided these subjects into two groups: the half experiencing greater conflict over objective aspects of the relationship and the half experiencing less conflict. Then he looked at how the answers to the *subjective* questions had changed between the two sessions. As dissonance theory would predict, the high-conflict group reported a greater positive increase in their subjective evaluations than did the low-conflict group. The subjects who perceived more problems with their relationship before becoming engaged reported a more fulfilling relationship after becoming engaged.

This finding suggests that, contrary to traditional social exchange principles, rewards and costs do not always tote up in some simple, additive way. When we know about negative aspects of the relationship but go ahead and commit ourselves to it even further, dissonance should be created. There is a discrepancy, a conflict, between thinking something is bad in some way and voluntarily sticking with it. We need to justify having made the commitment. One way to do this is to increase our attention to positive aspects of the relationship, particularly those positive aspects that are "subjective" and not directly contradicted by harsh reality. People can and do say with total conviction: "Of course we don't get along at all, but I love him/her very much." In the social exchange world of rational cost accounting, this could not happen. In the real world, it happens all the time, and dissonance theory lets us understand one way it can come about.

COMMITMENT TO THE RELATIONSHIP

Regardless of how we get there—through different stages or phases, by means of the various components of social exchange, or as a way to reduce dissonance—*commitment* is the bottom line of relationship development. Commitment refers to the strength of one's intentions to continue the relationship. The factors that produce commitment will vary in different relationships (Surra, 1987). But, in general, the more freely, frequently, and publicly we act, the more we become committed to the action itself and to the attitudes it implies (Kiesler, 1971; see Table 6.3).

The importance of commitment has been demonstrated in research on dating couples. As you would expect, commitment is higher among those who say they are "in love" than among those who do not report being in love (Hendrick & Hendrick, 1988). There was also a gender difference in commitment among these subjects. Women reported greater commitment to their present relationship than did men. In a

TABLE 6.3 FACTORS THAT INCREASE THE DEGREE OF COMMITMENT

1. *The explicitness of the behavior.* Publicly expressing an opinion is a stronger commitment than privately expressing your views.
2. *The importance of the behavior.* Expressing an opinion to your boss is a stronger commitment than expressing your views to a stranger.
3. *The degree of irrevocability.* Expressing an opinion in a published statement is a stronger commitment than expressing your views over the phone (as long as you are not being "bugged"!).
4. *Number of actions.* Expressing an opinion over and over again is a stronger commitment than expressing it only once.
5. *Degree of volition.* Expressing an opinion of your own free will is a stronger commitment than expressing it because someone makes you do it.
6. *Effort.* Going to a lot of trouble to express an opinion is a stronger commitment than when you can express it easily.

An exercise for the study of intimate relationships: Go back through the above factors, but for the words "expressing an opinion," substitute "expressing your love for your partner." Can you see how you would begin to feel more committed to the relationship as you express yourself publicly, to people who matter, in a way you cannot change?

SOURCE: Adopted from Kiesler, 1971.

Public identification as a couple strengthens commitment to
the relationship. (Alan Carey/The Image Works)

two-month longitudinal study of dating couples, the commitment they
expressed at the beginning of the study was the best single predictor of
whether they were still together at the end of the study (Hendrick,
Hendrick, & Adler, 1988). Indeed, commitment was a better predictor of
endurance of the relationship than either investments made in the
relationship or satisfaction with the relationship.

One reason why commitment has such powerful effects is that it
freezes our actions and thoughts. As long as we have not committed
ourselves, we are free to change. But once we have made a strong,
public commitment, change is much more difficult and much less likely.
When we are committed to a relationship, our interest in other possible
partners declines (Johnson & Rusbult, 1989; Leik & Leik, 1977; Rosenblatt, 1977). Should others try to convince us that we are wrong in our
commitment, we resist (Kiesler, 1971). Commitment can also affect how
we respond to our partner. If we are committed to a relationship with
that person, we are more likely to agree with him or her and less likely to
react against the partner's attempts to influence us (Kiesler, 1971; Pallak

& Heller, 1971). Thus, commitment tends to wed us to a relationship—as we cut off outside options, resist efforts by outsiders to make us change our position, and become more susceptible to influence from the partner.

When Commitment Fails

All of this begins to sound as though once we have entered into a commitment, we are forever bound. We know, however, that this is not true. Not all committed relationships last forever. In spite of elaborate and expensive wedding ceremonies, public identification as a couple, joint bank accounts, and the presence of several children, marriages can still end in divorce. Perhaps, then, the most interesting aspect of commitment to a relationship is not that it works, but that it sometimes fails to work. Is there anything about commitment itself that might actually damage a relationship?

The answer is yes. There are many positive aspects of commitment (affection, attachment, loyalty, faithfulness), but commitment is not necessarily a completely positive experience (Fehr, 1988). Some ties bind—painfully. Commitment can be experienced as a crushing burden of obligation, entrapment, and limited options. When we are committed to a relationship, we look forward to continuing to be with that person. As long as things are going well, this expectation for the future is pleasant to think about. But what if things are going badly? Then every negative aspect of the relationship has not just an existence in the present but a potential existence throughout the future. Tolerating something we dislike for a short period is not so hard, but thinking that we will have to tolerate it forever is distinctly unsettling.

Commitment can also open up fears about future vulnerability across a variety of issues. Imagine that you are having an argument with someone you never expect to see again. If you decide to "give in," it is a relatively small price to pay for some peace and quiet. After all, it is a one-time cost. But giving in to someone to whom we are committed has an entirely different connotation. If we give in now, does that mean that we will have to give in on future occasions? In a committed relationship, today's actions always have implications for the future. If these implications are viewed as threatening important future freedoms, commitment can make it more difficult to make compromises and reach a mutually acceptable arrangement (Brehm & Brehm, 1981).

This possibility seems to form the basis for the old story about a marriage breaking up because the husband couldn't stand the way his wife squeezed the toothpaste tube in the middle, instead of rolling it up from the bottom the way he did. Ridiculous as it sounds, that old story contains a good deal of wisdom about human behavior. Just picture the situation. Every morning that husband had to think about facing a squashed toothpaste tube for every coming morning of his life. And, standing in the bathroom, only half awake, he thinks, "First, the toothpaste . . . then what?"

Fortunately, most marriages do not break up over a disagreement about how to squeeze toothpaste. Most people do understand that every relationship has its costs, and, usually, they are able to separate important aspects of the relationship from trivial ones. Indeed, what may be more crucial than any single aspect of the relationship is its overall context. As we will see in the next chapter, the question of fairness plays a major role in creating that larger context.

CHAPTER SUMMARY

Stage Theories of Relationship Development

Stage theories maintain that relationships go through a certain set of stages in a certain order. Various stage theories have been proposed, involving two or more stages. There is, however, very little evidence for a fixed sequence of stages in intimate relationships. Instead, there are a variety of different patterns of development.

A Social Exchange Model of Relationship Development

Social exchange theory is based on an economic model of human behavior; it assumes that people are motivated by the desire to maximize profits and minimize losses in social interactions. The various components of social exchange are diagrammed in Figure 6.2.

Rewards and Costs. In the terms of social exchange, the outcome of a relationship is determined by rewards minus costs. It is generally true that happy couples behave in more rewarding ways toward each other than do unhappy couples. Rewards also contribute to the endurance of a relationship. Costs may be less important in the early days of a relationship than after it has been established. Both rewards and costs—as well other aspects of social exchange processes—are based on subjective assessments of reality. These assessments are subject to bias and distortion, and partners may disagree about their assessments of behavior in the relationship. An individual who displays an egocentric bias overestimates his or her own contribution to a particular outcome relative to the perceived contribution made by the partner. Partners may also disagree about how much an item or activity is worth, making it more difficult to provide effective rewards to each other.

Expectations. The comparison level (CL) refers to the average, overall outcome an individual expects in a relationship. From a social exchange perspective, satisfaction is determined by both the individual's initial CL and the outcome of the relationship. The lower the CL, the less rewarding the relationship need be to produce satisfaction.

Alternatives. The comparison level for alternatives (CL_{alt}) refers to the average, overall outcome an individual expects from an alternative relationship or lifestyle. CL_{alt} affects commitment to the relationship. The higher the CL_{alt}, the less commitment there should be to the existing relationship. Table 6.2 displays various combinations of outcomes, CL, and CL_{alt}. Some overall levels of CL_{alt} are set by broad societal trends, such as sex ratios. Sex ratios indicate the overall availability of potential opposite-sex partners within a given population. When there are more men than women, sex ratios are high; when there are fewer men than women, sex ratios are low. Baby boomers (those born between 1945 and 1957) experienced low sex ratios, due to the yearly increase in births and the tendency of women to marry slightly older men. Whites born in the 1970s will experience high sex ratios. However, white women over 40 and black women of all ages will still tend to face a scarcity of available male partners.

Investments. An investment is something an individual puts into a relationship that could not be recovered should that relationship end. In general, investments strengthen commitment. When investments in a relationship produce rewards from that relationship, commitment is increased by satisfaction with the relationship. But when heavy investments produce little satisfaction, individuals may become entrapped in the relationship. In entrapment, commitments to a failing course of action are increased in an effort to justify investments already made. Dissonance theory provides a broad theoretical framework that can account for entrapment effects. Dissonance is an uncomfortable state that arises from inconsistencies among thoughts, feelings, and behaviors. *Involuntary* actions that are inconsistent with thoughts and feelings do *not* create dissonance, but voluntary actions do. It is dissonant to voluntarily agree to engage in difficult, effortful behavior that produces unsatisfying consequences. But we can reduce dissonance by changing our attitude toward these consequences. Thus, subjects who engaged in effortful activities to become part of a boring group made more positive evaluations of the group than subjects who had expended little or no effort to join the group. It is also dissonant to know about problems in a relationship but go ahead and make a commitment to that relationship anyway. To reduce dissonance, we can increase our positive attitude toward the partner. Thus, newly engaged students who were aware of more problems before they became engaged reported a more fulfilling relationship after the engagement than did students who were aware of fewer problems. From the perspective of dissonance theory, we come to love that for which we have suffered in the past *and* that from which we suspect we will suffer in the future.

Commitment to the Relationship

Commitment refers to the strength of one's intentions to continue the relationship. In general, the more freely, frequently, and publicly we act, the more we become committed to the action and to the attitudes it implies. Among college students engaged in dating relationships, commitment was the best single predictor of the endurance of their relationship across a two-month period. Commitment to a relationship increases the endurance of that relationship because we cut off outside options, resist efforts by outsiders to make us change our position, and become more susceptible to influence from the partner.

When Commitment Fails. But commitment is no guarantee that a relationship will last a lifetime. Indeed, commitment can have some negative effects. In a committed relationship, total expected rewards are higher, but so are total expected costs—as both rewards and costs are anticipated to continue in the future. And it may be more difficult to make compromises and accommodations in a committed relationship because of fears that giving in now may imply the need to give in later as well.

7

Fairness, Selfishness, and Altruism

❖

Reciprocity ◆ Equity Theory ◆ *The Distress of Inequity* ◆ *Ways to Restore Equity* ◆ *Equity versus Equality versus Reward Level* ◆ *The Question of Fairness* ◆ Terms of Exchange ◆ *Interpersonal Orientation* ◆ *Exchange versus Communal Relationships* ◆ *The Question of Selfishness* ◆ Altruism ◆ Chapter Summary

T hink about your own experience. Do you try to treat others fairly? How do you feel if someone treats you *unfairly*? For most people, fairness is an important aspect of their intimate relationships. This chapter describes several approaches to fairness. As you will see, the question "What's fair?" has a number of different answers. We will also explore some fundamental questions about human motivation. Even when people give to another, is there always some self-centered bottom line? Or is it possible for people to act selflessly, concerned only about another's well-being? These are age-old issues—pondered by philosophers, theologians, and ordinary men and women in the course of their daily lives. The answers we give to these questions reveal how we view the basic nature of human relationships.

*R*ECIPROCITY

Reciprocity refers to transactions in which we give what we have received and receive what we have given. As described in Chapter 3 on interpersonal attraction, reciprocity is a basic law of social interaction: We like those we believe like us. Besides influencing initial attraction, reciprocity may also play a role in relationship development. But before we consider this possibility, we have to be more precise about how we define reciprocity in terms of its content and its timing.

Reciprocal social interactions can involve a number of different things to be exchanged. Sometimes tangible goods (such as money and food) are given or received; sometimes the items are intangible (such as affection and sympathy). Exchanges can be observable (overt) or hidden from the view of others (covert). An argument, for example, can involve overt exchanges (yelling, hitting, cursing) as well as covert ones (feelings of anger, physiological arousal). The degree of similarity between what is exchanged also varies. A strict in-kind exchange involves the giving and receiving of exactly the same kind of item: a smile for a smile, a frown for a frown. A reciprocal exchange of moderate similarity would involve behaviors that are of the same class but are not identical to each other: a hug in response to a smile, turning away in response to a frown.

The timing of reciprocal exchanges can differ as well. Some investigators emphasize immediate reciprocity (Gottman, 1979). In this kind of reciprocity, the behavior of one person has a direct impact on the behavior of another person. Suppose, for example, that Janice has a certain average tendency to yell at people, say about once an hour. Now Stuart comes into the picture. We notice that as long as Stuart is not yelling, Janice keeps to her once-an-hour yelling schedule. But when Stuart yells at her, Janice usually yells right back, even though this is off schedule from her usual yelling tendencies. Such, very roughly, is what Gottman calls a *probability change in behavior*. Stuart's negative behavior has an immediate impact on Janice's; each time he yells, there is an increased likelihood that she will too.

This kind of immediate, lockstep trading of behaviors is different from *similarities in the rate of behavior*. To illustrate rate similarity, imagine that we simply count the number of yells that Janice and Stuart emit over the course of a day. At the end of several days, we can look at their behavioral similarities in either of two ways:

A. We could take the number of Janice's yells and the number of Stuart's yells for each day we observe. If we find that these daily totals change in a similar fashion (e.g., on a day when Janice's yells increased, so did Stuart's), we could conclude that Janice and Stuart are reciprocal in their yelling behavior.

B. We can add up all of Janice's yells and divide by the number of days and then do the same for Stuart's yells. If we find that these two averages are similar, we could conclude that Janice and Stuart have reciprocal rates of yelling behavior.

It is important to note that both of these methods of determining rate similarity are based on totals (either for each period of observation as in A or across the entire time as in B). We cannot know from total scores how closely one person's behavior followed another's. When considerable time elapses between Stuart's yell and Janice's, it is possible that something other than Stuart's behavior caused Janice to yell. This difficulty in determining causal connections has led some investigators, such as Gottman, to argue that similar rates of behavior cannot be interpreted as evidence for behavioral reciprocity. On the other hand, it is quite possible that intimate relationships are, in fact, characterized by reciprocal exchanges that do not take place immediately but occur hours or days or years after the initiating behavior. Thus, while probability change is a more precise way to measure reciprocity in social interactions, its limited time perspective may mean that it misses the most important reciprocal exchanges that are occurring. Figure 7.1 illustrates these different patterns of the timing of reciprocity.

Most of the research on reciprocal exchanges in established relationships has focused on similar but not identical content (usually, broad categories of positive versus negative behaviors). When we focus on short periods of time, there is considerable evidence that reciprocity in negative behaviors is more likely and more impactful than reciprocity in positive behaviors (Gottman & Levenson, 1988; Halford, Hahlweg, & Dunne, 1990). In laboratory studies, unhappy couples display more reciprocity in negative, nonverbal behaviors (Type I) than do happy couples; the two types of couples tend not to differ in immediate, positive-affect reciprocity (Billings, 1979; Gottman, 1979; Margolin & Wampold, 1981; Pike & Sillars, 1985). Daily self-recordings of behavior provided by married couples also show greater negative reciprocity (Type IIA) than positive reciprocity (Wills et al., 1974). Thus, the expression of discontent appears to exert a powerful pull on the other person's behavior, especially between unhappy partners (Margolin, John, & O'Brien, 1989).

But what happens over the long run? Are quid pro quo negative exchanges always more common? Perhaps not. Research examining overall levels of positive and negative behaviors across time (Type IIB) has found that married couples are more similar in their rates of positive behaviors than in their rates of negative behaviors (Huston, McHale, & Crouter, 1986; Wills, Weiss, & Patterson, 1974). Moreover, couples who believe that positive reciprocity exists in their relationship may have more satisfying partnerships. Among dating couples in one study, those who perceived both partners as making equal contributions toward maintaining the relationship reported more happiness in the relationship when contacted two months later than did those who had initially perceived their contributions to be unequal (Fletcher, Fincham, Cramer, & Herson, 1987).

These findings suggest that there may be a crucial difference between immediate and long-term reciprocity. On a moment-by-moment basis, it is hard to ignore a frown, a glare, or a voice raised in anger. We

I. Probability Change
  Most of the time during the four-minute conversation observed in the
  laboratory, Janice yells only in response to Stuart's yelling.

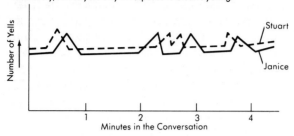

II. Similarity in Rates of Behavior
  Type A
    Janice and Stuart have similar daily changes in their rates of yelling
    during the four-day period they observe each other in their home.

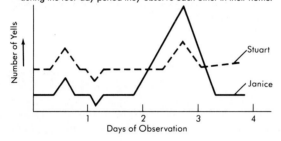

  Type B
    Janice and Stuart have similar average rates of yelling across the
    four-day period they observe each other in their home.

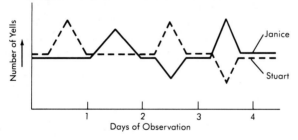

FIGURE 7.1
Different types of reciprocity.

tend to snap right back. The need to respond immediately to a positive
behavior is not so compelling. Over time, however, establishing a balance in the good things we do for each other may have a major impact
on the quality of the relationship.

    But even a couple's style of immediate reciprocity may have some
long-term implications for the relationship. This possibility was exam-

ined by Levenson and Gottman (1985), who conducted a three-year follow-up on a group of married couples. In an initial session, various aspects of the couples' interaction were examined—including their levels of positive- and negative-affect reciprocity and their degree of marital satisfaction (Levenson & Gottman, 1983). Then, three years later, those couples who were still married indicated their current satisfaction with the marriage. Upon examining the change in marital satisfaction over time, it was found that a decline in marital satisfaction was predicted by *more* reciprocity of the husband's negative affect by the wife in the initial session and by *less* reciprocity of the wife's negative affect by the husband. In this research, then, long-term effects were best predicted by a gender difference in negative-affect reciprocity. Those couples whose marital satisfaction declined over the years usually included a highly responsive woman and a highly unresponsive man. As we shall see in Chapter 8 on communication, a mismatch in emotional responsiveness is a common pattern among unhappy couples.

*E*QUITY THEORY

Despite variations in content and timing, reciprocity is a relatively simple basis for fairness in social interactions. Giving begets receiving and vice versa. Equity theory offers a more complex perspective on what is fair (Adams, 1965; McClintock, Kramer, & Keil, 1984; Messick & Cook, 1983; Walster, Walster, & Berscheid, 1978). According to equity theory, people are most satisfied with a relationship when the ratio between the benefits derived from a relationship and the contributions made to the relationship is similar for both partners. Simply stated (see Farkas & Anderson, 1979, for a more precise mathematical model), this means that in an equitable relationship,

$$\frac{\text{Your benefits}}{\text{Your contributions}} = \frac{\text{Your partner's benefits}}{\text{Your partner's contributions}}$$

Benefits from a relationship are positive when rewards exceed costs or negative when costs exceed rewards. Contributions can also be positive or negative; an individual can make more positive than negative contributions or more negative than positive ones. Some examples of relational benefits and contributions are given in Table 7.1.

Equity is different from equality between the partners. In equity terms, it is the balance that counts. If one partner obtains more benefits from the relationship but also makes a greater contribution, the relationship is still equitable. Imagine, for example, that we rate benefits

TABLE 7.1 BENEFITS AND CONTRIBUTIONS IN INTIMATE
RELATIONSHIPS: SOME EXAMPLES

Benefits	Rewards	Costs
Personal	Having a partner who is socially skilled	Having a partner who is socially inept
Emotional	Being loved by the partner	Not being loved by the partner
Day to day	Having a partner who provides satisfying companionship	Having a partner who does not provide satisfying companionship
Opportunities	The positive life experiences that depend on being in a relationship	Giving up certain opportunities in order to maintain the relationship

Contributions	Positive	Negative
Personal	Being socially skilled	Not being socially skilled
Emotional	Loving your partner	Not loving your partner
Day to day	Providing satisfying companionship to your partner	Not providing satisfying companionship to your partner

SOURCE: Based on Walster, Walster, & Berscheid, 1978.

and contributions on a 0-to-100-point scale and come up with the following three relationships—all of which are equitable:

	Partner X		Partner Y
(a)	80/100	=	80/100
(b)	20/100	=	20/100
(c)	30/60	=	50/100

   In relationships (a) and (b) both partners are receiving equal benefits
and making equal contributions, but the level of satisfying benefits is
much higher for the partners in relationship (a) than for those in relationship (b). Equity theory emphasizes the importance of the relative
level of benefits to contributions, not the absolute level of benefits.
Thus, according to the theory, both relationships (a) and (b) are equitable and should be satisfying to the partners.
   Relationship (c) is an especially interesting example of how equity
can occur when partners do *not* make equal contributions and derive
equal benefits. In (c), partners X and Y differ dramatically in how much
they put into the relationship and how much they get out of it. The
critical point for equity theory, however, is that their benefits and
contributions are still proportional, one to the other. Partner X is getting

According to equity theory, people should be most satisfied with a relationship when the ratio of benefits to contributions is similar for both partners. (Lawrence Migdale/Stock, Boston)

1 unit of benefit for every 2 units of desirable contribution, and so is partner Y.

In an inequitable relationship, benefits and contributions are not proportional between the partners. Thus, using our scale of 0 to 100, the following relationship would be considered as inequitable:

	Partner X		Partner Y
(d)	80/100	≠	20/100

Equity theorists use the terms "overbenefited" and "underbenefited" to describe partners in an inequitable relationship. In relationship (d), partner X would be viewed as overbenefited (for every 5 units of contribution to the relationship, he or she receives 4 units of benefit); partner Y is underbenefited (for every 5 units of contribution, he or she receives but 1 unit of benefit).

The Distress of Inequity

According to equity theory, both underbenefited and overbenefited partners should feel distressed, and both should want to restore equity. It is easy to see why an underbenefited person would want to restore equity: This person should feel cheated and deprived. On the other hand, it is somewhat difficult to see why a change should also be desired by the overbenefited. If, as social exchange models assume, we all want to maximize our rewards at the smallest possible price, the over-benefited person would seem to have done just that. Equity theorists usually suggest that there is a cultural norm of equitable fair play that makes an overbenefited person feel uncomfortable.

Inequity seems particularly likely to cut both ways when it comes to a person's mood and emotional state. Among college-age dating couples, individuals who perceived their relationships as equitable reported feeling happy and content (Walster, Walster, & Traupmann, 1978). In contrast, those who felt underbenefited reported being angry, and the overbenefited said they felt guilty. Inequity has also been shown to produce negative moods among married couples (Schafer & Keith, 1980) and in the friendships of elderly widows (Rook, 1987).

This sharp division between equity, on the one hand, and inequity (both overbenefit and underbenefit), on the other, has not always been so apparent. Indeed, equity theorists acknowledge that inequity is far more acceptable if you are overbenefited than if you are underbenefited (Austin & Walster, 1974). As described in Chapter 5, research on sexual satisfaction and extramarital affairs has found that only the *under-benefited* seem to suffer; the overbenefited have levels of satisfaction and contentment similar to those in equitable relationships (Hatfield, Greenberger, Traupmann, & Lambert, 1982; Traupmann, Hatfield, & Wexler, 1983; Walster, Traupmann, & Walster, 1978). This same pattern has also been obtained in research on the marital satisfaction of new-lyweds (Traupmann, Petersen, Utne, & Hatfield, 1981; Utne, Hatfield, Traupmann, & Greenberger, 1984).

Ways to Restore Equity

Equity theory proposes that when a person is in an inequitable relationship, he or she will want to change its terms to an equitable exchange. In light of the research just mentioned, it appears that this desire will often be stronger for those who feel underbenefited than for those who feel overbenefited. There are, in fact, a great many ways that an underbenefited individual might try to restore equity (Adams, 1965; Walster, Walster, & Berscheid, 1978).

First, a person can try to restore actual equity. For example, suppose Harriet feels underbenefited in her relationship with Larry. To restore equity, Harriet could reduce her contributions to the relationship. If benefits stayed constant, equity would be achieved. Or Harriet could demand more benefits to compensate for her present contributions. Attempts to restore actual equity may, however, fail. If Harriet reduces her contributions to the relationship, Larry may reduce the benefits he gives her. If she maintains her high level of contribution and asks for more benefits, her request may go unheeded.

When efforts at actual changes do not succeed, people may engage in an effort to restore psychological equity: to convince themselves that, in fact, equity does exist, even though benefits and contributions remain the same. One way for a person who feels underbenefited to do this is to believe that his or her partner deserves the better deal (McDonald, 1981). Harriet could, for example, convince herself that Larry was somehow a special person who deserved a high rate (higher than hers) of return on his contributions to the relationship; Larry's "specialness" thus becomes in itself a major contribution. Psychological equity can also be achieved by changing one's comparison standard. Though equity theory usually assumes that partners in a relationship compare themselves with each other, it is also possible to compare yourself with people in other relationships. Harriet could continue to believe that Larry gets the better deal in their relationship but feel equitably treated relative to other women she knows.

The third alternative response to an inequitable relationship is "to leave the field"—to leave the relationship, psychologically or in fact. As described in Chapter 5 on sexuality, underbenefited individuals may be particularly likely to engage in extramarital affairs (Walster, Traupmann, & Walster, 1978). But a person can have an extramarital affair without ending a marriage. What about commitment to the existing relationship? Do those who perceive their relationship as inequitable feel less committed to stay in it? Here the evidence is mixed. In one study of married couples, husbands and wives who perceived their marriage as an equitable one reported the strongest commitment to the marriage (Sabatelli & Cecil-Pigo, 1985). On the other hand, research on dating couples found no direct relationship between perceived equity and commitment (Michaels, Acock, & Edwards, 1986). These results suggest that equity might be a more important factor in long-term, enduring relationships such as marriage than in the early stages of dating and getting to know each other. But some research has found a different pattern. In a study by Lloyd, Cate, and Henton (1982), equity was more closely associated with satisfaction among casual daters than among more intimately involved couples. Thus, it appears that equity can be an important issue at some periods in a relationship and less important at other times in that relationship. However, we do not as yet have a firm understanding of what relational characteristics intensify equity concerns.

Personal characteristics may also influence reactions to equity or the lack of it. It is possible, for example, that different types of inequity may affect men and women differently. When newlyweds were asked whether they ever thought about getting divorced, the men in this study who felt underbenefited were more likely to say they had (Hatfield,

Utne, & Traupmann, 1979). Among women, however, the over-benefited were more likely to say that they had thought of divorce. These results are consistent with research on social power (see Chapter 9) suggesting that women often are uncomfortable with being in the dominant role in a heterosexual relationship.

Equity versus Equality versus Reward Level

Determining whether a relationship is equitable is a complicated process. You have to tally up your own benefits and contributions, compute your partner's benefit-contribution ratio, and compare the two. Some researchers have wondered whether individuals might rely on simpler calculations. Perhaps, for example, satisfaction with and commitment to a relationship are influenced more by equality than by equity. As described in the previous section on reciprocity, couples do appear to establish an equal balance in their exchanges—in both short-term negative interactions and long-term positive transactions. Research by Peterson (1981) on married couples suggested that equality may be more satisfying than equity. Those who perceived equality in benefits and contributions tended to be happier and more committed than those who perceived their relationship as equitable but unequal (as in relationship (c) on page 182).

Some other investigations, however, have indicated that even equality may be less important than the simple principle of reward. Perhaps it does not matter what your partner gives or gets as long as your own benefits are high enough. A series of studies by Cate and his colleagues has emphasized the role of the absolute level of benefits (Cate & Lloyd, 1988). These researchers found that the absolute level of rewarding outcomes was a better predictor of relationship satisfaction and endurance than was either equality of benefits or equity of benefits and contributions (Cate, Lloyd, & Henton, 1985; Cate, Lloyd, Henton, & Larson, 1982; Cate, Lloyd, & Long, 1988). In these studies, the best rule was the simplest one: The more good things people said they received from the relationship, the better they felt about the relationship. Research on couples living in married-student housing obtained similar findings. Reward level was a better predictor of satisfaction than either equality or equity (Martin, 1985).

The Question of Fairness

Taken as a whole, research on equity raises some crucial issues about fairness in a relationship. Some studies suggest that fairness is *not* an important factor in satisfaction with and endurance of intimate relationships. Other studies imply that fairness is important for some kinds of relationships but not for others. Although additional research is needed to help resolve these issues, some possible ways to reconcile such apparently contradictory findings can be suggested. First, the way that fairness (be it equity or equality) is measured may influence the results obtained. In earlier, experimental work on equity theory, equity was manipulated in an objective fashion—for example, by varying how much people were paid for a given task (see reviews in Walster, Berscheid, & Walster, 1973; Walster, Walster, & Berscheid, 1978). In studies of equity in intimate relationships, however, only *perceived* equity is measured. People are asked to estimate their benefits and contributions, as well as those of their partners. We do not know the accuracy of these perceptions. Nor do we know the causal processes involved when equity effects are found. Perhaps *in*equity diminishes satisfaction, but it could go the other way around. It has been suggested that equity assessments are not a necessary aspect of relationships but come into play primarily in response to relationship *dis*satisfaction (Holmes, 1981). When rewards are in high supply, equity may not matter. But if costs begin to mount, the individual may become concerned about who deserves to get what. Ironically, obsessive tracking of benefits and contributions may then serve to increase dissatisfaction even further. When we look for what might be wrong in a relationship, we are likely to find something.

Spouses who perceive the division of household labor and childcare as fairly distributed report greater marital satisfaction. (Steve Takatsuno/The Picture Cube)

Another possible reason for why measures of fairness, such as equity or reward equality, may not always be associated with relationship satisfaction or endurance involves the topic on which fairness is assessed. Fairness in some areas of life may be more important to people than fairness in other areas. There is, for example, growing evidence that the perception of fairness in the division of household tasks and child care has a strong association with marital satisfaction. Spouses who perceive the division of family work as fairly distributed report greater satisfaction (Benin & Agostinelli, 1988; Yogev & Brett, 1985). Fairness in this division of labor may, however, be particularly difficult for women to obtain. Research has indicated that employed wives contribute two times as much to household activities as their husbands (Atkinson & Huston, 1984; Maret & Finlay, 1984). Overall, according to Hochschild (1989), wives have 15 fewer hours of leisure each week than husbands, and this inequity can produce considerable strain and conflict in the relationship.

Finally, we need to realize that there are different answers to the question "What is fair?" Sometimes, people differ in the answers they give, regardless of the type of relationship involved. In other cases, different kinds of relationships prompt different definitions of fairness. The next section considers how the terms of exchange can vary depending on the individual and the relationship.

TERMS OF EXCHANGE

In Chapter 6, we examined the basic factors involved in social exchange: rewards, costs, expectations about relational outcomes, available alternatives, and investments. The effects of these factors on satisfaction with and commitment to the relationship were described. From a social exchange perspective, individuals are motivated to maximize their rewards. Social exchange theories view human behavior as selfish behavior in the pursuit of personal profit. But concerns about fairness place an outer limit on selfish acts. The principle of reciprocity, as well as equity models of human behavior, assumes that people are motivated to maximize their own rewards so long as those rewards can be obtained fairly. In the world of social exchange, there is only one person to be concerned about—oneself. In the world of fairness, the outcomes of both parties to the transaction must be taken into account. Note, however, that there is nothing necessarily selfish about fairness. If we assume that acting unfairly makes people feel guilty, then unfairness simply becomes a cost to be entered in the social exchange ledger. By this reasoning, unfair actions are avoided *not* because they hurt the other person, but because they make *us* feel bad. Thus, both reciprocity and equity can be considered as versions of social exchange, and neither necessarily contradicts the assumption that people strive to protect their own self-interest.

A number of social scientists have raised objections to the purely selfish perspective offered by social exchange. Rubin (1973), for example, has argued that in at least some relationships, there is "selfless concern for the welfare of others" (p. 83). Schwartz and Marten (1980) distinguish between the principle of economic rationality embodied in social exchange notions and the principles of harmony and trust to be found in relationships based on "solidarity." Even Lederer and Jackson (1968), whose book on marriage adopts a very practical approach, prefer not to define love in terms of pure gain for self. Instead, they endorse the definition offered by psychiatrist Harry Stack Sullivan: "When the satisfaction or the security of another person becomes as significant to one as is one's own satisfaction or security, then the state of love exists" (Sullivan, 1947, p. 20).

Leading theorists in the social exchange tradition itself have also been reluctant to think of intimate relationships as based solely on selfish gain. Blau (1964) states that while in the economic world relationships are merely ends to external rewards (e.g., money, power), in the world of relationships rewards become the "means for reaffirming and sustaining the association itself" (p. 36). Both Kelley (1979) and Levinger (1979b) have proposed that successful relationships move toward what Levinger calls "a more permanent peace," in which one's own needs and the needs of one's partner are both involved in determining one's actions.

Research on the possibility that not all social interactions are based on the purely selfish desire to maximize personal gains has taken a number of different approaches. In this section, we examine how individuals may differ in the terms of exchange they expect and desire in their relationships, and we look at how the type of relationship can also affect what terms are expected and desired. Then, in the concluding section of this chapter, we consider the more radical proposition that under some circumstances people can behave in a truly selfless way, seeking to benefit another regardless of the consequences for themselves.

Interpersonal Orientation

Murstein, whose SVR theory was discussed in Chapter 6, defines two orientations to social interactions (Murstein, Cerreto, & MacDonald, 1977). A person who has an *exchange orientation* wants and expects strict reciprocity in a relationship—a quid pro quo, where every action by one partner is met with a "similarly weighted action" by the other. In contrast, a person with a *nonexchange orientation* endorses the notion that "to love another is to forgive his transgressions and to accept him unconditionally" (p. 544). Research based on Murstein's approach to interpersonal orientations indicates that individuals who have a nonex-

TABLE 7.2 THE INTERPERSONAL ORIENTATION SCALE

Answer each question on a 5-point scale ranging from 1 = strongly disagree to 5 = strongly agree.

1. I would rather think about a personal problem by myself than discuss it with others.*
2. I consider myself a forgiving person.
3. Other people are the source of my greatest pleasure and pain.
4. I am interested in knowing what makes people tick.
5. When I receive a gift, I find myself thinking about how much it must be worth.*
6. Under no circumstances would I buy something I suspected had been stolen.
7. I am greatly influenced by the moods of the people I am with.
8. Sometimes the most considerate thing one person can do for another is to hide a bit of the truth.
9. Sometimes simply talking aloud about things that bother me makes me feel better—regardless of who, if anyone, hears these thoughts.
10. My friends and I seem to share the same musical interests.
11. I am reluctant to talk about my personal life with people I do not know well.*
12. I generally view myself as a person who is not terribly interested in what other people are really like.*
13. Sometimes I think I take things that other people say to me too personally.
14. It's important for me to work with people with whom I get along well, even if that means I get less done.
15. I often find myself wondering what my professors are really like.
16. If I were to share an apartment with somebody, I would want to find out about the person's family background, hobbies, and so forth.
17. I would prefer to do poorly on an exam that is machine scored rather than do equally poorly on one that is graded by the instructor.

change orientation report more satisfaction with their marriages or cohabiting arrangements than individuals who have an exchange orientation (Broderick & O'Leary, 1986; Milardo & Murstein, 1979; Murstein et al., 1977). On the other hand, an exchange orientation appears to have a stronger association with satisfaction in a friendship than does a nonexchange orientation (Murstein et al., 1977).

In their approach to individual differences in social interactions, Swap and Rubin (1983) developed the Interpersonal Orientation Scale, displayed in Table 7.2. High scores on this scale are obtained by individuals who say that they are very interested in and extremely responsive to others; low scores are obtained by those who indicate that they are less interested in and responsive to other people, as well as more concerned about their own personal gain. Overall, then, individuals

18. I tend to like people who are good looking.
19. What others think about my actions is of little or no consequence to me.*
20. The more other people reveal about themselves, the more inclined I feel to reveal things about myself.
21. When someone does me a favor I don't usually feel compelled to return it.*
22. Sitting on a bus or a subway, I sometimes imagine what the person sitting next to me does for a living.
23. The more I am with others, the more I tend to like them.
24. I would rather be given a simple and thoughtful gift than a more extravagant one that involved less thought and care.
25. I am very sensitive to criticism.
26. When people tell me personal things about themselves, I find myself feeling close to them.
27. One good turn does not necessarily deserve another.*
28. I can be strongly affected by someone smiling or frowning at me.
29. I find myself wondering what telephone operators are really like.

To determine your score on this scale, first reverse your scores on the items marked with an *—score each 1 as a 5; score each 2 as a 4; leave 3s the same; score each 4 as a 2; score each 5 as a 1. Then add up your scores for all items.

Swap and Rubin indicate that an average score is about 100. If your score is quite a bit higher than this (say about 15 points or more), this suggests that you are even more sensitive and responsive to others than is typical. If your score is quite a bit lower than the average, this suggests that you take a more matter-of-fact, businesslike approach to social relationships.

SOURCE: Swap & Rubin, 1983.

with high interpersonal orientation (IO) scores appear to resemble those classified by Murstein as having a nonexchange orientation, while people with low IO scores are similar to Murstein's subjects who had an exchange orientation.

Both high- and low-IO subjects participated in a laboratory study conducted by Swap and Rubin. Half of the subjects were led to believe that they had done quite well on an experimental task, much better than two other people they thought were also taking part in the experiment. The other half were told that they had done very poorly, much worse than their two supposed partners. All subjects then decided how much to reward themselves and their partners for their task performance. As Swap and Rubin had expected, low-IO subjects based their reward allocation on equity—giving themselves a greater share for a superior performance and a smaller share for an inferior performance. High-IO subjects, on the other hand, distributed rewards on the basis of equality—giving themselves and their partners roughly equal rewards, regardless of their own level of performance. Although subsequent research indicated that situational factors can modify how individuals allocate rewards to themselves and others (Major & Adams, 1983), it does appear that people who differ in their orientations to social interactions also differ in what kinds of behavior they consider fair.

Investigations of the role of interpersonal orientation are necessarily correlational in nature: An individual's score is correlated with a self-report or observed behavior. Such a correlational strategy cannot demonstrate that the interpersonal orientation involved actually caused the obtained differences in relational quality or reward-allocation behavior. In order to overcome these limits on causal analysis, it would be necessary to experimentally manipulate a person's interpersonal orientation, which is precisely what one group of researchers attempted to do.

All the subjects in this study by Seligman, Fazio, and Zanna (1980) were involved in dating relationships. As part of the experimental procedures, some subjects were reminded of the extrinsic rewards they might obtain from dating their partners (e.g., "My partner knows important people"; "My friends think more highly of me"). Other subjects were reminded of rewards intrinsic to the relationship itself (e.g., "We have a good time together"). In effect, the experimenters attempted to influence some subjects to adopt an exchange or low-IO perspective and others to adopt a nonexchange or high-IO perspective. A third group of subjects served as a control condition and were not reminded of any rewards available in the relationship. All subjects then indicated how much love they felt for their partner. As you might expect in light of the research described earlier in this section, extrinsic-reward subjects expressed less love than intrinsic-reward subjects. There was, however, no difference between intrinsic-reward subjects and the control group. Thus, an exchange orientation decreased love, but a nonexchange orientation did not increase it.

Exchange versus Communal Relationships

Up to this point, we have concentrated on differences between individuals, either existing before the study or produced during the study. But what about differences between relationships? By far the most sustained and systematic investigation on this issue has been conducted by Clark and her associates (Clark & Mills, 1979; Berg & Clark, 1986). Clark's distinction between *exchange* and *communal* relationships is similar to Murstein's two kinds of interpersonal orientations. According to Clark, exchange relationships are governed by the desire for and expectation of immediate, quid pro quo, tit-for-tat repayment for benefits given. Thus, costs should be quickly offset by compensating rewards, and the overall balance should remain at zero. In contrast, communal relationships are governed by the desire for and expectation of mutual responsiveness to each other's needs. Clark considers both close friendships and meaningful romantic attachments as communal relationships—differing from Murstein, who regards an exchange orientation as making a positive contribution to friendships. For Clark, exchange relationships are usually restricted to superficial, often brief, relatively task-oriented encounters between strangers or acquaintances.

In their research, Clark and her associates have found a number of differences in the way people behave in exchange and communal relationships (Clark, 1984; Clark & Mills, 1979; Clark, Mills, & Corcoran, 1989; Clark, Mills, & Powell, 1986; Clark & Waddell, 1985; Williamson & Clark, 1989). As summarized in Table 7.3, people in exchange relationships stick to the rules of social exchange. They expect benefits given

TABLE 7.3 DIFFERENCES BETWEEN EXCHANGE AND COMMUNAL RELATIONSHIPS

Situation	Exchange Relationships	Communal Relationships
When we do the other person a favor	We like the other person to pay us back immediately.	Our liking for the person who pays us back immediately may decrease.
When the other person does us a favor	We don't like the person who does not ask for immediate repayment.	We like the person who does not ask for immediate repayment.
When we are working with the other person on a joint task	We want to make sure that our contribution can be distinguished from the other person's contribution.	We don't make any clear distinction between the work of the other person and our own work.
When the other person may need some help	We keep track of the other person's needs only when we expect that person to have an opportunity in the near future to take care of our needs.	We keep track of the other person's needs even when that person will not have an opportunity in the near future to take care of our needs.
When we help the other person	Our mood and our self-evaluation show little change.	Our mood becomes more cheerful and our self-evaluation more positive.

SOURCE: Based on the results of Clark, 1984; Clark & Mills, 1979; Clark, Mills, & Corcoran, 1989; Clark, Mills, & Powell, 1986; Clark & Waddell, 1985; Williamson & Clark, 1989. Partially reprinted from Brehm & Kassin, 1990.

or received to be repaid immediately; they perceive each other's contributions as separate and keep track of them; they monitor the other person's needs only when they think it might lead to an opportunity for personal gain; and they experience little of a boost in mood and self-evaluation after helping the other person. But individuals involved in, or desiring the development of, a communal relationship avoid strict cost accounting. They do not respond favorably to immediate repayment; they do not make a clear distinction between their work and that of the other person; they monitor the other person's needs even when they see no opportunity for personal gain; and their mood and self-evaluation become more positive after helping the other person.

Most of Clark's research has involved experimental manipulations of exchange and communal relationships. Rather than examine how behavior differs, for example, between friends versus between strangers, she has usually manipulated the desire for one or the other type of relationship. In essence, this manipulation varies the availability of the other person for the development of a closer relationship. Subjects are told that the other subject in the study (who is actually a confederate and often presented on a videotape rather than in person) is either available (e.g., single, similar in life circumstances, interested in the experiment) or unavailable (e.g., married, very different in life circumstances, in a great hurry to finish the experiment). The advantage of this kind of approach is that it allows an experimental investigation of cause and effect. The disadvantage is that it cannot rule out the possibility that people could behave differently when they are hoping to develop a communal relationship than they would in an established relationship. Recognizing this problem, Clark (1986) has made a strong argument for the validity of her procedures. Moreover, the results of research conducted on subjects' actual relationships, though still limited, have been entirely consistent with Clark's conceptual model (Clark, 1984; Clark et al., 1989).

The Question of Selfishness

The research described in this section makes two important points. First, it illustrates that both correlational and experimental research strategies have advantages and disadvantages. As was emphasized in Chapter 2 on research methods, there is no single, perfect, research strategy. The ideal solution is to examine the same issue with a variety of different research methods. When the same results hold up across different methods, one has more confidence in the results. Of course, one also runs the risk that results will not hold up. For example, when individuals involved in long-term relationships were asked about the intrinsic rewards (e.g., "We always have fun together") and extrinsic rewards (e.g., "He/she has the right connections") available in their relationship, those who perceived a greater number of intrinsic rewards reported more love for the partner (Rempel, Holmes, & Zanna, 1985). Perception of extrinsic rewards, however, had no association with degree of love expressed—a failure to replicate the negative effect on love produced by awareness of extrinsic rewards in the experiment by Seligman et al. (1980). In another correlational study, happiness and satisfaction with a relationship were positively associated with the perception of important intrinsic rewards for being in the relationship but negatively associated with only some kinds of extrinsic rewards (Blais, Sabourin, Boucher, & Vallerand, 1990).

Despite the fact that the results of correlational studies and experimental research do not always coincide, the research on orientations to relationships does suggest that these orientations differ and that this difference matters. An exchange orientation—considered either as personal characteristics enduring across different kinds of relationships or as a response to a specific type of relationship—reflects the social exchange processes described in Chapter 6 and the concerns for fairness embodied in reciprocity and equity. At least within the bounds of fair play, the individual has selfish motives. The behavior of individuals with a nonexchange (or high-IO) orientation and of partners in a communal relationship appears, at first glance, to be less selfish. But is it? Immediate repayment in kind is neither expected nor desired. But what about long-term repayment in similar, though not identical, form? Even Clark (1981) has suggested that the difference between exchange and communal relationships is not that one is based on social exchange and the other is not, but that the two types of relationships involve two different types of exchanges. In more businesslike relationships, exchanges are expected to be immediate in timing and similar in content. In more intimate relationships, there are more degrees of freedom. One can wait for repayment, and what one does to meet the partner's needs may involve very different actions from what the partner does to meet one's own needs. If the difference between exchange and communal relationships (or exchange and nonexchange interpersonal orientations) is simply the difference between a short-term and a long-term loan, then both are equally selfish.

It is possible, of course, that the bottom line in a communal relationship is different from that in an exchange relationship. Perhaps those involved in a communal relationship take a more balanced approach—seeking to benefit themselves and to benefit the partner. But why? Are they responding to a state of *interdependence*, in which benefits for one are also rewarding for the other? If so, this may be prudent, but it is still selfish. The farmer who cultivates his or her fields, instead of burning them out on one large cash crop, is not usually viewed as behaving altruistically. It makes good, selfish sense to take good care of something—or someone—we depend upon to meet our needs. Are, then, people always "looking out for number one"?

ALTRUISM

A good many social scientists would answer *yes* to the question just posed. As Wallach and Wallach (1983) describe, most psychological theories stress the selfish origins of human behavior. But for some, the answer is *no*. The strongest evidence that altruism, an unselfish concern for another's welfare, exists has been provided by Batson and his colleagues (Batson, 1987; Batson, Fultz, & Schoenrade, 1987). According to the *empathy-altruism hypothesis* proposed by Batson, people experience some combination of two emotional responses when they witness someone in need of assistance: personal distress and empathic concern. Personal distress refers to feeling alarmed, troubled, upset, worried. Empathic concern is more tender-hearted, involving sympathy and compassion. Batson maintains that if personal distress predominates in reaction to a person in need, people will be egoistically motivated to reduce their own distress. If, however, empathic concern predominates, they will be altruistically motivated to reduce the other person's distress. Figure 7.2 outlines the basic components of the empathy-altruism hypothesis.

But how do we tell the difference between selfish, egoistic motives and unselfish, altruistic motives? In both cases, the person helps—though for different reasons. According to Batson, the crucial factor involves the ease of escaping from the situation. If escape is easy such that one can avoid having further contact with the needy person, those who are egoistically motivated will often choose to leave the scene rather than stay around and help. The motive to reduce one's own distress can be satisfied either way: Help the other, or if it is easier, get away from the sight of what is upsetting—out of sight, out of mind. But those who

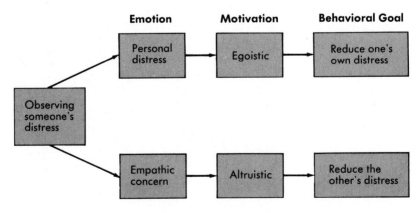

FIGURE 7.2
The empathy-altruism hypothesis. (Based on Batson, Fultz, & Schoenrade, 1987.)

are altruistically motivated will not leave even if escape is easy. The motive to reduce the other person's distress can only be satisfied by helping the other person.

In a series of studies, Batson and his colleagues have repeatedly found that helping depends on the degree of empathic concern and the ease of escape from witnessing the victim's suffering (Batson, Duncan, Ackerman, Buckley, & Birch, 1981; Batson, O'Quin, Fultz, Vanderplas, & Isen, 1983; Toi & Batson, 1982). Those with low empathic concern help more when escape is difficult than when it is easy; those with high empathic concern help just as much when escape is easy as when it is difficult (see Figure 7.3). Not all researchers have accepted Batson's formulation, and there is a continuing debate about whether he has, in fact, demonstrated that helping can occur for altruistic rather than ego-istic motives (Brehm & Kassin, 1990). Nevertheless, there is substantial evidence in support of the empathy-altruism hypothesis.

This hypothesis may have particularly important implications for intimate relationships. Empathic concern, the reaction that prompts altruistic motives, is strengthened by perceived similarity between the person in need and the potential helper (Batson et al., 1981; Krebs, 1975). Since, as described in Chapter 3 on interpersonal attraction, we tend to perceive those to whom we are attracted as similar to us and since actual similarity increases attraction, close friendships and roman-tic relationships would typically be characterized by high levels of sim-ilarity. Thus, observing a loved one in distress seems especially likely to

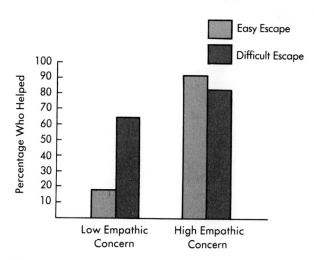

FIGURE 7.3
Percentage of those who helped a person in need.
(Results from Batson, Duncan, Ackerman, Buckley, & Birch, 1981.)

produce altruistic motives and helpful behavior based on a genuine desire to reduce the other's suffering.

Intimate relationships may also provide the necessary conditions for altruism in *nondistress* situations. It has been suggested that just as empathy leads to altruism in distress situations, so does emotional attachment lead to altruism when the other person is not suffering or in need of assistance (Schoenrade, Batson, Brandt, & Loud, 1986). Although this attachment-altruism hypothesis has only begun to be examined, it raises the possibility that there may be love beyond the bounds of social exchange principles, standards of fairness, or even a compassionate response to another's plight. For example, imagine that you cook a special dinner for your very best friend. You could do this because you want to put your friend in a good mood in order to get some help studying for a difficult upcoming exam. Or you could cook the meal to pay your friend back for loaning you some money several weeks ago. Or perhaps you are trying to help your friend get over the breakup of a romantic relationship. Or maybe you just want to make your friend happy. That last motive looks so simple and yet is so hard to demonstrate convincingly. But it has the most profound implications for our understanding of how we love and care about other human beings.

CHAPTER SUMMARY

Reciprocity

Reciprocity refers to transactions in which giving begets receiving and vice versa. Reciprocal exchanges can involve tangible goods, or they can involve intangibles such as affection and sympathy; exchanges can be observable or covert. In an in-kind exchange, the exact same kind of item is traded. Reciprocal exchanges can also involve items that are similar, but not identical, to each other. The timing of exchanges can differ as well (see Figure 7.1): immediate reciprocity, parallel day-by-day changes, similar rates across time. In the short run, negative behaviors are more likely to be reciprocal than positive ones. Unhappy couples, in particular, are characterized by reciprocal exchanges of nonverbal expressions of negative feelings. In the long run, however, rates of positive behavior may be more similar than rates of negative behavior, and the perception of positive reciprocity may contribute to relationship satisfaction. There is some evidence that couples in which there is a gender difference in negative-affect reciprocity (the wife reciprocates the husband's negative affect, but the husband does not reciprocate the wife's negative affect) may suffer a long-term decline in marital satisfaction.

Equity Theory

According to equity theory, people are most satisfied with a relationship in which the ratio of benefits to contributions is similar for both partners. In an inequitable relationship, one partner is overbenefited, while the other is underbenefited.

The Distress of Inequity. Perceived inequity in a close relationship is associated with negative moods such as anger (for the underbenefited) and guilt (for the overbenefited). However, only the underbenefited report low levels of satisfaction and contentment in the relationship.

Ways to Restore Equity. There are three major ways that an underbenefited person could restore equity: (1) Restore actual equity by reducing contributions or obtaining increased benefits; (2) restore psychological equity by convincing oneself that the partner deserves more or by comparing one's relationship with others who have an even lower ratio; and (3) leave the relationship psychologically by seeking satisfaction elsewhere or terminate the inequitable relationship entirely. Research evidence is inconsistent on whether equity is more important early in a relationship or later on. Among newlyweds, underbenefited men and overbenefited women were most likely to say they had thought of divorce.

Equity versus Equality versus Reward Level. Equity is a complicated process, and it has been suggested that simpler calculations are more often involved in people's feelings about a relationship. Equality of benefits and contributions, created by reciprocal exchanges, may have a greater impact than equity. But the absolute level of rewards may be more important than either equality or equity.

The Question of Fairness. In research on equity in intimate relationships, only perceived equity is measured. These findings are, therefore, correlational and cannot demonstrate what causal processes take place. Does inequity produce dissatisfaction? Or does dissatisfaction produce perceived inequity? It is likely that fairness (be it defined as equality or as equity) is a more pressing concern in some areas than in others. For example, the perception of fairness in the division of labor on household tasks and child care appears to have a strong association with marital satisfaction. Since employed wives continue to contribute far more to household activities than do employed husbands, a fair arrangement may be difficult for couples to work out.

Terms of Exchange

Interpersonal Orientation. Murstein distinguishes between two orientations that people take toward relationships. Those with an exchange orientation expect strict reciprocity; those with a nonexchange orientation accept the other unconditionally. In research on these orientations, having an exchange orientation was associated with less satisfaction among married and cohabiting couples and with more satisfaction among friendship pairs. The Interpersonal Orientation Scale also measures personal orientations toward relationships: High scorers on this scale say they are responsive to others, while low scorers say they are primarily concerned with personal gain. At least in private settings, high IOs allocate rewards equally, while low IOs allocate equitably.

Exchange versus Communal Relationships. When subjects involved in dating relationships were reminded of *extrinsic* rewards available in their relationships, they reported *less* love for their partners than subjects reminded of intrinsic rewards or not reminded of any kind of rewards. However, subsequent correlational studies found stronger and more consistent evidence for the *positive* effects of *intrinsic* rewards or attachment. In her examination of how different rules of fairness may apply to different types of relationships, Clark distinguishes between exchange relationships (in which strict and immediate reciprocity is expected) and communal relationships (in which mutual responsiveness to each other's needs is expected). People behave in different ways in these two types of relationships (see Table 7.3). Since much of Clark's research has focused on the desire for a communal relationship rather than on actual communal relationships, we do not know whether all the communal behaviors listed in Table 7.3 would also be found in established relationships.

The Question of Selfishness. Do people with a nonexchange or high IO orientation, or in a communal relationship, act in a selfless manner? The answer is no if (1) the terms of the exchange have simply changed to more long-term accounting procedures or (2) our helpful actions are designed to take good care of someone we depend on for our own well-being.

Altruism

The answer is yes if people are, in fact, concerned about the other's welfare, independent of the consequences for themselves. According to the empathy-altruism hypothesis, empathic concern in response to a person in need elicits an altruistic motive to reduce the other's distress, while personal distress in response to the needy individual prompts an egoistic motive to reduce one's own distress. The strongest evidence in support of the empathy-altruism hypothesis has been obtained in studies that vary the ease of escape from having to witness the other person's distress. Subjects low in empathic concern tend not to help when they can easily get away from the situation; subjects high in empathic concern help just as much when escape is easy as when it is difficult. It has also been suggested that emotional attachment to another may elicit altruistic motives even when that person is not suffering distress.

PART FOUR

———— ❖ ————

Relationship Issues

8

Communication

———— ❖ ————

The Role of Communication in Relationship Development • *The Theory of Social Penetration* • *Is It Always Gradual?* • Gender Differences in Communication • *Self-Disclosure* • *Expressive versus Instrumental Communication Styles* • *Nonverbal Communication* • Improving Communication • *Can Fighting Be Good for a Relationship?* • Chapter Summary

The vital importance of communication in intimate relationships has long been recognized. Chapter 5 described how frank and open communication can play a major role in sexual satisfaction. But the effects of communication are certainly not restricted to sexual interactions. Communication is a crucial factor in the development of all aspects of a relationship. Good communication can promote relationship satisfaction and endurance, while communication problems can contribute to dissatisfaction and the breakup of a relationship (Dindia & Fitzpatrick, 1985). From the beginning and, sometimes, to the end of a relationship, communication is a central ingredient.

Some of the most dramatic evidence for the importance of communication comes from a longitudinal study by Markman (1981). Markman kept in touch with nine couples over a period of 5½ years, beginning when they were planning marriage and continuing until after they had been married for several years. When these couples participated in an initial assessment during their engagement, they completed a self-report measure of their satisfaction with the relationship and rated the intensity of any problems they were experiencing. They also were asked to discuss some of these problems at a "talk table." This table was equipped so that each person could rate the other person's statements on a scale, ranging from 1 (= supernegative) to 5 (= superpositive). Both partners made ratings, but they did not know what the other's ratings were.

In Markman's first follow-up a year later, both initial satisfaction and problem intensity were correlated with the subjects' reports of marital adjustment, but there was no association of adjustment with the early ratings of communication impact. However, at subsequent follow-ups of 2½ as well as 5 years after the initial assessment, *only* the communication-impact measure predicted marital adjustment. Those couples who had indicated before they were married that their communications were more positive were more likely to have a happy marriage five years later. These results, indicating that some simple ratings made while couples were engaged could predict the quality of their relationship across half a decade, offer a powerful testimony to the importance of communication in intimate relationships.

THE ROLE OF COMMUNICATION IN RELATIONSHIP DEVELOPMENT

Dramatic as it is, the Markman study focused only on established relationships—beginning with couples committed to getting married and following them through the early years of their marriage. To understand fully the role of communication in intimate relationships, it is necessary to take an earlier starting point—when people are just beginning to get to know each other.

The Theory of Social Penetration

In their theory of social penetration, Altman and Taylor (1973) propose that the development of a relationship is closely tied to systematic changes in communication. According to this theory, social interactions move gradually from superficial to more intimate exchanges. For example, people who have just met may feel free to talk with each other about only a few, impersonal topics: "Where's your hometown?" "How do you like your French class?" "Don't you think the weather is awful today?" If this kind of superficial interaction is rewarding for the individuals involved, they can move closer to each other by increasing two aspects of their communication:

1. *Its breadth:* The variety of topics they discuss
2. *Its depth:* The personal significance of the topics they discuss

The theory of social penetration predicts that if we study people who are getting to know each other, we will find that their interaction can be diagrammed as a wedge (see Figure 8.1). Initially, the wedge is both narrow (few topics being discussed) and shallow (impersonal topics). As the relationship develops, the wedge should become broader (more topics being discussed) and deeper (more topics of personal significance being included).

Altman and Taylor intend their theory of social penetration to apply to all aspects of the communication process within developing relationships. They indicate that all interactive behaviors, such as sharing material possessions and communicating by nonverbal means, should proceed the same way—from initially superficial to increasingly intimate areas of exchange. However, most of their research on social penetration has concentrated on self-disclosure: our willingness to disclose personally revealing (and sometimes personally embarrassing) information about ourselves.

Self-disclosure has been an area of considerable interest to social scientists studying communication (Chelune, 1979; Derlega & Berg, 1987; Jourard, 1964). Indeed, our willingness to tell another person about our most intimate thoughts and feelings may be one of the clearest indicators of how we really feel about our relationship with that person. For Altman and Taylor, self-disclosure should follow the orderly principles laid out in their theory. Initially disclosure should be superficial (e.g., "I like sports, Bette Midler, and spaghetti"), with gradual but

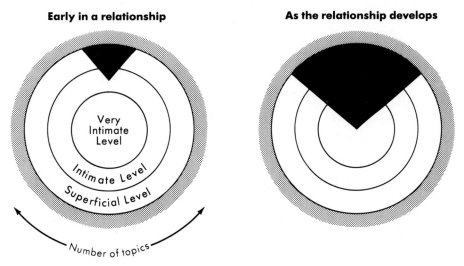

FIGURE 8.1
Altman and Taylor's wedge of social penetration.

increasing willingness to talk about very personal concerns (e.g., "My mother is an alcoholic"). Like other perspectives on relationship development (Berger, 1988), the theory of social penetration assumes that, at least to some extent, progress in a relationship depends on uncertainty reduction. As others tell us about themselves, our uncertainty about them declines and we gain sufficient confidence to tell them about our own thoughts and feelings.

In general, Altman and Taylor have found good support for their theoretical position. As people get to know each other, they expand the number of topics they discuss and the personal nature of what they reveal to each other. However, the rate of changes in breadth differs from the rate of changes in depth. As you can see from Figure 8.2, the rate of increase in superficial topics is at first greater than the rate of increase in intimate topics: The wedge becomes broader before it becomes deeper. Then intimate self-disclosure grows faster: The wedge becomes deeper without much change in breadth. In addition to describing changes in communication that take place as a relationship develops, the theory of social penetration also predicts that more extensive and intimate self-disclosure will be associated with more rewarding relationships. And, indeed, partners who self-disclose more to each other report greater emotional involvement in dating relationships (Rubin et al., 1980) and greater satisfaction in marriage (Hansen & Schuldt, 1984; Hendrick, 1981).

Overall, then, it appears that the more that people self-disclose to each other, the more progress is made in their relationship and the better the quality of that relationship. But there are also some specific patterns of self-disclosure that characterize different phases of a rela-

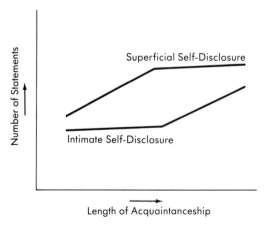

FIGURE 8.2
Changes in the rate of self-disclosure over time.

tionship. An initial encounter between strangers often involves *self-disclosure reciprocity*. New acquaintances match each other's level of self-disclosure, disclosing more if the other person does so and drawing back if the other person's self-disclosure declines (Cunningham, Strassberg, & Haan, 1986). Self-disclosure reciprocity appears to be useful in building a relationship.

Once a relationship is well established, however, immediate, quid pro quo reciprocity occurs less frequently (Altman, 1973; Derlega, Wilson, & Chaikin, 1976). Not only do partners in an established relationship have a different sense of the time available to them for responding to each other, but they may value responsiveness more than strict reciprocity. When we receive an intimate self-disclosure, we can reply by revealing something about ourself, or we can respond by expressing support and understanding (Archer, 1979). Partners in an established relationship are also likely to be concerned about privacy as well as about self-disclosure (Altman, Vinsel, & Brown, 1981). No relationship is able to sustain total openness and intimacy over long periods of time. And no two partners should want to. People need their privacy even in a close, intimate relationship. In the long run, it may be the balance between self-disclosure and respect for privacy that sustains an intimate attachment (Baxter, 1988).

Among couples whose relationship is in trouble, there are a variety of self-disclosure patterns. For some, both breadth and depth decrease, as partners withdraw from their relationship (Baxter, 1987). For others, breadth of self-disclosure contracts as satisfaction declines, but depth of self-disclosure increases—because of the barrage of negative feelings that distressed couples often express to each other (Tolstedt & Stokes, 1984). In this case, the social *de*penetration process in a distressed relationship does not resemble the sliver of a superficial relationship or the wedge of a satisfying intimate relationship, but rather a long, thin dagger of words designed to hurt.

Is It Always Gradual?

The theory of social penetration describes a gradual process of communication change and relationship development. But not all relationships develop gradually. Sometimes, people meet each other and, before they hardly know each other's names, bare their souls and tell all. There seem to be two major types of these "quick revelation encounters." The first is the legendary stranger-on-the-train (or plane, or bus) phenomenon. Settling down next to a stranger while embarking on a long journey, you soon find yourself telling this person things you would never mention even to your very best friend. Does this phenomenon contradict social penetration theory? Altman and Taylor think not. They believe that this kind of "intimacy" is only possible because you think you will never see the other person again. Such circumstances let you talk over your concerns with another human being, without having to worry about any long-term consequences. If, as many believe, confiding in others has positive benefits for psychological and perhaps even physical health (Pennebaker, 1989; Pennebaker, Colder, & Sharp, 1990), then the stranger-on-the-train phenomenon offers an opportunity to obtain a real benefit at virtually no cost.

But then there is love—and self-revelation—at first sight. Unlike the stranger-on-the-train phenomenon, here there is often every intention of creating a long-lasting relationship. Altman and Taylor do not deny that such immediate intimate self-disclosure occurs, but they caution against it. The two individuals have not built up a base of knowledge about each other, nor have they established a base of trust. While a speeded-up process of self-revelation can be exhilarating, the possibility of running into severe conflict is considerable. Moreover, the probability that the relationship will be able to withstand and resolve such conflict is rather low. In essence, Altman and Taylor view immediate intimacy experiences as "boom-and-bust" encounters. At first, everything goes right, far beyond our wildest dreams. But then there is a good chance that everything will go wrong.

College roommates who participated in a study by Berg (1984) appear to have experienced this boom-and-bust cycle. Those who indicated high levels of self-disclosure after living together for the first two weeks of the fall semester reported *less* liking for each other six months later in the spring semester. Similar findings were obtained among Navy men assigned to live for four days in isolated quarters with another Navy man whom they had not met before (Taylor, Altman, & Wheeler, 1972). Subjects were told they could withdraw from the study if they became too uncomfortable, and a number of subjects did withdraw. When Taylor et al. studied the communication patterns of the subjects who withdrew before the study was completed, they found there was a general tendency for these subjects (especially on their first day in isolation) to self-disclose to their partners at a very high rate. Taylor et al. suggested that the stress of the requirements of the experiment may have stimulated this self-disclosure, as an attempt to reduce anxiety. Unfortunately, however, the self-disclosure itself may then have added to the person's stress, leading him eventually to withdraw from the research and the relationship.

If there is some risk that early self-disclosure can be a case of "too much, too soon," should we conclude that relationship development is, as the theory of social penetration would have it, usually gradual and, for safety's sake, should be that way? Not necessarily. For example, one study on the development of friendships found that "the rate of emergence of intimate behavior was not as gradual as might be expected by social penetration theory'' (Hays, 1985, p. 914). More generally, some researchers have argued that people make relatively early distinctions between those relationships they desire to become close and those they are content to leave as superficial (Berg & Clark, 1986). It seems, then, there is a great deal of variation in the rate of self-disclosure. Sometimes, as with strangers on the train and in boom-and-bust encounters, highly intimate self-disclosure takes place very rapidly. Other times, self-disclosure may develop very slowly. In some relationships, however, self-disclosure may stall out at quite low levels, while in still others, self-disclosure may proceed at a relatively fast clip without becoming excessive. As we have seen before in this book, people's behavior in social interactions covers a tremendous range, and we should be cautious about trying to reduce it to any one simple formula.

GENDER DIFFERENCES IN COMMUNICATION

The difficulty men and women have in talking to each other is widely recognized. When Professor Henry Higgins cries out in *My Fair Lady*, "Why can't a woman be more like a man?" we all know he's not talking about anatomy. He is in love with Eliza, but he can't really understand her. He is an expert in languages and has taught Eliza how to speak English his upper-class way, but he can't really talk with her.

Henry Higgins is not alone. Almost every man and every woman has at some point despaired of ever "getting through" to the opposite sex. Why is there this "communication gap" between men and women? One possible reason is that they have quite different styles of communication (Tannen, 1990). This section will examine a number of gender differences in communication.

Self-Disclosure

On the average, women self-disclose more than do men (Cohn & Strassberg, 1983; Cozby, 1973). But this gender difference is by no means invariant. Specific situational factors as well as some general cultural norms have strong effects on self-disclosure (Hill & Stull, 1987; Wheeler, Reis, & Bond, 1989). In this section, we focus on two particularly important variables in gender differences in self-disclosure: the topic of disclosure and the gender of the person to whom one is disclosing during an initial encounter.

When Rubin et al. (1980) studied the self-disclosure patterns of dating couples in the Boston Couples Study (described in Chapter 5), they found that gender differences in self-disclosure were greatest on the following items:

- Females self-disclosed more than males about:
    feelings toward parents
    feelings toward closest friends
    feelings toward classes
    the things in life I am most afraid of
    my accomplishments
- Males self-disclosed more than females about:
    my political views
    the things about myself that I am most proud of
    the things I like most about my partner

Females, then, tend to disclose material that is personal and feeling-oriented and that may involve negative emotions. Males, on the other hand, disclose more readily when the information is factual and relatively neutral or positive in emotional tone. Often, while the women are discussing love, the men are talking about sports (Aries & Johnson, 1983).

A similar pattern of gender differences in self-disclosure was found in a study of married couples. Morton (1978) was interested in two types of self-disclosure. In *descriptive self-disclosure,* intimacy is determined by the content: giving out facts that are private as opposed to giving out facts that are already publicly known. In contrast, *evaluative self-disclosure* involves intimacy of feelings and judgments: revealing one's own feelings on a matter as opposed to not mentioning feelings and/or giving the feelings of other people. Subjects in Morton's study engaged in conversations that were observed and scored in terms of four categories:

1. High descriptive and high evaluative self-disclosure
2. High descriptive self-disclosure
3. High evaluative self-disclosure
4. Low descriptive and low evaluative self-disclosure

The results of this study indicated that, in general, females disclosed more than did males. They made more statements that were high in both descriptive and evaluative intimacy (Category 1), more that were high in evaluative intimacy (Category 3), and fewer that were low in both descriptive and evaluative intimacy (Category 4). However, males and females did not differ in the number of statements that were high in descriptive intimacy only (Category 2). Thus, when males did self-disclose, most of what they said was factual and nonemotional.

Men and women also differ on the reasons why they *avoid* self-disclosure. When researchers asked married couples why they disclosed to each other, husbands and wives gave similar answers (Burke, Weir, & Harrison, 1976). When, however, these researchers asked the couples why they did *not* disclose to each other, husbands' and wives' responses differed greatly (see Table 8.1).

Looking over the types of reasons spouses gave for avoiding self-disclosure, you can see that wives were primarily concerned about getting a negative reaction from the husband (being a burden) or getting no reaction at all (having the husband be unresponsive). Husbands, however, felt that work and family are separate and that their wives would be unable to help them solve the problem that was worrying them. It seems, then, that when people make a disclosure, they want to receive a similar response. Females make more emotional disclosures and want an emotional response. Males disclose more factual material and want a factual, practical response. Self-disclosure is avoided when women believe they will get an unemotional response and when men believe they will get an uninformed one.

The subjects participating in the research described so far were all involved in reasonably well-established heterosexual relationships. But what about new acquaintances? Research on self-disclosure between people who have just met each other indicates that, under these circumstances, the gender of the person receiving the disclosure is crucial.

TABLE 8.1 REASONS WHY HUSBANDS AND WIVES AVOID SELF-DISCLOSING TO EACH OTHER

Reason	Percentage Endorsing Reason	
	Wives	*Husbands*
Doesn't want to burden or worry spouse	48.4	18.3
Spouse unresponsive to my problems	22.6	9.8
Compartmentalizes home and work	0.0	25.4
Spouse lacks knowledge relevant to problem	0.0	19.7
Prefers to solve own problems	9.7	7.0
Own problems are trivial	9.7	1.4
Prefers not to replay negative experiences	6.4	8.4
Disclosure will lead to negative interaction with spouse	0.0	4.2
Spouse is physically inaccessible	0.0	1.4
Other	3.2	4.2

SOURCE: Burke et al., 1976.

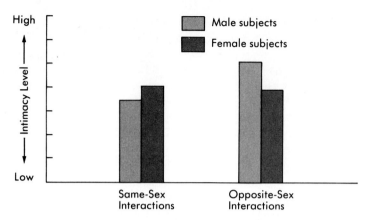

FIGURE 8.3
Gender differences in self-disclosure. (Data from Derlega, Winstead, Wong & Hunter, 1985.)

Consider, for example, a study by Derlega, Winstead, Wong, and Hunter (1985). These researchers found that although male college students disclosed less than did female college students in same-sex interactions, men exceeded women in self-disclosure to the opposite sex (see Figure 8.3). These results are strikingly similar to those obtained by Rubin (1974) in research involving airline travelers waiting in the departure lounges at an airport. In this study, male and female travelers were approached by either a male or female research assistant. Some travelers were asked to participate in a study of self-disclosure. As you can see from Figure 8.4, women were more willing than men to disclose in same-sex interactions, while men were somewhat more willing than women to disclose in opposite-sex interactions.

Overall, this research indicates that self-disclosure is best considered in terms of the relationship between two people rather than simply the product of the capacities of a single individual (Miller, 1990; Miller & Kenny, 1986; Wright & Ingraham, 1986). For individuals of the same sex, the social norms of our society encourage intimacy between women but discourage it between men. Thus, newly acquainted women are more apt to act in a warm, friendly, self-disclosing manner than are newly acquainted men. Later in this book (Chapter 13), we will consider the implications of these social norms for the development of same-sex friendships. Between opposite-sex individuals, however, the social norms for initial encounters are quite different. Men are expected to take the initiative, and women are expected to be more cautious in their response. Chapter 9 on power will examine some of the determinants and consequences of this social norm of male dominance in heterosexual relationships.

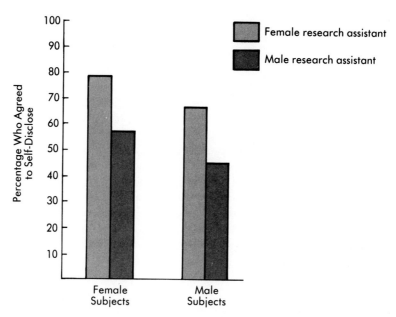

FIGURE 8.4
Percentage of agreements to self-disclose in airport study. (Data from
Rubin, 1974.)

Expressive versus Instrumental Communication Styles

For the purposes of the present chapter, the most important findings
from research on self-disclosure are those indicating that women tend to
be more and men to be less emotional in their social interactions. This
distinction has been given many different labels: femininity versus masculinity (Bem, 1974; Spence & Helmreich, 1978); communion versus
agency (Bakan, 1966); expressive versus instrumental (Parsons & Bales,
1955). The latter terms seem to capture best the gender difference in
communication to be discussed in this section. On the average, women
express their own emotions more readily and seem more sensitive to the
emotions of others. In contrast, men tend to be more concerned with
reaching objective, practical goals for themselves and for others. This
difference between the sexes occurs in a large number of cultures (Block,
1973; D'Andrade, 1966).

   What needs to be emphasized, however, is that the same communication style can be evaluated favorably or unfavorably. A highly expressive, emotional style can be seen as warm and responsive *or* as
hysterical and flighty. A highly instrumental, practical style can be seen
as steady and calm *or* as cold and unresponsive. Let us look at both sides
of each communication style.

Expressiveness: Pros and cons. There is considerable evidence that women are more socially sensitive than men. In terms of nonverbal communication, women are better than men at reading nonverbal cues (Hall, 1978) and are superior as senders of clear, communicative nonverbal messages to others (Rosenthal & DePaulo, 1979). Women also are more attentive listeners (Miller, Berg, & Archer, 1983), are more skillful in consoling those in distress (Burleson, 1982), and think more about relationship issues than do men (Pratt, Golding, Huster, & Sampson, 1989). In addition, women may more readily empathize with another person's feelings (Hoffman, 1977), though the evidence for this gender difference is not entirely consistent (Eisenberg & Lennon, 1983).

It is also the case, however, that women are more likely to display strong negative affect during conflict (Gottman, 1979; Noller, 1982; Notarius & Johnson, 1982; Raush, Barry, Hertel, & Swain, 1974). Moreover, women may use psychologically coercive tactics more than men (attempting to force the partner to comply by power plays, guilt, or verbal attack) and be more likely to reject efforts at reconciliation (Barnes & Buss, 1985; Raush et al., 1974). But the finding that women are more demanding than men during conflict may reflect women's desire for more changes in the relationship. When husbands and wives each tried to change the other's position during two conflict situations simulated in the laboratory, both spouses were equally demanding in their behavior (Christensen & Heavey, 1990). In terms of the relationship between verbal and nonverbal behavior, it appears that women are more likely to send double messages. Noller (1982) found that wives in unhappy marriages often sent a positive message visually (e.g., a smile) and a negative message verbally (e.g., "You're a really terrible person!"). Such double messages can be very confusing to the other person and make it difficult to know how to respond.

Instrumentality: Pros and cons. Although women may usually be more socially sensitive, they do not necessarily help others more than men do. It depends on the kind of help that is needed. When a female stranger needs assistance in a situation where there may be some degree of physical danger involved, men are more likely to try to help than are women (Eagly & Crowley, 1986). Husbands are also more likely to stay calm and problem-oriented when discussing areas of conflict with their wives (Gottman, 1979) and make more efforts to find a compromise solution (Raush et al., 1974). When taken to extremes, however, a "cool, calm, and collected" approach to conflict can become cold, emotionally withdrawn, and unresponsive to the other's concerns. Men's lack of emotional responsiveness has been noted by numerous investigators and may play a central role in marital dissatisfaction (Christensen & Heavey, 1990; Dosser, Balswick, & Halverson, 1986; Fishman, 1978; Gottman & Levenson, 1988; Margolin & Wampold, 1981; Roberts & Krokoff, 1990). A personals ad appearing in a recent issue of *The New*

York Review of Books illustrates how, even in an enduring marriage, many wives may long for a more expressive spouse:

> MENTALLY, EMOTIONALLY, PHYSICALLY FIT WF married 3 + decades to a good man of few words, wishes mental connection with good man of more words.

The problem of different wavelengths. This discussion of the differences between an expressive and an instrumental style indicates that neither has cornered the market on virtue. There are good aspects, and bad ones, to both. The real problem, it seems, is that men and women tend to exhibit different styles, a tendency that may intensify during conflict (Jones & Gallois, 1989). As with all gender differences in social behavior, this tendency is not absolute (Deaux, 1984). Some women will be more instrumental than some men; and some men will be more expressive than some women. Nevertheless, on average, men and women can easily get trapped on different wavelengths and have serious difficulty communicating with each other. When she is always saying "Warm up" and he is always saying "Calm down," it is hard for them to get together.

Nonverbal Communication

But what we say to each other is only part of the communication process. How we say it—with a smile, or a shrug, or a frown, or a glare—can be just as important, sometimes more. We frequently convey our emotions through nonverbal means of communication, and our emotional meaning can have a greater impact than the meaning of our words (Fletcher & Fitness, 1990). Some of the various functions that nonverbal behaviors can serve in intimate relationships are described in Table 8.2. Nonverbal communication has been mentioned before in this book and in this chapter. You may recall the discussion in Chapter 7 of how unhappy couples tend to immediately reciprocate nonverbal expressions of negative affect. In this chapter, it has been noted that women are more skillful at sending and decoding nonverbal cues, as well as more likely to send messages in which these cues contradict their words. This section explores the connections between nonverbal communication and relationship satisfaction, with a special emphasis on the gender of the communicators.

Like so many other aspects of intimate relationships, these connections depend a great deal on what kind of relationship we examine. As relationships endure, various aspects of nonverbal communication change. We can see these changes by tracing the path of nonverbal communication from dating relationships to newlyweds to established marriages.

TABLE 8.2 FUNCTIONS OF NONVERBAL BEHAVIORS IN INTIMATE
RELATIONSHIPS

Category	Description	Example
Providing information	Actor's behavior patterns permit an observer to make inferences about the actor's states, traits, or reactions to people or to the environment.	A subtle change in a husband's facial expression may lead his wife to judge that he is upset, but the same cues would not be useful to a stranger.
Regulating interaction	Changes in nonverbal behavior serve as cues to regulate the efficient give-and-take of interactions.	Close friends and family members are more likely than mere acquaintances to anticipate when a partner will start or stop speaking by knowing the partner's idiosyncratic pattern of gaze changes or postural adjustments.
Expressing intimacy	Increased intimacy between partners is indicated by higher levels of nonverbal involvement.	Lovers are more likely to stand close, touch, and gaze towards one another more than do mere acquaintances.
Social control	Social control involves goal-oriented behavior designed to influence another person.	As a person requests a favor from his close friend, he leans forward, touches him on the arm, and gazes intently.
Presentational function	A behavior pattern is managed by an individual, or a couple, to create or enhance an image.	When a quareling couple arrive at a party, they may cover their conflict by holding hands and smiling at one another.
Affect management	The experience of affect, especially strong affect, leads to changing patterns of nonverbal involvement.	Unexpected good fortune (winning the lottery) leads to sharing the news with family and friends. Hugs, kisses, and other forms of touching are likely in celebrating the good fortune with others.
Service-task function	Patterns of nonverbal involvement are determined primarily by service or task goals in an interaction.	The close approach, touch and gaze initiated by a physician towards a patient does *not* reflect interpersonal affect.

SOURCE: From Patterson, 1988.

Dating couples. A study by Sabatelli, Buck, and Dreyer (1980) examined nonverbal communication and relationship satisfaction among undergraduate dating couples. These investigators found that dating partners did *not* do better than independent judges at reading the nonverbal messages sent by their partners. In addition, increased psychological involvement in the relationship was *not* associated with greater sensitivity to one another's nonverbal cues. However, it was found that women who were quite good in general at reading other people's nonverbal messages (i.e., good decoders of strangers' messages as well as of their partners' communications) had male partners who expressed more love for them on Rubin's (1973) Loving Scale. Based on these results, Sabatelli et al. concluded that a man's love for his dating partner does not reflect her specific ability to read his nonverbal communications, but is enhanced if the woman is generally sensitive to nonverbal cues.

Newlyweds. Sabatelli and his colleagues have also examined the nonverbal communication process among newlywed couples (Sabatelli, Buck, & Dreyer, 1982). In contrast to dating couples, newlyweds were better able than judges to read each other's nonverbal messages. Moreover, the nonverbal skills of the female continued to be an important element in the relationship. First, on the sending side, it was found that wives who were in general good senders of nonverbal communications (i.e., good encoders of nonverbal messages that were read by strangers as well as by their husbands) had husbands who expressed relatively few marital complaints. Second, on the receiving side, wives who were especially skilled in decoding their husband's poorly expressed nonverbal messages (i.e., messages that independent judges found difficult to read) had husbands with relatively few marital complaints, and also had fewer marital complaints themselves.

Another examination of the nonverbal communication styles of newlyweds looked at physical orientation toward the partner (Beir & Sternberg, 1977). In this research, newlywed couples completed a questionnaire about their relationship. On the basis of their self-reports, they were divided into two groups: agreeing couples (i.e., those who had a relatively harmonious relationship) and disagreeing couples (i.e., those who reported significant areas of disagreement and conflict). All couples were then interviewed, and their physical orientation toward each other during the interview was observed. The differences between the two groups of couples were striking.

- Agreeing couples sat closer to each other than disagreeing couples.
- Agreeing couples looked at each other more often and longer than disagreeing couples.
- Agreeing couples turned toward each other more than did disagreeing couples.
- Agreeing couples sat with their legs in more open, sprawled positions than did disagreeing couples.

These findings are consistent with previous work indicating that physical closeness and visual regard reflect people's feelings of affection for each other (Bakken, 1979; see also Chapter 4 on "the lover's gaze"). It seems, then, that it is fairly easy for outside observers to tell how a relationship is going just by observing such simple things as how people sit and how often they look at each other. One wonders if the partners in the relationship are also able to read these signs of affection or discontent.

Married couples. Perhaps the most extensive research on nonverbal communication and relationship satisfaction has been conducted with married couples. Not surprisingly, distressed marital couples send fewer positive and more negative nonverbal signals than do happy marital couples (Gottman, 1979; Gottman, Markman, & Notarius, 1977; Noller, 1982, 1985). Unhappy couples are also characterized by the negative-affect reciprocity described in Chapter 7. When discussing topics that create conflict within the marriage, distressed wives engage in more reciprocity—in response to both positive and negative nonverbal messages—than do distressed husbands (Gottman, 1979). And, as noted in Chapter 7, couples in which the wife reciprocates negative affect but the husband doesn't are particularly likely to experience a decline in marital satisfaction over time (Levenson & Gottman, 1985). This lack of symmetry in nonverbal reciprocity creates a corresponding lack of symmetry in control over the interaction. When the wife engages in greater reciprocity of nonverbal cues of emotion than the husband, then the husband's feelings determine the tone of the interaction. The wife just keeps things going in the direction he initiates.

Further indications of the husband's major role has come from research on how married couples send and read their nonverbal communications. Gottman and Porterfield (1981) found that husbands who had highly satisfied wives could read their wives' nonverbal communications better than strangers could. In sharp contrast, husbands who had wives who were unhappy were less able to read their wives' nonverbal cues than were strangers. These investigators found no relationship between marital satisfaction and the wives' nonverbal communication skills. Noller's (1980) work obtained similar results. Classifying married couples according to their level of marital adjustment, she found that husbands in the poorly adjusted couples sent fewer clear messages and made more errors in reading their wives' nonverbal cues than husbands in well-adjusted couples. Again, the nonverbal communication skills of the wives were not related to marital satisfaction. Based on these results, Noller concluded that "the communication skill of the husband discriminates best between couples high and low in marital adjustment" (Noller, 1987, p. 172).

In a particularly interesting follow-up study, Noller (1981) compared the receiving abilities of married couples under two conditions: when they were reading the nonverbal messages of their spouses versus when they were reading the nonverbal messages of strangers. It was found that low-marital-adjustment couples (husbands *and* wives) had the greatest differences between these two conditions. This pattern of results suggests that individuals in unhappy marriages might be able to read nonverbal communications perfectly well but fail to do so when interacting with each other. When asked to predict how well their spouse could read their nonverbal messages, wives seemed more aware of the decline in decoding these messages that occurs among unhappy couples (Noller & Venardos, 1986). Compared with wives in happy couples, those in unhappy couples expected that their husband would be less accurate in the decoding task, which was the case. Husbands in unhappy couples, however, were off target in their predictions of their wife's decoding accuracy. Indeed, their predictions of her accuracy were somewhat more optimistic than those of more happily married men, exactly the opposite of the actual accuracy displayed.

Overview. Taken as a whole, research on nonverbal communication in intimate relationships highlights three basic themes and conclusions. First, there is some indication that nonverbal sensitivity does increase with increased depth of or commitment to the relationship. The study by Sabatelli et al. (1980) on dating couples did not find that these couples were better than judges at reading each other's nonverbal messages. But the second study by Sabatelli et al. (1982) did find that married couples did better than judges. Thus, when relationships that differ significantly in closeness are compared (i.e., dating couples versus married couples), increased closeness is associated with increased nonverbal sensitivity. When, however, the differences are less dramatic— for example, differences in how long people have been dating each other, how long a couple has been married, or how involved dating couples are with each other—then we do not find this association between greater closeness and greater nonverbal sensitivity.

Second, the connections among gender, nonverbal communication, and relationship satisfaction seem to change across these different relationships. For dating couples and newlyweds; the female's nonverbal skills appear to be more important in terms of satisfaction with the relationship. For married couples, however, it is the nonverbal skills of the male that seem more important. Thus, it may be that women's nonverbal skills are essential in the development of intimacy in a relationship, while men's abilities to communicate nonverbally are critical for maintaining intimacy within an established relationship.

Finally, let us examine the issue of exactly how nonverbal communication and relationship satisfaction affect each other. Here are two possibilities:

1.   Nonverbal skills will determine relationship satisfaction. Poor skills will lead to poor relationships; good skills will lead to good relationships.
2.   Relationship satisfaction will determine nonverbal communication. Poor relationships will produce poor communication; good relationships will produce good communication.

Actually, there is evidence for both of these propositions. In the studies by Sabatelli and his colleagues, females' *general* receiving and sending skills were associated with increased love by the partner and fewer marital complaints. Since these are general skills (displayed with strangers as well as partners), it is unlikely that they are caused by the state of the relationship. Here, it would appear, nonverbal skills may well play some causal role in determining relationship satisfaction.

However, when we find indications that nonverbal skills *specific* to the relationship are related to satisfaction, then the state of the relationship may be the determining factor. For instance, it is possible that the satisfied wives of satisfied husbands in Sabatelli et al.'s (1982) study of newlyweds made more effort to read their husbands' poorly expressed messages than did the wives in less happy marriages. In addition, it seems quite possible based on Noller's (1981) research that both the distressed husbands and wives in her research were capable of more skillful nonverbal communication than they showed with each other. Their discontent with their relationship, however, may have caused them to withdraw and not try hard enough to understand their spouse.

This issue of whether we are dealing with a *skill deficit* or a *performance deficit* is very important when we study communication in intimate relationships. If it is a skill deficit—a person does not know how to communicate clearly—then we can improve the relationship by teaching the skill. If, on the other hand, it is a performance deficit—the person knows how to communicate clearly but does not do so with this particular person—then attempts to improve the skill will presumably have no effect on the relationship.

In their book *A Couple's Guide to Communication*, Gottman and his colleagues (1976) refer to some relationship problems as "hidden agendas." These are usually problems of closeness in the relationship that lie behind apparent communication difficulties. For example, there may be too little closeness, so that at least one partner feels alone and isolated. Or there may be too much closeness, so that at least one partner feels invaded and overwhelmed. In such cases, the couple's real problems— their hidden agendas—will not go away simply by improving the communication between them.

This is a crucial point if we are to understand how communication and relationship satisfaction affect each other. On the one hand, there are some relationships that do suffer primarily from communication problems, and for these relationships, a concerted effort by both partners to improve their verbal and nonverbal communication should result in greater happiness and relationship satisfaction. On the other hand, there are some relationships that suffer primarily from other problems, and better communication will not provide a "cure." However, even with these relationships, better communication will enable the couple to focus more clearly on what their problems really are. Given the massive confusion that can exist when a relationship is in trouble, this is a significant benefit.

*I*MPROVING COMMUNICATION

Since improved communication is likely to be beneficial to all couples, regardless of the kinds of difficulties they experience, we turn now to some possible ways to develop better communication. But first we need a broader view of what good communication is. One excellent source for this broader view comes from the extensive research on communication in intimate relationships conducted by Gottman and his colleagues (Gottman, 1979; Gottman, Notarius, Gonso, & Markman, 1976). When they compared the communication patterns of couples in distressed marriages with those of couples who have satisfying and happy marriages, they observed the following patterns:

- *Intent of the communication.* Here, Gottman and his colleagues have found very few differences. Distressed marital partners usually do not intend to make their spouses unhappy, or angry, or upset.

- *Impact of the communication.* But distressed partners frequently do make their spouses unhappy. The rate of negative impact is much higher for distressed couples than for satisfied couples.

- *Getting problems out into the open (agenda building for a discussion).* This is an important phase of the discussion process. For distressed couples it is characterized by a lot of "cross-complaining"; The husband may say he does not like the way his wife spends money on clothes; the wife may say she does not like the way the husband spends money on stereo equipment. In contrast, satisfied couples make complaints but also recognize the validity of the other person's feelings and point of view (Koren, Carlton, & Shaw, 1980).

- *Negotiating an agreement.* The differences in this part of the discussion are similar to those in the agenda-building phase. Distressed couples offer each other counterproposals. Satisfied couples engage in "contracting": They indicate some acceptance of the partner's proposal as well as making one of their own. In other words, satisfied couples attempt to find compromise solutions; distressed couples seem locked into win-or-lose battles.

- *Mindreading.* Mindreading refers to those times when, instead of asking, we tell another person why he or she did something; it is just so easy for partners in an established relationship to think they know more about each other than they actually do (Shapiro & Swenson, 1969). Indeed, Gottman found that all married couples mindread. But distressed couples mindread in an emotionally negative way; they are critical and hostile. Satisfied couples mindread with more neutral or positive affect, not accusing each other of bad motives.

- *Metacommunication.* Metacommunications are communications about the communication. For example, when a person says "I don't think we're getting anywhere in this discussion," that person has made a metacommunicational statement. Asking "Why did you say that?" is a metacommunicational question. Again, Gottman did not find that distressed and satisfied couples differed in their frequency of metacommunications. He did find, however, that for distressed couples, metacommunications were all-absorbing and difficult to get beyond. In contrast, satisfied couples would make a metacommunication and then go easily on to something else. These findings by Gottman on metacommunications are similar to some clinical observations reported by Murphy and Mendelson (1973). The distressed couples they observed had a clear tendency to focus more on relationship issues (who is going to do what when) than on the task they were supposed to work on. Thus, distressed couples have difficulty in cooperation and coordination. They are so busy trying to figure out what each person should do, and making sure that no one "gets away" with anything, that they fail to get much else accomplished.

- *Self-summarizing.* Self-summarizing means that a person keeps summarizing what he or she has said. It is not communicative; it is repetitious and ignores the other person. Gottman and his colleagues have found that individuals in distressed marriages make many more self-summarizing statements than do individuals in satisfied marriages. They also describe a "self-summarizing syndrome" that includes almost all the elements of poor communication discussed in this section. The types of communication problems involved in this syndrome are outlined in Table 8.3, which gives some examples of the kinds of things that might be said.

TABLE 8.3 THE SELF-SUMMARIZING SYNDROME

EARLY STAGES OF THE SYNDROME

Both partners feel hurt and not listened to
   "You never hear what I say. I think you just don't care what I say."

Neither feels that the other sees his or her point of view
   "You never try to understand how I feel about this."

Conversation keeps drifting "off beam"
   "You never do what I ask. Just like your mother never does what I ask her
   to, and you always take your mother's side."

So the conversation never stays on one problem long enough to resolve it
   "I thought we were talking about how I spend too much money. Now
   we're talking about my mother. We've been through all this before, and we
   never get anywhere."

Mindreading occurs
   "You got drunk at the party just to make me mad, just to get back at me
   for yesterday."

*As does "kitchensinking," where everything but the kitchen sink gets dragged into the
argument*
   "It's not only your carelessness, it's the way you never check with me
   about anything, those friends you hang out with, your lousy attitude about
   what goes on in this house."

MIDDLE STAGES OF THE SYNDROME

Yes-butting
   "Yes, I could try to do that, but I'm sure it wouldn't work."

Cross-complaining
   "I hate the way you let dishes pile up in the sink."
   "I hate the way *you* leave *your* clothes on the floor."

Conversations end without resolution of the problem
   "There's no point in fighting about this again. We just can't get anywhere
   on it."

Interruptions are frequent
   "I think that what we should . . ."
   "Now, what we really should do is what I said before."

Frustration is enormous
   "Sometimes I get so mad about all this, I think I could just explode."

LATER STAGES OF THE SYNDROME

*The "standoff" occurs: Each person thinks it will be absolutely disastrous if he or she
"gives in"*
   "I will not give in to you on this. I always give in to you. You're
   destroying me."

Quarrels become more and more violent
   "Don't you dare hit me!"

And when not fighting, there is only heavy silence . . .

SOURCE: Adapted from Gottman, Notarius, Gonso, & Markman, 1976.

Obviously, no one wants to engage in the self-summarizing syndrome. Yet when we are angry, or resentful, or anxious, it is all too easy to find ourselves cross-complaining, kitchensinking, and all the rest. How can we avoid this trap of poor communication that only leaves us and our partners feeling worse?

Many of those who study communication and relationships have emphasized the importance of understanding and validation (Gottman et al., 1976; deTurck & Miller, 1986; Honeycutt, 1986; Reis & Shaver, 1988). To see the reason for this emphasis, look back at Table 8.3. The early stages of the self-summarizing syndrome involve resentment that builds up because people do not feel listened to. It is possible that if people did feel listened to, some of the later stages would never occur. Thus, it is vital to listen, to try to see the other person's point of view, and to communicate this to the other person.

Understanding and validation are not, however, the same as total agreement or acceptance. You may see the other person's perspective but still disagree with it. Compare the following three responses:

Cross-complaining	CHRIS:	I hate it when you act that way.
	SALLY:	And I hate it when you get drunk.
Agreement	SALLY:	Yes. I agree. It's not a nice way to act. I'll try to change.
Understanding and validation	SALLY:	Yes. I can understand that, and I don't blame you. But I want you to try to understand what I'm feeling too.

By trying to understand what the other person has said and indicating that you can appreciate (though not necessarily agree with) the other's point of view, you signal that you want a dialogue with the other person. This approach breaks through the self-summarizing syndrome, in which there is only the desire for a monologue. It is not easy to listen to another in the heat of a quarrel. Nor is it ever easy to validate the person when you do not accept the person's argument. But it is possible and could have a substantial effect on what happens to the relationship *after* the quarrel is over. The process of understanding and validating may be particularly important during conflicts between heterosexual couples. As we saw earlier in this chapter, men and women can get stuck on different wavelengths when they communicate with each other: the woman expressing emotion, the man concentrating on practical solutions. It can sometimes seem they are talking in different languages. Making a good-faith effort to try to understand the other's language and remembering to validate the person even though the person's style might be different from your own can help bridge the gap. Understanding and validation may also be crucial steps in the development of a common language, spoken with equal fluency by both men and women.

Another important aspect of good communication involves the way we express our own point of view. Patton and Ritter (1976) have listed several factors that promote openness in communication between intimate partners. These factors, described in Table 8.4, relate to the need for us to be specific (avoiding kitchensinking and not going off beam) as well as responsible (our feelings and perceptions are ours; we should acknowledge that we own them in our communications). By being specific and responsible, we choose to have a discussion that offers hope for resolution of the problem and that avoids personal attack on the other person. We choose, in other words, to have a discussion that can further the relationship rather than damage it.

TABLE 8.4 WAYS TO INCREASE OPEN COMMUNICATION

1. Statements should be mutually relevant with a focus on the here and now.

    Good communication: Paul, I feel very bad when you act the way you're behaving now. I want you to listen to me and feel happy for my having done so well on that exam. But it seems to me that you just want to talk about what happened to you today.

    Poor communication: Paul, you never listen to me. Even when you went home with me to visit Mom and Dad, you talked all the time. Never gave me a chance to say anything. None of you listened to me.

2. It is important to own one's feelings.

    Good communication: Joan, I feel very angry when you say you don't care what my friends think.

    Poor communication: Joan, you are making me very angry.

3. It is also important to specify what has caused one's feelings.

    Good communication: Dan, I feel very sad when you turn away from me like that.

    Poor communication: Dan, I feel sad.

4. Perceptions should be owned.

    Good communication: Mary, sometimes I think you act like that because you're mad at your boss, not really at me.

    Poor communication: Mary, you just act like that because you're mad at your boss.

5. Behavior should be identified as clearly and concretely as possible.

    Good communication: Tom, I feel really put down when you act like that. I start to say something, and you interrupt me and give your opinion.

    Poor communication: Tom, you make me feel really put down when you act so pushy.

SOURCE: Adapted from Patton & Ritter, 1976.

Can Fighting Be Good for a Relationship?

Even if we admit that conflict is inevitable in an intimate relationship, most of us probably still feel that it would be better not to have the unpleasantness of quarrels, disagreements, and arguments. But perhaps this negative view of conflict is mistaken. An increasing number of social scientists are coming to believe that conflict is an essential aspect of *promoting* intimacy. According to this perspective, it is the handling of conflict—not its absence—that allows relationships to grow and prosper (Holmes & Boon, 1990; Knudson, Sommers, & Golding, 1980; Peterson, 1983; Rands, Levinger, & Mellinger, 1981).

In their book *The Intimate Enemy*, Bach and Wyden (1968) consider this proposition in great detail, urging that, when fairly and skillfully done, fighting increases intimacy. Many of their suggestions for how to "fight fair" have already been described (e.g., listening, validating, owning our feelings), but Bach and Wyden go beyond providing rules for how to fight. They also provide guidelines for the results that should occur: a "fight effects profile." The categories in this profile are shown in Table 8.5. A "good fight" (i.e., one that is fair and skillful) should have the positive effects listed in this table and, thereby, contribute to the growth of a good relationship.

Many social scientists believe that conflict is an inevitable aspect of interpersonal intimacy and that the way a couple handles conflict will play a major role in determining the quality of their relationship. (Jean Boughton/Stock, Boston)

TABLE 8.5 THE FIGHT EFFECTS PROFILE

Each fight is scored by each individual from his or her point of view. In a good fight, both partners win. That is, both partners have considerably more positive outcomes than negative ones.

Category	Positive Outcome	Negative Outcome
Hurt	Person feels less hurt, weak, or offended	Person feels more hurt, weak, or offended
Information	Person gains more information about relationship or partner's feeling	Person learns nothing new
Resolution	Open conflict has made it more likely the issue will be resolved	Possibility of a solution is now less likely
Control	Person has gained more mutually acceptable influence over the partner's behavior	Person now has less mutually acceptable influence over the partner
Fear	Fear of fighting and/or the partner is reduced	Fear has increased
Trust	Person has more confidence that the partner will deal with him or her "in good faith, with good will, and with positive regard"	Person has less confidence in partner's goodwill
Revenge	Intentions to take revenge are not stimulated by the fight	Intentions to take revenge are stimulated by the fight
Reconciliation	Person makes active efforts to undo any harm he or she has caused and welcomes similar efforts by the partner	Person does not attempt or encourage reconciliation
Centricity	Person feels he or she is more central to the other's concern and interest	Person feels he or she "counts less" with partner
Self-Count	Person feels better about himself or herself: more confidence, more self-esteem	Person feels worse about himself or herself
Catharsis	Person feels cleared of tension and aggression	Person feels at least as much tension and aggression as before the fight
Cohesion-Affection	Closeness with and attraction to the partner has increased	Closeness with and attraction to the partner have decreased

SOURCE: Adapted from Bach & Wyden, 1968.

Bach and Wyden believe that there is no acceptable substitute for making every effort to have a "good fight" when disagreements arise. The available alternatives, they contend, are much worse. "Bad fighting" is one of these unacceptable alternatives. Here, the partners go at each other, with no holds barred. The results of bad fights can range from psychological distress to severe physical injury or even death. In the next chapter, on power, we will consider a range of potential causes of physical abuse in intimate relationships. It is possible that the lack of communication skills necessary to handle conflict and keep it within bounds makes a significant contribution to the escalation of conflict that can end in physical violence (Dutton, 1987).

Another alternative to having a good fight is to avoid fighting altogether. If there are no disagreements, fight avoidance seems reasonable. It is, however, unlikely that individuals involved in an intimate relationship, particularly those who live together, could have a lasting partnership without any disagreements. More often, fight avoidance serves to paper over problems and avoid serious issues in the relationship that couples are afraid to confront (Baxter & Wilmot, 1985; Gottman & Krokoff, 1989). At best, such avoidance tactics can create a relatively comfortable, though, perhaps, increasingly superficial, relationship. At worst, the partners collect "gunnysacks" of unresolved complaints that at some point burst open with explosive rage.

Bach and Wyden do not underestimate how hard it is to fight fair and have a "good" fight. It requires strong self-discipline and genuine caring about the other person. But the outcome is worth the effort. Instead of being seen as a dreadful problem, conflict can be seen as a challenging opportunity—the chance to learn about both partner and self, the possibility for the relationship to grow in strength and intimacy. Try to remember what you have learned about fighting fair the next time conflict puts your communication skills to the test.

CHAPTER SUMMARY

Communication is an important factor in the development and quality of a relationship. Research indicates that good communication early in a relationship is associated with long-term satisfaction with the relationship.

The Role of Communication in Relationship Development

The Theory of Social Penetration. According to the theory of social penetration, social interactions move gradually from superficial to intimate exchanges. As a relationship develops, both the breadth and depth of self-disclosure increase. Participants cover more topic areas and reveal more personally meaningful information. Breadth appears to increase first and then depth. In general, more extensive and intimate self-disclosure is associated with more rewarding relationships. There are also some more specific patterns of self-disclosure. For example, self-disclosure reciprocity is more common between strangers than between intimates. And for some couples in a troubled relationship, breadth of self-disclosure decreases, but depth increases—reflecting the intense negative emotions expressed during conflict.

Is It Always Gradual? Sometimes people disclose highly personal information soon after they first meet. In the "stranger-on-the-train" phenomenon, quick self-disclosure is safe because people don't expect ever to meet again. But where an enduring relationship is possible, too much self-disclosure too soon may damage the long-term prospects of the relationship. It is possible, however, that without going to extremes people may make relatively early distinctions between relationships they desire to become close and those they want to leave superficial. Self-disclosure may proceed much more rapidly in the former than in the latter.

Gender Differences in Communication

Self-Disclosure. On average, women self-disclose more than men, particularly in regard to material that is personal and feeling-oriented and that involves negative emotions. When males self-disclose, much of what they say is factual and nonemotional. There are also gender differences in avoidance of self-disclosure. Men tend to avoid self-disclosure when they believe they will obtain an uninformed response; women avoid it when they believe they will obtain an unemotional response. In initial interactions between strangers, self-disclosure is greater to female targets. Women tend to self-disclose more to same-sex partners than do men, while men tend to self-disclose more to opposite-sex partners than do women.

Expressive versus Instrumental Communication Styles. On average, women have a more emotionally expressive communication style, while men have a more practical, goal-oriented communication style. Women tend to be socially sensitive to the communications of others, but they also express more strong negative affect during conflict. In contrast, men tend to stay calm and problem-oriented when discussing areas of conflict, but they can become emotionally withdrawn and unresponsive to the other's concerns. This tendency for men and women to employ different styles of communication can create a communication gap between them. The highly expressive woman and the highly instrumental man are stuck on different wavelengths and often have trouble getting through to each other.

Nonverbal Communication. Three overall themes and conclusions emerge from research on nonverbal communication in intimate relationships. First, there is some indication that sensitivity to nonverbal cues does increase with increased longevity of and commitment to the relationship. Second, the woman's nonverbal skills appear more important early in the development of a heterosexual relationship, while the man's nonverbal skills may be more important for the quality of a well-established relationship. Third, it is necessary to distinguish between a skill deficit and a performance deficit in communication. A lack of skills can be remedied by training. But skills training will not directly improve a relationship for an individual who already possesses adequate skills but lacks the motivation to use them.

Improving Communication

Research by Gottman and his colleagues indicates that distressed couples cross-complain, make counterproposals, use a hostile and critical type of mindreading, become mired in all-absorbing metacommunications, and make self-summarizing statements. In contrast, happy couples validate each other, try to find compromise solutions, mindread with a positive attitude, can get away from metacommunications more easily, and avoid self-summarizing statements. In short, unhappy couples get locked into the full self-summarizing syndrome (see Table 8.3). Satisfied couples, on the other hand, focus on understanding the other person's position and validating the other person's worth as an individual. Good communication also requires being specific in our communications and taking responsibility for our own feelings and perceptions.

Can Fighting Be Good for a Relationship? It has been suggested that a good fight, fought fairly and with respect for the other participant, can promote intimacy (see Table 8.5). The alternatives to having a good fight are to have bad ones or avoid having any fights at all. Bad fights can produce psychological and, sometimes, physical damage to the participants. Fight avoidance can create superficial relationships, where people fear to tread into sensitive areas, or relationships where resentments build up and then explode. It is possible to view conflict as an opportunity to learn more about oneself and one's partner and as a way to strengthen the relationship.

9

Social Power

———— ❖ ————

Power as a Social Exchange Process ✦ *The Bases of Power* ✦ *The Process of Power* ✦
The Outcome of Power ✦ Power and Personality ✦ Power and Understanding ✦
Understanding Stereotypes ✦ Power and Violence ✦ *Why Don't They Leave?* ✦ *Violence
in Premarital Relationships* ✦ The Uses of Power ✦ Chapter Summary

S ocial power is the ability to influence the behavior of others and to resist
their influence on us (Bannester, 1969; Huston, 1983). It affects all relationships—between friends as well as lovers, at work as well as in the
family, in superficial as well as close encounters. This chapter describes some of
the basic factors involved in social power as they apply to intimate relationships.

POWER AS A SOCIAL EXCHANGE PROCESS

Although there are a number of different ways to analyze social power, one of
the most widely adopted perspectives is that of social exchange (Burgess &
Nielsen, 1977; Emerson, 1962; Thibaut & Kelley, 1959). If you have read Chapter
6, you are already familiar with the basic principles of social exchange. In this
chapter, the role of power in the social exchange process will be examined in
terms of the "three faces of power": the *bases* on which power is built, the
processes by which power is wielded, and the *outcome* produced by the use of
power (Olson & Cromwell, 1975).

The Bases of Power

From a social exchange perspective, power is based on the control of valuable resources. If A possesses something B wants, B will be motivated to comply with A's wishes in order to secure the resource from A. Thus, A will have power over B. There are three major factors involved in this view of social power.

First, the person possessing resources does not have to possess the desired resources directly; it is enough if he or she controls access to them. Money gives us a vivid example of the difference between actual possession and control of access. Imagine that you want a fabulous pair of running shoes but do not have the money to buy them. Does that mean that only the owner of the shoe store will have power over you? Obviously not; anyone who has the required sum of money and who you think might give it to you has at least some degree of power over you.

The running shoes example can also be used to illustrate the second factor related to power based on resources. Resource power can only exist if the other person values the resource, and the amount of power should directly reflect the amount of the other person's desire. If you have only a mild desire for the shoes, your friend who might lend you the money to buy them has only a little power. But if you want those shoes desperately, your friend has a great deal of power over you—unless, of course, there are other people who also have the necessary money.

This availability of alternative sources of desired resources is the third critical factor in the social exchange perspective on power. As described in Chapter 6, a person's relationship alternatives (called CL_{alt}) affect commitment to an existing relationship. Individuals with few alternatives (a low CL_{alt}) outside the existing relationship will tend to be more committed to that relationship than those with many alternatives (a high CL_{alt}). Without the prospect of other options, people are more *dependent* on what they already have. Thus, dependency depends on a person's own alternatives. A person's power, however, is affected by the other person's options. If there are many people who would loan you the money you need to buy the running shoes, then you are not very dependent on any one of them, and no one of them has much power over you.

In a relationship between just two people, power and dependency are *inversely* related: the less dependency, the more power. If you are less dependent on the relationship than is your partner, then you have more power over your partner than he or she has over you. Some rather depressing "laws" about intimate relationships put it this way:

> *The Law of Personal Exploitation*: In any sentimental relation the one who cares less can exploit the one who cares more. (Ross, 1921, p. 136)

The Principle of Least Interest: That person is able to dictate the conditions of association whose interest in the continuation of the affair is least. (Waller & Hill, 1951, p. 191)

These statements may seem harsh, but they point to an enduring reality in human relationships. Whenever we want something badly (be it running shoes or love) and believe we cannot get it elsewhere, the person who has what we want has the power to exert control over us.

Differences in available alternatives have been cited as one possible explanation for why husbands in most societies have more power than wives. Employment outside the home allows men to develop alternative sources of desired resources; women who do not work outside their homes have considerably fewer such opportunities (Levinger, 1976). Women with young children are particularly likely to be dependent on their husbands both financially and, often, socially (Laws, 1971). Moreover, Huston (1983) has noted that not only can alternatives affect power, but power can affect alternatives. It is possible for high-power individuals to prevent people with low power from developing alternative sources of the resources they desire. For instance, an economically more powerful husband can insist that his wife not pursue a career and thereby maintain the existing power structure in their relationship. There is some evidence, for example, that a husband's achievements serve to set a ceiling on his wife's accomplishments, ensuring that she is unlikely to surpass him (Philliber & Vannoy-Hiller, 1990).

Types of resources. If power is based on the resources we possess, what kinds of resources are involved? Table 9.1 defines and illustrates a classification of types of resource power developed by French and Raven (1959) and widely used in research on social power (Frost & Stahelski, 1988; Podsakoff & Schriesheim, 1985). The French and Raven classification focuses on the type of power produced by general categories of resources. Other classifications have emphasized more specific types of resources that contribute to social power. One classification scheme, for example, views power resources as including socio-economic resources, love and affection, expressions of understanding and support, companionship, sex, and services (Safilios-Rothschild, 1976b). Another includes status, money, goods, love, services, and information (Foa, 1971; Foa & Foa, 1980). These specific resources fit easily within the more general French and Raven typology. Reward power, for instance, can be based on virtually any one of them.

But are all resources equal in terms of social power? This question has provoked considerable debate. An early and highly influential version of the social exchange, resource-based view of social power held that socioeconomic resources are particularly important (Blood & Wolfe, 1960). According to this perspective, the person in a family who has more socioeconomic resources will have more influence on family deci-

TABLE 9.1 TYPES OF RESOURCE POWER

Type of Power	Resource	Gets People to Do What You Want Them to Do Because:
Reward power	Rewards	You can do something to them they like or take away something they don't like.
Coercive power	Punishments	You can do something to them they don't like or take away something they like.
Legitimate power	Authority: governmental, social status, religious	They recognize your authority to tell them what to do.
Referent power	Respect and/or love	They identify with you, feeling attracted and wanting to remain close.
Expert power	Expertise	You have the broad understanding they desire.
Informational power	Knowledge	You possess some specific knowledge they desire.

SOURCE: Based on French & Raven, 1959.

sions. Research guided by this version of resource theory has typically found that husbands have more power than do wives and that husbands with greater socioeconomic resources have more power than husbands with fewer socioeconomic resources.

But this latter finding has not always been replicated in cross-cultural research. In Greece and Yugoslavia, for example, husbands with greater socioeconomic resources appear to have *less* power in their families' decisions compared with husbands who have fewer such resources. Trying to account for these cross-cultural differences, Rodman (1972) proposed a *normative theory of power*. According to Rodman, gaining greater socioeconomic resources creates two, opposing, effects on social power. First, as husbands acquire these resources, their power in the family is increased just as resource theory says it should be. Second, however, gaining socioeconomic resources and status is also associated with coming to adopt a more egalitarian norm about sharing power in the family.

Rodman combined these two effects to create a four-stage *normative theory of power*. In the first stage—*patriarchy*—the husband is the authority in the family and has the greatest power regardless of his socioeconomic status. The second stage—*modified patriarchy*—involves cultures such as Greece and Yugoslavia, where the upper classes have more egalitarian beliefs than lower socioeconomic classes about power in the family. In the third stage—*transitional egalitarianism*—the culture does not clearly dictate who should have power, and, therefore, power will be based directly on possession of resources such as money and job prestige. Rodman classified most of the highly industrialized countries in the Western world, including the United States, as in this third stage. Finally, the fourth stage—*egalitarian*—is found in cultures that endorse the equal sharing of power, so that power is not affected by socioeconomic resources. Sweden and Denmark were cited as examples of such fourth-stage cultures.

Rodman's approach emphasizes the importance of cultural norms. According to his view, resource power only works where the culture is unclear about how power should be allocated. Where the culture—or the subgroup in the culture—has a clear norm about power, it is the norm that matters and resources are irrelevant.

However, it is possible that there is no necessary conflict between normative theory and the social exchange emphasis on resources. Instead, the critical factor may be how cultural norms influence what resources are valued (Sprey, 1975). Patriarchal societies value the male gender above all other resources, thus creating what Gillespie (1976) has called the "caste/class" system of male dominance. In modified patriarchal cultures, other resources besides gender are valued, at least in the upper levels of the society. Safilios-Rothschild (1976b) emphasizes, for example, the power of love in upper-class Greek society. Those women who thought their husbands were more in love with them also believed they had more power than did women who felt their husbands were more indifferent. Thus, within the upper classes of these modified patriarchal societies, the interplay of a variety of resources should determine the power that each spouse has.

But what about the last two stages? Why would socioeconomic resources be so important as a power base in some highly industrialized societies (like the United States) and not have that much effect in other industrialized societies (like Sweden)? One possibility is that the relative importance of socioeconomic resources reflects the values of the particular society. Where socioeconomic resources are valued more, they will play a greater role in determining individual power. Cultures, then, do develop norms, and these norms do affect power. Norms may directly allocate power in the society (as Rodman emphasizes), and/or they may indirectly distribute power through cultural beliefs about what is valuable in life.

So far, we have concentrated on the way the social exchange model of power applies to married couples. But what about unmarried couples? What about homosexual couples? Do the principles of social exchange affect the balance of power in these relationships too? The answer is a clear yes; the basic processes of social exchange apply regardless of marital status or sexual orientation. The Principle of Least Interest, for example, was as relevant for the lesbian couples studied by Caldwell and Peplau (1984) as for heterosexual dating couples in the

Boston Couples Study (Peplau, 1979). The less involvement people felt, the more power they believed they had. Economic resources were also important for both homosexual and heterosexual women. Lesbians who had more money and more education reported having more power, just as more career-oriented heterosexual women reported having greater power.

Social power does not, however, always operate in the same way for men and women. In a study of dating couples, women who reported being more involved in the relationship also reported having less power—as would be predicted by the Principle of Least Interest (Sprecher, 1985). But there was no association between level of involvement and self-reported power among men. On the other hand, men who said they had greater access to alternative relationships reported more power, but there was no association between alternatives and power among female subjects. And among those heterosexual couples who took part in the Boston Couples Study, only the women appeared to regard sexual activities with the partner as a social resource. Women who reported they had *not* had intercourse said they had more power in the relationship than did those who stated they had engaged in intercourse with their partner. The notion that women, but not men, can increase their power in a heterosexual relationship by withholding sexual favors is consistent with a traditional view of the resources controlled by each gender. According to this perspective, men have power based on money and status, whereas women have power based on love and sex. But what does this mean for social power between the genders? Is it possible for equal power to be based on the control of different resources?

In the abstract, this seems a reasonable proposition. Surely, love can matter at least as much as money in a relationship. In practice, however, the issue becomes more complex. First, we have to examine societal values again. While some individuals clearly value love more than money, it is doubtful whether one could characterize most of our own society this way. If resources are valued differentially, it is difficult to have an equal exchange and, therefore, hard to establish equal power.

A second point has to do with the "tradability" of resources. Foa and Foa (1980) describe some resources (e.g., money) as "universalistic" and others (e.g., love) as "particularistic." Universalistic resources can be exchanged with anyone; whoever owns them automatically has a certain freedom in deciding with whom he or she will exchange them. Particularistic resources are more limited; it is not clear who else will want them. Thus, some resources (such as socioeconomic ones) carry with them, virtually automatically, the possibility of being used in alternative relationships; other resources (such as love) may be relatively unique to the present relationship. As we have seen, having more alternatives is associated with having more power.

And, then, there is the matter of ultimate control over the resource. The ownership of money is clear-cut. The person who has it controls it. The vulnerability of money is also clear-cut. Money can be stolen, can be taken away by superior force. Love, in contrast, is far more complicated. On the one hand, it cannot be taken by force. As Blau (1964) has stated, "We cannot force others to give us their approval, regardless of how much power we have over them, because coercing them to express this admiration or praise would make their expression worthless" (p. 17). The power of love is that it must be given spontaneously.

On the other hand, love, like any other resource, must be valued to be effective in creating power. Our love, then, is only powerful when the other person loves us. As described by Scott Spencer (1980) in his novel *Endless Love*, when *their* love dies so does *our* power:

> There had been a time when Rose had felt she could protect her position in the marriage . . . by simply (and it *was* simple) withholding her love. But now that her love was no longer sought there was no advantage to be gained in rationing it. It was clear that the power she once had was not real power—it had been bestowed upon her, assigned. It had all depended on Arthur's wanting her, depended on his vulnerability to every nuance of rejection. He had, she realized now, chosen her weapon for her. He had given her a sword that only he could sharpen. (pp. 66–67)

Overall, then, both love and money are resources that can contribute to social power. But the types of power based on each of these resources are not identical and may, therefore, not be truly equal.

The Process of Power

The second face of power is the process by which it is expressed. The kinds of behaviors that can be used to get our way with others seem almost infinite. Some people use physical violence; others plead. Sometimes power is exercised by talking more than anyone else; at other times, the one who is silent is exerting his or her will most effectively. Although general rules about the process of power are hard to come by (Szinovacz, 1981), it does appear that the way we get our way is affected by the resources we possess as well as by culturally determined norms about how we should behave. In this section, we consider three possible ways in which power could be expressed: language, touch, and general styles of power.

Language and touch. Our use of language may be one of the most subtle and pervasive processes of power. How we talk to another person may be strongly influenced by the balance of power between us. Social scientists have observed that patterns of verbal communication can serve to maintain and enhance the more powerful position of males in heterosexual interactions (Thoren & Henley, 1975). Consider, for example, a study in which conversations between college students were surreptitiously recorded in public places (Zimmerman & West, 1975). Permission to analyze the recordings for research purposes was obtained from subjects after their conversation was completed. In these analyses, the language patterns of same-sex couples (male and female) were compared with those of opposite-sex couples. For same-sex couples, conversational structure was much the same regardless of whether two males or two females were talking. Cross-sex couples, however, displayed a distinctive gender-based pattern. First, males interrupted their female partners much more often than their female partners interrupted them. Interrupting someone is usually associated with having greater social power (Kollock, Blumstein, & Schwartz, 1985). Second, females were more silent than were males. As described by Zimmerman and West, females were getting "cut off at the pass" during these conversations. The cutoffs could be explicit or implicit. That is, when a woman would make a statement, the man might interrupt her before she was through, or he might let her finish but then just give her a minimum response ("um"). These cutoffs may have contributed to the greater silence among women. What's the point in talking if he isn't interested?

In a subsequent study, West and Zimmerman (1983) examined the cross-sex conversations of unacquainted couples who talked with each other in a laboratory setting. Again, males interrupted females far more often than females interrupted males. Taken together, these two studies suggest that various aspects of conversational style between heterosexual couples (both those who know each other and those who have just met) serve to ensure that males have more active control over the conversation than do females. Although conversational dominance appears to be affected by the topic of discussion, men are more likely to dominate discussions of neutral topics as well as of traditionally masculine topics, while women are more likely to dominate only when traditionally feminine topics are being discussed (Brown, Dovidio, & Ellyson, 1990).

Although research findings on power and language have been reasonably consistent, the relationship between power and physical touch is much less certain. In her influential book on this issue, entitled *Body Politics*, Henley (1977) maintained that men touch women more than vice versa and that this difference reflects the use of touch as an expression of higher status and greater power. Recent research confirms a gender difference in touch but indicates that both age and situation influence its occurrence (Major, Schmidlin, & Williams, 1990). Among the adults in this study, but not among the children, males touched females more than females touched males—especially in public, nonintimate settings. In addition, there was more cross-sex touching than same-sex touching among adults and more touching between female pairs in nonintimate settings than between male pairs. Major et al. doubt that any such complicated set of findings can be explained in terms of touch as a "top-down" expression of social power. Instead, like other investigators (Stier & Hall, 1984; Thayer, 1988), they emphasize that "touch serves multiple functions and has multiple meanings" (Major et al., p. 641). Touch can, of course, be intrusive or demeaning, and it can serve to reinforce dominance over the person being touched. But it can also act as a signal of interest in sexual activities, and it can function as a gesture of solidarity, indicating warmth and concern for the person being touched. An adequate understanding of the meaning of touch requires an appreciation of the context in which it occurs.

Styles of power. Another way to look at the process of power is to examine the styles people use when they try to influence others. Like verbal interactions, styles of power may reflect gender differences. Johnson (1976, 1978) has proposed that women are particularly likely to use personal power (e.g., appeals to affection and/or sexuality) and manipulative power (e.g., appeals based on helplessness). According to Johnson, men are more likely to use more direct forms of power (e.g., coercion, authority) as well as personal power based on competence (e.g., expertise, information).

The findings from a study on marital power appear to support Johnson's contentions. In this research, husbands and wives were asked why they did things their spouses asked them to do (Raven, Centers, & Rodrigues, 1975). The possible answers to this question involved the first five types of power listed in Table 9.1. Most wives indicated two reasons why they complied with their husband's wishes: his superior knowledge (expert power); and the fact that they were both members of the same family and, therefore, should see eye-to-eye on such matters (referent power). Most husbands, in contrast, only cited referent power as the major reason they complied with what their wives wanted them to do. While this study does not tell us directly about the styles of power people use, it does tell us about people's attitudes and beliefs in this area. Wives were viewed by husbands as wielding only personal power (based on their marital relationship): husbands were seen by wives as having both personal power and power based on impersonal expertise.

Styles of power among heterosexual and homosexual couples have also been investigated (Falbo & Peplau, 1980). Subjects in this study were male and female, gay and straight; they all responded to instructions to describe "How I get my partner to do what I want." Falbo and Peplau found that two dimensions characterized most of their subjects' replies. The first dimension involved direct power styles (e.g., asking, telling, talking) versus indirect styles (e.g., hinting, being nice, pouting), similar to Johnson's distinction between direct and manipulative power. The second dimension was that of bilateral styles (e.g., attempting persuasion, bargaining, etc.) versus unilateral ones (e.g., withdrawing, just letting each person do what he or she wants).

Comparisons were first made on the basis of sexual orientation and gender. On these analyses, homosexual individuals did not differ in their styles of power from heterosexuals. Among the homosexual subjects, males did not differ from females. However, among the heterosexual individuals, males and females differed sharply. Heterosexual males reported much more use of direct and bilateral styles than did heterosexual females. In contrast, heterosexual females reported extensive use of indirect and unilateral styles.

Falbo and Peplau then made two additional comparisons that are very important for interpreting their results. Including all their subjects (male and female, gay and straight) in their analyses, they looked at the association between power styles and subjects' reports of both power and satisfaction in their relationships. It was found that people who reported having greater power in the relationship also reported greater use of a bilateral power style. Greater satisfaction was associated with greater use of a direct power style. Thus, the power styles reported as most characteristic of heterosexual females were also the styles that were used by power*less* and *dis*satisfied individuals, regardless of gender or sexual orientation. By including homosexual couples, Falbo and Peplau were able to show that different power styles were not simply a matter of gender. Gay males did not differ from lesbians in terms of which styles of power they used more often. In this study, gender differences in power styles were restricted to heterosexual couples.

The research by Falbo and Peplau generated considerable interest and prompted a number of subsequent studies. The results of these studies, however, have not always agreed with those obtained by Falbo and Peplau (Cowan, Drinkard, & MacGavin, 1984; Offermann & Schrier, 1985). For example, although research on several hundred heterosexual and homosexual couples in well-established relationships did find that men reported receiving more indirect power tactics such as manipulation and supplication than did women, men and women did *not* differ in their reports of being the target of direct tactics such as bargaining (Howard, Blumstein, & Schwartz, 1986). It has also been noted that the type of power styles people use can be affected by cultural background (Belk et al., 1988), social norms (Belk & Snell, 1988), and stereotypes about male sexuality (Snell, Hawkins, & Belk, 1988).

Research by Gruber and White (1986) emphasizes the need to distinguish between people's general beliefs about who uses what type of power style and their views of their own behavior. These investigators found that both male and female undergraduates agree that men are more likely to use styles stereotypically defined as "masculine" (such as using reason, being assertive, claiming superior knowledge) and that women are more likely to use styles stereotypically defined as "feminine" (such as compromising, being a nuisance, using flattery). Subjects' descriptions of their *own* power tactics did not, however, always agree with the stereotypes. According to their self-reports, men used masculine power styles more often than women, but feminine power styles were used equally often by both genders. Gruber and White suggest that these findings are best considered in terms of freedom and constraint. Men, they propose, are free to adjust the tactic they employ to the circumstances they face, calling upon whatever approach seems most likely to work. But women, it is argued, are more constrained by social norms, and they restrict their power tactics to those seen as socially acceptable for females.

Although it is important to determine whether men and women employ different ways to get their way, an even more fundamental issue involves the effects of various power styles. How are speakers who use a certain style perceived by their listeners? Does it matter whether the speaker, or the listener, is male or female? Early research on this topic suggested that both genders may pay a social price for speaking "out of role" (Falbo, Hazen, & Linimon, 1982). In this study, women who used an expert style and men who used a helpless presentation style were liked less by their listeners than were women and men who adopted power styles more in keeping with traditional notions about the behavior of women and men. More recent research, however, raises the possibility that the social cost of speaking out of role may be greater for women than for men (Carli, 1990). After listening to a male or female speaker who spoke in either an assertive or a tentative manner, subjects rated the speaker on a variety of characteristics. In general, the tentative speaker was seen as less confident and less powerful than the assertive speaker, but only the tentative female speaker was perceived as less competent and less knowledgeable. The presentation style of male speakers did not affect their perceived competence and knowledge, nor did it determine their ability to influence the opinions of their audience. For female speakers, however, their influence depended on both their style and gender of the listener. Compared with assertive female speakers, tentative female speakers were *more* influential with male listeners and *less* influential with female listeners. Similarly, male listeners liked the tentative female speaker more, while female listeners responded more positively to the assertive female speaker. Taken together, these studies indicate that women still face a difficult dilemma when attempting to influence others. For them, the power styles that create respect (being an expert, behaving assertively) may well decrease liking and influence, especially among the men with whom they interact.

The Outcome of Power

The third face of power is its outcome. Most studies on power have defined the outcome of power in terms of which person gets his or her way in decisions made by the couple or family. However, this focus on explicit decision making has been criticized as both too narrow and possibly misleading. Consider, for example, the difference between "implementation" power and "orchestration" power (Safilios-Rothschild, 1976a). The person with orchestration power decides who will decide; the person with implementation power simply carries out delegated power. And whenever power is delegated, it can be recalled. Perhaps, then, studies of decision-making power are only measuring the lower level of implementation power without finding out who controls the decision maker. Research on decision making also has been faulted for not examining more carefully the types and importance of the decisions being studied (Brinkerhoff & Lupri, 1978; Safilios-Rothschild, 1970). Having the power to make trivial decisions is not the same as having the power to make important ones.

These distinctions involving the level of power and the importance of the decisions being made are particularly crucial when we examine the power that wives have in their marriages. Unless these distinctions are taken into account, studies of decision-making power may *overestimate* the power that wives have. A striking example of this possibility was provided in some research on Japanese-American wives in Hawaii (Johnson, 1975). When these wives filled out the typical questionnaire asking who makes the decisions in a number of areas relevant to married life, they did not indicate a single area where their husbands dominated, though they did report a drastic decline in their own power when "major decisions" were made (see Table 9.2). However, when these same women were interviewed in detail about how decisions were made in their families, their responses (as coded by judges) indicated a great deal of husband dominance (also shown in Table 9.2). It appears that much of the power these women had was delegated by their husbands and restricted to relatively minor, everyday decisions.

On the other hand, research on decision-making power may sometimes *underestimate* the power of wives. This possibility can be demonstrated by comparing the two most popular ways to measure marital power: (1) self-reports, usually questionnaires but sometimes interviews, and (2) laboratory observations of couples or families carrying out assigned decision-making tasks. Both these methods of research have specific advantages and disadvantages (see Chapter 2), but what is of concern here is that they seldom give the same picture of the marital power structure (Hadley & Jacob, 1976; Olson, 1977; Olson & Cromwell, 1975; Turk & Bell, 1972).

TABLE 9.2 IMPLEMENTATION POWER VERSUS ORCHESTRATION POWER

Daily Decisions (Based on Wives' Questionnaire Responses)	Husband-Dominated	Egalitarian	Wife-Dominated
Financial	37%	18%	45%
Social	12	60	28
Child rearing	2	40	58
Major decisions (e.g., changing jobs or residences)	48	50	2
Authority in the Home (Based on In-Depth Interviews)			
Husband-dominated	54%		
Egalitarian	39		
Wife-dominated	7		

SOURCE: Data from Johnson, 1975.

A study on marital power during early marriage (Corrales, 1975) provides a good illustration of the different findings that can result from these two approaches to studying power. In this study, when decision making was observed in the laboratory, wives had a great deal more power than was indicated when husbands and wives answered a questionnaire about who made various decisions in their families (see Table 9.3). This apparent increase in wife-power when we go from self-report data to observed interactions is fairly common in those studies that have used both types of measures (Olson & Cromwell, 1975).

TABLE 9.3 TWO METHODS OF STUDYING POWER

Self-Reports of Who Usually Decides	Husbands' Reports	Wives' Reports
Husband-dominated	58.4%	62.0%
Egalitarian	31.1	31.6
Wife-dominated	10.5	6.4
Observed Interactions in the Laboratory		
Husband-dominated	28.7%	
Egalitarian	46.9	
Wife-dominated	24.4	

SOURCE: Data from Corrales, 1975.

Trying to figure out what such a difference might mean, we run into two, completely contradictory possibilities. Probably the most common explanation is that in self-reports people are giving their "authority expectations" (McDonald, 1980). These expectations may well be heavily influenced by social norms, such as the greater social acceptability of male dominance. Since interactions in the lab are more like "real behavior," they should be less easily influenced by such norms and should give us a more accurate picture of decision-making power than do self-reports. This reasoning, then, would lead us to conclude that wives are actually a great deal more powerful than they or their husbands realize.

However, the opposite argument can also be made. Huston (1983) has described the power of deciding "when to win" as a higher level of power (somewhat akin to orchestration power). It could be that in the laboratory sessions, where only make-believe decisions are being made, husbands are heavily influenced by the social norm of gallantry. They may decide, since it doesn't really matter, to make their wives happy by letting them win the little game they are playing for the researchers. Husbands acting in this fashion would have good intentions, but their generosity would be firmly based on secure power.

To complicate the matter even further, husbands' and wives' self-reports about how much power each has in the relationship often do not agree (Olson & Cromwell, 1975; Safilios-Rothschild, 1970). Turk and Bell (1972) suggest that many self-reports of power will display what we might call a "powerlessness bias"; each person tends to overestimate the partner's power while underestimating his or her own power. Such a bias may reflect a fundamental distortion in the way we view power in our intimate relationships. We may all be quite sensitive to and aware of the power of our partners, and relatively unaware of our own power. In any event, the disagreements that have been found between methods of studying power (self- report versus observational) and between the self-reports of the partners indicate how difficult it can be to capture the reality of the outcome of power.

Female dominance: A taboo? Despite these difficulties, however, there is one major conclusion about the outcome of power that is well supported by the research evidence. Even today, female dominance in a heterosexual relationship is less acceptable *to both parties* than is male dominance. Although both men and women enjoy the benefits of having power and control (Horwitz, 1982; Madden, 1987), they are more comfortable when the balance of power in their relationship is tilted in the male direction than when it is tilted in the female direction. The evidence for this continuing discomfort with female dominance comes from a variety of sources.

You may recall from Chapter 5 on sexuality that typical gender scripts call for the man's taking the initiative and the female's making the response: The male proposes, the female disposes—as the saying goes. Although depictions of sexual initiation and dominance by females can be found in some pornographic materials, it appears that the appeal of the fantasy does not often translate into a desire for the reality (Kelley & Rolker-Dolinsky, 1987). The socially prescribed roles of a male initiator and a female responder seem widespread in sexual, or at least potentially sexual, heterosexual interactions (Folkes, 1982; Poppen & Segal, 1988). As described in Chapter 8, men self-disclose more than women in initial encounters with the opposite sex (Derlega, Winstead, Wong, & Hunter, 1985). In these encounters, self-disclosure is a means of taking the initiative. Since men are expected to be active, dominant, and forceful, they are perceived as more attractive when they display these characteristics than when they do not (Sadalla, Kenrick, & Vershure, 1987). Both men and women seem more comfortable when the man is masterful and the lady is in distress than when these roles are reversed (Zillmann, Weaver, Mundort, & Aust, 1986). Even physical characteristics may reflect a preference for male dominance. Among heterosexual couples, the man is typically older than the woman; and most men prefer dating shorter women, while most women prefer dating taller men (Shepperd & Strathman, 1989).

The greater acceptability of male rather than female dominance is not restricted to initial heterosexual encounters. Research on marital satisfaction has consistently found that both men and women are less satisfied in female-dominated relationships than in either egalitarian or male-dominated relationships (Centers, Raven, & Rodrigues, 1971; Corrales, 1975; Gray-Little & Burks, 1983). Indeed, in one study, a public display of female dominance was the single best predictor of relationship endurance and satisfaction (Filsinger & Thoma, 1988). These investigators observed the verbal interactions of 31 dating couples and then were able to keep in touch with 21 of them over a five-year period. To measure female dominance at the time of the initial laboratory session, Filsinger and Thoma classified couples in terms of whether the woman had interrupted the man at that time. As noted earlier in this chapter, interrupting someone is usually associated with having greater power (Kollock et al., 1985). Five years after this conversation in the laboratory had taken place, a full 80 percent of the couples in which the woman interrupted the man had broken up! And among those couples still together, most of them now married, the more often the woman had interrupted the man five years earlier, the less satisfied both partners were with their relationship. Just as female leaders in mixed-sex groups appear to elicit more negative reactions than male leaders (Butler & Geis, 1990), the rather astonishing results of the study by Filsinger and Thoma suggest that intimate relationships in which the female publicly displays dominance are particularly vulnerable to dissatisfaction and dissolution. Despite the increasing acceptance of an egalitarian norm for heterosexual relationships (Altrocchi & Crosby, 1989; Rogler & Procidano, 1989), the two forms of *non*egalitarian relationships are not held in equal regard. It seems, then, reasonable to propose that the way in which men and women respond to female dominance is a highly sensitive measure of the degree of gender equality in a society. So long as female dominance is less acceptable than male dominance, true equality has not been achieved.

POWER AND PERSONALITY

Thus far, we have looked at power as a process of social exchange and examined the way that resources, norms, and gender affect this process. This section describes another way to examine power: in terms of individual personality characteristics. According to personality theorists, individuals differ on how much they are motivated to obtain power, with some having a strong power motive and others a relatively weak one.

Initial research in this area was conducted by Veroff and his colleagues (Veroff & Feld, 1971; Veroff & Veroff, 1972). Based on the way these investigators measured the need for power, they concluded that this need reflected concerns about weakness; feeling weak and insecure, a person desires power in order to gain strength and security. This interpretation allowed Veroff and Veroff (1972) to account for some striking gender differences they obtained in their research. They found, for example, that for men, increasing education was associated with a decreasing need for power, whereas for women, it was associated with an increasing need for power. Single women had the highest need for power in the entire sample. According to the Veroffs, this pattern of results is determined by two factors. First, women who are single violate the cultural norm that places high value on marriage for women. Second, women who have more education are likely to be competing against men in "a man's world" and may feel that being female is a handicap in this situation. Both factors would undermine feelings of security and, from the Veroffs' perspective, result in an increased need for power.

The second major research effort on the need for power has been conducted by Winter and his associates. These investigators tried to create a more "positive" measure of the need for power than that used by Veroff. Specifically, Winter's (1973) measure of the need for power is designed to reflect an interest in strong, vigorous action; a desire to produce strong emotional effects in others; and a concern about reputation and position. (It is possible to suggest, of course, that these are exactly the interests, desires, and concerns that would be felt by someone who also felt weak and insecure.)

Winter's major example of a person strong in the need for power is the literary figure of Don Juan, who used the sexual conquest of women to prove his manhood and flaunt his power. Some of the research that has been conducted with Winter's measure of the need for power implies that Don Juan may be alive and well in the United States. The first of these studies (Stewart & Rubin, 1976) involved a subset of the couples participating in the Boston Couples Study (see Chapter 5). Although these men and women were equal in their general need for power, the power motive was much more important for the men's relationships than for the women's. For men, a high need for power was associated with low relationship satisfaction (both their own and that of their partners), low love for their partners, and a high number of anticipated problems in the relationship. Among women, need for power affected only the number of anticipated problems. In addition, men high in need for power were more likely than other men to indicate being interested in someone else, and they reported having had a larger number of previous relationships. Upon follow-up two years later, men high in need for power were more likely to have broken up with their partners and less likely to have married them. There was no relationship between need for power and any of these measures for women. Furthermore, even though need for power predicted a great deal about men's heterosexual relationships, this need was not related to their plans for future education or their career aspirations.

But what happens to Don Juan when he gets married? Of course, the literary one never did, and, presumably, the modern ones will try not to. But marriage is so highly valued in our society that maybe even Don Juans cannot avoid it. The married life of Don Juan has, in fact, been explored in a longitudinal study (Winter, Stewart, & McClelland, 1977). First measured in 1960 on their need for power when they were college students, male subjects were contacted 14 years later and asked about their current circumstances; among the questions (for those who were married) were some about their wives' careers. Men who were high in need for power when they were undergraduates were less likely to have wives with full-time careers than were men who were low in need for power during their undergraduate days. These results suggest that modern, married Don Juans may seek to exercise their power over women economically rather than (or, in addition to) sexually. There is also some indication that among both married and dating couples, men high in the need for power may inflict more physical abuse on their female partner than men low in the need for power (Mason & Blankenship, 1987). No association was found for women between the amount of physical abuse they reported inflicting on their male partner and the strength of their need for power.

It is important not to overemphasize the difference between men and women in their need for power. Among both sexes, the need for

According to research by Winter, women usually express their need for power by engaging in socially responsible actions. Men, on the other hand, express their need for power in both socially responsible and irresponsible behaviors. (Jerry Howard/Stock, Boston)

power varies—with some individuals having a strong need and others a weak one. In addition, the average intensity of the need as defined by Winter is similar for both sexes, and many of the activities associated with the power motive (holding office, seeking a power-related career, displaying visible signs of wealth and prestige) are similar among men and women (Winter, 1988). The difference between the way the power motive operates for men and women seems restricted to two general areas: intimate relationships and what Winter calls "profligate behaviors." As we have seen, men's need for power is closely related to their behavior in intimate relationships, but these associations are not found for women (Stewart & Chester, 1982). Moreover, only among men does a high need for power predict such "profligate behaviors" as drinking, drug use, aggression, and gambling (Winter, 1988).

Winter has suggested that these differences are not a matter of gender per se, but rather a reflection of the different socialization practices applied to males and females (Winter, 1988; Winter & Barenbaum, 1985). According to this perspective, girls receive more training in behaving in a responsible manner than do boys. This training, says Winter, prompts women with a high need for power to channel this need into socially responsible actions, while men express their need for power in both socially responsible *and* socially irresponsible ways. Winter's emphasis on the importance of responsibility training leads him to focus on other social factors besides gender that might affect how the need for power is expressed. He proposes, for example, that growing up with younger siblings promotes a greater sense of social responsibility and should strengthen the responsible exercise of power. And Winter believes that having children should also tend to increase the socially responsible use of power among both men and women. But if the root of the problem is socialization, then perhaps a full cure requires a change in socialization practices. If Winter's analysis is correct, providing social responsibility training to boys similar to what girls receive should help reduce the destructive effects of the power motive.

POWER AND UNDERSTANDING

Having examined power as part of the social exchange process and as a personality characteristic, let us turn to a third way to look at power in intimate relationships. This approach defines power in a relationship in terms of which of the two individuals has more influence on how the relationship progresses and on whether it is satisfying for both partners. Murstein (1976b)—one of the strongest advocates of this way of viewing power—argues that men have more impact on, and thus more power in, heterosexual relationships.

A key aspect of Murstein's proposal about power in heterosexual relationships involves who needs to understand whom. According to Murstein, the weak need to understand the strong if the relationship is to progress successfully. Since the more powerful partner is in a position to demand more rewards, the less powerful person has to understand the other in order to develop ways to please that person. This view of the relationship between power and understanding has also been suggested by a number of feminist scholars (Adams, 1971; Glazer-Malbin, 1975). As Miller (1976) put it, "subordinates . . . know much more about the dominants than vice-versa. They have to" (p. 10). The formulation itself is gender-free: Whoever (male or female) has less power will need to understand whoever (male or female) has more power. Since, however, it is usually assumed that, on the average, men have more power than women, the typical prediction is that women's understanding of their male partner will have a stronger association with relationship satisfaction than will men's understanding of their female partner.

Much of the research on the relationship between gender and understanding has involved a procedure where subjects first make ratings from their own point of view and then attempt to adopt the viewpoint of their partners. Murstein's approach is typical of, but somewhat more elaborate than, that used by other researchers. He has subjects fill out a questionnaire eight separate times! First, they describe themselves in terms of a number of different personality characteristics; then for the same set of characteristics they describe their ideal self (the way they would like to be), then their partner (the way they believe he or she really is), and then their ideal spouse. After all this, subjects go back through the same questionnaire predicting how their partner would have described self, ideal self, partner, and ideal spouse.

From the data generated by this procedure, Murstein developed two measures: confirmation and prediction. Confirmation refers to matches between a person's views of self and ideal self in relation to the partner's views of the person and desired ideal spouse. Prediction, on the other hand, involves how well the two partners can predict each other's ratings. Figure 9.1 diagrams these various comparisons. On the whole, Murstein's research on confirmation and prediction has tended to support his notions about women needing to understand men more than vice versa (Murstein, 1972a, 1976b; Murstein & Beck, 1972). For both premarital and marital couples, confirmation and prediction by the female of the male's views of himself were associated with enhanced relationship progress and satisfaction. Confirmation and prediction by the male of the female's view of herself showed no such association.

However, there is one major problem with these findings. As Murstein acknowledges, his results could reflect not the power of any individual man himself, but the importance and power of the masculine stereotype. Perhaps what is being confirmed and predicted by women is simply the way that men are supposed to be.

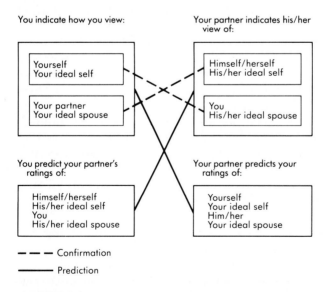

FIGURE 9.1
Murstein's measures. (Murstein, 1976.)

Understanding Stereotypes

The influence of the masculine stereotype in this kind of research was clearly demonstrated in an early study by Corsini (1956). He used a similar, but less extensive, procedure than that adopted later by Murstein: Married couples individually rated themselves and their partners and then predicted their partners' ratings. Corsini's results were similar to Murstein's. Marital adjustment was positively associated with the ability of the wife to predict her husband's view of himself, but not with the ability of the husband to predict his wife's view of herself.

Most investigators would have stopped right there, but Corsini took an interesting further step. He randomly paired questionnaire responses of men and women in his study, creating a set of "partners" who had never met. And these random pairings gave him exactly the same results as those he had obtained for actual married couples! Partners, randomly paired together, were happier in their marriages (to other people, not each other) when the woman could "predict" the man's view of himself. Obviously, this has nothing to do with understanding; you cannot "understand" a perfect stranger. Trying to figure out what was going on here, Corsini compared the self-description of each individual in his study with the self-descriptions of all the other people in the study of the same sex. High scores on this "conformity index" meant that the person viewed himself or herself similarly to the way that others of the same sex viewed themselves. In the final twist to this story, Corsini found that men who scored high on the conformity index tended to have happy marriages; no such relationship was found for women.

Corsini's results strongly suggest that wive's predictions are related to relationship success not because husbands are powerful and wives need to be understanding, but rather because both partners respond favorably to the stereotyped masculine role. To see how this process works, let's take up the pieces one by one. First, happy husbands rate themselves in a stereotyped way, though maybe they really do embody that stereotype in their behavior. Second, happy wives predict that their husbands will rate themselves in accordance with the masculine stereotype. Then, when you put a happy husband from one marriage with a happy wife from another marriage, it will look like she is able, miraculously, to predict how this unknown man views himself! She can't. She is just saying, for example, "My husband says he's strong and silent." And, sure enough, that unknown man from another (happy) marriage says, "As for me, I'm strong and silent."

Unfortunately, not everyone has attended to the potential role of stereotypes in affecting partners' ratings of each other. In addition to Murstein, a host of researchers have claimed that a wife's understanding of her husband makes a greater contribution to marital happiness than a husband's understanding of his wife (Dean, 1966; Kotlar, 1965; Sicoly & Ross, 1978; Stuckert, 1963; Taylor, 1967). None of these studies included random pairings to check for the possible influence of stereotyped concepts. But even if all the research results on the relationship between understanding a spouse and having a happy marriage are a matter of stereotypes, an important question remains. Why does agreement on the male stereotype—but *not* on the female stereotype—distinguish happy from unhappy couples? We know from the previous discussion of the taboo against female dominance in a heterosexual relationship that stereotyped expectations about female behavior do play an important role in relationship satisfaction. And yet from the research described in this section, happy and unhappy couples do not appear to differ in their ability to access the female stereotype so as to create the appearance of husbandly "understanding." Perhaps future research will generate some cogent reasons for why agreement on the male stereotype is particularly characteristic of happy couples. Or, perhaps, future research will discover that this pattern is no longer so widespread. In more recent studies, predictive accuracy and perspective-taking by *both* spouses were positively correlated with marital satisfaction (Arias & O'Leary, 1985; Long & Andrews, 1990). These results suggest that either it is becoming important for happy couples to agree on the female stereotype as well as the male one, or that happy couples have learned to understand each other as real, live people and not just as representations of a socially approved stereotype.

POWER AND VIOLENCE

In a 1971 article, sociologist William Goode made a rather startling assertion: "Like all other social units or systems, the family is a power system. All rest to some degree on force or its threat whatever else may be their foundations" (p. 624). What was startling about Goode's statement was not that he emphasized the role of power in the family; research on family—especially marital—power had been going on for years. Power was, at least to social scientists, an acceptable part of family life. But "force"—physical force and, therefore, in some cases physical violence—was a different matter entirely. In fact, until the 1970s, there was little attention paid to the role of physical abuse and violence in families; it was an almost unthinkable topic. When, however, investigators did begin to examine family violence, they rapidly discovered that it was both more common aand more severe than anyone would have thought (Van Hasselt, Morrison, Bellack, & Hersen, 1988).

The use of physical force in families occurs both across generations (between parents and children) and within generations (between spouses as well as among siblings). Here, we focus primarily on violence between husbands and wives. Because so much of family life occurs in private, it is difficult to obtain accurate statistics on the extent of spouse abuse. Perhaps the best estimates come from two national surveys conducted by Murray Straus and his colleagues (Hampton, Gelles, & Harrop, 1989; Straus & Gelles, 1986; Straus, Gelles, & Steinmetz, 1980). Those who participated in these surveys were asked to indicate how frequently they engaged in each of the eight types of physical aggression included in the Conflict Tactics Scale (see Figure 9.2). The rates of spouse abuse reported in the two surveys are summarized in Figure 9.3. Although the absolute numbers differ across the two surveys, these differences are probably only chance variations (Stocks, 1988). Between 1975 and 1985, spouse abuse remained relatively constant—and high. The 1985 rate of *severe* violence among couples means that over 3 million couples reported violent interactions in their lives.

For many people, one of the most surprising aspects of the data collected by Straus and his colleagues is the high level of wife-to-husband abuse. In terms of *severe* violence, the level of wife-to-husband abuse was higher in both surveys than the level of husband-to-wife abuse. Longitudinal research on aggression during early marriage has also found a greater prevalence of wife-to-husband abuse, though most of the abuse reported was relatively low in severity—e.g., pushing, slapping, shoving (Malone, Tyree, & O'Leary, 1989; O'Leary et al., 1989). The higher rates of wife-to-husband abuse were especially pronounced directly before marriage (with 44 percent of the women reporting having aggressed physically against their male partner compared

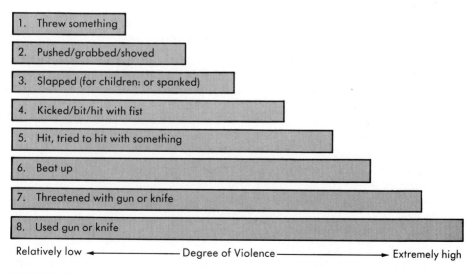

FIGURE 9.2
The Conflict Tactics Scale: Physical violence. (Straus, 1979.)

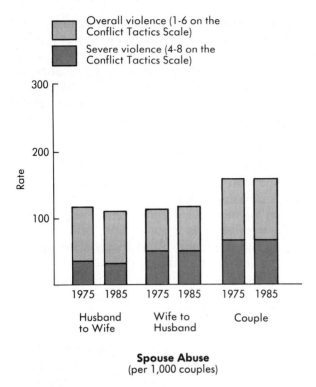

FIGURE 9.3
Spouse abuse in the United States, 1975 and 1985.
(Data from Straus & Gelles, 1986.)

with 31 percent of the men who reported having aggressed physically against their female partner) and after 18 months of marriage (36 percent versus 27 percent). By 30 months of marriage, the same trend remained but was no longer statistically significant (32 percent versus 25 percent).

This greater prevalence of wife-to-husband abuse has been the subject of considerable controversy (Steinmetz & Lucca, 1988; Straus, 1990). For instance, the Conflict Tactics Scale does not assess whether the violence involved was offensive or defensive in nature. According to some researchers, wife-to-husband abuse is often a defense against, or provoked by, husband-to-wife abuse (Browne, 1986; Russell, 1982; Walker & Browne, 1985). The Conflict Tactics Scale also does not include questions about the severity of injury resulting from abuse incidents, and most investigators believe that women are more likely than men to be seriously injured by domestic violence (Breines & Gordon, 1983; Browning & Dutton, 1986). Research by Stets and Straus (1990) indicates that women victims suffer serious injury more frequently than do men victims, and women are twice as likely as men to be killed by their spouse (O'Leary & Vivian, 1990). In general, women are far more vulnerable to violent attack from someone they know intimately (family member, former spouse, current or former romantic partner) than are men. Among the female victims included in national crime surveys conducted from 1973 ato 1987, 24.5 percent knew their attacker intimately, compared with only 3.9 percent of male victims who had a close relationship with the person who attacked them (Bureau of Justice Statistics, 1991).

Spouse abuse is not restricted to any one social class, race, or ethnic background; it occurs throughout society (Lockhart, 1987). But there are a number of specific factors associated with increased rates of spouse abuse (Barling, 1990; Fergusson, Horwood, Kershaw, & Shannon, 1986; Gelles & Straus, 1988; Straus et al., 1980):

- Stressful events such as unemployment and unplanned pregnancy
- Low socioeconomic status involving such factors as low income and little education
- Family background, including growing up in a violent family

That last factor, family background, has received particular attention from researchers and, recently, the mass media. There is reasonably consistent evidence of a *cycle of family violence* (Gelles, 1980; Kalmuss & Seltzer, 1986; O'Leary, 1988; Rosenbaum & O'Leary, 1986; Steinmetz, 1978; Stets, 1990). Adults who witnessed parental violence during their childhood are more likely to be involved in spouse abuse, as an abuser and perhaps as a victim. They are also more likely to abuse their own children. The long-term effects on spouse abuse of having been abused as a child are less well understood and may not be a major factor in the cycle of family violence (DeMaris, 1990). Regardless of the exact determinants of this intergenerational transmission of aggression, it is important to realize that it is not inevitable (Zigler, Rubin, & Kaufman, 1988). Most people who witness or experience abuse in their families of origin are not abused or abusive in their families of procreation (Emery, 1989). The cycle of violence refers to an average tendency not an absolute certainty. But even an average tendency in this matter is most disturbing, as it translates into enormous suffering for large numbers of individuals. In the cycle of family violence, the evil that people do does, in fact, live after them.

Why Don't They Leave?

Perhaps one of the most puzzling aspects of marital violence is why its victims so often remain in the relationship. Research on this issue has pointed to two particularly important factors (Gelles, 1976; Strube,

Shelters for battered women and their children provide physical safety as well as personal and financial counseling. (Mark Antman/The Image Works)

1988). First, the victim's economic status is crucial. Women who leave abusing relationships are more likely to be employed than women who stay. Second, commitment to the relationship can turn into entrapment (see Chapter 6). In one study of abused women, those in longer-lasting relationships were less likely to leave than those in more short-term relationships (Strube & Barbour, 1983). Moreover, women who spontaneously cited "love" as a reason for staying were less likely to leave. The more these women had invested in terms of both time and affection, the greater was their commitment to the relationship and the harder it was for them to leave it. In addition to economic dependence and psychological commitment, fear of even greater violence may also prevent the victims of spouse abuse from leaving the relationship. Dutton (1987) describes what he calls "abandonment panic" among some assaultive husbands who may react with extreme anger against the wife if she attempts to leave. The possibility of such violent reactions, says Dutton, "argues strongly for maximum protection of women who are attempting to leave abusive relationships" (p. 247).

Violence in Premarital Relationships

Research on family violence has made it clear that the use of physical power to control others is not restricted to the battlefield. Nor is the use of physical force restricted to married couples. Recently, there has been increasing concern with physical violence among dating couples. It appears that dating violence is widespread. In one study, for example, 22.3 percent of 355 undergraduates surveyed reported that violence had occurred in their relationship (Cate, Henton, Koval, Christopher, & Lloyd, 1982). The vast majority of these students indicated that only mild or moderate levels of violence had occurred (types 1 to 5 on the Conflict Tactics Scale shown in Figure 9.2). None reported the use of a knife or gun, but a few did state that beatings or threats with a weapon had taken place. The majority of those who indicated that violence had occurred in their relationships said this violence was reciprocal, with both partners engaging in physical force. Among subjects who said that only one person had used force, more females (22 percent) were said to have used force than males (10 percent).

Another study conducted on a different college campus found dating violence to be even more extensive (Sigelman, Berry, & Wiles, 1984). Among the 504 college students who participated in this survey, 53.6 percent of the men and 52.1 percent of the women stated that they had used some kind of physical force in their relationships. Although men and women were equally likely to report having used force in their relationships, more men (58.9 percent) than women (47.8 percent) indicated that their partners had used force against them. For both men and women, cohabitation was associated with having been the victim of physical violence. Indeed, it appears that cohabiting couples are more violent than either noncohabiting dating couples or married couples (Stets & Straus, 1989). Although the exact reasons for the association between cohabitation and physical violence are not clear, the in-between status of cohabitation could be an important factor. On the one hand, cohabiting couples have more extensive contact and, therefore, more opportunity for conflict than do noncohabiting dating couples. On the other hand, cohabitation is legally and, often, socially a less committed state than marriage. It seems possible that this combination of more contact but less commitment could create a greater risk for violent altercations.

Research on violence in dating relationships has also begun to focus on sexual coercion. Although exact figures differ from study to study, two general conclusions can be drawn (Muehlenhard & Linton, 1987; Poppen & Segal, 1988; Sigelman et al., 1984). First, more men than women report having used some kind of coercive behavior (psychological or physical) in an effort to obtain sex, and more women than men report having been coerced. Thus, while both men and women use physical force in their intimate relationships (and, under some circumstances at least, women may be more likely to use force than men), coercive sexual behavior appears much more prevalent among men than women. The second general conclusion that can be drawn from research on premarital sexual coercion is that more people (men *and* women) report having been coerced than having used coercion. In one study, for example, 56 percent of the men and 14 percent of the women reported they had used one or more of a set of coercive strategies (for example, "lies," "threats to end the relationship," "physical force") to initiate sexual activities in a heterosexual relationship (Poppen & Segal, 1988). But 44 percent of the men and 74 percent of the women said that at least one of these strategies had been used against them. Earlier in this chapter, it was noted that people seem to have a "powerlessness bias," being more sensitive to the power of others than to their own power. Similarly, people seem to be more aware of being coerced than of their own coercive actions.

This apparent lack of sensitivity to one's own use of coercion could contribute to a serious problem on many college campuses today: date rape (Shotland, 1989). Sometimes, of course, there is nothing subtle about rape. When a person is confronted with a gun, a knife, or a fist and told to submit sexually, this is clearly rape—regardless of whether it occurs on a date, in a marriage, or in a back alley. But coercion is not always so clear-cut. A woman can feel physically forced when the man believes he is only being appropriately sexually assertive. And a man can believe that a woman has "led him on" to a point where he should not be expected to stop. Moreover, while men do not usually think of themselves as "raped" by a woman, men can feel coerced by a woman into having sex when they don't really want to. Put two young people with healthy sexual appetites together with some alcohol, inadequate understanding of each other's concerns, and a fair amount of insecurity about their own self-worth, and you have a situation ready-made for date rape. But what if we change that scenario? What if both people agree in advance that each of them has veto power over sex? Could date rape be reduced if dating partners fully accepted that *no* really does mean *no* and puts an end to the discussion. Perhaps so. Unfortunately, it is a lot easier to get people to say the right thing than to do it. So long as our society regards male sexual activity as a form of conquest, encourages women to "play" hard-to-get, and finds it exceedingly difficult to formulate basic principles of responsible sexuality, date rape and other forms of sexual coercion will probably continue to turn the joy of sex into exploitation and abuse.

THE USES OF POWER

Throughout much of this chapter we have considered the damage that those who lack power can suffer at the hands of those who have it. Since power is always problematic and often dangerous, one might be tempted to conclude that human beings would be better off without it. But such a conclusion ignores the moral complexities of power. When we judge the *means* of power, we can find good (expert power based on broad-based understanding of a problem) and evil (physical force). Similarly, the *ends* to which power is directed can be good (to help another person develop to his or her fullest potential) or evil (to crush another person and make him or her submit to our will). If, then, we could eliminate power from human affairs, we would eliminate the power to do good as well as the power to do evil. In any event, we have no choice in the matter. Power is a fundamental aspect of the human condition; we cannot eliminate power any more than we can eliminate conflict. What we can do is to try to use whatever power we have wisely and humanely for the common good.

CHAPTER SUMMARY

Social power is the ability to influence the behavior of others and resist their influence on us.

Power as a Social Exchange Process

The Bases of Power. From a social exchange perspective, power is based on the control of valuable resources. A powerful person does not need to have direct control over these resources; indirect control can be sufficient. But power based on resources requires that the person over whom power is held values the resource. Resource power also depends on the availability of alternative sources of the resource. The greater your alternatives, the less dependent you are on any one person and the less power any one person has over you. In a dyadic relationship, power and dependency are inversely related: The one who is more dependent has less power. Many different types of resources can serve as the basis for many different types of power (see Table 9.1). The social norms within a culture also affect power. These norms may directly allocate power in the society, or they may indirectly distribute power through cultural beliefs about what is valuable in the society. Resource-based power does not necessarily operate the same way for both men and women. Traditionally, it has been expected that men would base their power on money and status, while women would base their power on love and sex. If power is based on different resources, can power be equal? To answer this question, we must consider whether the resources are equally valued, equally easy to exchange across various social inter-actions, and equally under control of the individual basing his or her power on it.

The Process of Power. The process of power refers to the way that power is expressed. Our use of language may be a subtle means of expressing power. For example, interrupting someone is usually associated with having greater social power, and males tend to interrupt females more than vice versa. The role of touch in expressing power is less clear, as touch can express dominance or solidarity. Men and women may use different power strategies. Some research has found that in heterosexual relationships, men are more likely to employ power styles that are direct and bilateral, while women are more likely to use indirect and unilateral styles. Not all research, however, has obtained this gender difference. In one study, the power styles of women were found to be more confined to stereotypically feminine tactics, while men appeared to have more freedom to use a wider variety of power styles— masculine and feminine. When men and women use nontraditional power styles, they may find themselves liked less than those who use the power styles traditionally associated with their gender. Women who speak in an assertive manner are respected more by both male and female listeners. Male listeners, however, are more influenced by a tentative female speaker than by an assertive one.

The Outcome of Power. The outcome of power can have different levels. Orchestration power refers to the authority to decide who will decide; implementation power refers to actions taken once power has been delegated. Research on decision making by husbands and wives has been criticized by some for overestimating the power of wives by mistaking implementation power for orchestration power. On the other hand, it is also possible that research, particularly that involving questionnaires, has underestimated the power of wives, since both husbands and wives may give stereotyped answers emphasizing the power of husbands. In estimating power in an intimate relationship, there may be a general tendency for people to overestimate the partner's power while underestimating their own. It is clear, however, that even today female dominance in a heterosexual relationship is less acceptable to both parties than is male dominance. Men are expected to take the initiative and women to take the role of responder. Both husbands and wives are more comfortable in either egalitarian or male-dominated relationships than in female-dominated marriages. In addition, it appears that heterosexual relationships in which the female publicly displays dominance may be less enduring.

Power and Personality

Individual differences in the need for power have been defined in two different ways. One approach defines need for power as reflecting concerns about weakness and has found that single women have an especially high need for power. Another approach defines need for power as an interest in strong, vigorous action that produces strong effects on others. On the basis of this definition of need for power, men and women have similar needs but may express them differently. In general, men's need for power has more connections with their intimate relationships than women's need for power. Among men, those high in need for power are less satisfied and less committed than those low in need for power. Men high in need for power when they were young were less likely to have wives with full-time careers when they were thirty-something. In addition, men high in need for power may inflict more physical abuse on their female partners. Men high in need for power are also more likely than men low in need for power to engage in "profligate behaviors" such as drinking and gambling; this association is not found for women. It has been suggested that women are more likely than men to express their need for power in socially constructive ways because women are socialized, more than men, to be socially responsible.

Power and Understanding

It is widely supposed that the weak need to understand the strong: That is, the one who has less power needs to understand the motives and desires of the one who has more power in order to please and placate the more powerful member of the relationship. If, then, males are more powerful in heterosexual relationships than females, there should be a positive association between female understanding of the male and progress in the relationship. This finding has been obtained in a number of studies. Most of these studies, however, failed to guard against an alternative explanation: the power of stereotypes.

Understanding Stereotypes. If both a man and a woman describe the man in a stereotyped manner, the woman will appear to understand him. This process accounts for why *randomly* paired partners were happier in their marriages when the woman could predict the man's view of himself. It is still not understood, however, why agreement on the male stereotype and *not* on the female stereotype distinguishes happy couples from unhappy ones. More recent research suggests that the gender difference in understanding may be a thing of the past.

Power and Violence

According to two national surveys conducted in 1975 and 1985, marital abuse has not changed across the decade, and it remains high. Surprisingly, a number of studies have indicated that wife-to-husband abuse is often higher than husband-to-wife abuse. It does appear that women victims are more likely to suffer serious injury than are men victims. Spouse abuse is associated with experiencing stressful events, having a low socioeconomic status, and growing up in a violent home. In the cycle of family violence, children who witness parental abuse are more likely as adults to be involved in spouse abuse (as abuser or victim) and to abuse their own children.

Why Don't They Leave? Research on spouse abuse indicates that victims are less likely to leave the relationship when they do not have adequate economic resources and when they have invested more (in terms of time and affection) in the relationship. In addition, victims may fear that if they try to leave, they will suffer even greater physical harm.

Violence in Premarital Relationships. Although different studies have obtained different estimates, it is clear that physical violence occurs in a large number of premarital relationships, especially between cohabiting couples. Sexual coercion, by physical or psychological means, is also widespread. More men than women report having used sexual coercion, but both sexes seem more aware of having been coerced by others than of their own coercive actions.

10

Jealousy

———— ❖ ————

Jealousy and Envy • The Causes of Jealousy • *Relational Factors* • *Sexual Exclusivity* • The Experience of Jealousy • *Types of Jealousy* • Gender Differences in Jealousy • *Becoming Jealous* • *Coping with Jealousy* • *Inducing Jealousy and Reacting to Rivalry* • *Perceiving a Partner's Motives* • Coping Constructively with Jealousy • Chapter Summary

*J*ealousy is like a San Andreas fault running beneath the smooth surface of an intimate relationship. Most of the time, its potential lies hidden. But when its rumblings begin, the destruction can be enormous. Consider, for example, the case of Jean Harris, once the respected headmistress of a prestigious private school. When her relationship with Herman Tarnower, known in the press as "the Scarsdale diet doctor," was threatened by his interest in a younger woman, Harris became increasingly distraught. Her work deteriorated as her jealous obsession took over more and more of her life. And, then, in a late-night confrontation at his house, she killed him. The intensity of her jealousy was apparent in a letter to Tarnower made public after his death.

HARRIS, IN LETTER TO LOVER, RAILS AT "YEARS OF BROKEN PROMISES"

The Scarscale Letter—a raging, eloquent, often obscene letter that Jean Harris sent Dr. Herman Tarnower last March 10, the day she shot him dead—was finally made public today, and its contents shocked a courtroom that by now would have seemed inured to shock.

There were charges that Lynne Tryforos, Harris' rival for Tarnower's affections, had not only destroyed $1,000 worth of Harris' clothing, but also had ruined a silk dress belonging to Harris by covering it with human excrement. There was the allegation that someone—probably Tryforos— had sent Harris a copy of Tarnower's will, with Harris' name "scratched out" and Tryforos' name written there instead.

There was, throughout, obscenity and loathing, both for herself and for the doctor. . . . Most of all there was rage directed at Tryforos, particularly at the news that the younger woman, not Jean Harris, was to be Tarnower's date for an upcoming testimonial dinner that spring.

Washington Post, February 5, 1981

The Harris-Tarnower case received massive press coverage because of the social prominence of those involved. Most jealousy-induced homicides get far less attention. A short paragraph in the newspaper or a 45-second sound-bite on the TV news is often all that is provided. Usually, the word "jealousy" is not even mentioned, but we can easily infer it from accounts such as, "Ex-husband shoots former wife, then kills self, during quarrel about ex-wife's new boyfriend."

Fortunately, jealousy-induced homicides and suicides are rare events that appear to be decreasing in our society (Stearns, 1989). Jealousy does not usually lead to a loss of life. It does, however, frequently create great psychological distress. Being jealous can be a state of torment and suspicion; being the focus of someone's jealousy can be a nightmare of unreasonable demands and uncertainty about what is coming next. Jealousy, says the *Song of Solomon*, "is cruel as the grave." It is also, in Shakespeare's phrase, a monster.

> O! beware, my lord, of jealousy;
> It is the green-eyed monster which doth
>   mock
> The meat it feeds on: that cuckold lives
>   in bliss
> Who, certain of his fate, loves not his
>   wronger;
> But, O! what damned minutes tells he
>   o'er
> Who dotes, yet doubts; suspects, yet
>   soundly loves!
>
>   William Shakespeare
>   *Othello*

In this chapter, we will examine some research that investigates the nature of this monster, and that may help us develop some ways to tame it.

JEALOUSY AND ENVY

According to Ellis and Weinstein (1986), jealousy can be viewed in terms of the potential disruption of a desired social exchange. They define jealousy as:

> . . . the emotion that people experience when control over valued resources that flow through an attachment to another person is perceived to be in jeopardy because their partner might want or might actually give and/or receive some of these resources from a third party. (p. 341)

In other words, jealousy is the emotional reaction to a perceived threat to an existing relationship. If you believe that your partner is only involved with you and is not interested in anyone or anything else, you cannot be jealous. More realistically, since virtually all partners do have at least some other interests, you will not be jealous as long as it is clear to you that you are considerably more important to your partner than these other interests. Jealousy becomes a possible reaction only when a person believes that some other interest may seriously detract from the relationship or replace it. Typically, jealousy is created by the perception that one's partner is attracted to someone else (Buunk & Bringle, 1987). But the threat is not always social. Female college students, for example, report feeling jealous about their boyfriend's time involvement with hobbies and family (Hansen, 1985).

Some investigators have argued that it is necessary to distinguish jealousy from other reactions such as envy and rivalry. For example, Bryson (1977) has distinguished among the three reactions by formulating the concise definitions that are illustrated in Figure 10.1. Jealousy is diagrammed in the first section of this figure: If person A and person C are already in a relationship, an attempt by person B to establish a relationship with C can cause A to be jealous. This process differs from envy, which is a person's desire to obtain something that someone else already possesses. Thus, where A is jealous in the first section of Figure 10.1, B would be envious; the second section of the figure reverses these roles, with A now envious and B jealous. Finally, there is rivalry, in which two people compete for something neither one possesses. In the third section of the figure, both persons A and B are rivals for the attention and affection of C.

Recently, the utility of a sharp distinction between envy and jealousy has been questioned. Salovey and Rodin (1986, 1989) agree with Bryson's description (as outlined in Figure 10.1) of the basic psychological conditions for envy and jealousy: the desire to have versus the possibility of losing. But they maintain that both envy and jealousy involve similar emotions, though the intensity of these emotions is

Jealousy

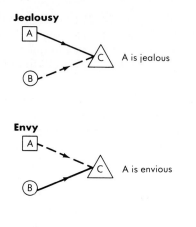

Envy

Rivalry

——— = An existing relationship

— — — = A desired relationship

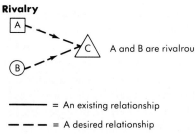

FIGURE 10.1
Jealousy, envy, and rivalry. (Adapted from Bryson, 1977.)

greater for jealousy than for envy. For these investigators, envy is best considered a special case of jealousy, "social comparison jealousy" in contrast to "social relations jealousy." This view of the relationship between envy and jealousy is controversial and conflicts with research results indicating that distinctly different clusters of emotions are involved (Smith, Kim, & Parrott, 1988).

Regardless of the degree of emotional similarity between envy and jealousy, Salovey and Rodin are surely correct in pointing out that the two are often intermingled. Although we describe Jean Harris as jealous in terms of her reaction to the threatened loss of her relationship with Herman Tarnower, we would also describe her as envious of Lynne Tryforos' apparent success in obtaining the doctor's affections. To see how envy is a necessary part of any love triangle, consider the pattern of events associated with envious reactions (Salovey & Rodin, 1984): a negative evaluation of your own performance in an important area of endeavor coupled with a good performance in this area by someone else. The more we value an *interpersonal* endeavor—such as a relationship—the more envy we should feel toward someone who replaces us in it.

The emphasis placed by Salovey and Rodin on the importance of the area of endeavor allows us to understand why we do not go around consumed with envy all the time. If you do not care about sports, you will not feel envious of someone who wins a gold medal at the Olympics. Even if you are a very good athlete in basketball, you probably will not feel envious of those who win the gold for track-and-field events. To feel envious, we must value what the other person has and want it for ourselves.

But the intensity of envious feelings may depend on more than the value we place on the other person's possession or accomplishment. According to the *self-evaluation maintenance* model, developed by Abraham Tesser (1988), our relationship with the other person is also important. Tesser maintains that strong feelings of envy are particularly likely when someone we are close to has a great success in an area of endeavor that we value highly for ourselves. The intensity of envy should be considerably less in regard to successful others with whom we do *not* have close ties. On the other hand, when someone we are close to has a great success in an area that is *not* relevant to our own feelings of self-esteem, we can BIRG—bask in the reflected glory (Cialdini et al., 1976). Tesser's model can be applied to both family dynamics and friendship choices (Campbell & Tesser, 1985). As expected, siblings have the most difficulty getting along when they are close in age and differ greatly on important abilities (Tesser, 1980). Unlike family members, friends are a matter of choice, and, consistent with Tesser's model, we prefer those who shine in *their* area but not in *ours* (Tesser, Campbell, & Smith, 1984).

Self-evaluation processes may also play a role in jealousy. There is some evidence that people experience jealousy and feel more anger when they lose a romantic partner to another person rather than when they lose a partner as a result of events such as rejection or geographical relocation (Mathes, Adams, & Davies, 1985). But not all losses to another person are equal. Which do you think would hurt more: losing a romantic partner to a perfect stranger or to a best friend? According to the SEM model, the latter should hurt more because such a loss would be a worse blow to our self-esteem. We compare ourselves more readily with those who are close to us, and if we are on the losing end, suffer more.

T*HE CAUSES OF JEALOUSY*

Just as the desire to protect self-esteem may influence reactions to a partner's attraction to someone else, so has the level of self-esteem been viewed as contributing to concerns about a partner's commitment to the existing relationship. According to this perspective, a person who has low self-esteem and thinks badly of himself or herself is more likely to fear that any existing relationship is vulnerable to threat: "Why would anyone stay with *me*?" Though such a relationship between the potential for jealousy and level of self-esteem seems a reasonable possibility, the evidence for it is not very strong. Some research has reported a general association between having low self-esteem and being jealous (Bringle & Evenbeck, 1979). But some studies have found this relationship only for males (White, 1981c) or only for females (Buunk, 1982); and some research has not been able to demonstrate any relationship at all between self-esteem and jealousy (White, 1981b).

Perhaps the reason for such confusing and contradictory results is that the hypothesis linking self-esteem to jealousy is *person specific* rather than *relationship specific*. Since jealousy can only occur within the context of a relationship, general self-esteem (based on our overall feelings about ourselves) may not be very informative. Instead, what should be important is relational self-esteem—how we feel about ourselves in regard to our intimate relationships.

Relational Factors

Research that has taken this approach has yielded more consistent findings. For example, White (1981b, 1981c) has found that jealousy is strongly related to feelings of inadequacy in a relationship. You may be a whiz at work or in school or on the athletic field, but if you have a feeling of inadequacy in an intimate relationship, you will be more likely to experience jealousy in regard to this relationship. Jealousy is also more likely to occur when one person believes that he or she is putting more effort into the relationship than the other person is (White, 1981b). When we feel we are more involved than our partner, we may be more vulnerable to jealousy because we have doubts about our partner's commitment.

Dependency on a relationship may be particularly important in setting the stage for jealousy (Bringle & Buunk, 1986). Berscheid maintains that regardless of our partner's involvement, the more we depend on the relationship to make us happy, the more susceptible to jealousy we will be (Berscheid, 1983; Berscheid & Fei, 1977). When a relationship matters a great deal to us, any threat to it can be more costly. Some supporting evidence for this contention comes from Buunk's research (1982). In his study, subjects who described themselves as more emotionally dependent on their relationships (e.g., "I can't imagine what my life would be without my partner"; "It would be difficult for me to find any other person with whom I would be so happy as with my present partner") were more likely to say that they would feel jealous if their partner became interested in someone else. Dependency on a relationship may also be closely related to possessiveness (Pinto & Hollandsworth, 1984; see Table 10.1). Presumably, this association goes both ways: Those who are dependent may be more likely to become

TABLE 10.1 THE POSSESSIVENESS SCALE

For each of the items below, indicate how you generally feel, think, or act in situations as they apply to a current personal relationship or a past relationship that was important to you at that time. If a certain situation has not occurred, answer as you think you would respond in that situation. There are no right or wrong answers. Your response should *not* reflect how you think you should act or how you would like to act. Please respond to each item by choosing one of the following descriptions:

Never or Rarely	Seldom	Sometimes	Often	Almost Always or Always
A	B	C	D	E

1. Even though we have a close relationship, I still see my old friends.*
2. I discourage him/her from developing interests of his/her own.
3. I feel jealous when he/she keeps in touch with old friends.
4. I encourage him/her to take off and do things by himself/herself.*
5. I encourage him/her to make new friends*.
6. When we are at a party with old friends, I feel OK even if he/she spends most of the time with other people.*
7. I feel that allowing him/her to maintain old friendships hurts our relationship.
8. When we are apart I feel unloved and lonely.
9. I feel secure about our relationship even though he/she makes new friends of the opposite sex.*
10. I feel hurt when he/she asks to be alone.
11. I feel that allowing him/her to maintain old friendships helps our relationship.*
12. When we are apart I worry that he/she will find someone new.
13. I discourage him/her from making new friends.
14. I find myself wanting to break off the relationship when he/she goes away for a week or more.
15. I do not like the idea of his/her going to a party if I cannot be there too.
16. I feel guilty about making new friends of the opposite sex.
17. I find it easy to trust him/her when we are apart for a few days.*
18. I find that making new friends helps our relationship.*
19. I get jealous when he/she develops interests on his/her own.
20. I gain personal satisfaction following interests on my own.*
21. I spend so much time with him/her that I do not have time to make new friends.

For items without an asterisk, score responses on a five-point scale ranging from "never or rarely" = 1 and "almost always or always" = 5. For items with an asterisk, score responses on the reversed scale: "never or rarely" = 5 and "almost always or always" = 1. Higher scores indicate higher levels of possessiveness.

SOURCE: From Pinto & Hollandsworth, 1984.

possessive, and those who are possessive may be more likely to become dependent. Either way, the need to maintain close and exclusive ties with the partner could increase the likelihood of jealousy.

Sexual Exclusivity

The desire for exclusive *sexual* ties with the partner often appears to play a crucial role in determining whether jealousy occurs. Compare, for example, the following two descriptions.

> Sandy and Chris are very good friends. They share an apartment together, spend lots of time together, and have many common interests. They also usually eat dinner together and enjoy telling each other about the day's events. One evening, however, Chris called Sandy about 6 P.M. to say that they would not be able to have dinner together that evening. Instead, Chris was going out with a former lover who had just returned to town.

> Sandy and Chris are lovers. They share an apartment together, spend lots of time together, and have many common interests. They also usually eat dinner together and enjoy telling each other about the day's events. One evening, however, Chris called Sandy about 6 P.M. to say that they would not be able to have dinner together that evening. Instead, Chris was going out with a former lover who had just returned to town.

Who do you think would be more likely to be jealous: Sandy the good friend or Sandy the lover? It seems obvious that most people would think that Sandy the lover would be more likely to be jealous. The inconvenience may be the same for both the friend and the lover; the actual disappointment at missing dinner together may also be the same. But only Sandy the lover could perceive a threat to the sexual exclusivity of the relationship with Chris. It is this kind of threat that seems to produce the most frequent feelings of jealousy, the most extreme emotional reactions to jealousy, and the most destructive behaviors as a result of jealousy (Reiss, 1986).

Since threat to sexual exclusivity appears such a crucial factor in inciting jealousy, a person's beliefs about sexual exclusivity should affect how likely he or she is to become jealous. People who value sexual exclusivity in their romantic relationships should be more likely to experience jealousy than people who feel comfortable with sexual *nonex-*clusivity. And, usually, this is the case. As people's desire for and expectation of sexual exclusivity increase, the likelihood that they will become jealous also increases (White 1981b, 1981c). But if people are involved or intend to become involved with someone else besides their primary partner, they are less likely to react jealously to their partner's extra-relationship involvements (Buunk, 1982). In addition, when asked how upset they would be about their partner's engaging in jealousy-provoking behavior with another person, individuals who had established relationships with partners who were already involved in another relationship reported a lower level of potential distress than those who were involved in what they believed to be a monogamous relationship (Bringle & Boebinger, 1990).

All of the studies just described examined people's reactions after a real or imagined jealously-provoking event had occurred. Thus, given a threat to a relationship, a stronger expectation of sexual exclusivity is associated with greater jealousy. But what if we approach this issue in the abstract, without tying it to any specific event? When Pines and Aronson (1983) surveyed people about their beliefs about relationships and their experiences of jealousy, they found that the more strongly people believed in monogamy, the *less* jealousy they reported. At first blush, this finding seems to contradict those obtained by other investigators. Actually, it doesn't. People who strongly believe in monogamy are likely to select partners who share this belief. In general, such couples will give each other less reason to feel jealous. Thus, a belief in monogamy and sexual exclusivity can cut both ways with jealousy. On the one hand, it should reduce the probability of selecting a partner who provokes jealousy by getting involved sexually with someone else. On the other hand, if such an involvement does take place, greater jealousy may well be experienced.

Although individuals differ a great deal in how important sexual exclusivity is to them, it is possible to view the value placed on sexual exclusivity as determined more by the culture than by the individuals who live within it. Some social scientists have suggested that sexual jealousy is essentially a cultural phenomenon, only occurring in societies that connect a sense of pride to the exclusivity of a sexual relationship (Bernard, 1977; Hatfield & Walster, 1978). Based on a survey of anthropological research records, Hupka's (1981) cross-cultural investigation provides some support for this notion. Hupka found that jealous behavior among males (there were insufficient data to examine female jealousy) was greater in those cultures that allowed personal ownership of property, valued sexual monogamy within marriage, and emphasized the importance of marriage for economic survival and social approval. In contrast, male jealousy was less severe in cultures that viewed property as belonging to the larger familial or communal group, placed few restrictions on sexual gratification before or after marriage, and believed that "matrimony was not a necessary condition for the individual to function effectively as an adult" (p. 331). Thus, being jealous appears to rest, at least in part, upon living in a society that promotes both individual ownership and intense pair-bonding.

*T*HE EXPERIENCE OF JEALOUSY

As we have seen, the causes of jealousy are complex, involving personal, relational, and cultural factors. The experience of jealousy is also a complex psychological process. White has outlined several major components in the experience of jealousy (White, 1981b: White & Mullen, 1989).

The first component in the experience of jealousy is "primary appraisal." Primary appraisal is the process by which an individual perceives that there is a threat to an existing relationship; it is affected by any and all factors that influence this perception. One way to think about primary appraisal is as a series of jealousy *thresholds,* or tolerance levels. When a given threshold is reached or exceeded, the experience of jealousy becomes more likely.

One set of thresholds involves the relationship factors already discussed. Certain *qualities of a relationship* (e.g., feeling insecure about it, feeling dependent on it) make it more likely that a person will perceive a threat to the relationship and, thus, feel jealous. The *type of relationship* is also important. As indicated, jealousy is more likely to occur with a lover than a friend: The threshold for the perception of threat to a romantic and/or sexual relationship appears to be lower than the threshold for the perception of threat to a friendship. Since we allow a friend more freedom in relationships with other people than we do a lover, we are less likely to perceive our friend's involvements with others as threatening that relationship.

Another set of thresholds involves characteristics of the threat. *Severity of the threat* can range from low to high. Consider, for example, the physical attractiveness of a person that our partner appears to be interested in. Most of us would be more likely to perceive a threat to our relationship if this other person were highly physically attractive than if the other person were quite unattractive physically. A variety of other characteristics can also contribute to the perceived severity of the threat: the other person's social style, intelligence, prestige, etc. In general, anything about the other person that makes him or her an especially desirable person to be with will increase the perceived severity of the threat that person can pose to our existing relationship. Jealousy is also affected by the *type of threat.* Sometimes we perceive the threat to be sexual in nature, believing our partner to be interested in a sexual relationship with the other person. Sometimes we perceive the threat to be to our emotional relationship with our partner; sometimes we perceive it to be to the time we spend with our partner in social activities. As noted earlier, the threat need not come from another individual. Nonsocial activities such as work, leisure, sports activities, and even household tasks can all threaten a relationship if we perceive them as taking time or interest away from our interaction with our partner.

The notion of a threshold is especially helpful when we consider the type of threat. Perceptions of sexual threats may have an especially low threshold: All we may need is the barest hint that our partner is interested in someone else sexually to become jealous. On the other hand, with the very same partner, our threshold for nonsocial threats may be fairly high. It may not be until we find ourselves sitting home alone night after night that we actually feel jealous of our partner's commitment to his or her work or studies.

During primary appraisal, our perceptions about the relationship and the threat will influence each other. If, for example, we feel very secure about a relationship, it will take a very strong threat for us to become jealous. On the other hand, if we feel uncertain and insecure about the relationship, we may become jealous in response to fairly weak threats. Indeed, it is possible for someone who feels very insecure about a very important relationship to perceive threats to the relationship when none actually exists.

Once a threat to an existing relationship is perceived, "secondary appraisal" begins. In secondary appraisal, we try to understand the situation better and begin to think about ways to cope with it. We may review our evidence that there actually is a threat (e.g., "Did he really seem all that interested in her?"; "Maybe she really was working late that evening"), and we may go over the "counterevidence" of our partner's enduring attachment to us (e.g., "We had such a wonderful time together last weekend"; "He was the one who wanted to live together").

When secondary appraisal is described in terms of reviewing the evidence and counterevidence, it sounds like a rational and constructive process. Unfortunately, secondary appraisal can also involve "catastrophic thinking," where the person rushes to the most extreme and worst possible conclusion. Here are some examples of catastrophic thinking in a jealousy situation:

> He was really interested in her. I'm sure of it. And now he'll leave me and never come back, and I'll be all alone, and I'll never be happy again.

> She wasn't at work. I'm sure she was out with someone else. She's cheating on me and making a fool of me. I bet everyone knows about it and is laughing at me.

Such catastrophic thinking goes far beyond the available evidence and is inherently irrational in its conclusions: "I'll *never* be happy again"; "*everyone* knows about it." But people experiencing jealousy are usually quite unaware that their thinking is irrational. For the individual, his or her thoughts become part of reality and, therefore, lead to extreme emotional reactions.

This emotional reaction is the third component of the jealousy experience. The possible emotional states involved in jealousy are enormously diverse. A person's emotional response can vary in intensity from mild twinges of feeling to total absorption in extreme jealousy. The type of emotion we feel when we are jealous can also vary. Most of us think of jealousy as involving only negative emotions: anger at the partner and/or the third party; anxiety about the possibility of losing the relationship with the partner; depression and sadness about the loss we experience. Although these may be the most typical emotional responses, the range of possible emotional responses is much larger.

In Pines and Aronson's (1983) extensive descriptive study of jealousy, their subjects reported having positive feelings when they were jealous (such as "excitement," "love," "feeling alive") as well as negative reactions ("emotional distress," "physical distress," "social embarrassment"). Being the focus of jealousy was also associated with a wide range of emotional responses: feeling good, anxious, happy, pitiful, angry, confused, superior, victimized, passionate. In fact, of the twenty-seven different feelings listed on the questionnaire that subjects com-

Jealousy sometimes involves catastrophic thinking in which the person rushes to the most extreme and worst possible conclusions. This kind of thinking may well increase the likelihood of destructive actions. (Harriet Gans/The Image Works)

pleted, every one was endorsed by at least one person as describing a way he or she had felt when the focus of jealousy. Thus, jealousy can produce a large and varied range of emotional reactions, and though it is more often experienced as a negative event than as a positive one, not all the feelings connected with jealousy are unpleasant.

After a person perceives a threat to an existing relationship (primary appraisal) and reacts cognitively (secondary appraisal) and emotionally (emotional reactions) to this threat, the next step in the jealousy experience is that of coping with the situation. Coping should be affected by all of the prior three components. We will cope differently with a severe threat than with a relatively weak one. We will cope differently if our assessment of the situation involves catastrophic thoughts than if we are more rational in our view of what is happening. Finally, our coping response will be affected by the type and intensity of the emotional response we are experiencing.

Though there are many specific ways that people can cope with jealousy, Bryson (1977) has suggested that all coping responses to jealousy can be categorized in terms of two major goal-oriented behaviors:

1. Attempts to maintain the relationship
2. Attempts to maintain self-esteem

Table 10.2 gives some examples of the way that this two-factor analysis would classify various types of behaviors that attempt to cope with jealousy. It should be apparent from these examples that neither type of coping is, in and of itself, more desirable than the other. Both can lead to positive, constructive behaviors or to negative, destructive behaviors.

The last component in the jealousy experience involves the outcome of the person's coping response. The outcome of coping must be considered at three different levels. First, what was the effect of the person's coping response on the perceived threat? Was the person able to reduce or eliminate the threat? Second, what was the effect of the person's

TABLE 10.2 TWO-FACTOR ANALYSIS OF COPING WITH JEALOUSY: TYPES OF BEHAVIORS

		RELATIONSHIP MAINTAINING	
		Yes	No
ESTEEM MAINTAINING	Yes	Negotiating a mutually acceptable solution	Verbal/physical attacks against the partner
	No	Clinging to the relationship	Self-destructive behaviors

SOURCE: Adapted from Bryson, 1977.

coping response on the individuals involved: the person, the partner, the other individual? And, third, coping must be evaluated in terms of its effects on the relationship. Has the relationship been maintained in its previous form, has it changed, or has it ended?

One of the most unfortunate aspects of jealousy and the way we try to cope with it is that we can easily end up winning the battle but losing the war. A jealous person who becomes enraged and violent can terrorize the partner into withdrawing from a potential alternative relationship. However, not only does this type of jealous behavior harm the partner, but in the long run, it is likely to make the partner even more interested in other relationships. Similarly, a jealous person can successfully beg and plead with the partner to give up another relationship, but such clinging will only decrease the person's feeling of self-worth and, in the long run, will probably reduce even further the partner's attraction to the existing relationship.

Thus, when we consider alternative ways to cope with jealousy, it is important to consider both the short-term and long-term consequences of our coping responses. A constructive coping response to jealousy will provide some immediate relief from the pain of jealousy, but it will also be sensitive to long-term effects such as the welfare of the inviduals who are involved and the quality of the relationship. In Bryson's terms, *both* self-esteem and the relationship are important.

Looking over White's model of the jealousy process, you can see that he includes cognitive (primary and secondary appraisal), emotional, and behavioral (coping) factors as contributing to the final outcome. Recently, Pfeiffer and Wong (1989) have developed what they call the Multidimensional Jealousy Scale (MJS) to measure these three factors. The items from this scale are reprinted in Table 10.3. When Pfeiffer and Wong correlated subjects' responses to the MJS with their responses on Rubin's (1973) Loving and Liking Scales, they found that increased loving and liking were associated with less frequent experiences of cognitive jealousy, and increased liking was associated with less frequent jealous actions. In general, then, the more we love or like a person, the less we will experience jealous thoughts or act in a jealous manner. The correlates of emotional jealousy are, however, more complex. As we would expect given the role of dependency and the desire for sexual exclusivity in the jealousy process, higher scores on the loving scale were associated with a higher MJS emotion score. Those who said they were more in love also said they would experience more distress if a romantic partner engaged in jealousy-provoking behavior. Interestingly, however, higher liking scores were associated with fewer jealous feelings. Thus, across all the components of jealousy measured by the MJS, liking was more strongly and consistently associated with lower levels of jealousy than was loving. Since subjects responded to all of the measures in terms of a person with whom they were having, or

TABLE 10.3 MULTIDIMENSIONAL JEALOUSY SCALE

Cognitive: How often do you have the following thoughts about X?

1. I suspect that X is secretly seeing someone of the opposite sex.
2. I am worried that some member of the opposite sex may be chasing after X.
3. I suspect that X may be attracted to someone else.
4. I suspect that X may be physically intimate with another member of the opposite sex behind my back.
5. I think that some members of the opposite sex may be romantically interested in X.
6. I am worried that someone of the opposite sex is trying to seduce X.
7. I think that X is secretly developing an intimate relationship with someone of the opposite sex.
8. I suspect that X is crazy about members of the opposite sex.

Emotional: How would you emotionally react to the following situations?

1. X comments to you on how great looking a particular member of the opposite sex is.
2. X shows a great deal of interest or excitement in talking to someone of the opposite sex.
3. X smiles in a very friendly manner to someone of the opposite sex.
4. A member of the opposite sex is trying to get close to X all the time.
5. X is flirting with someone of the opposite sex.
6. Someone of the opposite sex is dating X.
7. X hugs and kisses someone of the opposite sex.
8. X works very closely with a member of the opposite sex (in school or office).

Behavioural: How often do you engage in the following behaviours?

1. I look through X's drawers, handbag, or pockets.
2. I call X unexpectedly, just to see if he or she is there.
3. I question X about previous or present romantic relationships.
4. I say something nasty about someone of the opposite sex if X shows an interest in that person.
5. I question X about his or her telephone calls.
6. I question X about his or her whereabouts.
7. I join in whenever I see X talking to a member of the opposite sex.
8. I pay X a surprise visit just to see who is with him or her.

SOURCE: Pfeiffer & Wong, 1989.

had had, a strong romantic relationship, this pattern of results does not reflect the difference between a loving romance and a liking friendship. Instead, it may parallel the distinction made in Chapter 4 between passionate and companionate love. Relationships built on trust and respect may well be more resistant to jealousy than those built on passionate attachment and obsessive desire.

Types of Jealousy

A number of different types of jealousy have been studied by social scientists. For example, White (1981b) emphasizes the difference between *chronic jealousy* and *relationship jealousy*. When we study chronic jealousy, we try to find people who identify themselves as feeling jealous across a variety of specific, actual relationships. The study of chronic jealousy is, then, the study of jealousy as a personality characteristic, which is stronger for some people than for others. Although it is probably true that some people tend to become jealous more easily (e.g., at a lower threshold of threat) and more frequently than others, dispositional factors appear to be relatively weak predictors of the cognitive and emotional responses involved in jealousy (Bringle & Evenbeck, 1979; Bush, Bush, & Jennings, 1988). In contrast, the study of relationship jealousy takes a more situational approach. This research focuses on those factors in a relationship that promote or inhibit feelings of jealousy. From this perspective, jealousy is not seen as a trait that some people have and others do not, but as a reaction that many people can have depending on the prevailing conditions in a relationship.

Two other types of jealousy are distinguished by Buunk (1982). *Actual jealousy* is the jealousy that a person is actually experiencing at the current time or has actually experienced sometime in the past. *Anticipated jealousy* is jealousy that a person expects to experience if jealousy-provoking events occurred in the relationship. When we study anticipated jealousy, we are studying people's predictions about how and why they would feel jealous. Although such predictions are interesting in their own right, they are not the same as the actual experience of jealousy. We may think some things would make us jealous that, when they actually occur, do not. We may also feel "Oh, that wouldn't make *me* jealous" but then later find out that, in fact, it does!

Finally, there is the difference between *naturally occurring jealousy* and *induced jealousy*. Naturally occurring jealousy just happens; no one intends it or makes an effort to bring it about. Induced jealousy, on the other hand, is deliberately created; a person acts in certain ways that are designed to make his or her partner jealous, presumably in order to increase the partner's attachment to the relationship. Induced jealousy will be considered in more detail in the following section on gender differences in jealousy.

GENDER DIFFERENCES IN JEALOUSY

Although all of us have probably experienced jealousy at some point in our lives, there is considerable evidence that such experiences may vary depending on whether we are male or female. Clinical observations, made by therapists during their work with clients who are experiencing jealousy, have long emphasized how jealousy differs between the sexes. Summarizing these clinical accounts, Clanton and Smith (1977) note five areas where males and females experience and cope with jealousy in different ways. From the presentation of their summary in Table 10.4, you can see that these differences closely follow more general sex-role stereotypes. According to these clinical observations, men react to jealousy in an active, angry, competitive way. Women, on the other hand, exhibit dependency and self-punishing reactions. This contrast in the ways that men and women experience jealousy has also been demonstrated in the more carefully controlled research described in the following sections.

Becoming Jealous

Buunk's (1982) finding that both men and women said they *expected* to be more jealous if they were highly dependent on the relationship has been noted. However, when White (1981b, 1981c) obtained people's reports of their actual jealousy experiences, his results indicated that different types of dependency on the relationship are important for men and women. For women, jealousy was associated with the expectation that it would be difficult to obtain another relationship if the current one should end. For men, jealousy was positively correlated with "self-evaluative dependency," the degree to which the man's self-esteem was affected by his partner's judgments.

TABLE 10.4 A SUMMARY OF CLINICAL OBSERVATIONS OF GENDER DIFFERENCES IN JEALOUSY

	Men	*Women*
Feelings of jealousy	Deny	Acknowledge
Expression of jealousy	Rage and violence (often followed by depression)	Depression (crying, lack of sleep, etc.)
Focus of jealousy	Sexual activity of partner	Emotional involvement of partner
Blame	Partner or other person	Self
Become	Competitive with other person	Cling to partner

SOURCE: Adapted from Clanton & Smith, 1977.

Thus, while relationship dependency is a major factor in jealousy for both men and women, their exact concerns are somewhat different. Women emphasize the notion of having *a* relationship. If they are confident they could obtain a satisfactory replacement, they are less likely to experience jealousy in the present relationship. Men, on the other hand, focus more directly on their own self-esteem. If they do not see their partner's attraction to others as implying anything negative about themselves (e.g., "She'll just go for whoever can sweet-talk her the most"), they are less likely to become jealous.

Coping with Jealousy

This distinction between a focus on the relationship versus a focus on self-esteem is exactly parallel to Bryson's (1977) two types of coping responses (see Table 10.2). Not surprisingly, then, it appears that the same pattern of gender-linked differences occurs when people cope with their feelings of jealousy. In one of the few experimental studies of jealousy, male and female subjects watched a videotape depicting a jealousy situation (Shettel-Neuber, Bryson, & Young, 1978). Males saw a film in which a male tried to take a female away from another male; females watched a film in which a female attempted to take a male away from another female. Half the subjects saw a film in which the third party was highly attractive physically; for the other half, the third party was shown as rather unattractive. All subjects were instructed to try to put themselves in the position of the person whose relationship was being threatened by the third party and to report how they would feel if they were this person.

There were a number of gender differences in subjects' reactions to the videotapes:

- Men were more likely than women to say that they would:
  be angry with themselves
  get drunk or high
  verbally threaten the other man
  feel flattered by the other man's attraction to the partner
  feel "turned on" by the partner
- Women were more likely than men to say that they would:
  cry when alone
  try to make themselves more attractive to the partner
  try to make the partner think they didn't care

Perhaps the most interesting finding in the study by Shettel-Neuber et al. was an interaction between sex of the subject and attractiveness of the rival. Specifically, this interaction was found on the reactions of (1) going out with other people and (2) becoming more sexually aggressive with other people. When the third party was unattractive (and, presumably, less of a threat), males and females did not differ in how likely they thought they would be to have these two reactions. When, however, the third party was attractive, men said they would be highly likely to start going out with and become more sexually aggressive with other women. Women said they would be *un*likely to try to get involved with other men.

Overall, the findings from this study suggest that males and females differ a great deal in the ways in which they cope with jealousy. The behavior of males appears "property-oriented"—getting angry because someone is trying to take away a valued "possession," but also feeling flattered that someone else sees this "possession" as valuable enough to try to get it. When, however, the threat is severe, men consider leaving the relationship, presumably trying to repair the damage to their self-esteem by establishing their attractiveness to others. In contrast, women seem to focus almost exclusively on trying to preserve the existing relationship, and the effect of a severe threat is to make them withdraw from even the possibility of having other relationships.

Inducing Jealousy and Reacting to Rivalry

The greater emphasis that women place on preserving an existing relationship is also reflected in attempts to induce jealousy. When White (1980a) asked subjects if they had ever tried to make their partners jealous, many more females than males said that they had tried to induce jealousy. Moreover, the women who were the most likely to report having tried to induce jealousy were those who said they were more involved in the relationship than their partners were. It seems, then, that when women feel insecure in their heterosexual relationships, they may try to increase their attractiveness to their partner by getting their partner to feel jealous.

Although no one has systematically studied the effects of induced jealousy, it seems unlikely to be a very successful tactic. First of all, an underinvolved man is, by definition, not very dependent on the relationship. He may well also not be very dependent on his partner's judgments, making it relatively easy for him to perceive her jealousy-inducing behavior as reflecting her poor taste rather than constituting a threat to his self-esteem. Second, what if it does work? The research we have just examined indicates that men frequently respond to jealousy by becoming more interested, not in their partner, but in other women. And, finally, what if it really works and the underinvolved man becomes more involved? The implication we could draw from this kind of involvement is that the man is *not* involved with his woman partner, but, instead, is rivalrous and competitive with the other man in the induced-jealousy scenario.

Thompson and Richardson (1983) have called such rivalry between males over a female the "rooster effect." In their research, male subjects were excluded from an interaction between two other supposed subjects (in fact, experimental confederates) whom they had never met before. The person who initiated the exclusion of the subject was in some cases a male, in others a female. Sometimes the third party (who went along with the exclusion but took no active part in it) was male, sometimes female. All subjects were then given an opportunity to retaliate against the pair that had excluded them. As part of what was presented as an experiment on reaction times, each subject was allowed to set the level of electric shock the pair would receive. In this situation, the rooster effect was a clear motive for revenge. The highest level of shock was administered by subjects when the initiator of the exclusion was male and the other person was female.

Thus, the script seems written in advance for the characters to play their assigned parts. Men react with anger when other men cut them out of an interaction with a woman—even when they have never met that woman and do not have any kind of relationship with her. Moreover, as we have seen, women try to elicit such anger, under the mistaken impression that it says something about their unique value to their male partner. During the experimental demonstration of the rooster effect, no one was hurt; the shocks were not harmful and, for the most part, not even painful. In real life, it may not work out that way.

Perceiving a Partner's Motives

One of the factors that may affect our experience of jealousy involves our perception of our partner's motives for being attracted to someone else. In his investigation of this issue, White (1981a) examined four possible motives:

1. The desire for sexual variety
2. Attraction to the nonsexual qualities of another person
3. Dissatisfaction with the existing relationship
4. The desire for a relationship that will involve more commitment than the existing one does

The heterosexual couples who volunteered to participate in this research were asked: How important would each of these factors be to your partner for dating or seeing someone of the opposite sex other than

Women appear to be more likely than men to become jealous about a partner's nonsexual relationships. (Richard Wood/The Picture Cube)

you? Subjects were also asked how jealous they were in their current relationships.

A number of gender differences were found on the two major topics of White's research. First, women were more likely than men to see sexual motives, nonsexual attraction, and dissatisfaction with the existing relationship as reasons why their partner would get involved with someone else. Male subjects were more likely to think that their partner would get involved with someone else as part of searching for a more committed relationship. Thus, women perceived their male partner as having multiple potential motives for becoming attracted to another person. Men, on the other hand, emphasized their partner's desires for a committed relationship, apparently believing that if they would not provide this, their partner might go elsewhere.

White then examined the association between perceived motives of the partner and one's own jealousy. For both men and women, the more important they thought that sexual attraction to others and dissatisfaction with the existing relationship would be in motivating their partner to become involved with someone else, the more jealous they said they were. However, the importance of nonsexual attraction to another person as a potential motive was related only to females' reported jealousy. These findings suggest that both men and women experience jealousy if they see their partner getting involved with another person for sexual reasons, and support the earlier description of the major role of sexual threat in eliciting a jealous reaction. Jealousy also seems more likely for both men and women if they see their partner as dissatisfied with the existing relationship. In this case, attraction to another person is probably viewed as being not just a "passing fancy," but, rather, an indication of the partner's desire to terminate the existing relationship.

But why were nonsexual attractions as a potential motive only related to females' jealousy? Women, it appears, are concerned about any attractive aspect of a potential rival: sexual or nonsexual. The men in White's study, however, seemed primarily concerned about sexual attraction. White suggests that this difference may be produced by women's placing more value on the emotional, nonsexual aspects of a relationship than do men. Men's more exclusive concern with sexual threats to their relationships may also reflect the way that our society has tied men's self-worth to their sexual control over women. Thus, a female partner's sexual interest in another man may be felt as especially humiliating and threatening.

COPING CONSTRUCTIVELY WITH JEALOUSY

Although men and women may become jealous for different reasons and may react differently once they are jealous, many people—male *and* female—want to gain more control over jealousy. Jealousy can sometimes seem romantic when we see it enacted in plays and movies and books. In reality, however, jealousy is more often an ugly, awful feeling that can result in terribly destructive behavior. What can we do to cope better with jealousy in our relationships and to help create a society where jealousy is less frequent and less harmful?

There are no easy and certain answers to this question, but many of those who have considered this issue have emphasized two major themes. First, we have to do away with the notion that jealousy is a sign of "true love." In fact, jealousy is a sign of an intense attachment to another person and of a strong desire to continue in an intimate relationship with that person. It is a reflection, therefore, of our own desires, our own self-interest. As the French philosopher La Rochefoucauld remarked: "In jealousy, there is more self-love than love." The first step in controlling jealousy is to learn to recognize it for what it is.

A second step is to work on reducing the connection between the exclusivity of a relationship and our own personal worth. If someone we love loves another, that can be extremely unpleasant and most un-welcomed. It can mean some real losses: being alone while your partner is with someone else, enduring sexual deprivation, having less time with your partner, facing the possibility of a drastic change in the type of relationship you have with your partner. It does not mean, however, that your partner is a horrible, worthless person—or that you are.

From the perspective of Albert Ellis (1977), this is the difference between a rational reaction to a threat to an intimate relationship and an irrational one. When we react irrationally, we act as though our self-worth totally depended on the relationship. We feel that without that relationship with that person, we amount to nothing. If the loss of a relationship is perceived as the annhilation of self, then it is not surpris-ing that violent, sometimes deadly, actions can occur. When we react rationally, we may suffer, but we can cope constructively. We can talk to our partner about our feelings and try to work out some solution that everyone can live with. Perhaps we misperceived the situation; or maybe our partner really is interested in someone else. Perhaps this new involvement is short-term; or maybe it's going to last. Perhaps we can stay lovers; or maybe we should try to be good friends. Perhaps we should go our separate ways. None of this is easy, and, in fact, all of it may be very painful, but it can be done.

Clinical approaches to the treatment of jealousy tend to focus on the need to reduce the sort of irrational beliefs described by Ellis, enhance the self-esteem of the jealous partner, improve communication skills, and increase equity in the relationship (White & Mullen, 1989). Al-though there has been little empirical research on coping with jealousy, the results of a study by Salovey and Rodin (1988) provide some support for the importance of a sense of independence and self-worth in coping with jealousy. Undergraduates were asked about their use of three general coping strategies. The strategy of *self-reliance* appeared the most effective. As defined by items on the questionnaire that subjects com-pleted, self-reliance involved a combination of increased effort ("Don't give up") and denial ("Don't think about the unfairness of the situa-tion"). Another strategy, called *selective ignoring,* involved attempts to minimize one's jealousy concerns ("Decide it isn't so important"). Selec-tive ignoring was also associated with reduced jealousy, but it was not as effective as self-reliance. The third strategy, *self-bolstering,* was based on giving oneself good experiences independent of the relationship ("Do something nice for myself"); this strategy was not related to reduc-tions in jealousy.

We should be careful not to overinterpret these results, which are correlational and based on self-reports. Nevertheless, they are consis-tent with the general idea that having a sense of self-confidence about one's ability to act, and to survive, independently is crucial in coping with jealousy. In order to help us react rationally to jealousy, perhaps we should imagine that there is a warning label attached to every romantic relationship:

> WARNING: It is dangerous to your health and to your partner's if you do not know—surely, clearly, and beyond a doubt—that you are a valuable and worthwhile human being with *and* without your partner's love.

If we take this warning to heart, we are probably in a much better position to face the green-eyed monster—and to tame it.

CHAPTER SUMMARY

Jealousy and Envy

Jealousy is an emotional reaction to a perceived threat to an existing relationship. Typically, that threat involves attraction to some other person, but nonsocial threats (such as time involvement with family and hobbies) can also create jealousy. Jealousy can be distinguished from envy, a person's desire to obtain something that someone else has, and from rivalry, competition between two individuals over something both desire but neither one has. According to some investigators, jealousy and envy are closely related and involve similar emotions, though emotional intensity is usually greater in jealousy. Other researchers, however, maintain that jealousy and envy involve distinctly different patterns of emotional response. The self-evaluation maintenance model provides a helpful framework for understanding envy. According to this model, envy is most likely when someone we are close to has a great success in an area of endeavor that we value highly for ourselves. When, however, someone we are close to has a great success in an area that is not relevant to our own feelings of self-esteem, we can BIRG—bask in the reflected glory.

The Causes of Jealousy

The research evidence that jealousy is more likely for those individuals with low self-esteem is mixed and inconsistent, perhaps because characteristics of the specific relationship are more important than general characteristics of the individual.

Relational Factors. Jealousy does appear to be strongly related to feelings of inadequacy in a relationship. It is also more likely when one person believes that he or she is putting more effort than the partner into maintaining the relationship. Dependency on a relationship may be particularly important in jealousy; those who are more dependent may be more prone to experience jealousy.

Sexual Exclusivity. A threat to sexual exclusivity appears to be a critical factor in inciting severe jealous reactions. Beliefs about sexual exclusivity are also involved. Those who believe in monogamy are likely to select partners who share this belief, and such couples should have a relatively low incidence of sexual interactions outside the relationship. Thus, in general, those who believe in monogamy should have fewer jealousy experiences. On the other hand, once sexual interactions outside the relationship have taken place, those who believe in monogamy may well experience greater jealousy. Just as individuals differ in how important sexual exclusivity is to them, so do cultures. Jealous reactions appear to be more likely in cultures that value sexual monogamy, allow personal ownership of property, and emphasize the socioeconomic rewards of marriage.

The Experience of Jealousy

Jealousy can be divided into five distinct components. The first component is that of primary appraisal, in which an individual perceives that there is a threat to an existing relationship. Factors that influence the perception of threat include relational qualities (such as feeling insecure about it), the type of relationship (such as sexual or not), the severity of the threat (such as a very physically attractive third party), and the type of threat (such as sexual versus emotional). In the next stage, secondary appraisal, people inspect the situation more carefully, reviewing the evidence that a threat does or does not exist. Sometimes, secondary appraisal involves catastrophic thinking, in which the person rushes to extreme judgments.

The third aspect of the jealousy experience consists of the emotional reaction that results. Both the intensity and type of jealousy emotions vary enormously. Emotional reactions can be mild or strong; feelings are usually negative but can be positive. After a threat is perceived, assessed, and reacted to emotionally, the person begins to cope with the jealousy situation. Two major classes of coping behaviors are elicited by jealousy: (1) attempting to maintain the relationship and (2) attempting to maintain self-esteem. Both types can involve either constructive or destructive actions. The final component of the jealousy experience involves the outcome produced by the person's coping response. Coping outcomes include effects on the person's perception of threat, on the individuals involved, and on the existing relationship. A constructive coping response produces emotional relief *and* protects the welfare of those involved.

When the three major factors involved in jealousy (thoughts, feelings, and behavior) were measured and compared with subjects' scores on Rubin's Loving and Liking Scales, it was found that the more love or liking that was expressed, the less likely were jealous thoughts or behaviors. Jealous feelings, however, were greater among those who said they were more in love and less frequent among those who emphasized how much they liked their romantic partner. Overall, liking was more strongly and more consistently associated with lower levels of jealousy than was loving.

Types of Jealousy. A number of different types of jealousy have been studied. Chronic jealousy is an individual difference characteristic; some individuals report feeling jealous across a variety of specific relationships. Relationship jealousy is a situational characteristic; some relationship factors are more likely than others to produce jealous reactions. Actual jealousy is the jealousy that a person actually experiences now or has experienced in the past. Anticipated jealousy refers to a person's expectations about when he or she would feel jealous. Induced jealousy is deliberately produced, whereas naturally occurring jealousy occurs spontaneously.

Gender Differences in Jealousy

Becoming Jealous. Although dependency on the relationship is an important factor for both men and women in experiencing jealousy, the type of dependency differs. For men, jealousy is associated with having one's self-esteem lowered by a negative judgment by the partner. For women, jealousy is associated with the belief that another relationship would be difficult to obtain should the current one end.

Coping with Jealousy. Men and women report different ways of coping with jealousy. Men say they are more likely to be angry with themselves, get drunk or aggressive, and feel "turned on" by the jealousy situation. In contrast, women say they are more likely to cry, try to make themselves more attractive to the partner, and pretend they don't care. Gender differences may be especially pronounced in response to a severe threat—with men making an effort to secure another relationship and women withdrawing from other relational possibilities.

Inducing Jealousy and Reacting to Rivalry. According to their self-reports, women are more likely than men to try to induce jealousy in their partners. On the other hand, men may be more likely than women to become rivalrous with another man over a woman. In a study on the "rooster effect," male subjects behaved more aggressively when a male stranger excluded them from an interaction with a female stranger.

Perceiving a Partner's Motives. Men and women also differ in the types of motives they believe are likely to be involved should their romantic partner become interested in someone else. Women are more likely to see the desire for sexual variety, nonsexual attraction, and relationship dissatisfaction as motivating interest in a third party; men are more likely to view their partners as motivated by the desire for a more committed relationship. For both genders, jealousy was associated with believing their partners could be motivated by sexual attraction and relational dissatisfaction. Only among women, however, was their own jealousy associated with emphasizing the importance of the partner's nonsexual attraction to another person.

Coping Constructively with Jealousy

People may be able to cope more constructively with jealousy if they recognize that jealousy is a reflection of their own desire to continue a rewarding relationship, *not* a sign of true love for the partner. It is also important to try to avoid irrational reactions in which a person feels that without that specific relationship, he or she has no self-worth. In general, having a sense of self-confidence about one's own ability to take care of oneself may be the most effective way to tame the green-eyed monster.

PART FIVE

———— ❖ ————

When a Relationship Ends

11

Conflict and Dissolution

—————— ❖ ——————

*I*magine that we have just received the world's largest research grant to fund a massive, worldwide study of intimate relationships. Money in hand, we train a cast of thousands of research assistants and examine all the intimate relationships on the planet. As the data come in, we discover that all these relationships are much alike in many ways. Virtually all of them have positive, rewarding aspects along with at least some negative features. They all involve power arrangements of some sort and the need to work out questions of fairness. In all these relationships, partners communicate with each other; and in many of them, partners experience feelings of jealousy. So far, we are having a hard time justifying having received all that money. But, then, we realize that there is something that is not the same, something that sharply distinguishes some relationships from others: Some last and others don't. Perhaps this is where we should focus our attention.

Although this global investigation of relationships exists only in our imagination, there has been considerable research on why relationships fail to endure. Some of the reasons for relationship dissolution are structural: characteristics of the individuals and their relationship that seem to promote or hinder staying together over a long time. Other reasons involve the process by which conflict is handled; depending on this process, conflict may either be resolved within a continuing attachment or split the relationship apart. This chapter examines a number of structural factors that may play a role in the breakup of a relationship and then describes some major aspects of the ways in which intimate partners handle conflict. In addition, we begin our consideration of how people cope with the end of a relationship, thus setting the stage for subsequent chapters on important postrelationship issues such as loneliness (Chapter 12) and a person's social network (Chapter 13).

STRUCTURAL FACTORS IN CONFLICT AND DISSOLUTION

Potentially, there are an enormous number of structural factors that could be associated with conflict and dissolution in intimate relationships (Laner, 1978; Newcomb & Bentler, 1981). We could look at age, income, education, religion, ethnic background, personality . . . and on and on. Although such associations are informative, they tell us little about the psychological perspective of the individuals involved. But there are some structural factors that appear to be more directly connected with how people think and feel about their relationships. In this chapter, we focus on four of these more immediately relevant characteristics: gender, duration of the relationship, the presence of children, and strains created by competing demands from work and family.

Gender Differences

As we have seen throughout this book, there are a number of differences between men and women in the way they create and sustain intimate relationships. Men and women also appear to differ in their perception of problems in the relationship. In general, women report more problems in their heterosexual relationships than do men (Burgess & Wallin, 1953; Levinger, 1979a; Macklin, 1978). Moreover, there is some evidence that the degree of female dissatisfaction with a relationship is a better predictor than males' unhappiness of whether the relationship will end (Burgess & Wallin, 1953; Rubin, Peplau, & Hill, 1981).

If we assume that the problems reported in these studies actually do exist, then these findings seem to indicate that women are more sensitive to and aware of relational problems than men are. Another possibility, however, is that men and women come to relationships with different expectations and desires concerning those relationships and that, on average, heterosexual relationships work better to fulfill the expectations and desires of men than those of women (Bernard, 1972). Consistent with this line of reasoning, there are gender differences in the *specific* type of problems reported. For example, although divorcing men and women are equally likely to cite communication problems as a cause for the divorce, women emphasize basic unhappiness and incompatibility more than men do (Cleek & Pearson, 1985). On the other hand, although "gender role conflicts" about appropriate activities for men and women are mentioned by both sexes as contributing to divorce (Kitson & Sussman, 1982), men are more likely than women to cite "women's liberation" as a specific cause (Cleek & Pearson, 1985). It is also possible that some behaviors, perhaps particularly sexual behaviors, are more upsetting depending on the gender of those involved. Buss (1989) has argued, for instance, that sexual withholding by a women is especially upsetting to a male partner, while sexual aggression by a man is especially upsetting to a female partner. In addition, men appear more likely than women to blame the end of a relationship on their partner's sexual involvement with another person (Buunk, 1987).

Regardless of these differences in men's and women's awareness of and likely responses to relational problems, it does appear that women are more likely than men to initiate the termination of a relationship. Marital separation and divorce are initiated more often by wives than by husbands (Fletcher, 1983; Hagestad & Smyer, 1982; Harvey, Wells, & Alvarez, 1978; Jacobson, 1983). Findings from the Boston Couples Study (see Chapter 5) indicate that the same gender difference often occurs in the breakup of dating relationships (Hill, Rubin, & Peplau, 1976; Rubin et al., 1981), though some research on undergraduate dating couples has found that men report leaving a relationship more than women do (Rusbult, Zembrodt, & Iwaniszek, 1986). But what does it mean when someone files for divorce or walks out the door? Goode (1956), who also found that women were more likely than men to ask for a divorce, believed that men actually wanted the divorce more and behaved in ways that drove their wives to ask for it. Weiss (1975) takes a more moderate, and probably more realistic, view when he notes that "in most separations the definition of which spouse is the more responsible for the separation appears to be largely arbitrary" (p. 63).

Responsibility is, indeed, hard to determine. Consider, for example, the following interaction:

PARTNER A: If you do not stop doing X, I will leave.
PARTNER B: I won't stop.
PARTNER A: I'm leaving.

Now, we can all agree that Partner A left Partner B. But who is responsible for the breakup? Is it A who left, or B who wouldn't change? Most breakups probably involve a whole series of such interactions, with each partner sometimes asking for change and other times being asked to change. Unless we had some way to tally the exact characteristics of each interaction each time it occurred, we would have a hard time coming up with a reasonable assessment of who, in fact, was responsible for the breakup. In most cases, it is probably impossible to reach an objective judgment about each partner's share of the responsibility for the breakup. This difficulty may be one reason why, as we will see later in this chapter, people spend so much time and energy after a breakup trying to develop an understanding of what happened and who was to blame.

As Time Goes By

Although we seldom notice the effects of the passage of time on a relationship while time is passing, we can often look back and realize how important a role time played in what happened. For example, the longer partners know each other before marriage, the more likely it is that they will be satisfied in the marriage (Burgess & Cottrell, 1939) and the less likely it is that they will divorce (Goode, 1956). On the other hand, the longer a relationship lasts, the more people blame their partners for negative events that occur (Christensen, Sullaway, & King, 1983). Presumably, knowing each other for a longer time allows people to arrive at better arrangements that can more easily endure—and part of getting to know each other involves perceiving the negative, undesirable qualities of a partner once the intensity of early romance has diminished.

Time actually spent with the partner is also important (Surra & Longstreth, 1990). Marini (1976) found that both the amount of time spent together and the number of pleasurable activities done together were positively correlated with the happiness of married couples. There was also an interaction between these two factors: When either one was low, the other became more important in predicting marital happiness. Although it seems likely that the causal connection here goes both ways—spending time together (either by doing something together or just by being together) increases happiness, and happiness with the marriage increases the desire to spend time together— this study raises the possibility that if partners do not have time available to spend with each other, their chances for marital success may be reduced.

The effects of time on intimate relationships have been most extensively studied by researchers interested in the life cycle of marriage and the family. Two major positions have been taken in regard to this issue.

Some research has emphasized the possibility of a linear decline in marital satisfaction (Blood & Wolfe, 1960; Cimbalo, Faling, & Mousan, 1976; Pineo, 1961). According to Pineo (1961), this decline comes about because of two basic processes in relationship development. First, there is the inevitable fading of the romantic "high" of the courtship before marriage. Second, Pineo suggests that when people marry, it is because they have obtained a "good fit" between themselves. If this is the "best fit" that these two individuals can manage, then any changes that occur in either one of them will reduce the compatibility of their relationship. Since people do change, at least to some extent, as they grow older, the odds would seem high that what went so well together at 22 will no longer fit quite so well at 40.

Graziano and Musser (1982) have proposed an interesting variation of Pineo's "best fit" notion. According to these investigators, people often get involved in relationships because they have doubts about their own worthiness as individuals. These doubts motivate them to find another individual whose love and attention would prove that they are worthy and admirable: "If Chris loves me, that must mean I'm pretty special." There may be, however, an unfortunate twist to this kind of mate selection. If basking in the partner's glory works—and the person does begin to feel better about himself or herself—what was a source of pride may turn into a cause for competition or envy. Thus, in line with Tesser's (1988) theory of self-maintenance, the initial good fit between a generous superior and a grateful inferior could become with time a conflict-ridden relationship between two equals vying for superiority.

Not all researchers, however, believe that the story of a marriage is its losing battle against time. Indeed, some research has indicated the possibility that after an initial decline during the earlier years of marriage, marital satisfaction may begin to increase (Burr, 1970; Rollins & Cannon, 1974; Rollins & Galligan, 1978). This U-shaped pattern appears to be closely associated with the arrival and departure of children: with marital satisfaction declining as children are born and grow up, but then increasing as the children mature and leave home.

In reviewing the evidence on the two marital life cycles described here (see Figure 11.1), Spanier, Lewis, and Cole (1975) concluded that the decline in marital satisfaction during the early years of marriage is well documented. What happens after that is, they believe, less clear. It does seem that the decline usually stops, but whether there is an increase or merely a leveling off remains debatable.

When we speak of the life cycle of a marriage, we are, of course, speaking in very general terms. Obviously, there will be many exceptions to any one pattern. Some married couples may experience no

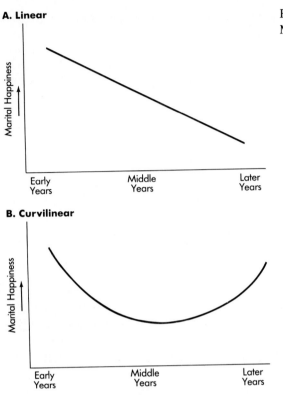

A. Linear

Marital Happiness

Early Years   Middle Years   Later Years

B. Curvilinear

Marital Happiness

Early Years   Middle Years   Later Years

FIGURE 11.1
Marital life cycles.

decline at all; other couples will ditch out in divorce the first year of marriage. Moreover, Gilford and Bengston (1979) have argued that it is oversimplified to talk in terms of global satisfaction. Instead, they suggest that one should look at two life cycles: the pattern of positive rewards and the pattern of negative costs. Their research on this issue indicates that the early years of marriage are a time of very high rewards *and* very high costs; there is great intensity in the relationship and great ambivalence. The middle years, according to Gilford and Bengston, see a decline in both, while the later years are characterized by a continuing decline in the negative aspects of marriage with an increase in the positive aspects. In his study of over 400 ever-married women living in Detroit, Whyte (1990) describes a somewhat different two-factor marital life cycle. For these individuals, marital quality declined over time and then stabilized. Marital problems, however, were low in the early years of marriage, increased with the arrival of children, and then declined when the children left home. Both of these two-factor models make the important point that the positive and negative aspects of married life should be considered as relatively independent processes that can develop differently over time.

When Two Become Three or More: Effects of Children on Marital Satisfaction

In describing the possible changes of marital satisfaction over time, it was noted how closely some of these changes seem to follow the arrival and departure of children. This suggests that there might be something about having children around that makes a satisfying relationship between the couple more difficult to sustain (Belsky, 1990; Steinberg & Silverberg, 1987). To investigate this issue, researchers have compared married couples who have children with childless couples married for similar lengths of time. With only a few exceptions (e.g., MacDermid, Huston, & McHale, 1990), such studies have obtained highly consistent results: Childless couples report greater satisfaction in their marriage (Glenn & McLanahan, 1982; Houseknecht, 1979; Ryder, 1973; Veroff, Douvan, & Kukla, 1981). There are, however, three important qualifications to this general conclusion. First, the negative effects of children are restricted to marital *satisfaction*. In terms of *duration* of the marriage, married couples with children stay together longer than those without children (Rankin & Manaker, 1985). Second, the reduction in marital satisfaction associated with having children seems to be stronger for wives than for husbands (Rollins & Galligan, 1978; Tucker, James, & Turner, 1985). Third, the quality of life is an important moderating factor. Having children is associated with a *severe* decline in marital satisfaction only among women who are already having a hard time managing the demands on their time and energy: low-income mothers employed full-time (Schumm & Bugaighis, 1986). Furthermore, when children are wanted and parent-child relationships are of good quality, negative effects of having children on parental well-being are much less likely (Rollins & Galligan, 1978; Umberson, 1989).

There have been some attempts to determine what age of the child is most likely to be associated with reduced marital satisfaction, but no strong pattern seems to emerge. Hoffman and Manis (1978) highlight the early years of parenthood, when everything (joys *and* frustrations) is more intense. Burr (1970) found that marital satisfaction was lowest during the time the children were in elementary school, while Rollins and his associates found that the decline in marital satisfaction continued into the period when there were teenage children in the family (Rollins & Cannon, 1974; Rollins & Galligan, 1978). Regardless of their age, it does appear that having a larger number of children is likely to increase the negative effect on marital satisfaction. And, as noted in the previous section, once the children leave home, marital satisfaction may increase for many couples (e.g., Rollins & Galligan, 1978; Skolnick, 1981). In one of the more detailed studies of postparental adjustment, Glenn (1975) found that postparental bliss was especially strong for wives, whose marital satisfaction increased substantially.

That having children could have a negative effect on the way a couple feels about each other flies in the face of many cherished beliefs about home and family. Certainly, it contradicts the expectations of most couples who are thinking about having children. The following section explores one possible explanation for why having children could make a marital relationship less satisfying.

Role Strain: Who Does What?

In every social organization, there are roles. In a classroom, there is the role of teacher and the role of student; in a business, there is the role of employer and the role of employee; and in a marriage, there is the role of husband and the role of wife. Although the roles of husband and wife have changed over time and differ across socioeconomic class (Anderson & Zinsser, 1988), the traditional, middle-class roles in Western industrialized nations were well defined. The husband's role was to earn money outside the home and act as an authority figure inside the home; the wife's role was to take care of the home, raise the children, and maintain appropriate social contacts. In such a system, there may have been a good many unhappy people, whose personal preferences did not match the requirements of their assigned roles, but there was clarity about what the roles were and who was to fill them.

Today, that clarity no longer exists in the United States and many other Western countries. In 1940, just over 27 percent of the women in the United States were employed; by 1987, a majority (56 percent) were in the work force. This change is most dramatic for women with children. In 1970, only 30 percent of women with children under the age of six were employed outside the home; by 1987, 57 percent were employed. Among women with children under the age of one, only 24 percent were employed in 1970, while 51 percent were employed by 1987. In a 1989 cover story entitled "Onward, Women!" *Time* magazine noted that 68 percent of women with children under the age of 18 were employed. It is estimated that by the year 2000, 81 percent of women aged 25 to 64 will be in the work force (Matthews & Rodin, 1989). When both spouses work, the fundamental basis for the traditional division of labor between the provider husband and the caretaker wife disappears.

Interestingly, however, while the basis for the traditional division of labor no longer exists, the traditional division of *household labor* continues. Despite their increasing participation in the work force outside

By the late 1980s, over 50 percent of women with children under the age of 1 year were employed outside the home. Many women experience considerable role strain as they try to meet their responsibilities at home and at work. (Elizabeth Crews/The Image Works)

the home, women still perform much more of the housework and child care than do men. This pattern does not appear to reflect factors other than gender:

> Women's employment, time availability, resources, conscious ideology, and power do not account for why wives still do the bulk of family work. More than any other factor, gender accounts for the amount and allocation of housework and childcare. (Thompson & Walker, 1989, p. 857)

Averaging across various studies, Hochschild (1989) concluded that, compared with men, women have 15 fewer hours of leisure each week; over a year, this amounts to an extra month of 24-hour days. Among the 50 two-job couples she interviewed, Hochschild found that 18 percent of the husbands shared about half (45–55 percent) of the household labor (including child care); 21 percent did between 30 percent and 45 percent; and 61 percent did 30 percent or less.

It seems likely that all of these developments are associated with considerable *role strain*—disagreements about who should perform various tasks and make various decisions—for both spouses. Wives who expect their husbands to be more involved in housework and child care are unhappy if these expectations are not satisfied (Ruble, Fleming, Hackel, & Stangor, 1988) and may experience a decline in marital satisfaction (Belsky, Lang, & Huston, 1986). Husbands who participate more in household labor than they expected to, or at least feel pressured by their wives to do so, may find the stresses of home spilling over into their performance at work (Bolger, DeLongis, Kessler, & Wethington, 1989). Indeed, many researchers believe that role strain is one of the major causes of marital conflict and dissolution (Frank, Anderson, & Rubinstein, 1979; Jacobson, Follette, & McDonald, 1982). According to Nettles and Loevinger (1983), "What differentiates problem marriages is not characterlogical problems with the couples . . . but different expectations and attitudes about the division of labor" (p. 685).

For some, this state of affairs provides an argument for returning to the traditional division of labor and the traditional roles of husband and wife. Economically, such a return seems unlikely, as most couples find that one income is simply not sufficient anymore. In addition, it seems unlikely that women will agree to forsake the educational and employment opportunities that have become available to them in recent years, and there is little indication that many men would agree to a role reversal in which they become the homemaker while only their wife works outside the home. Multiple roles—for both men and women—are probably here to stay.

Fortunately, multiple roles are not necessarily a bad development. Consider, for example, the debate between researchers who propose a *scarcity hypothesis* in regard to social roles (Goode, 1960) and those who advocate the *enhancement hypothesis* (Marks, 1977; Sieber, 1974). According to the scarcity hypothesis, more roles mean more stress since time and energy are stretched thin. In contrast, the enhancement hypothesis maintains that a greater number of roles will reduce stress, as disappointments in one area of life can be compensated for by success in another. In general, the evidence favors the enhancement hypothesis: Having multiple roles is usually associated with increased well-being (Repetti & Crosby, 1984; Rodin & Ickovics, 1990; Sorensen & Verbrugge, 1987; Thoits, 1983). Despite their having to balance the demands of household labor with those of their paid employment, employed women typically experience less psychological distress and better physical health than do unemployed women (Aneshensel & Pearlin, 1987; Spitze, 1988; Verbrugge, 1987). It should be emphasized, however, that the benefits of multiple roles depend on the quality of those roles (Barnett & Baruch, 1985). Among married women, employment is clearly beneficial only for those who have positive attitudes toward that employment (Repetti, Matthews, & Waldron, 1989). Indeed, work satisfaction appears to influence whether a women's employment is associated with positive or negative effects on marriage. According to Greenstein (1990), "It may be the case that employment reduces the risk of marital disruption for women who have a strong career orientation and enjoy their work, but increases the risk for women who have little work commitment and who are dissatisfied with the type of work they are doing" (p. 675).

Another factor that may have a major impact on whether multiple roles are experienced as stressful is the social support provided by one's partner (Repetti, 1989; Scarr, Phillips, & McCartney, 1989). In more traditional times, the expectations about social support were probably just as clear-cut as those about social roles. The wife was expected to support the husband's efforts at work and the husband to support the wife's work at home. Now, both partners need to be able to support each other in all of their multiple roles. The difficulties in doing this should not be underestimated, but neither should the potential advantages be overlooked. As the traditional social roles of husband and wife become increasingly irrelevant, couples will gain the freedom to work out that balance of paid employment and household labor that works best for them—as a couple and as individuals. Although it is easier to follow a blueprint based on gender to decide who does what, it is potentially much more satisfying to create your own division of labor based on individual talent and mutual support.

THE PROCESS OF CONFLICT AND DISSOLUTION

Structural factors, like those we have just examined, can be thought of as increasing the probability of conflict. For example, spouses trying to juggle the demands of multiple roles are more likely to find themselves with incompatible goals. He wants an early dinner in order to get to a late meeting; she wants a late dinner in order to have time to finish a project at work. The life circumstances embedded in structural factors do not, however, determine the outcome of conflict. The clash of incompatible goals can be resolved in a peaceful, loving manner—or in a hostile, antagonistic fashion (Stillars, 1981). What is crucial is the process of conflict—how partners deal with the conflict they experience.

The process of conflict is complicated, involving words, actions, and feelings. In Chapter 8, we explored various patterns of communication that can contribute to a constructive solution of conflict or to a destructive escalation of anger and resentment. Here, we focus on a different issue: the role of thoughts and beliefs in the process of conflict. Recent research on intimate relationships has suggested that the interpretations we make of our own and our partner's behavior during conflict may be just as important as what is actually said and done (Fincham, in press; Fincham, Bradbury, & Grych, 1990).

Attributions: A General Scenario

In their pioneering work on cognitive factors involved in intimate conflict, Orvis, Kelley, and Butler (1976) focused on the *causal attributions* (explanations for why something happened) people make during conflict. They offered the following propositions.

1. Attributional processes will be more active during conflict than at other times. When disagreements arise, people are motivated to search for the causes of their own and others' behavior. When people agree, the reasons for why they agree don't much matter. Subsequent research by Holtzworth-Munroe and Jacobson (1985, 1988) has confirmed this comparison. Married couples make more attributions for negative, unpleasant events in their relationships than for positive, enjoyable ones.

2. During conflict, each individual will take a benign view of the causes of his or her own behavior. According to Orvis et al., there is a definite tilt in the way we think about the causes of behavior during conflict. Attributional processes at such times are not objective and impartial; instead, they reflect a self-serving bias. Most of the time, most of us believe that our motives are good, and we almost always have a good excuse for our less admirable behaviors (Snyder, Higgins, & Stucky, 1983).

3. Attributions made during conflict can create attributional conflict—disagreement about motives—which is usually irresolvable. Most conflict initially concerns the facts about specific behaviors—who did what to whom. But as Orvis et al. point out, disagreements about facts often turn into conflict over motives. Instead of arguing about what people did, attributional arguments focus on why they did it. These sorts of disputes about motives are extremely difficult to resolve. Not only are the participants biased toward acceptable explanations for their own behavior, but each is susceptible to a phenomenon called the "actor-observer difference." The actor-observer difference refers to the tendency for individuals to see their own behavior as caused by situational factors and the behavior of others as caused by dispositional factors (Jones & Nisbett, 1972). Although there are exceptions to this general difference in perspective (Monson & Snyder, 1977), it does seem pervasive in many aspects of our lives (Watson, 1982). Since we know our own history and are aware of how our behavior changes in different situations, we can be sensitive to momentary, situational influences on what we do ("Hey, I was just going along with the crowd."). On the other hand, we do not have such detailed information about other people, and, besides, dispositional attributions seem to offer an efficient

way to predict people's behavior: "You're always doing that; you're just that sort of person." During conflict, it is easy for us to believe that anything that we did wrong was a temporary response to the situation, easily modifiable in the future, while anything that our partner did wrong was caused by a permanent feature of his or her personality.

Attributions: Differences between Happy and Unhappy Couples

It is important to realize, however, that not all couples make the same sorts of attributions. As indicated by research on married couples, attributions often reflect the overall state of the relationship (Bradbury & Fincham, 1990; Holtzworth-Munroe & Jacobson, 1987). Happy couples make *relationship-enhancing* attributions. Positive behavior by the partner is viewed as characteristic of that person, stable across time, and likely to be repeated in other areas of the relationship. In short, happy couples make internal, stable, and global attributions for each other's positive behaviors. For negative behaviors, the reverse pattern occurs, with happy couples making external, unstable, and specific attributions. Negative actions by the partner are discounted as a reflection of situational influences, seen as temporary in nature, and viewed as unlikely to extend to other areas of the relationship. Satisfied partners exaggerate the good and minimize the bad.

In contrast, distressed couples make *distress-maintaining* attributions. Among these couples, positive behaviors are discounted through the use of external, unstable, and specific attributions. Negative behaviors, however, are viewed as internal, stable, and global. Overall, unhappy couples exaggerate the bad and minimize the good. The different types of causal attributions made by happy and unhappy couples are displayed in Figure 11.2.

Responsibility attributions also differ according to the state of a couple's relationship (Bradbury & Fincham, 1990). Whereas causal attributions involve deciding on the factors that produce an event, attributions of responsibility indicate a person's accountability for an event. These two types of attributions are not the same (Shaver, 1985). It is possible, for instance, to cause something to happen but not be held responsible because of mitigating factors such as not intending it to happen. In general, unhappy couples are more likely than happy couples to regard the partner as selfishly motivated and behaving with negative intent. Here, too, unhappy couples seem predisposed to emphasize the bad and ignore the good. For them, the glass is always half empty rather than half full.

The findings on the causal and responsibility attributions made by happy and unhappy couples suggest that these attributions act as a

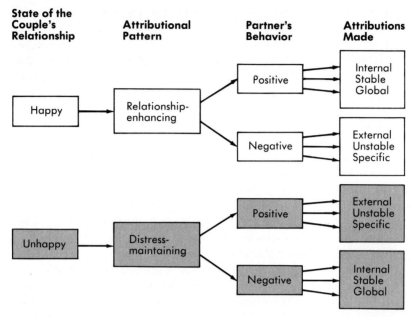

FIGURE 11.2
Attributions made by happy and unhappy couples. (Brehm & Kassin, 1990.)

screen—magnifying behaviors consistent with the state of the relationship while filtering out discrepant relationships. Over time, such a screen should intensify the initial emotional quality of the relationship: The happy should get happier, and the miserable more miserable. This interpretation assumes that attributions can produce differences in satisfaction. But there are some other possibilities. Perhaps, for instance, attributions are simply produced by the state of the relationship without having any direct influence themselves.

One way to examine the relationship between attributions and relational satisfaction is to look at effects over time. In a longitudinal study by Fincham and Bradbury (1987), married couples completed questionnaires about their relationship at two different times a year apart. On both occasions, those who made internal, stable, and global attributions for negative behavior by the partner also reported less marital satisfaction. In addition, for wives in the study, those who initially made more distress-maintaining attributions when the study began reported less marital satisfaction a year later. No such long-term effect of attributions was found for husbands. In another study, however, early attributions predicted marital satisfaction over a 12-month period only for husbands (reported in Fincham, Bradbury, & Scott, 1990). Although the reasons for this inconsistent pattern of gender difference are not clear, these two studies do raise the possibility that causal attributions for the partner's behavior can have an influence on subsequent satisfaction with the relationship.

There is, however, another possible causal connection that needs to be considered. There is considerable evidence that dissatisfaction with one's marriage is associated with depression (Gotlib & Hooley, 1988; Smolen, Spiegel, Shaukat, & Schwartz, 1988; Ulrich-Jakubowski, Russell, & O'Hara, 1988). Could it be that the distress-maintaining attributions made by unhappy couples stem from their depressed mood? Research by Fincham and his colleagues (1989) indicates that this is unlikely. Regardless of whether they were depressed or not, maritally dissatisfied wives were more likely than maritally satisfied wives to emphasize the negative aspects of their husband's motives. But Fincham et al. note that, over time, distress-maintaining attributions may, in fact, become associated with depression. In their view, such attributions are likely to increase hostile, noncooperative behavior during conflict, thereby intensifying stress and creating depression.

Putting these various research findings together, we are still left with a basic question about distress-maintaining attributions: What causes them? Does an unhappy, conflict-ridden relationship produce these attributions, which then can increase relational distress even further? Or are there certain behaviors by the partner that are particularly likely to trigger the distress-maintaining pattern of attributions? Or are some individuals especially prone to developing such a pattern in the face of even minor problems in the relationship? As is the case with most complex human behaviors, the type of attributions people make during relationship conflict is probably multiply determined and involves a variety of factors. It is, however, worth noting that conflict in intimate relationships, and perhaps the pattern of attributions that accompany it, may be more predictable than we might think. In a two-year longitudinal study of 21 couples, it was found that early, premarital reports of conflict were the best predictor of later, marital conflict (Kelly, Huston, & Cate, 1985). Perhaps the conflict·ial relationships in this study were simply bad matches to begin with. Or perhaps at least one of the partners had an enduring, attributional style that served to maintain and intensify conflict (Baucom, Sayers, & Duhe, 1989; Doherty, 1982). In any case, the study by Kelly et al. does suggest that it may be wise to pay close attention to conflict early in a relationship; what you see early on may be just what you get later on.

Volatility: A Problem and an Opportunity

Taken as a whole, research on the attributions made by distressed couples depicts an ever-tightening, increasingly vicious circle. Those experiencing marital distress are more likely to make the kind of attributions that increase the possibility of further distress. Caught in a trap, they cannot get out. Or can they? There is some evidence of another characteristic of distressed couples that may sometimes help them counteract the tendency to exaggerate the bad and minimize the good.

Consider, for example, a study by Fincham and Bradbury (1988) on distressed and nondistressed couples. From each couple, one spouse served as an experimental confederate, writing a negative description of his or her partner based on materials provided by the experimenter. The other spouse read the description. Half of these individuals were told that the negative description had been requested by the experimenter, while the other half were led to believe that their spouse had spontaneously written such an unfavorable description. Spouses then engaged in a 5-minute conversation, which was observed by the researchers. (After the experiment was completed, subjects were fully informed about the fact that some subjects had been misled about why their partner had written the unfavorable description. They were also told to call one of the researchers if they wanted to discuss the experiment further. Although it is claimed that "no adverse effects were reported" [p. 153], the lack of a systematic follow-up prevents an adequate assessment of whether there were any long-term consequences.)

The results of this study depended on couples' initial level of marital satisfaction. The presence or absence of an excuse for writing a negative description (that is, the experimenter's request to do so) had no significant effect on the behavior of nondistressed couples. Among distressed couples, however, those who believed that their partner had spontaneously written this description behaved more negatively toward the partner than those who believed the description to have an external cause. Surprisingly, spouses from distressed marriages also behaved more *positively* toward the partner they believed had spontaneously written a negative description than toward the one they believed had complied with the experimenter's instructions. Were these positive behaviors by distressed spouses simply an effort to try to compensate for their negative actions and to appear more reasonable in front of the observing researchers? Or are distressed couples more emotionally volatile, more reactive in positive *and* negative ways to emotionally arousing events?

Research by Jacobson, Follette, and McDonald (1982) raises a similar interpretational dilemma. These investigators had happy and unhappy couples report on daily events and indicate their overall satisfaction with their marriage. Among happy couples, the number of negative events that had occurred during a day had only a weak relationship with their overall satisfaction with the marriage. As predicted, however, this relationship was quite strong among unhappy couples: A greater number of negative events was associated with less marital satisfaction. But again there was a surprise in store. Unhappy couples were also more responsive to *positive* events. The number of positive events that had occurred during the day had a much stronger association with increased satisfaction among unhappy couples than among happy ones. Was this impression management for the researchers to whom they were reporting? Or were unhappy couples actually more responsive to both negative *and* positive events?

Although the possibility of deliberate impression management cannot be dismissed, the results of these two studies—using very different kinds of research methods—may well indicate that unhappy couples are particularly volatile in their emotional reactions. Given a negative event (an "unexcused" negative description of them by their partner), they react with a flurry of negative and positive behaviors. As we would expect, negative daily events lower their satisfaction with the relationship, but positive daily events also raise their satisfaction. Happy couples appear far more stable (Margolin, John, & O'Brien, 1989). They don't throw in the towel because of any single negative event, and they don't burst into euphoria because their partner does something nice. In many ways, the stability of happy couples and the volatility of unhappy couples work to the disadvantage of the latter. Relatively minor negative events that would not faze a happy couple may cause a tremendous explosion in an already distressed relationship. But volatility can create an opportunity for unhappy partners to break out of the trap of distress-maintaining attributions. Despite their tendency to dismiss positive behaviors by the partner, a positive emotional response can open the door to improving the relationship. Volatility means things are not fixed. They could get worse, but the opportunity also exists for them to get better.

COPING WITH THE END OF A RELATIONSHIP

As emphasized in Chapter 8 on communication, conflict does not necessarily lead to the dissolution of a relationship. Indeed, handled skillfully with genuine concern for the partner, conflict can strengthen an intimate attachment. But, sometimes, partners are unable to actively channel conflict in a more constructive direction. Instead, they may become passive—hoping things will get better but fearing they will get worse. Although a passive response to conflict may suffice in some circumstances, often it does not. The omission of a positive response can, at times, be as damaging to a relationship as the commission of a negative action (Gaelick, Bodenhausen, & Wyer, 1985; Rusbult, Johnson, & Morrow, 1986; Williams, 1979). If conflict continues, one or both of the partners may decide to leave the relationship. Thus, as diagrammed in Figure 11.3, there appear to be four basic responses to conflict and

FIGURE 11.3
Dimensions of response to dissatisfaction with a relationship. (Rusbult, 1987.)

dissatisfaction in a relationship (Rusbult & Zembrodt, 1983; Rusbult, Zembrodt, & Gunn, 1982):

1. *Voice:* Actively trying to improve the relationship
2. *Loyalty:* Passively waiting for things to get better
3. *Neglect:* Passively allowing things to get worse
4. *Exit:* Leaving the relationship

The end of an intimate relationship can be a traumatic experience (Bloom, Asher, & White, 1978; Menaghan & Lieberman, 1986; Stroebe & Stroebe, 1986). But not everyone is devastated by the loss of an intimate partner; over time, many people make a good adjustment (Hansson, Stroebe, & Stroebe, 1988b; McCrae & Costa, 1988). In this section, we consider some of the factors that influence how people cope with the end of a relationship. Subsequent chapters examine other postrelationship issues such as loneliness (Chapter 12) and social networks (Chapter 13).

Cognitive Aspects of Coping

Think about the last time you experienced the end of an intimate relationship: the loss of a romantic partner; the breakup of a friendship. Did you just accept it and go on with your life? Or did you find yourself thinking about it, trying to figure out what caused it? For many people, the end of a relationship creates an intense need to understand why it ended. This need appears to develop regardless of the circumstances involved. Widows go over the events leading up to the death of their husband (Glick, Weiss, & Parkes, 1974). After a marital separation, people engage in an "incessant causal analysis" (Harvey et al., 1978) and generate elaborate, detailed "accounts"—coherent stories that tie together the sequence of events that ended in the separation (Weiss, 1975). Why does all this cognitive activity take place after a relationship has ended?

The answer to this question lies in people's reactions to negative or unexpected events. When unpleasant things take place, or when events occur that we did not anticipate, we want to know why (Hastie, 1984; Weiner, 1985). You will recall that earlier in this chapter it was noted that people make more causal attributions for negative than positive events. Since the end of a relationship is often a distinctly unpleasant experience, it isn't surprising that people try to find an explanation for it. If, in addition, the end was unexpected, the need for an account should be even greater.

But let us push the question one step further: Why is it more important for us to have explanations for negative or unexpected events than for pleasant or anticipated outcomes? Sometimes, our need for an explanation may really be a need for a face-saving excuse; we want an account that puts us in the most favorable light. There is, however, another reason why we have such a strong desire to be able to explain why negative or unexpected events took place: control (Pittman & Pittman, 1980; Swann, Stephenson, & Pittman, 1981). If we can understand why something occurred, we may be able to use this knowledge to control whether or not it occurs in the future. The loss of a relationship that is viewed as outside of our control is more upsetting than one we feel some control over (Peterson, Rosenbaum, & Conn, 1985). If we can develop an account that helps us understand why the loss occurred, we can reassure ourselves that, next time, we will not let it happen again. As Harvey, Agostinelli, and Weber (1989) put it, "If one can develop an explanation that identifies a solvable problem within a past failed relationship . . . , then one's expectations for future relationships may be influenced by these accounts" (p. 54).

Initiator status. This analysis of the psychological needs that can be served by accounts suggests that people who develop accounts that reflect well on them or that give them a sense of control should cope better with the end of a relationship. One such potentially beneficial account would be to believe that you did the leaving, rather than that you were left. It is best to regard this report of "initiator status" as a subjective account rather than an objective fact, because, as mentioned earlier in this chapter, the responsibility for leaving is difficult to determine. Moreover, former partners do not always agree in their reports about who initiated the breakup (Hill et al., 1976).

At first, research on the effects of initiator status did indicate that those who said they left fared better than those who said they were left (Goode, 1956; Hill et al., 1976). Subsequently, however, a careful study by Pettit and Bloom (1984) raised questions about this conclusion. Pettit and Bloom divided 144 newly separated men and women into two categories: initiators (who reported having had primary responsibility for the decision to separate or who said that the separation was based on a mutual decision by the two spouses) and noninitiators (who attributed primary responsibility for the decision to their spouse). When first assessed, initiators appeared to be coping better than noninitiators, but follow-up assessments 6 and 18 months later obtained few differences between the two groups. Among a large number of measures administered over the course of this study, only two effects of initiator status were stable throughout the research. Male and female initiators held a more positive attitude toward being divorced than did noninitiators, and female initiators perceived more benefits from being divorced than did female noninitiators. Overall, Pettit and Bloom concluded that initiator status plays, at most, only a minor role in people's adjustment after the end of a marriage.

Interpersonal attributions. You may be surprised that Pettit and Bloom combined those who said they had initiated the separation with those who reported that the separation was a joint decision. These two accounts would seem to be quite different psychologically. Indeed, one study found that divorced men who reported mutual initiation appeared to be better adjusted than those who reported initiation by *either* self or spouse; initiator status was not related to the adjustment of the divorced women participating in this research (Thompson & Spanier, 1983). Newman and Langer (1988) draw a similar distinction between *dispositional attributions* to stable characteristics of the self or partner and *interpersonal attributions* involving interactions between both individuals. In a 1981 study of divorced women, Newman and Langer found that those who explained the breakup of their marriage in terms of negative characteristics of their spouse appeared to be coping less well than those who emphasized the unsatisfying nature of the marital interaction. Interpersonal attributions for the end of a relationship also correlated with reduced distress among men, but not among women, in a study of nonmarital relationships (Stephen, 1987). However, such an association between interpersonal attributions and good adjustment was not obtained in some other studies on divorced individuals (Fletcher, 1983) and on married couples (Baucom et al., 1989).

Self-attributions of responsibility. At this point, you may find yourself wondering whether postbreakup accounts are useful after all. Based on the research evidence currently available, there is no overwhelming support for the benefits of either perceiving yourself as the initiator of the breakup or explaining the breakup in terms of the interaction between yourself and your former partner. But what about seeing yourself as responsible for the relationship's ending, regardless of who actually walked out the door? The psychological implications of this sort of self-attribution are somewhat complicated. On the one hand, if you see yourself as responsible for the breakup, this could make you feel guilty and damage your self-esteem. On the other hand, self-attribution maximizes a sense of control; it says that you were in charge. There is some evidence that a sense of control can be more important after a breakup than feelings of blame and guilt. Among a group of 62 divorced and separated men and women, those who gave more causal responsibility to themselves for the end of the marriage reported coping better than those who gave less causal responsibility to themselves (Fletcher, 1983). In another study, an association between good adjustment after the separation and self-blame for the dissolution of the relationship was found for women but not for men (Spanier & Thompson, 1984).

In an intimate relationship, assigning more responsibility to the self often means assigning less responsibility to the partner, but these studies do not indicate which of the two types of attributions is more important. Sometimes, however, both enter into the equation. When married women were asked about how much they would blame themselves for marital conflict versus how much they would blame their husbands, those who blamed themselves more than they blamed their husbands reported more satisfaction in the marriage than women who blamed their husbands more than they blamed themselves (Madden & Janoff-Bulman, 1981). Absolute level of self-blame was not correlated with marital satisfaction. There is also another line of research on the association between blame and adjustment that may shed some light on this issue. Among individuals recovering from injuries and disease, self-blame is sometimes associated with better adjustment (Bulman & Wortman, 1977) and sometimes with poorer adjustment (Nielson & Mac-Donald, 1988). A more consistent pattern has been obtained for "other-blame"; those who blame others for their own distress are usually less well adjusted (Affleck, Tennen, Croog, & Levine, 1987; Taylor, Lichtman, & Wood, 1984; Tennen & Affleck, 1990).

It is ironic that despite the prevalence of obsessive reviews and account making after the end of a relationship, it has proved difficult to establish exactly what kinds of explanations are associated with better coping in this situation. You would think that something so common would have more dramatic effects. Presently, the best estimate is that blaming the partner may have negative effects on adjustment, while blaming the self may possibly have some benefits—at least in the short run. But possibly the influence of attributional accounts on coping has been overestimated. Perhaps traumatic events simply produce both psychological distress and attributional concerns, without either one affecting later developments in the other (Downey, Silver, & Wortman, 1990). According to this perspective, the explanation we come up with for the end of a relationship is a symptom of our distress but will not help us feel better—or worse—in the long run.

Emotional Aspects of Coping

In studies of coping after the end of a relationship, many investigators have commented on the intense emotional reactions that often occur (Glick et al., 1974; Jacobson, 1983; Spanier & Casto, 1979; Weiss, 1975). The death of a spouse, divorce, or the loss of a steady dating partner can often produce great distress and anguish. What has been perhaps less obvious is that, in fact, emotional reactions vary a great deal. Not everyone is lost in despair after the end of a relationship. Some people feel better than they did while the relationship was intact; some have no strong emotional response, positive or negative. Indeed, friends, family, and those involved in the relationship are often surprised by the emotional aftermath. Why is it that partners in a conflict-ridden, unsatisfying relationship sometimes experience great distress when the relationship ends? And how could it be that partners in a great romance sometimes seem not to miss it all that much?

According to Berscheid (1983), a careful application of Mandler's (1984) theory of emotion can help us understand some of the reasons for people's emotional reactions after the end of a relationship. Mandler's theory maintains that we experience an emotion in response to an *interruption* of our ongoing goal-directed activities. The emotional response can be negative or positive. When Debbie wants Mark to cuddle up and whisper "sweet nothings" in her ear but Mark insists on watching a basketball game on TV, Mark has interfered with Debbie's getting what she wants. Depending on how much she wanted Mark's love and attention, Debbie should feel at least irritated and perhaps very angry. On the other hand, suppose that Debbie is working hard on a school project and dreading having to make her fourth trip to the library for some reference materials. If at this point Mark walks in the door with reference books in hand, Debbie should feel a surge of gratitude and affection toward Mark for his unexpected assistance. In both these cases, Debbie's goal-directed activities have been interrupted, but in the first instance, Mark's behavior has interfered with Debbie's getting what she wanted, while in the second, Mark's behavior has facilitated it.

Berscheid believes that Mandler's interruption principle is extremely valuable in understanding the emotional reactions people have toward intimate relationships. First, it explains why the early stages in a relationship are likely to be highly emotional. As partners share more and more of their lives with each other, each one has more and more opportunities to affect the goals of the other: either in an interfering way or in a facilitative way. Unanticipated assistance brings us joy; unanticipated interference may cause rage.

All these emotional responses, however, rest on the unexpected nature of the partner's behavior. Once we come to know our partners well and are able to anticipate what they will do in many situations, their behavior no longer can serve as an interruption: For better or worse, we anticipate what they will do. This process of adaptation makes it very difficult to judge the actual worth a relationship has for the people involved. For example, consider a relationship in which each partner provides great assistance to the other. They give each other affection and support; they help each other out with the necessary tasks of everyday life. If, however, this mutual facilitation has been going on for a long time, the partners will no longer experience an emotional response in reaction to all the benefits the relationship provides them. They will take this facilitation for granted and, as time passes, may become unaware of how much they rely on each other. To both outsiders and the partners themselves, the relationship may seem tranquil or even dull. Thus, the lack of emotional response can mislead us about how much actual benefit the partners receive.

Berscheid, then, urges us to make a distinction between our emotional response to a relationship and the actual amount of facilitation present in the relationship. In long-term relationships, it is quite possible for a partner to provide us with great assistance in reaching our emotional and practical goals, but for us to fail to recognize how much assistance we are receiving. On the other hand, a relationship filled with intense positive emotions may, in fact, be providing us very little; the emotional intensity may reflect the unexpected nature of the benefits we receive, not their actual amount.

From Berscheid's perspective, it is this distinction between emotional response and actual amount of benefit received that makes it so difficult to predict the emotional reaction when a relationship breaks up. It is possible for people to feel madly in love and, then, when the relationship is over, realize they do not really miss it very much. It is also possible to feel that a relationship is deadly dull and, then, when it is over, feel overwhelmed with regret and longing. Berscheid's model (diagrammed in Table 11.1) proposes that a person's emotional response after a breakup will reflect the actual amount of facilitation from the partner that has been lost rather than the perceived emotional quality of the relationship while it lasted.

Berscheid, Snyder, and Omoto (1989a) have elaborated Berscheid's model of emotional response to the loss of a relationship in terms of the closeness of that relationship. Their Relationship Closeness Inventory (RCI) measures the frequency of contact that partners have with each other (the amount of time they typically spend alone with each other), the diversity of the activities that partners engage in with each other,

TABLE 11.1 REACTIONS TO THE LOSS OF A RELATIONSHIP

		TOTAL AMOUNT OF BENEFIT ("FACILITATION") RECEIVED	
		High	Low
		The growth-oriented relationship	The exciting relationship
		If it ends—	If it ends—
TOTAL AMOUNT OF UNEXPECTED BENEFIT ("FACILITATION") RECEIVED = TOTAL AMOUNT OF POSITIVE EMOTIONAL RESPONSE IN THE RELATIONSHIP	High	*Expected distress:* great *Actual distress:* great	*Expected distress:* great *Actual distress:* little
		"We expected to miss it, and we do."	"We expected to miss it, but we don't."
		The tranquil relationship	The nothing relationship
		If it ends—	If it ends—
	Low	*Expected distress:* little *Actual distress:* great	*Expected distress:* little *Actual distress:* little
		"We miss it much more than we expected to."	"We didn't expect to miss it and we don't."

and the reported impact (current and future) that partners have on each other's activities, decisions, and plans. These three measures (frequency, diversity, and strength of impact) are then summed to yield a total closeness score. Two studies have used the RCI to try to predict the stability of a relationship over time and the distress experienced after the end of a relationship.

In an initial investigation, Simpson (1987) obtained RCI scores from undergraduate subjects involved in dating relationships. Three months later, 42 percent of these relationships had broken up. When all of the various factors assessed in the study were taken into account, subjects' RCI scores did not predict whether their relationship was still intact after three months. Among those subjects whose relationship had ended, RCI scores did predict the intensity and duration of the distress they experienced. The closer the relationship had been, the greater was their emotional distress. In another study using the RCI, undergraduates involved in dating relationships were contacted three months and then nine months after the initial session at which they completed the RCI (Berscheid, Snyder, & Omoto, 1989b). Among those who could be contacted at both follow-ups, 49 percent of these relationships had ended. Although couples with high RCI scores were more likely to still be together after nine months, RCI scores did not predict the level of emotional distress experienced by those subjects whose relationship had ended. Thus, in one study, the Relationship Closeness Inventory predicted distress but not dissolution, while in another it predicted dissolution but not distress.

The exact reason for this mixed set of results is not known, but it might be noted that the RCI does not directly measure the amount of facilitation that partners provide to each other in a relationship. Spending time with each other across a diverse array of activities certainly offers the opportunity for facilitation to occur but does not guarantee that it will. Moveover, viewing the partner as having a strong impact on one's activities, decisions, and plans does not specify whether that impact is facilitative or interruptive. According to Berscheid's (1983) theoretical analysis, facilitation creates a condition of social dependency: Person X is dependent on person Y's actions to reach a goal desired by person X, or at least to reach it more quickly or easily. And yet the RCI does not ask about goals or about the effect of the partner on achieving them.

Dependency. Actually, it is clear that dependency on the partner does influence coping with the end of a relationship. Take, for example, money. Because women typically earn less than men, divorced and widowed women suffer considerably more financial hardship than their male counterparts (Guidubaldi & Cleminshaw, 1985; Weitzman, 1985). More generally, research by Chiriboga and Thurner (1980) found that individuals who reported having been less dependent on their spouse's skills and interests were happier after separation from a spouse than those who reported having been more dependent. If only one partner can do something that both partners need (pay the bills, cook, fix a leaky faucet, keep the house clean), then life for the one who lacks the necessary skills is going to be difficult after the breakup.

Berscheid's notion of facilitation in intimate relationships goes beyond such obvious instances of potentially costly dependency. Partners can facilitate the reaching of practical goals, but they can also assist in the reaching of more subtle socioemotional goals. According to Stephen (1984), partners can also contribute to the attainment of general philosophical or metaphysical goals. In a six-month longitudinal study, Stephen found that those undergraduates who reported having a "shared view of the world" with their dating partner (which Stephen called "symbolic interdependence") when first assessed were more distressed after the relationship broke up than were those who initially reported less similarity in world views. Presumably, sharing a view of the world with one's partner provides basic support for one's overall approach to life and other people. Losing such support could be a serious blow.

Expectations. Expectations also play a major role in reactions to facilitation or the loss of it (Riordan, Quigley-Fernandez, & Tedeschi, 1982). As Berscheid emphasizes, expected facilitation is often taken for granted and produces little if any emotional response. The unexpected loss of facilitation provided by the partner can, however, create great distress. For example, adjustment to the loss of an intimate relationship is often more difficult if the partner dies unexpectedly (Glick et al., 1974; Hansson, Stroebe, & Stroebe, 1988a) or if the partner's desire for a divorce was not anticipated (Jordan, 1988; Weiss, 1975).

An interesting study on the adjustment of widows to the loss of their husbands suggests that expectations influence coping through their effects on actual behavior (Remondet, Hansson, Rule, & Winfrey, 1987). Among these individuals, retrospective reports of having thought through the implications of their impending widowhood before their husband's death were associated with *greater* emotional disruption afterward. In contrast, retrospective reports of having actually engaged in preparatory behaviors (e.g., beginning to do things on their own; planning and making decisions for the future) were associated with *reduced* emotional disruption after their husband's death. These findings suggest that mere anticipation of the loss of a relationship is not the key factor involved in improving adjustment after the loss. Instead, anticipation will be helpful to the extent that it allows the individual to engage in coping behaviors before the loss has actually occurred. Since people who do not anticipate a loss cannot engage in such behaviors, they may have more difficulty adjusting once the loss occurs.

Gender. In principle, dependency and expectations should have similar effects on the emotional responses of both men and women. As a practical matter, however, there are important differences in the type of dependency experienced by many men and women, and this difference may affect their preparedness for the loss of a relationship. Just as women tend to be more financially dependent than men in heterosexual relationships, so do men tend to be more emotionally dependent than

Compared with married women, married men disclose less to friends. This lack of close friendships may make it more difficult for men to adjust to the loss of their spouse. (Michael Silik/The Image Works)

women (Powers, Keith, & Goudy, 1975; Stroebe & Stroebe, 1983). For example, in a national survey, 72 percent of married men compared with 58 percent of married women said they talked about their worries only with their spouse (Veroff et al., 1981). Another study comparing married and unmarried individuals obtained similar results (Tschann, 1988). Married men disclosed less to friends than did married women. Indeed, married men had the lowest disclosure to friends among the four groups participating in the study (married and unmarried; men and women). This difference between married men and women in the quality and extent of their friendships occurs among both first-married and remarried couples (Kurdek, 1989b).

The different types of dependency that men and women experience in marriage may influence their preparedness for the difficulties they would face should the relationship end (Brehm, 1987). Since financial dependency is usually considerably more visible than socioemotional dependency, women should be able to make a more realistic assessment of their potential losses. Such an assessment is unlikely to be perfectly accurate, and many women are startled by the enormous range of problems they encounter after a divorce (Arendell, 1988). Nevertheless, gender differences in dependency suggest that women would experience more anxiety and distress than men during the preseparation period as they focus on their anticipated losses, while men would experience more anxiety and distress than women during the postseparation period as they try to cope with losses that are much more upsetting than they had expected. And, indeed, the pattern predicted by this line of reasoning has been found in a number of studies of divorce (Bloom & Caldwell, 1981; Chiriboga & Cutler, 1977; Green, 1983; Hagestad & Smyer, 1982; Jacobson, 1983). In general, the worst time for women is before a marital separation, whereas for men the worst time is afterward.

Despite these differences between men and women in the type of loss that causes them the greatest difficulty and the timing of when they experience their greatest distress, we should not forget the similarities. When it comes to the end of a relationship, suffering is not confined to any one gender. Male and female, it hurts to lose someone you care about. Male and female, it takes considerable courage and strength of character to put your life back together again.

CHAPTER SUMMARY

Structural Factors in Conflict and Dissolution

Gender Differences. In general, women report more problems in their heterosexual relationships than do men, and female dissatisfaction with a relationship is a better predictor of whether the relationship will end. There are also gender differences in specific types of problems reported. For example, women emphasize basic unhappiness and incompatibility more than men do, while men are more likely than women to blame the end of a relationship on their partner's sexual involvement with another person. Although women are more likely than men to formally initiate the termination of a relationship, the responsibility for ending a relationship is usually difficult to determine.

As Time Goes By. Marital satisfaction is higher for those who knew each other longer before marriage, and satisfied partners spend more time with each other. Research on the life cycle of a marriage has emphasized two different possibilities. Some investigators believe that there is a linear decline in marital satisfaction over time. Other investigators, however, suggest that after an initial decline, marital satisfaction begins to increase—creating a U-shaped relationship between time and satisfaction. It is also possible that the developmental sequence of the positive rewards of marriage differs from that of the negative costs.

When Two Become Three or More: Effects of Children on Marital Satisfaction. In general, childless couples report greater satisfaction than couples with children. This negative effect of children appears stronger for wives than for husbands and is most pronounced for low-income mothers employed full-time. Children are less likely to have a negative effect on marital satisfaction when they are wanted and parent-child relationships are good.

Role Strain: Who Does What? The traditional roles of husband and wife in Western industrialized nations are fast disappearing due to the increased participation by women in paid employment outside the home. It is estimated that by the year 2000, 81 percent of women aged 25 to 64 will be in the work force. However, the increased employment of women has not resulted in a comparable increase in husbands' assuming responsibility for household chores and child care. On average, women have approximately 15 fewer hours of leisure each week than do men. All of these developments create role strain, as men and women engaged in multiple roles are more likely to disagree about who should be doing what. Two different views of the relationship between multiple roles and stress have been taken. According to the scarcity hypothesis, multiple roles increase stress because they stretch time and energy thin. In contrast, the enhancement hypothesis proposes that multiple roles reduce stress because disappointments in one area of life can be compensated for by success in another area. In general, the evidence favors the enhancement hypothesis: Multiple roles are usually associated with enhanced well-being, especially when these roles are evaluated favorably by the individual. Social support by one's partner can help ensure that multiple roles enhance one's life rather than diminish it.

The Process of Conflict and Dissolution

Attributions: A General Scenario. People are more active in their search for explanations during conflict than during more pleasant, peaceful interactions. During conflict, people will tend to take a benign view of the causes of their own behavior, easily finding excuses for what they do. Although conflict may start as a dispute about facts, it can readily turn into an attributional conflict over motives. Because of the actor-observer bias, partners will often disagree about each other's motives. The actor will view his or her behavior as situationally caused while regarding the partner's behavior as produced by the partner's enduring personal characteristics.

Attributions: Differences between Happy and Unhappy Couples. Despite these general trends in attributional behavior during conflict, there are major differences in the pattern of attributions exhibited by happy as compared with unhappy couples. Happy couples make relationship-enhancing causal attributions: emphasizing the good by making internal, stable, and global attributions for positive behavior by the partner and discounting the bad by making external, unstable, and specific attributions for negative behavior by the partner. Unhappy couples make distress-maintaining causal attributions, which are the mirror image of those made by happy couples (see Figure 11.2). Attributions of responsibility (indicating a person's accountability for an event) also differ depending on the state of the relationship. Unhappy couples are more likely than happy ones to regard the partner as selfishly motivated and behaving with negative intentions. There is some evidence that distress-maintaining attributions can precede, and perhaps make a causal contribution to, marital dissatisfaction. Although marital dissatisfaction is associated with depression, the connection between marital dissatisfaction and distress-maintaining attributions occurs among both depressed and nondepressed individuals.

Volatility: A Problem and an Opportunity. Distressed couples appear highly volatile in their emotional reactions: emitting a flurry of positive and negative behaviors in response to a negative behavior by the spouse; increasing in overall satisfaction with the relationship in response to positive daily events and decreasing in response to negative daily events. In contrast, happy couples seem more stable, less affected by the partner's behavior. Although volatility can produce emotional blowups, the presence of positive emotional responses may contribute to improvement of the relationship.

Coping with the End of a Relationship

In response to conflict and dissatisfaction, intimate partners can respond actively or passively, positively or negatively—creating the four basic responses of voice, loyalty, neglect, and exit. Although the end of a relationship is often traumatic, many people make a good adjustment.

Cognitive Aspects of Coping. After a relationship ends, people often spend considerable time and energy coming up with an organized account of what happened and why. This process reflects the general human tendency to want to explain negative or unexpected events; such explanations can serve to put our role in a positive light and give us a sense of control over future experiences. Research on coping with the end of a relationship has concentrated on several kinds of accounts. Though the findings are mixed, initiator status (seeing yourself as an active participant in making the decision to leave) appears to play only a minor role in adjustment after a separation. Some research suggests that interpersonal attributions of responsibility for the end of the relationship are associated with better adjustment than attributions to either the self or the partner; not all research findings, however, are consistent with this conclusion. It does appear that blaming the partner for the dissolution of the relationship can be associated with difficulties in coping, while blaming the self may sometimes be associated with better coping.

Emotional Aspects of Coping. Berscheid's model of emotional response in intimate relationships emphasizes dependency and expectations. When a partner facilitates our reaching a goal, we are dependent upon the partner. If, however, facilitation is taken for granted, we may not respond emotionally to that assistance. Thus, a well-established, highly facilitative relationship may be emotionally tranquil but create great distress if it ends. On the other hand, a highly emotional relationship, based on a low quantity of *unexpected* facilitation, may not cause much distress if it is terminated. Studies using the Relationship Closeness Inventory have been only partially successful in predicting the emotional distress people experience at the end of the relationship. It is clear, however, that dependency in practical areas such as finances and skills can influence coping, and the unexpected loss of a relationship is usually more debilitating than when the end was anticipated. Because women's financial dependency on men is more visible than men's socioemotional dependency on women, women may have more realistic views of and be more prepared for the difficulties they will face on their own. It does appear that the worst time for women in the process of conflict and dissolution is before the separation, while the worst time for men is afterward.

12

Loneliness

— ❖ —

L oneliness is a universal human experience. It is hard even to imagine someone who has not at sometime felt lonely. After the end of an intimate relationship, feelings of loneliness can be intense and extremely painful. But loneliness occurs in many other situations as well: trying to get to know people in a new school or on a new job; traveling alone in a foreign country; finding yourself at loose ends on a Saturday night. In this chapter, we examine the experience of being lonely, factors that may cause or intensify loneliness, and some possible ways to cope with lonely feelings.

WHAT IS LONELINESS?

Loneliness is not the same as physical isolation; people can feel happy as a clam in complete solitude but lonely in a crowd. Instead, loneliness is a feeling of deprivation and dissatisfaction produced by a discrepancy between the kind of social relations we want and the kind of social relations we have (Perlman &

Peplau, 1981). We feel lonely when we are alone *if* we would rather be with someone. We feel lonely when we are with other people *if* we would rather be with someone else.

Weiss (1973) has suggested that there are two different types of loneliness. In *social isolation*, people are dissatisfied and lonely because they lack a social network of friends and acquaintances. In *emotional isolation*, people are dissatisfied and lonely because they lack a single intense relationship. According to Weiss, it is not possible to ease one type of loneliness by substituting the other type of relationship. So, for example, if a couple has just moved to a new town where they do not know anyone, they will experience the loneliness of social isolation even though they have a close relationship with each other. On the other hand, a person can have an extensive social network and a very active social life but still feel lonely if he or she does not have a romantic partner. Since these two types of loneliness share a common emotional core, there is some debate about how clearly we can distinguish between them (Russell, Cutrona, Rose, & Yurko, 1984; Vaux, 1988a). Nevertheless, the general principle is an important one. If we lack the kind of relationship we desire, we can be lonely despite having other, quite rewarding social interactions.

How Does It Feel to Be Lonely?

When we are lonely, we feel dissatisfied, deprived, and distressed. This does not mean, however, that feelings of loneliness are all the same. In fact, different people in different situations may have different kinds of feelings when they are lonely. A study on the loneliness of widows illustrated how many kinds of emotions and desires can become bound up with the experience of being lonely (Lopata, 1969). For these women, loneliness was associated with one or more of the following:

- Desiring to be with the husband
- Wanting to be loved by someone
- Wanting to love and take care of someone
- Wanting to share daily experiences with someone
- Wanting to have someone around the house
- Needing someone to share the work
- Longing for previous form of life
- Experiencing loss of status
- Experiencing loss of other people as consequence of having lost husband
- Fearing inability to make new friends

Thus, loneliness included longing for the past, frustration with the present, and fears about the future.

Even for individuals who have not experienced the often devastating blow of losing a spouse, loneliness can involve many different kinds of feelings. Based on a survey of loneliness in the general population, Rubenstein, Shaver, and Peplau (1979) described four different sets of feelings that people say they have when they are lonely: desperation, impatient boredom, self-deprecation, and depression. The specific feelings reported in each of these clusters are given in Table 12.1. Though there are huge differences between some of these feelings (e.g., desperation versus boredom), loneliness is complex enough to encompass all of them.

Measuring Loneliness

Research on loneliness has taken two major approaches to defining and measuring loneliness (Shaver & Brennan, 1990). Some investigators have viewed loneliness as an enduring personality *trait*: Lonely people are those individuals who report a long history of frequent and intense feelings of loneliness. The New York University Loneliness Scale (Rubenstein & Shaver, 1982), displayed in Table 12.2, is primarily a trait measure of loneliness. Other researchers have defined loneliness as a

TABLE 12.1 FEELINGS WHEN LONELY

Desperation	*Impatient Boredom*
Desperate	Impatient
Helpless	Bored
Afraid	Desire to be elsewhere
Without hope	Uneasy
Abandoned	Angry
Vulnerable	Unable to concentrate
Self-Deprecation	*Depression*
Feeling unattractive	Sad
Down on self	Depressed
Stupid	Empty
Ashamed	Isolated
Insecure	Sorry for self
	Melancholy
	Alienated
	Longing to be with one special person

SOURCE: Rubenstein, Shaver, & Peplau, 1979.

TABLE 12.2 THE NYU LONELINESS SCALE

For each question below, circle the most appropriate answer. Then add up the numbers that correspond to the answers you chose. Your total score should fall between 80 (not at all lonely) and 320 (very lonely).

1. When I am completely alone, I feel lonely:

Almost never	(10)
Occasionally	(16)
About half the time	(24)
Often	(32)
Most of the time	(40)

2. How often do you feel lonely?

Never, or almost never	(10)
Rarely	(11)
Occasionally	(17)
About half the time	(23)
Quite often	(29)
Most of the time	(34)
All the time, or almost all the time	(40)

3. When you feel lonely, do you usually feel:

I never feel lonely	(10)
Slightly lonely	(13)
Somewhat lonely	(20)
Fairly lonely	(27)
Very lonely	(33)
Extremely lonely	(40)

4. Compared to people your own age, how lonely do you think you are?

Much less lonely	(10)
Somewhat less lonely	(16)
About average	(24)
Somewhat lonelier	(32)
Much lonelier	(40)

psychological *state*, which different people may experience for different lengths of time at different points in their lives. The University of California at Los Angeles Loneliness Scale (Russell, Peplau, & Cutrona, 1980), examples from which are shown in Table 12.3, is primarily a state measure of loneliness.

In looking over these two scales, you should note that it is possible for a person who is classified as lonely on the UCLA scale not to be so classified on the NYU scale. People can experience the state of loneliness

5. I am a lonely person

    Strongly disagree   (10)
    Disagree   (20)
    Agree   (30)
    Strongly agree   (40)

6. I always was a lonely person

    Strongly disagree   (10)
    Disagree   (20)
    Agree   (30)
    Strongly agree   (40)

7. I always will be a lonely person

    Strongly disagree   (10)
    Disagree   (20)
    Agree   (30)
    Strongly agree   (40)

8. Other people think of me as a lonely person

    Strongly disagree   (10)
    Disagree   (20)
    Agree   (30)
    Strongly agree   (40)

Loneliness scores on this scale: Average loneliness among respondents to newspaper surveys was about 170.

Rubenstein and Shaver suggest that

    80–132 = least lonely
    133–170 = less lonely than average
    171–206 = more lonely than average
    207–320 = most lonely

SOURCE: Rubenstein & Shaver, 1982.

without having had the chronic history of loneliness characteristic of the personal trait of loneliness. To see this difference, imagine that you have just moved away from a warm, secure social life into a new and unfamiliar situation where the people you meet seem cold and distant. Now answer the items from both scales. Your answers will indicate that although you are lonely in your present situation (high scores on the UCLA scale), you have not always been lonely (low scores on the NYU scale). As we will see later in this chapter, this difference between a

TABLE 12.3 EXAMPLES FROM THE REVISED UCLA LONELINESS SCALE

When people complete this scale, they indicate how often they feel the way described in each of the following statements:

Never = 1   Rarely = 2   Sometimes = 3   Often = 4

1. There is no one I can turn to.
2. I am no longer close to anyone.
3. No one really knows me well.
4. People are around me but not with me.

SOURCE: Russell, Peplau, & Cutrona, 1980.

chronic and enduring loneliness characteristic of some *people* and a more temporary state of affairs created by some *situations* is an important issue in research on the beliefs and behavior of lonely people.

Who Are the Lonely?

Regardless of whether we conceptualize loneliness as a trait or as a state, are there some people who are more vulnerable to loneliness than others? The answer is yes, with the major differences involving age, marital status, and gender.

Age. There is a stereotype in our society of the lonely old person. Both young and old agree that the older one gets, the lonelier one becomes (Rubenstein & Shaver, 1982). When we ask people about their own experiences of loneliness, however, we discover that this stereotype is dead wrong. In the United States, the loneliest people are adolescents and young adults (Peplau, Bikson, Rook, & Goodchilds, 1982; Rubenstein & Shaver, 1982). Loneliness actually declines with age (see Figure 12.1), at least until people are well into the later stages of old age, when it may begin to increase (Peplau et al., 1982; Schultz & Moore, 1984). This effect of age is so strong that even among a very restricted age range of young people (14–20), the younger people reported more loneliness (Ostrov & Offer, 1980).

Although this association between youth and loneliness goes against our stereotype of the elderly lonely, it is not really so surprising when we think about it. Young people face the enormously difficult task of defining their own identity as individuals. Without a solid sense of self, it is all too easy to feel unappreciated and unloved by others. Moreover, young people are constantly having to develop new relationships as they go through school and into employment settings; each new social situation creates the possibility of feeling lonely. Finally, it

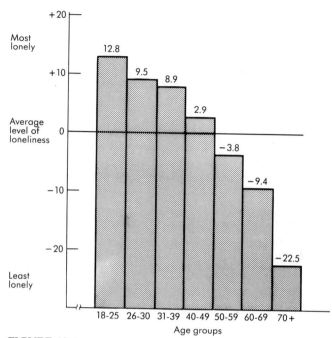

FIGURE 12.1
Loneliness scores by age groups. (Rubenstein, Shaver, & Peplau, 1979.)

may be that younger people have greater expectations about their relationships than do older people, who have learned to live with less than
perfect understanding and compatibility.

Marital status. In general, married people are less lonely than unmarried individuals (Freedman, 1978; Perlman & Peplau, 1981). However, most of this difference is accounted for by the greater loneliness of
the separated, divorced, and widowed (Perlman & Peplau, 1981;
Rubenstein & Shaver, 1982). When we compare people who have never
married with those who are presently married, these groups report
similar levels of loneliness (Perlman & Peplau, 1981). Thus, loneliness
seems to be a reaction to the loss of a marital relationship rather than a
response to its absence.

Gender. Although many studies of loneliness do not indicate any
overall difference between men and women, some research using the
UCLA scale has found that men have higher loneliness scores than do
women (Schultz & Moore, 1986, 1988; Stokes & Levin, 1986). According
to Borys and Perlman (1985), however, the gender difference you get
will depend upon the kind of question you ask. When these investiga-

tors combined loneliness scores on the UCLA scale from 28 different subject samples, they also found that men reported greater loneliness than did women. But when they combined 11 different samples in which subjects provided self-ratings of loneliness, they obtained exactly the opposite result: Here, women reported greater loneliness than men. For Borys and Perlman, the critical difference between the UCLA scale and self-ratings boils down to one word: loneliness. The UCLA scale never uses the word; subjects never have to state directly whether they are lonely. Self-ratings (as well as the NYU scale) do require this direct statement. Borys and Perlman believe that it is more difficult for males to explicitly acknowledge that they are lonely—and with good reason. When they had undergraduates read a brief description of a lonely person, identified either as a man or as a woman, the man was evaluated more negatively than the woman. The social price of admitting loneliness appears, then, to be higher for men than for women, and men may learn to avoid this "L-word." But when asked about their experiences without the word "lonely" being used, men's responses often indicate that they suffer more loneliness than women do.

In addition to overall differences between men and women, gender also interacts with marital status. Among married couples, wives report greater loneliness than do husbands (Freedman, 1978; Peplau et al., 1982; Rubenstein & Shaver, 1982). On the other hand, men report greater loneliness than women when they have never married, are separated or divorced, or are widowed (Peplau et al., 1982; Rubenstein & Shaver, 1982). These findings suggest that men and women may differ in their vulnerability to the two types of loneliness described earlier. Men, it appears, are most likely to be lonely when they experience the emotional isolation of not having an intimate partner. Women, however, may be most susceptible to loneliness if the intimate tie of marriage reduces their access to a larger social network (Fischer & Phillips, 1982). This kind of social isolation would seem particularly likely for wives who are unemployed, who have left their friends and family because of a change in the location of their husband's job, and who have young children.

Other background characteristics. In their survey on loneliness, Rubenstein and Shaver (1982) found a number of background characteristics that did *not* correlate with loneliness. There were no apparent differences in loneliness between people who lived in rural settings and those who lived in urban areas. In addition, people who had moved a number of times in their lives did not indicate that they experienced more loneliness than people who had seldom moved. However, Rubenstein and Shaver did find one very interesting background characteristic that was a strong predictor of loneliness. People whose parents had been divorced reported feeling more lonely than people whose parents had not divorced (see also Shaver & Rubenstein, 1980). More-

FIGURE 12.2

Loneliness scores by age at parents' divorce.
(Rubenstein, Shaver, & Peplau, 1979.)

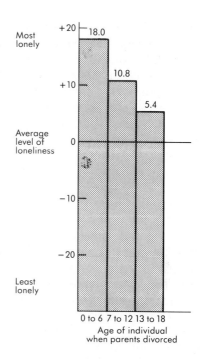

over, the younger the person was when his or her parents divorced, the more loneliness the person experienced as an adult (see Figure 12.2). This difference did not apply to people who had lost a parent by death: People who had been bereaved during childhood reported no more loneliness as adults than did people whose family remained intact throughout their childhood and adolescence. Thus, there seems something specific to the divorce process itself that increases the potential for feelings of loneliness as an adult. (See Chapter 13 for an extended discussion of the effects of divorce on children.)

SOME POSSIBLE CAUSES OF LONELINESS

Just as there are many different feelings involved in loneliness, so are there many different causes of loneliness (deJong-Gierveld, 1987). This section will review the possible causes of loneliness that have received the most attention from social scientists.

Inadequacies in Our Relationships

There are any number of reasons why we might feel dissatisfied with the relationships that we have. Rubenstein and Shaver (1982) found that most of the reasons that the people in their survey gave for being lonely could be classified into five major categories:

1. *Being unattached:* Having no spouse; having no sexual partner; breaking up with spouse or lover
2. *Alienation:* Feeling different; being misunderstood; not being needed; having no close friends
3. *Being alone:* Coming home to an empty house; being alone
4. *Forced isolation:* Being housebound; being hospitalized; having no transportation
5. *Dislocation:* Being far from home; starting in a new job or school; moving too often; traveling often

The first two categories parallel Weiss's distinction between loneliness based on emotional isolation (being unattached) and loneliness due to social isolation (alienation). There also appears to be an important difference between relationship deficits that are produced purely by the situation (forced isolation; dislocation) versus those (being unattached; alienation; being alone) that could come about in a variety of ways—such as being caused by characteristics of the other people in the lonely person's environment or by characteristics of the lonely person.

Changes in What We Want from a Relationship

Loneliness can also develop because of changes in our ideas about what we want out of our relationships. At one time in our life, our social relations may be quite satisfying and so we do not feel lonely. These relationships may then continue but at some point fail to be satisfying because we have changed in what we want. Peplau and her associates have noted that these changes can come from many different sources (Peplau, Russell, & Heim, 1979; Perlman & Peplau, 1981). Our moods change, and the kind of relationships we want when we are happy may be different from those we want when we are sad. As we age, we go through developmental changes that may affect our relational desires. The kind of friendship that was very satisfying when we were 15 may fail to satisfy us when we are 25. Situational changes also can be involved. Many people do not want a close, emotional involvement when they are preparing for their careers. Later on, however, when their careers are established, they may feel a great need for an emotionally committed relationship. Whatever the reason, we do change our minds about what we want from relationships, and if our relationships do not also change accordingly, we may experience loneliness.

Self-Esteem and Causal Attributions

Although it seems reasonable to believe that certain circumstances (e.g., the loss of an intimate partner; a move to a new place) as well as changes in what we want out of a relationship could *cause* us to feel lonely, the causal connection gets considerably more problematic when we consider personal and social characteristics of the individual. For example, the feeling of alienation cited by respondents in the survey by Rubenstein and Shaver (1982) could be a *direct cause* of loneliness (feeling alienated from others makes you feel lonely too), an *indirect cause* (people who feel alienated act in ways that drive others away and, thus, become lonely); or an *effect* of loneliness (feeling lonely makes you feel alienated too). There probably are some personal characteristics that make it more likely that a person who has them will experience loneliness. But loneliness does not occur in a psychological vacuum, and feeling lonely will have personal and social consequences. In the following pages, we examine some factors whose connection with loneliness could go either way: as a cause or as an effect.

Whatever the causal relationship involved, loneliness is associated with having low self-esteem (Peplau, Miceli, & Morasch, 1982; Rubenstein & Shaver, 1980). People who report themselves as lonely also tend to regard themselves as unworthy and unlovable. Perhaps because of this lack of self-esteem, lonely people expect to be uncomfortable in risky social situations (Vaux, 1988b). This anticipated discomfort may motivate lonely people to reduce their social contacts, which could make it more difficult for these individuals to establish the kinds of relationships they need in order not to be lonely anymore.

Explanations for the cause of loneliness might also serve to lock loneliness in place. According to Peplau and her colleagues, loneliness is apt to be especially intense and long-lasting when people believe that their own enduring characteristics cause their loneliness (Michela, Peplau, & Weeks, 1982; Peplau et al., 1979). This kind of internal, stable attribution paints a depressing picture—we are the cause of our own misery, and things are unlikely to change—and may discourage people from trying to meet people and make friends. In contrast, explanations for loneliness that rely on attributions that are external, unstable, or both offer some hope that things can change for the better (see Table 12.4). This more hopeful attitude may, in turn, reduce emotional distress and promote more active, constructive efforts to cope with feelings of loneliness. The results of research by Cutrona (1982) on the loneliess experienced by new college students were consistent with this line of reasoning. Those who made internal, stable attributions for their loneliness in the fall semester (saying they were lonely because of shyness, their personality, their fear of being rejected, and their not knowing what to do to start a relationship) were more likely to still be lonely in

TABLE 12.4 EXPLANATIONS OF LONELINESS

	LOCUS OF CAUSALITY	
	Internal	*External*
STABILITY *Stable*	I'm lonely because I'm unlovable, I'll never be worth loving.	The people here are cold and impersonal; none of them share my interests. I think I'll move.
Unstable	I'm lonely now, but I won't be for long. I'll stop working so much and go out and meet some new people.	The first semester in college is always the worst, I'm sure things will get better.

SOURCE: Based on Shaver & Rubenstein, 1980. From Brehm & Kassin, 1990.

the spring than were those students who made other kinds of attributions in the fall. Some investigators have noted, however, that we cannot be sure about the causal pathways involved in Cutrona's study (Shaver, Furman, & Buhrmester, 1985). Did the causal attributions that subjects made for their first-semester loneliness cause some to stay lonely and others to get over it? Or might those who made internal, stable attributions for their first-semester loneliness have had different prior experiences or different personalities that made them more likely to generate these attributions *and* more likely to stay lonely over the course of the year? As emphasized in the beginning of this section, it is often difficult to sort out cause from effect in research on the personal characteristics associated with loneliness.

Interpersonal Behaviors

This difficulty of distinguishing cause from effect also occurs in research on the interpersonal behavior of lonely people. As you will see, lonely people behave differently from nonlonely people in a variety of ways. But why? Does being lonely cause us to act differently? Or does acting differently create the social circumstances that produce loneliness? We don't know, though it seems likely that causation here goes in both directions. What we do know is that the interpersonal behavior of lonely people makes it harder for them to establish rewarding relationships with others.

Compared with people who are not lonely, lonely people evaluate others more negatively (Jones, Freemon, & Goswick, 1981; Jones, Sansome, & Helm, 1983; Wittenberg & Reis, 1986). They don't like others very much (Rubenstein & Shaver, 1980); mistrust others (Vaux, 1988b); interpret others' actions and intentions negatively (Hanley-Dunn, Maxwell, & Santos, 1985); and are more likely to hold hostile attitudes (Check, Perlman, & Malamuth, 1985; Sermat, 1980).

Lonely people also lack social skills in their behavior with others (Solano & Koester, 1989). They are more passive than nonlonely people in social interactions, hesitating to express their opinions in public (Hansson & Jones, 1981). In addition, lonely people tend to be socially unresponsive and insensitive. During conversations between lonely and nonlonely people, lonely people made fewer statements focusing on their conversational partners, asked fewer questions of their partners, were slower to respond to statements made by their partners, and were less likely to continue discussing the topic initiated by their partner (Jones, Hobbs, & Hackenbury, 1982). Lonely people also appear slow to develop intimacy in their relations with others, and their level of self-disclosure is low (Davis & Franzoi, 1986; Sloan & Solano, 1984; Solano, Batten, & Parish, 1982; Williams & Solano, 1983). Finally, there is some evidence that lonely men are more likely than nonlonely men to behave in physically aggressive ways (Check et al., 1985).

Given these negative attitudes and socially inept or undesirable behaviors, you might expect that lonely people would elicit negative reactions from others. And in some circumstances, though not all, this is the case (Jones, 1990; Jones, Cavert, Snider, & Bruce, 1985; Rook, 1988). The conversational partners of lonely people feel they do not know the person very well (Solano et al., 1982) and regard the lonely person as socially incompetent (Spitzberg & Canery, 1985). Overall, then, lonely people seem caught in a downward social spiral. They reject others, lack social skills in their behavior with others, and, at least in some instances, are rejected by others (see Figure 12.3). Regardless of where this pattern begins, all of its components reinforce each other and make social life more difficult and less rewarding.

Social anxiety and shyness. Loneliness is only one of a number of common problems that involve personal distress and social dissatisfaction. Another such problem, social anxiety, refers to feelings of discomfort in the presence of others (Leary, 1983). There are many different types of social anxiety—including fear of public speaking (called "speech anxiety") and shyness, which combines social inhibition and avoidance along with feelings of discomfort in interpersonal interactions (Jones, Cheek, & Briggs, 1986; Zimbardo, 1977). A self-report scale measuring shyness is reprinted in Table 12.5. Loneliness, shyness, and social anxiety are all interrelated; those suffering from one often suffer from the others as well (Bruch, Gorsky, Collins, & Berger, 1989; Cheek &

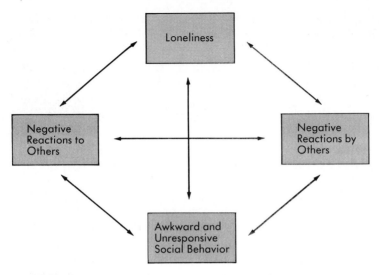

FIGURE 12.3
Loneliness: A vicious circle.

Busch, 1981; Jones & Carpenter, 1986; Solano & Koester, 1989). In particular, the interpersonal behaviors of shy and socially anxious people closely resemble those of lonely people: negative attitudes toward others, passive and unresponsive behavior with others, and negative reactions from others in some circumstances (Gurtman, Martin, & Hintzman, 1990; Jones & Carpenter, 1986; Langston & Cantor, 1989).

Socially anxious feelings can arise from a number of different sources (Leary, 1987). They can be a learned response to an unpleasant social encounter; social difficulties in the past can contribute to social anxiety in the future. Social anxiety also appears to have an important cognitive component. People who are anxious about social encounters often believe that they lack the skills necessary for social success (Maddux, Norton, & Leary, 1988). Even if, in fact, they have such skills, their belief that they lack them is likely to cause concern. When a person wants to make a favorable impression on others but is convinced that he or she is unable to do so, awareness of this discrepancy can create considerable anxiety (Schlenker & Leary, 1982).

Depression. In an attempt to discriminate among a variety of problems in living, Anderson and Harvey (1988) examined the relationship among a number of self-report scales measuring loneliness, social anxiety, shyness, and depression. These four scales yielded three basic factors: loneliness, social anxiety/shyness, and depression. And all three were positively correlated with each other. Thus, just as loneliness is

TABLE 12.5 THE REVISED CHEEK AND BUSS SHYNESS SCALE

Indicate the degree to which the following statements apply to you by responding to each one in terms of the following scale:

	Agree	1	2	3	4	5	Disagree

1. I am socially somewhat awkward.*
2. I don't find it hard to talk to strangers.
3. I feel tense when I'm with people I don't know well.*
4. When in a group of people, I have trouble thinking of the right things to talk about.*
5. I feel nervous when speaking to someone in authority.*
6. I am often uncomfortable at parties and other social functions.*
7. I feel inhibited in social situations.*

8. I have trouble looking someone right in the eye.*
9. I am more shy with members of the opposite sex.*
10. I do not find it difficult to ask other people for information.
11. It does not take me long to overcome my shyness in new situations.
12. It is hard for me to act natural when I am meeting new people.*
13. I have no doubts about my social competence.

For items without an asterisk, higher scores (disagreement) mean more shyness. For items with an asterisk, lower scores (agreement) mean more shyness.

SOURCE: From Cheek, 1983.

associated with social anxiety and shyness, so it is associated with depression (Lobdell & Perlman, 1986). Depression is characterized by negative mood (such as feelings of sadness and despair), low self-esteem, pessimism, lack of initiative, and slowed thought processes (Holmes, 1991). It may involve disturbances in sleeping and eating patterns along with reduced sexual desire. Approximately 5 percent of the population will experience a major depression sometime during their lives (Robins et al., 1984), but many more will suffer from brief, relatively mild bouts with the "blues."

Like those suffering from loneliness or social anxiety, depressed individuals seem caught in an ever-worsening, downward spiral of interpersonal behaviors. Depressed individuals reject others, exhibit awkward or inadequate social skills, and are rejected by others (Burchill & Stile, 1988; Gurtman et al., 1990; Hokanson, Loewenstein, Hedeen, & Howes, 1986; Strack & Coyne, 1983). In addition, depressed individuals are similar to lonely people in their discomfort with, and avoidance of, risky social interactions (Pietromonaco & Rook, 1987). Depression is also associated with a pattern of causal attributions for negative events that resembles the attributions for loneliness made by the college students who stayed lonely across their freshman year in Cutrona's (1982) study. In general, depressed individuals are prone to explain their negative experiences in terms of causes that are internal (to the self rather than the situation), stable (constant across time rather than varying), and global (affecting many different areas of life rather than just one specific area). In other words, depressed people tend to blame enduring personal characteristics for the bad things that happen to them—just as those students who stayed lonely blamed enduring personal characteristics for their lonely condition. The association between depression and this "depressive attributional style" has been well documented (Sweeney, Anderson, & Bailey, 1986), although, as is the case with loneliness, the causal connections involved remain a matter of dispute (Barnett & Gotlib, 1988).

Although depression and loneliness frequently occur together, they are not identical conditions. Consider, for example, these findings from another study of college freshmen (Bragg, 1979; Weeks, Michela, Peplau, & Bragg, 1980). First, while dating (even in a very casual way) was associated with less loneliness and with less depression, knowing people was associated only with less loneliness. Second, in terms of satisfaction with their lives, lonely students indicated low satisfaction only with their social lives, but depressed students reported low satisfaction with both the social and nonsocial aspects of the way they were living. Taken together, these results suggest that depression is a more global state of dissatisfaction and discontent that can be particularly sensitive to success or failure in romantic relationships. On the other hand, loneliness appears more specifically interpersonal in nature, but affected by a broader range of social interactions. Despite these differences, however, the close connection between depression and loneliness is evident. When the first-semester college students in this study were recontacted five weeks after their initial participation, those who were still lonely had become even more depressed than they were initially. It's depressing to stay lonely, and being depressed makes it harder to engage in an active effort to improve our social life.

COPING WITH LONELINESS

In this section, we examine the process of coping with loneliness. First, we consider the actions, constructive and destructive, that people engage in when they are lonely. Then, we turn to some specific coping responses that might be useful in reducing feelings of loneliness. Some closing comments offer a somewhat different perspective: that loneliness can make a positive contribution to personal growth and intimacy with others.

TABLE 12.6 WHAT PEOPLE DO WHEN THEY FEEL LONELY

Sad Passivity	Active Solitude
Cry	Study or work
Sleep	Write
Sit and think	Listen to music
Do nothing	Exercise, walk
Overeat	Work on a hobby
Take tranquilizers	Go to a movie
Watch TV	Read
Get drunk or stoned	Play music
Social Contact	Distractions
Call a friend	Spend money
Visit someone	Go shopping

SOURCE: Rubenstein & Shaver, 1982.

What Do People Do When They Are Lonely?

As we know from our own experience and the observation of others, there are many different reactions to loneliness. Table 12.6 summarizes the four major types of responses to loneliness mentioned by participants in the survey conducted by Rubenstein and Shaver (1982). As you can see, two of these categories involve positive, constructive coping behaviors: social contact and active solitude. In contrast, some of the behaviors categorized as "sad passivity" are potentially self-destructive. The distractions of going shopping and spending money are harder to classify. A moderate spree based on a flush bank account seems a reasonable way to get your mind off things, but self-induced impoverishment created by reckless spending is unlikely to be an effective cure for social dissatisfaction.

In their discussion of the self-help strategies of lonely people, Rook and Peplau (1982) distinguish between cognitive and behavioral coping strategies. Various examples of these two types are listed in Tables 12.7 and 12.8, which also indicate the extent to which they were used by the college students surveyed. The majority of these strategies are positive and constructive: e.g., reminding yourself that you actually do have good relationships with other people; trying to find new ways to meet people. But some negative, self-destructive reactions (e.g., taking your mind off feeling lonely by using drugs or alcohol) were also reported fairly frequently.

TABLE 12.7 COGNITIVE STRATEGIES COLLEGE STUDENTS USED TO COPE WITH LONELINESS

Strategy	Never	Sometimes	Often
Thought about things you could do to overcome your loneliness	4%	52%	44%
Reminded yourself that you actually do have good relationships with other people	7	33	60
Tried to figure out why you were lonely	7	54	39
Thought about good qualities that you possess (such as being warm, intelligent, sensitive, self-sufficient, etc.)	7	68	25
Told yourself that your loneliness would not last forever, that things would get better	10	38	52
Thought about things you can do extremely well (excelling at schoolwork, athletics, artwork, gourmet cooking, etc.)	10	47	23
Told yourself that most other people are lonely at one time or another	11	56	33
Taken your mind off feeling lonely by deliberately thinking about other things (anything other than your loneliness)	13	61	26
Told yourself that you were over-reacting, that you shouldn't be so upset	14	62	24
Thought about possible benefits of your experience of loneliness (such as telling yourself that you were learning to be self-reliant, that you would grow from the experience, etc.)	21	42	37
Changed your goals for social relationships (such as telling yourself that it is not that important to be popular, that at this point in your life it's all right not to have a boyfriend or girlfriend, etc.)	22	55	23

SOURCE: Rook & Peplau, 1982.

What Helps People Feel Less Lonely?

It is obvious that mindlessly watching TV, drinking to excess, or eating when you are not even hungry are all poor ways to cope with loneliness. These activities do not produce a more satisfying social life and, indeed, could well make it more difficult to establish good relationships. It is clearly better to cope actively and positively with loneliness (Rook, 1984). But how can we do this? The actions reported by participants in

TABLE 12.8 BEHAVIORAL STRATEGIES COLLEGE STUDENTS USED TO COPE WITH LONELINESS

Strategy	Never	Sometimes	Often
Tried harder to be friendly to other people (such as making an effort to talk to people in your classes, etc.)	2%	62%	36%
Taken your mind off feeling lonely through some mental activity (such as reading a novel, watching TV, going to a movie, etc.)	6	60	34
Worked particularly hard to succeed at some activity (such as studying extra hard for an exam, putting extra effort into practicing an instrument, pushing yourself on an athletic skill, etc.)	7	53	40
Done something helpful for someone else (such as helping a classmate with homework, doing volunteer work, etc.)	7	64	29
Done something you are very good at (schoolwork, athletics, artwork, etc.)	7	66	27
Taken your mind off feeling lonely through some physical activity (such as jogging, playing basketball, shopping, washing the car, etc.)	12	51	37
Tried to find new ways to meet people (such as joining a club, moving into a dorm, going to dances, etc.)	18	64	18
Done something to make yourself more physically attractive to others (going on a diet, buying new clothes, changing your hairstyle, etc.)	20	61	19
Done something to improve your social skills (such as learning to dance, learning to be more assertive, improving conversational skills, etc.)	25	66	9
Talked to a friend or relative about ways to overcome your loneliness	40	45	15
Taken your mind off feeling lonely by using drugs or alcohol	74	25	1
Talked to a counselor or therapist about ways to overcome your loneliness	91	6	3

SOURCE: Rook & Peplau, 1982.

the surveys just summarized offer some suggestions, some of them quite helpful. On the basis of their research, social scientists have also come up with some ideas.

Earlier in this chapter, four self-defeating characteristics of lonely people (and of those who are socially anxious or depressed) were described:

1. Expecting discomfort in socially risky situations
2. Making internal, stable attributions for unpleasant experiences and feelings
3. Having negative attitudes toward others
4. Behaving in passive and unresponsive ways with others

Regardless of whether these characteristics cause or are produced by loneliness, they make it difficult to establish the kind of rewarding social relationships needed to get over being lonely. It would, therefore, seem to be important for people experiencing loneliness to try to counteract these thoughts and behaviors. Here are some suggestions for how to do so.

1. If the fear of possible social failure is keeping you from getting involved in some potentially interesting social interactions, try some rational cost analysis. If you go to that party, for example, and don't meet anyone, are you any worse off than you were? But if you go and have some enjoyable interactions, aren't you much better off than you were? Isn't the potential benefit worth the risk?

2. If you find yourself blaming your own inadequacies for feeling lonely, look around. Are you the *only* lonely person in your current situation? Usually, if you look really carefully, you will discover that the answer is no; others are lonely too, which suggests that situational factors are involved. The sometimes extremely strong impact of the situation on loneliness was illustrated in the study of first-semester college freshmen mentioned earlier (Bragg, 1979; Weeks et al., 1980). At the first testing session two weeks after classes started, 75 percent of the more than 300 subjects who participated reported experiencing at least occasional loneliness, and 43 percent said they were moderately or severely lonely. Five weeks later, loneliness had decreased, but the prevalence of loneliness was still very high: 66 percent reported occasional loneliness, and 30 percent indicated that they were experiencing moderate or severe loneliness. Significant numbers of these students blamed their own inadequacies for being lonely, and yet, obviously, the situation of being new at school was by far the most important factor. The next time you are tempted to blame yourself for being lonely, think about this research and look for some situational influences that might be involved.

3. Identifying situational influences does not, however, mean that you should just sit back and wait for things to get better. The situation may be the root cause for loneliness, but often it takes individual effort

to turn things around (Peplau et al., 1979; Revenson, 1981). Sometimes, as noted above, that effort involves taking some social risks. But attitudes are also important. Do you find yourself getting more and more critical about others? Home alone, do you think of them as selfish, shallow, and uncaring? Such negative attitudes can have the force of a self-fulfilling prophecy: What you expect is what you get. Armed with negative, even hostile, attitudes about others, your behavior is unlikely to be all sweetness and light—and their reaction is unlikely to be the warm acceptance you desire. Taking a more positive approach—actively looking for others' good qualities—has a much better chance of success.

4. But what if you dutifully do "all of the above" and you are still lonely? Does this mean that, despite your good intentions, you are being tripped up by inadequate social skills? Possibly. Some people can benefit from social skills training provided by therapists, counseling centers, or various community groups. But there is another possible factor involved. What sort of relationship are you looking for? In Cutrona's (1982) study of freshmen who did or did not stay lonely across their entire first year in college, those who stayed lonely seemed to believe that only a successful romance could reduce their loneliness. However, the students who became less lonely as the school year progressed placed greater emphasis on the satisfaction that could be derived from friendship. Other investigators have also highlighted the role of friendship in reducing or preventing loneliness (Rook & Peplau, 1982; Schmidt & Sermat, 1983). Putting some effort into deepening and enriching our relationships with our friends may be a better way of coping with loneliness than desperately seeking Mr. or Ms. Right.

Loneliness as a Growth Experience

Thus far we have concentrated on how to reduce or avoid loneliness by improving our social relations. One possible implication of this approach might be that loneliness should always be avoided or reduced. Actually, that is a false assumption. There may be times when loneliness can be transformed into a constructive experience for the individual.

One transformation process involves turning the negative, unpleasant state of loneliness into the positive, enjoyable state of solitude. Too often our reaction to even mild feelings of loneliness is to immediately seek companionship or to try to kill time by mindless activities. As an alternative, we might consider those examples of "active solitude" listed in Table 12.6, particularly those that are pleasure-oriented rather than work-related. We all have things we really like to do but never seem to have the time for. When we start feeling bored, restless, and lonely, this can be a signal that now we do have the time. Perhaps we like long,

To turn the unpleasant state of loneliness into the positive state of solitude, it is important to have things to do that we enjoy doing by ourselves. (Charles Kennard/ Stock, Boston)

leisurely bubble baths, perhaps walking in the woods, or perhaps just sitting around and daydreaming about the future. In order to turn loneliness into solitude, it is not the specific activity we engage in that matters; what counts is our attitude toward the activity. If we seek distraction or oblivion, we have not found solitude. But if we immerse ourselves in the activity, enjoying it for its own sake, then we can appreciate our moment of solitude without fretting over being lonely.

One of the great benefits of being able to enjoy solitude is that we learn that we can take good care of ourselves and need not always depend on other people to make us happy. Such an awareness is not a barrier to having intimate ties with others. Indeed, the ability to be comfortably alone with one's self may enhance our capacity to love others (Branden, 1980; Moustakas, 1972; Safilios-Rothschild, 1981). If we always require rewarding interactions with other people in order to be happy, this places a terrible burden on them—one they may not be willing or able to bear. Furthermore, being alone (physically *or* psycho-logically) can be used to develop an understanding of our own needs, feelings, and perspective on life. And, it is hoped, the more self-knowledge we have, the better equipped we are to have realistic, accepting, and loving relationships with others. It is by no means easy to face ourselves and our aloneness in the world; it can, however, be an enormously enriching experience. As the British historian Edward Gibbon once remarked, "I was never less alone than when by myself."

These two strategies of transformation—turning loneliness into solitude and using aloneness to gain self-knowledge—provide a balance to reducing loneliness through improving or extending our social relations. Much of healthy personal growth consists of promoting such a balance—of trying to develop satisfying relationships with other people *and* of trying to create a secure, internal base of satisfaction within ourselves.

CHAPTER SUMMARY

What Is Loneliness?

Loneliness is not the same as physical isolation. Instead, it is a feeling of deprivation and dissatisfaction produced by a discrepancy between the kind of social relations one has and the kind one desires. Two different types of loneliness have been identified: social isolation created by lack of a social network, and emotional isolation based on the lack of a single intense relationship.

How Does It Feel to Be Lonely? A variety of emotions and desires can be bound up with the experience of being lonely. In one survey, respondents reported four major categories of feelings they have when lonely: desperation, impatient boredom, self-deprecation, and depression.

Measuring Loneliness. The NYU Loneliness Scale measures the personality trait of loneliness; high scorers on this scale report a long history of frequent and intense feelings of loneliness. In contrast, the UCLA Loneliness Scale measures the state of loneliness, which varies across time and different situations.

Who Are the Lonely? In general, loneliness decreases with age, as adolescents and young adults report the greatest amount of loneliness. Married people are less lonely than those who have experienced the loss of a relationship through separation, divorce, or death of the partner. When responding to the UCLA Loneliness Scale (which does not use the word "lonely"), men tend to report greater loneliness than do women. When providing self-ratings of loneliness, however, women tend to report greater loneliness than do men. Since lonely men are evaluated more negatively than lonely women, men may be reluctant to explicitly acknowledge their lonely feelings. Among married couples, wives report greater loneliness than husbands. Among those who are not married, men report greater loneliness than women. In regard to other background characteristics, people whose parents were divorced report feeling greater loneliness than those from intact families. Loneliness does not, however, appear to be associated with having suffered the death of a parent during one's childhood.

Some Possible Causes of Loneliness

Inadequacies in Our Relationships. The reasons participants in one survey gave for being lonely involved five major categories: being unattached, alienation, being alone, forced isolation, and dislocation. These reasons cover a broad range, with some being situational in nature and others possibly reflecting personal characteristics of the lonely person.

Changes in What We Want from a Relationship. As people change (in their mood, their age, or their external situation), what they want from their relationships may also change. If their relationships do not change accordingly, they may experience loneliness.

Self-Esteem and Causal Attributions. Loneliness is associated with having low self-esteem. Lonely people also expect to be uncomfortable in risky social situations; these expectations may serve to maintain loneliness by motivating lonely people to avoid certain social contacts. Explanations for loneliness may also increase its duration. In one study, college freshmen who made internal, stable attributions for their loneliness in the fall semester were more likely to still be lonely in the spring than were those who employed different kinds of attributions.

Interpersonal Behaviors. Lonely people appear caught in a downward social spiral. Relative to nonlonely people, they hold more negative attitudes toward others, are more passive and unresponsive in their social interactions, and sometimes elicit more negative reactions from others. Each of these components reinforces the others and makes it more difficult for the lonely person to establish the rewarding social relationships necessary to eliminate loneliness. Another problem in living, social anxiety, involves feelings of discomfort in the presence of others. Shyness includes feelings of discomfort in social situations along with social inhibition and avoidance. Social anxiety and shyness are often associated with each other, and each is frequently associated with loneliness. The interpersonal behavior of socially anxious and shy individuals closely resembles that of lonely people. Socially anxious concerns can be a learned response to an unpleasant social encounter; they may also reflect the belief, accurate or not, that the individual is not capable of obtaining the social success that he or she desires. Depression is also associated with loneliness, and with shyness and social anxiety as well. Like those who are lonely, depressed individuals experience difficulties in their social interactions, are uncomfortable with risky social situations, and tend to blame themselves for negative events. Depression and loneliness are not, however, identical psychological conditions. Depression is a more global state of dissatisfaction, while loneliness is more specifically interpersonal in nature. Depressed individuals, at least those of college age, may be particularly sensitive to success or failure in romantic relationships, while loneliness is affected by a broad range of social interactions.

Coping with Loneliness

What Do People Do When They Are Lonely? According to their responses to survey questions, people appear to engage in a wide variety of behaviors when they are lonely. Some of these behaviors involve active, constructive coping; others are potentially self-destructive.

What Helps People Feel Less Lonely? In addition to the active, constructive coping behaviors reported in surveys, some suggestions for coping with loneliness can be derived from the research described in this chapter. Possible ways to reduce loneliness would include (1) doing a rational cost analysis of risky social situations to decide whether the potential gain warrants taking the risk, (2) looking for situational causes of loneliness, rather than blaming your own enduring personal characteristics, (3) maintaining a positive attitude toward others, and (4) concentrating on enriching friendships rather than searching for a romantic partner.

Loneliness as a Growth Experience. Loneliness does not always have to be reduced or avoided; sometimes it can be transformed into a constructive experience. One such transformation involves turning loneliness into solitude by using alone time to engage in pleasurable behaviors. It is also possible that learning to be alone with oneself can contribute to self-knowledge, which may strengthen our capacity for establishing intimate relationships with others. It is suggested that healthy personal growth consists of establishing a balance between satisfying relationships with others and a secure base of satisfaction within ourselves.

13

The Social Network

❖

When Parents Get Divorced ✦ *What Happens after a Divorce?* ✦ *Adjustment after a Divorce* ✦ *What Is a Family?* ✦ Friendship ✦ *Gender Differences in Same-Sex Friendships* ✦ *Individual Differences in Friendship* ✦ *Friendship and Stress* ✦ *Social Support: Is It Useful?* ✦ Chapter Summary

When an intimate relationship goes through a time of conflict and dissolution, it often becomes the center of our existence. We go over and over what is happening, and when it ends, we feel the loneliness of losing what seems to be the most important relationship we have. At some point, however, most of us wake up from this two-person universe and begin to realize that we are embedded in a more extensive social network. We remember that there are other people we care about: friends, relatives, and—for some—children.

This chapter will examine the ways that our larger social network is affected by the loss of a relationship as well as the ways this network may help us recover from this loss. First, we will consider the vertical network: how divorce affects parents, children, and the parent-child relationship. Then, we will look at the horizontal network: the role of friendship in men's and women's lives. Both of these sections emphasize that all our intimate relationships are interrelated. Major changes in any one part of the social network often have effects on all the other parts of that network.

348

WHEN PARENTS GET DIVORCED

There was a time when children whose parents were divorced felt different from the rest of their peers. Divorce used to be rare enough that having divorced parents was a distinct burden for a child. Being a child of divorce is still a burden, but it is no longer very distinctive. Compared with 73 percent in 1960, it is estimated that in 1990 only 56 percent of American children under the age of 18 will live with both their biological parents, each of whom has been married only once (Jacobson, 1987). Most of the others will live in single-parent families or in step-families (Hernandez, 1988). In 1987, approximately one-fourth of the 60 million children in the United States under the age of 18 lived with only one parent. Over 40 percent of single-parent families are maintained by a divorced parent, and 90 percent of single parents are women (Norton, 1987). Just as divorce contributes to the increase in single-parent families, so does it influence the rise in the number of stepfamilies. By the mid-1980s, some 20 percent of married-couple households in the United States involved at least one spouse who had been divorced (Cherlin &

Approximately one-fourth of children in the United States under the age of 18 live with only one parent, and 90 percent of single-parents are women. Here, a teenage daughter makes lunch, while her divorced working mother checks the day's schedule. (Ellis Herwig/Stock, Boston)

McCarthy, 1985), and in 16 percent of U.S. married-couple families at least one spouse had a child by a former marriage (Norton, 1987). Though specific facts and figures like these can be hard to keep track of, the general conclusion is overwhelmingly clear. Divorce has a major impact on the lives of millions of adults and children in our society today. Although each person's experience with divorce is unique, there are some general patterns that often occur. In this chapter, we consider some of these patterns as they apply to Mom, Dad, and the kids.

What Happens after a Divorce?

To those involved, the end of a marriage can be a time of complete chaos and confusion. So much is happening that everything begins to blur together, and life becomes separated into two large chapters: before and after. In fact, however, there are some specific areas of change that are particularly important and can be particularly difficult to handle. Here, we examine three such areas: economic changes, parental relationships, and remarriage.

Economic changes. It may seem crass to say so, but some of the greatest problems caused by divorce are a matter of money. Imagine, for instance, the following scenario:

> Bill and Ann were married for nine years. He is 36; she is 34. They have one child, Susan, who is 7 years old. Bill is a certified public accountant employed by a law firm; while Ann was married, she taught math at a church-run elementary school. Their joint financial assets consisted of two cars, a house and furnishings, and some savings. Under the terms of their separation agreement, these assets were divided equally. Each kept one car; they divided the savings equally; and they sold the house so that they could split the equity they had invested in it. Bill moved to a one-bedroom apartment close to where he works. Ann received custody of Susan, and they moved to a two-bedroom apartment some distance from where they used to live. Even though Bill contributes child support, Ann soon discovered that she could not support herself and Susan on her current salary. She took a job in the public schools for more money. Susan enrolled in a new school, closer to where she is now living. In just a few short months, all three changed their residence, Ann changed her job, and Susan changed schools.

Many people who have gone through a divorce, as adults or as children, will recognize parts of this scenario. It is not at all unusual, and the economics of divorce account for most of it. In her 1985 book *The Divorce Revolution*, Leonore Weitzman spells out the full financial impact of divorce.

First, why did Bill and Ann sell their house? If, for example, Ann and Susan had continued to live there, then they would have avoided the stress of moving to and living in a new place; Susan would have remained in the same school and kept her same friends. Yet, as Weitzman points out, selling the house is increasingly required in order to allow equal division of property held jointly by the spouses. And an equal division of "community property" is an increasingly common feature of "no-fault" divorce. Beginning in the 1970s, many states adopted no-fault divorce laws as a replacement for, or alternative to, the former legal requirement to determine guilt in a divorce proceeding. A no-fault approach to divorce has much to recommend it—being less expensive, more honest, and less demeaning than the old divorce trials. What was not anticipated, however, was how much no-fault would influence the economic aspects of divorce. Since, by definition, there is no guilty party in a no-fault divorce, it seems reasonable simply to split the family's assets. But you cannot split a house unless you sell it and divide the proceeds. Thus, one of the unexpected consequences of no-fault divorce was the increasing tendency for court-approved divorce settlements to include the sale of the family's home, which, in turn, precipitates other major changes in family members' lives.

Another unexpected consequence was what Weitzman calls "the systematic impoverishment of divorced women and children" (p. xiv). She estimates that, on average, divorced women suffer a 73 percent decline in their standard of living, while divorced men experience a 42 percent increase in their standard of living. Not surprisingly, the financial hardship experienced by many divorced women is associated with increased psychological distress for them and their children (Braver, Gonzalez, Wolchik, & Sandler, 1989; Emery, 1988). There are a number of reasons for the dramatic discrepancy between men's and women's postdivorce economic status. First, think back to our hypothetical couple, Ann and Bill. Like most married couples, Bill's income was greater than Ann's. As long as Ann was married, she didn't need to maximize her earnings because the two incomes combined were sufficient. On her own, however, Ann discovered that her salary would not cover her expenses, which were greater than Bill's because she had custody of Susan. In short, if women make less than men do, then women will have more financial problems after divorce than men do. Such problems are intensified when, as is usually the case, the children of divorce live with their mother instead of their father.

But this is nothing new. What is new is that the traditional way of compensating women for that income differential—alimony—has virtually disappeared. According to Weitzman, only about 17 percent of divorcing women are awarded alimony, and the average duration of the award is two years. It is very unlikely that a young, well-educated, employed woman like Ann would either ask for or receive alimony. And then there is child support. When Weitzman wrote her book on the financial consequences of no-fault divorce, child support was a national scandal. Studies indicated that a majority (around 53 percent) of women awarded court-ordered child support did not receive full payment, and a sizable minority (25 to 33 percent) did not receive a penny. In 1988, Congress attempted to rectify this situation by passing a law with much stricter provisions for the assessing and collecting of child-support payments. Employers will now be notified of court-awarded support payments and will be required to deduct the appropriate amount from the employee's paycheck. It is expected that these and other revisions in the Child-Support Enforcement Program will greatly improve the compliance rate with court orders (Rich, 1989). Since, however, court-ordered child-support payments are usually too low to cover the actual cost of raising a child (Peterson & Nord, 1990), then the financial strains faced by divorced mothers and the children who live with them will have been eased but not eliminated.

Even if the current levels of child-support payments stipulated in divorce agreements are not sufficient to meet the financial problems faced by many divorced mothers, such payments may have some important, and potentially beneficial, side effects. Increased child-support payments by noncustodial fathers are associated with more frequent visits with their children, raising the possibility that mandatory increases in one kind of involvement might result in increases in the other kind:

> Noncustodial parents who pay support may feel more uncomfortable about playing only part of the parent role than they do about avoiding parental responsibilities altogether, so if they pay child support they are more likely to visit as well. (Seltzer, Schaeffer, & Charng, 1989, p. 1027)

Parental relationships. Continued contact with a noncustodial parent may, however, run into an interpersonal roadblock—continued conflict between the ex-spouses (Hetherington, Stanley-Hagan, & Anderson, 1989). If every visit involves a fight, why visit? In one of the saddest ironies of divorce, the end of the marriage does not necessarily mean the end of the acrimony. One study, for example, found that about half of the divorced couples with children who participated in the research had an angry, hostile relationship; only a small proportion could be regarded as friends (Ahrons & Wallisch, 1987). Upon finding a similar pattern, another researcher concluded that "post-marital harmony was a minority phenomenon" (Ambert, 1988, p. 327).

The psychological costs of a bad relationship between ex-spouses can be quite high for everyone involved. Conflict with the ex-spouse is associated with poor adjustment for both divorced men and women (Tschann, Johnston, & Wallerstein, 1989). Children, especially boys, exposed to continued conflict between their biological parents have more difficulty adjusting to divorce (Demo & Acock, 1988; Emery, 1988; Tschann, Johnston, Kline, & Wallerstein, 1989). Within nondivorced families, parental conflict also has negative effects on children (Grych & Fincham, 1990). Indeed, children have a better adjustment in a calm, harmonious single-parent family or stepfamily than they do in biological families of origin where conflict is high (Hetherington, Cox, & Cox, 1982; Lamb, 1977; Long & Forehand, 1987; Stolberg, Camplair, Currier, & Wells, 1987). The level of parental conflict has greater effects on children than does the structure of the family. Thus, the inability of many divorced couples to resolve their differences, even after they have dissolved their marriage, can make it much harder for them and their children to construct a rewarding new life.

Remarriage. By far, the most popular way to construct that new life is to remarry: Half of all recent marriages involve at least one previously married individual (Bumpass, Sweet, & Castro Martin, 1990). Overall, some 80 percent of divorced individuals remarry (Norton, 1987). Men, however, are more likely to remarry than women. The rate of remarriage among men is around 83 percent, while women's remarriage rate may be as low as 70 percent (Norton & Moorman, 1987). In addition, remarriage appears to work better for men than for women: Remarried men report greater marital satisfaction than do remarried women (Vemer, Coleman, Ganong, & Cooper, 1989). Although most research has found that second marriages fail sooner and at a faster rate than do first ones (Cherlin, 1983; Furstenberg & Spanier, 1984), these differences may reflect the greater likelihood of remarriage for individuals who have an especially high rate of divorce (those who first married at a very young age and who have low levels of education). When age at first marriage and level of education are taken into account, remarriages appear to have no greater risk of disruption than first marriages (Castro Martin & Bumpass, 1989).

Some types of remarriage, however, may be easier to manage than others. Married couples involved in "simple" stepfamilies, in which only one of the adults brings children into the marriage, report greater marital satisfaction than do those in "complex" stepfamilies, in which both adults bring children into the marriage (Vemer et al., 1989). But all stepfamilies face some daunting problems. As noted in a *Newsweek* article entitled "Step by Step," just diagramming the family tree can be an advanced test in genealogy:

> The original plot goes like this: first comes love. Then comes marriage. Then comes Mary with a baby carriage. But now there's a sequel: John and Mary break up. John moves in with Sally and her two boys. Mary takes the baby Paul. A year later Mary meets Jack, who is divorced with three children. They get married. Paul, barely 2 years old, now has a mother, a father, a stepmother, a stepfather, and five stepbrothers and stepsisters—as well as four sets of grandparents (biological and step) and countless aunts and uncles. And guess what? Mary's pregnant again. (Kantrowitz & Wingert, 1990, p. 24)

Besides the difficulty of simply keeping track of the characters, both adults and children often encounter problems adjusting to their new roles (Bray, 1988). Though family relationships tend to improve over time, stepparents usually remain less active as parents than biological parents who have custody (Hetherington et al., 1989). Stepmothers, however, may be more active than stepfathers (Santrock & Sitterle, 1987). And, whether as a cause or an effect of this more active involvement, stepmother families appear to encounter more difficulties than do stepfather families (Hetherington et al., 1989). But stepfathers do not necessarily have an easy time of it. Although stepsons usually adjust to the presence of a stepfather and benefit from their relationship with him, it is considerably harder for stepfathers to gain acceptance by a stepdaughter (Hetherington, 1987). Children in complex remarriages, where, as noted before, there are children in the home from the previous marriages of *both* spouses, have particularly high levels of behavior problems (Hetherington et al., 1989).

Remarriage, of course, is not limited to custodial parents, but the remarriage of noncustodial parents seems to have only slight effects on their involvement with their children (Furstenberg, 1988). By and large, those who had little involvement remain disengaged, while those who stayed in close contact continue to do so. And how does a close relationship with a noncustodial parent affect the child's relationship with his or her stepparent? Here, too, it appears that stepmothers may face more problems than stepfathers. Active involvement by a noncustodial father seems unlikely to damage, and may benefit, the relationship between a stepfather and a child (Maccoby, Depner, & Mnookin, 1990). In contrast, frequent visits by a noncustodial mother are associated with greater difficulties in the relationship between a stepmother and, especially, a stepdaughter (Brand, Clingempeel, & Bowen-Woodward, 1988). The child's own personal adjustment, however, may benefit from continued contact with the noncustodial mother (Zill, 1988).

Overall, then, current research describes a number of problems that stepfamilies may have to deal with. But such difficulties should not be exaggerated. According to Furstenberg (1987), stepfamily life is a "mixed picture." Relationships between stepchildren and stepparents may not be as close as those between biological parents and their children, but "the vast majority of stepfamilies appear to function quite well" (p. 56). On the whole, children in stepfamilies differ remarkably little from children who reside with both their biological parents (Ganong & Coleman, 1987). Moreover, the divorce rate for remarriages with children is no higher than that for remarriages without them (Castro Martin & Bumpass, 1989). Having children involved can make a remarriage both more complicated *and* more rewarding.

Adjustment after a Divorce

We have seen how three major factors (economic changes, parental relationships, and remarriage) can influence the postdivorce experiences of children and adults. Now, let us step back and take a broader view of the divorce process and its effects on adjustment. What happens in the short term and in the long run?

Longitudinal studies of divorce. Although a number of investigators have conducted longitudinal studies of divorce (studying divorced couples and their children across some period of time), two such studies are especially well known and widely cited (see Table 13.1). The longitudinal study by Wallerstein and her colleagues began with 60 families with a total of 131 children (Wallerstein & Blakeslee, 1989; Wallerstein & Kelly, 1980). Family members were first interviewed 6 months after the parents had separated. Follow-ups were conducted at 18 months, 5 years, and 10 years after separation. (There has also been a 15-year follow-up, but these data have not yet been systematically analyzed and reported.) In the 10-year follow-up, members of 52 families were interviewed, with information obtained on 113 parents and 116 children. The

TABLE 13.1 LONGITUDINAL STUDIES OF DIVORCE

	Wallerstein and Her Colleagues	Hetherington and Her Colleagues
Initial Sample of Subjects	60 separated families with a total of 131 children	144 families—half nondivorced, half divorced, mother-custody
Time of First Interview	6 months after separation	2 months after divorce
Follow-up Assessments	18 months, 5 years, 10 years, 15 years	1 year, 2 years, 6 years
Sample of Subjects at Last (Analyzed) Follow-up	Members of 52 families: information obtained on 113 parents and 116 children	124 of the original families; 56 new families added
Design of the Study	No control group of nondivorced families	Three groups at the last follow-up: 1. Remarried mother and stepfather 2. Mother-custody, nonremarried 3. Nondivorced

longitudinal study by Hetherington and her colleagues began with 144 families, half of whom were nondivorced and half divorced with the mother having custody (Hetherington, 1987, 1988; Hetherington et al., 1982). The first interviews were conducted 2 months after the divorced families had divorced, with subsequent follow-ups at 1 year, 2 years, and 6 years. In the 6-year follow-up, 124 of the original families participated and a new cohort of families was added to yield a total of 180. These families included 30 daughters and 30 sons in each of three family types: (1) remarried mother and stepfather; (2) mother-custody, nonremarried; and (3) nondivorced.

It is important to note the differences between these studies. In Wallerstein's research, families were contacted earlier in the divorce process (after *separation* rather than after the divorce was legally granted) and have been followed longer. On the other hand, Hetherington's research employs a more careful design with equal numbers of male and female children, as well as types of families. Moreover, only Hetherington includes a nondivorced control group.

Despite the differences in their research strategies and procedures, both Wallerstein and Hetherington agree that the early period after a separation or divorce is much worse than later on. Hetherington (1987) calls the first two years a "crisis period" during which both parents and children experience severe adjustment problems. Wallerstein and Kelly (1980) depict their families at six months after separation as traumatized. Many of the parents were depressed; some were suicidal. Many of the children exhibited psychological problems such as anxiety, sleep disturbances, phobias, and depression. And two-thirds of the mother-child relationships had deteriorated from those reported for the preseparation period. By two years, however, the divorced families studied by Hetherington had greatly improved, and the families participating in Wallerstein's research showed major gains in adjustment at 18 months and even more at the 5-year follow-up. Although the passage of time is not some kind of magical cure-all for the stresses and strains of divorce, still, for most people, things do get better as time goes on (Emery, 1988).

But how much better do they get, and for whom? In addressing these questions, Wallerstein focuses primarily on the former and Hetherington on the latter. Based on the experiences of the families she has studied, Wallerstein draws a rather pessimistic conclusion, as indicated by these quotes from her 1989 book with Blakeslee describing the results of the 10-year follow-up:

> The effects of divorce are often long-lasting. Children are especially affected because divorce occurs during their formative years. (pp. 297–298)

> In this study, . . . almost half the children entered adulthood as worried, underachieving, self-deprecating, and sometimes angry young men and women. (p. 299)

Feelings, especially angry feelings and feelings of hurt and humiliation, can remain in full force for many years after divorce. (p. 301)

Some adults are at greater risk than others. Women with young children, especially if they are driven into poverty by divorce, face a Herculean struggle to survive emotionally and physically. (p. 301)

Many older men and women going out of long-term marriages are alone and unhappy, facing older age with rising anxiety. (p. 301)

Many a father seems to have lost the sense that his children are part of his own generational continuity, his defense against mortality. This blunting of the father's relationship to his children is a stunning surprise. (p. 302)

Wallerstein also emphasizes the good adjustment of some of her subjects, calling some of the children "compassionate, courageous, and competent" (p. 298), noting that many adults "show striking growth in competence and self-esteem" (p. 300), and commending the "heroic measures of loyalty, selflessness, and devotion to their children" shown by some parents and stepparents (p. 302). Nevertheless, her concern is evident. From her perspective, divorce is a major trauma with severe, long-lasting consequences for many, or even most, of those who experience it. Perhaps. But it is also possible that the lack of a control group of nondivorced families leads Wallerstein to exaggerate the negative effects of divorce. How many children of intact families also enter adulthood worried, underachieving, self-deprecating, and sometimes angry? How many nondivorced men and women face aging with rising anxiety? Without a nondivorced control group, it is impossible to determine which life problems are uniquely associated with divorce and which are shared among a wider population of those who have experienced divorce and those who have not. Although not all of the possible long-term effects described by Wallerstein have been investigated more systematically, it does appear that her concerns about a lack of generational continuity between divorced fathers and their children are well founded. When compared with their never-divorced peers, middle-aged men who had been divorced had far fewer contacts with their adult children (Cooney & Uhlenberg, 1990). This lack of contact was most pronounced for fathers whose children were young when the divorce occurred. Fathers whose children were older or were adults when they were divorced were considerably more likely to stay in touch. A good many of Wallerstein's other findings may well stimulate this kind of more controlled research needed to test them adequately. Thus, Wallerstein's greatest contribution may consist of her formulation of general hypotheses that can serve to guide further research.

The design of Hetherington's study allows her to be more specific in the questions she asks and the results she reports. First, she notes the "pervasive" loneliness of the divorced, nonremarried women who participated in her study. According to Hetherington, this loneliness stems from the lack of an intimate, romantic relationship. Consistent with this interpretation, the adjustment of remarried women was quite similar to that of nondivorced women. Second, Hetherington finds that many of the divorced, nonremarried mothers continue to be locked in a power struggle with their sons:

> Although the divorced mothers are as physically and verbally affectionate with their children as are mothers in the other family groups, they more often get involved with their sons in angry, escalating coercive cycles. . . . It should be noted that the sons of divorced women recognize their own aggressive, noncompliant behaviors and report that their mothers have little control over their behavior; however, they also report and exhibit high levels of warmth toward their mothers. It might be best to view this relation between divorced mothers and sons as intense and ambivalent rather than purely hostile and rejecting. (Hetherington, 1987, p. 193)

In contrast, the relationship between divorced mothers and their daughters was usually quite positive, not differing from that between nondivorced mothers and their daughters. Finally, Hetherington's research documents the difficulties in the stepfather-stepdaughter relationship, as described earlier in this chapter. Although Hetherington's overall view of the consequences of divorce is more positive than Wallerstein's, she is sensitive to the difficulties involved. A consistent theme throughout her research is that cross-sex adult-child relationships (divorced mothers and their sons; stepfathers and their stepdaughters) may pose greater adjustment problems than same-sex adult-child relationships (divorced mothers and their daughters; stepfathers and stepsons). This pattern raises the question of how well the sons and daughters of divorce will fare with their adult heterosexual relationships, an issue we will address in the next section.

Thanks to the research conducted by Wallerstein, Hetherington, and other investigators, we are beginning to develop an increasingly clear picture of those factors that are associated with children's adjustment to their parents' divorce. According to Emery (1988), four factors are particularly strong predictors:

1. *The passage of time.* As we have seen, the adjustment to divorce of both children and adults improves over time. Children's adjustment to remarriage shows the same pattern.

2. *Quality of children's relationship with their residential parent(s).* The children of divorce are like any other children. They are more likely to have a sound psychological and social development in a stable, secure, and loving home environment—regardless of whether they live with one parent or two (Baldwin, Cole, & Baldwin, 1982; Rutter, 1979).

3. *Parental conflict.* As indicated earlier in this chapter, parental conflict between spouses or between ex-spouses is often damaging to their children's well-being.

4. *Economic standing of children's residential family.* Again, children of divorce are just like other children. Poverty creates conditions (e.g., malnutrition, lack of adequate medical care, overstressed parents who may fail to provide sufficient love and attention, inadequate housing, fewer educational opportunities, feelings of deprivation and personal inadequacy) that can have profound, negative consequences on a child's development.

It is, of course, easier to list such factors than it is to make sure that children receive what they need. Nevertheless, divorcing or remarrying parents may find it helpful to remember that with children the basics are what count: a little time, a lot of love, peace between parents, and freedom from poverty.

Adults whose parents were divorced. At present, there is much more research available on the adjustment of children under 18 to a divorce than on the adjustment of adults whose parents were divorced. It seems likely, however, that research on adults whose parents divorced will increase in the coming years as the offspring of the "divorce explosion" that started in the late 1960s move into adulthood. Until then, our conclusions should be tentative, but there is some indication that parental divorce may affect adult adjustment.

In fact, there is consistent evidence that the children of divorce are more likely to experience divorce themselves, an effect that is strongest among white females (Glenn & Kramer, 1987; Keith & Finlay, 1988). The increased rate of divorce experienced by adults whose parents were divorced cannot be accounted for in terms of the absence of a parent. Adults who suffered the death of a parent during childhood do not have a higher rate of divorce than those who grew up in intact families (Glenn & Kramer, 1985). Although the exact causes for the specific effect of parental divorce are not known, a number of possibilities have been cited (Glenn & Kramer, 1987). Perhaps, for example, children of divorce learn more about initiating and maintaining marital conflict than about how to reduce it; this learning may then carry over into their own behavior as a spouse. Or perhaps because their parents divorced, the children of divorce find divorce easier to resort to when they are unhappy in their marriages. Yet a third possibility involves a lower commitment to marriage. Having seen a bad marriage up close, children of divorce may be apprehensive about all that can go wrong in a marriage and withhold their full commitment to it.

Whatever factors are involved in creating a greater probability of divorce, children of divorce do not appear to have radically different attitudes toward divorce and marriage than children whose parents did not divorce (Amato, 1988; Franklin, Janoff-Bulman, & Roberts, 1990; Kinnaird & Gerrard, 1986). They are more accepting of alternatives to traditional family structures as well as of divorce; they are less optimistic about the success of their own future marriage and anticipate placing less trust in a future spouse; and they idealize marriage less. On the other hand, they value marriage just as much as adults from non-divorced families of origin, and there is no evidence of any kind of wholesale rejection or disparagement of the married state.

Indeed, some studies of college students suggest that the children of divorce may be more likely to run toward intimate relationships than away from them. One study found that male and female students whose parents had divorced cohabited more often, dated more frequently, and were more likely to have had premarital sexual relationships than those whose parents had not divorced (Booth, Brinkerhoff, & White, 1984). An association between parental divorce and increased sexual experi-ence was also obtained among a sample of female college students (Kinnaird & Gerrard, 1986). However, the intimate relationships of young adults whose parents divorced may be more complicated than a simple eagerness to become sexually involved. It is possible, for in-stance, that children who benefited from a divorce-induced decline in parental conflict later developed more rewarding social lives as adults (Slater & Calhoun, 1988). On the other hand, those who were un-prepared for the divorce and regarded it as unnecessary may feel more compelled to establish adult romantic attachments, even ones that are not particularly rewarding.

Divorce, however, is not unique in its potential to affect the long-term social outcomes of those children who experience it. As empha-sized earlier, parental conflict within an intact marriage can also have negative effects on children. Indeed, Booth and Edwards (1989) main-tain that "remaining in an unhappy marriage has many more adverse, and stronger, effects on the next generation than parental divorce does" (p. 41). Analyzing the responses of a national sample of married persons who were asked about their parents' relationship, this study found that those whose parents had divorced reported more marital problems than those whose parents had not divorced. Among subjects whose parents had *not* divorced, however, parental marital unhappiness was associ-ated with difficulties in both the subjects' own marriages and their own relationships with their children. It also appears that generalized dis-trust of others is particularly likely among those adults who report *continuing* conflict between their divorced parents—after the divorce as well as before it (Franklin et al., 1990). For both the short-term and the long-run, the quality of the parental relationship has a greater influence on a child's development than does the structure of the family unit.

What Is a Family?

Although dramatic, the changes in family life in the United States should not be exaggerated out of all proportion. There have always been many different kinds of families. The changes that have occurred in the last generation seem enormous because they happened so rapidly, creating a huge discrepancy between people's expectations and the reality they face. Even today, when people talk about "the family" and being "family-oriented," they often are referring to the nuclear family: Mom, Dad, and their (biological) children. No divorce. No single parents. No stepfamilies. Frequently, these different arrangements aren't even seen as "real families."

People are, of course, entitled to their preferences, and a loving, harmonious nuclear family has much to recommend it. But the discrepancy between an idealized image of the way things should be and the reality of the way they are may have made it more difficult to take care of the families we actually have. There are, in fact, some very clear signs that many families are having a hard time. At present, some 25 percent of U.S. children under the age of 18 live in poverty. For children in single-mother families, the rate is much higher: An astonishing 60 percent live in poverty (Norton, 1987). Or consider day care. Although the percentage of mothers with young children who work outside the home almost doubled in just 17 years (1970 to 1987), finding adequate day care is still a nightmarish ordeal for many parents (Wingert & Kantrowitz, 1990). What is available is often not affordable, and what is affordable is often not desirable. These are family issues of the utmost urgency, and yet they may not be seen as such if family is defined solely in terms of the 1950s ideal of an intact marriage and a full-time homemaker.

A narrow definition of family may also make it harder to develop a new ideal of family life, one less bound by structure and more responsive to the quality of the relationships involved. At some level, this is an easy adjustment to make. A "good family" has always been defined in terms of love, commitment, and responsibility—not just biology. At a deeper level, however, many people are probably reluctant to grant the same respect to "nonnuclear families" that they give almost automatically to the nuclear structure. The nuclear family seems more secure, more permanent; the others seem more temporary, more makeshift. And, therein, lies a major problem: How can single-parent families or stepfamilies become as secure and permanent as nuclear families if no one (including those involved) expects them to be this way? If we expect instability and lack of commitment, that is what we are likely to get. But if we focus on the quality of family life and commend good families no matter how they came about, we can offer support to all families in their efforts to provide love and security to their members. It will be interesting to see if the 1990s become the decade, not of *"the* American family," but of *all* the families in our society.

FRIENDSHIP

Just as family can be a vital source of love and security, so can friends. Curiously, however, our own society now places relatively little emphasis on the value of friendship. Compared with the immense importance of friendship in earlier eras of the United States and in many other countries today, current regard for friends in our society seems weak and lukewarm. Often, friendship is something we appreciate mainly in its absence. When we move to a new place and have no friends, then we realize how much having friends contributes to our lives. Or when we suffer the loss of other significant relationships, then we are aware of how much we need good friends (Milardo, Johnson, & Huston, 1983). The problem with such an approach to friendship is that if we do not make the effort to maintain our friendships during good times, we may find ourselves without friends during those bad times when our need for them is greatest.

As we examine the role that friendship plays in people's lives, and especially its importance after the end of a romantic relationship (Sermat, 1980), we should keep in mind that friendship is not a medicine that one stores on the shelf and gets out to help cure a bout of lovesickness. Instead, the ability to make and keep friends requires a continuing, active, pro-friend attitude along with continuing, active, pro-friend behaviors. Dawley's (1980) Friendship Potential Inventory (see Table 13.2) provides a good example of this kind of positive approach to a friendship. You might want to see how you score on this inventory, and you might want to think about whether your score would be influenced to any large extent by your involvement in a romantic relationship.

Gender Differences in Same-Sex Friendships

According to Davis and Todd (1985), the recipe for friendship includes a long list of good ingredients such as acceptance, trust, respect, support, intimacy, and enjoyment. But not everyone puts these ingredients together in the same way. Consider, for example, the following two descriptions of some same-sex friendships:

> Sarah and Janet are very close friends. Often, they stay up half the night talking about love and life and how they feel about everything and everyone. In times of trouble, each is always there for the other to lean on. When

TABLE 13.2 THE FRIENDSHIP POTENTIAL INVENTORY†

This questionnaire is designed to measure your friendship potential. To complete this questionnaire, assign a value to each statement by choosing from the answers below the number (from +2 to −2) which indicates the extent to which you agree or disagree with the statement. For example, if you "completely agree" with a statement, you would write "+2" in the blank before it, or, if you moderately disagree, you would write "−1" in the blank. Be sure to fill in all blanks.

+2 = Completely agree
+1 = Moderately agree
  0 = Neither agree nor disagree
−1 = Moderately disagree
−2 = Completely disagree

_____ 1. Most people seem to have more friends than I do.*

_____ 2. I often compliment my friends on their nice appearance.

_____ 3. I'd rather use public transportation than ask a friend for a ride.*

_____ 4. I shy away from meeting new people because I'm afraid they won't like me.*

_____ 5. I'm the type of person who likes people.

_____ 6. In times of trouble I count on my friends for help.

_____ 7. People tend to feel good when they are around me.

_____ 8. I'd help a friend who was in a jam even if it was inconvenient for me to do so.

_____ 9. I hold back from criticizing people and their ideas.

_____ 10. When I like someone, I try to let them know it.

_____ 11. I'm too busy to have many friends.*

_____ 12. When I see someone I know, I greet them with a smile and a cheerful "hello."

_____ 13. I am reluctant to confide in others.*

_____ 14. I'll occasionally give a gift to a friend just because I want to.

_____ 15. Very seldom will I call a friend just to chat.*

_____ 16. I'm reluctant to lend money no matter how small the amount.*

_____ 17. I like to spend my free time socializing with friends.

_____ 18. If a close friend told me a confidential secret, there's a good chance that I would tell someone else.*

_____ 19. I'm not likely to help a person if it involves much trouble for me.*

_____ 20. There are other things that are more important to me than making friends.*

Cont.

† Acknowledgment is given to Chris Harper, Catherine Musham, Dale General, and Michael Waldo for their assistance in developing this questionnaire.
SOURCE: Dawley, 1980.

TABLE 13.2 *Cont.*

_____ 21. If a friend asked my opinion about an unflattering hairstyle, I would give an honest answer.

_____ 22. One or a few close friends are worth many not-so-close friends.

_____ 23. I believe that most people really don't need or want my friendship.*

_____ 24. When in a group, I let others keep the conversation going.*

_____ 25. I'll go out of my way to keep in touch with old friends, even if they live far away.

_____ 26. My friendships tend to get better with the passage of time.

_____ 27. I tend to be a "wallflower" at parties.*

_____ 28. One of my difficulties in making friends is my fear of rejection.*

* Reverse score.

Scoring: You determine your friendship potential score by:

1. Reverse the sign (+ or −) on questions 1, 3, 4, 11, 13, 15, 16, 18, 19, 20, 23, 24, 27, and 28.
2. Add up all *positive* scored questions and write this figure below.
3. Add total of all positively answered questions to factor of 56.
4. Add up all negative scored questions and subtract this number from the total.
5. The resultant number is your friendship potential score.

Total Positive Score _____
Plus Correction Factor ___56___
Equals _____
Subtract Total of Negative Score _____
Your Friendship Potential Score _____

People with scores of 85 and above are defined as having above average friendship potential. Scores between 67 and 85 are in the Average Range. People with scores of 67 or below fall in the category of below average in Friendship Potential.

they experience any problems in their romantic relationships, they immediately get on the phone with each other, asking for, and getting, all the advice and consolation they need. Sarah and Janet feel that they know everything about each other.

Larry and Bob are very close friends. Often, they stay up half the night playing cards or tinkering with Bob's old car, which is constantly breaking down. In times of trouble, they always help each other out. Bob will loan Larry money whenever he runs short; Larry will give Bob a ride home from work whenever their best efforts have failed to revive Bob's beloved 1960 Chevy. They go everywhere together—to the bars, to play basketball, on double dates. Larry and Bob feel they are the best of buddies.

Do these two descriptions seem reasonable to you? Based on your own experience and your observation of others, do you believe that women's friendships tend to be like Sarah and Janet's, while men's friendships tend to be like Larry and Bob's? If so, you are in agreement with most research on gender differences in friendship. According to this research, women's friendships are based primarily on emotional sharing and men's friendships on engaging in common activities (Barth & Kinder, 1988; Hays, 1988; Sherrod, 1989; Winstead, 1986). There are exceptions to the rule, and all close friendships involve some of both elements (Wright, 1988). Nevertheless, Wright's (1982) terms remain pithy and accurate descriptors of two different, gender-related approaches to friendships: Women's are "face-to-face," while men's are "side-by-side." These differences between male and female friendships parallel more general differences between all-male and all-female interactions. Female interactions are characterized by more agreement and less overt conflict; whereas male interactions are characterized by more disagreement and more confrontational behaviors. These very different styles of interacting with other members of the same sex have been observed among children as well as adults (Carli, 1989; Maccoby, 1990).

In addition to having more intimate same-sex friendships, women also regard these friendships more favorably than do men (Rose, 1985; Wheeler, Reis, & Nezlek, 1983). This more positive evaluation of same-sex friendships by women appears at different ages and in various cultures: with adolescents as well as adults (Wright & Keple, 1981) and for students from New Zealand and Hong Kong as well as from the United States (Aukett, Richie, & Mill, 1988; Wheeler, Reis, & Bond, 1989). But what accounts for the gender difference in same-sex friendships? Is it a matter of capacity or choice? Are men less capable of forming intimate friendships with each other or less willing?

To answer such questions, it is helpful to recall a related phenomenon described earlier in this book: the general tendency for women to engage in intimate self-disclosure more than men. As noted in Chapter 8 on communication, social norms appear to play a greater role than basic capability in the gender difference in self-disclosure. Under circumstances where it is considered socially appropriate, men self-disclose more than women do (Derlega, Winstead, Wong, & Hunter, 1985). A similar conclusion was reached by Reis, Senchak, and Solomon (1985) after a series of studies on possible reasons for the greater intimacy of female same-sex friendships. These researchers maintain that men are fully capable of forming intimate friendships with other men, but they choose not to do so—presumably because such male-to-male intimacy is less socially acceptable than female-to-female intimacy. This lack of social support for close, confiding male friendships could contribute to the greater socioemotional dependency on their spouse experienced by married men as compared with married women, which (as indicated in Chapter 11) may make it more difficult for divorced men to cope with the end of their marriage.

It is also possible that not only are men more restricted in the range of their intimate attachments than are women, but that men view even cross-sex attachments as potentially dangerous and threatening. In a highly controversial study, Pollak and Gilligan (1982) found that men were more likely than women to include violent images when writing stories in response to pictures depicting relationships between men and women. Women, on the other hand, were more likely to include violent images in the stories they wrote in response to pictures of individual achievement. On the basis of these findings, Pollak and Gilligan concluded that men tended to be characterized by a fear of intimacy and a sensitivity to the dangers of entrapment, while women tended to be characterized by a fear of separation and a sensitivity to the dangers of social isolation.

The publication of this research produced a heated debate between Pollak and Gilligan (1983, 1985) and their critics (Benton et al., 1983; Weiner et al., 1983). However, a subsequent study by Helgeson and Sharpsteen (1987) appears to offer some comfort to both sides of this controversy. On the one hand, their results confirmed the basic pattern obtained by Pollak and Gilligan: Violent imagery appeared more often for men in response to pictures of intimacy and affiliation, and more often for women in response to pictures of individual achievement. On the other hand, Helgeson and Sharpsteen emphasize that violent imagery was relatively infrequent across all the research (including their own) conducted on this issue. Thus, these investigators suggest that pictorial representations of social situations will trigger strong feelings of anxiety and hostility among only a small proportion of men and women, but that among those who do have such reactions, the gender differences found by Pollak and Gilligan appear to hold. Of course, we should be cautious about generalizing from how people respond to pictures to how they actually respond in real-life situations.

Given these caveats, however, the basic notion that intimacy is more anxiety-producing for men and individual achievement is more anxiety-producing for women is not so farfetched. After all, it is only very recently in a small number of countries that the idea of granting equal educational and occupational opportunity for women has been taken seriously. And, even now, young women who act in a self-aggrandizing, immodest way are evaluated more negatively than young men who behave in that manner (Hetherington, Crown, Wagner, & Rigby, 1989). In light of such long-standing, deeply ingrained prohibitions on women's achievements, it would be quite surprising if women were not more likely than men to have some anxious concerns in this area. It would also be quite surprising if men were not sensitive to cultural prohibitions against free and open expression of their emotional attachments. Although such prohibitions differ across societies, the research described in this book certainly suggests that they continue to exist in the United States. And one of the most telling consequences of such prohibitions is the difficulty men face in forming emotionally significant friendships with other men.

Individual Differences in Friendship

Besides the effects of gender, people also take different approaches to friendship on the basis of their personal needs. Consider, for example, two motives that prompt individuals to seek out social contact (McAdams, 1982):

1. *The need for affiliation (N_{aff}):* The desire to maintain many rewarding interpersonal relationships
2. *The need for intimacy (N_{int}):* The preference for warm, close, communicative relationships

Although both of these needs are associated with increased involvement with others, the type of involvement differs. The need for affiliation is associated with more active, controlling social behavior across a large number of social contacts. Relative to those with a low N_{aff}, individuals with a high N_{aff} communicate more with other people, find social activities more enjoyable, and react more positively to the company of others (McClelland, 1985). On the other hand, the need for intimacy is associated with more passive, less controlling social behavior that emphasizes the depth and quality of social relations. Relative to those with a low N_{int}, those with a high N_{int} are more trusting and confiding in their relationships and experience a greater sense of well-being (McAdams & Bryant, 1987; McAdams, Healy, & Krause, 1984).

According to McAdams (1985, 1988), the need for intimacy may play a particularly important role in the development of close friendships. The friendships of individuals high in the need for intimacy involve high levels of self-disclosure, the desire to avoid separation, and a belief in the importance of loyalty between friends. There is also some evidence that the need for intimacy may contribute to long-term positive life outcomes. In a longitudinal study, McAdams and Vaillant (1982) compared the social motives of a group of male college graduates at age 30 and their psychosocial adjustment almost two decades later. Youthful need for affiliation did not predict middle-age adjustment, but there was an association between need for intimacy in young adulthood and adjustment status years later. Those who had been high in N_{int} when young were better adjusted when older. These findings suggest that, in the long run, the quality of one's relationships may be considerably more important than their quantity.

Friendship and Stress

After the loss of an intimate relationship, people often seek out others—friends, family, professional help. This desire to "reach out and touch someone" is part of a more general tendency for people to want to be with others when they are under stress. Though widespread, such a tendency is not universal. For example, when people anticipate an upcoming physically painful experience, they will prefer to be with other people rather than wait by themselves; this preference is particularly strong when the other people are awaiting a similar, painful experience (Schachter, 1959). In contrast, when people anticipate an upcoming personally embarrassing experience, their desire to be with others in a similar predicament declines; they would rather be alone or wait with others who do not have any knowledge about the individual's embarrassing experience (Firestone, Kaplan, & Russel, 1973; Sarnoff & Zimbardo, 1961). Thus, those in fearful misery love the company of similarly fearful others, while those in embarrassed misery prefer solitude or the company of uninformed others. Why the difference?

According to Rofé (1984), the answer is *utility*. Rofé asserts that stress will increase the desire to be with others only when being with others is expected to be useful in reducing stress. In turn, the expected utility of affiliating under stress will depend on a variety of factors (see Table 13.3). First, there is the type of stress. There are several reasons why people would expect that waiting with others before a painful experience would help them feel better. They would have the opportunity to compare their emotional reactions with those of others to help judge how appropriate their own feelings are. Better yet, they could have a chance to obtain information from knowledgeable others about how to cope with the impending threat (Kulik & Mahler, 1989). Being with others before, or after, an embarrassing experience is much more

TABLE 13.3 AFFILIATION UNDER STRESS

	Factors That Increase Affiliation under Stress	Factors That Decrease Affiliation under Stress
Type of Stress	• Manageable fear	• Unmanageable fear • Embarrassment
Characteristics of the Person Experiencing the Stress	• First-born • Female	• Later-born • Male
Characteristics of the Potential Affiliate	• Similar to the person experiencing stress • Able to handle the stressful situation	• Dissimilar to the person experiencing stress • Unable to handle the stressful situation

SOURCE: From Brehm & Kassin, 1990. Based on Rofé, 1984.

problematic. Embarrassment is a form of *social* anxiety, and being with others seems likely to increase this type of stress rather than reduce it. For example, individuals who have been rejected by a romantic partner for someone else may be reluctant to seek consolation from others because they fear they will feel humiliated and embarrassed if they let others know what happened.

Rofé notes that personal characteristics can also influence the desire to affiliate under stress. Some individuals (females and those who are the firstborn in their family of origin) are more likely than others (males and later-borns) to affiliate in stressful circumstances. Perhaps those who prefer affiliation have had life experiences, such as social approval for dependency and lots of parental attention, that have led them to believe that others can help them adjust to stress. In any event, it does appear that women rely more on friends during stressful periods than do men. During the stressful first semester of college, women interact more frequently with their same-sex best friends than men do (Wheeler & Nezlek, 1977). After a divorce, women report more reliance on others than do men, especially on friends (Chiriboga, Coho, Stein, & Roberts, 1979).

As we have seen, another factor influencing the desire to affiliate under stress involves the characteristics of those who are present. If our goal is to compare our emotional reaction with that of other people, those other people need to be in an emotional state similar to ours. If our goal is to obtain information to help us cope, we must have some confidence that they are competent to manage the stressful situation. In other words, sometimes we want to be with someone who is just as stressed out as we are, while at other times, we want to be with someone who has had a similar experience and has overcome it. The first person reassures us that it's okay to feel the way we do; the second offers some hope that we too can feel better, and perhaps some specific advice for how to get there.

Social Support: Is It Useful?

Rofé's model addresses the issue of when people will want to be with others during stress—when they believe it will be useful. Research on social support examines the other side of the equation. Is it, in fact, useful to have others around during stressful periods? From a quick reading of the massive research on social support that has been conducted since the mid-1970s, one would think that the answer must be a resounding yes. Consider just a few examples of the findings. Divorced parents involved in more social participation outside the home report less stress (Raschke, 1977), and divorced individuals who experience major disruptions in their social network during the divorce process have more difficulty coping (Daniels-Mohring & Berger, 1984; Wilcox, 1981). Widows involved with neighbors and friends feel better about themselves and their lives (Arling, 1976). Women who have an intimate relationship with a spouse or boyfriend are less likely to become depressed (Brown & Harris, 1978; Costello, 1982). College students who report more adequate social support have higher levels of secretory immunoglobulin A, a major antibody which reduces the risk of infectious disease (Jemmott & Magloire, 1988). People who have more social contacts live longer (Berkman & Syme, 1979). The message seems loud and clear: Social support is good for you.

Actually, a closer look at the message being sent by research on social support indicates that things are not quite that clear-cut. There are major questions about when social support is useful, for whom it is useful, and the tradeoff between the utility of social support and its costs.

When is social support useful? Early concepts of social support assumed that it would provide a buffer against stress (Cassel, 1974; Cobb, 1976). When stress was low, social support should be irrelevant, but when stress was high, those who had the support of others should fare better than those without it. In a "buffer effect," those who experience high stress *and* have little social support should be the worst off. Despite its prominence in these early theories, this concept of social support as a buffer against stress has been criticized on various conceptual and methodological grounds (Gore, 1984; Thoits, 1982). An alternative view of social support sees it as having direct effects on psychological and physical well-being. According to this perspective, people who have high levels of social support should always be better off than those who have low levels—regardless of the amount of stress they are experiencing. So which is it? Is social support only beneficial when you are under stress, or is it always helpful? Based on the research evidence, it appears that benefits can occur *either* as a buffer or directly, depending on the specific kind of social support involved (Cohen & Wills, 1985). Slack and Vaux (1988) suggest that the way social support affects adjustment may also be influenced by gender. These investigators found that for men depression was directly related to social support (those men who had less social support were more depressed), but that there was a buffer effect for women (those who had experienced more negative life events *and* had less social support were more depressed).

For whom is social support useful? It is not, however, the case that, one way or another, social support is always useful for everyone. As Keinan and Hobfoll (1989) note:

> Whereas social support was originally viewed as a panacea for all stress-related ills, more recent research points to the conceptualization of social

support as one of a number of social and personal resources that may be mobilized during times of need. For . . . [some people] other resources may be more appropriate and therefore more effective for them. (pp. 40–41)

A similar conclusion was reached in a study of divorce and relationships with relatives (Gerstel, 1988). Although men and women relied on their relatives for assistance during the divorce process, only for women was this reliance associated with better coping. Among men, increased reliance was associated with increased psychological distress.

Does this mean that the social support received by these divorcing men actually harmed them? We don't know. Because these results are correlational, we cannot determine the cause-and-effect relationships involved. Perhaps women who relied on their kin received a more welcoming response than did men. Or perhaps only those men who were in very bad shape to begin with relied on their relatives for help. It is often very difficult to disentangle the actual effects of social support from a host of other factors, including people's effectiveness in eliciting the support they seek and their adjustment status before seeking support (Conn & Peterson, 1989; Cutrona, 1989; Heller, 1979; Hobfoll & Stokes, 1988; Sarason, Sarason, Hacker, & Basham, 1985).

The costs of social support. Nevertheless, it is clear that social support is not a free lunch. Costs are involved, and sometimes these costs may outweigh the benefits (Coyne & Bolger, 1990; Rook & Pietromonaco, 1987). If a desire for social support keeps people attached to a stressful relationship, the negative consequences may well be greater than the positive ones (Manne & Zautra, 1989; Rook, 1984). Even positive, rewarding relationships can be a source of stress. When those we love are in trouble, we share their distress and make an effort to help them (Hobfoll & London, 1986; Riley & Eckenrode, 1986). For example, in a study of people's reaction to the 1979 accident at the Three Mile Island nuclear power plant, the men who lived nearby experienced less stress if they had a good relationship with their wife (Solomon, Smith, Robins, & Fischbach, 1987). But women who had a good marital relationship showed *more* indications of stress, suggesting that for them strong attachments in this situation were stress-inducing rather than stress-buffering. Such differential costs for social ties may occur both within marriage (Whiffen & Gotlib, 1989) and outside of it. According to some researchers, women's greater tendency to share the distress experienced by members of their social network may account for why women have higher rates of various psychological disorders (such as depression and anxiety) than men do (Kessler, McLeod, & Wethington, 1985).

Friendship revisited. Social support is a very broad term, used to refer to all sorts of assistance (emotional, informational, material) from

Like any kind of social support, friendship is most likely to be beneficial when there is a good fit between the needs of the individual and the resources provided by friends. (Gale Zucker/Stock, Boston)

all sorts of people (relatives and romantic partners as well as friends). In terms of friendship, two implications of the research described in this section seem particularly valuable. First, like any kind of social support, the benefits of friendship will depend on a fit between the needs of the individual and the resources provided by the friend. Sometimes, a person needs a friend who will listen to and share intimate concerns. At other times, however, a person needs a buddy, to go out and pal around with. In other words, people need *both* face-to-face and side-by-side friendships—as different aspects of the same relationship or with different people. Unfortunately, the gender construction of friendship is such that women are more likely to get the former and men to get the latter. A more "liberated" view of friendship would include the recognition that both types are useful for both men and women.

The second implication for friendship that can be drawn from research on social support has to do with the costs of sustaining a relationship. If you are carrying a heavy load at work or school and involved in a serious romantic relationship or married with children, where do you get the time and energy for friends? No doubt, many people decide they don't have the time or energy, and they let their friendships fade away. In the short run, this may be a reasonable strategy. Over time, however, there may be some drawbacks. In Chapter 11, it was noted that multiple social roles have generally been found to be more beneficial than a single role. Similarly, research on the way we view ourself indicates that having a complex self-concept involving many different identities (e.g., student, lover, film buff, jogger, environmentalist) is associated with better psychological and physical well-being (Linville, 1987). Both sets of findings suggest that, despite placing greater demands on a person's time and energy, diversification is an advantage. This advantage may stem from avoiding the vulnerability of being overly dependent on one role or one self-identity: If you only have one, what do you do if you lose it? But there is a more positive explanation as well. Multiple roles, identities, and relationships require energy to sustain, but they also create energy in return. Friendship is, then, not just good insurance to lay away in case a romantic relationship ends; it is also a source of personal enrichment and growth. Friendship does not have to be seen as taking energy away from a romantic relationship; it can be viewed as enlarging the pool of energy available. This compatibility was nicely demonstrated in a study of over 2000 residents of Washington State, all married and 55 or older (Lee, 1988). For both men and women, having *friends* was the best predictor of being satisfied in their *marriage*!

As we have seen throughout this chapter, people don't just have a set of isolated, independent relationships. They have social networks, in which a variety of relationships are interconnected. Such interconnections make it difficult to contain negative effects; all too often, parental conflict spills over and affects their children's lives. But such interconnections also make it possible to magnify positive effects. A good relationship between parents usually promotes better parent-child relations; a good friendship can contribute to a satisfying marriage. Like a stringed instrument, the whole social network tends to reverberate with the single note that is struck.

CHAPTER SUMMARY

When Parents Get Divorced

Increasingly, American children live in many different kinds of families: with both biological parents, who have been married only once; in single-parent families, usually with their mother; and in stepfamilies in which at least one parent has been married before and brought at least one child into the new family. The high rate of divorce in the United States has contributed to the increase in both single-parent families and stepfamilies.

What Happens after a Divorce? Although no-fault divorce laws have made it easier, and less humiliating, for people to obtain a divorce, they have also had some unintended consequences. Because an equal division of tangible assets is often part of a no-fault divorce, divorcing couples frequently sell their home and split the proceeds. The sale of the home means that everyone has to move, and moving to a new residence—and for children, a new school—can be a very stressful part of the divorce process. The most striking unintended consequence of no-fault divorce laws has been the severe economic disadvantage experienced by many divorcing women, especially those awarded custody of the children. Alimony, which in the past served to compensate women for their lower earnings relative to men's, has virtually disappeared. Though child support is still often awarded, the amount stipulated by the court is frequently inadequate and often not paid. Stricter provisions for collecting child-support payments were instituted by Congress in 1988 and should improve the collection rate. Increased child-support payments are associated with increased visits by the noncustodial parent. Research has indicated that continued contact with a noncustodial father has positive effects on children, especially boys. Continued contact, however, is less likely when ex-spouses have a conflictual relationship. Conflict between ex-spouses is also associated with poorer postdivorce adjustment for both adults and children. Another major issue faced by many divorced adults and their children is the creation of a stepfamily. Though stepfamily relationships improve over time, stepparents tend to remain less active in their parental role than custodial parents. Stepmothers seem to face particular difficulties, while stepfathers have a harder time gaining acceptance from stepdaughters than from stepsons.

Adjustment after a Divorce. Two major longitudinal studies of the divorce process have been conducted by Wallerstein and by Hetherington. Both agree that adults and children experience great emotional distress and turmoil immediately after a separation or divorce. These two investigators also agree that, over time, things improve for most individuals. Wallerstein, however, maintains that many adults and children continue to experience serious adjustment problems, even years after the divorce. The lack of a nondivorced control group to compare with her group of divorced families makes it difficult to evaluate Wallerstein's findings. According to Hetherington, whose research included a nondivorced control group, continuing problems are most likely among divorced women who have not remarried, between single-parent mothers and their sons, and between stepfathers and stepdaughters. In general, four factors are particularly strong predictors of children's adjustment after a divorce: passage of time, quality of their relationship with their residential parents, parental conflict, and economic standing of their residential family. The most well-documented long-term effect of divorce is an increased divorce rate among adults whose parents were divorced.

What Is a Family? To be family-oriented and child-centered in the 1990s will require sustained efforts to reduce poverty and increase adequate day care. It will also require developing more positive expectations about the ability of single-parent families and stepfamilies to provide love and security to their members.

Friendship

For many people today, friends are something they come to appreciate only when they don't have them. A more positive approach takes a more active, continuing interest in maintaining friendships.

Gender Differences in Same-Sex Friendships. In general, women's friendships are based on emotional sharing (face-to-face) and men's on engaging in common activities (side-by-side). Women also regard their same-sex friendships more favorably than men regard theirs. It is likely that male friendships are less intimate because, at least in the United States, such intimacy is less socially acceptable. Societal norms that discourage male-to-male intimacy may contribute to the greater socioemotional dependency on their spouse experienced by married men. Since men are not granted the same freedom to express their emotional attachments as are women, some men may develop a fear of intimacy. Similarly, since women have traditionally been denied the freedom to achieve on their own, some women may develop a fear of the separation from others created by individual achievement.

Individual Differences in Friendship. The needs for affiliation and for intimacy are two social motives that prompt individuals to seek out social contact. N_{aff} involves the desire to maintain many rewarding interpersonal relationships; it is associated with more active, controlling social behavior across a large number of social contacts. N_{int} involves the preference for warm, close, communicative relationships; it is associated with more passive, less controlling social behavior that emphasizes depth and quality of social relations. The need for intimacy may play a particularly important role in the development of close friendships and may contribute to long-term adjustment.

Friendship and Stress. According to Rofé, the desire to be with others while enduring a stressful experience depends on whether the presence of others is expected to be useful in reducing stress. Factors that influence this expectation include the type of stress (the desire to affiliate is greater when people anticipate physical pain than when they are embarrassed), characteristics of the individual (females and first-borns affiliate under stress more than males and second-borns), and characteristics of the people with whom one could affiliate (similar others and those who are competent to handle the stress are more desirable).

Social Support: Is It Useful? There is massive evidence that social support is associated with better adjustment. However, many questions remain about how and when social support is beneficial. Sometimes, social support is associated with better adjustment *only* when stress is high (a buffer effect); at other times, social support is associated with better adjustment regardless of the level of stress. Social support is not, however, useful for everyone. The costs of social support may detract from its benefits. Even positive, rewarding relationships can be a source of stress, as people share the distress of their loved ones and try to help them. Research on social support has two major implications for friendship. First, the benefits of friendship depend upon a fit between the needs of the individual and the resources provided by a friend. Second, the costs of sustaining a friendship are real. These costs may, however, be offset by the advantage of having multiple close relationships rather than concentrating on only one intense partnership.

PART SIX

— ❖ —

Improving Intimate Relationships

14

Therapeutic Interventions

--- ❖ ---

*I*f we want to improve our intimate relationships—strengthen them, work on problems that have arisen—there are many ways to do this. Often, by working only with our partner, we can accomplish the changes we want. When sources of help in addition to the partner are sought, there are numerous possibilities: talking to friends and family, reading books on the subject, or attending classes relevant to relationships. These are all essentially "self-help" efforts and often will suffice. Sometimes, however, self-help is not enough, and couples will feel the need for professional assistance. This chapter describes the extensive variety of professional services that are available to couples.

There are probably many couples who could benefit from professional assistance but never seek it out. One reason for this may be a misconception that people have about the role of professional assistance for relationship problems: They may believe that such assistance should be obtained only when the relationship is in serious trouble. Actually, mental health professionals are becoming increasingly interested in working with couples *before* there are any serious problems in the relationship. Besides the more traditional role of helping couples in distress, professional assistance can be valuable in preventing problems and enriching relationships that are already rewarding.

In this chapter, the full range of professional services available to couples will be described. Reflecting this range, the chapter is organized in terms of the developmental sequence of relationships from early in a relationship to later on, with a final section on therapeutic interventions relevant to the dissolution of relationships. Before embarking on this survey, it is important to take note of the kind of terminology that will be used throughout this chapter. The vast majority of the work described here has focused on the institution of marriage. Thus, we have the terms "premarital" and "marital enrichment" programs, "marital" and "divorce" therapy. These terms do not mean, however, that the value of these programs and therapies is restricted to married couples or to heterosexual individuals. Many of the interventions described here can be useful for any significant intimate relationship, regardless of the legal status of that relationship or the sexual orientation of the partners.

EARLY IN THE RELATIONSHIP: PREMARITAL PROGRAMS

The high divorce rate in the United States has led to a growing recognition of the need to prepare people better for the long-term commitment of marriage. Religious groups have strengthened and expanded their traditional role in premarital counseling. Since, however, there is serious question about the effectiveness of the standard premarital lectures offered by many churches (Olson, Russell, & Sprenkle, 1980), many mental health professionals (from both the religious and secular communities) have become interested in premarital programs requiring more active learning by the participants. A number of structured, systematic programs for premarital counseling have been developed. The following are some examples of these sorts of programs.

Based on the assumption that the best way to prevent later marital problems is to teach premarital couples better communication skills, the Couples Communication Program (CCP) concentrates on four major areas of the communication process (Miller, Nunnally, & Wackman, 1976).

1. Training in awareness and expression of thoughts, feelings, and intentions.
2. Training in better communication through the sender-receiver-clarification sequence:
   • The sender states his or her feelings or beliefs.
   • The receiver listens carefully and summarizes what the sender has said.

- The sender clarifies for the receiver if the summary is inaccurate or incomplete.
3. Training in various types of communications that can occur in a relationship so that partners can understand the options available to them in communicating with each other and the impact of each type of communication on each of them.
4. Training in ways to build one's own self-esteem and that of the partner.

The Premarital Relationship Improvement by Maximizing Empathy and Self-Disclosure (PRIMES) program is similar to CCP in its emphasis on developing better communication skills as a way to prevent problems in the relationship (Ginsberg & Vogelsong, 1977). PRIMES also has four major areas of concentration, with the first two bearing a close resemblance to the first two areas of CCP.

1. Training in the expressive mode of communication. The skills taught here are very similar to those guidelines for good communication discussed in Chapter 8: Express feelings; be clear that they are your feelings ("I feel . . . " rather than "You make me feel . . . "); make positive statements as much as possible; be specific about your feelings and about any changes you ask your partner to make.
2. Training in empathic responding: Put yourself in your partner's shoes; try to feel the way he or she does; reflect back to your partner what you think he or she said and how you think he or she feels; do not interrupt, make judgments, or ask for new information.
3. Training in how and when to switch from the expressive mode to the responding mode.
4. Training in how to facilitate good communication on the part of other people.

The Premarital Relationship Enhancement Program (PREP) seeks to apply the principles of behavioral marital therapy (described later in this chapter) to premarital relationships (Markman & Floyd, 1980; Markman, Floyd, & Dickson-Markman, 1982; Markman, Floyd, Stanley, & Lewis, 1986). In this program, couples are taught communication and conflict-resolution skills and are introduced to some of the basic features of the behavioral approach, such as:

- Monitoring their own and their partner's behaviors
- Learning what behaviors please or displease the partner
- Making contractual agreements about changes in behavior

An Overview

All these programs take an educational approach to premarital counseling. Typically, the programs are carried out by a trainer (or cotrainers) working with a group of couples. The trainer explains the rationale of the program, models the skills to be learned, and encourages and coaches the participants in their efforts. Participants actively engage in communication with others in the group, role-play specific problem areas, read a text discussing how to improve relationship skills, and practice their skills at home with each other. All three programs are intensive, highly structured, and time-limited (e.g., five to eight weeks). The effectiveness of these programs in teaching skills and promoting more satisfying relationships will be discussed in the following section on enrichment programs.

LATER IN THE RELATIONSHIP: MARITAL ENRICHMENT PROGRAMS

Marital enrichment programs share the preventative philosophy of premarital programs: Relationship improvement now will reduce problems later. In addition, enrichment programs take a purely positive, growth-oriented approach to long-term relationships, maintaining that every relationship can become more satisfying and more meaningful. Here, too, religious groups have played a leading role (Garland, 1983). One church-sponsored program, the multidenominational Marriage Encounter program, involves a 44-hour experience held over a single weekend (Lester & Doherty, 1983). Among secular groups, the largest organization involved in marital enrichment is the Association of Couples for Marriage Enrichment (ACME). ACME provides organizational support for retreats and growth groups of interested couples (Mace & Mace, 1976). Though these groups do not have any structured program specified in advance, the usual goals are for partners to experience and express more positive feelings and to formulate growth plans for their relationship.

There are also a number of structured programs that have been designed for enrichment purposes. CCP, for example, is used as an enrichment program, as is the Conjugal Relationship Enhancement (CRE) program (Guerney, 1977; Guerney, Brock, & Coufal, 1986)—the latter being the original "parent" program from which its premarital offspring, PRIMES, evolved.

A more behavioral approach to enrichment has been developed by Harrell and Guerney (1976). Their behavioral-exchange program puts particular emphasis on learning conflict-management skills. The program consists of nine major steps:

The multidenominational Marriage Encounter program encourages partners to experience more positive feelings for each other and to develop plans for the continued enrichment of their relationship. (Spencer Grant/Stock, Boston)

1. Listen carefully—summarize what your partner said.
2. Locate a relationship issue, something that both partners want to change.
3. Identify your own contribution to this issue.
4. Identify alternative solutions, more than one.
5. Evaluate these alternative solutions.
6. Make an exchange: Select one behavior change for each partner.
7. Place conditions on this exchange—bonuses for making the behavior change; penalties for not making it.
8. Implement the exchange: Keep trying; keep records.
9. Renegotiate to see if additional or alternative behavior changes are necessary.

General reviews of the effectiveness of various premarital and marital enrichment programs suggest that, on the average, these programs are modestly successful (Giblin, Sprenkle, & Sheehan, 1985; Gurman & Kniskern, 1977). It appears that improvement in communication skills may be the most enduring change (Wampler, 1982). On the other hand, there is some evidence that increases in relationship satisfaction and a sense of intimacy are often short-lived (Joanning, 1982; Wampler, 1982). Although some distressed couples may benefit from enrichment programs (Giblin et al., 1985), there is concern about a small proportion of couples for whom these programs may have damaging effects on their relationship and their personal well-being (Lester & Doherty, 1983). Because of this possibility for harm, highly distressed couples should be identified before their participation in an enrichment program and given a referral to appropriate therapeutic services (Doherty & Walker, 1982). Even couples with a more stable and satisfying relationship should be cautioned against exaggerated expectations about the benefits of participating in a premarital or marital enrichment program. These programs can assist many couples in developing a better relationship, but they cannot create happiness or guarantee endurance.

An Enrichment Program for Sexual Interaction

The pioneering work by Masters and Johnson (1970) in the treatment of sexual dysfunction resulted in two important principles that have been generally adopted by clinicians. First, Masters and Johnson developed systematic, behavioral treatment programs for specific sexual problems. In addition to this improved treatment technology, however, Masters and Johnson emphasized that sexuality occurs in the context of a relationship. With committed partners, both individuals need to be involved in the treatment, even if only one of them has a specific sexual problem. Some researchers in the area of human sexual functioning have questioned the extremely high improvement rates reported by Masters and Johnson (Heinman & Verhulst, 1990) and have urged the need for more carefully controlled research to evaluate treatment effectiveness (Heiman, LoPiccolo, & LoPiccolo, 1981). On the whole, however, the behavioral techniques and relationship approach advocated by Masters and Johnson "have received significant empirical support and should be considered the treatment of choice" (Gurman & Kniskern, 1981, p. 749; see also, Heiman, 1986).

Sexuality may be an especially appropriate focus for enrichment efforts. In an interesting expansion of the Masters and Johnson approach, Maddox (1976) described such an enrichment program for sexual interaction. This program consists of four major components:

1. Sexual attitudes reassessment
2. Sexual communication groups
3. Body awareness sessions
4. Behavioral home assignments

Though the long-term effects of sexual enrichment programs have yet to be adequately documented, their potential seems promising.

*L*ATER IN THE RELATIONSHIP: MARITAL THERAPY

The history of marital therapy in the United States dates to the late 1920s when professional marriage counselors first became available for couples having difficulties in their relationship (Broderick & Schrader, 1981; Humphrey, 1983; Prochaska & Prochaska, 1978). Marital therapy has always involved a number of different disciplines—such as marriage and family counseling, pastoral counseling, psychiatry, psychology, social work, and sociology. Moreover, marital therapy is essentially a "grass roots" movement. Professionals began to offer marital therapy in response to clients who came and asked for help. Family therapy, on the other hand, developed primarily in response to professional concern. During the 1950s, while working with severely disturbed young people, a number of therapists became convinced that adequate treatment was only possible when the entire family unit was involved in therapy. This decision to focus on the family system rather than the psychopathology of the individual who was identified as "sick" marked the beginning of family therapy as a distinct form of treatment.

Because of these different developmental histories, there were initially some important differences between marital therapy and family therapy. Marital therapists usually worked with the two marital partners, neither of whom was severely disturbed. Family therapists typically worked with at least three family members (parents and child), at least one of whom was severely disturbed. Over time, however, these differences have tended to fade as the originally parallel fields of marital therapy and family therapy began to merge. Many marital therapists have adopted the systems approach (discussed later in the chapter) that was the hallmark of family therapy, and many family therapists work primarily with the marital dyad, even when the identified patient is the child. Both marital and family therapies can be distinguished from individual therapies by their focus on relationships. In these therapies, the relationship between the individuals receives at least as much attention as the individuals themselves (Whitaker, 1975).

Since this book focuses primarily on intimate relationships between two adults, the present chapter will only describe therapeutic interventions appropriate for couples and will not review interventions specifically designed for parents and children. Consistent with the increasing overlap between the domains of marital and family therapy, however, many of the therapeutic perspectives and techniques discussed here are also highly relevant to the treatment of families.

Formats

Even when we restrict our discussion to couples' therapy, there are a surprisingly large number of ways that therapy can take place:

- *Individual.* One therapist and one client discuss together the client's relationship.
- *Collaborative.* Each of two clients has his or her individual therapist, and the two therapists consult each other about their clients.
- *Concurrent.* One therapist sees each of the two clients in separate, individual sessions.
- *Conjoint.* One therapist sees both clients together in the same session. Sometimes, there are cotherapists (frequently one male and one female) involved in the conjoint sessions.
- *Conjoint group.* One therapist (or a pair of therapists) works with a group of couples in group sessions.

As you read this list of the different types of therapeutic modalities used in marital therapy, you may have noticed that they line up on a dimension running from more individually oriented to more relationally oriented. In many ways, this dimension reflects the development of the field, as more individually oriented approaches have given way to the more relationally oriented formats. Presently, conjoint therapy is the most frequently adopted format, with the use of conjoint groups increasing.

Theoretical Orientations

Theoretical discussions about therapy often resemble theological disputes during the Middle Ages: passionate, seemingly endless, and sometimes extraordinarily obscure. They are, however, also necessary, as therapists try to find some guidelines to help them in the incredibly complicated task of trying to help other people. Let us consider briefly some of the major theoretical frameworks adopted by marital therapists.

Psychodynamic approaches. Orthodox psychoanalysis as developed by Sigmund Freud in the early twentieth century was a resolutely one-at-a-time process. There was one therapist (the "analyst") and one client—and this arrangement was seen as critical to the effectiveness of the treatment. The client was expected to transfer his or her central unconscious conflicts onto the relationship with the analyst (the "transference neurosis"); only by working through this transference relationship could the client gain insight and be in a position to change his or her feelings and behavior. It was believed that if other people were present during therapy, the transference relationship would be damaged and therapeutic improvement would not occur.

Many of the founders of family therapy came from psychoanalytic backgrounds, and their insistence on seeing more than one client at a time represented a dramatic break with the analytic tradition. In recent years, however, it has become more accepted that basic Freudian and more general psychodynamic principles can coexist with a relational focus and a conjoint modality (Dare, 1986).

Most marital therapists working from a psychodynamic orientation stress three fundamental propositions:

1. In the way they choose a mate and the manner in which they interact in marriage, individuals are frequently acting out their unconscious conflicts.
2. Many unconscious conflicts stem from events that took place in a person's family of origin.
3. The major therapeutic goal is for the clients to gain insight into their unconscious conflicts—to understand why they feel and act the way they do, in order that they may have the freedom to choose to feel and act differently.

Table 14.1 provides an example of marital therapy from a psychodynamic perspective.

Rogerian approaches. Based on work by Carl Rogers, Rogerian (or "client-centered") therapy views psychological difficulties as caused by faulty socialization. As people grow up, they can become engulfed by the need to gain love and approval; thus, they may grow away from their true needs and desires, substituting instead a "false self" designed to win social acceptance. Rogerian therapists attempt to assist their clients to discover their "true selves"—their true feelings and needs—by providing clients with acceptance ("unconditional positive regard") and empathic understanding. This acceptance is directed toward the person and does not mean that the Rogerian therapist approves or encourages destructive behavior. Indeed, helping clients to make the distinction between respect for a person and reaction to his or her behavior is one of the major goals of client-centered therapy. Although Guerney's (1977) Conjugal Relationship Enhancement program is more structured and directive than most Rogerian approaches, the aim of the CRE program to increase warmth, acceptance, and empathy between partners fits well within the Rogerian perspective.

TABLE 14.1 A PSYCHODYNAMIC APPROACH TO MARITAL THERAPY

. . . A common problem presented more and more by couples is the dispute over who is to assume how many and which household tasks. Although the wife may be operating from a vantage point of equality and symmetry, neither she nor her husband may recognize that a shaky sense of masculine identity underlies his stubborn resistance to sharing the household duties. The therapist must keep in mind that any adequate solution must consider both spouses' positions.

Negotiating cannot be a simple matter of working out percentages of time or availability of each. Since unconscious feelings play a part in creating the problem, a purely cognitive negotiating approach is doomed to failure. Absolutely essential is that at least the therapist have some awareness of the contributing problems. Without necessarily working toward greater awareness of the threat posed to the husband by his wife's requests, the therapist may guide them toward some resolution wherein more feminine related duties are undertaken by the wife and those less feminine by the husband. In this way the therapist, through added awareness, can prevent the negotiating approach from completely failing.

The following example is one which on the surface would appear open to negotiating but where initially it failed completely. In one session the spouses were disputing the wife's opening of her husband's mail. Because of the intensity of their convictions, these seemed like irreconcilable differences not open for compromise since each spouse remained fixed in the "rightness" of his or her position.

Any simple and immediately obvious compromise solution, such as the husband agreeing to let his wife see his mail after *he* had opened it, was no solution for either. The wife felt she had a right to share her husband's mail; he felt she was intruding on his rights. Obviously, reality negotiations concerning how to deal with the letter-opening disagreements were not going to work. Much more was necessary for the spouses to understand what their disagreement was all about. It is axiomatic, when obvious solutions are not grasped, that the therapist must point the couple toward the task of understanding why not.

The therapist began by encouraging both to discuss their feelings and thoughts with respect to the problem. After some time and effort both spouses began to better understand reasons for the intensity of each other's feelings, and each became less entrenched in maintaining his or her own view. The husband's reluctance was expressed as feeling like a child again with "mother" snooping into his affairs. Once his wife viewed his protest from this context, her own attitude and stance changed; she had previously interpreted the behavior as her husband's wish not to share things with her. Being able to understand his behavior as not aimed at her allowed her to feel less need to press for "inclusion" in this way. At the same time it opened up an opportunity for them to discuss her feelings of "being left out" more than she wished, and allowed them to explore more acceptable ways of alleviating both of these feelings. Examples like these stress how superficial the therapeutic work *may* be if it stays with and focuses only on a solution to the surface problem without promoting an understanding of what needs are served by the resistances to negotiating.

SOURCE: Ables & Brandsma, 1977.

Systems approaches. When family therapists decided they needed to see the whole family in therapy, they also realized they needed a different conceptualization of psychological problems. Instead of locating the problem in a person, they attempted to see the problem as part of the entire family system. Thus, symptomatic behavior on the part of one individual in the family (e.g., a drug-abusing teenager) was viewed:

- *Not* as an individual problem—e.g., the emotional disturbance of the teenager
- *Not* as an individual problem caused by the social environment— e.g., by the poor parenting of a resentful mother and withdrawn father
- But as behavior that is *functional* for the entire family system— e.g., the mother and father are able to feel closer to each other as they try to manage the child, and the child receives the attention of both parents.

This concept of the family—or any other relational unit—as a system that is maintained by the behaviors (both healthy and unhealthy) of its members is shared by all existing family system theories (Aylmer, 1986; Todd, 1986). Beyond this basic concept, however, these theories differ widely. Steinglass (1978, 1987), for example, has examined some of the considerable variation in both practice and belief among system theorists. The range of this variation is strikingly evident in Hoffman's (1981) survey of the field, where she describes five major "schools" of family system theories *and* five "great originals"—charismatic leaders in the family therapy movement who each established separate approaches of their own. Looking for shared assumptions is a dangerous enterprise in the face of such diversity, but a few constants do seem to emerge.

- A focus on the individual's differentiation from the family system—that is, on the need to learn how to be both separate *and* close in relationships.
- An emphasis on the process of communication, as communication both reflects how the system operates and serves to stabilize its operation.
- An emphasis on the structure of the relationship system: the roles people play, the coalitions they form, their places in the family intergenerational hierarchy.
- The assumption that unhealthy individuals reflect unhealthy but stable relationship systems. Thus, a major goal of systems therapy is to destabilize the system so that healthier, more flexible relationships can develop.

An example of marital therapy from a systems approach is presented in Table 14.2.

TABLE 14.2 A SYSTEMS APPROACH TO MARITAL THERAPY

A couple was seen in conjoint therapy after one interview with the woman triggered a stormy depression, which was accompanied by bursts of unbearable anxiety and somatic symptoms such as daily vomiting, headaches, and abdominal pain. The proposition of the therapist that there was some behavior in the nonsymptomatic partner that preceded and contributed to explain the [wife's] symptoms was met with total incredulity by both partners. In a subsequent crisis of the symptomatology that followed a period of quiescence, the therapist was able to detect and show to both members that when the husband started to experience anxiety due to mounting responsibilities in his complex job, the wife would respond to that cue with a flare of symptoms. Immediately, the husband would become involved in taking care of her and simultaneously his anxiety would vanish, freeing him for an effective performance at work (which became quite shaky due to his anxiety once when she was on vacation and a new requirement of his job took place). As a result of this observation, the therapist expressed his worries about what would happen to the husband if her symptoms subsided . . . , suggested to her that she produce symptoms out of phase . . . and centered his attention on the husband's anxiety, acknowledging the wife's valuable contribution whenever she reported experiencing symptoms. . . . The whole symptomatic pattern broke within three months, after five years of plaguing the couple's life, as they replaced their hidden homeostatic agreement with one that was more mutual and did not require the presence of symptoms.

SOURCE: Sluzki, 1978.

Behavioral approaches. As with psychodynamic and Rogerian approaches, behavioral marital therapy (BMT) evolved from an individual approach into a set of techniques to be used with couples. The behavioral approach to marital therapy was first described in a 1969 article by Stuart, in which he established its fundamental principles. For Stuart and the behavioral marital therapists who came after him, a distressed marriage is defined in terms of a low level of reinforcing exchanges between the partners. Because they do not reinforce positive behavior toward each other, the partners either withdraw from the marital interaction or attempt to control each other's behavior in coercive, punishing ways. BMT attempts to increase the level of positive, reinforcing exchanges between the two individuals, as well as to decrease their negative, punishing exchanges.

Although BMT has many variations (Weiss, 1978), there does seem to be a set of three common procedures that are used by most behavioral marital therapists to increase reinforcing exchanges (N. S. Jacobson & Margolin, 1979; Liberman, Wheeler, de Visser, Kuehnel, & Kuehnel, 1980; Stuart, 1980):

1. *Direct instructions by the therapist to increase positive behaviors that are desired by the partners.* These positive behaviors can be those specifically requested by one of the partners ("I really enjoy it when you rub my back") or can be generated by more general

efforts to please the partner. For example, on "love days" (Weiss, Hops, & Patterson, 1973), one partner deliberately sets out to please the other partner in as many different ways as he or she can think of.

2. *Teaching the partners communication and problem-solving skills.* Communication skills training in BMT is similar to that used in the PRIMES program described earlier. In contrast to the PRIMES program, however, the emphasis in BMT is on the *instrumental* value of communication as a necessary ingredient for good problem solving. BMT also directly teaches problem-solving skills, such as those included in Harrell and Guerney's (1976) behavioral-exchange enrichment program.

3. *Working out contracts.* The last step in problem solving during behavioral marital therapy is making a written agreement about behavior change. Often such contracts are unilateral, noncontingent ones—where one partner agrees to perform a certain behavior on specified occasions without any reward for performance or penalty for noncompliance. BMT may also include contingency contracts. Some behavioral therapists advocate a quid pro quo contingency contract, in which behavior change by one partner is directly linked to behavior change by the other (Jacobson & Margolin, 1979). Other BMT therapists, concerned about the "who's going to change first" dilemma, suggest the alternative of "good-faith" contracts—parallel agreements in which the behavior change of each partner is reinforced by privileges earned (Weiss, Birchler, & Vincent, 1974). An example of the difference between quid pro quo and good-faith contracts is provided in Table 14.3. Table 14.4 describes a marital therapy case from the behavioral perspective.

Cognitive approaches. The importance of beliefs and expectations in affecting behavior is central to rational-emotive therapy as developed by Albert Ellis. In their 1961 book, Ellis and Harper applied this perspective to marital problems. At first, the response to this kind of cognitive approach to marital difficulties was less than overwhelming. During the 1980s, however, the "cognitive revolution" in all of psychology began to have a major effect on therapeutic interventions with couples (Epstein, 1982; Fincham, Bradbury, & Beach, 1990). Many therapists from differing theoretical orientations are now sensitive to cognitive factors. Among behaviorally oriented therapists, the combination of behavioral and cognitive approaches to marital difficulties is called cognitive behavioral marital therapy (CBMT). Two cognitive factors that are commonly addressed in marital therapy are unrealistic expectations and causal attributions (Baucom & Epstein, 1990; Beck, 1988; Margolin, 1987).

TABLE 14.3 TWO DIFFERENT TYPES OF CONTINGENCY CONTRACTS

Quid pro Quo
Husband agrees to clean the bathroom every Saturday. *Wife* agrees to do laundry every Sunday. Wife does laundry on Sunday only when husband has cleaned bathroom on Saturday. Husband cleans bathroom only if wife did laundry on previous Sunday.

Good Faith

Contract A

Husband agrees to clean bathroom every Saturday. On those Saturdays when he does, he chooses the activity for the evening, and the wife assumes responsiblity for reservations and a babysitter.

Contract B

Wife agrees to do laundry every Sunday. When and only when she does, husband will assume all responsibility for children on Sunday nights, including baths, undressing, and putting to bed.

SOURCE: Jacobson & Margolin, 1979.

According to Ellis and Harper (1961), marital problems come about when a person's unrealistic expectations for perfection on the part of his or her spouse are disconfirmed by the actual behavior of that individual. This disconfirmation leads to irrational and catastrophic thoughts about the self ("I must be worthless for him or her to act like this") or the partner ("He or she is a terrible, vicious person to act like this"). Such thoughts trigger an intense emotional reaction of rage and despair, as well as an escalating level of irrational behavior toward the partner.

In developing their Relationship Belief Inventory, Eidelson and Epstein (1982) identified five dysfunctional expectations about intimate relationships:

1. *Disagreement is destructive.* The belief that any kind of disagreement between intimate partners is necessarily harmful and destructive to their relationship.
2. *Mindreading is expected.* The belief that partners who truly love each other should be able to sense each other's needs without direct communication.
3. *Partners cannot change.* The belief that individuals cannot change, and, therefore, the relationship is also fixed and unchangeable.
4. *Sexual performance must be perfect.* The belief that one's sexual performance must always be perfect and without flaw.
5. *The sexes are different.* The belief that men and women differ so radically in their personalities and in what they want in relationships that they cannot find common ground.

TABLE 14.4 A BEHAVIORAL APPROACH TO MARITAL THERAPY

Mr. and Mrs. O'Sullivan were referred to the Stony Brook marital therapy program by a local mental health clinic which had a lengthy waiting list. They presented themselves as follows in the initial interview.

Sharon: An attractive 32-year-old woman who said that the major marital problems were lack of communication, lack of mutual interests, sexual naïveté, and decreasing affection. She felt that she had a low tolerance for frustration and that she was depressed. She was a housewife with three children, aged eight, five, and three. Sharon was very dissatisfied with the marriage, she reported feeling like a prisoner, and she resented her husband's "over-involvement" in Alcoholics Anonymous.

Paul: A neat, reserved 35-year-old salesman who noted only one major marital problem, lack of communication. However, he reported that his wife displayed misdirected anger and had a minimal tolerance for the shortcomings of others. Paul had been a heavy drinker since his college graduation and throughout their 12 years of marriage. Fortunately, he had been abstinent for the past three years during which he was an active member of A.A.

This couple was seen for a total of 10 conjoint sessions and one initial one-hour interview with each spouse. Therapy was deemed successful by the therapist and both clients. The major treatment procedures included:

1. Teaching communication skills—particular emphasis was placed on listening without interrupting and minimizing punitive statements and questions which sounded like declarations.
2. Encouraging Sharon to engage in more activities outside the home (for example, a prayer group, a women's group, and Al Anon) to increase the positive feedback she might obtain from people other than her husband.
3. Encouraging both Sharon and Paul to volunteer to do things which satisfied each other's needs. They were asked to sign a weekly therapy plan sheet to indicate that they understood the nature of their behavior change agreements and that they were committed to making these changes. The necessity of mutual compromise as a vehicle for alleviating distress was emphasized.
4. Prompting Paul to display some form of affectionate behavior once per day as improvements were made in the relationship.
5. Helping Sharon learn to ask Paul directly to meet more of her needs—especially her needs for his affection. In brief, she was encouragd to be more expressive of her needs.
6. Asking Sharon and Paul to entertain the notion that her criticism of A.A. and Paul's involvement in it (for example, "Most of the members are sick," and "You spend too much time there") resulted from his failure to be affectionate and to tell her at least several hours before going to an A.A. meeting that he needed to go that evening.
7. Having Sharon contemplate the possibility that when Paul went to bed before she did and politely said "Good night," he was not putting her down and she need not feel jealous.

In summary, the treatment procedures included:

1. Communication training.
2. Negotiation and compromise.
3. Therapist's suggestions that Sharon find social reinforcers outside the marriage.
4. Therapist's suggestion that Paul be more affectionate.
5. Insight, that is, reinterpretation or relabeling of certain behaviors.

SOURCE: O'Leary & Turkewitz, 1978a.

Many of these beliefs, and the problems they can create, have been discussed in previous chapters in this book. In their research, Eidelson and Epstein found that reduced marital satisfaction was associated with each of them. The belief that disagreement is destructive had a particularly high association with marital dissatisfaction among both distressed and nondistressed couples. Satir (1967), a leading family systems therapist, has vividly described the way that some families expect that total love will equal total agreement. When, inevitably, disagreement arises, it cannot be acknowledged openly because it threatens the security of all the members of the family and, thus, must go "underground." Such hidden disagreements are then revealed only indirectly through destructive patterns of behavior and communication within the family.

For therapists who emphasize the role of irrational expectations in contributing to marital distress, one of the major goals of therapy is to replace irrational beliefs with more rational ones. Typically, this involves helping the couple to realize that both have unrealistic expectations and standards, to understand the damage that such beliefs can cause, and to develop more explicit and flexible perspectives.

Causal attributions are a second cognitive factor associated with marital dissatisfaction. As described in Chapter 11 on conflict and dissolution, distressed couples are more likely to rely on "distress-maintaining" attributions, blaming unchangeable characteristics of the partner for his or her negative behaviors and discounting the partner's positive behavior in terms of temporary, situational influences. Distress-maintaining attributions involve both the locus of attribution (internal to the partner versus external) and the stability of the perceived cause (enduring versus temporary). In his discussion of the role of cognitive factors in marital therapy, Hurvitz (1970) placed particular emphasis on the stability dimension. According to Hurvitz, one of the major problems in distressed marriages is that partners generate "terminal hypotheses" for each other's behavior, blaming the behavior on unchangeable factors either in themselves or from outside the marriage. Such hypotheses are terminal because they are a dead end for the relationship, indicating that change and improvement are not possible. In contrast, "instrumental hypotheses" link the current behavior to causes that are subject to change. Hurvitz proposed that a major goal in marital therapy is to help guide the couple away from their terminal hypotheses into considering and exploring instrumental hypotheses.

Some support for Hurvitz's formulation was obtained in the research by Eidelson and Epstein (1982) on irrational beliefs. Among nondistressed couples in their sample, the belief that partners cannot change was not associated with marital satisfaction. However, among the distressed couples, who were all beginning marital therapy, the belief that partners cannot change was strongly associated with lower levels of marital satisfaction. For these couples, a "terminal hypothesis" of the impossibility of change may have been doubly stressful. Not only were they regarding the many negative events in their troubled marriage as unchangeable, but they may well have been applying the same hypothesis to therapy itself. Thus, they found themselves committed to a process of change without having much, if any, hope that change could occur. It seems reasonable to suppose that before therapy can be effective, those participating in it must believe that it has some chance of working.

The Effectiveness of Marital Therapy

But is such a belief warranted? How effective is marital therapy; does it work? Such questions are more easily asked than answered. The study of the effectiveness of psychotherapy has always been marked by dispute and controversy. Over the last three decades, there have usually been two opposing sides in most considerations of this issue: the behaviorists and the "nonbehaviorists" (including psychodynamic, client-centered, and systems approaches). Typical criticisms made by each camp can be summarized as follows (Gurman, Knudson, & Kniskern, 1978; Jacobson & Weiss, 1978).

Behavioristically inclined researchers have criticized nonbehavioristic studies of therapy outcomes for:

- Relying too much on self-reports, especially self-reports of therapists, as the measure of effectiveness
- Failing to compare therapy outcomes with what happens to people who have similar problems but are not in therapy (waiting-list control group)
- Failing to compare therapy outcomes with what happens to people who have similar problems, who have similar expectations for improving with treatment, and who receive just as much attention from a therapist—but who do not receive the specific, active elements of the treatment program (attention-placebo control group)
- Failing to compare various elements of the treatment program to see which ones are most effective (component analysis of the therapeutic intervention)

Nonbehaviorally inclined researchers have responded with the following criticisms of behavioral outcome research as:

- Relying too much on volunteer subjects who have not sought treatment (analogue studies with nonclinical populations)
- Failing to use experienced therapists

- Changing trivial behaviors that may not occur in real-life situations and, if they do, may not matter

And each criticizes the other for failing to carry out follow-up studies of sufficient duration to determine whether therapeutic improvement is enduring or only transitory.

During the 1980s, however, the atmosphere became more tolerant and integrative (Jacobson & Gurman, 1986). Behavior therapists made a serious effort to expand their therapeutic vision and procedures, asking such questions as "Is there a place for passion, play, and other non-negotiable dimensions?" in marital therapy (Margolin, 1983). Similarly, psychodynamic and family therapists became more comfortable with using behaviorally based training programs to improve communication and problem-solving skills (Robin & Foster, 1989). And, today, marital therapists of all persuasions are relying more on systems theory and focusing more on cognitive factors. A comprehensive examination of the effectiveness of marital and family therapy by Gurman, Kniskern, and Pinsof (1986) reflects this more integrative approach. Consistent with an earlier review (Gurman & Kniskern, 1978), Gurman et al. make a case for the value of nonbehavioral marital therapies. They acknowledge, however, "that there has been very little controlled empirical study of any of the 'nonbehavioral' marital therapies" (p. 584). In their consideration of behavioral marital therapy, Gurman et al. join with long-time proponents of BMT such as Jacobson (1978; Jacobson, Follette, & Elwood, 1984) to emphasize the far superior empirical base for BMT. However, they also join with these proponents to raise some questions about the specific effects of BMT, which appears to be more successful in decreasing negative behaviors than in increasing positive ones, and about the magnitude of change produced by BMT (see also Baucom & Hoffman, 1986). Overall, Gurman et al. conclude that both nonbehavioral and behavioral marital therapies are superior to no treatment, though the evidence for BMT's effectiveness is considerably stronger.

Another aspect of the more constructive dialogue occurring among therapists and researchers from different theoretical backgrounds involves their recognition of "nonspecific" factors that influence the course of all therapies. Most would agree that two such factors are particularly important in marital therapy. First, couples need to learn and use methods of good communication. As emphasized in Chapter 8, clear and constructive communication is essential for a good relationship. The second factor is the therapist's skill in establishing a positive, working relationship with both partners. Regardless of the therapist's theoretical inclination, if such a relationship is not established, therapy is unlikely to be effective. These two factors are essential in marital therapies where the couple desires to bring their relationship back from the brink of dissolution. And they are just as important in therapies where dissolution has already occurred. In the next section, we examine therapeutic approaches to the end of a relationship.

WHEN THE RELATIONSHIP ENDS: DIVORCE THERAPY AND MEDIATION

The field of marital therapy has had a hard time dealing with divorce. In simpler, if more oppressive, times, marital therapists could put their hearts and skills into helping preserve their clients' marriages and just chalk up divorce as a therapeutic failure. More recently, however, this view has been changing. Most marital therapists today take a more neutral position toward the marital relationship—recognizing that some clients will benefit from an improved marriage while others will benefit from the dissolution of the marriage. Although this perspective seems reasonable enough, enormous practical problems are involved for marital therapists who adopt it. On the one hand, how can the therapist help clients give the marriage a chance without pressuring them to stay in it? On the other hand, how can the therapist make clear the clients' freedom to terminate the marriage without pushing them toward divorce? And, perhaps most difficult of all, what is the therapist's role when one client wants a divorce and the other does not—how does the therapist avoid taking sides?

Regardless of how these issues are resolved by the specific therapist and the specific couple, at some point marital therapy ends. That point may signal a stronger, more rewarding partnership between the two individuals. Or it may indicate that the couple has made a definite decision to divorce. The end of the marriage does not, however, necessarily mean the end of the therapy. Many people going through a divorce seek out professional help. For some, the divorce is one of a number of problems they address in therapy. But there is an increasing desire for therapy that is specifically designed to help people through the emotional turmoil of the divorce process (Rice & Rice, 1985). This kind of therapeutic endeavor is generally known as divorce therapy.

Just like marital therapy, divorce therapy takes place in a variety of formats. Though most therapists advocate individual therapy for the divorcing partners (with the same therapist or with different ones), many therapists see the couple together on occasion. Group therapy for divorcing individuals (usually without their partners) is often recommended. Research on the effectiveness of such groups indicates that many participants experience an increase in self-esteem (Sprenkle & Storm, 1983).

But perhaps the most widely used form of assistance to divorcing couples is unique to the divorce process: divorce mediation (Coogler, 1978; Haynes, 1981; Milne, 1986). Created as an alternative to the adversarial model of the legal system—"You get your lawyer; I'll get mine; and we'll settle this in court"—mediation emphasizes open communication, negotiation, and mutual resolution of the emotional, financial, and child-related issues in divorce. Mediators are typically from legal or behavioral science backgrounds and need to be knowledgeable in both these fields. Agreements formulated during the course of mediation are put in written form, in order to serve as the basis for the divorce petition to the court. Mediators do not, however, serve as the lawyers in the divorce action itself, and most mediators require their clients to have separate legal counsel to inspect all agreements resulting from mediation.

Though divorce mediation is a new field and is still defining itself in terms of personnel and procedures, preliminary research on its effectiveness is encouraging (Emery & Wyer, 1987; Pearson & Thoennes, 1982; Sprenkle & Storm, 1983). As summarized by Emery (1988), research findings suggest the following conclusions:

> (1) Court-based mediation programs, which focus almost exclusively on child-rearing issues, lead to a significant reduction in custody hearings—50 to 75% of parents are diverted from court by successful mediation; (2) the content of agreements reached in mediation and in litigation do not differ greatly, except that joint legal custody is a more frequent outcome of mediation; (3) compliance with agreement reached in mediation appears to be somewhat better than with settlements reached through adversarial procedures; and (4) parents, especially fathers, are generally more satisfied with their experiences with mediation than with adversarial procedures. (p. 134)

Although further research is needed on the long-term adjustment of families using divorce mediation instead of adversarial proceedings, mediation does appear to offer a less acrimonious, more constructive approach to the divorce process. As such, it may help protect both adults and children from the sometimes disastrous consequences of an embittered, embattled divorce.

As we have seen in this chapter, couples therapy is expanding into "cradle-to-grave" coverage for relationships. Whereas once the focus was almost exclusively on preserving committed relationships, now couples therapy is available before making that commitment and after that commitment has been terminated. And, indeed, some want to take it even further. Framo (1982) has suggested that "postdivorce therapy" should be available for couples who have ended their committed, living-together arrangement but still want a positive, healthy relationship. Some couples can, of course, work this out on their own, but some may need professional assistance. The idea of postdivorce therapy probably strikes many people as a little strange. But 25 years ago, divorce therapy would have seemed just as odd. In a time of transition it is hard to predict what is ahead. As this chapter has indicated, however, when relational needs develop, therapeutic services to help meet those needs will become available.

CHAPTER SUMMARY

Early in the Relationship: Premarital Programs

Both religious and secular groups provide premarital programs, which range from lectures to more active learning experiences for the participants. The more structured programs emphasize improvement in communication skills; behavioral programs also teach basic features of the behavioral approach such as how to make contractual agreements about changes in behavior.

An Overview. Typically, the more structured educational programs are carried out by a trainer (or cotrainers) working with a group of couples. Procedures include role plays, assigned reading, and practicing at home.

Later in the Relationship: Marital Enrichment Programs

Both religious and secular groups provide marital enrichment programs, which aim to prevent problems before they develop and to enhance the relationship as a whole. There are a number of more structured marital enrichment programs; some emphasize communication skills, while others are more behavioral in their approach. On average, premarital and marital enrichment programs appear to be modestly effective, with communication skills showing the most lasting improvement. These programs are probably not suitable for highly distressed couples, who should be referred to more appropriate therapeutic services.

An Enrichment Program for Sexual Interaction. The approach to sexual dysfunction developed by Masters and Johnson includes both systematic behavioral techniques and an emphasis on the relational context in which sexual problems occur. It has been suggested that these two components could serve as the basis for an enrichment program for sexual interaction.

Later in the Relationship: Marital Therapy

Marital therapy developed in response to clients who came and asked for help. Family therapy, on the other hand, developed in response to professional concerns that adequate treatment of an individual family member required the participation of all family members. Both marital and family therapies can be distinguished from individual therapies by their focus on relationships.

Formats. There are many different formats for marital therapy. Presently, conjoint therapy (where one therapist or two cotherapists see both clients together in the same session) is widely used. The use of conjoint groups (where a group of couples participate in group sessions) is also quite common.

Theoretical Orientations. Some of the major theoretical orientations adopted by marital therapists include the following. The psychodynamic approach emphasizes the role of unconscious conflicts in influencing behavior and the need for insight into these conflicts as a prerequisite for change. The Rogerian (or client-centered) approach views therapy as a process during which the therapist provides acceptance and empathic understanding in order to help clients regain a sense of their true feelings and needs. In a systems approach to therapy, it is assumed that unhealthy behavior by an individual reflects an unhealthy but stable relational system; for change to occur, the system must be destabilized. Behavioral approaches define a distressed relationship in terms of a low level of reinforcing exchanges between the partners. Contracting is a behavioral technique used to increase positive exchanges. Contracts may be noncontingent—where one partner agrees to perform a certain behavior desired by the other partner without any reward or penalty—or contingent. Contingency contracts may be quid pro quo, in which behavior change by one partner is directly linked to behavior change by the other; or they may be good-faith parallel agreements, in which the behavior change of each partner is reinforced by earned privileges. Cognitive approaches to marital therapy emphasize the role of unrealistic expectations and causal attributions in contributing to marital distress. Some of the irrational beliefs associated with low levels of marital satisfaction include assuming that disagreement is always destructive and that change is impossible. The irrational belief that change is impossible is similar to a certain kind of causal attribution: "terminal hypotheses," in which negative behaviors are attributed to unchangeable factors within the partners or outside the marriage. A more hopeful kind of causal attribution, "instrumental hypotheses," views current behavior as produced by causes that are subject to change.

The Effectiveness of Marital Therapy. There is continued debate between behaviorists and nonbehaviorists about the most appropriate ways to study the effectiveness of psychotherapy. In general, the behaviorists emphasize the need for rigorous experimental procedures and designs, while the nonbehaviorists emphasize the need for studies focusing on the serious problems of actual clients. Despite their differences, however, behaviorists and nonbehaviorists also share some concerns and some techniques. Overall, it appears that both behavioral and nonbehavioral marital therapies are superior to no treatment, though the evidence for the effectiveness of behavioral approaches is considerably stronger. Both behaviorists and nonbehaviorists recognize the importance of nonspecific factors such as clear, constructive communication between partners and the development of a trusting relationship between the therapist and both partners.

When the Relationship Ends: Divorce Therapy and Mediation

Therapy that is specifically designed to help people through the turmoil of the divorce process is called divorce therapy. Just like marital therapy, divorce therapy takes place in many different formats. Most therapists advocate individual therapy for divorcing partners, though they may see the couple together on occasion. Group therapy for divorcing individuals is also often recommended; participation in such groups is associated with increased self-esteem. Divorce mediation addresses both the psychological and legal aspects of divorce—emphasizing open communication, negotiation, and mutual resolution of emotional, financial, and child-related issues. Preliminary research on the effectiveness of divorce mediation indicates that it is associated with fewer custody hearings, increased joint custody agreements, better compliance with agreements reached, and increased satisfaction, especially among fathers. Thus, mediation may be more effective than adversarial proceedings in reducing acrimony and destructiveness during the divorce process. In addition to the more well-established approaches described in this chapter (premarital programs, marital enrichment programs, marital therapy, divorce therapy, divorce mediation), it has been suggested that postdivorce therapy should be available for couples who no longer live together but want to maintain a positive relationship.

15

$\mathcal{R}$elationships $\mathcal{T}$omorrow

— ❖ —

Changing Roles ◆ Changing the Rules ◆ Changing the Requirements ◆ Changing
Reality ◆ Chapter Summary

B y this point, you probably feel that you have a reasonably good understanding of the state of relationships today. But what about the relationships of tomorrow? Will they change radically from what we have
now, or will they remain pretty much the same? Obviously, no one has a crystal
ball to give us definitive answers to such questions about the future. It is,
however, an interesting exercise to make some informed guesses. Actually, it is
more than interesting; it is important. Once we believe that certain changes in
intimate relationships *could* occur, we may begin to act in ways that increase the
possibility that these changes *will* occur. Such self-fulfilling prophecies about
intimate relationships probably go on all the time, without people ever realizing
it. As you read through the issues raised in this chapter, you have the opportunity to consider your own beliefs and expectations about relationships in a
more deliberate fashion.

Before trying to peer into the future, let us focus on a few facts about the
present. If forced to come up with the two major changes that have taken place
in heterosexual relationships over the past generation, most people would
probably nominate some aspect of two basic developments: increased egalitarianism and serial monogamy. *Increased egalitarianism* refers to changes in
attitudes and behaviors related to men's and women's social roles. While many
differences remain in what men and women actually do, as well as in what they
are expected to do, these differences have narrowed considerably over the last
25 years. More than ever before, men and women in the United States face equal

opportunities and similar problems. The other major development, *serial monogamy*, refers to the increasing number of intimate relationships that people experience, one by one (Brody, Neubaum, & Forehand, 1988). Today, dating begins at an early age, cohabitation before marriage is commonplace, the age at which people marry keeps rising, the divorce rate is high, and the remarriage rate is even higher. For most people, their lifetime total of romantic relationships is greater than one, sometimes much greater. Whatever shape intimate relationships take in the future will be strongly influenced by what happens to egalitarianism and serial monogamy.

CHANGING ROLES

My own best guess is that the trend toward egalitarianism in education and employment is irreversible. By 1986, women outnumbered men in college enrollments among black, Hispanics, and whites (Hacker, 1989). Only among Asians did male college enrollments outnumber female enrollments, and here too the proportion of women was increasing. As described in Chapter 11, women's participation in the work force increased steadily throughout the 1980s, and it shows no signs of slowing down. Indeed, women and minorities will constitute a majority of the work force in the twenty-first century, as white male workers become a minority. Although women are still seriously underrepresented in the top echelons of private and public organizations, there is no indication that the educational and employment opportunities already secured will be given up or taken away. In the future, then, we can expect that most heterosexual relationships will involve men and women of roughly comparable education and employment status.

Interestingly, however, this equality is based on changes in only one direction. Women have gained access to what was formerly a male preserve. Changes in the other direction have been minimal or nonexistent. More men have entered professions that were once viewed as almost exclusively reserved for women (e.g., nursing), but this is a far smaller shift in comparison with women's entrance into professions that were once viewed as reserved for men (e.g., law, medicine). And, as indicated in Chapter 11, the movement of married women into the work force has not generated an equivalent movement of married men into housework and child care. Psychologically, we could say that women have been allowed to become more masculine in their behavior (independent, competitive, aggressive), while men have not been allowed to become more feminine (emotionally expressive, nurturant, sensitive).

And, indeed, masculinity has its advantages. People who describe themselves as possessing these characteristics report better personal adjustment and coping skills than people who do not describe them-

Although society now supports women's participation in economic and political roles once reserved for men, men have not gained equal support to participate in family-oriented roles once emphasized more for women. In the twenty-first century, the quality of heterosexual intimate relationships may well depend on both men's and women's having the freedom to work and to love. (Deborah Kahn Kalas/Stock, Boston)

selves as possessing them (Spence, Deaux, & Helmreich, 1985). On the other hand, people who describe themselves as possessing traditional feminine characteristics appear to have more satisfying intimate relationships (Antill, 1983; Peterson, Baucom, Elliott, & Farr, 1989). Taken together, these findings would seem to imply that the best solution would be for a person to possess both masculine and feminine characteristics—to be androgynous (Bem, 1974; Spence & Helmreich, 1978). Although the concept of androgyny has intuitive appeal to many people, its benefits have been surprisingly hard to demonstrate (Cook, 1985). One reason for this difficulty may lie in the need to take account of the interaction between personal characteristics and situational demands. Being masculine *and* feminine across *all* situations may not be particularly beneficial. For example, a person who experiences the urge to be both competitive and nurturant in the same situation may experience considerable internal conflict (Kelly & Worell, 1977). Instead, the ability to be flexible—to be masculine in some situations and feminine in other situations—may be more advantageous. Although Bem (1975) emphasized the notion of flexibility in her early work, researchers have yet to adequately examine this approach to androgyny (Cook, 1985).

And, indeed, in real life as well as in research designs, flexibility is not an easy proposition. Today, many women feel overburdened by the combination of job and family responsibilities. Part of this burden involves the sheer exhaustion of trying to do too much in too little time, but another part of it concerns the difficulty in shifting from "boss" at work to "loving wife and mother" at home. Men also find this transition difficult, as William Novak (1983) found out when he asked some men in their thirties and forties what they thought women really wanted. One man put it this way:

> Some women understand that I have to be driven at work, but then they want me to be a totally different person with them. They're looking for somebody who's John D. Rockefeller at the office and Dr. Benjamin Spock at the dinner table. But that's impossible because one set of qualities cancels out the other. I'm sorry, but I'm only one person, not two.

That, of course, is exactly the problem. Each of us is only one person, not two, and yet most of us have two goals: occupational achievement and interpersonal intimacy. If these two goals are, in fact, incompatible, then a great many people (men as well as women, homosexuals as well as heterosexuals) are going to end up feeling like a failure in a major aspect of their life. The unidirectional movement described above, in which women have moved toward men's roles without a compensating movement of men toward women's roles, suggests that more of these failures will take place in interpersonal than in occupational commitments. Since Mom and Pop are both busy minding the store, who is going to mind their relationship—and who is going to take care of their children?

Americans are clearly worried about that last issue. In a *Newsweek* poll conducted in October 1989 ("For Better or Worse?"), 68 percent of the adults sampled stated that it was more important for a family "to make some financial sacrifices so that one parent can stay home to raise the children" rather than "to have both parents working so the family can benefit from the highest possible income." But the rejected alternative was badly worded: Most parents do not feel as if they work in order to "benefit from the highest possible income." They believe they work in order to make ends meet, to provide important advantages to their children, or to fulfill long-standing and deeply meaningful career interests. Thus, the wish that somebody (who?) would stay home seems destined to remain unrealized for many couples.

One possible future is, then, a rather bleak prospect: all work and little love. But there is another option. What if the demands made by the two settings of work and home were more compatible, so that bridging the gap could be less of a strain for both men and women? In fact, that gap is probably not nearly so wide as we sometimes believe it to be. During the 1970s and 1980s when many middle-aged women entered the work force for the first time, we discovered that running an office was not much different from running a home. They both require organizational ability, interpersonal skills, patience, and dedication. Similarly, the emphasis on the hard-driving, ruthless competitiveness needed to "make it" on the job is much overplayed. Most jobs call for teamwork rather than shootouts at the O.K. Corral, tact rather than confrontation, and a sense of timing and pace rather than relentless pressure. The hyperfeminine home and the hypermasculine job are products of our imagination. These imaginary products were compatible with the traditional division of labor that assigned paid employment to men and homemaking to women. But this division is fast disappearing, and it is time to change our images of the qualities required in both settings.

It is probably also time to change the structure of home and work, although that will be more difficult. You can, however, picture the possibilities. What if large enterprises (both public and private) provided day care and schooling on the premises? Smaller enterprises could band together to provide similar facilities. What if apartment houses provided communal services to cook meals, wash the laundry, and clean the apartments? Neighborhoods of single-family dwellings could band together to provide similar services. Today, we ask men and women to somehow fit job and family into structures designed for a former way of life. We need to change course and start rearranging those structures in order to help both men and women get what they both really want.

CHANGING THE RULES

Changing some of the structural aspects of the way we live would help reduce some of the stresses and strains experienced by men and women committed to both their loved ones and their occupation. But even these changes would not solve all the problems created by the transition from a gender-based division of labor to egalitarian relationships. Take, for example, the social paradox that as power becomes more equal, sensitivity to unequal power increases. When there are huge power differentials, most people accept them because they seem inevitable. But as the balance of power shifts, people who before had little power now begin to think of themselves as having freedom and rights; their vision of what they deserve expands. You can see this process at work during times of political change. The people losing power become hypersensitive about any erosion of their prerogatives; those gaining power become hypersensitive about continuing inequalities; and both may resort to coercive means to protect their position.

The same analysis can be applied to heterosexual relationships today. As men and women move toward equality in the society and with each other, women, who have greater freedom now than ever before, are also more aware of areas where equality has not yet been established. Some men feel threatened by women's gains and may try to block their further progress. Many men, however, are supportive of women's efforts but may be puzzled by the paradox described here: As equality grows, demands for more equality increase. In intimate relationships as in politics, the transition from unequal power to equality is a delicate moment. Tensions run high; people feel edgy and confused; the potential for conflict escalates. This association between increasing equality and increased potential for conflict was demonstrated in a study on dual-career (both spouses had full-time professional careers) and single-career (the wife was primarily a homemaker) marriages (Sexton & Perlman, 1989). On the one hand, this study found that dual-career spouses perceived their contributions to the marriage as more equal than did single-career spouses (though, for both types of couples, the wife was viewed as making a greater contribution than the husband). On the other hand, the dual-career spouses also made more frequent attempts to influence each other than did the single-career spouses. Such influence attempts probably reflect the more equal status of the married partners, but they may also create a greater potential for conflict. Thus, it seems possible that heterosexual intimate relationships will experience relatively high levels of conflict and instability so long as equality is coming closer but is not yet achieved.

But what will happen when it is achieved—within the society as a whole or, at least, among certain couples? Fitzpatrick's (1988) work on communication in marriage suggests that even here the association between equality and conflict will remain. In her research, couples who had more egalitarian beliefs about appropriate roles for men and women engaged in more overt conflict than couples who had more traditional beliefs about gender roles. One could argue, of course, that the egalitarian couples who participated in this study were still approaching equality, rather than having attained it. But I suspect that there is, in fact, a close association between conflict and equality.

Strong differences in power not only reduce sensitivity to inequality; they also provide a script for how people should behave. Traditional gender roles (men go to work, while women stay home; men are independent and assertive, while women are dependent and nurturant) told men and women what to do. So long as both parties complied with their assigned roles, conflict was reduced. But equality throws out the script. Men and women who do not subscribe to traditional gender roles have to figure out what to do. This does not mean that they do exactly the same thing—that would be another script. Instead, they have to consider their own and their partner's talents, interests, skills, and needs. Every relationship becomes a unique product, rather than being cloned from a master blueprint. Creating a unique product is a harder task; it is always more difficult to grow your own. And creating a unique relationship between two fully equal partners will always involve more conflict, as individual couples have to develop their own set of rules for reconciling their differences.

If you believe that conflict is inherently bad, then this is a rather discouraging view of the future of relationships. But if you take the more positive perspective on conflict described in Chapter 8, the beneficial aspects of this future are readily apparent. Conflict between equals is more likely to be a fair fight, rather than a state of coercive oppression and smoldering resentment. Conflict between equals is also more likely to yield creative solutions, rather than stale repetitions of outdated approaches. And conflict is, of course, only part of a relationship between equals, not the whole of it. I would also make the case that love between equals is particularly rich and satisfying. When there is inequality, the loving act of the subordinate can easily be perceived as flattery in the service of self-protection, while the loving act of the superior can easily be seen as patronizing and demeaning. Equality frees the individuals involved to express their love freely and spontaneously and to trust that the response they receive will be given freely and spontaneously. Intimate relationships in an egalitarian future will take more time and effort to sustain, but the benefits should be well worth the investment.

CHANGING THE REQUIREMENTS

Consider the following two scenarios:

> Marsha and Jonathan are very close friends. They love to go places together or just sit around and talk. Marsha thinks Jonathan is an extraordinarily nice person: kind, considerate, interesting, with a great sense of humor. Jonathan thinks Marsha is one of the best people he has ever met: thoughtful, caring, great fun to be with, and absolutely reliable. Despite their fondness for each other, however, Marsha and Jonathan would never think of marrying each other. They are just good friends.

> Cathy and Bill are lovers. Their relationship sometimes seems like something out of a movie. They have tremendous arguments but then make up and have tremendous sex. Bill often has fits of jealousy; he doesn't like Cathy to talk to other men and often accuses her of flirting. Cathy says he is just too possessive. She also thinks he takes her too much for granted. He can keep her waiting for hours, while he is busy at school or out with some buddies. Bill says Cathy is unreasonable. With their very different interests, they even get into fights about what to do when they are together. But, still, they love each other and intend to get married.

One really has to wonder what is going on here. Is there something wrong with the way people choose the person they marry? Marsha and Jonathan seem far better suited for each other than Cathy and Bill. And yet we have all known people like Marsha and Jonathan who don't marry, and people like Cathy and Bill who do. One very important issue for the future of intimate relationships involves the requirements people set for selecting a marital partner. No doubt about it; romantic, passionate love is one of the greatest experiences on earth. There is, however, much doubt about whether it is a reasonable basis on which to select someone with whom you intend to spend the next 50 or so years of your life. In his usual provocative style, George Bernard Shaw ridiculed this kind of selection process:

> When two people are under the influence of the most violent, most insane, most delusive and most transient of passions, they are required to swear that they will remain in that excited, abnormal and exhausting condition continuously until death do them part. (1963, p. 335)

Actually, most people probably *don't* expect to remain continuously in that abnormal and exhausting condition. What they often do expect is some kind of smooth transition from romantic excitement to tranquil commitment. In the terms used in Chapter 4, they expect passionate love to develop naturally into companionate love. It is not clear, however, that this is a reasonable assumption. Although we cannot be sure about cause and effect, we do know that the rise in the divorce rate in the United States has paralleled an increase in people's stated intention to marry only someone they are in love with (Simpson, Campbell, & Berscheid, 1986).

These developments suggest that heterosexuals may have drawn too sharp a distinction between committed romantic attachments and friendships. In contrast, gay men and lesbians seem less likely to strictly segregate friends from lovers and more likely to adopt a "best friends" model of committed relationships (Harry & DeVall, 1978; Larson, 1982; Vetere, 1982). When considering the heterosexual split between romance and friendship, two different questions are involved. First, why do people like Cathy and Bill get married? The answer to this question seems obvious: They mistake lust for love. It is easy for us, as outside observers, to disparage such a mistake; probably none of us would want to bet on the longevity of such a marriage. But if you have ever been in a relationship similar to the one described between Cathy and Bill, you know that things don't seem so simple to the participants. Their attraction to each other is so powerful that they want to believe that it will suffice to get them over all their problems. Sometimes, it will. But, more often, it will not.

The second question is more difficult. Why do people like Marsha and Jonathan *not* get married? They have, without marriage, what most people expect and desire to get from marriage: companionate love with its shared intimacy, fun in being together, and mutual respect. What they probably don't have, however, is immediate, spontaneous sexual attraction. And it appears that many people make the assumption that if sexual attraction is not present within a relatively short time after meeting someone, it will not, or cannot, develop later. In other words, it seems easier to believe that sex (passionate love) can develop into friendship (companionate love) than to believe that friendship can develop into sexual attraction.

In societies where arranged marriages are common, a different set of assumptions prevails. Here, it is assumed that once people of similar backgrounds and interests are married, love will follow. I am not arguing in favor of arranged marriages, although I would contend that a marry-for-love society with a 50 percent divorce rate should not be too quick to condemn other types of arrangements. It does seem to me, however, that it might be helpful to start breaking down that distinction between romance and friendship—*before* making a long-term commitment. Since many successful long-term relationships look like friendships, then it seems reasonable to look for friendship in the first place. At a minimum, being friends prior to a romantic involvement may help couples who break up remain on friendlier terms (Metts, Cupach, & Bejlovec, 1989). Having grown up during the divorce explosion of recent decades, today's young adults have a great deal of information about successful and unsuccessful relationships. It is hoped that this information will allow them to create a better selection process than the "excited, abnormal and exhausting condition" of passionate love.

CHANGING REALITY

If it seems so logical to emphasize friendship, or companionate love, as a sound basis for long-term commitments, why do we focus so much on romantic, passionate love? According to some social scientists, the preoccupation with romantic love has its roots in a fundamental aspect of our society—individualism (Bellah, Madsen, Sulliven, Swindler, & Tipton, 1985; Dion & Dion, 1988). Individualism refers to the tendency to place one's own personal goals and preferences above the goals and preferences of a group. It is usually contrasted with collectivism, the tendency to subordinate personal desires to the desires of the group. Throughout its history, the United States has been viewed as a highly individualistic society—soon after its founding (Tocqueville, 1840) as well as today (Bellah et al., 1985; Hofstede, 1980; Triandis, Bontempo, Villareal, Asai, & Lucca, 1988). Canada, along with Northern and Western Europe, is also considered to be an individualistic society, while societies in most of the rest of the world are usually seen as reflecting some form of collectivism (Triandis et al., 1988).

As the 1990s began, we witnessed what appears to be a rapid and massive change in Eastern Europe and perhaps in the U.S.S.R. away from collectivism toward more individualistic political and economic structures. At the same time, however, there was increasing concern about whether the United States would be able to compete with the economic prowess of the more collectivist Japanese society. Someone trying to read the tea leaves of history might well have been confused. Is individualism, U.S. style, the wave of the future? Or is it collectivism, Japanese style?

Trying to predict the future of intimate relationships, we encounter the same contradictory indicators. On the one hand, as described in Chapter 1, our attitudes toward and behavior in relationships have become increasingly individualistic. On the other hand, many people are troubled by the lack of stability in sexual and marital relationships, especially when children are involved. Similar concerns about the potentially damaging effects of unrestrained individual choice are often expressed about many other problems in our society today—such as drug addiction, violent crime, insider-trading on Wall Street, and the exploitation of natural resources. It is quite remarkable how the same basic dimension dominates the discussion in so many different arenas: international affairs, domestic public policy, and intimate relationships. What is the appropriate balance between individual free choice and one's obligation to others?

Such a balance lies at the very heart of adult intimate relationships. In these relationships, we choose to make a commitment to someone else. But what is the nature of that commitment? Since we choose it because it makes us feel good, do we then discard it if it makes us feel bad? That's free choice, and one of proven value to individuals who have fled abusive relationships. No benefits are to be gained from turning relationships into prisons. But individual choice is not always beneficial to everyone. Romantic love is often viewed as an example of individual hedonism, based more on the lover's desires than on a genuine concern for the beloved (Bellah et al., 1985; Brehm, 1988; Peele, 1988). As noted at the beginning of this section, the individualistic character of romantic love may account for its great popularity in the United States today. In any event, romantic love can certainly run into conflict with existing commitments to others. And when it does, what is the right thing to do? Should love conquer all, even when this means leaving behind a spouse and children? Or should the commitment be upheld, even when this means the loss of passionate love? In light of the current divorce rate, it appears that many people in the United States prefer the first option to the second one.

Moreover, when they leave a relationship they tend to do it thoroughly. After a divorce, most people have either acrimonious interactions or no interaction at all. In his research on stepfamilies, Furstenberg (1988) notes the extremely low levels of involvement by many noncustodial parents. Indeed, some research suggests that a clean break, with no lingering attachment (positive *or* negative) to the former spouse, is associated with better adult adjustment (Berman, 1988; Tschann, Johnston, & Wallerstein, 1989). Another study, however, found that remarried husbands who had more positive attitudes toward their former wife were also more satisfied in their new marriage (Guisinger, Cowan, & Schuldberg, 1989). Though such a small number of studies does not allow us to draw any firm conclusions, they do serve to raise some important issues.

First, it is not particularly surprising that *negative* feelings about the ex-spouse are associated with poorer adjustment and less marital satisfaction in the second marriage. There are many possible reasons for this correlation. Perhaps personality traits of the divorced individual contribute to all of these effects: the divorce itself, negative feelings about the ex-spouse, poor adjustment after the divorce, and low levels of satisfaction in the remarriage. Or perhaps the stresses and strains of continued hostile relations with the ex-spouse damage both individual adjustment and satisfaction in the remarriage. What is more puzzling is the possibility that *positive* thoughts and feelings about the ex-spouse might also be associated with poorer adjustment. Perhaps these positive responses simply reflect the divorced individual's continuing longing for the relationship; if so, such thoughts and feelings would provide a continuing source of frustration.

It is also possible, however, that positive responses to an ex-spouse or ex-romantic partner are particularly difficult, and even painful, in a culture that so strongly endorses independence and self-sufficiency. After all, the United States was built on the notion of cutting your losses and moving on to the new frontier. People who would prefer to absorb their losses and stay in touch may interpret their preference as some sort of personal inadequacy, as a weakness. But one can interpret such an inclination as a sign of great strength. In an age of serial monogamy, Kelley's (1983) distinction between a commitment to the relationship and a commitment to the person may be especially valuable. When these two commitments are packaged together, the end of a relationship necessarily means the end of the commitment between the two individuals. Most people adopt this perspective when they think of romantic and marital relationships. And yet we have always had a model for regarding the two commitments as separate—right in our own families. Parents and children start out in one kind of relationship, in which children depend on their parents to take care of them, but this relationship ends once the children have grown up. A new kind of relationship then develops, which often resembles a close friendship. Later, aging parents often depend on their children to take care of them. Over time, the parent-child relationship changes drastically, but this does not end their commitment to each other. Thus, it is possible to make commitments to other people that can, if necessary, outlast any specific form of relationship with them. The question is whether we care enough to do so.

In my judgment, the highly individualistic nature of our society today makes it hard for many people to care enough. The culture we live in teaches us what is desirable and what is not. In the United States, we are taught to look out for number one and to make it on our own. Obviously, these lessons are exaggerated. Most everyone looks out for

In families, the personal commitment between parents and children endures despite many changes in the characteristics of their relationship. (Elizabeth Crews/ The Image Works)

somebody else too, and no one ever makes it completely on his or her own. Nevertheless, the fundamental principle has a powerful hold on people's beliefs and goals. Independence and self-reliance are seen as desirable; conformity and dependency as undesirable. This principle influences our view of ourselves and our relationships with others. It amounts to what social scientists have called an "assumptive world" (Parkes, 1975), a "personal theory of reality" (Epstein, 1984), or a "life scheme" (Thompson & Janigian, 1988). Regardless of the label being used, individualism is a good example of a general perspective on life that serves to organize the way we perceive reality.

To suggest that as a society we have veered too far in this direction and need to strengthen our sense of social obligation is not merely to recommend a few minor shifts in behavior: a little more kindness here, a tad more gentleness there. If such a change of direction is to be meaningful, it will require the reconstruction of reality as we see it. We will have to learn some new lessons about just how much each of us relies on others; to realize that the solutions to so many of the tasks we will face in the twenty-first century must be based on teamwork and cooperation; and to develop ways to maintain our commitments to others even if the forms of our relationships with them vary over time. No small agenda, and yet one on which the future of our intimate relationships may well depend.

CHAPTER SUMMARY

Two of the major changes that have occurred in heterosexual relationships over the past generation are increased egalitarianism (greater similarity between men and women in expectations and actual behavior) and serial monogamy (increased number of romantic relationships over the course of a lifetime). It is suggested that further developments in these trends will influence the future of intimate relationships.

Changing Roles

Increasingly, women have access to educational and employment opportunities equal to those available to men. But the movement of married women into the work force has not produced an equivalent involvement by married men in household and child-care responsibilities. Psychologically, then, women seem to have been allowed to become more masculine in their behavior, while men have *not* been allowed to become more feminine in their behavior. In general, masculinity is associated with better personal adjustment and coping, and femininity is associated with having more satisfying intimate relationships. Combining masculine and feminine characteristics, called adrogyny, may be most advantageous when people have the flexibility to be masculine in some situations and feminine in other situations. Both men and women, however, often find it difficult to switch from behaving in more masculine ways at work to behaving in more feminine ways at home. Because of the emphasis on work and financial success in our society, there is growing concern about a loveless future, in which children are neglected and relationships fail because of lack of attention. Two possible approaches are suggested for creating a more balanced and satisfying life for both men and women. First, we should recognize that the difference between home and work may have been exaggerated. A more realistic recognition of the similar qualities required may make it easier to meet the demands of both settings. Second, many existing societal structures are based on a traditional division of labor (man at work; woman at home) that is rapidly disappearing. New structures need to be developed in order to help men and women meet their dual goals of occupational achievement and interpersonal intimacy.

Changing the Rules

In intimate relationships as well as in politics, a fundamental shift in the balance of power creates tension and conflict. The people losing power resent the loss of their prerogatives; those gaining power resent continuing inequalities. Dual-career couples, for example, may have more equality in their relationship than single-career couples, but they may also experience greater conflict about those areas where inequalities still remain. Indeed, it is possible that the association between egalitarianism and conflict in intimate relationships will continue even when full equality is achieved. The traditional division of labor provided a script that determined who would do what. In an egalitarian relationship, there is no such script. Individual couples have to work out their own set of rules for reconciling differences in their needs and desires. It is suggested, however, that conflict in an egalitarian relationship can be more constructive than destructive. In addition, love between equals should be particularly rich and satisfying.

Changing the Requirements

There is a serious question about whether passionate, romantic love is a reasonable basis on which to choose a partner for a long-term committed relationship. Do people expect that passionate love ("that excited, abnormal and exhausting condition") will last a lifetime? Or do they expect that as passionate love fades, companionate love will take its place? The current divorce rate in the United States makes one wonder how often either expectation holds true. It does appear that it may be easier for people to maintain optimistic expectations about the fate of passionate love than to believe that nonsexual friendship can develop, over time, into sexual attraction. And, yet, looking for friendship first may be the best way to secure an enduring love later.

Changing Reality

Throughout its history, the United States has been viewed as a highly individualistic society in which people place their personal goals and preferences above those of a group. Ironically, however, while Eastern Europe and the U.S.S.R. seem to be becoming more individualistic, many in the United States worry about competing economically with the more collectivist Japanese society and are troubled by the damage caused by unrestrained individual choice. Adult intimate relationships involve both free choice and obligation to others, and achieving a healthy balance between the two can be difficult. Under what circumstances should one leave a relationship? And when the relationship has ended, does that mean that the commitment to the individual must also end? It is suggested that our society may have placed too great an emphasis on independence and self-reliance and that our personal theories of reality may need to be revised to make more room for the importance of building community, establishing solidarity, and caring about others.

References

---------- ❖ ----------

Abbey, A. (1982). Sex differences in attributions for friendly behavior: Do males misperceive females' friendliness? *Journal of Personality and Social Psychology, 42*, 830–838.

Abbey, A., & Melby, C. (1986). The effects of nonverbal cues on gender differences in perceptions of sexual intent. *Sex Roles, 15*, 283–298.

Abbott, A. R., & Sebastian, R. J. (1981). Physical attractiveness and expectations of success. *Personality and Social Psychology Bulletin, 7*, 481–485.

Ables, B. S., & Brandsma, J. M. (1977). *Therapy for couples.* San Francisco: Jossey-Bass.

Adams, J. S. (1965). Inequity in social exchange. In L. Berkowitz (Ed.), *Advances in experimental social psychology* (Vol. 2, pp. 267–299). New York: Academic Press.

Adams, M. (1971). The compassion trap. In V. Gornick & B. K. Moran (Eds.), *Woman in sexist society* (pp. 401–416). New York: Basic Books.

Affleck, G., Tennen, H., Croog, S., & Levine, S. (1987). Causal attribution, perceived control, and recovery from a heart attack. *Journal of Social and Clinical Psychology, 5*, 339–358.

Ahrons, C. R., & Wallisch, L. S. (1987). The relationship between former spouses. In D. Perlman & S. Duck (Eds.), *Intimate relationships: Development, dynamics, and deterioration* (pp. 269–296). Newbury Park, CA: Sage.

Ainsworth, M., Blehar, M. C., Waters, E., & Wall, S. (1978). *Patterns of attachment: A psychological study of the strange situation.* Hillsdale, NJ: Erlbaum.

Allen, J. B., Kenrick, D. T., Linder, D. E., & McCall, M. A. (1989). Arousal and attribution: A response facilitation alternative to misattribution and negative-reinforcement models. *Journal of Personality and Social Psychology, 57*, 261–270.

Altman, I. (1973). Reciprocity of interpersonal exchange. *Journal of Theory of Social Behavior, 3*, 249–261.

Altman, I., & Taylor, D. A. (1973). *Social penetration: The development of interpersonal relationships.* New York: Holt, Rinehart & Winston.

Altman, I., Vinsel, A., & Brown, B. A. (1981). Dialectic conceptions in social psychology: An application to social penetration and privacy regulation. In L. Berkowitz (Ed.), *Advances in experimental social psychology* (Vol. 14, pp. 107–160), New York: Academic Press.

Altrocchi, J., & Croxby, R. D. (1989). Clarifying and measuring the concept of traditional vs. nontraditional roles in marriage. *Sex Roles, 20*, 639–648.

Amabile, T. M. (1983). Brilliant but cruel: Perceptions of negative evaluators. *Journal of Experimental Social Psychology, 19,* 146–156.

Amato, P. R. (1988). Parental divorce and attitudes about marriage and family life. *Journal of Marriage and the Family, 50,* 453–461.

Ambert, A. (1988). Relationship between ex-spouses: Individual and dyadic perspectives. *Journal of Social and Personal Relationships, 5,* 327–346.

Anderson, B. S., & Zinsser, J. P. (1988). *A history of their own: Women in Europe* (Vol. 1). New York: Harper & Row.

Anderson, C. A., & Harvey, R. J. (1988). Discriminating between problems in living: An examination of depression, loneliness, shyness, and social anxiety. *Journal of Social and Clinical Psychology, 6,* 482–491.

Andres, D., Gold, D., Berger, C., Kinch, R., & Gillett, P. (1983). Selected psychosocial characteristics of males: Their relationship to contraceptive use and abortion. *Personality and Social Psychology Bulletin, 9,* 387–396.

Aneshensel, C. S., & Pearlin, L. I. (1987). Structural contexts of sex differences in stress. In R. C. Barnett, L. Biener, & G. K. Baruch (Eds.), *Gender and stress* (pp. 75–95). New York: Free Press.

Antill, J. K. (1983). Sex role complementarity versus similarity in married couples. *Journal of Personality and Social Psychology, 45,* 145–155.

Archer, R. L. (1979). Role of personality and the social situation. In G. J. Chelune (Ed.), *Self-disclosure* (pp. 28–58). San Francisco: Jossey-Bass.

Archer, R. P., & Cash, T. F. (1985). Physical attractiveness and maladjustment among psychiatric inpatients. *Journal of Social and Clinical Psychology, 3,* 170–180.

Arendell, T. (1988). *Mothers and divorce.* Berkeley: University of California Press.

Arias, H., & O'Leary, K. D. (1985). Semantic and perceptual discrepancies in discordant and nondiscordant marriages. *Cognitive Therapy and Research, 9,* 51–60.

Aries, E. J., & Johnson, F. L. (1983). Close friendship in adulthood: Conversational content between same-sex friends. *Sex Roles, 9,* 1183–1197.

Arling, G. (1976). The elderly widow and her family, neighbors, and friends. *Journal of Marriage and the Family, 38,* 757–768.

Aron, A. (1988). The matching hypothesis reconsidered again: Comment on Kalick and Hamilton. *Journal of Personality and Social Psychology, 54,* 441–446.

Aron, A., Dutton, D. G., Aron, E. N., & Iverson, A. (1989). Experiences of falling in love. *Journal of Social and Personal Relationships, 6,* 243–257.

Aronson, E., Brewer, M., & Carlsmith, J. M. (1985). Experimentation in social psychology. In G. Lindzey & E. Aronson (Eds.), *Handbook of social psychology* (3d ed., Vol. 1, pp. 441–486). New York: Random House.

Aronson, E., & Cope, V. (1968). My enemy's enemy is my friend. *Journal of Personality and Social Psychology, 8,* 8–12.

Aronson, E., & Mills, J. (1959). The effect of severity of initiation on liking for a group. *Journal of Abnormal and Social Psychology, 59,* 177–181.

Aronson, E., & Worchel, S. (1966). Similarity versus liking as determinants of interpersonal attractiveness. *Psychonomic Science, 5,* 157–158.

Atchley, R. C. (1975). Dimensions of widowhood in later life. *Gerontologist, 15,* 176–178.

Atchley, R. C. (1977). *The social forces in later life*. Belmont, CA: Wadsworth.

Atkinson, J., & Huston, T. L. (1984). Sex role orientation and division of labor early in marriage. *Journal of Personality and Social Psychology, 46*, 330–345.

Aukett, R., Richie, J., & Mill, K. (1988). Gender differences in friendship patterns. *Sex Roles, 19*, 57–66.

Austin, W., & Walster, E. (1974). Reactions to confirmations and disconfirmations of expectancies of equity and inequity. *Journal of Personality and Social Psychology, 30*, 208–213.

Aylmer, R. C. (1986). Bowen family systems marital therapy. In N. S. Jacobson & A. S. Gurman (Eds.), *Clinical handbook of marital therapy* (pp. 107–148). New York: Guilford.

Bach, G. R., & Wyden, P. (1968). *The intimate enemy*. New York: Morrow.

Backer, T. E., Batchelor, W. F., Jones, J. M., & Mays, V. E. (1988). Special issue: Psychology and AIDS. *American Psychologist, 43* (11).

Backman, C. W., & Secord, P. F. (1959). The effect of perceived liking on interpersonal attraction. *Human Relations, 12*, 379–384.

Bakan, D. (1966). *The duality of human existence*. Boston: Beacon Press.

Bakken, D. (1979). Regulation of intimacy in social encounters: The effects of sex of interactants and information about attitude similarity. In M. Cook & G. Wilson (Eds.), *Love and attraction*. Oxford: Pergamon Press.

Baldwin, A. L., Cole, R. E., & Baldwin, C. P. (1982). Parental pathology, family interaction, and the competence of the child in school. *Monographs of the Society for Research in Child Development, 47*, No. 5.

Bandura, A., Ross, D., & Ross, S. A. (1963). A comparative test of the status envy, social power, and secondary reinforcement theories of identificatory learning. *Journal of Abnormal and Social Psychology, 67*, 527–534.

Bannester, E. M. (1969). Sociodynamics: An integrative theorem of power, authority, interfluence and love. *American Sociological Review, 34*, 374–393.

Bardis, P. D. (1979). Homeric love. In M. Cook & G. Wilson (Eds.), *Love and attraction* (pp. 255–260). Oxford: Pergamon Press.

Barling, J. (1990). Employment and marital functioning. In F. D. Fincham & T. N. Bradbury (Eds.), *The psychology of marriage: Basic issues and applications* (pp. 201–225). New York: Guilford.

Barnes, M. L., & Buss, D. M. (1985). Sex differences in the interpersonal behavior of married couples. *Journal of Personality and Social Psychology, 48*, 654–661.

Barnett, L. R., & Nietzel, M. T. (1979). Relationship of instrumental and affectional behaviors and self-esteem to marital satisfaction in distressed and nondistressed couples. *Journal of Consulting and Clinical Psychology, 47*, 946–957.

Barnett, P. A., & Gotlib, I. H. (1988). Psychosocial functioning and depression: Distinguishing among antecedents, concomitants, and consequences. *Psychological Bulletin, 104*, 97–126.

Barnett, R. C., & Baruch, G. K. (1985). Women's involvement in multiple roles and psychological distress. *Journal of Personality and Social Psychology, 49*, 135–145.

Barry, W. A. (1970). Marriage research and conflict: An integrative review. *Psychological Bulletin, 73*, 41–54.

Bar-Tal, D., & Saxe, L. (1976). Perceptions of similarly and dissimilarly attractive couples and individuals. *Journal of Personality and Social Psychology, 33,* 772–781.

Barth, R. J., & Kinder, B. N. (1988). A theoretical analysis of sex differences in same-sex friendships. *Sex Roles, 19,* 349–363.

Batson, C. D. (1987). Prosocial motivation: Is it ever truly altruistic? In L. Berkowitz (Ed.), *Advances in experimental social psychology* (Vol. 20, pp. 65–122). Orlando, FL: Academic Press.

Batson, C. D., Duncan, B. D., Ackerman, P., Buckley, T., & Birch, K. (1981). Is empathic emotion a source of altruistic motivation? *Journal of Personality and Social Psychology, 40,* 290–302.

Batson, C. D., Fultz, J., & Schoenrade, P. A. (1987). Distress and empathy: Two qualitatively distinct vicarious emotions with different motivational consequences. *Journal of Personality, 55,* 19–39.

Batson, C. D., O'Quin, K., Fultz, J., Vanderplas, M., & Isen, A. M. (1983). Influence of self-reported distress and empathy on egoistic versus altruistic motivation to help. *Journal of Personality and Social Psychology, 45,* 706–718.

Baucom, D. H., & Epstein, N. (1990). *Cognitive-behavioral marital therapy.* New York: Brunner/Mazel.

Baucom, D. H., & Hoffman, J. A. (1986). The effectiveness of marital therapy: Current status and application to the clinical setting. In N. S. Jacobson & A. S. Gurman (Eds.), *Clinical handbook of marital therapy* (pp. 597–620). New York: Guilford.

Baucom, D. H., Sayers, S. L., & Duhe, A. (1989). Attributional style and attributional patterns among married couples. *Journal of Personality and Social Psychology, 56,* 596–607.

Bauman, L. J., & Siegel, K. (1987). Misperception among gay men of the risk for AIDS associated with their sexual behavior. *Journal of Applied Social Psychology, 17,* 329–350.

Baxter, L. A. (1987). Self-disclosure and relationship disengagement. In V. Derlega & J. H. Berg (Eds.), *Self-disclosure: Theory, research, and therapy* (pp. 155–174). New York: Plenum.

Baxter, L. A. (1988). A dialectical perspective on communication strategies in relationship development. In S. Duck (Ed.), *Handbook of personal relationships* (pp. 257–273). New York: Wiley.

Baxter, L. A., & Wilmot, W. W. (1985). Taboo topics in close relationships. *Journal of Social and Personal Relationships, 2,* 253–269.

Beach, S. R. H., & Tesser, A. (1988). Love in marriage: A cognitive account. In R. J. Sternberg & M. L. Barnes (Eds.), *The psychology of love* (pp. 330–355). New Haven, CT: Yale University Press.

Beck, A. T. (1988). *Love is never enough.* New York: Harper & Row.

Beir, E. G., & Sternberg, D. P. (1977). Marital communication. *Journal of Communication, 27,* 92–103.

Bell, A. P., & Weinberg, M. S. (1978). *Homosexualities.* New York: Simon and Schuster.

Bellah, R. N., Madsen, R., Sullivan, W. M., Swindler, A., & Tipton, S. M. (1985). *Habits of the heart: Individualism and commitment in American life.* Berkeley: University of California Press.

Belk, S. S., & Snell, W. E., Jr. (1988). Avoidance strategy use in intimate relationships. *Journal of Social and Clinical Psychology, 7,* 80–96.

Belk, S. S., Snell, W. E., Jr., Garcia-Falconi, R., Hernandez-Sanchez, J. E., Hargrove, L., & Holtzman, W. H., Jr. (1988). Power strategy use in the intimate relationships of women and men from Mexico and the United States. *Personality and Social Psychology Bulletin, 14,* 439–447.

Belsky, J. (1990). Children and marriage. In F. D. Fincham & T. N. Bradbury (Eds.), *The psychology of marriage: Basic issues and applications* (pp. 172–200). New York: Guilford.

Belsky, J., Lang, M., & Huston, T. L. (1986). Sex typing and division of labor as determinants of marital change across transition to parenthood. *Journal of Personality and Social Psychology, 50,* 517–522.

Bem, S. L. (1974). The measurement of psychological androgyny. *Journal of Consulting and Clinical Psychology, 42,* 155–162.

Bem, S. L. (1975). Sex role adaptability: One consequence of psychological androgyny. *Journal of Personality and Social Psychology, 31,* 634–643.

Benin, M. H., & Agostinelli, J. (1988). Husbands' and wives' satisfaction with the division of labor. *Journal of Marriage and the Family, 50,* 349–361.

Bennett, N., Blanc, A., & Bloom, D. (1988). Commitment and the modern union. Assessing the link between premarital cohabitation and subsequent marital stability. *Sociological Review, 53,* 997–1008.

Bentler, P. M., & Huba, G. J. (1979). Simple minitheories of love. *Journal of Personality and Social Psychology, 37,* 124–130.

Benton, C. J., Hernandez, A. C. R., Schmidt, A., Schmitz, M. D., Stone, A. J., & Weiner, B. (1983). Is hostility linked with affiliation among males and with achievement among females? A critique of Pollak and Gilligan. *Journal of Personality and Social Psychology, 45,* 1167–1171.

Berardo, F. M. (1970). Survivorship and social isolation: The case of the aged widower. *The Family Coordinator, 19,* 11–15.

Berg, J. H. (1984). Development of friendship between roommates. *Journal of Personality and Social Psychology, 46,* 346–356.

Berg, J. H., & Clark, M. S. (1986). Differences in social exchange between intimate and other relationships: Gradually evolving or quickly apparent? In V. J. Derlega & B. A. Winstead (Eds.), *Friendship and social interaction* (pp. 101–128). New York: Springer-Verlag.

Berg, J. H., & McQuinn, R. D. (1986). Attraction and exchange in continuing and noncontinuing dating relationships. *Journal of Personality and Social Psychology, 50,* 942–952.

Berger, C. R. (1988). Uncertainty and information exchange in developing relationships. In S. Duck (Ed.), *Handbook of personal relationships* (pp. 239–255). New York: Wiley.

Berger, D. G., & Wenger, M. G. (1973). The ideology of virginity. *Journal of Marriage and the Family, 35,* 666–676.

Berkman, L., & Syme, S. (1979). Social networks, host resistance, and mortality: A nine year followup study of Alameda County residents. *American Journal of Epidemiology, 109,* 186–204.

Berman, W. H. (1988). The role of attachment in the post-divorce experience. *Journal of Personality and Social Psychology, 54,* 496–503.

Bernard, J. (1972). *The future of marriage.* New York: World.

Bernard, J. (1976). Homosociality and female depression. *Journal of Social Issues*, *32*, 213–238.

Bernard, J. (1977). Jealousy and marriage. In G. Clanton & L. G. Smith (Eds.), *Jealousy* (pp. 141–150). Englewood Cliffs, NJ: Prentice-Hall.

Bernstein, W. M., Stephenson, B. O., Snyder, M. L., & Wicklund, R. A. (1983). Causal ambiguity and heterosexual affiliation. *Journal of Experimental Social Psychology*, *19*, 78–92.

Berscheid, E. (1983). Emotion. In H. H. Kelley, E. Berscheid, A. Christensen, J. H. Harvey, T. L. Huston, G. Levinger, E. McClintock, L. A. Peplau & D. R. Peterson (Eds.), *Close relationships* (pp. 110–168). New York: Freeman.

Berscheid, E. (1985). Interpersonal attraction. In G. Lindzey & E. Aronson (Eds.), *Handbook of social psychology* (3d ed., Vol. 2, pp. 413–484). New York: Random House.

Berscheid, E., Dion, K., Walster, E., & Walster, G. W. (1971). Physical attractiveness and dating choice: A test of the matching hypothesis. *Journal of Experimental Social Psychology*, *7*, 173–189.

Berscheid, E., & Fei, J. (1977). Romantic love: Sexual jealousy. In G. Clanton & L. G. Smith (Eds.), *Jealousy* (pp. 101–109). Englewood Cliffs, NJ: Prentice-Hall.

Berscheid, E., & Peplau, L. A. (1983). The emerging science of relationships. In H. H. Kelley, E. Berscheid, A. Christensen, et al. (Eds.), *Close relationships* (pp. 1–19). New York: Freeman.

Berscheid, E., Snyder, M., & Omoto, A. M. (1989a). Issues in studying close relationships: Conceptualizing and measuring closeness. In C. Hendrick (Ed.), *Review of personality and social psychology: Vol. 10. Close relationships* (pp. 63–91). Newbury Park, CA: Sage.

Berscheid, E., Snyder, M., & Omoto, A. M. (1989b). The relationship closeness inventory: Assessing the closeness of interpersonal relationships. *Journal of Personality and Social Psychology*, *57*, 792–807.

Berscheid, E., & Walster, E. (1974a). A little bit about love. In T. Huston (Ed.), *Foundations of interpersonal attraction* (pp. 355–381). New York: Academic Press.

Berscheid, E., & Walster, E. (1974b). Physical attractiveness. In L. Berkowitz (Ed.), *Advances in experimental social psychology* (Vol. 7, pp. 157–215). New York: Academic Press.

Berscheid, E., Walster, E., & Campbell, R. (1972). "Grow old along with me." Unpublished manuscript, Department of Psychology, University of Minnesota.

Billings, A. (1979). Conflict in distressed and nondistressed married couples. *Journal of Consulting and Clinical Psychology*, *47*, 368–376.

Birchler, G. R., & Webb, L. J. (1977). Discriminating interaction behavior in happy and unhappy marriages. *Journal of Consulting and Clinical Psychology*, *45*, 494–495.

Birchler, G. R., Weiss, R. L., & Vincent, J. P. (1975). Multimethod analysis of social reinforcement exchange between maritally distressed and nondistressed spouse and stranger dyads. *Journal of Personality and Social Psychology*, *31*, 349–360.

Black, H., & Angelis, V. B. (1974). Interpersonal attraction: An empirical investigation of platonic and romantic love. *Psychological Reports, 34,* 1243–1246.

Blais, M. R., Sabourin, S., Boucher, C., & Vallerand, R. J. (1990). Toward a motivational model of couple happiness. *Journal of Personality and Social Psychology, 59,* 1021–1031.

Blau, P. M. (1964). *Exchange and power in social life.* New York: Wiley.

Block, J. H. (1973). Conceptions of sex role: Some cross-cultural and longitudinal perspectives. *American Psychologist, 28,* 512–526.

Blood, R. O., & Wolfe, D. M. (1960). *Husbands and wives: The dynamics of married living.* New York: Free Press.

Bloom, B., Asher, S. J., & White, S. W. (1978). Marital disruption as a stressor: A review and analysis. *Psychological Bulletin, 85,* 867–894.

Bloom, B. L., & Caldwell, R. A. (1981). Sex differences in adjustment during the period of marital separation, *Journal of Marriage and the Family, 43,* 693–701.

Bolger, N., DeLongis, A., Kessler, R. C., & Wethington, E. (1989). The contagion of stress across multiple roles. *Journal of Marriage and the Family, 51,* 175–183.

Borys, S., & Perlman, D. (1985). Gender differences in loneliness. *Personality and Social Psychology Bulletin, 11,* 63–76.

Booth, A., Brinkerhoff, D. B., & White, L. K. (1984). The impact of parental divorce and courtship. *Journal of Marriage and the Family, 46,* 85–94.

Booth, A., & Edwards, J. N. (1989). Transmission of marital and family quality over the generations: The effect of parental divorce and unhappiness. *Journal of Divorce, 13,* 41–58.

Boyden, T., Carroll, J. S., & Maier, R. A. (1984). Similarity and attraction in homosexual males: The effects of age and masculinity-femininity. *Sex Roles, 10,* 939–948.

Bradbury, T. N., & Fincham, F. D. (1990). Attributions in marriage: Review and critique. *Psychological Bulletin, 107,* 3–33.

Brand, E., Clingempeel, W. G., & Bowen-Woodward, K. (1988). Family relationships and children's psychological adjustment in stepmother and stepfather families. In E. M. Hetherington & J. D. Arasteh (Eds.), *Impact of divorce, singleparenting, and stepparenting on children* (pp. 299–324). Hillsdale, NJ: Erlbaum.

Branden, N. (1980). *The psychology of romantic love.* Los Angeles: Tarcher.

Braver, S. L., Gonzalez, N., Wolchik, S. A., & Sandler, I. N. (1989). Economic hardship and psychological distress in custodial mothers. *Journal of Divorce, 12,* 19–34.

Bray, J. H. (1988). Children's development during early remarriage. In E. M. Hetherington & J. D. Arasteh (Eds.), *Impact of divorce, singleparenting, and stepparenting on children* (pp. 279–298). Hillsdale, NJ: Erlbaum.

Bragg, M. (1979). "A comparative study of loneliness and depression." Unpublished doctoral dissertation, University of California, Los Angeles.

Breault, K. D., & Kposowa, J. (1987). Explaining divorce in the United States: A study of 3,111 counties, 1980. *Journal of Marriage and the Family, 49,* 549–558.

Brehm, J. W. (1966). *A theory of psychological reactance.* New York: Academic Press.

Brehm, J. W., & Cohen, R. A. (1962). *Explorations in cognitive dissonance*. New York: Wiley.

Brehm, S. S. (1987). Coping after a relationship ends. In C. R. Snyder & C. E. Ford (Eds.), *Coping with negative life events* (pp. 191–212). New York: Plenum Press.

Brehm, S. S. (1988). Passionate love. In R. J. Sternberg & M. L. Barnes (Eds.), *The psychology of love* (pp. 232–263). New Haven, CT: Yale University Press.

Brehm, S. S., & Brehm, J. W. (1981). *Psychological reactance: A theory of freedom and control*. New York: Academic Press.

Brehm, S. S., & Kassin, S. M. (1990). *Social psychology*. Boston: Houghton Mifflin.

Breines, W., & Gordon, L. (1983). The new scholarship on family violence. *Signs, 8*, 490–531.

Briggs, S. R., & Cheek, J. M. (1988). On the nature of self-monitoring: Problems with assessment, problems with validity. *Journal of Personality and Social Psychology, 54*, 663–678.

Brindle, D. (1989, December 31), Most couples now try living together before marriage. *Manchester Guardian Weekly*, p. 3.

Bringle, R. G., & Boebinger, K. L. G. (1990). Jealousy and the "third" person in the love triangle. *Journal of Social and Personal Relationships, 7*, 119–133.

Bringle, R. G., & Buunk, B. (1986). Examining the causes and consequences of jealousy: Some recent findings and issues. In R. Gilmour & S. Duck (Eds.), *The emerging field of personal relationships* (pp. 225–240). Hillsdale, NJ: Erlbaum.

Bringle, R. G., & Evenbeck, S. (1979). The state of jealousy as a dispositional characteristic. In M. Cook & G. Wilson (Eds.), *Love and attraction* (pp. 201–204). Oxford: Pergamon Press.

Brinkerhoff, M., & Lupri, E. (1978). Theoretical and methodological issues in the use of decision-making as an indicator of conjugal power: Some Canadian observations. *Canadian Journal of Sociology, 3*, 1–20.

Brislin, R. W., & Lewis, S. A. (1968). Dating and physical attractiveness: Replication. *Psychological Reports, 22*, 976.

Brockner, J., & Rubin, J. Z. (1985). *Entrapment in escalating conflicts: A social psychological analysis*. New York: Springer-Verlag.

Broderick, C. B., & Schrader, S. S. (1981). The history of professional marriage and family therapy. In A. S. Gurman & D. P. Kniskern (Eds.), *Handbook of family therapy*. (pp. 5–35). New York: Brunner/Mazel.

Broderick, J. E., & O'Leary, K. D. (1986). Contributions of affect, attitudes, and behavior to marital satisfaction. *Journal of Consulting and Clinical Psychology, 54*, 514–517.

Brody, G. H., Neubaum, E., & Forehand, R. (1988). Serial marriage: A heuristic analysis of an emerging family form. *Psychological Bulletin, 103*, 211–222.

Brooks-Gunn, J., & Furstenberg, F. F., Jr. (1989). Adolescent sexual behavior. *American Psychologist, 44*, 249–257.

Brown, C. E., Dovidio, J. F., & Ellyson, S. L. (1990). Reducing sex differences in visual displays of dominance: Knowledge is power. *Personality and Social Psychology Bulletin, 16*, 358–368.

Brown, G. W., & Harris, T. (1978). *Social origins of depression: A study of psychiatric disorder in women*. New York: Free Press.

Brown, L. S., & Zimmer, D. (1986). An introduction to therapy issues of gay and lesbian couples. In N. S. Jacobson & A. S. Gurman (Eds.), *Clinical handbook of marital therapy* (pp. 451–468). New York: Guilford.

Browne, A. (1986). Assault and homicide at home: When battered women kill. In M. J. Saks & L. Saxe (Eds.), *Advances in applied social psychology* (Vol. 3, pp. 57–79). Hillsdale, NJ: Erlbaum.

Browning, J., & Dutton, D. (1986). Assessment of wife assault with the Conflicts Tactics Scale: Using complex data to quantify the differential reporting effect. *Journal of Marriage and the Family, 48,* 375–379.

Bruch, M. A., Gorsky, J. M., Collins, T. M., & Berger, P. A. (1989). Shyness and sociability examined: A multicomponent analysis. *Journal of Personality and Social Psychology, 57,* 904–915.

Brundage, J. A. (1987). Law, sex, and Christian society in medieval Europe. Chicago: University of Chicago Press.

Bryson, J. B. (1977). Situational determinants of the expression of jealousy. In H. Sigall (Chair), *Sexual jealousy.* Symposium presented at the Annual Meeting of the American Psychological Association, San Francisco.

Bulman, R. J., & Wortman, C. B. (1977). Attribution of blame and coping in the "real world": Severe accident victims react to their lot. *Journal of Personality and Social Psychology, 35,* 351–363.

Bumpass, L., Sweet, J., & Castro Martin, T. (1990). Changing patterns of remarriage. *Journal of Marriage and the Family, 52,* 747–756.

Burchill, S. A. L., & Stile, W. B. (1988). Interactions of depressed college students with their roommates: Not necessarily negative. *Journal of Personality and Social Psychology, 55,* 410–419.

Bureau of Justice Statistics. (1991). Female crime victims. Washington, D C: U.S. Department of Justice.

Burger, J. M., & Burns, L. (1988). The illusion of unique invulnerability and use of effective contraception. *Personality and Social Psychology Bulletin, 14,* 264–270.

Burgess, E. W., & Cottrell, L. S. (1939). *Predicting success or failure in marriage.* New York: Prentice-Hall.

Burgess, E. W., & Wallin, P. (1953). *Engagement and marriage.* Philadelphia: Lippincott.

Burgess, R. L. (1981). Relationships in marriage and the family. In S. Duck & R. Gilmour (Eds.), *Personal relationships. 1: Studying personal relationships* (pp. 179–196). New York: Academic Press.

Burgess, R. L., & Nielsen, J. M. (1977). Distributive justice and the balance of power. In J. H. Kunkel (Ed.), *Behavioral theory in sociology* (pp. 139–169). New Brunswick, NJ: Transaction Books.

Burke, R. J., Weir, T., & Harrison, D. (1976). Disclosure of problems and tensions experienced by marital partners. *Psychological Reports, 38,* 531–542.

Burleson, B. R. (1982). The development of comforting communication skills in childhood and adolescence. *Child Development, 53,* 1578–1588.

Burr, W. R. (1970). Satisfaction with various aspects of marriage over the life cycle: A random middle class sample. *Journal of Marriage and the Family, 32,* 29–37.

Bush, C. R., Bush, J. P., & Jennings, J. (1988). Effects of jealousy threats on relationship perception and emotions. *Journal of Social and Personal Relationships, 5,* 285–303.

Buss, D. A. (1989). Conflict between the sexes: Strategic interference and the evocation of anger and upset. *Journal of Personality and Social Psychology 56,* 735–747.

Buss, D. M. (1988a). The evolution of human intrasexual competition: Tactics of mate attraction. *Journal of Personality and Social Psychology, 54,* 616–628.

Buss, D. M. (1988b). The evolutionary biology of love. In R. J. Sternberg & M. L. Barnes (Eds.), *The psychology of love* (pp. 100–118). New Haven, CT: Yale University Press.

Buss, D. M. (1989). Sex differences in human mate preferences: Evolutionary hypotheses tested in 37 cultures. *Behavioral and Brain Sciences, 12,* 1–14.

Buss, D. M., & Barnes, M. (1986). Preferences in human mate selection. *Journal of Personality and Social Psychology, 50,* 559–570.

Butler, D., & Geis, F. L. (1990). Nonverbal affect responses to male and female leaders: Implications for leadership evaluations. *Journal of Personality and Social Psychology, 58,* 48–59.

Buunk, B. (1982). Anticipated sexual jealousy: Its relationship to self-esteem, dependency, and reciprocity. *Personality and Social Psychology Bulletin, 8,* 310–316.

Buunk, B. (1987). Conditions that promote breakups as a consequence of extra-dyadic involvements. *Journal of Social and Clinical Psychology 5,* 271–284.

Buunk, B., & Bringle, R. G. (1987). Jealousy in love relationships. In D. Perlman & S. Duck (Eds.), *Intimate relationships: Development, dynamics, and deterioration* (pp. 123–147). Newbury Park, CA: Sage.

Byrne, D. (1971). *The attraction paradigm.* New York: Academic Press.

Byrne, D., & Clore, G. L. (1970). A reinforcement model of evaluative processes. *Personality: An International Journal, 1,* 103–128.

Byrne, D., Clore, G. L., & Smeaton, G. (1986). The attraction hypothesis: Do similar attitudes affect anything? *Journal of Personality and Social Psychology 51,* 1167–1170.

Byrne, D., Ervin, C. E., & Lamberth, J. (1970). Continuity between the experimental study of attraction and real-life computer dating. *Journal of Personality and Social Psychology, 16,* 157–165.

Byrne, D., & Fisher, W. A. (1983). *Adolescents, sex, and contraception.* Hillsdale, NJ: Erlbaum.

Byrne, D., London, O., & Reeves, K. (1968). The effects of physical attractiveness, sex and attitude similarity on interpersonal attraction. *Journal of Personality, 36,* 259–271.

Byrne, D., & Murnen, S. K. (1988). Maintaining loving relationships. In R. J. Sternberg & M. L. Barnes (Eds.), *The psychology of love* (pp. 293–310). New Haven, CT: Yale University Press.

Byrne, D., & Rhamey, R. (1965). Magnitude of positive and negative reinforcements as a determinant of attraction. *Journal of Personality and Social Psychology, 2,* 884–889.

Caldwell, M. A., & Peplau, L. A. (1984). The balance of power in lesbian relationships. *Sex Roles, 10,* 587–599.

Campbell, A. (1981). *The sense of well being in America: Patterns and trends.* New York: McGraw-Hill.

Campbell, J. D., & Tesser, A. (1985). Self-evaluation maintenance process in relationships. In S. Duck & D. Perlman (Eds.), *Understanding personal relationships: An interdisciplinary approach* (pp. 107–135). London: Sage.

Cantor, J. R., Zillmann, D., & Bryant, J. (1975). Enhancement of experienced sexual arousal in response to erotic stimuli through misattribution of unrelated residual arousal. *Journal of Personality and Social Psychology, 32,* 69–75.

Caporael, L. R. (1989). Mechanisms matter: The difference between sociobiology and evolutionary psychology. *Behavioral and Brain Sciences, 12,* 17–18.

Cargan, L., & Melko, M. (1982). *Singles: Myths and realities.* Beverly Hills, CA: Sage Publications.

Carli, L. L. (1989). Gender differences in interaction style and influence. *Journal of Personality and Social Psychology, 56,* 565–576.

Carli, L. L. (1990). Gender, language, and influence. *Journal of Personality and Social Psychology, 59,* 941–951.

Carroll, L. (1988). Concern with AIDS and the sexual behavior of college students. *Journal of Marriage and the Family, 50,* 405–411.

Cash, T. F., & Derlega, V. J. (1978). The matching hypothesis: Physical attractiveness among same-sex and friends. *Personality and Social Psychology Bulletin, 4,* 240–243.

Caspi, A., & Harbener, E. S. (1990). Continuity and change: Assortive marriage and the consistency of personality in adulthood. *Journal of Personality and Social Psychology, 58,* 250–258.

Cassel, J. (1974). Psychosocial processes and "stress": Theoretical formulation. *International Journal of Health Services, 6,* 471–482.

Castro Martin, T., & Bumpass, L. L. (1989). Recent trends in marital disruption. *Demography, 26,* 37–51.

Catania, J. A., Gibson, D. R., Chitwood, D. D., & Coates, T. J. (1990). Methodological problems in AIDS behavioral research: Influences on measurement error and participation bias in studies of sexual behavior. *Psychological Bulletin, 108,* 339–362.

Cate, R. M., Henton, J. M., Koval, J., Christopher, F. S., & Lloyd, S. (1982). Premarital abuse: A social psychological perspective. *Journal of Family Issues, 3,* 79–90.

Cate, R. M., & Lloyd, S. A. (1988). Courtship. In S. Duck (Ed.), *Handbook of personal relationships* (pp. 409–427). New York: Wiley.

Cate, R. M., Lloyd, S. A., & Henton, J. M. (1985). The effect of equity, equality, and reward level on the stability of students' premarital relationships. *Journal of Social Psychology, 125,* 715–721.

Cate, R. M., Lloyd, S., Henton, J. M., & Larson, J. (1982). Fairness and reward level as predictors of relationship satisfaction. *Social Psychology Quarterly, 45,* 177–181.

Cate, R. M., Lloyd, S. A., & Long, E. (1988). The role of rewards and fairness in developing premarital relationships. *Journal of Marriage and the Family, 50,* 443–452.

Centers, R., Raven, B. H., & Rodrigues, A. (1971). Conjugal power structure: A reexamination. *American Sociological Review, 36,* 264–278.

Chaiken, S. (1979). Communicator physical attractiveness and persuasion. *Journal of Personality and Social Psychology, 37,* 1387–1397.

Check, J. V. P., Perlman, D., & Malamuth, N. M. (1985). Loneliness and aggressive behavior. *Journal of Social and Personal Relationships, 2,* 243–252.

Cheek, J. M. (1983). The Revised Cheek and Buss Shyness Scale. Unpublished manuscript, Wellesley College.

Cheek, J. M., & Busch, C. M. (1981). The influence of shyness on loneliness in a new situation. *Personality and Social Psychology Bulletin, 7,* 572–577.

Chelune, G. J. (1976). Reactions to male and female disclosure at two levels. *Journal of Personality and Social Psychology, 34,* 1000–1003.

Chelune, G. J. (Ed.). (1979). *Self-disclosure.* San Francisco: Jossey-Bass.

Cherlin, A. (1983). The trends: Marriage, divorce, remarriage. In A. S. Skolnick & J. H. Skolnick (Eds.), *Family in transition* (4th Ed., pp. 128–137). Boston: Little, Brown.

Cherlin, A., & McCarthy, J. (1985). Remarried couple households: Data from the June 1980 current population survey. *Journal of Marriage and the Family, 47,* 23–30.

Chiriboga, D. A., Coho, A., Stein, J. A., & Roberts, J. (1979). Divorce, stress and social supports: A study in help-seeking behavior. *Journal of Divorce, 3,* 121–135.

Chiriboga, D. A., & Cutler, L. (1977). Stress responses among divorcing men and women. *Journal of Divorce, 7,* 67–81.

Chiriboga, D. A., Roberts, J., & Stein, J. A. (1978). Psychological well-being during marital separation. *Journal of Divorce, 2,* 21–36.

Chiriboga, D. A., & Thurner, M. (1980). Marital lifestyles and adjustment to separation. *Journal of Divorce, 3,* 379–390.

Christensen, A. (1979). Naturalistic observation of families: A system for random audio recordings. *Behavior Therapy, 10,* 418–427.

Christensen, A., & Heavey, C. L. (1990). Gender and social structure in the demand/withdraw pattern of marital conflict. *Journal of Personality and Social Psychology, 59,* 73–81.

Christensen, A., Sullaway, M., & King, C. (1983). Systematic error in behavioral reports of dyadic interaction: Egocentric bias and content analysis. *Behavioral Therapy, 5,* 129–140.

Cialdini, R. B., Borden, R. J., Thorne, A., Walker, M. R., Freeman, S., & Sloan, L. R. (1976). Basking in reflected glory: Three (football) field studies. *Journal of Personality and Social Psychology, 34,* 366–375.

Cimbalo, R. S., Faling, V., & Mousan, P. (1976). The course of love: A cross-sectional design. *Psychological Report, 38,* 1292–1294.

Clanton, G., & Smith, L. G. (Eds.). (1977). *Jealousy.* Englewood Cliffs, NJ: Prentice-Hall.

Clark, A. L., & Wallin, P. (1964). The accuracy of husbands' and wives' reports of the frequency of marital coitus. *Population Studies, 18,* 165–173.

Clark, M., & Reis, H. T. (1988). Interpersonal processes in close relationships. *Annual Review of Psychology 39,* 609–672.

Clark, M. S. (1981). Noncomparability of benefits given and received: A cue to the existence of friendship. *Social Psychology Quarterly, 44,* 375–381.

Clark, M. S. (1984). Record keeping in two types of relationships. *Journal of Personality and Social Psychology, 47,* 549–577.

Clark, M. S. (1986). Evidence of the effectiveness of manipulations of communal and exchange relationships. *Personality and Social Psychology Bulletin, 12,* 414–425.

Clark, M. S., & Mills, J. (1979). Interpersonal attraction in exchange and communal relationships. *Journal of Personality and Social Psychology, 37,* 12–24.

Clark, M. S., Mills, J., & Powell, M. C. (1986). Keeping track of needs in communal and exchange relationships. *Journal of Personality and Social Psychology, 51,* 333–338.

Clark, M. S., Mills, J. R., & Corcoran, D. M. (1989). Keeping track of needs and inputs of friends and strangers. *Personality and Social Psychology Bulletin, 15,* 533–542.

Clark, M. S., & Waddell, B. (1985). Perceptions of exploitations in communal and exchange relationships. *Journal of Social and Personal Relationships, 2,* 403–418.

Clarke, A. C. (1968). *2001: A space odyssey.* New York: New American Library.

Clarke-Stewart, K. A., & Bailey, B. L. (1989). Adjusting to divorce: Why do men have it easier? *Journal of Divorce, 13,* 75–94.

Cleek, M. G., & Pearson, T. A. (1985). Perceived causes of divorce: An analysis of interrelationships. *Journal of Marriage and the Family, 47,* 179–183.

Clore, G. L., & Byrne, D. (1974). A reinforcement-affect model of attraction. In T. L. Huston (Ed.), *Foundations of interpersonal attraction* (pp. 143–170). New York: Academic Press.

Cobb, S. (1976). Social support as a moderator of life stress. *Psychosomatic Medicine, 38,* 300–314.

Cochran, S. D., & Mays, V. M. (1989). Women and AIDS-related concerns: Roles for psychologists in helping the worried well. *American Psychologist, 44,* 529–535.

Cohen, R. S., & Christensen, A. (1980). Further examination of demand characteristics in marital interaction. *Journal of Consulting and Clinical Psychology 48,* 121–123.

Cohen, S., & Wills, T. A. (1985). Stress, social support, and the buffering hypothesis. *Psychological Bulletin, 98,* 310–357.

Cohn, N. B., & Strassberg, D. S. (1983). Self-disclosure reciprocity among preadolescents. *Personality and Social Psychology Bulletin, 9,* 97–102.

Collins, N. L., & Read, S. J. (1990). Adult attachment, working models, and relationship quality in dating couples. *Journal of Personality and Social Psychology 58,* 644–663.

Condon, J. W., & Crano, W. D. (1988). Inferred evaluation and the relation between attitude similarity and interpersonal attraction. *Journal of Personality and Social Psychology, 54,* 789–797.

Conn, M. K., & Peterson, C. (1989). Social support: Seek and ye shall find. *Journal of Social and Personal Relationships, 6,* 345–358.

Coogler, O. J. (1978). *Structured mediation in divorce settlement.* Lexington, MA: Lexington Books.

Cook, E. P. (1985). *Psychological androgyny.* Elmsford, NY: Pergamon Press.

Cook, T. D., & Campbell, D. T. (1979). *Quasi-experimentation: Design and analysis issues for field settings.* Chicago: Rand McNally.

Coombs, R. H., & Kenkel, W. F. (1966). Sex differences in dating aspirations and satisfaction with computer-selected partners. *Journal of Marriage, 28,* 62–66.

Cooney, T. M., & Uhlenberg, P. (1990). The role of divorce in men's relations with their adult children after mid-life. *Journal of Marriage and the Family, 52*, 677–688.

Cooper, J., & Fazio, R. H. (1984). A new look at dissonance theory. In L. Berkowitz (Ed.), *Advances in experimental social psychology* (Vol. 17, pp. 229–267). New York: Academic Press.

Corliss, R. (1989, July 31). When humor meets heartbreak. *Time*, pp. 65 & 67.

Cornell, L. L. (1989). Gender differences in remarriage and divorce in Japan and the United States. *Journal of Marriage and the Family, 51*, 457–463.

Corrales, C. G. (1975). Power and satisfaction in early marriage. In R. E. Cromwell & D. H. Olson (Eds.), *Power in families* (pp. 197–216). New York: Wiley.

Corsini, R. J. (1956). Understanding and similarity in marriage. *Journal of Abnormal and Social Psychology, 52*, 327–342.

Costello, C. G. (1982). Social factors associated with depression: A retrospective community study. *Psychological Medicine, 12*, 329–339.

Cowan, G., Drinkard, J., & MacGavin, L. (1984). The effects of target, age, and gender on use of power strategies. *Journal of Personality and Social Psychology, 47*, 1391–1398.

Coyne, J. C., & Bolger, N. (1990). Doing without social support as an explanatory concept. *Journal of Social and Clinical Psychology 9*, 148–158.

Cozby, P. C. (1973). Self-disclosure: A literature review. *Psychological Bulletin, 79*, 73–91.

Cramer, R. E., Weiss, R. F., Steigleder, M. K., & Balling, S. S. (1985). Attraction in context: Acquisition and blocking of person-directed action. *Journal of Personality and Social Psychology 49*, 1221–1230.

Critelli, J. W., & Waid, D. R. (1980). Physical attractiveness, romantic love, and equity restoration in dating relationships. *Journal of Personality Assessment, 44*, 624–629.

Crohan, S. E., & Veroff, J. (1989). Dimensions of marital well-being among white and black newlyweds. *Journal of Marriage and the Family, 51*, 373–383.

Cromwell, R. E., & Olson, D. G. (1975). Multidisciplinary perspectives of power. In R. E. Cromwell & D. H. Olson (Eds.), *Power in families* (pp. 15–37). New York: Wiley.

Crowne, D. P., & Marlowe, D. (1964). *The approval motive.* New York: Wiley.

Cunningham, J. A., Strassberg, D. S., & Haan, B. (1986). Effects of intimacy and sex-role congruency on self-disclosure. *Journal of Social and Clinical Psychology, 4*, 393–401.

Cunningham, J. D., & Antill, J. K. (1981). Love in developing romantic relationships. In S. Duck & R. Gilmour (Eds.), *Personal relationships. 2: Developing personal relationships* (pp. 27–51). New York: Academic Press.

Cupach, W. R., & Comstock, J. (1990). Satisfaction with sexual communication in marriage: Links to sexual satisfaction and dyadic adjustment. *Journal of Social and Personal Relationships, 7*, 179–182.

Curran, J. P., & Lippold, S. (1975). The effects of physical attraction and attitude similarity on attraction in dating dyads. *Journal of Personality, 43*, 528–539.

Curtis, R. C., & Miller, K. (1986). Believing another likes or dislikes you: Behaviors making the beliefs come true. *Journal of Personality and Social Psychology, 51*, 284–290.

Cutrona, C. (1989). Ratings of social support by adolescents and adult informants: Degree of correspondence and prediction of depressive symptoms. *Journal of Personality and Social Psychology, 57*, 723–730.

Cutrona, C. E. (1982). Transition to college: Loneliness and the process of social adjustment. In L. A. Peplau & D. Perlman (Eds.), *Loneliness: A sourcebook of current theory, research, and therapy* (pp. 291–309). New York: Wiley Interscience.

Dailey, D. M. (1979). Adjustment of heterosexual and homosexual couples in pairing relationships: An exploratory study. *Journal of Sex Research, 15*, 143–157.

D'Andrade, R. G. (1966). Sex differences and cultural institutions. In E. Maccoby (Ed.), *The development of sex differences* (pp. 174–204). Stanford, CA: Stanford University Press.

Daniels-Mohring, D., & Berger, M. (1984). Social network changes and the adjustment to divorce. *Journal of Divorce, 8*, 17–32.

Dare, C. (1986). Psychoanalytic marital therapy. In N. S. Jacobson & A. S. Gurman (Eds.), *Clinical handbook of marital therapy* (pp. 13–28). New York: Guilford.

Darley, J. M., & Fazio, R. H. (1980). Expectancy confirmation processes arising in the social interaction sequence. *American Psychologist, 35*, 867–881.

Davis, K. E., & Todd, M. J. (1982). Friendship and love relationships. In K. E. Davis & T. Mitchell (Eds.), *Advances in descriptive psychology* (Vol. 2, pp. 79–122). Greenwich, CT: JAI Press.

Davis, K. E., & Todd, M. J. (1985). Assessing friendship: Prototypes, paradigm cases, and relationship description. In S. Duck & D. Perlman (Eds.), *Understanding personal relationships: An interdisciplinary approach* (pp. 17–38). London: Sage.

Davis, M. H., & Franzoi, S. L. (1986). Adolescent loneliness, self-disclosure, and private self-consciousness: A longitudinal investigation. *Journal of Personality and Social Psychology, 51*, 595–608.

Davis, M. H., & Oathout, H. A. (1987). Maintenance of satisfaction in romantic relationships: Empathy and relational competence. *Journal of Personality and Social Psychology, 53*, 397–410.

Dawley, H. H. (1980). *Friendship.* Englewood Cliffs, NJ: Prentice-Hall.

Dean, D. G. (1966). Emotional maturity and marital adjustment. *Journal of Marriage and the Family, 28*, 454–457.

Deaux, K. (1984). From individual differences to social categories: Analysis of a decade's research on gender. *American Psychologist, 39*, 105–116.

Deaux, K., & Hanna, R. (1984). Courtship in the personals column: The influence of gender and sexual orientation. *Sex Roles, 11*, 363–375.

DeBuono, B. A., Zinner, S. H., Daamen, M., & McCormack, W. M. (1990). Sexual behavior of college women in 1975, 1986, and 1989. *The New England Journal of Medicine, 322*, 821–825.

DeLamater, J. (1987). Gender differences in sexual scenarios. In K. Kelly (Ed.), *Females, males, and sexuality: Theories and research* (pp. 127–139). Albany: State University of New York Press.

DeMaris, A. (1990). The dynamics of generational transfer in courtship violence: A biracial exploration. *Journal of Marriage and the Family, 52*, 219–231.

DeMaris, A., & Leslie, G. R. (1984). Cohabitation with the future spouse: Its influence upon marital satisfaction and communication. *Journal of Marriage and the Family, 46*, 77–84.

Demo, D. H., & Acock, A. C. (1988). The impact of divorce on children. *Journal of Marriage and the Family, 50,* 619–648.

DePaulo, B. M., Tang, J., & Stone, J. I. (1987). Physical attractiveness and skill at detecting deception. *Personality and Social Psychology Bulletin, 13,* 177–187.

Derlega, V. J., & Berg, J. H. (1987). *Self-disclosure: Theory, research, and therapy.* New York: Plenum.

Derlega, V. J., & Chaikin, A. L. (1976). Norms affecting self-disclosure in men and women. *Journal of Consulting and Clinical Psychology, 44,* 376–380.

Derlega, V. J., Wilson, M., & Chaikin,, A. L. (1976). Friendship and disclosure reciprocity. *Journal of Personality and Social Psychology, 34,* 578–587.

Derlega, V. J., Winstead, B. A., Wong, P. T. P., & Hunter, S. (1985). Gender effects in an initial encounter: A case where men exceed women in disclosure. *Journal of Social and Personal Relationships, 2,* 25–44.

Dermer, M., & Pyszczynski, T. A. (1978). Effects of erotica upon men's loving and liking responses for women they love. *Journal of Personality and Social Psychology, 36,* 1302–1309.

Dermer, M., & Thiel, D. L. (1975). When beauty may fail. *Journal of Personality and Social Psychology, 31,* 1168–1176.

de Rougemont, D. (1956). *Love in the Western world.* New York: Harper & Row.

deTurck, M. A., & Miller, G. R. (1986). The effects of husbands' and wives' social cognition on their marital adjustment, conjugal power, and self-esteem. *Journal of Marriage and the Family, 48,* 715–724.

Dindia, K., & Fitzpatrick, M. A. (1985). Marital communication: Three approaches compared. In S. Duck & D. Perlman (Eds.), *Understanding personal relationships: An interdisciplinary approach* (pp. 137–157). London: Sage.

Dion, K. K. (1986). Stereotyping based on physical attractiveness: Issues and conceptual perspectives. In C. P. Herman, M. P. Zanna, & E. T. Higgins (Eds.), *The Ontario Symposium: Vol. 3. Physical appearance, stigma, and social behavior* (pp. 7–21). Hillsdale, NJ: Erlbaum.

Dion, K. K., Berscheid, E., & Walster, E. (1972). What is beautiful is good. *Journal of Personality and Social Psychology, 24,* 285–290.

Dion, K. K., & Dion, K. L. (1985). Personality, gender, and the phenomenology of romantic love. In P. Shaver (Ed.), *Review of personality and social psychology: Vol. 6. Self, situations, and social behavior* (pp. 209–239). Beverly Hills, CA: Sage.

Dion, K. K., & Stein, S. (1978). Physical attractiveness and interpersonal influence. *Journal of Experimental Social Psychology, 14,* 97–108.

Dion, K. L. (1983). Personal communication.

Dion, K. L., & Dion, K. K. (1973). Correlates of romantic love. *Journal of Consulting and Clinical Psychology, 41,* 51–56.

Dion, K. L., & Dion, K. K. (1975). Self-esteem and romantic love. *Journal of Personality, 43,* 39–57.

Dion, K. L., & Dion, K. K. (1976a). The Honi phenomenon revisited: Factors underlying the resistance to perceptual distortion of one's partner. *Journal of Personality and Social Psychology, 33,* 170–177.

Dion, K. L., & Dion, K. K. (1976b). Love, liking and trust in heterosexual relationships. *Personality and Social Psychology Bulletin, 2,* 187–190.

Dion, K. L., & Dion, K. K. (1979). Personality and behavioral correlates of romantic love. In M. Cook & G. Wilson (Eds.), *Love and attraction* (pp. 213–220). Oxford: Pergamon Press.

Dion, K. L., & Dion, K. K. (1988). Romantic love: Individual and cultural perspectives. In R. J. Sternberg & M. L. Barnes (Eds.), *The psychology of love* (pp. 264–289). New Haven, CT: Yale University Press.

Doherty, W. J. (1982). Attribution style and negative problem solving in marriage. *Family Relation, 31,* 201–205.

Doherty, W. J., & Walker, B. J. (1982). Marriage encounter casualties: A preliminary investigation. *American Journal of Family Therapy, 10,* 15–25.

Dosser, D. A., Jr., Balswick, J. O., & Halverson, C. F., Jr. (1986). Male inexpressiveness and relationships. *Journal of Social and Personal Relationships, 3,* 241–258.

Downey, G., Silver, R. C., & Wortman, C. B. (1990). Reconsidering the attribution-adjustment relation following a major negative event: Coping with the loss of a child. *Journal of Personality and Social Psychology, 59,* 925–940.

Driscoll, R., Davis, K. W., & Lipetz, M. E. (1972). Parental interference and romantic love. *Journal of Personality and Social Psychology, 24,* 1–10.

Duck, S. W. (1977). *The study of acquaintance.* Westmead, Farnborough, Hants., England: Saxon House, Teakfield Limited.

Durkheim, E. (1951). *Suicide.* Glencoe, IL.: Free Press. (Originally published in French in 1897.)

Dutton, D. G. (1987). Wife assault: Social psychological contributions to criminal justice policy. In S. Oskamp (Ed.), *Applied social psychology annual: Vol. 7. Family process and problems: Social psychological aspects* (pp. 238–261). Newbury Park, CA: Sage.

Dutton, D. G., & Aron, A. P. (1974). Some evidence for heightened sexual attraction under conditions of high anxiety. *Journal of Personality and Social Psychology, 30,* 510–517.

Dwyer, J. (1983). *Statistical models for the social and behavioral sciences.* New York: Oxford University Press.

Eagly, A. H., & Crowley, M. (1986). Gender and helping behavior: A meta-analytic review of the social psychological literature. *Psychological Bulletin, 100,* 283–308.

Ebbesen, E. B., Kjos, G. L., & Konecni, V. J. (1976). Spatial ecology: Its effects on the choice of friends and enemies. *Journal of Experimental Social Psychology, 12,* 505–518.

Edmonds, V. H. (1967). Marriage conventionalization: Definition and measurement. *Journal of Marriage and the Family, 29,* 681–688.

Edmonds, V. H., Withers, G., & Dibatista, B. (1972). Adjustment, conservatism, and marital conventionalization. *Journal of Marriage and the Family, 34,* 96–103.

Eidelson, R. J., & Epstein, N. (1982). Cognition and relationship maladjustment: Development of a measure of dysfunctional relationship beliefs. *Journal of Consulting and Clinical Psychology, 50,* 715–720.

Eisenberg, N., & Lennon, R. (1983). Sex differences in empathy and related capacities. *Psychological Bulletin, 94,* 100–131.

Elder, G. H., Jr. (1969). Appearance of education in marriage mobility. *American Sociological Review, 34,* 519–533.

Ellis, A. (1977). Rational and irrational jealousy. In G. Clanton & L. G. Smith (Eds.), *Jealousy* (pp. 170–179). Englewood Cliffs, NJ: Prentice-Hall.

Ellis, A., & Harper, R. (1961). *Creative marriage*. New York: Lyle Stuart.

Ellis, C., & Weinstein, E. (1986). Jealousy and the social psychology of emotional experience. *Journal of Social and Personal Relationships, 3*, 337–357.

Elwood, R. W., & Jacobson, N. S. (1982). Spouses' agreement in reporting their behavioral interactions: A clinical replication. *Journal of Consulting and Clinical Psychology, 50*, 783–784.

Emerson, R. (1962). Power-dependence relations. *American Sociological Review, 27*, 31–41.

Emery, R. (1988). *Marriage, divorce, and children's adjustment*. Newbury Park, CA: Sage.

Emery, R. E. (1989). Family violence. *American Psychologist, 44*, 321–328.

Emery, R. E., & Wyer, M. M. (1987). Divorce mediation. *American Psychologist, 42*, 472–480.

Epley, S. W. (1974). Reduction of the behavioral effects of aversive stimulation by the presence of companions. *Psychological Bulletin, 81*, 271–283.

Epstein, N. (1982). Cognitive therapy with couples. *The American Journal of Family Therapy, 10*, 5–16.

Epstein, S. (1984). Controversial issues in emotion theory. In P. Shaver (Ed.), *Review of personality and social psychology: Emotions, relationships, and health* (pp. 64–88). Beverly Hills, CA: Sage.

Ericsson, K. A., & Simon, H. A. (1980). Verbal reports on data. *Psychological Review, 87*, 215–251.

Espenshade, T. J. (1979). The economic consequences of divorce. *Journal of Marriage and the Family, 41*, 615–625.

Falbo, T., Hazen, M. D., & Linimon, D. (1982). The costs of selecting power bases associated with the opposite sex. *Sex Roles, 8*, 147–158.

Falbo, T., & Peplau, L. A. (1980). Power strategies in intimate relationships. *Journal of Personality and Social Psychology, 38*, 618–628.

Farina, A., Fischer, E. H., Sherman, S., Smith, W. T., Groh, T., & Mermin, P. (1977). Physical attractiveness and mental illness. *Journal of Abnormal Psychology, 86*, 510–517.

Farkas, A. J., & Anderson, N. H. (1979). Multidimensional input in equity theory. *Journal of Personality and Social Psychology, 37*, 879–896.

Farrell, J., & Markman, H. J. (1986). Individual and interpersonal factors in the etiology of marital distress: The example of remarital couples. In R. Gilmour & S. Duck (Eds.), *The emerging field of personal relationships* (pp. 251–263). Hillsdale, NJ: Erlbaum.

Feeney, J. A., & Noller, P. (1990). Attachment style as a predictor of adult romantic relationships. *Journal of Personality and Social Psychology, 58*, 281–291.

Fehr, B. (1988). Prototype analysis of the concepts of love and commitment. *Journal of Personality and Social Psychology, 55*, 557–579.

Feingold, A. (1988). Matching for attractiveness in romantic partners and same-sex friends: A meta-analysis and theoretical critique. *Psychological Bulletin, 104*, 226–235.

Feingold, A. (1990). Gender differences in effects of physical attractiveness on romantic attraction: A comparison across five research paradigms. *Journal of Personality and Social Psychology, 59,* 981–993.

Fengler, A. P. (1974). Romantic love in courtship: Divergent paths of male and female students. *Journal of Comparative Family Studies, 5,* 134–139.

Fergusson, D. M., Horwood, L. J., Kershaw, K. L., & Shannon, F. T. (1986). Factors associated with reports of wife assault in New Zealand. *Journal of Marriage and the Family, 48,* 407–412.

Festinger, L. (1951). Architecture and group membership. *Journal of Social Issues, 7,* 152–163.

Festinger, L. (1957). *A theory of cognitive dissonance.* Evanston, IL: Row, Peterson.

Festinger, L., Schachter, S., & Back, K. W. (1950). *Social pressures in informal groups: A study of human factors in housing.* New York: Harper & Brothers.

Filsinger, E. E., & Thoma, S. J. (1988). Behavioral antecedents of relationship stability and adjustment: A five-year longitudinal study. *Journal of Marriage and the Family, 50,* 785–795.

Fincham, F. D. (in press). Understanding close relationships: An attributional perspective. To appear in S. Zelen (Ed.), *New models-new extension of attribution theory.* New York: Springer-Verlag.

Fincham, F. D., Beach, S. R. H., & Bradbury, T. N. (1989). Marital distress, depression, and attributions: Is the marital distress-attribution relationship an artifact of depression? *Journal of Consulting and Clinical Psychology, 57,* 768–771.

Fincham, F. D., & Bradbury, T. N. (1987). The impact of attributions in marriage: A longitudinal analysis. *Journal of Personality and Social Psychology, 53,* 510–517.

Fincham, F. D., & Bradbury, T. N. (1988). The impact of attributions in marriage: An experimental analysis. *Journal of Social and Clinical Psychology, 7,* 147–162.

Fincham, F. D., & Bradbury, T. N. (1989). Perceived responsibility for marital events: Egocentric or partner-centric bias? *Journal of Marriage and the Family, 51,* 27–35.

Fincham, F. D., Bradbury, T. N., & Beach, S. R. H. (1990). To arrive where we began: A reappraisal of cognition in marriage and in marital therapy. *Journal of Family Psychology, 4,* 167–184.

Fincham, F. D., Bradbury, T. N., & Grych, J. H. (1990). Conflict in close relationships: The role of interpersonal phenomena (pp. 161–184). In S. Graham & V. S. Folkes (Eds.), *Attribution theory: Applications to achievement, mental health, and interpersonal conflict* (pp. 161–184). Hillsdale, NJ: Erlbaum.

Fincham, F. D., Bradbury, T. N., & Scott, C. K. (1990). Cognition in marriage. In F. D. Fincham & T. N. Bradbury (Eds.), *The psychology of marriage: Basic issues and applications* (pp. 118–149). New York: Guilford.

Firestone, I. J., Kaplan, K. J., & Russel, J. C. (1973). Anxiety, fear, and affiliation with similar state vs. dissimilar state others: Misery sometimes loves nonmiserable company. *Journal of Personality and Social Psychology, 26,* 409–414.

Fischer, C. S., & Phillips, S. L. (1982). Who is alone? Social characteristics of people with small networks. In L. A. Peplau & D. Perlman (Eds.), *Loneliness: A sourcebook of current theory, research, and therapy* (pp. 21–39). New York: Wiley Interscience.

Fishbein, M. D., & Thelen, M. H. (1981). Psychological factors in mate selection and marital satisfaction: A review. *JSAS: Catalog of Selected Documents in Psychology, 11*, 84 (MS #2374).

Fisher, W. A. (1986). A psychological approach to human sexuality: The sexual behavior sequence. In D. Byrne & K. Kelley (Eds.), *Alternative approaches to the study of sexual behavior* (pp. 131–171). Hillsdale, NJ: Erlbaum.

Fishman, P. N. (1978). Interaction: The work women do. *Social Problems, 25*, 397–406.

Fiske, D. W. (1975). A source of data is not a reassuring instrument. *Journal of Abnormal Psychology, 84*, 20–23.

Fitzpatrick, M. A. (1988). *Between husbands and wives: Communication in marriage.* Newbury Park, CA: Sage.

Fletcher, G. J. O. (1983). Sex differences in causal attributions for marital separation. *New Zealand Journal of Psychology, 12*, 82–89.

Fletcher, G. J. O., Fincham, F. D., Cramer, L., & Heron, N. (1987). The role of attributions in the development of dating relationships. *Journal of Personality and Social Psychology, 53*, 481–489.

Fletcher, G. J. O., & Fitness, J. (1990). Occurrent social cognition in close relationship interaction: The role of proximal and distal variables. *Journal of Personality and Social Psychology, 59*, 464–474.

Foa, E. B., & Foa, U. G. (1980). Resource theory: Interpersonal behavior as exchange. In K. J. Gergen, M. S. Greenber, & R. H. Willis (Eds.), *Social exchange: Advances in theory and research* (pp. 77–94). New York: Plenum.

Foa, U. G. (1971). Interpersonal and economic resources. *Science, 171*, 345–351.

Folkes, V. S. (1982a). Communicating the reasons for social rejection. *Journal of Experimental Social Psychology, 18*, 235–252.

Folkes, V. S. (1982b). Forming relationships and the matching hypothesis. *Personality and Social Psychology Bulletin, 8*, 631–636.

Folkes, V. S., & Sears, D. O. (1977). Does everybody like a liker? *Journal of Experimental Social Psychology, 13*, 505–519.

Footlick, J. K. (1990, Winter/Spring). What happened to the family? *Newsweek Special Edition,* pp. 14–20.

For better or worse? (1990, Winter/Spring), *Newsweek Special Edition,* p. 18.

Framo, J. L. (1982). *Explorations in marital and family therapy.* New York: Springer.

Frank, E., Anderson, C., & Rubinstein, D. (1978). Frequency of sexual dysfunction in "normal" couples. *New England Journal of Medicine, 299*, 111–115.

Frank, E., Anderson, C., & Rubinstein, D. (1979). Marital role strain and sexual satisfaction. *Journal of Consulting and Clinical Psychology, 217*, 1096–1103.

Franklin, K. M., Janoff-Bulman, R., & Roberts, J. E. (1990). Long-term impact of parental divorce on optimism and trust: Changes in general assumptions or narrow beliefs? *Journal of Personality and Social Psychology, 59*, 743–755.

Freedman, J. (1978). *Happy people: What happiness is, who has it, and why.* New York: Harcourt Brace Jovanovich.

French, J. R. P., Jr., & Raven, B. H. (1959). The bases of social power. In D. Cartwright (Ed.), *Studies in social power* (pp. 150–167). Ann Arbor: University of Michigan Press.

Freud, S. (1922/1951). *Group psychology and the analysis of the ego*. New York: Liveright.

Fromm, E. (1956). *The art of loving*. New York: Harper & Row.

Frost, D. E., & Stahelski, A. J. (1988). The systematic measurement of French and Raven's bases of social power in workgroups. *Journal of Applied Social Psychology, 18,* 375–389.

Furstenberg, F. F., Jr. (1987). The new extended family: The experience of parents and children after remarriage. In K. Pasley & M. Ihinger-Tallman (Eds.), *Remarriage and stepparenting* (pp. 42–61). New York: Guilford.

Furstenberg, F. F., Jr. (1988). Child care after divorce and remarriage. In E. M. Hetherington & J. D. Arasteh (Eds.), *Impact of divorce, singleparenting, and stepparenting on children* (pp. 245–261). Hillsdale, NJ: Erlbaum.

Furstenberg, F. F., Jr., Brooks-Gunn, J., & Chase-Lansdale, L. (1989). Teenage pregnancy and childbearing. *American Psychologist, 44,* 313–320.

Furstenberg, F. F., Jr., & Spanier, G. B. (1984). The risk of dissolution in remarriage: An examination of Cherlin's hypothesis of incomplete institutionalization. *Family Relations, 33,* 433–441.

Gadlin, H. (1977). Private lives and public order: A critical view of the history of intimate relations in the United States. In G. Levinger & H. L. Raush (Eds.), *Close relationships: Perspectives on the meaning of intimacy* (pp. 33–72). Amherst: University of Massachusetts Press.

Gaelick, L., Bodenhausen, G. V., & Wyer, R. S., Jr. (1985). Emotional communication in close relationships. *Journal of Personality and Social Psychology, 49,* 1246–1265.

Ganong, L. H., & Coleman, M. (1987). Effects of parental remarriage on children. In K. Pasley & M. Ihinger-Tallman (Eds.), *Remarriage and stepparenting* (pp. 94–140). New York: Guilford.

Ganong, L. H., Coleman, M., & Mapes, D. (1990). A meta-analytic review of family structure stereotypes. *Journal of Marriage and the Family, 52,* 287–297.

Garland, D. S. R. (1983). *Working with couples for marriage enrichment: A guide to developing, conducting, and evaluating programs:* San Francisco: Jossey-Bass.

Gathorne-Hardy, J. (1981). *Marriage, love, sex and divorce.* New York: Summit Books.

Geis, B. D., & Gerrard, M. (1984). Predicting male and female contraceptive behavior: A discriminant analysis of groups high, moderate, and low in contraceptive effectiveness. *Journal of Personality and Social Psychology, 46,* 669–680.

Geiselman, R. E., Haight, N. A., & Kimata, L. G. (1984). Context effects in the perceived physical attractiveness of faces. *Journal of Experimental Social Psychology, 20,* 409–424.

Gelles, R. J. (1976). Abused wives: Why do they stay? *Journal of Marriage and the Family, 38,* 659–668.

Gelles, R. J. (1980). Violence in the family: A review of research in the family. *Journal of Marriage and the Family, 42,* 873–885.

Gelles, R. J., & Straus, M. A. (1988). *Intimate violence.* New York: Simon and Schuster.

Gelman, D. (1987, October 26). Not tonight dear. *Newsweek,* pp. 64–66.

Gerard, H. B., & Mathewson, G. C. (1966). The effects of severity of initiation on liking for a group: A replication. *Journal of Experimental Social Psychology, 2,* 278–287.

Gerrard, M. (1987a). Emotional and cognitive barriers to effective contraception: Are males and females really different? In K. Kelley (Ed.), *Females, males, and sexuality: Theories and research* (pp. 213–242). Albany: State University of New York Press.

Gerrard, M. (1987b). Sex, sex guilt, and contraceptive use revisited: The 1980s. *Journal of Personality and Social Psychology, 52,* 975–980.

Gerstel, N. (1988). Divorce and kin ties: The importance of gender. *Journal of Marriage and the Family, 50,* 209–219.

Giblin, P., Sprenkle, D., & Sheehan, R. (1985). Enrichment outcome research: A meta-analysis of premarital, marital, and family interventions. *Journal of Marital and Family Therapy, 11,* 257–271.

Gifford, R., & Gallagher, T. M. B. (1985). Sociability: Personality, social context, and physical setting. *Journal of Personality and Social Psychology, 48,* 1015–1023.

Gilford, R., & Bengston, V. (1979). Measuring marital satisfaction in three generations: Positive and negative dimensions. *Journal of Marriage and the Family, 41,* 387–398.

Gillespie, D. L. (1976). Who has the power? The marital struggle. In S. Cox (Ed.), *Female psychology: The emerging self* (pp. 192–211). Chicago: Science Research Associates.

Ginsberg, B. G., & Vogelsong, E. (1977). Premarital relationship improvement by maximizing empathy and self-disclosure. The PRIMES program. In B. Guerney (Ed.), *Relationship enhancement* (pp. 268–288). San Francisco: Jossey-Bass.

Gladue, B. A., & Delaney, H. J. (1990). Gender differences in perception of attractiveness of men and women in bars. *Personality and Social Psychology Bulletin, 16,* 378–391.

Glass, S. P., & Wright, T. L. (1985). Sex differences in type of extramarital involvement and marital dissatisfaction. *Sex Roles, 12,* 1101–1120.

Glazer-Malbin, N. (1975). Man and woman: Interpersonal relationships in the marital pair. In N. Glazer-Malbin (Ed.), *Old family/new family* (pp. 27–66). New York: Van Nostrand.

Glenn, N. D. (1975). Psychological well-being in the post-parental stage: Some evidence from national surveys. *Journal of Marriage and the Family, 37,* 105–110.

Glenn, N. D., & Kramer, K. B. (1985). The psychological well-being of adult children of divorce. *Journal of Marriage and the Family, 47,* 905–912.

Glenn, N. D., & Kramer, K. B. (1987). The marriages and divorces of the children of divorce. *Journal of Marriage and the Family, 49,* 811–825.

Glenn, N. D., & McLanahan, S. (1982). Children and marital happiness: A further specification of the relationship. *Journal of Marriage and the Family, 44,* 63–72.

Glenn, N. D., & Weaver, C. N. (1988). The changing relationship of marital status to reported happiness. *Journal of Marriage and the Family, 50,* 317–324.

Glick, I. O., Weiss, R., & Parkes, C. M. (1974). *The first year of bereavement.* New York: Wiley.

Glick, P. (1985). Orientation toward relationships: Choosing a situation in which to begin a relationship. *Journal of Experimental Social Psychology, 21,* 544–562.

Glick, P. S., & Spanier, G. B. (1981). Cohabitation in the U.S. In P. J. Stein (Ed.), *Single life: Unmarried adults in social context* (pp. 194–209). New York: St. Martin's Press.

Goldfarb, L., Gerrard, M., Gibbons, F. X., & Plante, T. (1988). Attitudes toward sex, arousal, and the retention of contraceptive information. *Journal of Personality and Social Psychology, 55,* 634–641.

Goldman, W., & Lewis, P. (1977). Beautiful is good. Evidence that the physically attractive are more socially skillful. *Journal of Experimental Social Psychology, 13,* 125–130.

Goldstein, M., Kilroy, M. C., & Van de Voort, D. (1976). Gaze as a function of conversation and degree of love. *Journal of Psychology, 92,* 227–234.

Goode, W. J. (1956). *After divorce.* Glencoe, IL: Free Press.

Goode, W. J. (1960). A theory of strain. *American Sociological Review, 25,* 483–496.

Goode, W. J. (1971). Force and violence in the family. *Journal of Marriage and the Family, 33,* 624–626.

Gore, S. (1984). Stress-buffering functions of social supports: An appraisal and clarification of research methods. In B. S. Dohrenwend & B. P. Dohren-wend (Eds.), *Stressful events and their contexts* (pp. 202–222). New Brunswick, NJ: Rutgers University Press.

Gotlib, I. H., & Hooley, J. M. (1988). Depression and marital distress: Current status and future directions. In S. Duck (Ed.), *Handbook of personal relationships: Theory, research, and interventions* (pp. 543–570). New York: Wiley.

Gottman, J., Markman, H., & Notarius, C. (1977). The topography of marital conflict: A sequential analysis of verbal and nonverbal behavior. *Journal of Marriage and the Family, 39,* 461–477.

Gottman, J., Notarius, C., Gonso, J., & Markman, H. J. (1976a). *A couple's guide to communication.* Champaign, IL: Research Press.

Gottman, J., Notarius, C., Markman, H., Banks, S., Yoppi, B., & Rubin, M. E. (1976b). Behavior exchange theory and marital decision making. *Journal of Experimental Social Psychology, 34,* 14–23.

Gottman, J. M. (1979). *Marital interaction.* New York: Academic Press.

Gottman, J. M., & Krokoff, L. J. (1989). Marital interaction and satisfaction: A longitudinal view. *Journal of Consulting and Clinical Psychology, 57,* 47–52.

Gottman, J. M., & Levenson, R. L. (1988). The social psychophysiology of marriage. In P. Noller & M. A. Fitzpatric (Eds.), *Perspectives on marital interaction* (pp. 182–200). Clevedon, England: Multilingual Matters LTD.

Gottman, J. M., & Porterfield, A. L. (1981). Communication dysfunction in the non-verbal behavior of marital couples. *Journal of Marriage and the Family, 43,* 817–827.

Gove, W. R. (1972a). Sex, marital status, and suicide. *Journal of Health and Social Behavior, 13,* 204–213.

Gove, W. R. (1972b). The relationship between sex roles, marital status, and mental illness. *Social Forces, 51,* 34–44.

Gove, W. R. (1973). Sex, marital status and mortality. *American Journal of Sociology, 79,* 45–67.

Grauerholz, E., & Serpe, R. T. (1985). Initiation and response: The dynamics of sexual interaction. *Sex Roles, 12,* 1041–1059.

Gray-Little, B., & Burks, N. (1983). Power and satisfaction in marriage: A review and critique. *Psychological Bulletin, 93,* 513–538.

Graziano, W. G., & Musser, L. M. (1982). The joining and the parting of the ways. In S. Duck (Ed.), *Personal relationships. 4: Dissolving relationships* (pp. 75–106). New York: Academic Press.

Green, R. G. (1983). The influence of divorce prediction variables on divorce adjustment: An expansion and test of Lewis' and Spanier's theory of marital quality and stability. *Journal of Divorce, 7,* 67–81.

Green, R. G., & Sporakowski, M. J. (1983). The dynamics of divorce: Marital quality, alternative attraction, and external pressure. *Journal of Divorce, 7,* 77–88.

Green, S. K., Buchanan, D. R., & Heuer, S. K. (1984). Winners, losers, and choosers: A field investigation of dating initiation. *Personality and Social Psychology Bulletin, 10,* 502–511.

Greenstein, T. N. (1990). Marital disruption and the employment of married women. *Journal of Marriage and the Family, 52,* 657–676.

Griffitt, W. (1987). Females, males, and sexual responses. In K. Kelley (Ed.), *Females, males, and sexuality: Theories and research* (pp. 141–173). Albany: State University of New York Press.

Griggs, L. (1990, July 2). A losing battle with AIDS. *Time* magazine, pp. 41–43.

Gruber, K. J., & White, J. W. (1986). Gender differences in the perceptions of self's and others' use of power strategies. *Sex Roles, 15,* 109–118.

Grych, J. H., & Fincham, F. D. (1990). Marital conflict and children's adjustment: A cognitive-contextual framework. *Psychological Bulletin, 108,* 267–290.

Guerney, B., Jr., Brock, G., & Coufal, J. (1986). Integrating marital therapy and enrichment: The relationship enhancement approach. In N. S. Jacobson & A. S. Gurman (Eds.), *Clinical handbook of marital therapy* (pp. 151–172).

Guerney, B. G. (1977). *Relationship enhancement.* San Francisco: Jossey-Bass.

Guidubaldi, J., & Cleminshaw, H. (1985). Divorce, family health, and child adjustment. *Family relations, 34,* 35–41.

Guisinger, S., Cowan, P. A., & Schuldberg, D. (1989). Changing parent and spouse relations in the first years of remarriage of divorced families. *Journal of Marriage and the Family, 51,* 445–456.

Gurman, A. S., & Kniskern, D. P. (1977). Enriching research on marital enrichment programs. *The Journal of Marriage and Family Counseling, 3,* 3–11.

Gurman, A. S., & Kniskern, D. P. (1978). Research on marital and family therapy: Progress, perspective, and prospect. In S. L. Garfield & A. E. Bergin (Eds.), *Handbook of psychotherapy and behavior change: An empirical analysis* (2nd ed., p. 817–902). New York: Wiley.

Gurman, A. S., & Kniskern, D. P. (1981). *Handbook of family therapy.* New York: Brunner/Mazel.

Gurman, A. S., Kniskern, D. P., & Pinsof, W. M. (1986). Research on marital and family therapies. In S. L. Garfield & A. E. Bergin (Eds.), *Handbook of psychotherapy and behavior change* (3rd ed., pp. 565–624). New York: Wiley.

Gurman, A. S., Knudson, R. M., & Kniskern, D. P. (1978). Behavioral marriage therapy: IV. Reply: Take two aspirin and call us in the morning. *Family Process, 17,* 165–180.

Gurtman, M. B., Martin, K. M., & Hintzman, N. M. (1990). Interpersonal reactions to displays of depression and anxiety. *Journal of Social and Clinical Psychology, 9,* 256–267.

Guttentag, M., & Secord, P. F. (1983). *Too many women? The sex ratio question.* Beverly Hills, CA: Sage.

Hacker, A. (1989, October 12). Affirmative action: The new look. *New York Review of Books*, pp. 63–68.

Hadley, T., & Jacob, T. (1976). The measurement of family power. *Sociometry, 39*, 384–395.

Hagestad, G. O., & Smyer, M. A. (1982). Dissolving long-term relationships: Patterns of divorcing in middle age. In S. Duck (Ed.), *Personal relationships, 4: Dissolving relationships* (pp. 155–188). New York: Academic Press.

Halford, W. K., Hahlweg, K., & Dunne, M. (1990). The cross-cultural consistency of marital communication associated with marital distress. *Journal of Marriage and the Family, 52*, 487–500.

Hall, E. T. (1966). *The hidden dimension*. Garden City, NY: Doubleday & Company.

Hall, J. A. (1978). Gender effects in decoding nonverbal cues. *Psychological Bulletin, 85*, 845–857.

Hamilton, G. V. (1929). *A research in marriage*. New York: Albert & Charles Boni.

Hampton, R. L., Gelles, R. J., & Harrop, J. W. (1989). Is violence in black families increasing? A comparison of 1975 and 1985 national survey rates. *Journal of Marriage and the Family, 51*, 969–980.

Hanley-Dunn, P., Maxwell, S. E., & Santos, J. F. (1985). Interpretation of interpersonal interactions: The influence of loneliness. *Personality and Social Psychology Bulletin, 11*, 445–456.

Hansen, G. L. (1985). Dating jealousy among college students. *Sex Roles, 12*, 713–721.

Hansen, J. E., & Schuldt, W. J. (1984). Marital self-disclosure and marital satisfaction. *Journal of Marriage and the Family, 46*, 923–926.

Hansson, R. O., & Jones, W. H. (1981). Loneliness, cooperation, and conformity among American undergraduates. *Journal of Social Psychology, 115*, 103–108.

Hansson, R. O., Stroebe, M. S., & Stroebe, W. (1988a). Bereavement and widowhood. *Journal of Social Issues, 44*, 73–52.

Hansson, R. O., Stroebe, M. S., & Stroebe, W. (1988b). In conclusion: Current themes in bereavement and widowhood research. *Journal of Social Issues, 44*, 207–216.

Haring-Hidore, M., Stock, W. A., Okun, M. A., & Witter, R. A. (1985). Marital status and subjective well-being: A research synthesis. *Journal of Marriage and the Family, 47*, 947–953.

Harrell, J., & Guerney, B. (1976). Training married couples in conflict negotiation skills. In D. H. Olson (ed.), *Treating relationships* (pp. 151–165). Lake Mills, IA: Graphic Publishing.

Harrison, A., & Saeed, L. (1977). Let's make a deal: An analysis of revelations and stipulations in lonely hearts advertisements. *Journal of Personality and Social Psychology, 35*, 257–264.

Harrison, A. A. (1977). Mere exposure. In L. Berkowitz (Ed.), *Advances in experimental social psychology* (Vol. 10, pp. 39–83). New York: Academic Press.

Harry, J., & DeVall, W. B. (1978). *The social organization of gay males*. New York: Praeger.

Harvey, J. H., Agostinelli, G., & Weber, A. L. (1989). Account-making and the formation of expectations about close relationships. In C. Hendrick (Ed.),

Review of personality and social psychology: Vol. 10. Close relationships (pp. 39–62). Newbury Park, CA: Sage.

Harvey, J. H., Christensen, A., & McClintock, E. (1983). Research methods. In H. H. Kelley, E. Berscheid, A. Christensen, et al. (Eds.), *Close relationships* (pp. 449–485). New York: Freeman.

Harvey, J. H., Flanary, R., & Morgan, M. (1986). Vivid memories of vivid loves gone by. *Journal of Social and Personal Relationships, 3*, 359–373.

Harvey, J. H., Hendrick, S. S., & Tucker, K. (1988). Self-report methods in studying personal relationships. In S. Duck (Ed.), *Handbook of personal relationships: Theory, research, and interventions* (pp. 99–113). New York: Wiley.

Harvey, J. H., Wells, G. L., & Alvarez, M. D. (1978). Attribution in the context of conflict and separation in close relationships. In J. H. Harvey, W. J. Ickes, & R. F. Kidd (Eds.), *New directions in attributional research* (Vol. 2, pp. 235–260). Hillsdale, NJ: Erlbaum.

Hastie, R. (1984). Causes and effects of causal attribution. *Journal of Personality and Social Psychology, 46*, 44–56.

Hatfield, E. (1988). Passionate and companionate love. In R. J. Sternberg & M. L. Barnes (Eds.), *The psychology of love* (pp. 191–217). New Haven, CT: Yale University Press.

Hatfield, E., Greenberger, E., Traupmann, J., & Lambert, P. (1982). Equity and sexual satisfaction in recently married couples. *Journal of Sex Research, 18*, 18–32.

Hatfield, E., & Rapson, R. L. (1987). Passionate love: New directions in research. In W. H. Jones & D. Perlman (Eds.), *Advances in personal relationships* (Vol. 1, pp. 109–139). Greenwich, CT: JAI Press.

Hatfield, E., & Sprecher, S. (1986a). Measuring passionate love in intimate relationships. *Journal of Adolescence, 9*, 383–410.

Hatfield, E., & Sprecher, S. (1986b). *Mirror, mirror . . . The importance of looks in everyday life*. Albany: State University of New York Press.

Hatfield, E., Traupmann, J., & Sprecher, S. (1984). Older women's perceptions of their intimate relationships. *Journal of Social and Clinical Psychology, 2*, 108–124.

Hatfield, E., Utne, M. K., & Traupmann, J. (1979). Equity theory and intimate relationships. In R. L. Burgess & T. L. Huston (Eds.), *Social exchange in developing relationships* (pp. 99–133). New York: Academic Press.

Hatfield, E., & Walster, G. W. (1978). *A new look at love*. Reading, MA: Addison-Wesley.

Hayduk, L. A. (1983). Personal space: Where we now stand. *Psychological Bulletin, 94*, 293–335.

Haynes, J. M. (1981). *Divorce mediation*. New York: Springer.

Hays, R. B. (1985). A longitudinal study of friendship development. *Journal of Personality and Social Psychology, 48*, 909–924.

Hays, R. B. (1988). Friendship. In S. Duck (Ed.), *Handbook of personal relationships: Theory, research, and intervention* (pp. 391–408). New York: Wiley.

Hazan, C., & Shaver, P. (1987). Romantic love conceptualized as an attachment process. *Journal of Personality and Social Psychology, 52*, 511–524.

Heaton, T. B. (1984). Religious homogamy and marital satisfaction. *Journal of Marriage and the Family, 46*, 729–733.

Heider, F. (1958). *The psychology of interpersonal relations.* New York: Wiley.

Heiman, J. R. (1986). Treating sexually distressed marital relationships. In N. S. Jacobson & A. S. Gurman (Eds.), *Clinical handbook of marital therapy* (pp. 361–385). New York: Guilford.

Heiman, J. R., LoPiccolo, L., & LoPiccolo, J. (1981). The treatment of sexual dysfunction. In A. S. Gurman & D. P. Kniskern (Eds.), *Handbook of family therapy* (pp. 631–661). New York: Brunner/Mazel.

Heiman, J. R., & Verhulst, J. (1990). Sexual dysfunction and marriage. In F. D. Fincham & T. N. Bradbury (Eds.), *The psychology of marriage: Basic issues and applications* (pp. 299–322). New York: Guilford.

Helgeson, V. X., & Sharpsteen, D. J. (1987). Perceptions of danger in achievement and affiliation situations: An extension of the Pollak and Gilligan versus Benton et al. debate. *Journal of Personality and Social Psychology, 53,* 727–733.

Heller, K. (1979). The effects of social support: Prevention and treatment implications. In A. P. Goldstein & F. H. Kanfer (Eds.), *Maximizing treatment gains: Transfer enhancement in psychotherapy* (pp. 353–382). New York: Academic Press.

Hendrick, C. (1988). Roles and gender relationships. In S. Duck (Ed.), *Handbook of personal relationships* (pp. 429–448). New York: Wiley.

Hendrick, C., & Hendrick, S. (1983). *Liking, loving, and relating.* Monterey, CA: Brooks/Cole.

Hendrick, C., & Hendrick, S. S. (1986). A theory and method of love. *Journal of Personality and Social Psychology, 50,* 392–402.

Hendrick, C., & Hendrick, S. S. (1988). Lovers wear rose-colored glasses. *Journal of Social and Personal Relationships, 5,* 161–183.

Hendrick, C., & Hendrick, S. S. (1989). Research on love: Does it measure up? *Journal of Personality and Social Psychology, 56,* 784–794.

Hendrick, S. S. (1981). Self-disclosure and marital satisfaction. *Journal of Personality and Social Psychology, 40,* 1150–1159.

Hendrick, S. S., & Hendrick, C. (1987). Love and sex attitudes: A close relationship. In W. H. Jones & D. Perlman (Eds.), *Advances in personal relationships* (Vol. 1, pp. 141–169). Greenwich, CT: JAI Press.

Hendrick, S. S., Hendrick, C., & Adler, N. L. (1988). Romantic relationships: Love, satisfaction, and staying together. *Journal of Personality and Social Psychology, 54,* 980–988.

Henley, N. M. (1977). *Body politics.* Englewood Cliffs, NJ: Prentice-Hall.

Hernandez, D. J. (1988). Demographic trends and the living arrangements of children. In E. M. Hetherington & J. D. Arasteh (Eds.), *Impact of divorce, singleparenting, and stepparenting on children* (pp. 3–22). Hillsdale, NJ: Erlbaum.

Hetherington, E. M. (1987). Family relations six years after divorce. In K. Pasley & M. Ihinger-Tallman (Eds.), *Remarriage and stepparenting* (pp. 185–205). New York: Guilford.

Hetherington, E. M. (1988). Parents, children, and siblings: Six years after divorce. In R. A. Hinde & J. Stevenson-Hinde (Eds.), *Relationships within families* (pp. 311–331). Oxford: Clarendon Press.

Hetherington, E. M., Cox, M., & Cox, R. (1982). Effects of divorce on parents and children. In M. Lamb (Ed.), *Nontraditional families* (pp. 233–288). Hillsdale, NJ: Erlbaum.

Hetherington, E. M., Stanley-Hagan, M., & Anderson, E. R. (1989). Marital transitions: A child's perspective. *American Psychologist, 44,* 303–312.

Hetherington, L., Crown, J., Wagner, H., & Rigby, S. (1989). Toward an understanding of social consequences of "feminine immodesty" about personal achievements. *Sex Roles, 20,* 371–380.

Hieger, L. J., & Troll, L. A. (1973). A three-generation study of attitudes concerning the importance of romantic love in mate selection. *Gerontologist, 13* (3, Part 2), 86.

Hill, C. T., Rubin, Z., & Peplau, L. A. (1976). Breakups before marriage. The end of 103 affairs. *Journal of Social Issues, 32,* 147–168.

Hill, C. T., & Stull, D. E. (1987). Gender and self-disclosure: Strategies for exploring the issues. In V. J. Derlega & J. H. Berg (Eds.), *Self-disclosure: Theory, research, and therapy* (pp. 81–100). New York: Plenum.

Hindy, C. G., Schwarz, J. C., & Brodsky, A. (1989). *If this is love, why do I feel so insecure?* New York: Atlantic Monthly Press.

Hinsz, V. B. (1989). Facial resemblance in engaged and married couples. *Journal of Social and Personal Relationships, 6,* 223–229.

Hobart, C. W. (1958). The incidence of romanticism during courtship. *Social Forces, 36,* 364–367.

Hobfoll, S. E., & London, P. (1986). The relationship of self-concept and social support to emotional distress among women during war. *Journal of Social and Clinical Psychology, 4,* 189–203.

Hobfoll, S. E., & Stokes, J. P. (1988). The process and mechanics of social support. In S. Duck (Ed.), *Handbook of personal relationships: Theory, research, and intervention* (pp. 497–517). New York: Wiley.

Hochschild, A. (1989). *The second shift.* New York: Viking.

Hofferth, S. L., Kahn, J. R., & Baldwin, W. (1987). Premarital sexual activity among U.S. teenage women over the past three decades. *Family Planning Perspectives, 19,* 46–53.

Hoffman, L. (1981). *Foundations of family life.* New York: Basic Books.

Hoffman, L. W., & Manis, J. D. (1978). Influences of children on marital interaction and parental satisfactions and dissatisfactions. In R. M. Lerner & G. B. Spanier (Eds.), *Child influences on marital and family interaction* (pp. 165–213).

Hoffman, M. L. (1977). Sex differences in empathy and related behaviors. *Psychological Bulletin, 84,* 712–722.

Hofstede, G. (1980). *Culture's consequences, international differences in work-related values.* Beverly Hills, CA: Sage.

Hokanson, J. E., Loewenstein, D. A., Hedeen, C., & Howes, M. J. (1986). Dysphoric college students and roommates: A study of social behaviors over a three month period. *Personality and Social Psychology Bulletin, 12,* 311–324.

Holmes, D. S. (1991). *Abnormal psychology.* New York: Harper & Row.

Holmes, J. G. (1981). The exchange process in close relationships: Microbehavior and macromotives. In M. J. Lerner & S. C. Lerner (Eds.), *The justice motive in social behavior* (pp. 261–284). New York: Plenum.

Holmes, J. G., & Boon, S. D. (1990). Developments in the field of close relationships: Creating foundations for intervention strategies. *Personality and Social Psychology Bulletin, 16,* 23–41.

Holmes, J. G., & Rempel, J. K. (1989). Trust in close relationships. In C.

Hendrick (Ed.), *Review of personality and social psychology: Vol. 10. Close relationships* (pp. 187–220). Newbury Park, CA: Sage Publications.

Holtzworth-Munroe, A., & Jacobson, N. S. (1985). Causal attributions of marital couples: When do they search for causes? What do they conclude when they do? *Journal of Personality and Social Psychology, 48,* 1398–1412.

Holtzworth-Munroe, A., & Jacobson, N. S. (1987). An attributional approach to marital dysfunction and therapy. In J. E. Maddux, C. D. Stoltenberg, & R. Rosenwein (Eds.), *Social processes in clinical and counseling psychology* (pp. 153–170). New York: Springer-Verlag.

Holtzworth-Munroe, A., & Jacobson, N. S. (1988). Toward a methodology for coding spontaneous causal attributions: Preliminary results with married couples. *Journal of Social and Clinical Psychology, 7,* 101–112.

Homans, G. C. (1961). *Social behavior.* New York: Harcourt, Brace & World.

Honeycutt, J. M. (1986). A model of marital functioning based on an attraction paradigm and social-penetration dimensions. *Journal of Marriage and the Family, 48,* 651–667.

Horney, K. (1939). *New ways in psychoanalysis.* New York: Norton.

Horwitz, A. V. (1982). Sex-role expectations, power, and psychological distress. *Sex Roles, 8,* 607–624.

Houseknecht, S. K. (1979). Childlessness and marital adjustment. *Journal of Marriage and the Family, 41,* 259–265.

Houts, A. C., Cook, T. D., & Shadish, W. R., Jr. (1986). The person-situation debate: A critical multiplist perspective. *Journal of Personality, 54,* 52–105.

Howard, J. A., Blumstein, P., & Schwartz, P. (1986). Sex, power, and influence tactics in intimate relationships. *Journal of Personality and Social Psychology, 51,* 102–109.

Howard, J. A., Blumstein, P., & Schwartz, P. (1987). Social or evolutionary theories? Some observations on preferences in human mate selection. *Journal of Personality and Social Psychology, 53,* 194–200.

Howard, J. W., & Dawes, R. M. (1976). Linear prediction of marital happiness. *Personality and Social Psychology Bulletin, 2,* 478–480.

Humphrey, F. G. (1983). *Marital therapy.* Englewood Cliffs, NJ: Prentice-Hall.

Hunt, M. M. (1959). *The natural history of love.* New York: Knopf.

Hupka, R. B. (1981). Cultural determinants of jealousy. *Alternative Lifestyles, 4,* 310–356.

Hurvitz, N. (1970). Interaction hypotheses in marriage counseling. *Family Coordinator, 19,* 64–75.

Huston, T. L. (1973). Ambiguity of acceptance, social desirability, and dating choice. *Journal of Experimental Social Psychology 9,* 32–42.

Huston, T. L. (1983). Power. In H. H. Kelley, E. Berscheid, A. Christensen, et al. (Eds.), *Close relationships* (pp. 169–219). New York: Freeman.

Huston, T. L., McHale,, S. M., & Crouter, A. C. (1986). When the honeymoon's over: Changes in the marriage relationship over the first year. In R. Gilmour & S. Duck (Eds.), *The emerging field of personal relationships* (pp. 109–132). Hillsdale, NJ: Erlbaum.

Huston, T. L., Surra, C. A., Fitzgerald, N. M., & Cate, R. M. (1981). From courtship to marriage: Mate selection as an interpersonal process. In S. Duck & R. Gilmour (Eds.), *Personal relationships. 2: Developing personal relationships* (pp. 53–88). New York: Academic Press.

Ickes, W., & Tooke, W. (1988). The observational method: Studying the interaction of minds and bodies. In S. Duck (Ed.), *Handbook of personal relationships: Theory, research, and interventions* (pp. 79–98). New York: Wiley.

Issacson, W. (1989, November 20). Should gays have marriage rights? *Time*, pp. 101–102.

Jacobs, L. E., Berscheid, E., & Walster, E. (1971). Self-esteem and attraction. *Journal of Personality and Social Psychology, 17*, 84–91.

Jacobson, D. S. (1987). Family type, visiting patterns, and children's behavior in the stepfamily: A linked family system. In K. Pasley & M. Ihinger-Tallman (Eds.), *Remarriage and stepparenting* (pp. 257–272). New York: Guilford.

Jacobson, G. F. (1983). *The multiple crises of marital separation and divorce.* New York: Grune & Stratton.

Jacobson, N. S. (1978). A review of the research on the effectiveness of marital therapy. In T. J. Paolino & B. S. McCrady (Eds.), *Marriage and marital therapy: Psychoanalytic, behavior and systems theory perspectives* (pp. 395–444). New York: Brunner/Mazel.

Jacobson, N. S., Follette, W. C., & Elwood, R. W. (1984). Outcome research on behavioral marital therapy: A methodological and conceptual reappraisal. In K. Hahlweg & N. Jacobson (Eds.), *Marital interaction: Analysis and modification* (pp. 113–129). New York: Guilford.

Jacobson, N. S., Follette, W. C., & McDonald, D. W. (1982). Reactivity to positive and negative behavior in distressed and nondistressed married couples. *Journal of Consulting and Clinical Psychology, 50*, 706–714.

Jacobson, N. S., & Gurman, A. S. (Eds.). (1986). *Clinical handbook of marital therapy.* New York: Guilford Press.

Jacobson, N. S., & Margolin, G. (1979). *Marital therapy: Strategies based on social learning and behavior exchange principles.* New York: Brunner/Mazel.

Jacobson, N. S., McDonald, D. W., Follette, W. C., & Berley, R. A. (1985). Attributional processes in distressed and nondistressed married couples. *Cognitive Therapy and Research, 9*, 35–59.

Jacobson, N. S., & Moore, D. (1981). Spouses as observers of the events in their relationships. *Journal of Consulting and Clinical Psychology, 49*, 269.

Jacobson, N. S., Waldron, H., & Moore, D. (1980). Toward a behavioral profile of marital distress. *Journal of Consulting and Clinical Psychology, 48*, 696–703.

Jacobson, N. S., & Weiss, R. L. (1978). Behavioral marriage therapy: III. Critique: The contents of Gurman et al. may be hazardous to our health. *Family Process, 17*, 149–164.

Jacoby, A. P., & Williams, J. D. (1985). Effects of premarital sexual standards and behavior on dating and marriage desirability. *Journal of Marriage and the Family, 47*, 1059–1065.

Jemmott, J. B., III, & Magloire, K. (1988). Academic stress, social support, and secretory immunoglobulin A. *Journal of Personality and Social Psychology, 55*, 803–810.

Jessor, R., Costa, F., Jessor, L., & Donovan, J. E. (1983). Time of first intercourse: A prospective study. *Journal of Personality and Social Psychology, 44*, 608–626.

Joanning, H. (1982). The long-term effects of the couple communication program. *Journal of Marital and Family Therapy, 8*, 463–468.

Johnson, C. L. (1975). Authority and power in Japanese-American marriage. In R. E. Cromwell & D. H. Olson (Eds.), *Power in families* (pp. 182–196). New York: Wiley.

Johnson, D. J., & Rusbult, C. E. (1989). Resisting temptation: Devaluation of alternative partners as a means of maintaining commitment in close relationships. *Journal of Personality and Social Psychology, 57,* 967–980.

Johnson, P. (1976). Women and power: Toward a theory of effectiveness. *Journal of Social Issues, 32,* 99–110.

Johnson, P. (1978). Women and interpersonal power. In I. H. Frieze, J. Parsons, P. B. Johnson, D. Ruble, & G. Zellman (Eds.), *Women and sex roles: A social psychological perspective* (pp. 301–320). New York: Norton.

Johnson-George, C., & Swap, W. (1982). Measurement of specific interpersonal trust: Construction and validation of a scale to assess trust in a specific order. *Journal of Personality and Social Psychology, 43,* 1306–1317.

Jones, E., & Gallois, C. (1989). Spouses' impressions of rules for communication in public and private marital conflicts. *Journal of Marriage and the Family, 51,* 957–967.

Jones, E. E., & Nisbett, R. E. (1972). *The actor and the observer: Divergent perceptions of the causes of behavior.* Morristown, NJ: General Learning Press.

Jones, R. A. (1985). *Research methods in the social and behavioral sciences.* Sunderland, MA: Sinauer Associates, Inc.

Jones, R. W., & Bates, J. E. (1978). Satisfaction in male homosexual couples. *Journal of Homosexuality, 3,* 217–224.

Jones, W. H. (1990). Loneliness and social exclusion. *Journal of Social and Clinical Psychology, 9,* 214–220.

Jones, W. H., & Carpenter, B. N. (1986). Shyness, social behavior, and relationships. In W. H. Jones, J. M. Cheek, & S. R. Briggs (Eds.), *Shyness: Perspectives on research and treatment* (pp. 227–238). New York: Plenum.

Jones, W. H., Cavert, C. W., Snider, R. L., & Bruce, T. (1985). Relational stress: An analysis of situations and events associated with loneliness. In S. Duck & D. Perlman (Eds.), *Understanding personal relationships: An interdisciplinary approach* (pp. 221–242). London: Sage.

Jones, W. H., Cheek, J. M., & Briggs, S. R. (Eds.). (1986). *Shyness: Perspectives on research and treatment.* New York: Plenum.

Jones, W. H., Freemon, J. E., & Goswick, R. A. (1981). The persistence of loneliness: Self and other determinants. *Journal of Personality, 49,* 27–48.

Jones, W. H., Hobbs, S. A., & Hackenbury, D. (1982). Loneliness and social skills deficits. *Journal of Personality and Social Psychology, 42,* 682–689.

Jones, W. H., Sansome, C., & Helm, B. (1983). Loneliness and interpersonal judgments. *Personality and Social Psychology Bulletin, 9,* 437–442.

Jong-Gierveld, J. de (1987). Developing and testing a model of loneliness. *Journal of Personality and Social Psychology, 53,* 119–128.

Jordan, P. (1988). The effects of marital separation on men. *Journal of Divorce, 12,* 57–82.

Jourard, S. M. (1964). *The transparent self.* New York: Van Nostrand.

Kaats, G. R., & Davis, K. E. (1970). The dynamics of sexual behavior of college students. *Journal of Marriage and the Family, 32,* 390–399.

Kalick, S. M. (1988). Physical attractiveness as a status cue. *Journal of Experimental Social Psychology, 24,* 469–489.

Kalick, S. M., & Hamilton, T. E., III (1986). The matching hypothesis revisited. *Journal of Personality and Social Psychology, 51,* 673–682.

Kalick, S. M., & Hamilton, T. E., III (1988). Closer look at a matching simulation: Reply to Aron. *Journal of Personality and Social Psychology, 54,* 447–451.

Kalmuss, D. (1984). The intergenerational transmission of marital aggression. *Journal of Marriage and the Family, 46,* 11–20.

Kalmuss, D., & Seltzer, J. A. (1986). Continuity of marital behavior in remarriage: The case of spouse abuse. *Journal of Marriage and the Family, 48,* 113–120.

Kandel, D. B. (1978). Similarity in real-life adolescent friendship pairs. *Journal of Personality and Social Psychology, 36,* 306–312.

Kanin, E. J., Davidson, K. D., & Scheck, S. R. (1970). A research note on male-female differentials in the experience of heterosexual love. *The Journal of Sex Research, 6,* 64–72.

Kantrowitz, B., & Wingert, P. (1990, Winter/Spring) Step by step. *Newsweek Special Edition,* pp. 24–34.

Kazdin, A. E. (1980). *Research design in clinical psychology.* New York: Harper & Row.

Keinan, G., & Hobfoll, S. E. (1989). Stress, dependency, and social support: Who benefits from husband's presence in delivery? *Journal of Social and Clinical Psychology, 8,* 32–44.

Keith, V. M., & Finlay, B. (1988). The impact of parental divorce on children's educational attainment, marital timing, and likelihood of divorce. *Journal of Marriage and the Family, 50,* 797–809.

Kelley, H. H. (1971). Attribution in social interaction. In E. E. Jones, D. E. Kanouse, H. H. Kelley, R. E. Nisbett, S. Valins, & B. Weiner (Eds.), *Attribution: Perceiving the causes of behavior* (pp. 1–26). Morristown, NJ: General Learning Press.

Kelley, H. H. (1977). An application of attribution theory to research methodology for close relationships. In G. Levinger & H. L. Raush (Eds.), *Close relationships: Perspectives on the meaning of intimacy* (pp. 87–113). Amherst: University of Massachusetts Press.

Kelley, H. H. (1979). *Personal relationships: Their structures and processes.* Hillsdale, NJ: Erlbaum.

Kelley, H. H. (1983). Love and commitment. In H. H. Kelley, E. Berscheid, A. Christensen, et al. (Eds.), *Close relationships* (pp. 265–314). New York: Freeman.

Kelley, K., & Rolker-Dolinsky, B. (1987). The psychosexology of female initiation and dominance. In D. Perlman & S. Duck (Eds.), *Intimate relationships: Development, dynamics, and deterioration* (pp. 63–87). Newbury Park, CA: Sage.

Kelly, C., Huston, T. L., & Cate, R. M. (1985). Premarital relationship correlates of the erosion of satisfaction in marriage. *Journal of Social and Personal Relationships, 2,* 167–178.

Kelly, J. A., & Worell, J. (1977). New formulations of sex roles and androgyny: A critical review. *Journal of Consulting and Clinical Psychology, 45,* 1101–1115.

Kenkel, W. F. (1961). Sex of observer and spousal roles in decision-making. *Marriage and Family Living, 23,* 185–186.

Kennedy, R. (1989). *Life choices* (2nd ed.). New York: Holt, Rinehart & Winston.

Kenny, D. A. (1988). The analysis of data from two-person relationships. In S. Duck (Ed.), *Handbook of personal relationships: Theory, research, and interventions* (pp. 57–78). New York: Wiley.

Kenrick, D. T., & Cialdini, R. B. (1977). Romantic attraction: Misattribution versus reinforcement explanations. *Journal of Personality and Social Psychology, 35,* 381–391.

Kenrick, D. T., & Gutierres, S. E. (1989). Influence of popular erotica on judgments of strangers and mates. *Journal of Experimental Social Psychology, 25,* 159–167.

Kenrick, D. T., & Trost, M. R. (1989). A reproductive exchange model of heterosexual relationships: Putting proximate economics in ultimate perspective. In C. Hendrick (Ed.), *Review of Personality and Social Psychology: Vol. 10. Close relationships* (pp. 92–118). Newbury Park, CA: Sage.

Kephart, W. (1967). Some correlates of romantic love. *Journal of Marriage and the Family, 29,* 470–479.

Keppel, G. (1982). *Design and analysis: A researcher's handbook* (2nd ed.). Englewood Cliffs, NJ: Prentice-Hall.

Kerckhoff, A. C., & Davis, K. E. (1962). Value consensus and need complementarity in mate selection. *American Sociological Review, 27,* 295–303.

Kerlinger, F. N. (1979). *Scientific behavioral research: A conceptual primer.* New York: Holt, Rinehart & Winston.

Kernis, M. H., & Wheeler, L. (1981). Beautiful friends and ugly strangers: Radiation and contrast effects in perceptions of same-sex pairs. *Personality and Social Psychology Bulletin, 7,* 617–620.

Kessler, R. C., McLeod, J. D., & Wethington, E. (1985). The costs of caring: A perspective on the relationship between sex and psychological distress. In I. G. Sarason & B. R. Sarason (Eds.), *Social support: Theory, research and applications* (pp. 491–506). Dordrecht, The Netherlands: Martinus Nijhoff Publishers.

Kessler, R. C., & McRae, J. A., Jr. (1984). A note on the relationships of sex and marital status to psychological stress. In J. R. Greenley (Ed.), *Research in community and mental health* (Vol. 4, pp. 109–130). Greenwich, CT: JAI Press.

Kidder, L. H., Fagan, M. A., & Cohn, E. S. (1981). Giving and receiving: Social justice in close relationships. In M. J. Lerner & S. C. Lerner (Eds.), *The justice motive in social behavior* (pp. 235–259). New York: Plenum.

Kiesler, C. A. (1971), *The psychology of commitment.* New York: Academic Press.

Kiesler, S. B., & Baral, R. L. (1970). The secret for a romantic partner: The effects of self-esteem and physical attractiveness on romantic behavior. In K. J. Gergen & D. Marlove (Eds.), *Personality and social behavior* (pp. 155–166). Reading, MA: Addison-Wesley.

Kihlstrom, J. F. (1987). Introduction to the special issue: Integrating personality and social psychology. *Journal of Personality and Social Psychology, 53,* 989–992.

Kinnaird, K. L., & Gerrard, M. (1986). Premarital sexual behavior and attitudes toward marriage and divorce among young women as a function of their mother's marital status. *Journal of Marriage and the Family, 48,* 757–765.

Kitson, G. C., & Sussman, M. B. (1982). Marital complaints, demographic characteristics, and symptoms of mental distress in divorce. *Journal of Marriage and the Family, 44,* 87–101.

Kleinke, C. L. (1979). Effects of personal evaluations. In G. J. Chelune (Ed.), *Self-disclosure* (pp. 59–79). San Francisco: Jossey-Bass.

Knowles, E. (1980). An affiliative-conflict theory of personal and group spatial behavior. In P. B. Paulus (Ed.), *Psychology of group influence* (pp. 133–188). Hillsdale, NJ: Erlbaum.

Knox, D., Jr. (1970). Conceptions of love at three developmental levels. *Family Coordinator, 19,* 151–156.

Knox, D. H., & Sporakowski, M. J. (1968). Attitudes of college students toward love. *Journal of Marriage and the Family, 30,* 638–642.

Knudson, R. M., Sommers, A. A., & Golding, S. L. (1980). Interpersonal perception and mode of resolution in marital conflict. *Journal of Personality and Social Psychology, 38,* 751–763.

Knupfer, G., Clark, W., & Room, R. (1966). The mental health of the unmarried. *American Journal of Psychiatry, 122,* 841–851.

Koestner, R., & Wheeler, L. (1988). Self-presentation in personal advertisements: The influence of implicit notions of attraction and role expectations. *Journal of Social and Personal Relationships, 5,* 149–160.

Kollock, P., Blumstein, P., & Schwartz, P. (1985). Sex and power in interaction: Conversational privileges and duties. *American Sociological Review, 50,* 34–46.

Koren, P., Carlton, K., & Shaw, D. (1980). Marital conflict: Relations among behaviors, outcomes, and distress. *Journal of Consulting and Clinical Psychology, 48,* 460–468.

Kotlar, S. L. (1965). Middle-class role perceptions and marital adjustments. *Sociology and Social Research, 49,* 283–293.

Krebs, D. (1975). Empathy and altruism. *Journal of Personality and Social Psychology, 32.* 1134–1146.

Krebs, D., & Adinolfi, A. A. (1975). Physical attractiveness, social relations, and personality style. *Journal of Personality and Social Psychology, 31,* 245–253.

Kulik, J. A., & Mahler, H. I. M. (1989). Stress and affiliation in a hospital setting: Preoperative roommate preferences. *Personality and Social Psychology Bulletin, 15,* 183–193.

Kurdek, L. A. (1989a). Relationship quality in gay and lesbian cohabiting couples: A 1-year follow-up. *Journal of Social and Personal Relationships, 6,* 39–59.

Kurdek, L. A. (1989b). Social support and psychological distress in first-married and remarried newlywed husbands and wives. *Journal of Marriage and the Family, 51,* 1047–1064.

Kurdek, L. A., & Schmitt, J. P. (1986). Relationship quality in heterosexual married, heterosexual cohabiting, and gay and lesbian relationships. *Journal of Personality and Social Psychology, 51,* 711–720.

Lamb, M. (1977). The effects of divorce on children's personality development. *Journal of Divorce, 1,* 163–174.

Laner, M. R. (1978). Love's labours lost: A theory of marital dissolution. *Journal of Divorce, 1,* 213–232.

Langlois, J. H. (1986). From the eye of the beholder to behavioral reality: Development of social behaviors and social relations as a function of physical attractiveness. In C. P. Herman, M. P. Zanna, & E. T. Higgins (Eds.), *The Ontario Symposium: Vol. 3. Physical appearance, stigma, and social behavior* (pp. 23–51). Hillsdale, NJ: Erlbaum.

Langston, C. A., & Cantor, N. (1989). Anxiety and social constraint: When making friends is hard. *Journal of Personality and Social Psychology, 56,* 649–661.

Larson, P. C. (1982). Gay male relationships. In W. Paul, J. D. Weinrich, J. C. Gonziorek, & M. E. Hotveldt (Eds.), *Homosexuality: Social, psychological, and biological issues* (pp. 219–232). Beverly Hills, CA: Sage Publications.

Lauer, J., & Lauer, R. (1985, June). Marriages made to last. *Psychology Today,* pp. 22–26.

Laws, J. (1971). A feminist review of marital adjustment literature: The rape of the Locke. *Journal of Marriage and the Family, 33,* 483–516.

Leary, M. R. (1983). *Understanding social anxiety: Social, personality, and clinical perspectives.* Beverly Hills, CA: Sage.

Leary, M. R. (1987). A self-presentation model for the treatment of social anxieties. In J. E. Maddux, C. D. Stoltenberg, & R. Rosenweig (Eds.), *Social processes in clinical and counseling psychology* (pp. 126–138). New York: Springer Verlag.

Lederer, W., & Jackson, D. O. (1968). *The mirages of marriage.* New York: Norton.

Lee, G. R. (1988). Marital satisfaction in later life: The effects of nonmarital roles. *Journal of Marriage and the Family, 50,* 775–783.

Lee, J. A. (1977). A typology of styles of loving. *Personality and Social Psychology Bulletin, 3,* 173–182.

Lee, J. A. (1988). Love-styles. In R. J. Sternberg & M. L. Barnes (Eds.), *The psychology of love* (pp. 38–67). New Haven, CT: Yale University Press.

Lehman, D. R., & Taylor, S. E. (1987). Date with an earthquake: Coping with a probable unpredictable disaster. *Personality and Social Psychology Bulletin, 13,* 546–555.

Leigh, G. K., Homan, T. B., & Burr, W. R. (1987). Some confusions and exclusions of the SVR theory of dyadic pairing: A response to Murstein. *Journal of Marriage and the Family, 49,* 933–937.

Leik, R. K., & Leik, S. K. (1977). Transition to interpersonal commitment. In R. Hamblin & J. H. Kunkel (Eds.), *Behavior theory in sociology* (pp. 299–322). New Brunswick, NJ: Transaction Books.

Lennox, R. D. (1988). The problem with self-monitoring: A two-sided scale and a one-sided theory. *Journal of Personality Assessment, 52,* 58–73.

Leonard, G. (1982, December). The end of sex. *Esquire,* p. 74.

Leslie, L. A., Huston, T. L., & Johnson, M. P. (1986). Parental reactions to dating relationships: Do they make a difference? *Journal of Marriage and the Family, 48,* 57–66.

Lester, M. E., & Doherty, W. J. (1983). Couples' long-term evaluations of their marriage encounter experience. *Journal of Marital and Family Therapy, 9,* 183–188.

Levenson, R. W., & Gottman, J. M. (1978). Toward the assessment of social competence. *Journal of Consulting and Clinical Psychology, 46,* 453–462.

Levenson, R. W., & Gottman, J. M. (1983). Marital interaction: Physiological linkage and affective exchange. *Journal of Personality and Social Psychology, 45,* 587–597.

Levenson, R. W., & Gottman, J. M. (1985). Physiological and affective predictors of change in relationship satisfaction. *Journal of Personality and Social Psychology, 49,* 85–94.

Levinger, G. (1976). A social psychological perspective on marital dissolution. *Journal of Social Issues, 32*, 21–47.

Levinger, G. (1977). Re-viewing the close relationship. In G. Levinger and H. L. Raush (Eds.). *Close relationships: Perspectives on the meaning in intimacy* (pp. 137–166). Amherst: University of Massachusetts Press.

Levinger, G. (1979a). Marital cohesiveness at the brink. The fate of applications for divorce. In G. Levinger and O. C. Moles (Eds.) *Divorce and separation* (pp. 137–150). New York: Basic Books.

Levinger, G. (1979b). A social psychological perspective on marital dissolution. In G. Levinger & O. C. Moles (Eds.), *Divorce and separation* (pp. 37–60). New York: Basic Books.

Levinger, G. (1988). Can we picture "love"? In R. J. Sternberg & M. L. Barnes (Eds.), *The psychology of love* (pp. 139–158). New Haven, CT: Yale University Press.

Levinger, G., & Huesmann, L. R. (1980). An "incremental exchange" perspective on the pair relationship: Interpersonal reward and level of involvement. In K. K. Gergen, M. S. Greenberg, & R. H. Willis (Eds.), *Social exchange: Advances in theory and research* (pp. 165–188). New York: Plenum.

Levinger, G., Senn, D. J., & Jorgensen, B. W. (1970). Progress toward permanence in courtship: A test of the Kerckhoff-Davis hypotheses. *Sociometry, 33*, 427–443.

Levy, M. B., & Davis, K. E. (1988). Love styles and attachment styles compared: Their relation to each other and to various relationship characteristics. *Journal of Social and Personal Relationships, 5*, 439–471.

Lewis, R. A. (1972). A developmental framework for the analysis of premarital dyadic formation. *Family Process, 11*, 17–48.

Lewis, R. A. (1973). A longitudinal test of a developmental framework for premarital dyadic formation. *Journal of Marriage and the Family, 35*, 16–25.

Liberman, R. P., Wheeler, E. C., deVisser, L. A. J. M., Kuehnel, J., & Kuehnel, T. (1980). *Handbook of marital therapy.* New York: Plenum.

Linton, R. (1936). *The study of man.* New York: Appleton-Century-Crofts.

Linville, P. (1987). Self-complexity as a cognitive buffer against stress-related illness and depression. *Journal of Personality and Social Psychology, 52*, 663–676.

Lloyd, K. Paulsen, J., & Brockner, J. (1983). The effects of self-esteem and self-consciousness on interpersonal attraction. *Personality and Social Psychology Bulletin, 9*, 397–404.

Lloyd, S., Cate, R., & Henton, J. (1982). Equity and rewards as predictors of satisfaction in casual and intimate relationships. *Journal of Psychology, 110*, 43–48.

Lloyd, S. A., Cate, R. M., & Henton, J. M. (1984). Predicting premarital relationship stability: A methodological refinement. *Journal of Marriage and the Family, 46*, 71–76.

Lobdell, J., & Perlman, D. (1986). The intergenerational transmission of loneliness. A study of college females and their parents. *Journal of Marriage and the Family, 48*, 589–595.

Locke, K. D., & Horowitz, L. M. (1990). Satisfaction in interpersonal interactions as a function of similarity in level of dysphoria. *Journal of Personality and Social Psychology, 58*, 823–831.

Lockhart, L. L. (1987). A reexamination of the effects of race and social class on the incidence of marital violence: A search for reliable differences. *Journal of Marriage and the Family, 49,* 603–610.

London, K. A., & Wilson, B. F. (1988, October). Divorce. *American Demographics,* pp. 22–26.

Long, C. J., & Andrews, D. W. (1990). Perspective taking as a predictor of marital adjustment. *Journal of Personality and Social Psychology, 59,* 126–131.

Long, N., & Forehand, R. (1987). The effects of parental divorce and marital conflict on children: An overview. *Journal of Developmental and Behavioral Pediatrics, 8,* 292–296.

Lopata, H. Z. (1969). Loneliness, forms and components. *Social Problems, 17,* 248–261.

Lott, A. J., & Lott, B. E. (1974). The role of reward in the formation of positive interpersonal attitudes. In T. Huston (Ed.), *Foundations of interpersonal attraction* (pp. 171–189). New York: Academic Press.

Lui, K., Darrow, W. W., & Rutherford, G. W., III, (1988). A model-based estimate of the mean incubation period for AIDS in homosexual men. *Science, 240,* 1333–1335.

Lund, M. (1985). The development of investment and commitment scales for predicting continuity of personal relationships. *Journal of Social and Personal Relationships, 2,* 3–23.

Lynch, J. J. (1977). *The broken heart: The medical consequences of loneliness.* New York: Basic Books.

Maccoby, E. E. (1990). Gender and relationships: A developmental account. *American Psychologist, 45,* 513–520.

Maccoby, E. E., Depner, C. E., & Mnookin, R. H. (1990). Coparenting in the second year after divorce. *Journal of Marriage and the Family, 52,* 141–155.

MacDermid, S. M., Huston, T. L., & McHale, S. M. (1990). Changes in marriage associated with the transition to parenthood: Individual differences as a function of sex-role attitudes and changes in the division of household labor. *Journal of Marriage and the Family, 52,* 475–486.

Mace, D., & Mace, V. (1976). Marriage enrichment—A preventitive group approach for couples. In D. H. Olson (Ed.), *Treating relationships* (pp. 321–336). Lake Mills, IA: Graphic Publishing.

Macklin, E. D. (1978). Review of research on nonmarital cohabitation in the United States. In B. I. Murstein (Ed.), *Exploring intimate lifestyles* (pp. 197–243). New York: Springer.

Macklin, E. D. (1980). Nontraditional family forms: A decade of research. *Journal of Marriage and the Family, 42,* 905–922.

Madden, M. E. (1987). Perceived control and power in marriage: A study of marital decision making and task performance. *Personality and Social Psychology Bulletin, 13,* 73–82.

Madden, M. E., & Janoff-Bulman, R. (1981). Blame, control, and marital satisfaction: Wives' attributions for conflict in marriage. *Journal of Marriage and the Family, 43,* 663–674.

Maddox, J. W. (1976). Sexual health: An enrichment and treatment program. In D. H. Olson (Ed.), *Treating relationships* (pp. 355–382). Lake Mills, IA: Graphic Publishing.

Maddux, J. E., Norton, L. W., & Leary, M. R. (1988). Cognitive components of social anxiety: An investigation of the integration of self-presentation theory and self-efficacy theory. *Journal of Social and Clinical Psychology, 6,* 180–190.

Major, B., & Adams, J. B. (1983). Role of gender, interpersonal orientation, and self-presentation in distributive-justice behavior. *Journal of Personality and Social Psychology, 45,* 598–608.

Major, B., Carrington, P. I., & Carnevale, P. J. D. (1984). Physical attractiveness and self-esteem: Attributions for praise from an other-sex evaluator. *Personality and Social Psychology Bulletin, 10,* 43–50.

Major, B., Schmidlin, A. M., & Williams, L. (1990). Gender patterns in social touch: The impact of setting and age. *Journal of Personality and Social Psychology, 58,* 634–643.

Malone, J., Tyree, A., & O'Leary, K. D. (1989). Generalization and containment: Different effects of past aggression for husbands and wives. *Journal of Marriage and the Family, 51,* 687–697.

Manchester Guardian Weekly. (1989, December 24). Tough fight ahead against AIDS, p. 14.

Mandler, G. (1984). *Mind and body.* New York: Norton.

Manne, S. L., & Zautra, A. S. (1989). Spouse criticism and support: Their association with coping and psychological adjustment among women with rheumatoid arthritis. *Journal of Personality and Social Psychology, 56,* 608–617.

Marecek, J. (1987). Counseling adolescents with problem pregnancies. *American Psychologist, 42,* 89–93.

Maret, E., & Finlay, B. (1984). The distribution of household labor among women in dual-earner families. *Journal of Marriage and the Family, 46,* 357–364.

Margolin, G. (1978). Relationships among marital assessment procedures: A correlational study. *Journal of Consulting and Clinical Psychology, 46,* 1556–1558.

Margolin, G. (1983). Behavioral marital therapy: Is there a place for passion, play, and other non-negotiable dimensions? *The Behavior Therapist, 6,* 65–68.

Margolin, G. (1987). Marital therapy: A cognitive-behavioral-affective approach. In N. S. Jacobson (Ed.), *Psychotherapists in clinical practice: Cognitive and behavioral perspectives* (pp. 232–285). New York: Guilford Press.

Margolin, G., John, G. S., & O'Brien, M. (1989). Sequential affective patterns as a function of marital conflict style. *Journal of Social and Clinical Psychology, 8,* 45–61.

Margolin, G., & Wampold, B. E. (1981). A sequential analysis of conflict and accord in distressed and nondistressed marital partners. *Journal of Consulting and Clinical Psychology, 49,* 554–567.

Margolin, L., & White, L. (1987). The continuing role of physical attractiveness in marriage. *Journal of Marriage and the Family, 49,* 21–28.

Marini, M. (1976). Dimensions of marriage happiness: A research note. *Journal of Marriage and the Family, 38,* 443–447.

Mark, M. M., & Miller, M. L. (1986). The effects of social permissiveness, target gender, subject gender, and attitude toward women on social perception: In search of the double standard. *Sex Roles, 15,* 311–322.

Markman, H. J. (1981). Prediction of marital distress: A 5-year follow-up. *Journal of Consulting and Clinical Psychology 49*, 760–762.

Markman, H. J., & Floyd, F. (1980). Possibilities for the prevention of marital discord: A behavioral perspective. *American Journal of Family Therapy, 8*, 29–48.

Markman, H. J., Floyd, F., & Dickson-Markman, F. (1982). Towards a model for the prediction and primary prevention of marital and family distress and dissolution. In S. Duck (Ed.), *Personal relationships. 4: Dissolving relationships* (pp. 233–261). New York: Academic Press.

Markman, H. J., Floyd, F. J., Stanley, S. M., & Lewis, H. C. (1986). Prevention. In N. S. Jacobson & A. S. Gurman (Eds.), *Clinical handbook of marital therapy* (pp. 173–195). New York: Guilford.

Marks, G., & Miller, N. (1982). Target attractiveness as a mediator of assumed attitude similarity. *Personality and Social Psychology Bulletin, 8*, 728–735.

Marks, S. R. (1977). Multiple roles and role strain: Some notes on human energy, time and commitment. *American Sociological Review, 42*, 921–936.

Marshall, G. D., & Zimbardo, P. G. (1979). Affective consequences of inadequately explained physiological arousal. *Journal of Personality and Social Psychology, 37*, 970–988.

Martin, M. W. (1985). Satisfaction with intimate exchange: Gender-role differences and the impact of equity, equality, and rewards. *Sex Roles, 12*, 597–605.

Maslach, C. (1979). Negative emotional biasing of explained arousal. *Journal of Personality and Social Psychology, 37*, 953–969.

Maslow, A. (1954). *Motivation and personality.* New York: Harper & Row.

Maslow, A. (1968). *Toward a psychology of being.* Princeton, NJ: Van Nostrand.

Mason, A., & Blankenship, V. (1987). Power and affiliation motivation, stress, and abuse in intimate relationships. *Journal of Personality and Social Psychology, 52*, 203–210.

Masters, W. H., & Johnson, V. E. (1970). *Human sexual inadequacy.* Boston: Little, Brown.

Masters, W. H., & Johnson, V. E. (1979). *Homosexuality in perspective.* Boston: Little, Brown.

Mathes, E. W., Adams, H. E., & Davies, R. M. (1985). Jealousy: Loss of relationship rewards, loss of self-esteem, depression, anxiety, and anger. *Journal of Personality and Social Psychology, 48*, 1552–1561.

Matthews, K. A., & Rodin, J. (1989). Women's changing work roles: Impact on health, family, and public policy. *American Psychologist, 44*, 1389–1393.

May, R. (1972). *Power and innocence.* New York: Norton.

McAdams, D. P. (1982). Intimacy motivation. In A. J. Stewart (Ed.), *Motivation and society* (pp. 133–171). San Francisco: Jossey-Bass.

McAdams, D. P. (1985). Motivation and friendship. In S. Duck & D. Perlman (Eds.), *Understanding personal relationships: An interdisciplinary approach* (pp. 85–105). London: Sage.

McAdams, D. P. (1988). Personal needs and personal relationships. In S. Duck (Ed.), *Handbook of personal relationships: Theory, research, and intervention* (pp. 7–22). New York: Wiley.

McAdams, D. P., & Bryant, F. B. (1987). Intimacy motivation and subjective mental health in a nationwide sample. *Journal of Personality, 55*, 395–414.

McAdams, D. P., Healy, S., & Krause, S. (1984). Social motives and friendship patterns. *Journal of Personality and Social Psychology, 47*, 828–838.

McAdams, D. P., & Vaillant, G. E. (1982). Intimacy motivation and psychosocial adjustment: A longitudinal study. *Journal of Personality Assessment, 46*, 586–593.

McCarthy, B. (1981). Studying personal relationships. In S. Duck & R. Gilmour (Eds.), *Personal relationships. 1: Studying personal relationships* (pp. 23–46). New York: Academic Press.

McClelland, D. (1985). How motives, skills, and values determine what people do. *American Psychologist, 40*, 812–825.

McClintock, C. G., Kramer, R. M., & Keil, L. J. (1984). Equity and social exchange in human relationships. In L. Berkowitz (Ed.), *Advances in experimental social psychology* (Vol. 17, pp. 183–228). New York: Academic Press.

McClintock, E. (1983). Interaction. In H. H. Kelley, E. Berscheid, A. Christensen, et al. (Eds.), *Close relationships* (pp. 68–109). New York: Freeman.

McCrae, R. R., & Costa, P. T., Jr. (1988). Psychological resilience among widowed men and women: A 10-year followup of a national sample. *Journal of Social Issues, 44*, 129–142.

McDonald, G. W. (1980). Family power: The assessment of a decade of theory and research. *Journal of Marriage and the Family, 42*, 841–854.

McDonald, G. W. (1981). Structural exchange and marital interaction. *Journal of Marriage and the Family, 43*, 825–839.

Menaghan, E. G., & Lieberman, M. A. (1986). Changes in depression following divorce: A panel study. *Journal of Marriage and the Family, 48*, 319–328.

Messersmith, C. E. (1976). Sex therapy and the marital system. In D. H. Olson (Ed.), *Treating relationships* (pp. 339–354). Lake Mills, IA: Graphic Publishing.

Messick, D. M., & Cook, K. S. (Ed.). (1983). *Equity theory: Psychological and sociological perspectives.* New York: Praeger.

Metts, S., Cupach, W. R., & Bejlovec, R. A. (1989). "I love you too much to ever start liking you": Redefining romantic relationships. *Journal of Social and Personal Relationships, 6*, 259–274.

Meyer, J. P., & Pepper, S. (1977). Need compatibility and marital adjustment in young married couples. *Journal of Personality and Social Psychology, 35*, 331–342.

Michaels, J. W., Acock, A. C., & Edwards, J. N. (1986). Social exchange and equity determinants of relationship commitment. *Journal of Social and Personal Relationships, 3*, 161–175.

Michela, J. L., Peplau, L. A., & Weeks, D. G. (1982). Perceived dimensions of attributions for loneliness. *Journal of Personality and Social Psychology, 43*, 929–936.

Mikulincer, M., Florian, V., & Tolmacz, R. (1990). Attachment styles and fear of personal death: A case study of affect regulation. *Journal of Personality and Social Psychology, 58*, 273–280.

Milardo, R. M., Johnson, M. P., & Huston, T. L. (1983). Developing close relationships: Changing patterns of interaction between pair members and social networks. *Journal of Personality and Social Psychology, 44*, 964–976.

Milardo, R. M., & Murstein, B. I. (1979). The implications of exchange orientation on the dyadic functioning of heterosexual cohabitation. In M. Cook &

G. Wilson (Eds.), *Love and attraction* (pp. 279–285). Oxford: Pergamon Press.

Miller, B. C., & Bingham, C. R. (1989). Family configuration in relation to the sexual behavior of female adolescents. *Journal of Marriage and the Family, 51*, 499–506.

Miller, D. T., & Turnbull, W. (1986). Expectancies and interpersonal processes. *Annual Review of Psychology, 37*, 233–256.

Miller, J. B. (1976). *Toward a new psychology of women.* Boston: Beacon Press.

Miller, L., Berg, J. H., & Archer, R. L. (1983). Openers: Individuals who elicit intimate self-disclosure. *Journal of Personality and Social Psychology, 44*, 1234–1244.

Miller, L. C. (1990). Intimacy and liking: Mutual influence and the role of unique relationships. *Journal of Personality and Social Psychology, 59*, 50–60.

Miller, L. C., & Kenny, D. A. (1986). Reciprocity of self-disclosure at the individual and dyadic levels: A social relations analysis. *Journal of Personality and Social Psychology, 50*, 713–719.

Miller, S., Nunnally, E. W., & Wackman, D. B. (1976). Minnesota Couples Communication Program (MCCP): Premarital and marital groups. In D. H. Olson (Ed.), *Treating relationships* (pp. 21–40). Lake Mills, IA: Graphic Publishing.

Milne, A. L. (1986). Divorce mediation: A process of self-definition and self-determination. In N. S. Jacobson & A. S. Gurman (Eds.), *Clinical handbook of marital therapy* (pp. 197–216). New York: Guilford.

Money, J. (1987). Sin, sickness, or status? Homosexual gender identity and psychoneuroendocrinology. *American Psychologist, 42*, 384–399.

Monson, T. C., & Snyder, M. (1977). Actors, observers, and the attribution process. Toward a reconstruction. *Journal of Experimental Social Psychology, 13*, 89–111.

Morgan, C. S. (1980). Female and male attitudes toward life: Implications for theories of mental health. *Sex Roles, 6*, 367–380.

Morton, T. U. (1978). Intimacy and reciprocity of exchange: A comparison of spouses and strangers. *Journal of Personality and Social Psychology, 36*, 72–81.

Moustakas, C. (1972). *Loneliness and love.* New York: Prentice-Hall.

Muehlenhard, C. L. (1988). Misinterpreted dating behaviors and the risk of date rape. *Journal of Social and Clinical Psychology, 6*, 20–37.

Muehlenhard, C. L., & Linton, M. A. (1987). Date rape and sexual aggression in dating situations: Incidence and risk factors. *Journal of Counseling Psychology, 34*, 186–196.

Mueser, K. T., Grau, B. W., Sussman, S., & Rosen, A. J. (1984). You're only as pretty as you feel: Facial expression as a determinant of physical attractiveness. *Journal of Personality and Social Psychology, 46*, 469–478.

Munro, B., & Adams, G. R. (1978). Love American style: A test of role structure theory on changes in attitudes toward love. *Human Relations, 31*, 215–228.

Murphy, D. C., & Mendelson, L. A. (1973). Communication and adjustment in marriage: Investigating the relationships. *Family Process, 21*, 317–326.

Murstein, B. I. (1972a). Person perception and courtship progress among premarital couples. *Journal of Marriage and the Family, 34*, 621–626.

Murstein, B. I. (1972b). Physical attractiveness and marital choice. *Journal of Personality and Social Psychology, 22*, 8–12.

Murstein, B. I. (1976a). The stimulus-value-role theory of marital choice. In H. Grunebaum & J. Christ (Eds.), *Contemporary marriage: Structures, dynamics, and therapy* (pp. 165–168). Boston: Little, Brown.

Murstein, B. I. (1976b). *Who will marry whom? Theories and research in marital choice.* New York: Springer.

Murstein, B. I. (1986). *Paths to marriage.* Beverly Hills, CA: Sage.

Murstein, B. I. (1987). A clarification and extension of the SVR theory of dyadic pairing. *Journal of Marriage and the Family, 49*, 929–933.

Murstein, B. I., & Beck, G. D. (1972). Person perception, marriage adjustment and social desirability. *Journal of Consulting and Clinical Psychology, 39*, 396–403.

Murstein, B. I., Cerreto, M., & MacDonald, M. G. (1977). A theory and investigation of the effect of exchange-orientation on marriage and friendship. *Journal of Marriage and the Family, 39*, 543–548.

Murstein, B. I., & Christy, P. (1976). Physical attractiveness and marital adjustment in middle-aged couples. *Journal of Personality and Social Psychology, 34*, 537–542.

Napoleon, T., Chassin, L., & Young, R. D. (1980). A replication and extension of "Physical attractiveness and mental health." *Journal of Abnormal Psychology, 89*, 250–253.

Neimeyer, G. J. (1984). Cognitive complexity and marital satisfaction. *Journal of Social and Clinical Psychology, 2*, 258–263.

Neimeyer, R. A., & Neimeyer, G. J. (1983). Structural similarity in the acquaintance process. *Journal of Social and Clinical Psychology, 1*, 146–154.

Nettles, E. J., & Loevinger, J. (1983). Sex role expectation and ego level in relation to problem marriages. *Journal of Personality and Social Psychology, 45*, 676–687.

Nevid, J. S. (1984). Sex differences in factors of romantic attraction. *Sex Roles, 11*, 401–411.

The New York Review of Books (1990, July 19). p. 55.

Newcomb, M. D. (1986). Cohabitation, marriage, and divorce among adolescents and young adults. *Journal of Social and Personal Relationships, 3*, 473–494.

Newcomb, M. D. (1987). Cohabitation and marriage: A quest for independence and relatedness. In S. Oskamp (Ed.), *Social Psychology Annual: Vol. 7. Family processes and problems: Social psychological aspects* (pp. 128–156). Beverly Hills, CA: Sage.

Newcomb, M. D., & Bentler, P. M. (1980). Assessment of personality and demographic aspects of cohabitation and marital success. *Journal of Personality Assessment, 4*, 11–24.

Newcomb, M. D., & Bentler, P. M. (1981). Marital breakdown. In S. Duck & R. Gilmour (Eds.), *Personal relationships. 3: Personal relationships in disorder* (pp. 57–94). New York: Academic Press.

Newcomb, M. D., Huba, G. J., & Bentler, P. M. (1986). Determinants of sexual and dating behaviors among adolescents. *Journal of Personality and Social Psychology, 50*, 428–438.

Newcomb, T. M. (1959). Individual systems of orientation. In S. Koch (Ed.), *Psychology: A study of a science* (Vol. 3, pp. 384–422). New York: McGraw-Hill.

Newcomb, T. M. (1961). *The acquaintance process.* New York: Holt, Rinehart & Winston.

Newcomer, S., & Udry, J. R. (1987). Parental marital status effects on adolescent sexual behavior. *Journal of Marriage and the Family, 49,* 235–240.

Newman, H. M., & Langer, E. J. (1981). Post-divorce adaptation and the attribution of responsibility. *Sex Roles, 7,* 223–232.

Newman, H. M., & Langer, E. J. (1988). Investigating the development and courses of intimate relationships. In L. Y. Abramson (Ed.), *Social cognition and clinical psychology: A synthesis* (pp. 148–173). New York: Guilford.

Nias, D. K. B. (1979). Marital choice: Matching or complementation. In M. Cook & G. Wilson (Eds.), *Love and attraction* (pp. 151–155). Oxford: Pergamon Press.

Nida, S. A., & Koon, J. (1983). They get better looking at closing time around here, too. *Psychological Reports, 52,* 657–658.

Nielson, W. R., & MacDonald, M. R. (1988). Attributions of blame and coping following spinal cord injury: Is self-blame adaptive? *Journal of Social and Clinical Psychology, 7,* 163–175.

Nisbett, R. E., & Wilson, T. D. (1977). Telling more than we can know: Verbal reports on mental processes. *Psychological Review, 84,* 231–259.

Noller, P. (1980). Misunderstandings in marital communication: A study of couples' nonverbal communications. *Journal of Personality and Social Psychology 39,* 1135–1148.

Noller, P. (1981). Gender and marital adjustment level differences in decoding messages from spouses and strangers. *Journal of Personality and Social Psychology, 41,* 272–278.

Noller, P. (1982). Channel consistency and inconsistency in the communications of married couples. *Journal of Personality and Social Psychology, 43,* 732–741.

Noller, P. (1985). Negative communications in marriage. *Journal of Social and Personal Relationships, 2,* 289–301.

Noller, P. (1987). Nonverbal communication in marriage. In D. Perlman & S. Duck (Eds.), *Intimate relationships: Development, dynamics, and deterioration* (pp. 123–147). Newbury Park, CA: Sage.

Noller, P., & Venardos, C. (1986). Communication awareness in married couples. *Journal of Social and Personal Relationships, 3,* 31–42.

Norton, A. J. (1987, July/August). Families and children in the year 2000. *Children Today,* pp. 6–9.

Norton, A. J., & Moorman, J. E. (1987). Current trends in marriage and divorce among American women. *Journal of Marriage and the Family, 49,* 3–14.

Notarius, C. I., & Johnson, J. S. (1982). Emotional expression in husbands and wives. *Journal of Marriage and the Family, 44,* 483–489.

Novak, W. (1983, February). What do women really want? *McCall's.*

Oberstone, A., & Sukoneck, H. (1976). Psychological adjustment and life style of single lesbians and single heterosexual women. *Psychology of Women Quarterly, 1,* 172–188.

Offermann, L. R., & Schrier, P. E. (1985). Social influence strategies: The impact of sex, roles, and attitudes toward power. *Personality and Social Psychology Bulletin, 11,* 286–300.

O'Grady, K. E. (1989). Physical attractiveness, need for approval, social self-esteem, and maladjustment. *Journal of Social and Clinical Psychology, 8,* 62–69.

O'Leary, K. D. (1988). Physical aggression between spouses: A social learning theory perspective. In V. B. Van Hasselt, R. L. Morrison, A. S. Bellack, & M. Hersen (Eds.), *Handbook of family violence* (pp. 31–55). New York: Plenum.

O'Leary, K. D., Barling, J., Arias, I., Rosenbaum, A., Malone, J., & Tyree, A. (1989). Prevalence and stability of physical aggression between spouses. A longitudinal analysis. *Journal of Consulting and Clinical Psychology, 57,* 263–268.

O'Leary, K. D., & Kent, R. (1972). Behavior modification for social action: Research tactics and problems. In L. A. Hamerlynck, L. C. Handy, & E. J. Mash (Eds.), *Behavior change: Methodology, concepts and practice* (pp. 69–96). Champaign, IL: Research Press.

O'Leary, K. D., & Turkewitz, H. (1978a). Marital therapy from a behavioral perspective. In T. J. Paolino & B. McCrady (Eds.), *Marriage and marital therapy: Psychoanalytic, behavioral and systems theory perspectives* (pp. 240–297). New York: Brunner/Mazel.

O'Leary, K. D., & Turkewitz, H. (1978b). Methodological errors in marital and child treatment research. *Journal of Consulting and Clinical Psychology, 46,* 747–758.

O'Leary, K. D., & Vivian, D. (1990). Physical aggression in marriage. In F. D. Fincham & T. N. Bradbury (Eds.), *The psychology of marriage: Basic issues and applications* (pp. 323–348). New York: Guilford.

Olson, D. H. (1969). The measurement of family power by self-report and behavioral methods. *Journal of Marriage and the Family, 31,* 545–550.

Olson, D. H. (1977). Insiders' and outsiders' views of relationships: Research strategies. In G. Levinger & H. L. Raush (Eds.), *Close relationships* (pp. 115–135). Amherst: University of Massachusetts Press.

Olson, D. H., & Cromwell, R. E. (1975). Methodological issues in family power. In R. E. Cromwell & D. H. Olson (Eds.), *Power in families* (pp. 131–150). New York: Wiley.

Olson, D. H., Russell, C., & Sprenkle, J. (1980). Marriage and family therapy: A decade review. *Journal of Marriage and the Family, 42,* 973–994.

Omoto, A. M., & Snyder, M. (1990). Basic research in action: Volunteerism and society's response to AIDS. *Personality and Social Psychology Bulletin, 16,* 152–165.

Onward, Women! (1989, December 4). *Time,* pp. 80–89.

O'Rourke, J. F. (1963). Field and laboratory: The decision making behavior of family groups in two experimental conditions. *Sociometry, 26,* 422–435.

Orvis, B. R., Kelley, H. H., & Butler, D. (1976). Attributional conflict in young couples. In J. H. Harvey, W. J. Ickes, & R. E. Kidd (Eds.), *New directions in attribution research* (Vol. 1, pp. 353–386). Hillsdale, NJ: Erlbaum.

Ostrov, E., & Offer, D. (1980). Loneliness and the adolescent. In J. Hartog, J. R. Audy, & T. A. Cohen (Eds.), *The anatomy of loneliness* (pp. 170–185). New York: International Universities Press.

Pallak, M. S., & Heller, J. F. (1971). Interactive effects of commitment to justice interaction and threat to attitudinal freedom. *Journal of Personality and Social Psychology, 17*, 325–331.

Pam, A., Plutchik, R., & Conte, H. R. (1975). Love: A psychometric approach. *Psychological Reports, 37*, 83–88.

Parkes, C. M. (1975). What becomes of redundant world models? A contribution to the study of adaptation to change. *British Journal of Medical Psychology, 43*, 131–137.

Parks, M. R., Stan, C. M., & Eggert, L. L. (1983). Romantic involvement and social network involvement. *Social Psychology Quarterly, 46*, 116–131.

Parsons, T., & Bales, R. F. (1955). *Family socialization and interaction process.* Glencoe, IL: Free Press.

Patterson, M. L. (1988). Functions of nonverbal behavior in close relationships. In S. Duck (Ed.), *Handbook of personal relationships: Theory, research, and interventions* (pp. 41–56). New York: Wiley.

Patton, B. R., & Ritter, B. (1976). *Living together . . . Female/male communication.* Columbus, OH: Charles E. Merrill.

Pearson, J., & Thoennes, H. (1982). Mediation and divorce: The benefits outweigh the costs. *Family Advocate, 4*, 25–32.

Pedhazur, E. J. (1982). *Multiple regression in behavioral research: Explanation and prediction* (2nd ed.). New York: Holt, Rinehart & Winston.

Peele, S. (1988). Fools for love: The romantic ideal, psychological theory, and addictive love. In R. J. Sternberg & M. L. Barnes (Eds.), *The psychology of love* (pp. 159–188). New Haven, CT: Yale University Press.

Pennebaker, J. W. (1989). Confession, inhibition, and disease. In L. Berkowitz (Ed.), *Advances in experimental social psychology* (Vol. 22, pp. 211–244). San Diego, CA: Academic Press.

Pennebaker, J. W., Colder, M., & Sharp, L. K. (1990). Accelerating the coping process. *Journal of Personality and Social Psychology, 58*, 528–537.

Pennebaker, J. W., Dyer, M. A., Caulkins, R. J., Litowitz, D. L., Ackerman, P. L., Anderson, D. B., & McGraw, K. M. (1979). Don't the girls get prettier at closing time: A country and western application to psychology. *Personality and Social Psychology Bulletin, 5*, 122–125.

Peplau, L. A. (1979). Power in dating relationships. In J. Freeman (Ed.), *Women: A feminist perspective* (2nd ed., pp. 106–121). Palo Alto, CA: Mayfield.

Peplau, L. A., Bikson, T. K., Rook, K. S., & Goodchilds, J. D. (1982). Being old and living alone. In L. A. Peplau & D. Perlman (Eds.), *Loneliness: A sourcebook of current theory, research, and therapy* (pp. 327–347). New York: Wiley Interscience.

Peplau, L. A., Cochran, S. D., Rook, K., & Padesky, C. (1978). Loving women: Attachment and autonomy in lesbian relationships. *Journal of Social Issues, 34*, 7–27.

Peplau, L. A., & Gordon, S. L. (1983). The intimate relationships of lesbians and gay men. In E. R. Allgeier & N. B. McCormick (Eds.), *Changing boundaries: Gender roles and sexual behavior* (pp. 226–244). Palo Alto, CA: Mayfield.

Peplau, L. A., & Gordon, S. L. (1985). Women and men in love: Gender differences in close relationships. In V. E. O'Leary, R. K. Unger, & B. S. Wallston (Eds.), *Women, gender, and social psychology* (pp. 257–291). Hillsdale, NJ: Erlbaum.

Peplau, L. A., Miceli, M., & Morasch, B. (1982). Loneliness and self-evaluation. In L. A. Peplau & D. Perlman (Eds.), *Loneliness: A sourcebook of current theory, research, and therapy* (pp. 135–151). New York: Wiley Interscience.

Peplau, L. A., Rubin, Z., & Hill, C. T. (1977). Sexual intimacy in dating relationships. *Journal of Social Issues, 33*, 86–109.

Peplau, L. A., Russell, D., & Heim, M. (1979). The experience of loneliness. In I. Frieze, D. Bar-Tal, & J. Carroll (Eds.), *New approaches to social problems: Applications of attribution theory* (pp. 53–78). San Francisco: Jossey-Bass.

Perlman, D., & Fehr, B. (1987). The development of intimate relationships. In D. Perlman & S. Duck (Eds.), *Intimate relationships: Development, dynamics, and deterioration* (pp. 13–42). Newbury Park, CA: Sage.

Perlman, D., & Oskamp, S. (1971). The effects of picture context and exposure frequency on evaluations of negroes and whites. *Journal of Experimental Social Psychology, 7*, 503–514.

Perlman, D., & Peplau, L. A. (1981). Toward a social psychology of loneliness. In S. Duck & R. Gilmour (Eds.), *Personal relationships. 3: Personal relationships in disorder* (pp. 31–56). New York: Academic Press.

Perloff, L. S. (1987). Social comparison and illusion of invulnerability to negative life events. In C. R. Snyder & C. E. Ford (Eds.), *Coping with negative life events: Clinical and social psychological perspectives* (pp. 217–242). New York: Plenum.

Person, E. S. (1988). *Dreams of love and fateful encounters.* New York: Norton.

Peterson, C. (1981). Equity, equality, and marriage. *Journal of Social Psychology, 113*, 283–284.

Peterson, C., Rosenbaum, A. C., & Conn, M. K. (1985). Depressive mood reactions to breaking up. Testing the learned helplessness model of depression. *Journal of Social and Clinical Psychology, 3*, 161–169.

Peterson, C. D., Baucom, D. H., Elliott, M. J., & Farr, P. A. (1989). The relationship between sex role identity and marital adjustment. *Sex Roles, 21*, 775–787.

Peterson, D. R. (1983). Conflict. In H. H. Kelley, E. Berscheid, A. Christensen, et al. (Eds.), *Close relationships* (pp. 360–396). New York: Freeman.

Peterson, J. L., & Nord, C. W. (1990). The regular receipt of child support: A multistage process. *Journal of Marriage and the Family, 52*, 539–551.

Pettit, E. J., & Bloom, B. L. (1984). Whose decision was it? The effects of initiator status on adjustment to marital disruption. *Journal of Marriage and the Family, 46*, 587–596.

Petty, R. E., & Mirels, H. L. (1981). Intimacy and scarcity of self-disclosure: Effects on interpersonal attraction for males and females. *Personality and Social Psychology Bulletin, 7*, 493–503.

Pfieffer, S. M., & Wong, P. T. P. (1989). Multidimensional jealousy. *Journal of Social and Personal Relationships, 6*, 181–196.

Phillips, R. (1988). *Putting asunder: A history of divorce in Western society.* Cambridge: Cambridge University Press.

Philliber, W. W., & Vannoy-Hiller, D. (1990). The effect of husband's occupational attainment on wife's achievement. *Journal of Marriage and the Family, 52*, 323–329.

Pietromonaco, P. R., & Rook, K. S. (1987). Decision style in depression: The contribution of perceived risk versus benefits. *Journal of Personality and Social Psychology, 52*, 399–408.

Pike, G. R., & Sillars, A. L. (1985). Reciprocity of marital communication. *Journal of Social and Personal Relationships, 2*, 303–324.

Pineo, P. C. (1961). Disenchantment in the later years of marriage. *Journal of Marriage and Family Living, 23*, 3–11.

Pines, A., & Aronson, E. (1983). Antecedents, correlates, and consequences of sexual jealousy. *Journal of Personality, 51*, 108–136.

Pinto, R. P., & Hollandsworth, J. G., Jr. (1984). A measure of possessiveness in intimate relationships. *Journal of Social and Clinical Psychology, 2*, 273–279.

Pistole, M. C. (1989). Attachment in adult romantic relationships: Style of conflict resolution and relationship satisfaction. *Journal of Social and Personal Relationships, 6*, 505–510.

Pittman, T. S., & Pittman, L. L. (1980). Deprivation of control and the attribution process. *Journal of Personality and Social Psychology, 39*, 377–389.

Podsakoff, P. M., & Schriesheim, C. A. (1985). Field studies of French and Raven's bases of power: Critique, reanalysis, and suggestions for future research. *Psychological Bulletin, 97*, 387–411.

Pollak, S., & Gilligan, C. (1982). Images of violence in Thematic Apperception scores. *Journal of Personality and Social Psychology, 42*, 159–167.

Pollak, S., & Gilligan, C. (1983). Differing about differences: The incidence and interpretation of violent fantasies in men and women. *Journal of Personality and Social Psychology, 45*, 1172–1175.

Pollak, S., & Gilligan, C. (1985). Killing the messenger. *Journal of Personality and Social Psychology, 48*, 374–375.

Poppen, P. J., & Segal, N. J. (1988). The influence of sex and sex role orientation on sexual coercion. *Sex Roles, 19*, 689–701.

Powers, E. A., Keith, P., & Goudy, W. H. (1975). Family relationships and friendships. In R. C. Atchley (Ed.), *Rural environments and aging* (pp. 67–90). Washington, DC: Gerontological Society.

Pratt, M. W., Golding, G., Huster, W., & Sampson, R. (1989). Sex differences in adult moral orientation. *Journal of Personality, 56*, 373–391.

Price, R. A., & Vandenberg, S. S. (1979). Matching for physical attractiveness. *Personality and Social Psychology Bulletin, 5*, 398–400.

Prochaska, J., & Prochaska, J. (1978). Twentieth century trends in marriage and family therapy. In T. J. Paolino & B. S. McCrady (Eds.), *Marriage and marital therapy: Psychoanalytic, behavioral and systems theory perspectives* (pp. 1–24). New York: Brunner/Mazel.

Radloff, L. (1975). Sex differences in depression: The effects of occupation and marital status. *Sex Roles, 1*, 249–269.

Radlove, S. (1983). Sexual response and gender roles. In E. R. Allgeier & N. B. McCormick (Eds.), *Changing boundaries: Gender roles and sexual behavior* (pp. 87–105). Palo Alto, CA: Mayfield.

Rands, M., Levinger, G., & Mellinger, G. (1981). Patterns of conflict resolution and marital satisfaction. *Journal of Family Issues, 2*, 297–321.

Rankin, R. P., & Manaker, J. S. (1985). The duration of marriage in a divorcing population: The impact of children. *Journal of Marriage and the Family, 47*, 43–52.

Raschke, H. J. (1977). The role of social participation in postseparation and postdivorce adjustment. *Journal of Divorce, 1*, 129–140.

Raush, H. L., Barry, W. A., Hertel, R. K., & Swain, M. A. (1974). *Communication, conflict and marriage.* San Francisco: Jossey-Bass.

Raven, B. H., Centers, R., & Rodrigues, A. (1975). The bases of conjugal power. In R. E. Cromwell & D. H. Olson (Eds.), *Power in families* (pp. 217–232). New York: Wiley.

Regan, M. C., & Roland, H. E. (1985). Rearranging family and career priorities: Professional women and men of the eighties. *Journal of Marriage and the Family, 47*, 985–992.

Reik, T. (1944/1957). A psychologist looks at love. In T. Reik (Ed.), *Of love and lust* (pp. 1–194). New York: Farrar, Straus, and Cudahy.

Reis, H. T., Nezlek, J., & Wheeler, L. (1980). Physical attractiveness in social interaction. *Journal of Personality and Social Psychology, 38*, 604–617.

Reis, H. T., Senchak, M., & Solomon, B. (1985). Sex differences in the intimacy of social interaction: Further examination of potential explanations. *Journal of Personality and Social Psychology, 48*, 1204–1217.

Reis, H. T., & Shaver, P. (1988). Intimacy as an interpersonal process. In S. Duck (Ed.), *Handbook of personal relationships* (pp. 367–389). New York: Wiley.

Reis, H. T., Wheeler, L., Spiegel, N., Kernis, M. H., Nezlek, J., & Perri, M. (1982). Physical attractiveness in social interaction: II. Why does appearance affect social experience? *Journal of Personality and Social Psychology, 43*, 979–996.

Reisenzein, R. (1983). The Schachter theory of emotion: Two decades later. *Psychological Bulletin, 94*, 239–264.

Reiss, I. L. (1960). Toward a sociology of the heterosexual love relationship. *Marriage and Family Living, 22*, 139–145.

Reiss, I. L. (1986). A sociological journey into sexuality. *Journal of Marriage and the Family, 48*, 233–242.

Remondet, J. H., Hansson, R. O., Rule, B., & Winfrey, G. (1987). Rehearsal for widowhood. *Journal of Social and Clinical Psychology, 5*, 285–297.

Rempel, J. K., Holmes, J. G., & Zanna, M. P. (1985). Trust in close relationships. *Journal of Personality and Social Psychology, 49*, 95–112.

Repetti, R. L. (1989). Effects of daily workload on subsequent behavior during marital interaction: The roles of social withdrawal and spouse support. *Journal of Personality and Social Psychology, 57*, 651–659.

Repetti, R. L., & Crosby, F. (1984). Gender and depression: Exploring the adult-role explanation. *Journal of Social and Clinical Psychology, 2*, 57–70.

Repetti, R. L., Matthews, K. A., & Waldron, I. (1989). Employment and women's health: Effects of paid employment on women's mental and physical health. *American Psychologist, 44*, 1394–1401.

Revenson, T. A. (1981). Coping with loneliness: The impact of causal attributions. *Personality and Social Psychology Bulletin, 7*, 565–571.

Rice, L. N., & Rice, D. G. (1985). *Divorce therapy*. New York: Guilford.

Rich, S. (1989, December 8). Child-support collections jump in '88. *The Washington Post*, p. A13.

Ridley, C., Peterman, D., & Avery, A. (1978). Cohabitation: Does it make for a better marriage? *Family Coordinator, 27*, 129–136.

Riley, D., & Eckenrode, J. (1986). Social ties: Subgroup differences in costs and benefits. *Journal of Personality and Social Psychology, 51*, 770–778.

Rindfuss, R. R., & Stephen, E. H. (1990). Marital noncohabitation: Separation does not make the heart grow fonder. *Journal of Marriage and the Family, 52*, 259–270.

Riordan, C. A., Quigley-Fernandez, B., & Tedeschi, J. T. (1982). Some variables affecting changes in interpersonal attraction. *Journal of Experimental Social Psychology, 18,* 358–374.

Riordan, C. A., & Tedeschi, J. T. (1983). Attraction in aversive environments: Some evidence for classical conditioning and negative reinforcement. *Journal of Personality and Social Psychology, 44,* 683–692.

Riskin, J., & Faunce, E. E. (1972). An evaluative review of family interaction research. *Family Process, 11,* 365–455.

Robbins, C., Kaplan, H. B., & Martin, S. S. (1985). Antecedents of pregnancy among unmarried adolescents. *Journal of Marriage and the Family, 47,* 567–583.

Roberts, L. J., & Krokoff, L. L. (1990). A time-series analysis of withdrawal, hostility, and displeasure in satisfied and dissatisfied marriages. *Journal of Marriage and the Family, 52,* 95–105.

Robin, A. L., & Foster, S. L. (1989). *Negotiating parent-adolescent conflict: A behavioral family systems approach.* New York: Guilford.

Robins, L. N., Helzer, J. E., Weissman, M. M., Orvaschel, H., Gruenberg, E., Burke, J. D., & Reigier, D. A. (1984). Lifetime prevalence of specific psychiatric disorders in three sites. *Archives of General Psychiatry, 41,* 949–958.

Rodin, J., & Ickovics, J. R. (1990). Women's health: Review and research agenda as we approach the 21st century. *American Psychologist, 45,* 1018–1034.

Rodin, M. (1982). Non-engagement, failure to engage, and disengagement. In S. Duck (Ed.), *Personal Relationships 4: Dissolving relationships* (pp. 31–49). New York: Academic Press.

Rodman, H. (1972). Marital power and the theory of resources in cultural context. *Journal of Comparative Family Studies, 3,* 50–69.

Rofé, Y. (1984). Stress and affiliation: A utility theory. *Psychological Bulletin, 91,* 235–250.

Rogler, L. H., & Procidano, M. E. (1989). Egalitarian spouse relations and wives' marital satisfaction in intergenerationally linked Puerto Rican families. *Journal of Marriage and the Family, 51,* 37–39.

Rollins, B., & Cannon, K. (1974). Marital satisfaction over the family life cycle: A reevaluation. *Journal of Marriage and the Family, 36,* 271–282.

Rollins, B. C., & Galligan, R. (1978). The developing child and marital satisfaction of parents. In R. M. Lerner & G. B. Spanier (Eds.), *Child influences on marital and family interaction* (pp. 71–105). New York: Academic Press.

Rook, K. (1984). Promoting social bonding: Strategies for helping the lonely and socially isolated. *American Psychologist, 39,* 1389–1407.

Rook, K. (1988). Toward a more differentiated view of loneliness. In S. Duck (Ed.), *Handbook of personal relationships: Theory, research, and interventions* (pp. 571–589). New York: Wiley.

Rook, K. S. (1984). The negative side of social interaction: Impact on psychological well-being. *Journal of Personality and Social Psychology, 46,* 1097–1108.

Rook, K. S. (1987). Reciprocity of social exchange and social satisfaction among older women. *Journal of Personality and Social Psychology, 52,* 145–154.

Rook, K. S., & Peplau, L. A. (1982). Perspectives on helping the lonely. In L. A. Peplau & D. Perlman (Eds.), *Loneliness: A sourcebook of current theory, research, and therapy* (pp. 351–378). New York: Wiley Interscience.

Rook, K. S., & Pietromonaco, P. (1987). Close relationships: Ties that heal or ties that bind? In W. H. Jones & D. Perlman (Eds.), *Advances in personal relationships* (Vol. 1, pp. 1–35). Greenwich, CT: JAI Press.

Rose, S. M. (1985). Same- and cross-sex friendships and the psychology of homosociology. *Sex Roles, 12*, 63–74.

Rosenbaum, A., & O'Leary, K. D. (1986). The treatment of marital violence. In N. S. Jacobson & A. S. Gurman (Eds.), *Clinical handbook of marital therapy* (pp. 385–405). New York: Guilford.

Rosenbaum, M. E. (1986). The repulsion hypothesis: On the nondevelopment of relationships. *Journal of Personality and Social Psychology, 51*, 1156–1166.

Rosenblatt, A., & Greenberg, J. (1988). Depression and interpersonal attraction: The role of perceived similarity. *Journal of Personality and Social Psychology, 55*, 112–119.

Rosenblatt, P. C. (1977). Needed research on commitment in marriage. In G. Levinger & H. L. Raush (Eds.), *Close relationships: Perspectives on the meaning of intimacy* (pp. 73–86). Amherst: University of Massachusetts Press.

Rosenthal, R., & DePaulo, B. (1979). Sex differences in eavesdropping on nonverbal cues. *Journal of Personality and Social Psychology, 37*, 273–285.

Ross, E. A. (1921). *Principles of sociology.* New York: Century.

Ross, M., & Sicoly, F. (1979). Egocentric biases in availability and attribution. *Journal of Personality and Social Psychology, 37*, 322–336.

Rotter, J. B. (1966). Generalized expectancies for internal versus external control of reinforcement. *Psychological Monographs, 80* (1, Whole No. 609).

Rubenstein, C. M., & Shaver, P. (1980). Loneliness in two northeastern cities. In J. Hartog, J. R. Audy, & Y. A. Cohen (Eds.), *The anatomy of loneliness* (pp. 319–337). New York: International Universities Press.

Rubenstein, C. M., & Shaver, P. (1982). *In search of intimacy.* New York: Delacorte Press.

Rubenstein, C. M., Shaver, P., & Peplau, L. A. (1979). Loneliness. *Human Nature, 2*, 58–65.

Rubin, Z. (1973). *Liking and loving.* New York: Holt, Rinehart & Winston.

Rubin, Z. (1974). Lovers and other strangers: The development of intimacy in encounters and relationships. *American Scientist, 62*, 182–190.

Rubin, Z., Hill, C. T., Peplau, L. A., & Dunkel-Schetter, C. (1980). Self-disclosure in dating couples: Sex roles and the ethic of openness. *Journal of Marriage and the Family, 42*, 305–317.

Rubin, Z., & Levinger, G. (1974). Theory and data badly rated: A critique of Murstein's SVR and Lewis's PDF models of mate selection. *Journal of Marriage and the Family, 36*, 226–231.

Rubin, Z., & Mitchell, C. (1976). Couples research as couples counseling: Some unintended effects of studying close relationships. *American Psychologist, 31*, 17–25.

Rubin, Z., Peplau, L. A., & Hill, C. T. (1981). Loving and leaving: Sex differences in romantic attachments. *Sex Roles, 7*, 821–835.

Ruble, D. N., Fleming, A. S., Hackel, L. S., & Stangor, C. (1988). Changes in the marital relationship during the transition to first time motherhood: Effects of violated expectations concerning division of household labor. *Journal of Personality and Social Psychology, 55*, 78–87.

Rusbult, C. E. (1980a). Commitment and satisfaction in romantic associations: A test of the investment model. *Journal of Experimental Social Psychology, 16,* 172–186.

Rusbult, C. E. (1980b). Satisfaction and commitment in friendships. *Representative Research in Social Psychology, 11,* 96–105.

Rusbult, C. E. (1983). A longitudinal test of the investment model: The development (and deterioration) of satisfaction and commitment in heterosexual involvement. *Journal of Personality and Social Psychology, 45,* 101–117.

Rusbult, C. E. (1987). Responses to dissatisfaction in close relationships: The exit-voice-loyalty-neglect model. In D. Perlman & S. Duck (Eds.), *Intimate relationships: Development, dynamics, and deterioration* (pp. 209–237). Newbury Park, CA: Sage.

Rusbult, C. E., Johnson, D. J., & Morrcw, G. D. (1986). Impact of couple patterns of problem solving on distress and nondistress in dating relationships. *Journal of Personality and Social Psychology, 50,* 744–753.

Rusbult, C. E., & Zembrodt, I. M. (1983). Responses to dissatisfaction in romantic involvement: A multidimensional scaling analysis. *Journal of Experimental Social Psychology, 19,* 274–293.

Rusbult, C. E., Zembrodt, I. M., & Gunn, L. K. (1982). Exit, voice, loyalty, and neglect: Responses to dissatisfaction in romantic involvements. *Journal of Personality and Social Psychology, 43,* 1230–1242.

Rusbult, C. E., Zembrodt, I. M., & Iwaniszek, J. (1986). The impact of gender and sex-role orientation on responses to dissatisfaction in close relationships. *Sex Roles, 15,* 1–20.

Russell, B. (1938). *Power.* London: Allen and Unwin.

Russell, D., Cutrona, C. E., Rose, J., & Yurko, K. (1984). Social and emotional loneliness: An examination of Weiss's typology of loneliness. *Journal of Personality and Social Psychology, 46,* 1313–1321.

Russell, D., Peplau, L. A., & Cutrona, C. E. (1980). The revised UCLA Loneliness Scale: Concurrent and discriminant validity evidence. *Journal of Personality and Social Psychology, 39,* 472–480.

Russell, D. E. (1982). *Rape in marriage.* New York: Macmillan.

Rutter, M. (1979). Maternal deprivation. 1972–1978: New findings, new concepts, new approaches. *Child Development, 50,* 283–305.

Ryder, R. G. (1973). Longitudinal data relating marriage satisfaction to having a child. *Journal of Marriage and the Family, 35,* 604–606.

Sabatelli, R. M., Buck, R., & Dreyer, A. (1980). Communication via facial cues in intimate dyads. *Personality and Social Psychology Bulletin, 6,* 242–247.

Sabatelli, R. M., Buck, R., & Dreyer, A. (1982). Nonverbal communication accuracy in married couples: Relationship with marital complaints. *Journal of Personality and Social Psychology, 43,* 1088–1097.

Sabatelli, R. M., & Cecil-Pigo, E. F. (1985). Relational interdependence and commitment in marriage. *Journal of Marriage and the Family, 47,* 931–937.

Sachs, D. H. (1976). The effects of similarity, evaluation, and self-esteem on interpersonal attraction. *Representative Research in Social Psychology, 7,* 44–50.

Sadalla, E. K., Kenrick, D. T., & Vershure, B. (1987). Dominance and heterosexual attraction. *Journal of Personality and Social Psychology, 52,* 730–738.

Saegert, S. C., Swap, W., & Zajonc, R. (1973). Exposure, context, and interpersonal attraction. *Journal of Personality and Social Psychology, 25,* 234–242.

Safilios-Rothschild, C. (1970). The study of family power structure: A review, 1960–1969. *Journal of Marriage and the Family, 32,* 535–552.

Safilios-Rothschild, C. (1976a). The dimensions of power distribution in the family. In H. Grunebaum & J. Christ (Eds.), *Contemporary marriage: Structure, dynamics and therapy* (pp. 275–292). Boston: Little, Brown.

Safilios-Rothschild, C. (1976b). A macro- and micro-examination of family power and love: An exchange model. *Journal of Marriage and the Family, 38,* 355–362.

Safilios-Rothschild, C. (1977). *Love, sex, sex roles.* Englewood Cliffs, NJ: Prentice-Hall.

Safilios-Rothschild, C. (1981). Toward a social psychology of relationships. *Psychology of Women Quarterly, 5,* 377–384.

Salovey, P., & Rodin, J. (1984). Some antecedents and consequences of social-comparison jealousy. *Journal of Personality and Social Psychology, 47,* 780–792.

Salovey, P., & Rodin, J. (1986). The differentiation of social-comparison jealousy and romantic jealousy. *Journal of Personality and Social Psychology, 50,* 1000–1112.

Salovey, P., & Rodin, J. (1988). Coping with envy and jealousy. *Journal of Social and Clinical Psychology, 7,* 15–33.

Salovey, P., & Rodin, J. (1989). Envy and jealousy in close relationships. In C. Hendrick (Ed.), *Review of personality and social psychology: Vol. 10. Close relationships* (pp. 221–246). Newbury Park, CA: Sage.

Santrock, J. W., & Sitterle, K. A. (1987). Parent-child relationships in stepmother families. In K. Pasley & M. Ihinger-Tallman (Eds.), *Remarriage and stepparenting* (pp. 273–299). New York: Guilford.

Sarason, B. R., Sarason, I. G., Hacker, T. A., & Basham, R. B. (1985). Concomitants of social support: Social skills, physical attractiveness, and gender. *Journal of Personality and Social Psychology, 49,* 469–480.

Sarnoff, I., & Zimbardo, P. (1961). Anxiety, fear, and social affiliation. *Journal of Abnormal and Social Psychology, 62,* 356–363.

Satir, V. (1967). *Conjoint family therapy.* Palo Alto, CA: Science and Behavior Books.

Scanzoni, J. (1979). Social processes and power in families. In W. R. Burr, R. Hill, F. I. Nye, and I. L. Reiss (Eds.), *Contemporary theories about the family: Research-based theories* (Vol. 1, pp. 295–316). New York: Free Press.

Scarr, S., Phillips, D., & McCartney, K. (1989). Working mothers and their families. *American Psychologist, 44,* 1402–1409.

Schachter, S. (1959). *The psychology of affiliation: Experimental studies of the sources of gregariousness.* Stanford, CA: Stanford University Press.

Schachter, S. (1964). The interaction of cognitive and physiological determinants of emotional state. In L. Berkowitz (Ed.), *Advances in experimental social psychology* (Vol. 1, pp. 49–80). New York: Academic Press.

Schachter, S., & Singer, J. E. (1979). Comments on the Maslach and Marshall-Zimbardo experiments. *Journal of Personality and Social Psychology, 37,* 989–995.

Schafer, R. B., & Keith, P. M. (1980). Equity and depression among married couples. *Social Psychology Quarterly, 43,* 430–435.

Schlenker, B. R., & Leary, M. R. (1982). Social anxiety and self-presentation: A conceptualization and model. *Psychological Bulletin, 92*, 641–669.

Schmidt, N., & Sermat, V. (1983). Measuring loneliness in different relationships. *Journal of Personality and Social Psychology, 44*, 1038–1047.

Schoenrade, P. A., Batson, C. D., Brandt, J. R., & Loud, R. E., Jr. (1986). Attachment, accountability, and motivation to benefit another not in distress. *Journal of Personality and Social Psychology, 51*, 557–563.

Schullo, S. A., & Alperson, B. L. (1984). Interpersonal phenomenology as a function of sexual orientation, sex, sentiment, and trait categories in long-term dyadic relationships. *Journal of Personality and Social Psychology, 47*, 983–1002.

Schultz, N. R., Jr., & Moore, D. (1984). Loneliness: Correlates, attributions, and coping among older adults. *Personality and Social Psychology Bulletin, 10*, 67–77.

Schultz, N. R., Jr., & Moore, D. (1986). The loneliness experience of college students: Sex differences. *Personality and Social Psychology Bulletin, 12*, 111–119.

Schultz, N. R., Jr., & Moore, D. (1988). Loneliness: Differences across three age levels. *Journal of Social and Personal Relationships, 5*, 275–284.

Schumm, W. R., & Bugaighis, M. A. (1986). Marital quality over the marital career: Alternative explanations. *Journal of Marriage and the Family, 48*, 165–168.

Schwartz, G., & Marten, D. (1980). *Love and commitment.* Beverly Hills, CA: Sage Publications.

Scoresby, A. L. (1977). *The marriage dialogue.* Reading, MA: Addison-Wesley.

Sears, D. O. (1986). College sophomores in the laboratory: Influences of a narrow data base on social psychology's view of human nature. *Journal of Personality and Social Psychology, 51*, 515–530.

Secord, P. F. (1983). Imbalanced sex ratios: The social consequences. *Personality and Social Psychology Bulletin, 9*, 525–543.

Segal, M. (1987, September). AIDS education. *FDA Consumer*, pp. 26–30.

Seligman, C., Fazio, R. H., & Zanna, M. P. (1980). Effects of salience of extrinsic rewards on liking and loving. *Journal of Personality and Social Psychology, 38*, 453–460.

Seligmann, J. (1990, Winter/Spring). Variations on a theme. *Newsweek Special Edition*, pp. 38–46.

Seltzer, J. A., Schaeffer, N. C., & Charng, H. (1989). Family ties after divorce: The relationship between visiting and paying child support. *Journal of Marriage and the Family, 51*, 1013–1031.

Sermat, V. (1980). Some situational and personality correlates of loneliness. In J. Hartog, J. R. Audy, & Y. A. Cohen (Eds.), *The anatomy of loneliness* (pp. 305–318). New York: International Universities Press.

Sexton, C. S., & Perlman, D. S. (1989). Couples' career orientation, gender role orientation, and perceived equity as determinants of marital power. *Journal of Marriage and the Family, 51*, 933–941.

Shapiro, A., & Swenson, C. (1969). Patterns of self-disclosure among married couples. *Journal of Counseling Psychology, 16*, 179–180.

Shaver, K. G. (1985). *The attribution of blame.* New York: Springer-Verlag.

Shaver, P., Furman, W., & Buhrmester, D. (1985). Transition to college: Network changes, social skills, and loneliness. In S. Duck & D. Perlman

(Eds.), *Understanding personal relationships: An interdisciplinary approach* (pp. 193–219). London: Sage.

Shaver, P., Hazan, C., & Bradshaw, D. (1988). Love as attachment: The integration of three behavioral systems. In R. J. Sternberg & M. L. Barnes (Eds.), *The psychology of love* (pp. 68–99). New Haven, CT: Yale University Press.

Shaver, P., & Rubenstein, C. (1980). Childhood attachment experience and adult loneliness. In L. Wheeler (Ed.), *Review of personality and social psychology* (Vol. 1, pp. 42–73). Beverly Hills, CA: Sage Publications.

Shaver, P. R., & Brennan, K. A. (1990). Measures of depression and loneliness. In J. P. Robinson, P. R. Shaver, & L. S. Wrightsman (Eds.), *Measures of personality and social psychological attitudes* (pp. 195–289). Orlando, FL: Academic Press.

Shaver, P. R., & Hazan, C. (1988). A biased overview of the study of love. *Journal of Social and Personal Relationships, 5*, 473–501.

Shaw, G. B. (1963). *Complete plays with prefaces* (Vol. 4). New York: Dodd, Mead.

Shephard, J. W., & Ellis, H. D. (1972). Physical attractiveness and selection of marriage partners. *Psychological Reports, 30*, 1004.

Shepperd, J. A., & Strathman, A. J. (1989). Attractiveness and height: The role of stature in dating preference, frequency of dating, and perceptions of attractiveness. *Personality and Social Psychology Bulletin, 15*, 617–627.

Sherrod, D. (1989). The influence of gender on same-sex friendships. In C. Hendrick (Ed.), *Review of personality and social psychology: Vol. 10. Close relationships* (pp. 164–186). Newbury Park, CA: Sage Publications.

Shettel-Neuber, J., Bryson, J. B., & Young, L. E. (1978). Physical attractiveness of the "other person" and jealousy. *Personality and Social Psychology Bulletin, 4*, 612–615.

Shilts, R. (1987). *And the band played on.* New York: St. Martin's Press.

Shotland, R. L. (1989). A model of the causes of date rape in developing and close relationships. In C. Hendrick (Ed.), *Review of personality and social psychology: Vol. 10. Close relationships* (pp. 247–270). Newbury Park, CA: Sage.

Sicoly, F., & Ross, M. (1978). "Interpersonal perceptions of division of labor and marital satisfaction." Unpublished paper, University of Waterloo, Toronto, Ontario.

Sieber, J. (1974). Toward a theory of role accumulation. *American Sociological Review, 39*, 567–578.

Sigall, H., & Landy, D. (1973). Radiating beauty: The effects of having a physically attractive partner on person perception. *Journal of Personality and Social Psychology, 28*, 218–224.

Sigall, H., & Michela, J. (1976). I'll bet you say that to all the girls: Physical attractiveness and reactions to praise. *Journal of Personality, 44*, 611–626.

Sigelman, C. K., Berry, C. J., & Wiles, K. A. (1984). Violence in college students' dating relationships. *Journal of Applied Social Psychology, 14*, 530–548.

Silverman, I. (1971, September). Physical attractiveness and courtship. *Sexual Behavior*, 22–25.

Simenquer, J., & Carroll, D. (1982). Singles: The new Americans. New York: Simon & Schuster.

Simpson, J. A. (1987). The dissolution of romantic relationships: Factors involved in relationship stability and emotional distress. *Journal of Personality and Social Psychology, 53*, 683–692.

Simpson, J. A. (1990). Influence of attachment styles on romantic relationships. *Journal of Personality and Social Psychology, 59*, 971–980.

Simpson, J. A., Campbell, B., & Berscheid, E. (1986). The association between romantic love and marriage: Kephart (1967) twice revisited. *Personality and Social Psychology Bulletin, 12*, 363–372.

Skolnick, A. (1978). *The intimate environment: Exploring marriage and the family* (2nd ed.). Boston: Little, Brown.

Skolnick, A. (1981). Married lives: Longitudinal perspectives on marriage. In D. Eichorn, J. Clausen, N. Haan, M. Honzik, & P. Mussen (Eds.), *Present and past in middle life* (pp. 269–298). New York: Academic Press.

Slack, D., & Vaux, A. (1988). Undesirable life events and depression: The role of event appraisals and social support. *Journal of Social and Clinical Psychology, 7*, 290–296.

Slater, E. J., & Calhoun, K. S. (1988). Familial conflict and marital dissolution: Effects on the social functioning of college students. *Journal of Social and Clinical Psychology, 6*, 118–126.

Slater, P. E. (1968). Some social consequences of temporary systems. In W. G. Bennes & P. E. Slater (Eds.), *The temporary society* (pp. 77–96). New York: Harper & Row.

Sloan, W. W., Jr., & Solano, C. (1984). The conversational styles of lonely males with strangers and roommates. *Personality and Social Psychology Bulletin, 10*, 293–301.

Sluzki, C. E. (1978). Marital therapy from a systems theory perspective. In T. J. Paolino, Jr., & B. S. McCrady (Eds.), *Marriage and marital therapy. Psychoanalytic, behavioral and systems theory perspectives* (pp. 366–394). New York: Brunner/Mazel.

Smeaton, G., Byrne, D., & Murnen, S. K. (1989). The repulsion hypothesis revisited: Similarity irrelevance or dissimilarity bias? *Journal of Personality and Social Psychology, 56*, 54–59.

Smith, E. R. (1978). Specifications and estimation of causal models in psychology: Comment on Tesser and Paulus. *Journal of Personality and Social Psychology, 36*, 34–38.

Smith, E. R., & Miller, F. S. (1978). Limits on perception of cognitive processes: A reply to Nisbett & Wilson. *Psychological Review, 85*, 355–362.

Smith, R. H., Kim, S. H., & Parrott, W. G. (1988). Envy and jealousy: Semantic problems and experiential distinctions. *Personality and Social Psychology Bulletin, 14*, 401–409.

Smolen, R. C., Spiegel, D. A., Shaukat, A. K., & Schwartz, J. F. (1988). Examination of marital adjustment and marital assertion in depressed and nondepressed women. *Journal of Social and Clinical Psychology, 7*, 284–289.

Snell, W. E., Jr., Hawkins, R. C., II, & Belk, S. S. (1988). Stereotypes about male sexuality and the use of social influence strategies in intimate relationships. *Journal of Social and Clinical Psychology, 7*, 42–48.

Snyder, C. R., Higgins, R. L., & Stucky, R. J. (1983). *Excuses: Masquerades in search of grace.* New York: Wiley.

Snyder, M. (1974). The self-monitoring of expressive behavior. *Journal of Personality and Social Psychology, 30*, 526–537.

Snyder, M., Berscheid, E., & Glick, P. (1985). Focusing on the exterior and the interior: Two investigations of the initiation of personal relationships. *Journal of Personality and Social Psychology, 48*, 1427–1439.

Snyder, M., & Gangestad, S. (1986). On the nature of self-monitoring: Matters of assessment, matters of validity. *Journal of Personality and Social Psychology, 51*, 125–139.

Snyder, M., & Ickes, W. (1985). Personality and social behavior. In G. Lindzey & E. Aronson (Eds.), *Handbook of social psychology* (3rd ed., Vol. 2, pp. 883–947). New York: Random House.

Snyder, M., & Simpson, J. A. (1984). Self-monitoring and dating relationships. *Journal of Personality and Social Psychology, 47*, 1281–1291.

Snyder, M., & Simpson, J. A. (1987). Orientations toward romantic relationships. In D. Perlman & S. Duck (Eds.), *Intimate relationships: Development, dynamics, and deterioration* (pp. 45–62). Newbury Park, CA: Sage.

Snyder, M., Simpson, J. A., & Gangestad, S. (1986). Personality and sexual relations. *Journal of Personality and Social Psychology, 51*, 181–190.

Snyder, M., Tanke, E. D., & Berscheid, E. (1977). Social perception and interpersonal behavior: On the self-fulfilling nature of social stereotypes. *Journal of Personality and Social Psychology, 35*, 656–666.

Solano, C. H., Batten, P. G., & Parish, E. A. (1982). Loneliness and patterns of self-disclosure. *Journal of Personality and Social Psychology, 43*, 524–531.

Solano, C. H., & Koester, N. H. (1989). Loneliness and communication problems: Subjective anxiety or objective skills? *Personality and Social Psychology Bulletin, 15*, 126–133.

Solomon, S. D., Smith, E. M., Robins, L. N., & Fischbach, R. L. (1987). Social involvement as a mediator of disaster-induced stress. *Journal of Applied Social Psychology, 17*, 1092–1112.

Somers, A. R. (1981). Marital status, health, and the use of health services: An old relationship revisited. In P. J. Stein (Ed.), *Single life: Unmarried adults in social context* (pp. 178–190). New York: St. Martin's Press.

Sorensen, G., & Verbrugge, L. M. (1987). Women, work, and health. *Annual Review of Public Health, 8*, 235–251.

South, S. J. (1988). Sex ratios, economic power, and women's roles: A theoretical extension and empirical test. *Journal of Marriage and the Family, 50*, 19–31.

Spanier, G. B., & Castro, R. F. (1979). Adjustment to separation and divorce: A qualitative analysis. In G. Levinger and O. C. Moles (Eds.), *Divorce and separation* (pp. 211–227). New York: Basic Books.

Spanier, G. B., Lewis, R. A., & Cole, C. L. (1975). Marital adjustment over the family life cycle: The issue of curvilinearity. *Journal of Marriage and the Family, 37*, 263–275.

Spanier, G. B., & Thompson, L. (1984). *Parting: The aftermath of separation and divorce*. Beverly Hills, CA: Sage.

Spaulding, C. (1970). The romantic love complex in American culture. *Sociology and Social Research, 55*, 82–100.

Spence, J., & Helmreich, R. (1978). *Masculinity and femininity: Their psychological dimensions, correlates, and antecedents*. Austin & London: University of Texas Press.

Spence, J. T., Deaux, K., & Helmreich, R. L. (1985). Sex roles in contemporary society. In G. Lindzey & E. Aronson (Eds.), *Handbook of social psychology* (3rd ed., Vol. 2, pp. 149–178). New York: Random House.

Spencer, S. (1980). *Endless love*. New York: Avon Books.

Spitzberg, B. H., & Canery, D. J. (1985). Loneliness and relationally competent communication. *Journal of Social and Personal Relationships, 2,* 387–402.

Spitze, G. (1988). Women's employment and family relations: A review. *Journal of Marriage and the Family, 50,* 595–618.

Sporakowski, M. J., & Hughston, G. A. (1978). Prescriptions for happy marriage: Adjustments and satisfactions of couples married for 50 or more years. *Family Coordinator, 27,* 321–327.

Sprecher, S. (1985). Sex differences in bases of power in dating relationships. *Sex Roles, 12,* 449–462.

Sprecher, S. (1989). The importance to males and females of physical attractiveness, earning potential, and expressiveness in initial attraction. *Sex Roles, 21,* 591–607.

Sprecher, S., DeLamater, J., Neuman, N., Neuman, M., Kahn, P., Orbuck, D., & McKinney, K. (1984). Asking questions in bars: The girls (and the boys) may not get prettier at closing time and other interesting results. *Personality and Social Psychology Bulletin, 10,* 482–488.

Sprecher, S., & Hatfield, E. (1982). Self-esteem and romantic attraction: Four experiments. *Recherches de Psychologie Sociale, 4,* 61–81.

Sprecher, S., & Metts, S. (1989). Development of the "Romantic Beliefs Scale" and examination of the effects of gender and gender-role orientation. *Journal of Social and Personal Relationships, 6,* 387–411.

Sprenkle, D. H., & Storm, C. L. (1983). Divorce therapy outcome research: A substantive and methodological review. *Journal of Marital and Family Therapy, 9,* 239–258.

Sprey, J. (1975). Family power and process: Toward a conceptual integration. In R. E. Cromwell & D. H. Olson (Eds.), *Power in families* (pp. 61–79). New York: Wiley.

Srole, L., Langner, T. S., Michael, S. T., Kirkpatrick, P., Opler, M. R., & Rennie, T. A. C. (1978). *Mental health in the metropolis: The midtown Manhattan study* (rev. ed.). New York: New York University Press.

Stack, S. (1989). The impact of divorce on suicide in Norway, 1951–1980. *Journal of Marriage and the Family, 51,* 229–238.

Stack, S. (1990). New micro-level data on the impact of divorce on suicide, 1959–1980: A test of two theories. *Journal of Marriage and the Family, 52,* 119–127.

Stall, R. D., Coates, T. J., & Hoff, C. (1988). Behavioral risk reduction for HIV infection among gay and bisexual men. *American Psychologist, 43,* 878–885.

Staples, R. (1981). Black singles in America. In P. J. Stein (Ed.), *Single life: Unmarried adults in social context* (pp. 40–51). New York: St. Martin's Press.

Stearns, P. N. (1989). *Jealousy: The evolution of an emotion in American history.* New York: New York University Press.

Steck, L., Levitan, D., McLane, D., & Kelley, H. H. (1982). Care, need, and conceptions of love. *Journal of Personality and Social Psychology, 43,* 481–491.

Steinberg, L., & Silverberg, S. B. (1987). Influences on marital satisfaction during the middle stages of the family life cycle. *Journal of Marriage and the Family, 49,* 751–760.

Steinglass, P. (1978). The conceptualization of marriage from a systems theory perspective. In T. J. Paolino & B. S. McCrady (Eds.), *Marriage and marital therapy: Psychoanalytic, behavioral and systems theory perspectives* (pp. 298–365). New York: Brunner/Mazel.

Steinglass, P. (1987). A systems view of family interaction and psychopathology. In T. Jacobs (Ed.), *Family interaction and psychopathology* (pp. 25–65). New York: Plenum.

Steinmetz, S. K. (1978). Violence between family members. *Marriage and Family Review, 1,* 1–16.

Steinmetz, S. K., & Lucca, J. S. (1988). Husband battering. In V. B. Van Hasselt, R. L. Morrison, A. S. Bellack, & M. Hersen (Eds.), *Handbook of family violence* (pp. 233–246). New York: Plenum.

Stephan, W., Berscheid, E., & Walster, E. (1971). Sexual arousal and heterosexual perception. *Journal of Personality and Social Psychology, 20,* 93–101.

Stephen, T. (1987). Taking communication seriously? A reply to Murstein. *Journal of Marriage and the Family, 49,* 937–938.

Stephen, T. D. (1984). Symbolic interdependence and post-breakup distress: A reformulation of attachment. *Journal of Divorce, 8,* 1–16.

Stephen, T. D. (1987). Attribution and adjustment to relationship termination. *Journal of Social and Personal Relationships, 4,* 47–61.

Sternberg, R. J. (1986). A triangular theory of love. *Psychological Review, 93,* 119–135.

Sternberg, R. J. (1988). Triangulating love. In R. J. Sternberg & M. L. Barnes (Eds.), *The psychology of love* (pp. 119–138). New Haven, CT: Yale University Press.

Stets, J. E. (1990). Verbal and physical aggression in marriage. *Journal of Marriage and the Family, 52,* 501–514.

Stets, J. E., & Straus, M. A. (1989). The marriage license as a hitting license: A comparison of assaults in dating, cohabiting, and married couples. *Journal of Family Violence, 41,* 33–52.

Stets, J. E., & Straus, M. A. (1990). Gender differences in reporting marital violence and its medical and psychological consequences. In M. A. Straus and R. J. Gelles (Eds.), *Physical violence in American families: Risk factors and adaptations to violence in 8,145 families* (pp. 151–165). New Brunswick, NJ: Transaction Publishers.

Stewart, A. J., & Chester, N. L. (1982). Sex differences in human social motives: Achievement, affiliation, and power. In A. J. Stewart (Ed.), *Motivation and society* (pp. 172–218). San Francisco: Jossey-Bass.

Stewart, A. J., & Rubin, Z. (1976). The power motive in the dating couple. *Journal of Personality and Social Psychology, 34,* 305–309.

Stier, D. S., & Hall, J. A. (1984). Gender differences in touch: An empirical and theoretical review. *Journal of Personality and Social Psychology, 47,* 440–459.

Stillars, A. L. (1981). Attributions and interpersonal conflict resolution. In J. H. Harvey, W. Ickes, & R. F. Kidd (Eds.), *New directions in attribution research* (pp. 279–305). Hillsdale, NJ: Erlbaum.

Stocks, J. T. (1988). Has family violence decreased? A reassessment of the Straus and Gelles data. *Journal of Marriage and the Family, 50,* 281–285.

Stokes, J., & Levin, I. (1986). Gender differences in predicting loneliness from social network characteristics. *Journal of Personality and Social Psychology, 51,* 1069–1074.

Stolberg, L. A., Camplair, C., Currier, K., & Wells, M. J. (1987). Individual, familial, and environmental determinants of children's post-divorce adjustment and maladjustment. *Journal of Divorce, 11*, 51–70.

Stone, L. (1988). Passionate attachments in the West in historical perspective. In W. Gaylin & E. Person (Eds.), *Passionate attachments: Thinking about love* (pp. 15–26). New York: The Free Press.

Storms, M., & Thomas, G. (1977). Reactions to physical closeness. *Journal of Personality and Social Psychology, 35*, 412–418.

Strack, S., & Coyne, J. C. (1983). Social confirmation of dysphoria: Shared and private reactions to depression. *Journal of Personality and Social Psychology, 44*, 798–806.

Straus, M. A. (1979). Measuring intrafamily conflict and violence: The conflict tactics (CT) scales. *Journal of Marriage and the Family, 41*, 75–88.

Straus, M. A. (1990). The Conflict Tactics Scale and its critics: An evaluation and new data on validity and reliability. In M. A. Straus & R. J. Gelles (Eds.), *Physical Violence in American Families: Risk factors and adaptations to violence in 8,145 families* (pp. 49–73). New Brunswick, NJ: Transaction Publishers.

Straus, M. A., Gelles, R. J., & Steinmetz, S. K. (1980). *Behind closed doors*. Garden City, NY: Anchor Books.

Stroebe, M. S., & Stroebe, W. (1983). Who suffers more? Sex differences in health risks of the widowed. *Psychological Bulletin, 93*, 279–301.

Stroebe, W., Insko, C. A., Thompson, V. D., & Layton, B. D. (1971). Effects of physical attractiveness, attitude similarity, and sex on various aspects of interpersonal attraction. *Journal of Personality and Social Psychology, 18*, 79–91.

Stroebe, W., Lenkert, A., & Jonas, K. (1988). Familiarity may breed contempt: The impact of student exchange on national stereotypes and attitudes. In W. Stroebe, A. W. Kruglanski, D. Bar-Tal, & M. Hewstone (Eds.), *The social psychology of intergroup conflict* (pp. 167–187). New York: Springer-Verlag.

Stroebe, W., & Stroebe, M. S. (1986). Beyond marriage: The impact of partner loss on health. In R. Gilmour & S. Duck (Eds.), *The emerging field of personal relationships* (pp. 203–224). Hillsdale, NJ: Erlbaum.

Strong, S. R., Hills, H. J., Kilmartin, C. T., DeVries, H., Lanier, K., Nelson, B. N., Strickland, D., & Meyer, C. W., III. (1988). The dynamic relations among interpersonal behaviors: A test of complementarity and anti-complementarity. *Journal of Personality and Social Psychology, 54*, 798–810.

Strube, M. J. (1988). The decision to leave an abusive relationship: Empirical evidence and theoretical issues. *Psychological Bulletin, 104*, 236–250.

Strube, M. J., & Barbour, L. S. (1983). The decision to leave an abusive relationship: Economic dependence and psychological commitment. *Journal of Marriage and the Family, 45*, 785–794.

Stuart, R. B. (1969). Operant interpersonal treatment for marital discord. *Journal of Consulting and Clinical Psychology, 33*, 675–682.

Stuart, R. B. (1980). *Helping couples change: A social learning appeal to marital therapy*. New York: Guilford Press.

Stuckert, R. P. (1963). Role perception and marital satisfaction—a configurational approach. *Marriage and Family Living, 25,* 415–419.

Sullivan, H. S. (1947). *Conceptions of modern psychiatry.* Washington, DC: William Alanson White Psychiatric Foundation.

Surra, C. A. (1987). Reasons for changes in commitment: Variations by courtship types. *Journal of Social and Personal Relationships, 4,* 17–33.

Surra, C. A., Chandler, M., Asmussen, L., & Wareham, J. (1987). Effects of premarital pregnancy on the development of interdependence in relationships. *Journal of Social and Clinical Psychology, 5,* 123–139.

Surra, C. A., & Huston, T. L. (1987). Mate selection as a social transition. In D. Perlman & S. Duck (Ed.), *Intimate relationships: Development, dynamics, and deterioration* (pp. 88–120). Newbury Park: CA: Sage Publications.

Surra, C. A., & Longstreth, M. (1990). Similarity of outcomes, interdependence, and conflict in dating relationships. *Journal of Personality and Social Psychology, 59,* 501–516.

Swann, W. B., Jr., Stephenson, B., & Pittman, T. S. (1981). Curiosity and control: On the determinants of the search for social knowledge. *Journal of Personality and Social Psychology, 40,* 635–642.

Swap, W. C., & Rubin, J. Z. (1983). Measurement of interpersonal orientation. *Journal of Personality and Social Psychology, 44,* 208–219.

Sweeney, P. D., Anderson, K., & Bailey, S. (1986). Attributional style in depression: A meta-analytic review. *Journal of Personality and Social Psychology, 50,* 974–991.

Szinovacz, M. E. (1981). Relationship among marital power measures. A critical review and an empirical test. *Journal of Comparative Family Studies, 12,* 151–169.

Tanfer, K. (1987). Patterns of premarital cohabitation among never-married women in the United States. *Journal of Marriage and the Family, 49,* 483–497.

Tannen, D. (1990). *You just don't understand: Women and men in conversation.* New York: William Morrow.

Taylor, A. E. (1967). Role perception, empathy, and marriage adjustment. *Sociology and Social Research, 52,* 22–34.

Taylor, D. A., Altman, I., & Wheeler, L. (1972). Self-disclosure in isolated groups. *Journal of Personality and Social Psychology, 26,* 39–47.

Taylor, S. E., Lichtman, R. R., & Wood, J. V. (1984). Attributions, beliefs about control, and adjustment to breast cancer. *Journal of Personality and Social Psychology, 46,* 489–502.

Tennen, H., & Affleck, G. (1990). Blaming others for threatening events. *Psychological Bulletin, 108,* 209–232.

Tennov, D. (1979). *Love and limerence: The experience of being in love.* New York: Stein and Day.

Terman, L. M., Buttenweiser, P., Ferguson, L. W., Johnson, W. B., & Wilson, D. P. (1938). *Psychological factors in marital happiness.* New York: McGraw-Hill.

Tesser, A. (1978). Self-generated attitude change. In L. Berkowitz (Ed.), *Advances in experimental social psychology* (Vol. 11, pp. 289–338). New York: Academic Press.

Tesser, A. (1980). Self-esteem maintenance in family dynamics. *Journal of Personality and Social Psychology, 39,* 77–91.

Tesser, A. (1988). Toward a self-evaluation maintenance model of social behavior. In L. Berkowitz (Ed.), *Advances in experimental social psychology* (Vol. 21, pp. 181–227). New York: Academic Press.

Tesser, A., & Brodie, M. (1971). A note on the evaluation of a "computer date." *Psychonomic Science, 23,* 300.

Tesser, A., Campbell, J., & Smith, M. (1984). Friendship choice and performance: Self-evaluation maintenance in children. *Journal of Personality and Social Psychology, 46,* 561–574.

Tesser, A., & Paulus, D. L. (1976). Toward a causal model of love. *Journal of Personality and Social Psychology, 34,* 1095–1105.

Tesser, A., & Paulus, D. L. (1978). On models and assumptions: A reply to Smith. *Journal of Personality and Social Psychology, 36,* 40–42.

Tharp, R. G. (1963). Psychological patterning in marriage. *Psychological Bulletin, 60,* 97–117.

Thayer, S. (1988, March). Close encounters. *Psychology Today,* pp. 30–36.

Thelen, M., Fishbein, M. D., & Tatten, H. A. (1985). Interspousal similarity: A new approach to an old question. *Journal of Social and Personal Relationships, 2,* 437–446.

Thibaut, J. W., & Kelley, H. H. (1959). *The social psychology of groups.* New York: Wiley.

Thoits, P. (1983). Multiple identities and psychological well-being: A reformulation and test of the social isolation hypothesis. *American Sociological Review, 48,* 174–187.

Thoits, P. A. (1982). Conceptual, methodological, and theoretical problems in studying social support as a buffer against life stress. *Journal of Health and Social Behavior, 23,* 145–159.

Thompson, A. P. (1984). Emotional and sexual components of extramarital relations. *Journal of Marriage and the Family, 46,* 35–42.

Thompson, D. (1990, January 22). The AIDS political machine. *Time,* pp. 24–25.

Thompson, H. L., & Richardson, D. R. (1983). The rooster effect: Same-sex rivalry and inequity as factors in retaliative aggression. *Personality and Social Psychology Bulletin, 9,* 415–425.

Thompson, L., & Spanier, G. B. (1983). The end of marriage and acceptance of marital termination. *Journal of Marriage and the Family, 45,* 103–113.

Thompson, L., & Walker, A. J. (1989). Gender in families: Women and men in marriage, work, and parenthood. *Journal of Marriage and the Family, 51,* 845–871.

Thompson, S., & Janigian, A. S. (1988). Life schemes: A framework for understanding the search for meaning. *Journal of Social and Clinical Psychology, 7,* 260–280.

Thompson, S. C., & Kelley, H. H. (1981). Judgments of responsibility for activities in close relationships. *Journal of Personality and Social Psychology, 41,* 469–477.

Thorne, B., & Henley, N. (Eds.). (1975). *Language and sex: Difference and dominance.* Rowley, MA: Newbury House.

Thornton, A. (1988). Cohabitation and marriage in the 1980s. *Demography, 25,* 497–508.

Thornton, A. (1989). Changing attitudes toward family issues in the United States. *Journal of Marriage and the Family, 51,* 873–893.

Thornton, A., & Freedman, D. (1982). "Changing attitudes toward marriage and single life." Unpublished manuscript, Institute for Social Research, University of Michigan, Ann Arbor.

Tocqueville, A. de (1840/1956). *Democracy in America.* (Vols. 1 & 2). New York: Knopf.

Todd, T. C. (1986). Structural-strategic marital therapy. In N. S. Jacobson & A. S. Gurman (Eds.), *Clinical handbook of marital therapy* (pp. 71–105). New York: Guilford.

Toi, M., & Batson, C. D. (1982). More evidence that empathy is a source of altruistic motivation. *Journal of Personality and Social Psychology, 43,* 281–292.

Tolstedt, B. E., & Stokes, J. P. (1984). Self-disclosure, intimacy, and the depenetration process. *Journal of Personality and Social Psychology, 46,* 84–90.

Too late for Prince Charming? (1986, June 2). *Newsweek,* pp. 54–57, 61.

Toomin, M. K. (1975). Structural separation for couples in conflict. In A. S. Gurman & D. G. Rice (Eds.), *Couples in conflict* (pp. 353–362). New York: Jason Aronson.

Traupmann, J., Hatfield, E., & Wexler, P. (1983). Equity and sexual satisfaction in dating couples. *British Journal of Social Psychology, 22,* 33–40.

Traupmann, J., Petersen, R., Utne, M., & Hatfield, E. (1981). Measuring equity in intimate relations. *Applied Psychology Measurement, 5,* 467–480.

Trent, K., & South, S. J. (1989). Structural determinants of the divorce rate: A cross-societal analysis. *Journal of Marriage and the Family, 51,* 391–404.

Triandis, H. C., Bontempo, R., Villareal, M. J., Asai, M., & Lucca, N. (1988). Individualism and collectivism: Cross-cultural perspectives on self-ingroup relationships. *Journal of Personality and Social Psychology, 54,* 323–338.

Triandis, H. C., McCusker, C., & Hui, C. H. (1990). Multimethod probe of individualism and collectivism. *Journal of Personality and Social Psychology, 59,* 1006–1020.

Triplett, R. G., & Sugarman, D. B. (1987). Reactions to AIDS victims: Ambiguity breeds contempt. *Personality and Social Psychology Bulletin, 13,* 265–274.

Trussell, J., & Rao, K. V. (1989). Premarital cohabitation and marital stability: A reassessment of the Canadian evidence. *Journal of Marriage and the Family, 51,* 535–540.

Tschann, J. M. (1988). Self-disclosure in adult friendship: Gender and marital status differences. *Journal of Social and Personal Relationships, 5,* 65–81.

Tschann, J. M., Johnston, J. R., Kline, M., & Wallerstein, J. S. (1989). Family process and children's functioning during divorce. *Journal of Marriage and the Family, 51,* 431–444.

Tschann, J. M., Johnston, J. R., & Wallerstein, J. S. (1989). Resources, stressors, and attachment as predictors of adult adjustment after divorce: A longitudinal study. *Journal of Marriage and the Family, 51,* 1033–1046.

Tucker, C. M., James, L. M., & Turner, S. M. (1985). Sex roles, parenthood, and marital adjustment: A comparison of blacks and whites. *Journal of Social and Clinical Psychology, 3,* 51–61.

Tucker, M. B., & Mitchell-Kernan, C. (1990). New trends in black American interracial marriage: The social structure context. *Journal of Marriage and the Family, 52,* 209–218.

Turk, J. L., & Bell, N. W. (1972). Measuring power in families. *Journal of Marriage and the Family, 34,* 215–227.

Ulrich-Jakubowski, D., Russell, D. W., & O'Hara, M. W. (1988). Marital adjustment and difficulties: Cause or consequence of depressive symptomatology? *Journal of Social and Clinical Psychology, 7*, 312–318.

Umberson, D. (1989). Relationships with children: Explaining parents' psychological well-being. *Journal of Marriage and the Family, 51*, 999–1012.

Utne, M. K., Hatfield, E., Traupmann, J., & Greenberger, D. (1984). Equity, marital satisfaction, and stability. *Journal of Social and Personal Relationships, 1*, 323–332.

Vallacher, R. R. (1983). "'Your cheating heart': The double-standard in extramarital relations." Paper presented at the Annual Meeting of the Midwestern Psychological Association.

Van Hasselt, V. B., Morrison, R. L., Bellack, A. S., & Hersen, M. (Eds.), (1988). *Handbook of family violence.* New York: Plenum.

van Ijzendoorn, M. H., & Kroonenberg, P. M. (1988). Cross-cultural patterns of attachment: A meta-analysis of the strange situation. *Child Development, 59*, 147–156.

Vargas Llosa, M. (1986). *The perpetual orgy.* Trs. Helen Lane. New York: Farrar, Straus, and Giroux.

Vaux, A. (1988a). Social and emotional loneliness: The role of social and personal characteristics. *Personality and Social Psychology Bulletin, 14*, 722–734.

Vaux, A. (1988b). Social and personal factors in loneliness. *Journal of Social and Clinical Psychology, 6*, 462–471.

Vemer, E., Coleman, M., Ganong, L. H., & Cooper, H. (1989). Marital satisfaction in remarriage: A meta-analysis. *Journal of Marriage and the Family, 51*, 713–725.

Verbrugge, L. M. (1987). Role responsibilities, role burdens, and physical health. In F. Crosby (Ed.), *Spouse, parent, worker: On gender and multiple roles* (pp. 154–166). New Haven, CT: Yale University Press.

Veroff, J., Douvan, E., & Kukla, R. A. (1981). *The inner American: A self-portrait from 1957 to 1976.* New York: Basic Books.

Veroff, J., & Feld, S. (1971). *Marriage and work in America: A study of motives and roles.* New York: Van Nostrand Reinhold.

Veroff, J., & Veroff, J. B. (1972). Reconsideration of a measure of power motivation. *Psychological Bulletin, 78*, 279–291.

Vetere, V. A. (1982). The role of friendship in the development and maintenance of lesbian love relationships. *Journal of Homosexuality, 8*, 51–65.

Vincent, J. P., Friedman, L. C., Nugent, J., & Messerly, L. (1979). Demand characteristics in observations of marital interaction. *Journal of Consulting and Clinical Psychology, 47*, 557–566.

Vincent, J. P., Weiss, R. L., & Birchler, G. R. (1975). Dyadic problem solving behavior as a function of marital distress and spousal vs. stranger interactions. *Behavior Therapy, 6*, 475–487.

Walker, L. E. A., & Browne, A. (1985). Gender and victimization by intimates. *Journal of Personality, 53*, 179–195.

Wallach, M. A., & Wallach, L. (1983). *Psychology's sanction for selfishness: The error of egoism in theory and therapy.* San Francisco: Freeman.

Waller, W. W., & Hill, R. (1951). *The family, a dynamic interpretation.* New York: Dryden Press.

Wallerstein, J. S., & Blakeslee, S. (1989). *Second chances: Men, women, and children a decade after divorce.* New York: Ticknor & Fields.

Wallerstein, J. S., & Kelly, J. B. (1980). *Surviving the breakup: How children and parents cope with divorce.* New York: Basic Books.

Walster, E. (1965). The effect of self-esteem on romantic liking. *Journal of Experimental Social Psychology, 1,* 184–197.

Walster, E. (1970). The effect of self-esteem on liking for data on various social desirabilities. *Journal of Experimental Social Psychology, 6,* 248–253.

Walster, E. (1971). Passionate love. In B. Murstein (Ed.), *Theories of attraction and love* (pp. 85–99). New York: Springer.

Walster, E., Aronson, V., Abrahams, D., & Rottman, L. (1966). The importance of physical attractiveness in dating behavior. *Journal of Personality and Social Psychology, 4,* 508–516.

Walster, E., Berscheid, E., & Walster, G. W. (1973). New directions in equity. *Journal of Personality and Social Psychology 25,* 151–176.

Walster, E., Traupmann, J., & Walster, G. W. (1978). Equity and extramarital sexuality. *Archives of Sexual Behavior, 7,* 127–141.

Walster, E., Walster, G. W., & Berscheid, E. (1978). *Equity: Theory and research.* Boston: Allyn & Bacon.

Walster, E., Walster, G. W., Piliavin, J., & Schmidt, L. (1973). "Playing hard-to-get": Understanding an elusive phenomenon. *Journal of Personality and Social Psychology, 26,* 113–121.

Walster, E., Walster, G. W., & Traupmann, J. (1978). Equity and premarital sex. *Journal of Personality, 36,* 82–92.

Wampler, R. S. (1982). Bringing the review of literature into the age of quantification: Meta-analysis as a strategy for integrating research findings in family studies. *Journal of Marriage and the Family, 44,* 1009–1023.

Warner, R. M., & Sugarman, D. B. (1986). Attributions of personality based on physical appearance, speech, and handwriting. *Journal of Personality and Social Psychology, 50,* 792–799.

Warren, B. L. (1966). A multiple variable approach to the assortive mating phenomenon. *Eugenics Quarterly, 13,* 285–298.

Watkins, J. D. (1988). *Report of the Presidential Commission on the Human Immunodeficiency Virus Epidemic.* Submitted to the President of the United States, June 24, 1988. Washington, DC: US Government Printing Office.

Watson, D. (1982). The actor and the observer: How are their perceptions of causality different? *Psychological Bulletin, 92,* 682–700.

Watson, R. E. L. (1983). Premarital cohabitation vs. traditional courtship: Their effects on subsequent marital adjustment. *Family Relations, 32,* 139–147.

Watson, R. E. L., & DeMeo, P. W. (1987). Premarital cohabitation vs. traditional courtship and subsequent marital adjustment: A replication and follow-up. *Family Relations, 36,* 193–197.

Webb, E. J., Campbell, D. T., Schwartz, R. D., Sechrest, L., & Grove, J. B. (1981). *Nonreactive measures in the social sciences* (2nd ed.). Boston: Houghton Mifflin.

Wedell, D. H., Parducci, A., & Geiselman, R. E. (1987). A formal analysis of ratings of physical attractiveness: Successive contrast and simultaneous association. *Journal of Experimental Social Psychology, 23,* 230–249.

Weeks, D. G., Michela, J. L., Peplau, L. A., & Bragg, M. E. (1980). The relation between loneliness and depression: A structural equation analysis. *Journal of Personality and Social Psychology, 39,* 1238–1244.

Weiner, B. (1985). "Spontaneous" causal thinking. *Psychological Bulletin, 97*, 74–84.

Weiner, B., Stone, A. J., Schmitz, M. D., Schmidt, A., Hernandez, A. C. R., & Benton, C. J. (1983). Compounding the errors: A reply to Pollak and Gilligan. *Journal of Personality and Social Psychology, 45*, 1176–1178.

Weingarten, H. R. (1985). Marital status and well-being: A national study comparing first-married, currently divorced, and remarried adults. *Journal of Marriage and the Family, 47*, 653–662.

Weiss, R. L. (1978). The conceptualization of marriage from a behavioral perspective. In T. J. Paolino & B. S. McCrady (Eds.), *Marriage and marital therapy: Psychoanalytic, behavioral and systems theory perspectives* (pp. 165–239). New York: Brunner/Mazel.

Weiss, R. L., Birchler, G. R., & Vincent, J. P. (1974). Contractual models for negotiating training in marital dyads. *Journal of Marriage and the Family, 36*, 321–330.

Weiss, R. L., Hops, H., & Patterson, G. R. (1973). A framework for conceptualizing marital conflict, a technology for altering it, some data for evaluating it. In L. A. Hamerlynck, L. C. Handy, & E. J. Mash (Eds.), *Behavior change: Methodology, concepts and practice* (pp. 309–342). Champaign, IL: Research Press.

Weiss, R. S. (1969). The fund of sociability. *Transaction, 7*, 36–43.

Weiss, R. S. (1973). *Loneliness.* Cambridge, MA: MIT Press.

Weiss, R. S. (1975). *Marital separation.* New York: Basic Books.

Weitzman, L. J. (1985). *The divorce revolution: The unexpected social and economic consequences for women and children in America.* New York: The Free Press.

West, C., & Zimmerman, D. H. (1983). Small insults: A study of interruptions in cross-sex conversations between unacquainted persons. In B. Thorne, C. Kramarge, & N. Henley (Eds.), *Language, gender and society* (pp. 102–117). Rowley, MA: Newbury House.

Wetzel, C. G., & Insko, C. A. (1982). The similarity-attraction relationship: Is there an ideal one? *Journal of Experimental Social Psychology, 18*, 253–276.

Wheeler, L., & Nezlek, J. (1977). Sex differences in social participation. *Journal of Personality and Social Psychology, 35*, 742–754.

Wheeler, L., Reis, H., & Nezlek, J. (1983). Loneliness, social interaction, and sex roles. *Journal of Personality and Social Psychology, 45*, 943–953.

Wheeler, L., Reis, H. T., & Bond, M. H. (1989). Collectivism-individualism in everyday social life: The middle kingdom and the melting pot. *Journal of Personality and Social Psychology, 57*, 79–86.

Whiffen, V. E., & Gotlib, I. H. (1989). Stress and coping in maritally distressed and nondistressed couples. *Journal of Social and Personal Relationships, 6*, 327–344.

Whitaker, C. A. (1975). A family therapist looks at marital therapy. In A. S. Gurman & D. G. Rice (Eds.), *Couples in conflict* (pp. 165–174). New York: Jason Aronson.

White, G. L. (1980a). Inducing jealousy: A power perspective. *Personality and Social Psychology Bulletin, 6*, 222–227.

White, G. L. (1980b). Physical attractiveness and courtship progress. *Journal of Personality and Social Psychology, 39*, 660–668.

White, G. L. (1981a). Jealousy and partner's perceived notion for attraction to a rival. *Social Psychology Quarterly, 49,* 24–30.

White, G. L. (1981b). A model of romantic jealousy. *Motivation and Emotion, 5,* 295–310.

White, G. L. (1981c). Some correlates of romantic jealousy. *Journal of Personality, 49,* 129–147.

White, G. L., Fishbein, S., & Rutstein, J. (1981). Passionate love: The misattribution of arousal. *Journal of Personality and Social Psychology, 41,* 56–62.

White, G. L., & Kight, T. D. (1984). Misattribution of arousal and attraction: Effects of salience of explanation of arousal. *Journal of Experimental Social Psychology, 20,* 55–64.

White, G. L., & Mullen, P. E. (1989). *Jealousy: Theory, research, and clinical strategies.* New York: Guilford Press.

White, J. M. (1987). Premarital cohabitation and marital stability in Canada. *Journal of Marriage and the Family, 49,* 641–647.

White, J. M. (1989). Reply to comment by Trussell & Rao: A reanalysis of the data. *Journal of Marriage and the Family, 51,* 540–544.

Whyte, M. K. (1990). *Dating, mating, and marriage.* New York: Aldine de Gruyter.

Whitley, B. F., Jr. (1988). The relation of gender-role orientation to sexual experience among college students. *Sex Roles, 19,* 619–638.

Wicklund, R. A., & Brehm, J. W. (1976). *Perspectives on cognitive dissonance.* Hillsdale, NJ: Erlbaum.

Wilcox, B. L. (1981). Social support in adjusting to marital disruption: A network analysis. In B. H. Gottlieb (Ed.), *Social networks and social support* (pp. 97–115). Beverly Hills, CA: Sage Publications.

Williams, A. M. (1979). The quantity and quality of marital interaction related to marital satisfaction: A behavioral analysis. *Journal of Applied Behavior Analysis, 12,* 665–678.

Williams, J. C., & Solano, C. H. (1983). The social reality of feeling lonely: Friendship and reciprocation. *Personality and Social Psychology Bulletin, 9,* 237–242.

Williams, J. D., & Jacoby, A. P. (1989). The effects of premarital heterosexual and homosexual experience on dating and marriage desirability. *Journal of Marriage and the Family, 51,* 489–497.

Williamson, G. M., & Clark, M. S. (1989). Providing help and desire relationship type as determinants of changes in moods and self-evaluations. *Journal of Personality and Social Psychology, 56,* 722–734.

Wills, T. A., Weiss, R. L., & Patterson, G. R. (1974). A behavioral analysis of the determinants of marital satisfaction. *Journal of Consulting and Clinical Psychology, 42,* 802–811.

Wilson, W. (1967). Correlates of avowed happiness. *Psychological Bulletin, 67,* 294–306.

Winch, R. F. (1958). *Mate selection: A theory of complementary needs.* New York: Harper & Brothers.

Winer, B. J. (1971). *Statistical principles in experimental design* (2nd ed.). New York: McGraw-Hill.

Wingert, P., & Kantrowitz, B. (1990, Winter/Spring). The day care generation. *Newsweek Special Edition,* pp. 86–92.

Winstead, B. A. (1986). Sex differences in same-sex friendships. In V. J. Derlega & B. A. Winstead (Eds.), *Friendship and social interaction* (pp. 81–99). New York: Springer-Verlag.

Winter, D. G. (1973). *The power motive.* New York: Free Press.

Winter, D. G. (1988). The power motive in women—and men. *Journal of Personality and Social Psychology, 54,* 510–519.

Winter, D. G., & Barenbaum, N. B. (1985). Responsibility and the power motive in women and men. *Journal of Personality, 53,* 335–355.

Winter, D. G., Stewart, A. J., & McClelland, D. C. (1977). Husband's motives and wife's career level. *Journal of Personality and Social Psychology, 35,* 159–166.

Wittenberg, M. T., & Reis, H. T. (1986). Loneliness, social skills, and social perception. *Personality and Social Psychology Bulletin, 12,* 121–130.

Women: Stretching their options. (1987, January 26). *Time,* p. 14.

Wood, W., Rhodes, N., & Whelan, M. (1989). Sex differences in positive well-being: A consideration of emotional style and marital status. *Psychological Bulletin, 106,* 249–264.

Wright, P. H. (1982). Men's friendships, women's friendships and the alleged inferiority of the latter. *Sex Roles, 8,* 1–20.

Wright, P. H. (1988). Interpreting research on gender differences in friendship: A case for moderation and a plea for caution. *Journal of Social and Personal Relationships, 5,* 367–373.

Wright, P. H., & Keple, T. W. (1981). Friends and parents of a sample of high school juniors: An exploratory study of relationship intensity and interpersonal rewards. *Journal of Marriage and the Family, 43,* 559–570.

Wright, R. A., & Contrada, R. J. (1986). Dating selectivity and interpersonal attractiveness: Toward a better understanding of the "elusive phenomenon." *Social and Personal Relationships, 3,* 131–148.

Wright, T. L., & Ingraham, L. J. (1986). Partners and relationships influence self-perceptions or self-disclosures in naturalistic interactions. *Journal of Personality and Social Psychology, 50,* 631–635.

Wright, T. L., Ingraham, L. J., & Blackmer, D. R. (1985). Simultaneous study of individual differences and relationship effects in attraction. *Journal of Personality and Social Psychology, 47,* 1059–1062.

Xiaohe, X., & Whyte, M. K. (1990). Love matches and arranged marriages: A Chinese replication. *Journal of Marriage and the Family, 52,* 709–722.

Yogev, S., & Brett, J. (1985). Perceptions of the division of housework and child care and marital satisfaction. *Journal of Marriage and the Family, 47,* 609–618.

Zajonc, R. B. (1968). Attitudinal effects of mere exposure. *Journal of Personality and Social Psychology Monograph Supplement, 9,* Part 2, 1–27.

Zajonc, R. B., Adelmann, P. K., Murphy, S. T., & Niedenthal, P. M. (1987). Convergence in physical appearance of spouses. *Motivation and Emotion, 11,* 335–346.

Zigler, E., Rubin, N., & Kaufman, J. (1988, May). Do abused children become abusive parents? *Parents,* pp. 100–104, 106.

Zilbergeld, B. (1978). *Male sexuality: A guide to sexual fulfillment.* Boston: Little, Brown.

Zill, N. (1988). Behavior, achievement and health problems among children in stepfamilies. In E. M. Hetherington & J. D. Arasteh (Eds.), *Impact of divorce, singleparenting, and stepparenting on children* (pp. 325–368). Hillsdale, NJ: Erlbaum.

Zillman, D. (1978). Attribution and misattribution of excitatory reactions. In J. H. Harvey, W. Ickes, & R. F. Kidd (Eds.), *New directions in attribution research* (Vol. 2, pp. 335–368). Hillsdale, NJ: Erlbaum.

Zillmann, D. (1984). *Connections between sex and aggression*. Hillsdale, NJ: Erlbaum.

Zillmann, D., Johnson, R. C., & Day, K. D. (1974). Attribution of apparent arousal and proficiency of recovery from sympathetic activation affecting excitation transfer to aggressive behavior. *Journal of Experimental Social Psychology, 10,* 503–515.

Zillmann, D., Weaver, J. B., Mundorf, N., & Aust, C. F. (1986). Effects of an opposite-gender companion's affect to horror on distress, delight, and attraction. *Journal of Personality and Social Psychology, 51,* 586–594.

Zimbardo, P. G. (1977). *Shyness*. New York: Jove.

Zimmerman, D. H., & West, C. (1975). Sex roles, interruptions and silences in conversations. In B. Thorne & N. Henley (Eds.), *Language and sex: Difference and dominance* (pp. 105–129). Rowley, MA: Newbury House.

$\mathcal{A}$cknowledgments

❖

The author and McGraw-Hill extend grateful thanks to the following for permission to quote from the indicated material:

pp. 7, 11, and 16: "Marriage Rates"; "Age at Marriage"; "Divorce Rates"; "Living Together." From NEWSWEEK, Winter/Spring, Special Edition, 1990 © 1990, Newsweek, Inc. All rights reserved. Reprinted by permission.

p. 9: Lauer, J. & Lauer, R. "What Keeps a Marriage Going." Reprinted with permission from *Psychology Today.* Copyright © 1985 (PT Partners, L.P.).

p. 23: Freedman, J. "The Ten Pillars of Happiness." © 1978. Reprinted by permission of the publishers, Harcourt Brace Jovanovich, Inc.

p. 46: Edmonds, V. H. "Marriage Conventionalization Scale." From "Marriage Conventionalization: Definition and Measurement," *Journal of Marriage and the Family, 29,* 681–688. Copyrighted 1967 by the National Council on Family Relations, 3989 Central Ave. N.E., Suite #550, Minneapolis, MN 55421. Reprinted by permission.

p. 61: Stills, Stephen. "Love the One You're With." © 1970 Gold Hill Music, Inc. Used by permission. All Rights Reserved.

p. 70: Snyder, M. & Gangestad, S. "The Self-Monitoring Scale." From "On the nature of self-monitoring: Matters of assessment, matters of validity," *Journal of Personality and Social Psychology, 51,* 125–129. Copyright 1986 by the American Psychological Association. Reprinted by permission of the authors.

p. 61: "Schematic Diagram of a Westgate West Building." Reprinted from *Social Pressures in Informal Groups* by Leon Festinger, Stanley Schachter, and Kurt Back, with the permission of the publishers, Stanford University Press. Copyright 1950 by Leon Festinger, Stanley Schachter, and Kurt Back.

pp. 78, 108, 109, 157, 182, 193, 212, 234, 306, 334, 368: "A Two-Step Model of the Attraction Process"; "Styles of Loving"; "The Triangular Theory of Love: Types of Relationships"; "Factors That Influence Satisfaction and Commitment in a Relationship"; "Benefits and Contributions in Intimate Relationships"; "Differences Between Exchange and Communal Relationships"; "Gender Differences in Self-Disclosure"; "Types of Resource Power"; "Attributions Made by Happy and Unhappy Couples"; "Explanations of Loneliness"; "Affiliation under Stress." From Brehm, Sharon S., & Saul Kassin, *Social Psychology*. Copyright © 1990 by Houghton-Mifflin Company. Used with permission.

p. 82: Buss, D. M. "The Top Ten Male and Female Acts Judged Most Effective in Attracting Opposite-Sex Partners." From "The evolution of human intrasexual competition: Tactics of mate attraction," *Journal of Personality and Social Psychology, 54,* 616–628. Copyright 1988 by the American Psychological Association. Reprinted by permission.

p. 92: Springsteen, B. Quote from "Crush on You." Reprinted by permission of the author.

p. 97: Rubin, Z. "Liking and Loving Scales." Reprinted from *Liking and Loving.* New York: Holt, Rinehart, and Winston, Inc., 1973. Used by permission of the author.

p. 99: Hatfield, E., & Rapson, R. L. "The Passionate Love Scale (Short Form)." From "Passionate love: New directions in research" in W. H. Jones and D. Perlman (Eds.), *Advances in Personal Relationships,* Vol. 1, (pp 109–139). Copyright © 1987 by JAI Press Inc., Greenwich, CT. Reprinted by Permission of JAI Press.

pp. 106–107: Johnson-George, C., & Swap, W. C. "The Specific Interpersonal Trust Scale." From "Measurement of Specific Interpersonal Trust," *Journal of Personality and Social Psychology, 43,* 1306–1317. Copyright 1982 by the American Psychological Association. Reprinted by permission of the authors.

p. 108: Shaver, P., Hazan, C., & Bradshaw, D. "Attachment Styles." From "Love as attachment: The integration of three behavioral systems" in R. Sternberg & M. L. Barnes (Eds.), *The Psychology of Love* (p. 80). Copyright © 1988 by Yale University Press, New Haven, CT.

p. 112: "Revision of the Gross Romanticism Scale." Reprinted from *Social Forces, 36,* 1958. From "The Incidence of Romanticism during Courtship" by C. W. Hobart. Copyright © by The University of North Carolina Press.

p. 112: Spaulding, C. (1970). "The Romantic Love Complex Scale." Reprinted by permission of *Sociology and Social Research, 55,* 82–100.

p. 113: Fengler, A. P. (1974). "The Romantic Idealist Factor." Reprinted by permission of the editor, *Journal of Comparative Family Studies, 5,* 134–139.

p. 144: Radlove, S. "The Fantasy Model of Sex." Reprinted by permission of Mayfield Publishing Company.

pp. 146–147 Scoresby, A. L., "Sexual Communication Problems and Some Possible Solutions." From *Marriage Dialogue* © 1977, Addison-Wesley Publishing Company, Inc., Reading, Mass. Pages 64–65, Table 2, reprinted with permission.

p. 155: Murstein, B. I. "Stages of Courtship in SVR Theory." From "A Clarification and Extension of the SVR Theory of Dyadic Pairing," *Journal of Marriage and the Family, 49,* 929–933. Copyrighted 1987 by the National Council on Family Relations, 3989 Central Ave. N.E., Suite #550, Minneapolis, MN 55421. Reprinted by permission.

pp. 190–191: Swap, W. C., & Rubin, J. Z. "The Interpersonal Orientation Scale." From "Measures of Interpersonal Orientation," *Journal of Personality and Social Psychology, 44,* 208–219. Copyright 1983 by the American Psychological Association. Reprinted with permission of the authors.

p. 196: Batson, C. D., & Fultz, J., and Schoenrade, P. A. "The Empathy-Attribution Hypothesis." From "Distress and Empathy: Two Qualitatively Distinct Vicarious Emotions with Different Motivational Consequences," *Journal of Personality, 55,* 19–39. Copyright © 1987.

p. 211: Burke, R. J., Weir, T., & Harrison, D. "Reasons Why Husbands and Wives Avoid Self-Disclosing to Each Other." Reprinted with permission of authors and publisher from "Disclosure of Problems and Tensions Experienced by Marital Partners." *Psychological Reports,* 1976, *38,* 531–542, Table 2.

p. 216: Patterson, M. L. "Functions of Nonverbal Behaviors in Intimate Relationships." In Duck, S. (Ed.), *Handbook of Personal Relationships: Theory, Research, and Interventions.* Copyright © 1988 John Wiley & Sons Inc.

p. 253: Straus, M. A. "The Conflict Tactics Scale." From "Measuring Intrafamily Conflict and Violence: The Conflict Tactics (CT) Scales," *Journal of Marriage and the Family, 41,* 75–88. Copyrighted 1979 by the National Council on Family Relations, 3989 Central Ave. N.E., Suite #550, Minneapolis, MN 55421. Reprinted by permission.

p. 263: "Mrs. Harris, in Letter to Lover, Rails at 'Years of Broken Promises'" (Feb. 5, 1981). Reprinted by permission of *The Washington Post.*

p. 269: Pinto, R. P., & Hollandsworth, J. G., Jr. "The Possessiveness Scale." From "A Measure of Possessiveness in Intimate Relationships," *Journal of Social and Clinical Psychology, 2,* 273–279. Copyright 1984. Reprinted by permission of Guilford Publications.

p. 277: Pfeiffer, S. M., & Wong, P. T. "Multidimensional Jealousy Scale." From "Multidimensional Jealousy," *Journal of Social and Personal Relationships, 6,* 181–196. Copyright © 1989 by Sage Publications. Reprinted by permission of Sage Publications Inc.

p. 310: Rusblut, C. E. "Dimensions of Response to Dissatisfaction with a Relationship." From D. Perlman, & S. Duck (Eds.), *Intimate Relationships: Development, Dynamics, and Deterioration* (pp. 209–237). Copyright 1987 by Sage Publications.

p. 325, 329, and 331: "Feelings When Lonely"; "Loneliness Scores by Age Groups"; "Loneliness Scores by Age at Parents' Divorce." From "Loneliness" by C. Rubenstein, P. Shaver, and L. A. Peplau from *Human Nature* magazine February 1979. Copyright © 1979 by Human Nature, Inc. Reprinted by permission of the publisher.

pp. 326–327 and 339: "The NYU Loneliness Scale"; "What People Do When They Are Lonely." From *In Search of Intimacy* by Carin Rubenstein, Phillip Shaver, copyright © 1982 by Carin Rubenstein, and Phillip Shaver. Used by permission of Dell Books, a division of Bantam, Doubleday, Dell Publishing Group, Inc.

p. 328: Russell, D., Peplau, L. A., & Cutrona, C. E. Items from "The UCLA Loneliness Scale: From "The Revised UCLA Loneliness Scale: Concurrent and

Discriminant Validity Evidence," *Journal of Personality and Social Psychology, 39,* 472–480. Copyright 1980 by The American Psychological Association. Reprinted with permisssion of the authors.

p. 337: Cheek, J. M. (1983). Unpublished manuscript. Wellesley College. "The Revised Cheek and Buss Shyness Scale."

p. 340 and 341: Rook, K. S., & Peplau, L. A. "Cognitive Strategies College Students Used to Cope with Loneliness"; "Behavioral Strategies College Students Used to Cope with Loneliness." From "Helping the Lonely," in L. A. Peplau & D. Perlman (Eds.) *Loneliness: A Sourcebook of Current Theory, Research and Therapy.* Copyright © 1982 John Wiley & Sons, Inc. Reprinted by permission of John Wiley & Sons, Inc.

p. 363: Dawley, H. H., Jr. "Friendship Potential Inventory." From *Friendship.* Copyright © 1980 by Prentice-Hall, Inc., Englewood Cliffs, N.J. Reprinted by permission of the author.

p. 388: Ables, B. S., & Brandsma, J. M. (1977). Illustrative case study material. Reprinted by permission of Jossey-Bass Publishers, San Francisco.

p. 390: Sluzki, E. C. (1978). Illustrative case study material. Reprinted by permission of Brunner/Mazel, Inc., New York.

p. 392: Jacobson, N. S., & Margolin, G. (1979). Illustrative case study material. Reprinted by permission of Brunner/Mazel, Inc., New York.

p. 393: O'Leary, K. D., & Turkewitz, H. (1978a). Illustrative case study material. Reprinted by permission of Brunner/Mazel, Inc., New York.

Name Index

Subject Index

❖

Satisfaction (*Cont.*)
fairness and, 188
nonverbal communication and, 219–221
Scarcity hypothesis, 302
Secure attachment, 105, 108, 113
Self-actualization, 119–121
Self-attributions and coping, 312–314
Self-blame, 313
Self-disclosure, 205–209
descriptive vs. evaluative, 210
gender differences in, 209–212, 245
privacy and, 207
rate of, 207–209
reciprocity, 207
Self-disclosure reciprocity, 207
Self-esteem
jealousy and, 267–268
loneliness and, 333–334
love and, 118–122
Self-generated attitude change, 102–103
Self-help, 221
Selfishness, 194–195
Self-reports, 43–46
problems of, 44–45
types of, 44
Self-summarizing syndrome, 222–224
Sequential observations, 48
Serial monogamy, 403
Setting, 41–43
Sex-role stereotypes
complementarity in, 79–82
physical attractiveness of, 80
Sexual attraction, fear as, 100–102
Sexual exclusivity, 270–271
Sexual intercourse
among dating couples, 135–136
frequency of, 133–134
gender-related attitudes toward, 130–132
Sexual revolution, 125
Sexual satisfaction, 132–138
of dating couples, 134–136
equity in, 136–138
of married couples, 133–134
Sexuality, 125–149
AIDS (acquired immune deficiency syndrome), 125, 128–130, 139–142
attitudes toward, 130–132
and drug users, 129, 141
among heterosexual young adults, 129
among homosexuals, 129, 139–142
the illusion of unique vulnerability, 130
communication and, 142–145
sexual satisfaction and, 142–145
contraception and safe sex, 128–130
enrichment programs for, 384–385
and homosexuals, 129, 138–142
factors of sexual satisfaction, 143
legal issues affecting, 139–140

Sexuality (*Cont.*):
relationship issues, 138–142
love and, 134–136
male "fantasy model" of, 144
marital happiness and, 133–134
predictors of premarital sexual activity, 126–130
sexual functioning efficiency in, 142
social attitudes toward, 125 126
subjective quality of, 142–143
Shyness, loneliness and, 335–336
Significant result, 52
Simulation studies, 43
Single life style, 19–24
advantages of, 21–24
casual factors of, 19
definition of, 20–21
disadvantages of, 21–24
effects of, 21–24
gender difference in, 21–23
and happiness, 23
rate, 19
Single men, problems of, 22–23
Single women, cultural stereotypes of, 22
Social exchange
alternatives, 163–167
outcomes, 163–164
sex ratios, 164–167
expectations, 162–163
investments, 167–171
power as, 231–246
bases of, 232–237
classification of, 233
dependence in, 232
language in, 237–238
normative theory of, 234
outcome, 242–246
and physical touch, 238–239
process of, 237
resources in, 232–233
styles of, 239–241
rewards and costs, 157–162
among dating couples, 159
and marital satisfaction, 158–159
perception of, 159–162
Social isolation, 324
Social network, 348–376
the family and divorce, 349–360
and friendship, 362–369, 372
utility of, 369–373
Social penetration theory, 204–207
Specific Interpersonal Trust Scale, 106–107, 115
Spouses
abuse of, 252–256
physical attractiveness of, 80
Stereotypes, and power, 251–252
Stimulus Value Role (SVR) theory, 154–155, 189